MICROSOFT
OFFICE
Advanced Concepts and Techniques

Course Two

WORD 6
EXCEL 5
ACCESS 2
POWERPOINT 4

Gary B. Shelly
Thomas J. Cashman
Misty E. Vermaat

Contributing Authors

Marvin M. Boetcher
Steven G. Forsythe
Sherry L. Green
Philip J. Pratt
James E. Quasney

boyd & fraser
publishing company

An International Thomson Publishing Company

Danvers • Albany • Bonn • Boston • Cincinnati • Detroit • London • Madrid • Melbourne
Mexico City • New York • Paris • San Francisco • Singapore • Tokyo • Toronto • Washington

MICROSOFT
OFFICE
Advanced Concepts and Techniques

WORD 6
EXCEL 5
ACCESS 2
POWERPOINT 4

Course Two

Special thanks go to the following reviewers of the Shelly Cashman Series Windows Applications textbooks:

Susan Conners, Purdue University Calumet; **William Dorin**, Indiana University Northwest; **Robert Erickson**, University of Vermont; **Deborah Fansler**, Purdue University Calumet; **Roger Franklin**, The College of William and Mary; **Roy O. Foreman**, Purdue University Calumet; **Patricia Harris**, Mesa Community College; **Cynthia Kachik**, Santa Fe Community College; **Suzanne Lambert**, Broward Community College; **Anne McCoy**, Miami-Dade Community College/Kendall Campus; **Karen Meyer**, Wright State University; **Mike Michaelson**, Palomar College; **Michael Mick**, Purdue University Calumet; **Cathy Paprocki**, Harper College; **Jeffrey Quasney**, Educational Consultant; **Denise Rall**, Purdue University; **Sorel Reisman**, California State University, Fullerton; **John Ross**, Fox Valley Technical College; **Lorie Szalapski**, St. Paul Technical College; **Susan Sebok**, South Suburban College; **Betty Svendsen**, Oakton Community College; **Jeanie Thibault**, Educational Dynamics Institute; **Margaret Thomas**, Ohio University; **Carole Turner**, University of Wisconsin; **Diane Vaught**, National Business College; **Dwight Watt**, Swainsboro Technical Institute; **Melinda White**, Santa Fe Community College; **Eileen Zisk**, Community College of Rhode Island; and **Sue Zulauf**, Sinclair Community College.

© 1995 boyd & fraser publishing company
One Corporate Place • Ferncroft Village
Danvers, Massachusetts 01923

International Thomson Publishing
boyd & fraser publishing company is an ITP company.
The ITP trademark is used under license.

Printed in the United States of America

For more information, contact boyd & fraser publishing company:

boyd & fraser publishing company
One Corporate Place • Ferncroft Village
Danvers, Massachusetts 01923, USA

International Thomson Publishing Europe
Berkshire House
168-173 High Holborn
London, WC1V 7AA, United Kingdom

Thomas Nelson Australia
102 Dodds Street
South Melbourne
Victoria 3205 Australia

Nelson Canada
1120 Birchmont Road
Scarborough, Ontario
Canada M1K 5G4

International Thomson Editores
Campos Eliseos 385, Piso 7
Colonia Polanco
11560 Mexico D.F. Mexico

International Thomson Publishing GmbH
Konigswinterer Strasse 418
53227 Bonn, Germany

International Thomson Publishing Asia
Block 211, Henderson Road #08-03
Henderson Industrial Park
Singapore 0315

International Thomson Publishing Japan
Hirakawa-cho Kyowa Building, 3F
2-2-1 Hirakawa-cho, Chiyoda-ku
Tokyo 102, Japan

ISBN 0-7895-0106-6 (perfect bound)
ISBN 0-7895-0116-3 (spiral bound)

2 3 4 5 6 7 8 9 10   BC   9 8 7 6 5

This book was designed using Windows 3.11, QuarkXpress 3.31 for Windows, and CorelDraw 3.0 & 5.0 for Windows.

ONTENTS

ADVANCED SPREADSHEETS USING MICROSOFT EXCEL 5 FOR WINDOWS   E1

▶ ## PROJECT ONE
Working with Templates and Multiple Worksheets in a Workbook   E2

▶ ## PROJECT TWO
Data Tables, Macros Using Visual Basic, and Scenario Manager   E71

ADVANCED DATABASE MANIPULATION USING MICROSOFT ACCESS 2 FOR WINDOWS   A1

ADVANCED PRESENTATION GRAPHICS USING MICROSOFT POWERPOINT 4 FOR WINDOWS   PP1

PREFACE

Microsoft Office: Advanced Concepts and Techniques was specifically developed for a one-quarter or one-semester advanced personal computer applications course. This book assumes that the student is familiar with the fundamentals of Microsoft Office, Microsoft Word, Microsoft Excel, Microsoft Access, Microsoft PowerPoint, and OLE. These fundamental topics are covered in the companion textbook, *Microsoft Office: Introductory Concepts and Techniques.* The objectives of this book are as follows:

▶ To extend the student's basic knowledge of Microsoft Office and the four application tools

▶ To acquaint the student with the proper way to solve personal computer application-type problems

▶ To use practical problems to illustrate personal computer applications

▶ To take advantage of the advanced capabilities of word processing, spreadsheet creation, database manipulation, and presentation graphics in a Windows environment

▶ To develop a learn-by-doing environment in which the student is less dependent on the instructor

When students complete a course using this textbook, they will have a firm knowledge of Microsoft Office and will be able to solve a variety of personal computer-related problems.

▶ THE SHELLY CASHMAN APPROACH

The Shelly Cashman Series Windows Applications books present word processing, spreadsheet, database, programming, presentation graphics, and Windows itself by showing the actual screens displayed by Windows and the applications software.
Because the student interacts with pictorial displays when using Windows, written words in a textbook does not suffice. For this reason, the Shelly Cashman Series emphasizes screen displays as the primary means of teaching Windows applications software. Every screen shown in the Shelly Cashman Series Windows Applications books appears in color, because the student views color on the screen. In addition, the screens display exactly as the student will see them. The screens in this book were captured while using the software. Nothing has been altered or changed except to highlight portions of the screen when appropriate.

The Shelly Cashman Series Windows Applications books present the material using a unique pedagogy designed specifically for the graphical environment of Windows. The textbooks are primarily designed for a lecture/lab method of presentation, although they are equally suited for a tutorial/hands-on approach wherein the student learns by actually completing each project following the step-by-step instructions. Features of this pedagogy include the following:

▶ **Project Orientation:** Each project in the book solves a complete problem, meaning that the student is introduced to a problem to be solved and is then given the step-by-step process to solve the problem.

▶ **Step-by-Step Instructions:** Each of the tasks required to complete a project is identified throughout the development of the project. For example, a task might be to change a chart type from a combination area and column chart to a 3-D column chart using Excel. Then, each step to accomplish the task is specified. The steps are accompanied by screens. The student is not told to perform a step without seeing the result of the step on a color screen. Hence, students learn from this book the same as if they were using the computer. This attention to detail in accomplishing a task and showing the resulting screen makes the Shelly Cashman Series Windows Applications textbooks unique.

▶ **Multiple Ways to Use the Book:** Because each step to accomplish a task is illustrated with a screen, the book can be used in a number of ways, including: (a) Lecture and textbook approach — The instructor lectures on the material in the book. The student reads and studies the material and then applies the knowledge to an application on a computer; (b) Tutorial approach — The student performs each specified step on a computer. At the end of the project, the student has solved the problem and is ready to solve comparable student assignments; (c) Reference — Each task in a project is clearly identified. Therefore, the material serves as a complete reference because the student can refer to any task to determine how to accomplish it.

▶ **Windows/Graphical User Interface Approach:** Windows provides a graphical user interface. All of the examples in the book use this interface. Thus, the mouse is used for the majority of control functions and is the preferred user communication tool. When specifying a command to be executed, the sequence is as follows: (a) If a button invokes the command, use the button; (b) If a button is not available, use the command from a menu; (c) If a button or a menu cannot be used, only then is the keyboard used to implement a Windows command.

▶ ORGANIZATION OF THIS TEXTBOOK

M *icrosoft Office: Advanced Concepts and Techniques* consists of three projects each on Microsoft Word 6, Microsoft Excel 5, and Microsoft Access 2 and two projects on Microsoft PowerPoint 4.

Advanced Word Processing Using Microsoft Word 6 for Windows

This textbook begins by providing detailed instruction on how to use the advanced commands and techniques of Microsoft Word 6. The material is divided into three projects as follows:

Project 1 – Creating a Document with Tables and Charts In Project 1, students work with tables and charts in a document. Students learn how to add a shadow box border with shading; add color to characters; change the space between characters; insert an existing document into an open document; insert a section break; save a document with a new filename; set and use tabs; create a table; add a caption to a table; sum rows in a table; format a table with Table AutoFormat; change column widths in a table; center a table; use the Format Painter button; change the alignment of table cell text; chart a table; add custom bullets to a list; and change the starting page number in a section.

Project 2 – Generating Form Letters, Mailing Labels, and Envelopes In Project 2, students learn how to generate form letters, mailing labels, and envelopes from a main document and a data file. Topics include creating and editing the three main documents and their associated data file; adding the system date to a document; inserting merge fields into the main document; using an IF field; displaying and printing field codes; merging and printing the documents; selecting data records to merge and print; sorting data records to merge and print; viewing merged data in the main document; and inserting a bar code on the mailing labels and envelopes.

Project 3 – Creating a Professional Newsletter In Project 3, students learn how to use Word's desktop publishing features to create a newsletter. Topics include adding ruling lines; adjusting shading in a paragraph; adding the bullet symbol; formatting the document into multiple columns; creating a dropped capital letter; framing and positioning graphics between columns; inserting a column break; adding a vertical rule between columns; creating a pull-quote; adding a box border around paragraphs; adding color to characters and lines; and changing the color of a graphic.

Advanced Spreadsheets Using Microsoft Excel 5 for Windows

Following the three advanced projects on Microcosft Word 6 for Windows, this textbook presents three advanced projects on Microsoft Excel 5. The topics presented are as follows:

Project 1 – Working with Templates and Multiple Worksheets   In Project 1, students learn to create a template and consolidate data into one worksheet. Topics include building and copying a template; multiple worksheets; 3-D references; adding notes; changing page setup characteristics; and finding and replacing data.

Project 2 – Data Tables, Macros Using Visual Basic, and Scenario Manager   In Project 2, students learn more about analyzing data in a worksheet and how to use macros. Topics include applying the PMT function to determine a monthly payment; analyzing data by (1) goal seeking, (2) creating a data table, and (3) creating a Scenario Summary Report worksheet; writing macros in VBA to automate worksheet activities; creating a button and assigning a macro to it; and protecting a worksheet.

Project 3 – Sorting and Filtering a Worksheet Database   In Project 3, students learn how to create, sort, and filter a database. Topics include using a data form to create and maintain a database; creating subtotals; finding, extracting, and deleting records that pass a test; applying database functions; and creating a pivot table.

Advanced Database Manipulation Using Microsoft Access 2 for Windows

Following the advanced projects on Microsoft Excel this textbook provides detailed instrucion on advanced topics in Microsoft Access 2. The topics are divided into three projects as follows:

Project 1 – Presenting Data: Reports and Forms   In Project 1, students learn to create custom reports and forms. Topics including creating queries for reports; using Report Wizards; modifying a report design; saving a report; printing a report; creating a report with grouping and subtotals; removing totals from a report; and changing the characteristics of items on a report. Other topics include creating an initial form using FormWizards; modifying a form design; moving fields; and adding fields and combo boxes. Students learn how to change a variety of special effects such as font styles, formats, and color.

Project 2 – Advanced Topics   In Project 2, students learn to use date, memo, and OLE fields. Topics include incorporating these fields in the structure of a database; updating the data in these fields and changing the table properties; creating a form that incorporates a one-to-many relationship between tables; manipulating subforms on a main form; incorporating date, memo, and OLE fields in forms; and incorporating various visual effects in forms. Students learn to use date and memo fields in a query.

Project 3 – Using Macros – Creating an Application System   In Project 3, students learn how to create a menu made up of buttons, which allows the user to select the table and forms to use to generate information. Topics include creating, associating, and running a macro; adding a combo box to a form; adding a Paintbrush picture to a form; modifying the properties of an option group; and using an application system.

Advanced Presentation Graphics Using Microsoft PowerPoint 4 for Windows

The final Microsoft Office software application covered in this textbook is Microsoft PowerPoint 4. The material is presented in two advanced projects as follows:

Project 1 – Embedded Visuals   In Project 1, students create a presentation from a Microsoft Word outline and then enhance it with embedded visuals. Topics include creating a special slide background using a clip art image; scaling an object to a precise size; resizing an object about center; stacking objects; embedding a Microsoft Excel chart; layering objects; grouping objects to create a new clip art image; embedding a picture; and creating a black closing slide.

Project 2 – Customizing a Presentation   In Project 2, students customize the presentation created in Project 1 by inserting a company logo and changing the color scheme. Topics include changing templates; selecting a new color scheme; drawing a company logo; adding shaded fill color; creating a graphic image from text using Microsoft WordArt; grouping the logo and graphic image into one logo object; and pasting the logo object to the Slide Master so it displays on each slide in the presentation. Other topics cover adding a border to a picture; linking and embedding "drill down" documents; adding captions; hiding a slide; creating speaker notes in Notes Pages view; and running a slide show using the PowerPoint Viewer.

END-OF-PROJECT STUDENT ACTIVITIES

Each project ends with a wealth of student activities including most or all of the following features:

- A list of key terms for review
- A Quick Reference that lists the ways to carry out a task using the mouse, menu, or keyboard shortcuts
- Student Assignments for homework and classroom discussion
- Computer Laboratory Exercises that usually require the student to load and manipulate a file, a document, a spreadsheet, a database, or a slide from the Student Diskette that accompanies this book
- Computer Laboratory Assignments that require the student to develop a complete project assignment; the assignments increase in difficulty from a relatively easy assignment to a case study

ANCILLARY MATERIALS FOR TEACHING FROM THE SHELLY CASHMAN SERIES WINDOWS APPLICATIONS TEXTBOOKS

A comprehensive instructor's support package accompanies all textbooks in the Shelly Cashman Series.

Annotated Instructor's Edition (AIE)   The AIE is designed to assist you with your lectures by suggesting illustrations to use, summarizing key points, proposing pertinent questions, offering important tips, alerting you to pitfalls, and by incorporating the answers to the Student Assignments. There are several hundred annotations throughout the textbook.

Computer-Based LCD Lecture Success System   The Shelly Cashman Series proudly presents the finest LCD learning material available in textbook publishing. The Lecture Success System diskette, together with a personal computer and LCD technology, are used in lieu of transparencies. The system enables you to explain and illustrate the step-by-step, screen-by-screen development of a project in the textbook without entering large amounts of data, thereby improving your students' grasp of the material. The Lecture Success System leads to a smooth, easy, error-free lecture.

The Lecture Success System diskette that accompanies the Instructor's Materials comes with files that correspond to key figures in the book. You load the files that pertain to a project and display them as needed. If the students want to see a series of steps a second time, simply reopen the file you want to start with and redo the steps. This presenttion system is available to adopters without charge.

Instructor's Materials   The instructor's ancillary contains the following:

▶ Detailed lesson plans including project objectives, project overview, and a three-column outline of each project that includes page references and illustration references
▶ Answers to all student assignments at the end of the projects
▶ A test bank of more than 600 True/False, Multiple Choice, and Fill-In questions
▶ Illustrations for every screen, diagram, and table in the textbook on CD-ROM — for selection and display in a lecture or to print and make transparencies
▶ An Instructor's Diskette that includes the projects and solutions to the Computer Laboratory Assignments at the end of each project
▶ A Lesson Plans and Test Bank Diskette that includes the detailed lesson plans and test bank for customizing to individual instructor's needs

MicroExam IV   MicroExam IV, a computerized test-generating system, is available free to adopters of any Shelly Cashman Series textbooks. It includes all of the questions from the test bank just described. MicroExam IV is an easy-to-use, menu-driven software package that provides instructors with testing flexibility and allows customizing of testing documents.

NetTest IV   NetTest IV allows instructors to take a MicroExam IV file made up of True/False and Multiple Choice questions and proctor a paperless examination in a network environment. The same questions display in a different order on each PC. Students have the option of instantaneous feedback. Tests are electronically graded, and an item analysis is produced.

▶ ACKNOWLEDGMENTS

The Shelly Cashman Series would not be the success it is without the contributions of outstanding publishing professionals. First, and foremost, among them is Becky Herrington, director of production and designer. She is the heart and soul of the Shelly Cashman Series, and it is only through her leadership, dedication, and untiring efforts that superior products are produced.

Under Becky's direction, the following individuals made significant contributions to these books: Ginny Harvey, series administrator and manuscript editor; Peter Schiller, production manager, Ken Russo, senior illustrator and cover art; Mike Bodnar, Greg Herrington, and Dave Bonnewitz, illustrators; Jeanne Black and Betty Hopkins, typographers; Tracy Murphy, series coordinator; Sue Sebok and Melissa Dowling LaRoe, copy editors; Marilyn Martin and Nancy Lamm, proofreaders; Henry Blackham, cover and opener photography; Dennis Woelky, glass etchings; and Christina Haley, indexer.

Special recognition for a job well done must go to Jim Quasney, who, together with writing, assumed the responsibilities as series editor. Particular thanks go to Thomas Walker, president and CEO of boyd & fraser publishing company, who recognized the need, and provided the support, to produce the full-color Shelly Cashman Series Windows Applications textbooks.

We hope you will find using the book an enriching and rewarding experience.

Gary B. Shelly
Thomas J. Cashman

▶ SHELLY CASHMAN SERIES – TRADITIONALLY BOUND TEXTBOOKS

The Shelly Cashman Series presents both Windows- and DOS-based personal computer applications in a variety of traditionally bound textbooks, as shown in the table below. For more information, see your ITP representative or call 1-800-423-0563.

COMPUTERS	
Computers	Using Computers: A Gateway to Information Using Computers: A Gateway to Information, Brief Edition
Computers and Windows Applications	Using Computers: A Gateway to Information and Microsoft Office (also available in spiral bound) Using Computers: A Gateway to Information and Microsoft Works 3.0 (also available in spiral bound) Complete Computer Concepts and Microsoft Works 2.0 (also available in spiral bound)
Computers and DOS Applications	Complete Computer Concepts and WordPerfect 5.1, Lotus 1-2-3 Release 2.2, and dBASE IV Version 1.1 (also available in spiral bound) Complete Computer Concepts and WordPerfect 5.1, Lotus 1-2-3 Release 2.2, and dBASE III PLUS (also available in spiral bound)
Computers and Programming	Using Computers: A Gateway to Information and Programming in QBasic

WINDOWS APPLICATIONS	
Integrated Packages	Microsoft Office: Introductory Concepts and Techniques (also available in spiral bound) Microsoft Office: Advanced Concepts and Techniques (also available in spiral bound) Microsoft Works 3.0 (also available in spiral bound) Microsoft Works 2.0 (also available in spiral bound)
Windows	Microsoft Windows 3.1 Introductory Concepts and Techniques Microsoft Windows 3.1 Complete Concepts and Techniques
Windows Applications	Microsoft Word 2.0, Microsoft Excel 4, and Paradox 1.0 (also available in spiral bound)
Word Processing	Microsoft Word 6* • Microsoft Word 2.0 WordPerfect 6.1* • WordPerfect 6* • WordPerfect 5.2
Spreadsheets	Microsoft Excel 5* • Microsoft Excel 4 Lotus 1-2-3 Release 5* • Lotus 1-2-3 Release 4* Quattro Pro 6 • Quattro Pro 5
Database Management	Paradox 5 • Paradox 4.5 • Paradox 1.0 Microsoft Access 2*
Presentation Graphics	Microsoft PowerPoint 4*

DOS APPLICATIONS	
Operating Systems	DOS 6 Introductory Concepts and Techniques DOS 6 and Microsoft Windows 3.1 Introductory Concepts and Techniques
Integrated Package	Microsoft Works 3.0 (also available in spiral bound)
DOS Applications	WordPerfect 5.1, Lotus 1-2-3 Release 2.2, and dBASE IV Version 1.1 (also available in spiral bound) WordPerfect 5.1, Lotus 1-2-3 Release 2.2, and dBASE III PLUS (also available in spiral bound)
Word Processing	WordPerfect 6.0 WordPerfect 5.1 Step-by-Step Function Key Edition WordPerfect 5.1 WordPerfect 5.1 Function Key Edition WordPerfect 4.2 (with Educational Software) WordStar 6.0 (with Educational Software)
Spreadsheets	Lotus 1-2-3 Release 4 • Lotus 1-2-3 Release 2.4 • Lotus 1-2-3 Release 2.3 Lotus 1-2-3 Release 2.2 • Lotus 1-2-3 Release 2.01 Quattro Pro 3.0 Quattro with 1-2-3 Menus (with Educational Software)
Database Management	dBASE 5 dBASE IV Version 1.1 dBASE III PLUS (with Educational Software) Paradox 4.5 Paradox 3.5 (with Educational Software)

PROGRAMMING AND NETWORKING	
Programming	Microsoft Visual Basic 3.0 for Windows* Microsoft BASIC QBasic
Networking	Novell NetWare for Users
Internet	The Internet: Introductory Concepts and Techniques (UNIX Version) The Internet: Introductory Concepts and Techniques (Mosaic Version)

*Also available as a Double Diamond Edition, which is a shortened version of the complete book

▶ SHELLY CASHMAN SERIES – Custom Edition PROGRAM

I f you do not find a Shelly Cashman Series traditionally bound textbook to fit your needs, boyd & fraser's unique **Custom Edition** program allows you to choose from a number of options and create a textbook perfectly suited to your course. The customized materials are available in a variety of binding styles, including boyd & fraser's patented **Custom Edition** kit, spiral bound, and note-book bound. Features of the **Custom Edition** program are:

▶ Textbooks that match the content of your course
▶ Windows- and DOS-based materials for the latest versions of personal computer applications software
▶ Shelly Cashman Series quality, with the same full-color materials and Shelly Cashman Series pedagogy found in the traditionally bound books
▶ Affordable pricing so your students receive the **Custom Edition** at a cost similar to that of traditionally bound books

The table on the right summarizes the available materials. For more information, see your ITP representative or call 1-800-423-0563.

COMPUTERS	
Computers	Using Computers: A Gateway to Information
	Using Computers: A Gateway to Information, Brief Edition
	Introduction to Computers (32-page)
OPERATING SYSTEMS	
Windows	Microsoft Windows 3.1 Introductory Concepts and Techniques
	Microsoft Windows 3.1 Complete Concepts and Techniques
DOS	Introduction to DOS 6 (using DOS prompt)
	Introduction to DOS 5.0 (using DOS shell)
	Introduction to DOS 5.0 or earlier (using DOS prompt)
WINDOWS APPLICATIONS	
Integrated Packages	Microsoft Works 3.0
	Microsoft Works 2.0
Microsoft Office	Using Microsoft Office (16-page)
	Object Linking and Embedding (OLE) (32-page)
Word Processing	Microsoft Word 6*
	Microsoft Word 2.0
	WordPerfect 6.1*
	WordPerfect 6*
	WordPerfect 5.2
Spreadsheets	Microsoft Excel 5*
	Microsoft Excel 4
	Lotus 1-2-3 Release 5*
	Lotus 1-2-3 Release 4*
	Quattro Pro 6
	Quattro Pro 5
Database Management	Paradox 5
	Paradox 4.5
	Paradox 1.0
	Microsoft Access 2*
Presentation Graphics	Microsoft PowerPoint 4*
DOS APPLICATIONS	
Integrated Package	Microsoft Works 3.0
Word Processing	WordPerfect 6.0
	WordPerfect 5.1 Step-by-Step Function Key Edition
	WordPerfect 5.1
	WordPerfect 5.1 Function Key Edition
	Microsoft Word 5.0
	WordPerfect 4.2
	WordStar 6.0
Spreadsheets	Lotus 1-2-3 Release 4
	Lotus 1-2-3 Release 2.4
	Lotus 1-2-3 Release 2.3
	Lotus 1-2-3 Release 2.2
	Lotus 1-2-3 Release 2.01
	Quattro Pro 3.0
	Quattro with 1-2-3 Menus
Database Management	dBASE 5
	dBASE IV Version 1.1
	dBASE III PLUS
	Paradox 4.5
	Paradox 3.5
PROGRAMMING AND NETWORKING	
Programming	Microsoft Visual Basic 3.0 for Windows*
	Microsoft BASIC
	QBasic
Networking	Novell NetWare for Users
Internet	The Internet: Introductory Concepts and Techniques (UNIX Version)
	The Internet: Introductory Concepts and Techniques (Mosaic Version)

* Also available as a mini-module

WORD PROCESSING

USING MICROSOFT WORD 6 FOR WINDOWS

MICROSOFT WORD 6 FOR WINDOWS

PROJECT ONE

▼

CREATING A DOCUMENT WITH TABLES AND CHARTS

OBJECTIVES You will have mastered the material in this project when you can:

- ▸ Add a box border with a drop shadow to selected paragraphs
- ▸ Shade inside the box border
- ▸ Add color to characters
- ▸ Change the spacing between characters
- ▸ Insert a section break
- ▸ Insert an existing document into an open document
- ▸ Save an active document with a new filename
- ▸ Set custom tabs

- ▸ Change alignment of tab stops
- ▸ Add a caption to a table
- ▸ Insert a table into a document
- ▸ Format a table
- ▸ Change the width of table columns
- ▸ Change alignment of data in table cells
- ▸ Sum the rows and columns in a table
- ▸ Use the Format Painter button
- ▸ Chart a table
- ▸ Customize the bullets in a list
- ▸ Create a header for a section

▶ INTRODUCTION

 I n all likelihood, sometime during your professional life you will find yourself placed in a sales role. You might be selling a tangible product like plastic or a service like interior decorating to a customer or client. Within the organization, you might be selling an idea, such as a benefits package to company employees, or a budget plan to upper management. To sell an item, whether tangible or intangible, you will often find yourself writing a proposal. Proposals vary in length, style, and formality, but all are designed to elicit acceptance from the reader.

A proposal may be one of three types: planning, research, or sales. A **planning proposal** offers solutions to a problem or improvement to a situation. A **research proposal** usually requests funding for a research project. A **sales proposal** offers a product or service to existing or potential customers.

▶ PROJECT ONE — SALES PROPOSAL

P roject 1 uses Word to produce the sales proposal shown in Figures 1-1a, 1-1b, and 1-1c below and on the next two pages. The sales proposal is designed to persuade prospective students to choose Blue Lake College for a post-high school education. The proposal has a colorful title page to grasp the reader's attention. The body of the sales proposal uses tables and a chart to present numeric data pictorially.

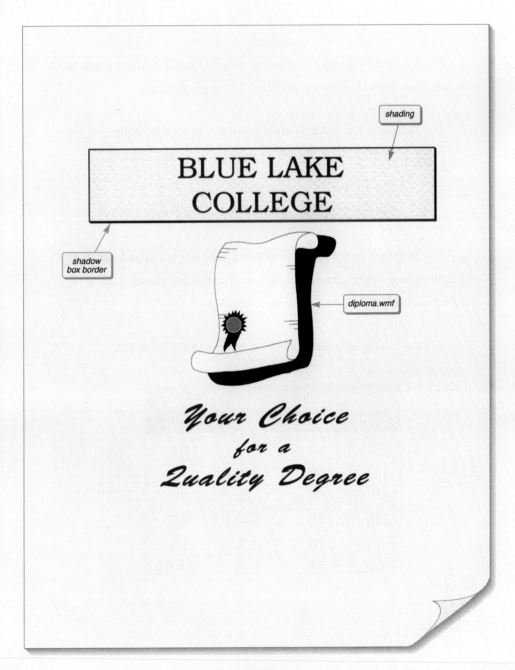

FIGURE 1-1a

Blue Lake College 1

Blue Lake College is committed to providing a high-quality education for the people of its surrounding communities. Thousands of people from all walks of life have graduated from Blue Lake and are now successfully achieving their career goals. We invite you to join our student body and realize your dreams too.

Blue Lake is small enough to give you personalized attention, yet large enough to meet your needs. Choose to attend our school on a full- or part-time basis.

Table 1: BLUE LAKE STUDENT STATUS BREAKDOWN ← *caption*

	% Female	% Male
Part-Time Students	55.2	44.8
Full-Time Students	47.8	52.2

data in table form →

With our diverse student population including recent high school graduates, single parents, senior citizens, housewives, new career seekers, and transfer students, you'll feel comfortable in our campus environment.

Table 2: AGE DISTRIBUTIONS OF BLUE LAKE STUDENTS ← *caption*
(in table form)

	# of Female Students	# of Male Students	Total # of Students
18-23	626	651	1277
24-29	678	646	1324
30-39	591	601	1192
40-50	576	555	1131
Over 50	220	201	421
Totals	2691	2654	5345

data in table form →

FIGURE 1-1b

Blue Lake College 2

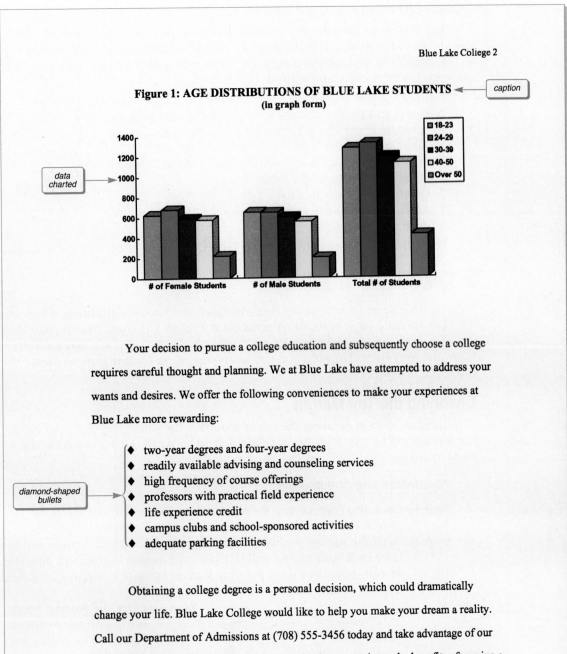

Figure 1: AGE DISTRIBUTIONS OF BLUE LAKE STUDENTS ← caption
(in graph form)

Your decision to pursue a college education and subsequently choose a college requires careful thought and planning. We at Blue Lake have attempted to address your wants and desires. We offer the following conveniences to make your experiences at Blue Lake more rewarding:

- ◆ two-year degrees and four-year degrees
- ◆ readily available advising and counseling services
- ◆ high frequency of course offerings
- ◆ professors with practical field experience
- ◆ life experience credit
- ◆ campus clubs and school-sponsored activities
- ◆ adequate parking facilities

Obtaining a college degree is a personal decision, which could dramatically change your life. Blue Lake College would like to help you make your dream a reality. Call our Department of Admissions at (708) 555-3456 today and take advantage of our one class free-of-charge program so you can begin to experience the benefits of earning a college degree.

FIGURE 1-1c

Document Preparation Steps

The following document preparation steps give you an overview of how the document in Figures 1-1a, 1-1b, and 1-1c on the previous pages will be developed in this project. If you are preparing the document in this project on a personal computer, read these steps without doing them.

1. Create a title page with a box border, shading, color, and clip art.
2. Insert an existing document beneath the title page in a new section.
3. Save the active document with a new filename.
4. Add a table to the document using custom tabs.
5. Add a table to the document using the Insert Table button.
6. Create a chart from the table.
7. Customize bullets in a list.
8. Add a header to the second section of the document.
9. Print the document.

The following pages contain a detailed explanation of each of these steps.

▶ CREATING A TITLE PAGE

A title page should be designed to catch the reader's attention. Therefore, the title page of the sales proposal in Project 1 (Figure 1-1a on page MSW3) uses a shaded box border with a shadow, color, clip art, and a variety of fonts and font sizes. The steps on the following pages outline how to create the title page in Project 1.

Changing the Top Margin

The first step in creating the cover letter for the sales proposal is to change the top margin to 2 inches. Because the default in Word is 1 inch, follow these steps to change the top margin to 2 inches.

TO CHANGE THE TOP MARGIN

Step 1: Click the Page Layout View button on the horizontal scroll bar to switch the document window to page layout view.

Step 2: With the mouse pointer on the top margin boundary, press and hold the ALT key and press and hold the left mouse button and drag the margin boundary until the gray shaded margin area reads 2". Release the left mouse button and the ALT key.

Step 3: Click the Normal View button on the horizontal scroll bar to switch back to normal view.

The top margin is set at 2" (Figure 1-2).

FIGURE 1-2

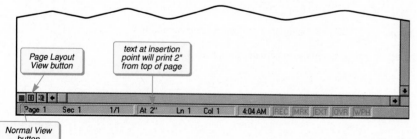

Page Layout View button

text at insertion point will print 2" from top of page

Normal View button

Entering the First Line of the Title Page

The next step in creating the title page is to enter the college name, which is centered and bold in the Bookman Old Style font with a font size of 36 (see Figure 1-3).

TO ENTER THE COLLEGE NAME ON THE TITLE PAGE

Step 1: Click the Center button on the Formatting toolbar.

Step 2: Click the Font box arrow on the Formatting toolbar and select Bookman Old Style (or a similar font) from the list of available fonts.

Step 3: Click the Font Size box arrow on the Formatting toolbar and select 36 from the list of available font sizes.

Step 4: Click the Bold button on the Formatting toolbar.

Step 5: Type BLUE LAKE and press the ENTER key.

Step 6: Type COLLEGE and press the ENTER key.

The title page now displays as shown in Figure 1-3.

FIGURE 1-3

Adding a Shadow Box Border with Shading

You can learned how to add a border to a paragraph using the Borders toolbar. In this project, you want a **shadow box border** surrounding the entire college name. That is, a shadow displays on the bottom and right edges of the box border. To do this, you must use the Borders and Shading command. Follow these steps to add a shadow box border to the college name and to shade inside the box border.

TO ADD A SHADOW BOX BORDER WITH SHADING ▼

STEP 1 ▶

Select the paragraphs to be bordered by dragging the mouse pointer in the selection bar to the left of the two lines. (Be sure not to select the paragraph mark on line 3.) Select the Format menu and point to the Borders and Shading command.

Word highlights the college name on lines 1 and 2 (Figure 1-4).

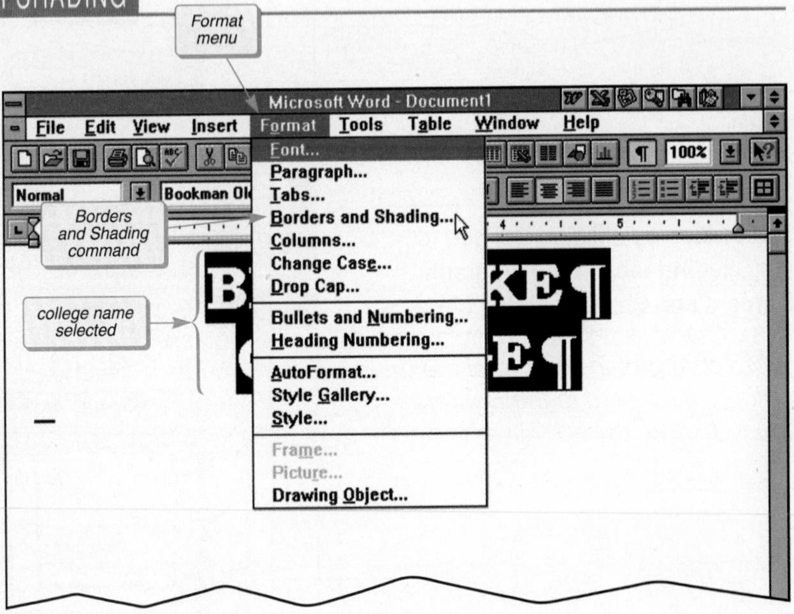

FIGURE 1-4

STEP 2 ▶

Choose the Borders and Shading command.

Word displays the Paragraph Borders and Shading dialog box (Figure 1-5). (If the options in the Borders tab do not display in your Paragraph Borders and Shading dialog box, click the Borders tab.)

STEP 3

In the Presets area of the Paragraph Borders and Shading dialog box, click the Shadow option. In the Line area, click 1 1/2 pt line style. Point to the Color drop-down list box arrow.

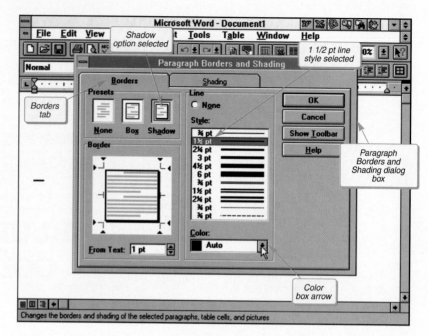

FIGURE 1-5

STEP 4 ▶

Click the Color box arrow. Point to Blue in the list of available colors.

Word displays a list of available border colors (Figure 1-6).

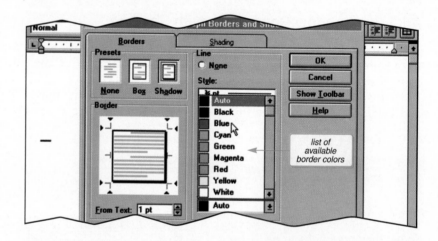

FIGURE 1-6

STEP 5 ▶

Select Blue by clicking it. Point to the Shading tab in the Paragraph Borders and Shading dialog box.

Word changes the colors of the options displayed in the Borders tab to blue (Figure 1-7).

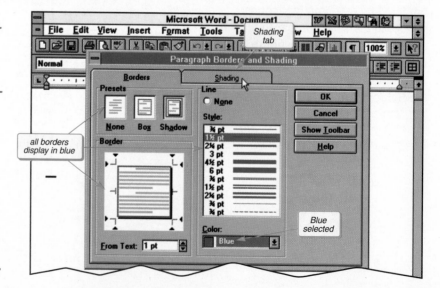

FIGURE 1-7

STEP 6 ▶

Click the Shading tab. Select 5% shading in the Shading list by clicking it. Point to the OK button.

Word displays the options in the Shading tab of the Paragraph Borders and Shading dialog box (Figure 1-8). The Preview area displays a sample of the selected shading.

FIGURE 1-8

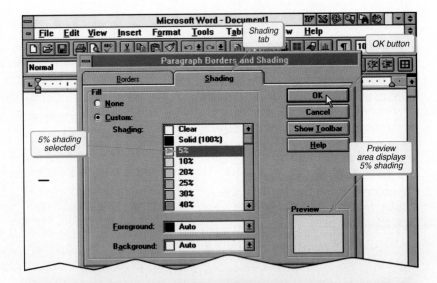

STEP 7 ▶

Choose the OK button in the Paragraph Borders and Shading dialog box. (Leave the college name selected for the next steps.)

Word draws a shadow box border with 5% shading around the college name (Figure 1-9).

FIGURE 1-9

You can add shading to a box border with the Borders button on the Formatting toolbar; you cannot, however, add a shadow box border or color with the Borders button. Thus, to add a shadow box border or color, use the Borders and Shading command from the Format menu.

Because you want the characters in the college name also to be blue (like the border) the next step is to color the characters as shown in these steps.

TO ADD COLOR TO CHARACTERS ▼

STEP 1 ▶

If the college name is not already highlighted, select it. With the mouse pointer positioned in the selection, click the right mouse button. Point to the Font command in the shortcut menu.

Word displays a shortcut menu that corresponds to the selection (Figure 1-10). The characters in the college name are selected.

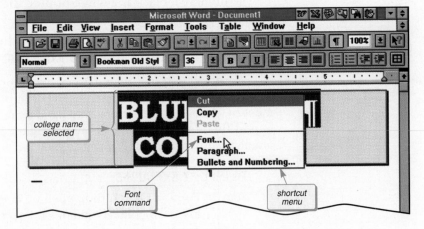

FIGURE 1-10

STEP 2 ▶

Choose the Font command. Change the font color to blue by clicking the Color box arrow and clicking Blue. Point to the OK button.

Word displays the Font dialog box (Figure 1-11). In the Font dialog box, you can set the font typeface, font style, font size, and color. (If the options in the Font tab do not display in your Font dialog box, click the Font tab.)

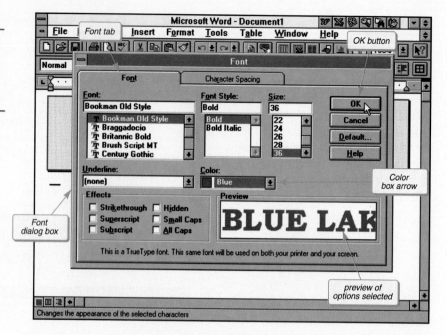

FIGURE 1-11

STEP 3 ▶

Choose the OK button. Click on the paragraph mark in line 3 to remove the selection.

Word colors the selected characters to blue (Figure 1-12).

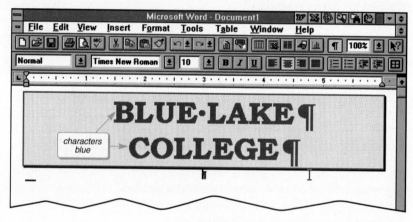

FIGURE 1-12

If you have a black-and-white printer, the colors other than black or white will print in shades of gray.

Importing a Graphic into the Title Page

Word for Windows includes a series of predefined graphics called clip art files or Windows metafiles, and you insert, or import, these graphics into a Word document by choosing the Picture command from the Insert menu. The next step is to import the diploma graphic shown in Figure 1-1a on page MSW3 into the document, as shown in the following steps.

TO IMPORT A GRAPHIC

Step 1: Position the insertion point on line 3 and press the ENTER key. The insertion point should be on line 4, the desired location of the diploma graphic.

Step 2: From the Insert menu, choose the Picture command.

Step 3: In the Insert Picture dialog box, point to the down arrow on the File Name list scroll bar and hold down the left mouse button until diploma.wmf displays.

Step 4: Select the filename diploma.wmf by clicking it. If the Preview Picture check box is off, click it to display the selected graphic (Figure 1-13).

Step 5: Choose the OK button in the Insert Picture dialog box.

Word inserts the selected graphic (Figure 1-1a on page MSW3) into the document at the location of the insertion point.

FIGURE 1-13

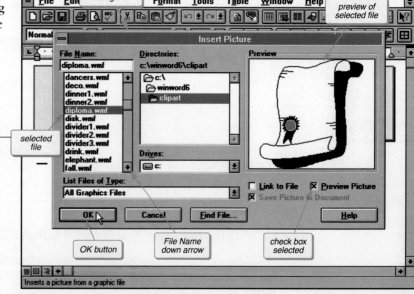

Formatting and Entering the College Slogan

The next step is to enter the college slogan beneath the graphic on the title page. The slogan is 36 point Brush Script MT font in italic and colored blue. Because you need to display the Font dialog box to color characters, you can change the font typeface, font style, and font size from the Font dialog box, instead of using the Formatting toolbar. Follow these steps to format the slogan from the Font dialog box and to enter it.

TO FORMAT AND ENTER THE COLLEGE SLOGAN ▼

STEP 1 ▶

Press the ENTER key twice. Position the mouse pointer to the right of the last paragraph mark in the document window (line 6) and click the right mouse button. From the shortcut menu, choose the Font command. In the Font dialog box, use the up or down arrow on the Font scroll bar to bring Brush Script MT (or a similar font) into the Font list and select it. Likewise, select Bold Italic in the Font Style list and select 36 in the Size list. Click the Color box arrow and select Blue in the Color list.

The Preview area in the Font dialog box reflects current selections (Figure 1-14).

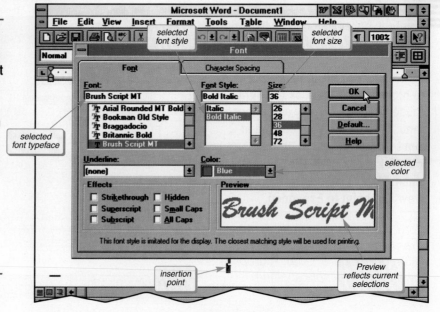

FIGURE 1-14

STEP 2 ▶

Choose the OK button. Type Your Choice and press the ENTER key. Change the font size to 28 by clicking the Font Size box arrow and selecting 28. Type for a and press the ENTER key. Change the font size back to 36 by clicking the Font Size box arrow and selecting 36. Type Quality Degree

Word displays the college slogan (Figure 1-15).

FIGURE 1-15

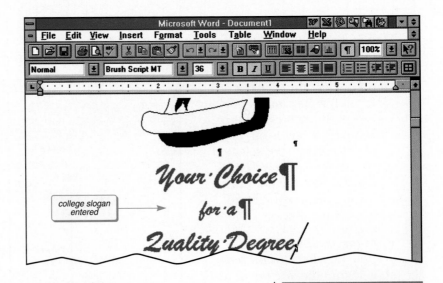

college slogan entered

Changing the Space Between Characters

The college slogan at the bottom of the title page in Figure 1-1a on page MSW3 is **expanded**; that is, there is extra space between each character. With Word, you can condense or expand the spacing between characters to create special effects. Word, by default, condenses or expands the space between characters by one point. Follow these steps to expand the space between the characters in the college slogan by 3 points (see Figure 1-18).

TO CHANGE THE SPACE BETWEEN CHARACTERS ▼

STEP 1 ▶

Select the college slogan on lines 6, 7, and 8 by dragging the mouse pointer in the selection bar to the left of the text. With the mouse pointer in the highlighted text, click the right mouse button to display a shortcut menu. Choose the Font command from the shortcut menu. In the Font dialog box, click the Character Spacing tab. Click the Spacing box arrow and point to Expanded.

Word displays the options in the Character Spacing tab of the Font dialog box (Figure 1-16). A drop-down list of available spacing options displays.

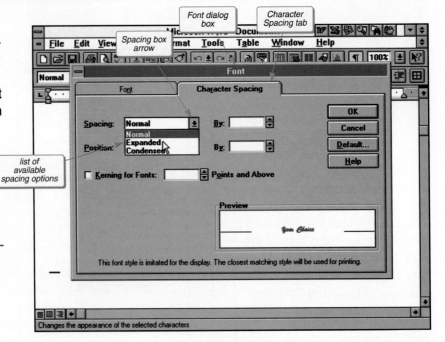

FIGURE 1-16

STEP 2 ▶

Select Expanded by clicking it.
Repeatedly click the up arrow in the
Spacing By box until it displays 3 pt.

*Expanded becomes the selected
spacing (Figure 1-17). The (Spacing) By box displays 3 pt as the
amount of space to place between
the selected characters.*

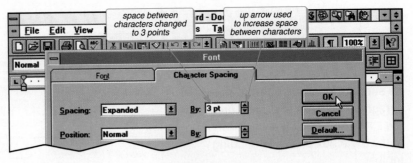

FIGURE 1-17

STEP 3 ▶

Choose the OK button. Click to the
right of the paragraph mark in line 8
to remove the highlight.

*Word expands the selected text by
3 points (Figure 1-18).*

FIGURE 1-18

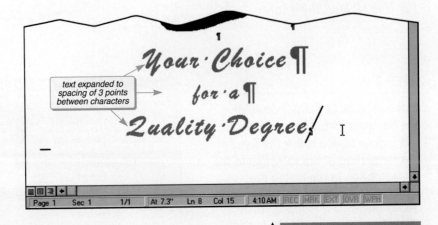

Saving the Title Page

Because you have finished the title page, you should save it by performing the
following steps.

TO SAVE A DOCUMENT

Step 1: Insert the data diskette into drive A. Click the Save button on the
Standard toolbar.

Step 2: Type the filename `proj1ttl` in the File Name box. Do not press the
ENTER key.

Step 3: If necessary, click the Drives box arrow and select drive A.

Step 4: Choose the OK button in the Save As dialog box.

The title page for the sales proposal is now complete. The next step is to
insert a draft of the proposal beneath the title page.

▶ INSERTING AN EXISTING DOCUMENT INTO AN OPEN DOCUMENT

Assume you have already prepared a draft of the body of the proposal and
saved it with the filename PROJ1DFT. You would like the draft to display
on a separate page beneath the title page. Once the two documents
appear on the screen together as one document, you would like to save this active
document with a new name so each of the original documents remains intact.

You want the inserted pages of the sales proposal to use the Times New
Roman font and be left-justified. That is, you want to return to the normal style.
Because the text to be entered at the insertion point is currently formatted for
centered, bold, and italicized 36 point Brush Script MT, the next step is to return
to the normal style, as shown in the steps on the next page.

TO RETURN TO THE NORMAL STYLE ▼

STEP 1 ▶

Be sure the insertion point is on the paragraph mark on line 8 and press the ENTER key. Click the word Normal in the Style box on the Formatting toolbar.

Word selects the word Normal in the Style box (Figure 1-19).

FIGURE 1-19

STEP 2 ▶

Move the mouse pointer down into the document window and click the left mouse button. Click the Return the formatting of the selection to the style? option in the dialog box.

Word displays a Reapply Style dialog box (Figure 1-20). In this dialog box, you can either create a new style based on the selection in the document window or return to the style displayed in the Style box.

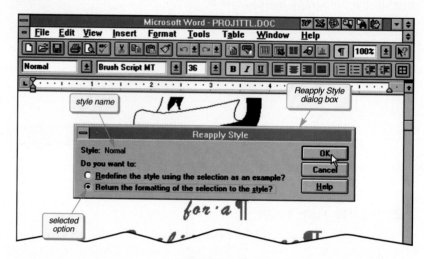

FIGURE 1-20

STEP 3 ▶

Choose the OK button.

Word returns the paragraph mark at the location of the insertion point to the normal style (Figure 1-21). That is, the paragraph mark is left-justified and the text to be entered is Times New Roman.

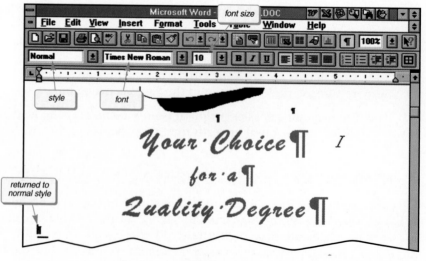

FIGURE 1-21

Inserting a Section Break

The draft of the sales proposal should appear on a separate page beneath the title page. The draft to be inserted requires different page formatting than the title page. Recall that you increased the top margin of the title page to 2 inches. The draft should have a top margin of 1 inch. To change margins for the draft of the proposal and retain the margins for the title page, you must insert a new section.

A Word document can be divided into any number of **sections.** All documents have at least one section. If, during the course of creating a document, you would like to change the margins, paper size, page orientation, page number position, contents or position of headers, footers, or footnotes, you must create a new section. Each section may be formatted differently from the others.

When you create a new section, a **section break** displays on the screen as a double dotted line separated by the words End of Section. Section breaks do not print. When you create a section break, you specify whether the new section should begin on a new page or not. Follow these steps to create a section break that begins on a new page.

TO CREATE A SECTION BREAK ▼

STEP 1 ▶

Be sure the insertion point is positioned on the paragraph mark on line 9. From the Insert menu, choose the Break command. In the Section Breaks area of the Break dialog box, select the Next Page option by clicking it. Point to the OK button.

Word displays the Break dialog box (Figure 1-22). The Next Page option instructs Word to create a new page for the new section.

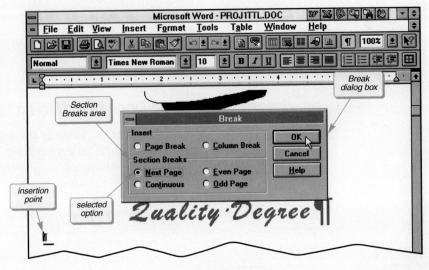

FIGURE 1-22

STEP 2 ▶

Choose the OK button.

Word creates a section break in the document (Figure 1-23). The insertion point and paragraph mark are placed in the new section. Notice the status bar indicates the insertion point is on page 2 in section 2.

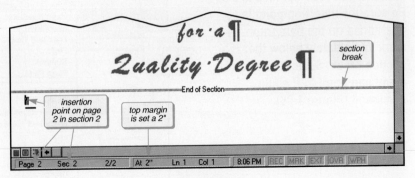

FIGURE 1-23

All section formatting is stored in the section break. You can delete a section break and all associated section formatting by selecting the section break and clicking the Cut button on the Standard toolbar. If you accidentally delete a section break, you can bring it back by clicking the Undo button on the Standard toolbar.

Notice in Figure 1-23 on the previous page that the top margin is set at 2 inches. Recall that the top margin of the new section containing the text of the draft of the sales proposal is to be set at 1 inch. Thus, follow these steps to change the top margin of section 2 to 1 inch.

TO CHANGE THE TOP MARGIN

Step 1: Be sure the insertion point is in section 2. Click the Page Layout View button on the scroll bar to switch to page layout view.

Step 2: With the mouse pointer on the top margin boundary, press and hold the ALT key and press and hold down the left mouse button and drag the margin boundary until the gray shaded margin area reads 1". Release the left mouse button and the ALT key.

FIGURE 1-24

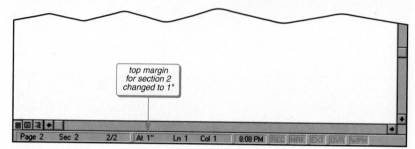

Step 3: Click the Normal View button on the scroll bar.

Step 4: Click the up arrow on the vertical scroll bar so you can see the bottom of the college slogan.

The top margin is set at 1" (Figure 1-24).

Inserting a Second Document into an Open Document

The next step is to insert the draft of the sales proposal beneath the section break. If you created the draft at an earlier time, you may have forgotten its name. Thus, you can display the contents of, or **preview**, any file before inserting it. Follow these steps to insert the draft of the proposal into the open document.

TO INSERT A SECOND DOCUMENT INTO AN OPEN DOCUMENT ▼

STEP 1 ►

Insert into drive A the Student Diskette that accompanies this book. Be sure the insertion point is positioned on the paragraph mark immediately below the section break. Select the Insert menu and point to the File command (Figure 1-25).

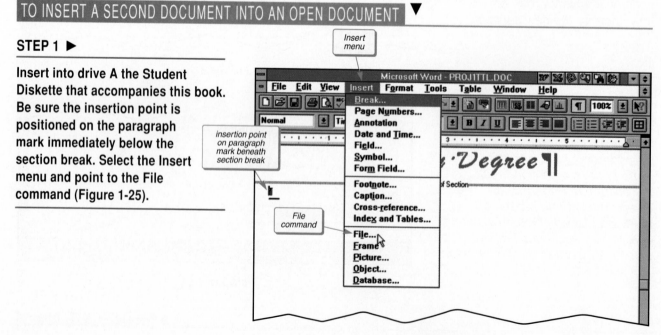

FIGURE 1-25

STEP 2 ▶

Choose the File command. In the File dialog box, click the Drives box arrow and select a:. Double-click the word subdirectory in the Directories list box. Point to the Find File (Find File...) button.

Word displays the File dialog box (Figure 1-26). A list of available files in the word subdirectory on drive A displays in the File Name list box.

FIGURE 1-26

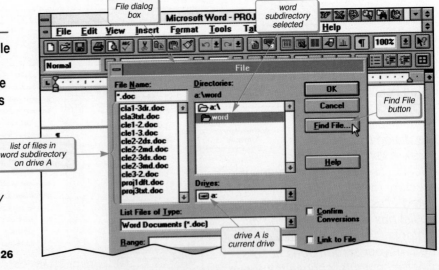

STEP 3 ▶

Choose the Find File button. When the Search dialog box displays, point to the Advanced Search (Advanced Search...) button.

Word displays the Search dialog box (Figure 1-27). Because Word documents have an extension of .doc, the default filename to search for is *.doc, which means all files with an extension of .doc. Because you want to search for *.doc files in the word subdirectory, you must choose the Advanced Search button, which allows you to specify subdirectories.

FIGURE 1-27

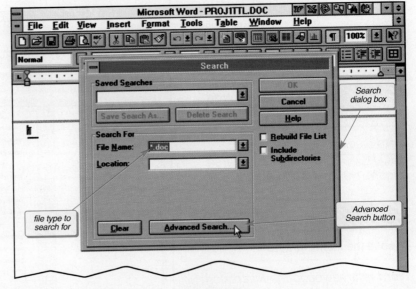

STEP 4 ▶

Choose the Advanced Search button. When the Advanced Search dialog box displays, choose the Add button (◄◄ Add).

Word displays the Advanced Search dialog box (Figure 1-28). The current drive and subdirectory display in the Directories list. The drive and subdirectory to be searched, a:\word, display in the Search In box. That is, you want to display files in the word subdirectory on drive A.

FIGURE 1-28

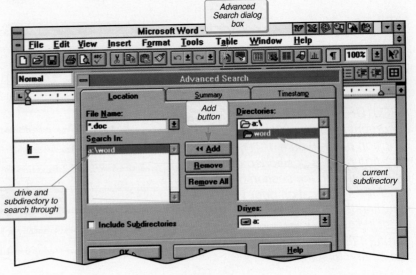

STEP 5 ▶

Choose the OK button in the
Advanced Search dialog box.
Choose the OK button in the Search
dialog box.

*Word displays the Find
File dialog box (Figure
1-29). A list of files on the
selected search drive (A) and subdirectory (word) displays in the
Listed Files list box. The first file in
the list box is highlighted, and its
contents display in the Preview of
area. (If your screen does not display file contents, choose the View
box arrow. Then, select Preview.)*

FIGURE 1-29

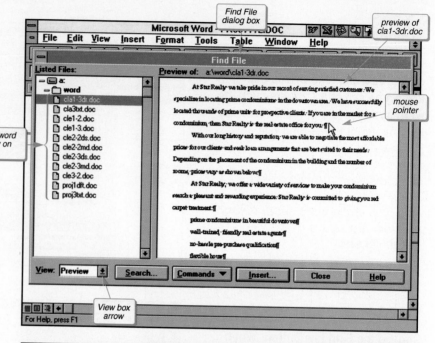

STEP 6 ▶

Select the filename proj1dft.doc by
clicking it. Point to the Insert button
(Insert...).

*Word displays the contents of
PROJ1DFT in the Preview of area
(Figure 1-30).*

STEP 7

Choose the Insert button.

*Word returns you to the File dialog
box.*

FIGURE 1-30

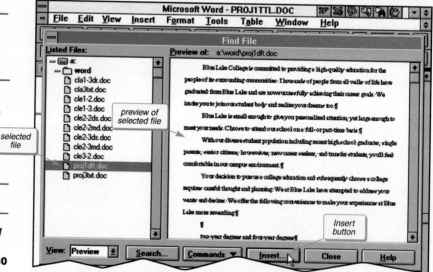

STEP 8 ▶

Choose the OK button in the File
dialog box. Press SHIFT+F5.

*Word inserts the file
PROJ1DFT into the open
document at the location of
insertion point (Figure 1-31). The
insertion point is positioned immediately beneath the section break,
which was its location prior to
inserting the new document.
Pressing SHIFT+F5 instructs Word
to return the insertion point to your
last editing location.*

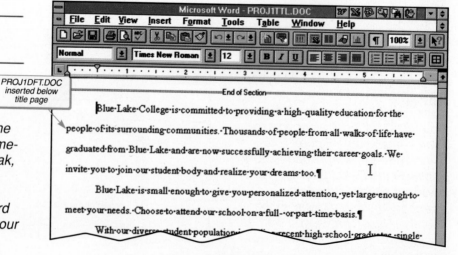

FIGURE 1-31

Word inserts the complete document immediately above the insertion point and positions the insertion point beneath the inserted document. If the insertion point is positioned in the middle of the first document, the first document continues after the end of the inserted document.

Previewing files before opening them is very useful if you have forgotten the name of a particular file. For this reason, you can choose the Find File command directly from the File menu. Once chosen, the Find File dialog box displays, as shown in Figure 1-29. The only difference is the Insert button is an Open button. Thus, you can open a file directly from the Find File command on the File menu, instead of using the File command on the Insert menu.

Word remembers your last three editing locations. Thus, you can press SHIFT+F5 up to three times to move the insertion point to prior editing locations in your document.

Saving the Active Document with a New Filename

The current filename in the title bar is PROJ1TTL.DOC, yet the active document contains both the title page and the draft of the sales proposal. Because you might want to keep the title page as a separate document called PROJ1TTL, you should save the active document with a new filename. If you save the active document by clicking the Save button on the Standard toolbar, Word will assign it the current filename. Thus, use the following steps to save the active document with a new filename.

TO SAVE AN ACTIVE DOCUMENT WITH A NEW FILENAME

Step 1: Insert the data disk into drive A.
Step 2: From the File menu, choose the Save As command.
Step 3: In the Save As dialog box, type the filename `proj1` in the File Name box. Do not press the ENTER key after typing the filename.
Step 4: If drive A is not the current drive, select it by clicking the Drives drop-down box arrow and selecting a:.
Step 5: Choose the OK button in the Save As dialog box.

Word saves the document with the filename PROJ1.DOC (see Figure 1-33 on page MSW21).

Printing the Document

To see a hardcopy of the newly formed file PROJ1, perform the following steps.

TO PRINT THE DOCUMENT

Step 1: Ready the printer.
Step 2: Click the Print button on the Standard toolbar.

When you remove the document from the printer, review it carefully. The printed document is shown in Figure 1-32 on the next page. (Depending on the printer driver you are using, your wordwrap may occur in different locations from what is shown in Figure 1-32.)

To make the body of the proposal more pleasing to the eye, you could add one or two tables, a chart, and a bulleted list. These enhancements to Project 1 are discussed in the following pages.

BLUE LAKE COLLEGE

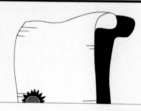

Blue Lake College is committed to providing a high-quality education for the people of its surrounding communities. Thousands of people from all walks of life have graduated from Blue Lake and are now successfully achieving their career goals. We invite you to join our student body and realize your dreams too.

Blue Lake is small enough to give you personalized attention, yet large enough to meet your needs. Choose to attend our school on a full- or part-time basis.

insert table here →

With our diverse student population including recent high school graduates, single parents, senior citizens, housewives, new career seekers, and transfer students, you'll feel comfortable in our campus environment.

insert table and chart here →

Your decision to pursue a college education and subsequently choose a college requires careful thought and planning. We at Blue Lake have attempted to address your wants and desires. We offer the following conveniences to make your experiences at Blue Lake more rewarding:

single-space and add diamond-shape bullets →

two-year degrees and four-year degrees

readily available advising and counseling services

high frequency of course offerings

professors with practical field experience

life experience credit

campus clubs and school-sponsored activities

adequate parking facilities

Obtaining a college degree is a personal decision, which could dramatically change your life. Blue Lake College would like to help you make your dream a reality. Call our Department of Admissions at (708) 555-3456 today and take advantage of our one class free-of-charge program so you can begin to experience the benefits of earning a college degree.

FIGURE 1-32

▶ SETTING AND USING TABS

Beneath the second paragraph of the sales proposal, you decide to add a table that displays the number of full-time and part-time students by gender at Blue Lake College. With Word, you can create tables by setting tab stops (like on a typewriter) or by using the Insert Table button (▦) on the Standard toolbar. For this first table, you will set tab stops; for the second table that will be added later, you will use the Insert Table button.

Recall that Word, by default, places tab stops at every .5-inch mark on the ruler. You can use these default tab stops or set your own custom tab stops. When you set a custom tab stop, Word clears all default tab stops to the left of the custom tab stop. You can also specify how the text will align at a tab stop: left, centered, right, or decimal. Tab settings are stored in the paragraph mark at the end of each paragraph. Thus, each time you press the ENTER key, the custom tab stops are carried forward to the next paragraph.

The first step in creating the table is to set custom tab stops for the heading lines in the table. The text in the first tab stop should be left-justified, the default; and the text in the last two tab stops should be centered. The steps on the following pages show how to set custom tab stops for the paragraph at the location of the insertion point.

TO SET CUSTOM TAB STOPS ▼

STEP 1 ▶

Position the insertion point at the end of the second paragraph (after the period following the word basis) and press the ENTER key twice. Point to the 1.25" mark on the ruler (Figure 1-33).

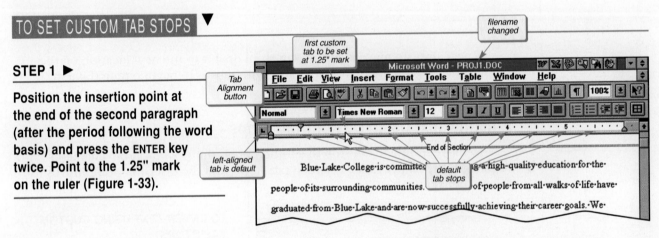

FIGURE 1-33

STEP 2 ▶

Click the left mouse button.

Word places a custom tab stop at the 1.25" mark on the ruler and removes the default tab stops at the .5" and 1" marks (Figure 1-34). The custom tab stop displays on the ruler as a small dark capital L (L), the same symbol inside the Tab Alignment button, which indicates the text entered at the tab stop will be left-justified. The next custom tab stop is to be centered.

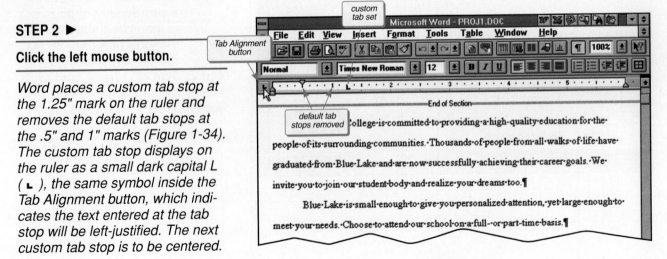

FIGURE 1-34

STEP 3 ▶

Click the Tab Alignment button. Click the 3.5" and 4.5" marks on the ruler.

The symbol inside the Tab Alignment button changes to an inverted capital T (▲), indicating the next custom tab stop set will be a centered tab stop (Figure 1-35). Word places a custom tab stop at the 3.5" and 4.5" marks on the ruler and removes the default tab stops between the 1.25" and 3.5" marks and between the 3.5" and 4.5" marks. The custom tab stops display on the ruler as inverted capital Ts, indicating text typed at the tab stops will be centered.

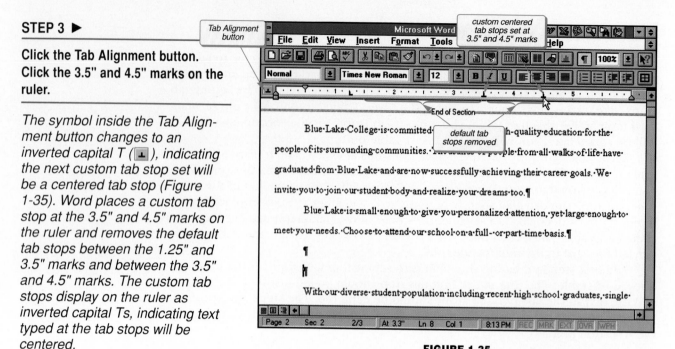

FIGURE 1-35

If necessary, to move a custom tab stop, drag it to the new location on the ruler. The next step in creating the table with tabs is to begin typing the text in the table.

Entering Text Using Custom Tab Stops

To move from one tab stop to another, press the TAB key. A tab character displays in the empty space between tab stops, and the insertion point moves to the next custom tab stop.

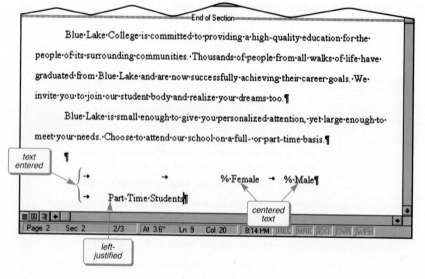

FIGURE 1-36

TO ENTER TEXT USING CUSTOM TAB STOPS

Step 1: Be sure the insertion point is positioned on the paragraph mark on line 8 in the sales proposal. Press the TAB key twice.

Step 2: Type % Female and press the TAB key.

Step 3: Type % Male and press the ENTER key.

Step 4: Press the TAB key and type Part-Time Students

The document window displays as shown in Figure 1-36.

Changing the Alignment of a Tab Stop

On the previous pages, you defined the tab stops at the 3.5" and 4.5" marks as centered tab stops because you wanted the titles of the table columns to be centered over the numbers in the table. The data in the table (the actual percentage values), however, have decimal points in the numbers. Typically, you align values such as these on the decimal point. To change the tab stops from centered tabs to decimal tabs, you must first clear the existing centered custom tabs and reset them to decimal tab stops. Then, you can finish the remaining entries in the table, as shown in the following steps.

TO CHANGE THE ALIGNMENT OF TAB STOPS ▼

STEP 1 ▶

Point to the 3.5" custom tab stop marker on the ruler (Figure 1-37).

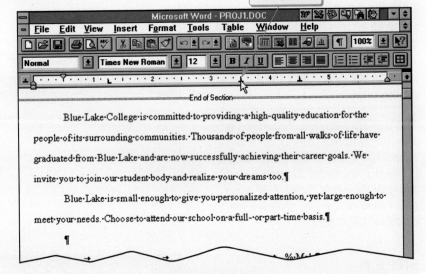

FIGURE 1-37

STEP 2 ▶

Drag the 3.5" custom tab stop marker down and out of the ruler. Point to the 4.5" custom tab stop marker on the ruler.

Word removes the 3.5" custom tab stop from the ruler (Figure 1-38).

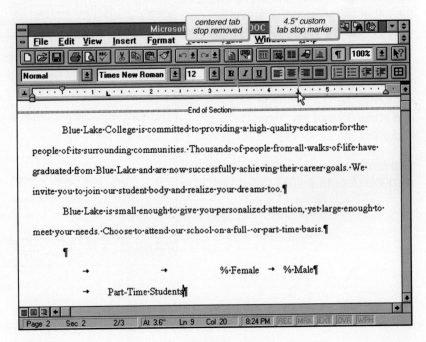

FIGURE 1-38

STEP 3 ▶

Drag the 4.5" custom tab
stop marker down and out of the
ruler. Point to the Tab Alignment
button on the ruler.

*Word removes the 4.5" custom tab
stop and fills to the right of the
1.25" mark with default tab stops
(Figure 1-39).*

STEP 4

Click the Tab Alignment button
twice so an inverted capital T with a
decimal point beside it displays on
the button's face ( ). Click the 3.5"
mark on the ruler. Click the 4.5" mark
on the ruler.

*Word places custom tab stops at
the 3.5" and 4.5" marks on the
ruler. The custom tab stops display
as inverted capital Ts with a decimal point beside them indicating
text typed at the tab stop will be
decimal-aligned.*

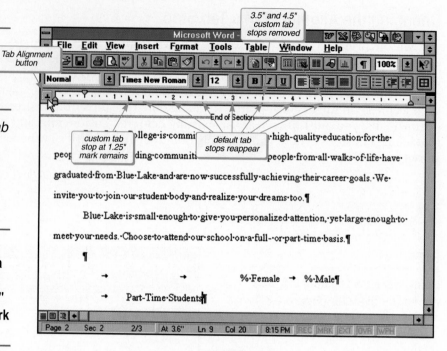

FIGURE 1-39

STEP 5 ▶

Be sure the insertion point is to
the left of the paragraph mark on
line 9. Press the TAB key, type `55.2`
and press the TAB key. Type `44.8`
and press the ENTER key. Press the
TAB key, type `Full-Time Students`
and press the TAB key. Type `47.8`
and press the TAB key. Type `52.2`
and press the ENTER key.

*The first table in the sales proposal
displays (Figure 1-40).*

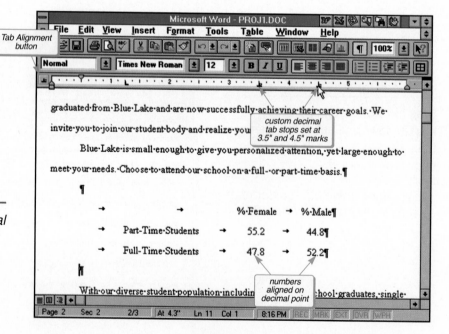

FIGURE 1-40

Adding a Caption to a Table

When you place tables into a document, you often put a title on the table. If you refer to the tables in the text of your document, it is convenient to add table numbers to your tables. Word provides a **caption** feature that keeps track of your table numbers. In this way, if you move, delete, or add a table, Word automatically renumbers the remaining tables in your document. Follow these steps to add a title to the table just created by using the Caption command.

TO ADD A CAPTION TO A TABLE ▼

STEP 1 ▶

Select the table to be titled by dragging the mouse pointer through the selection bar to the left of lines 8, 9, and 10 in the sales proposal. Select the Insert menu and point to the Caption command.

Word highlights the table to be captioned (Figure 1-41).

FIGURE 1-41

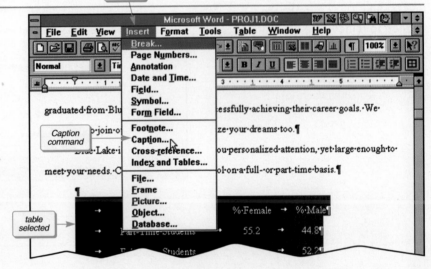

STEP 2 ▶

Choose the Caption command. In the Caption dialog box, click the Label box arrow and point to Table.

Word displays the Caption dialog box (Figure 1-42). In addition to tables, Word allows you to caption equations and figures. The default label is Figure.

FIGURE 1-42

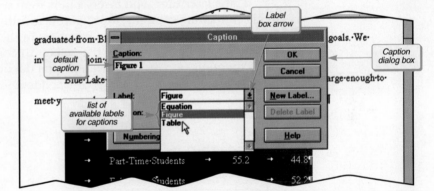

STEP 3 ▶

Select Table by clicking it. Click in the Caption box.

Word changes the caption label to Table 1 (Figure 1-43). The insertion point is in the Caption box.

STEP 4

Type : BLUE LAKE STUDENT STATUS BREAKDOWN and choose the OK button.

Word adds the caption above the table and places a square to the left of the caption.

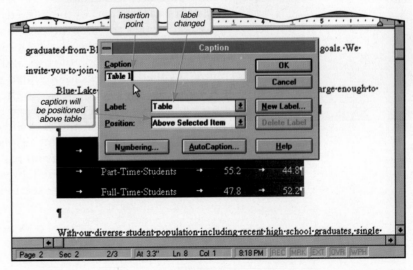

FIGURE 1-43

STEP 5 ▶

Select the caption by clicking in the selection bar to its left. Change its font size to 12 by clicking the Font Size box arrow on the Formatting toolbar and selecting 12 from the list. Center the caption by clicking the Center button on the Formatting toolbar. Click outside the caption to remove the highlight.

The caption for the table is complete (Figure 1-44).

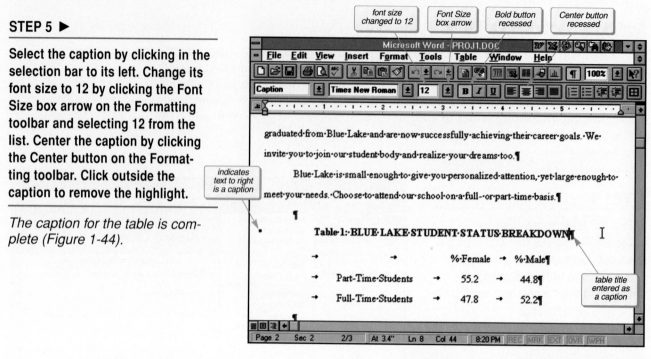

FIGURE 1-44

If, at a later time, you insert a new item with a caption or move or delete items containing captions, Word automatically updates caption numbers internally. To display the updated caption numbers in the document window, select the entire document by choosing the Select All command from the Edit menu, then press function key **F9**. When you print a document, Word automatically updates the caption numbers, regardless if the document window displays the updated caption numbers or not.

▶ CREATING A TABLE

Beneath the third paragraph of the sales proposal draft (Figure 1-32 on page MSW20), you decide to add another table. This time, however, you want to place a chart of the table data immediately below the table. One easy way to chart data is to enter the data into a Word table. Thus, you will use the Insert Table button to create this second table.

A Word **table** is a collection of rows and columns. The intersection of a row and a column is called a **cell**. Cells are filled with data. The data you enter within a cell wordwraps just as text does between the margins of a document.

Within a table, you can easily rearrange rows and columns, change column widths, sort rows and columns, and sum the contents of rows and columns. You can use Table Format to make the table display in a professional manner. You can also perform all character formatting and paragraph formatting to table data. For these reasons, many Word users create tables with the Insert Table button, instead of using tabs as discussed in the prior section.

Inserting an Empty Table

The first step is to insert an empty table into the document. When inserting a table, you must specify the total number of rows and columns, called the **dimension** of the table. Referring to Figure 1-45, this table contains seven rows and four columns, called a 7 x 4 (pronounced 7 by 4) table. If you initially insert a table with too few or too many rows and/or columns, you can easily add or delete rows and/or columns to or from the table.

Follow the steps below to insert a 7 x 4 table into Project 1.

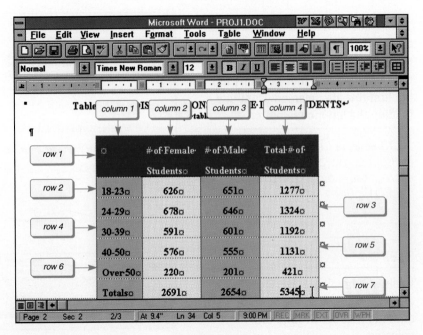

FIGURE 1-45

TO INSERT AN EMPTY TABLE ▼

STEP 1 ▶

Position the insertion point after the period following the word environment and press the ENTER key twice. Drag the first-line indent marker to the left margin. Click the Insert Table button on the Standard toolbar. Point to the upper left cell in the grid. Press and hold down the left mouse button.

Word displays a grid to define the dimensions of the desired table (Figure 1-46). The data in the table cells will be left-aligned with no first-line indent. If, when you drag the first-line indent marker, the document window scrolls to the left, click to the right of the scroll box on the horizontal scroll bar, then click to the left of the scroll box.

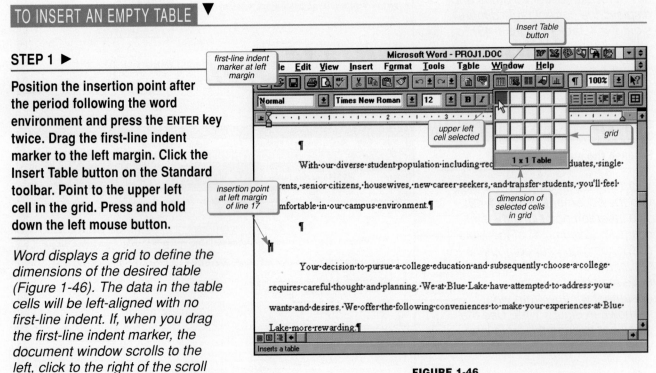

FIGURE 1-46

STEP 2 ▶

While still holding down the left mouse button, drag the mouse to the right until the first four columns in the first row are selected. Continue holding the left mouse button.

Word selects the first four columns in the first row and displays the current table dimension, 1 × 4 Table (Figure 1-47).

FIGURE 1-47

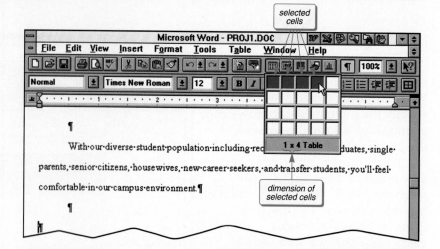

STEP 3 ▶

While still holding down the left mouse button, drag the mouse down until the first seven rows are selected.

Word selects a rectangular area of seven rows and four columns and displays the current table dimension: 7 × 4 Table (Figure 1-48).

FIGURE 1-48

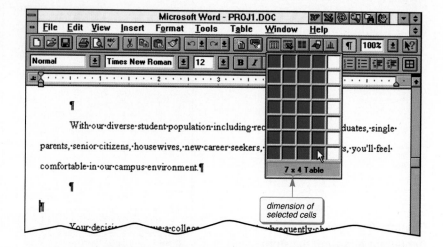

STEP 4 ▶

Release the mouse button.

Word inserts an empty 7 × 4 table into the document (Figure 1-49). The insertion point is in the first cell (row 1 column 1) of the table. (Depending on your computer's setup, more or less of the table may display in the document window from what is shown in Figure 1-49. Use the scroll bar to bring the table into view.)

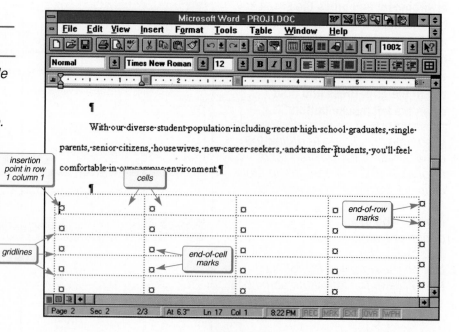

FIGURE 1-49

The table displays on the screen with dotted **gridlines**. If your table does not have gridlines, choose the Gridlines command from the Table menu. Word does not print the table with gridlines; instead, the gridlines display to help you identify in which row and column you are working. Each row has an **end-of-row mark**, which is used to add columns to the right of a table. Each cell has an **end-of-cell mark**, which is used to select a cell. A cell is the intersection of a row and a column. Notice the end-of-cell marks are currently left-justified within each cell, indicating the data will be left-justified within the cells.

Entering the Data into the Table

The first step is to enter the data into the table. To advance from one column to the next, press the TAB key. To advance from one row to the next, also press the TAB key; do not press the ENTER key. The ENTER key is used to begin new paragraphs within a cell. Perform the following steps to enter the data into the table.

TO ENTER DATA INTO THE TABLE

Step 1: With the insertion point in row 1 column 1, press the TAB key. Type # of Female Students and press the TAB key. Type # of Male Students and press the TAB key. Type Total # of Students and press the TAB key.

Step 2: Type 18-23 and press the TAB key. Type 626 and press the TAB key. Type 651 and press the TAB key twice.

Step 3: Type 24-29 and press the TAB key. Type 678 and press the TAB key. Type 646 and press the TAB key twice.

FIGURE 1-50

Step 4: Type 30-39 and press the TAB key. Type 591 and press the TAB key. Type 601 and press the TAB key twice.

Step 5: Type 40-50 and press the TAB key. Type 576 and press the TAB key. Type 555 and press the TAB key twice.

Step 6: Type Over 50 and press the TAB key. Type 220 and press the TAB key. Type 201 and press the TAB key twice.

Step 7: Type Totals

The table data displays (Figure 1-50).

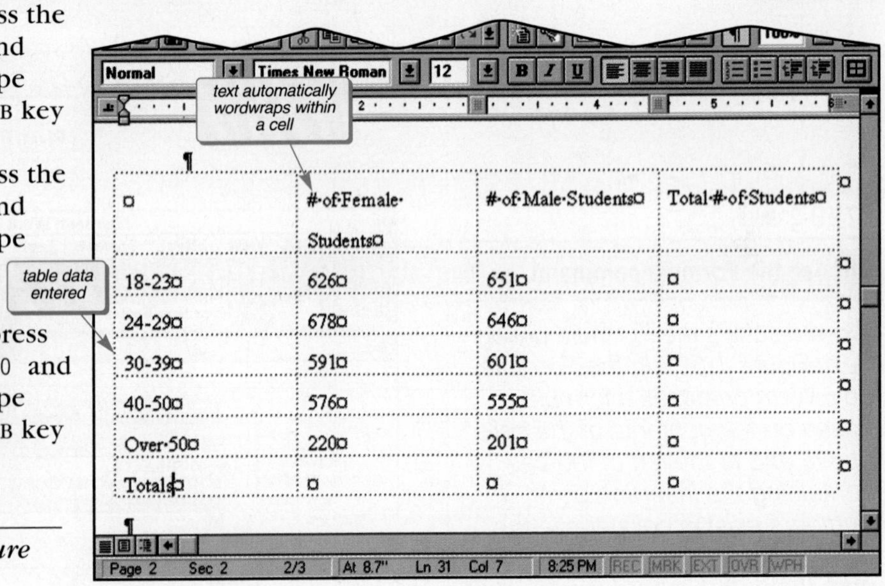

You modify the contents of cells just as you modify text in a document. To delete the contents of a cell, select the cell contents and press the DELETE key. To modify text within a cell, position the insertion point in the cell by clicking in the cell; then, correct the entry. You can double-click the OVR indicator on the status bar to toggle between insert and overtype modes. You may also drag and drop or cut and paste the contents of cells.

Because the TAB key advances you from one cell to the next in a table, press **CTRL+TAB** to insert a tab into a cell.

Summing Rows and Columns in a Table

Word can add together, or **SUM**, the contents of cells in a table. Follow these steps to sum the number of female and male students in rows 2 through 6 (see Figure 1-55).

TO SUM THE CONTENTS OF CELL ROWS ▼

STEP 1 ▶

Position the insertion point in the cell where you want the sum to display (row 2 column 4) by clicking in the cell. Select the Table menu and point to the Formula command.

The insertion point is in row 2 column 4 to calculate the total number of students in the 18-23 age range (Figure 1-51).

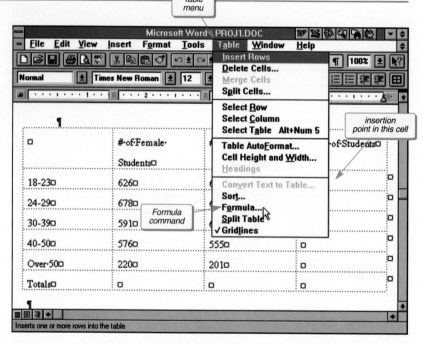

FIGURE 1-51

STEP 2 ▶

Choose the Formula command.

Word displays the Formula dialog box (Figure 1-52). In the Formula box, Word proposes a formula based on the contents of the cells above and to the left of the cell containing the insertion point. If numbers exist in cells above the insertion point, Word proposes to sum them. If numbers exist in cells to the left of the insertion point, Word suggests to sum them. If numbers exist in cells above and to the left of the insertion point, Word guesses which cells to sum. You can change Word's formula proposal.

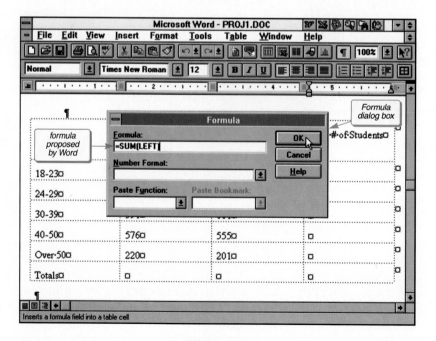

FIGURE 1-52

STEP 3 ▶

Choose the OK button in the Formula dialog box. Position the insertion point in the next cell to contain a sum, row 3 column 4 (total students in 24-29 age range).

Word places the sum 1277 in the Total # of Students column for the age range 18-23 (Figure 1-53).

FIGURE 1-53

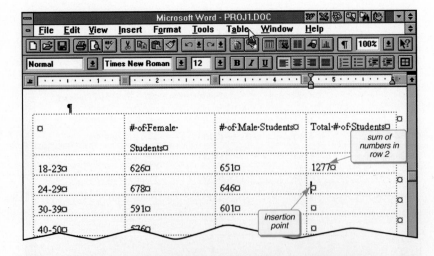

STEP 4 ▶

From the Table menu, choose the Formula command. In the Formula dialog box, select the word ABOVE by dragging the mouse pointer through it. Be sure not to select the parentheses surrounding the word ABOVE.

Word suggests to sum the cells above the insertion point (Figure 1-54). You want to sum cells to the left of the insertion point.

STEP 5

Type left and choose the OK button in the Formula dialog box.

Word sums the numbers in the third row of the table for the age range 24-29.

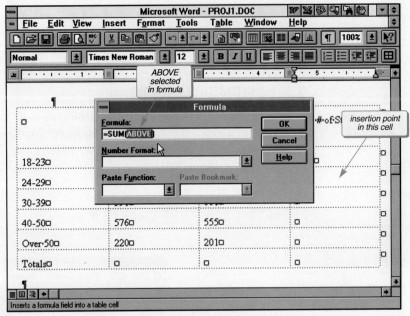

FIGURE 1-54

STEP 6 ▶

Repeat the procedures in Steps 4 and 5 for the Total # of Students column in rows 4 through 6.

The row totals display (Figure 1-55).

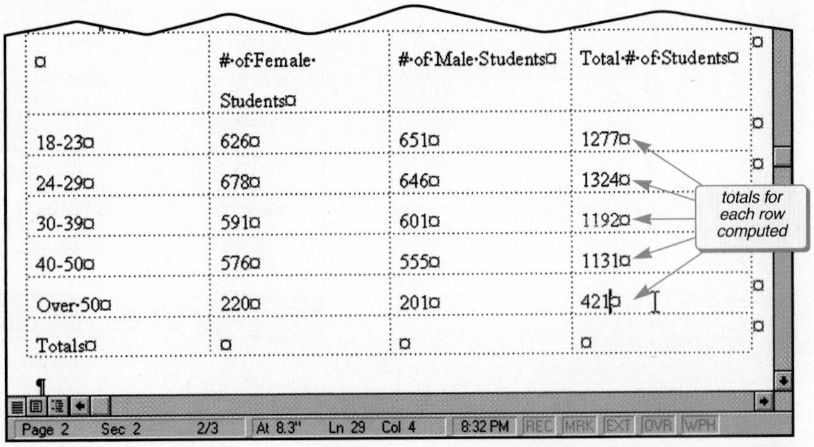

FIGURE 1-55

The next step is to sum the contents of columns 2, 3, and 4, as shown in the following steps.

FIGURE 1-56

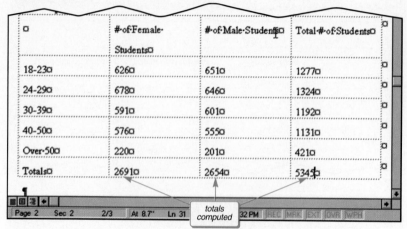

TO SUM THE CONTENTS OF COLUMNS

Step 1: Click in the cell to contain the total (row 7 column 2).

Step 2: From the Table menu, choose the Formula command.

Step 3: Choose the OK button in the Formula dialog box.

Step 4: Repeat Steps 1 through 3 for columns 3 and 4 of row 7.

The column totals display (Figure 1-56).

Formatting a Table

Instead of formatting a table yourself, Word provides thirty-four predefined formats for tables. These predefined formats vary the borders, shading, colors, and font for the cells within a table. Follow these steps to format the table with the Table AutoFormat command.

TO FORMAT A TABLE WITH TABLE AUTOFORMAT ▼

STEP 1 ►

With the mouse pointer somewhere in the table, click the right mouse button to display a shortcut menu. Point to the Table AutoFormat command in the shortcut menu.

Word displays a shortcut menu for tables (Figure 1-57).

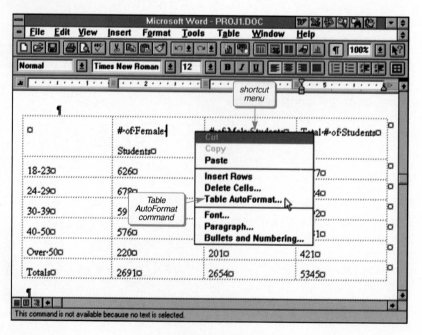

FIGURE 1-57

STEP 2 ▶

Choose the Table AutoFormat command. In the Table AutoFormat dialog box, click the Color check box to turn color on for the table. Point to the Formats list down scroll arrow.

Word displays the Table AutoFormat dialog box (Figure 1-58). The first predefined table format, Simple 1, is selected in the Formats list, and a preview of the selected format displays in the Preview area.

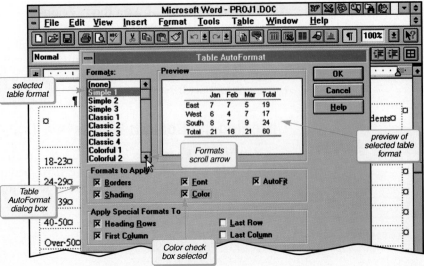

FIGURE 1-58

STEP 3 ▶

Hold down the left mouse button while pointing to the Formats list down scroll arrow until the Columns 3 format displays. Select Columns 3 by clicking it. Point to the OK button.

Word displays a preview of the Columns 3 format (Figure 1-59).

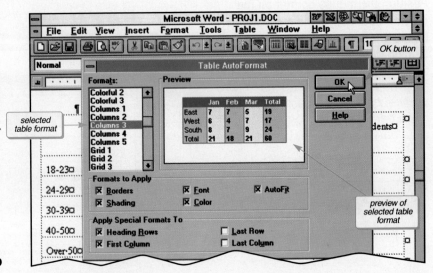

FIGURE 1-59

STEP 4 ▶

Choose the OK button.

Word formats the table according to the Columns 3 format (Figure 1-60).

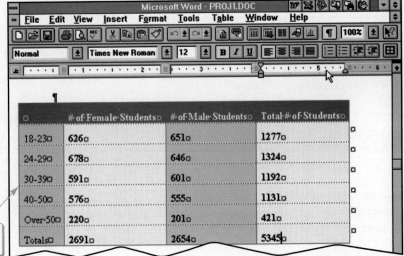

FIGURE 1-60

Notice in Figure 1-60 on the previous page that Word changed the widths of the columns in the table. Because the AutoFit check box was selected (Figure 1-59 on the previous page) in the Table AutoFormat dialog box, Word redefines column widths based on the cell containing the longest data item. Thus, the column widths are now equal to the column titles. The next step is to change these column widths.

Changing the Column Widths in a Table

You adjust the widths of columns in a table by dragging the column boundaries. A **column boundary** is the vertical gridline immediately to the right of a column. The following steps show how to change the column widths in a table.

TO CHANGE THE COLUMN WIDTHS IN A TABLE ▼

STEP 1 ▶

Position the mouse pointer on the column boundary to be moved; that is, the gridline to the right of the # of Female Students column.

The mouse pointer changes to two vertical bars with an arrow next to each bar (◄||►) when on a column boundary (Figure 1-61).

FIGURE 1-61

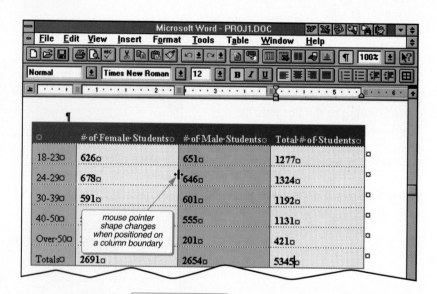

STEP 2 ▶

Press and hold down the ALT key while you drag the column boundary until the column width measurement on the ruler reads approximately 0.85".

Because you press the ALT key while dragging the column boundary, Word displays the width of the columns in inches on the ruler (Figure 1-62). A vertical dotted line moves with the mouse pointer so you can see the new column width.

FIGURE 1-62

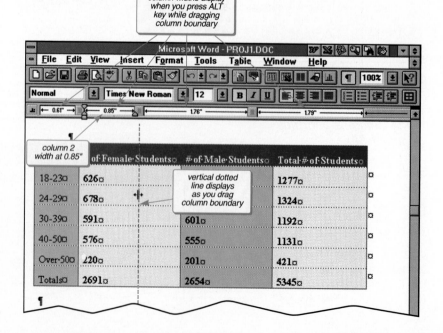

STEP 3 ▶

Release the mouse and the ALT key.

Word resizes column 2 to be 0.85"
(Figure 1-63).

STEP 4

Point to the column boundary to the right of the # of Male Students column.

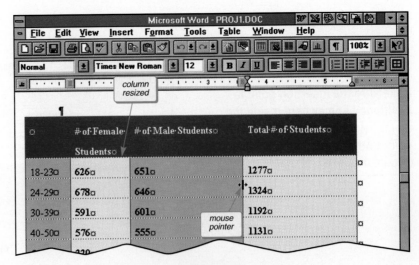

FIGURE 1-63

STEP 5 ▶

Press and hold down the ALT key while you drag the column boundary until the column width measurement on the ruler reads approximately 0.85". Point to the column boundary to the right of the Total # of Students column. Press and hold down the ALT key while you drag the column boundary until the column width measurement on the ruler reads approximately 0.85".

All of the columns in the table are resized (Figure 1-64).

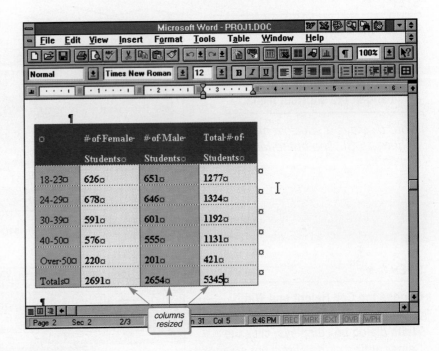

FIGURE 1-64

The next step is to center the table between the left and right margins of the document.

Centering a Table

The table is currently positioned at the left margin. According to Figure 1-1b on page MSW4, the table should be centered between the left and right margins. You cannot use the Center button on the Formatting toolbar to center the table because this button is used to center the contents of the cells. To center the entire table, you must first select it and then center it using the Cell Height and Width command, as shown in the steps on the next page.

TO CENTER A TABLE ▼

STEP 1 ▶

Make sure the insertion point is positioned somewhere inside the table. Select the Table menu and point to the Select Table command (Figure 1-65).

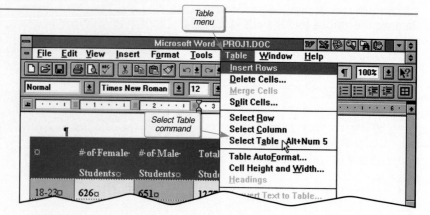

FIGURE 1-65

STEP 2 ▶

Choose the Select Table command. Click the right mouse button in the table to display a shortcut menu. Point to the Cell Height and Width command in the shortcut menu.

Word displays a shortcut menu (Figure 1-66). The entire table is highlighted.

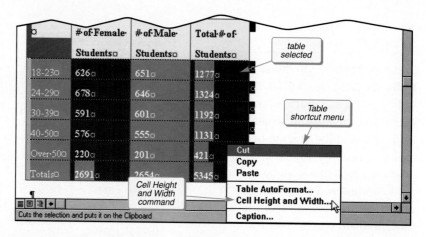

FIGURE 1-66

STEP 3 ▶

Choose the Cell Height and Width command. When the Cell Height and Width dialog box displays, click the Center option in the Alignment area.

Word displays the Cell Height and Width dialog box (Figure 1-67). The Center option in the Alignment area is selected.

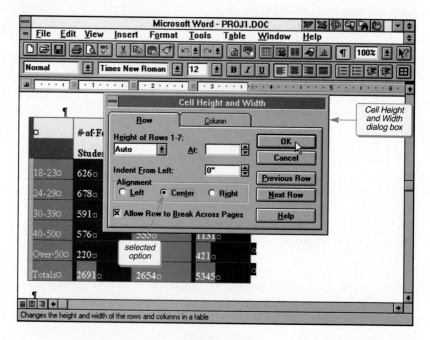

FIGURE 1-67

STEP 4 ▶

Choose the OK button in the Cell Height and Width dialog box. Click in the table to remove the selection.

Word centers the table between the left and right margins of the document (Figure 1-68).

FIGURE 1-68

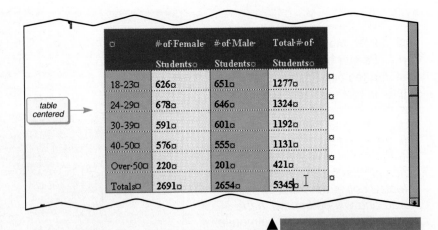

When looking at the table in Figure 1-68, you decide the age ranges in column 1 should be bold, like the rest of the data in the table. One method of accomplishing this task would be to select each of the cells and then click the Bold button on the Formatting toolbar. Another technique is to use the Format Painter button, which copies existing formatting from a specified location to another.

Using the Format Painter Button

Because the data in row 2 column 2 is bold and you want to bold the data in column 1 cells, you can copy the bold format from the cell at row 2 column 2 to the cells in column 1. To do this, you must first select the cell that contains the formatting to be copied. You select a cell by pointing to the **cell selection bar,** which is an unmarked area about 1/4" wide at the left edge of the cell, and clicking the left mouse button. When the mouse pointer is in the cell selection bar, it changes to a right-pointing block arrow. Because the cells you are copying the formatting to are in a column, you select the entire column by pointing to the **column selection bar,** which is an unmarked area about 1/4" wide above the gridline at the top of the column. When the mouse pointer is in the column selection bar, it changes to a downward-pointing arrow (↓). Follow these steps to use the Format Painter button on the Standard toolbar to copy formatting.

TO USE THE FORMAT PAINTER BUTTON ▼

STEP 1 ▶

Point in the cell selection bar of the cell formatting to be copied (row 2 column 2).

The mouse pointer changes to a right-pointing block arrow when in the cell selection bar (Figure 1-69).

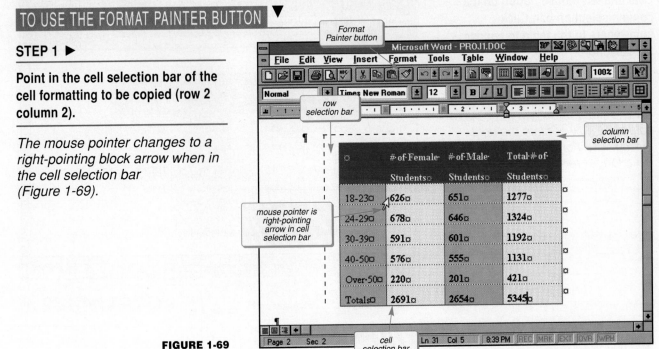

FIGURE 1-69

STEP 2 ▶

Click the left mouse button. Click the Format Painter button on the Standard toolbar. Position the mouse pointer in the document window.

Word highlights the cell at row 2 column 2 (Figure 1-70). The Format Painter button is recessed, indicating the format in the selected cell is temporarily being stored and will be copied to the next cell(s) you select. The mouse pointer changes to an I-beam with a small paint brush () when the Format Painter button is recessed.

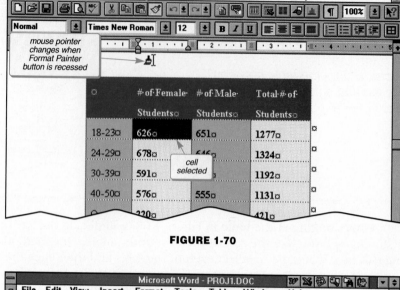

FIGURE 1-70

STEP 3 ▶

Point to the column selection bar at the top of column 1.

The mouse pointer changes to a downward-pointing arrow on the column selection bar (Figure 1-71).

FIGURE 1-71

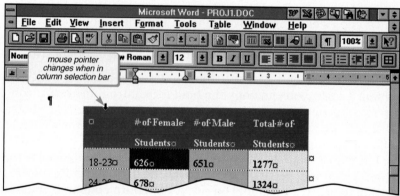

STEP 4 ▶

Click the left mouse button on the column selection bar. Click somewhere in the table to remove the selection.

Word copies the selected formatting to the selected column (Figure 1-72). All of the data in the cells of column 1 now contain the bold format. The Format Painter button is no longer recessed.

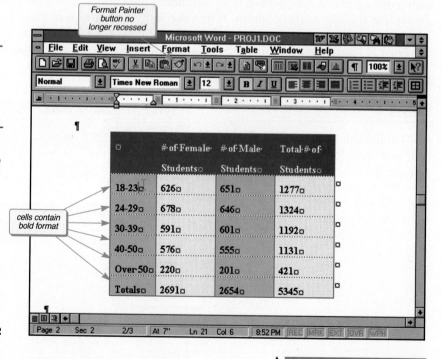

FIGURE 1-72

If you want to copy character formatting to multiple locations in a document, double-click the Format Painter button. Select each location to which you want the format copied. When you are finished copying the character formatting, click the Format Painter button again to restore the normal I-beam pointer.

Just as with paragraphs, you can left-align, center, or right-align the end-of-cell marks in a table. The next step is to center the number of students in the cells.

Changing the Alignment of Text Within Cells

The data you enter into the cells is by default left-aligned. You can change the alignment just as you would for a paragraph. You must first select the cell(s) before changing its alignment. Follow these steps to center the end-of-cell marks ( ) for cells that contain the number of student values (see Figure 1-74).

TO CENTER END-OF-CELL MARKS ▼

STEP 1 ▶

Point to the first end-of-cell mark to be centered (row 2 column 2). Drag the mouse to highlight all the cells to be centered (columns 2, 3, and 4 of rows 2 through 7).

Word selects columns 2, 3, and 4 of the last six rows in the table (Figure 1-73). The mouse pointer points to the bottom right cell in the table (row 7 column 4).

FIGURE 1-73

STEP 2 ▶

Click the Center button on the Formatting toolbar. Click in the table to remove the highlight.

Word centers the end-of-cell marks in the selected area (Figure 1-74). The Center button is recessed.

FIGURE 1-74

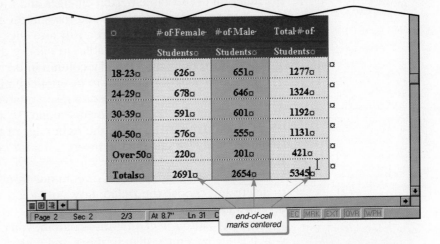

The final step in creating the table is to add a caption to it, as shown in the steps on the next page.

TO ADD A CAPTION TO A TABLE

Step 1: Be sure the insertion point is somewhere in the table. Select the table by choosing the Select Table command from the Table menu.

Step 2: With the mouse pointer in the selection, click the right mouse button to display a shortcut menu. From the shortcut menu, choose the Caption command.

Step 3: In the Caption dialog box, if Table is not displayed in the Label box, click the Label box arrow and select Table.

Step 4: In the Caption dialog box, click in the Caption box and type : AGE DISTRIBUTIONS OF BLUE LAKE STUDENTS and choose the OK button.

Step 5: Select the caption by clicking in the selection bar to its left. Click the Center button on the Formatting toolbar. Change the font size to 12 by clicking the Font Size box arrow and selecting 12 in the list.

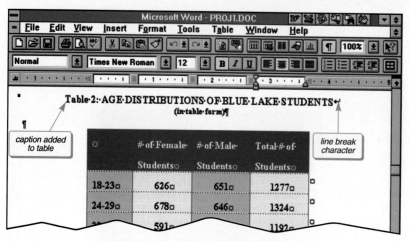

FIGURE 1-75

Step 6: Click outside the selection to remove the highlight. Move the insertion point to the end of the caption (immediately following the last S in STUDENTS). Press SHIFT+ENTER to create a line break. Change the font size to 10 by clicking the Font Size box arrow and selecting 10. Type (in table form) and press the ENTER key.

The caption displays above the table (Figure 1-75).

At times, you might want to add additional rows or columns to a table. To add a row to the end of a table, position the insertion point in the bottom right corner cell and press the TAB key. Depending on the task you want to perform in a table, the function of the Table button changes and the commands in the Table and associated shortcut menu change. To add rows in the middle of a table, select the row below where you want to insert a row and click the Insert Rows button (the same button you clicked to insert a table) or choose the Insert Rows command from the Table or shortcut menu. To add a column in the middle of a table, select the column to the right of where you want to insert a column and click the Insert Columns button (the same button you clicked to insert a table) or choose the Insert Columns command from the Table or shortcut menu. To add a column to the right of a table, select the end-of-row marks at the right edge of the table, then click the Insert Columns button or choose the Insert Columns command from the Table or shortcut menu.

If you want to delete rows or columns from a table, select the rows or columns to delete and choose the Delete Rows or Delete Columns command from the Table or shortcut menu.

Recall that to select an entire column, you click in the column selection bar, which is the area immediately above and including the gridline at the top of a column. The mouse pointer changes to a solid down-pointing arrow when in the column selection bar. To select an entire row, you click in the **row selection bar,** which is an unmarked area about 1/4" wide to the left of a row gridline. The mouse pointer changes to a right-pointing arrow in the row selection bar.

▶ CHARTING A TABLE

When you use the Insert Table button to create a table, Word can easily convert the data you enter in the table into a chart by using an embedded charting application called **Microsoft Graph**. With Microsoft Graph, you can chart all or part of a table. Because Microsoft Graph is an embedded application, it has its own menus and commands. With these commands, you can easily change the appearance of any chart. The following steps illustrate how to chart the Age Distributions table just created (see Figure 1-83 on page MSW43).

NOTE: If your installation is Microsoft Office 4.2 or you have Excel 5, a Chart-Wizard dialog box may display instead of the Microsoft Graph window. If this happens, follow the steps outlined on page MSW43.

TO CHART A TABLE ▼

STEP 1 ▶

Select the first six rows of the table by dragging the mouse pointer through the row selection bar to the left of each of the first six rows. Point to the Insert Chart button (📊) on the Standard toolbar.

Word highlights the first six rows in the table (Figure 1-76).

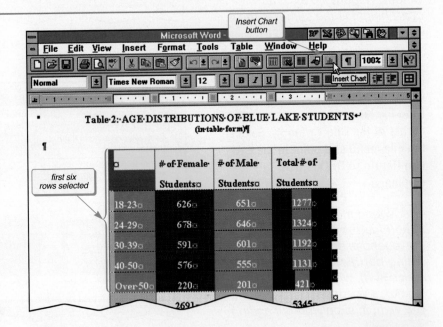

FIGURE 1-76

STEP 2 ▶

Choose the Insert Chart button. Move the mouse pointer to the left border of the Chart window.

*Word opens the Microsoft Graph application (Figure 1-77). The selected rows in the table display in a **Datasheet window**, and the chart of the datasheet displays in a **Chart window**. The document window displays in a window behind the Microsoft Graph window. The mouse pointer changes to a double-headed arrow when on the border of a window. If your screen displays a ChartWizard dialog box, go to the steps on page MSW43.*

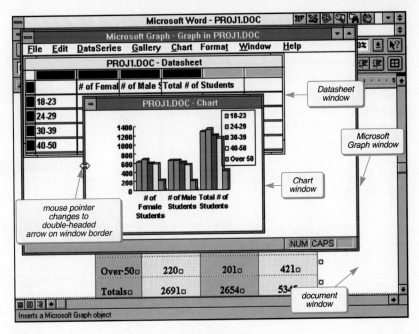

FIGURE 1-77

STEP 3 ▶

Drag the mouse to the left edge of the Microsoft Graph window. Drag the right edge of the Chart window to the right edge of the Microsoft Graph window. Drag the top edge of the Chart window to the top edge of the Datasheet window. Move the mouse pointer into the legend in the Chart window.

The chart width is now the same as the Microsoft Graph window (Figure 1-78). The chart height is the same as the Datasheet window.

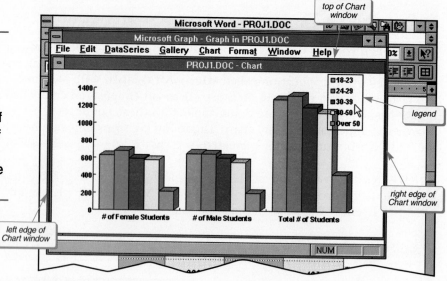

FIGURE 1-78

STEP 4 ▶

Drag the legend to the upper right corner of the Chart window. Select the File menu and point to the Exit and Return to PROJ1.DOC command.

The legend moves to the right (Figure 1-79). When the legend is selected, it displays **sizing handles**, *which are used to resize it. (If, when you drag the legend, it is not positioned where you want it, simply drag it again.)*

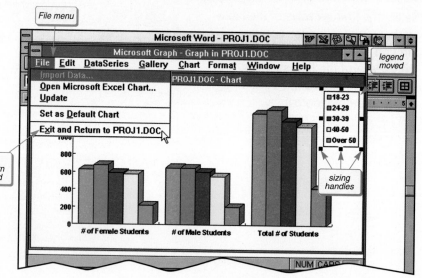

FIGURE 1-79

STEP 5 ▶

Choose the Exit and Return to PROJ1.DOC command. Point to the Yes button.

Word displays a Microsoft Graph dialog box, asking if you want to place the chart into PROJ1.DOC (Figure 1-80).

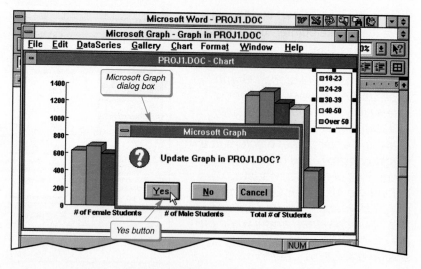

FIGURE 1-80

STEP 6 ▶

Choose the Yes button.

Word closes the Microsoft Graph application and places the chart beneath the table in PROJ1.DOC (Figure 1-81).

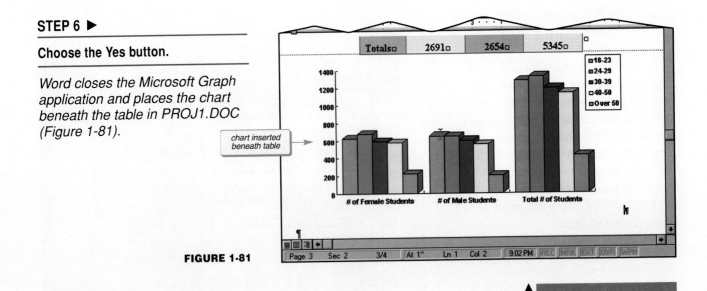

FIGURE 1-81

To modify an existing chart in the document, double-click on the chart to reopen the Microsoft Graph application. Then, you can make any necessary changes to the chart. When you close the Microsoft Graph window, Word displays the Microsoft Graph dialog box in Figure 1-80 to confirm that you want the changes to take effect in your document.

If, when you click the Insert Chart button, your screen displays a ChartWizard dialog box, you have Microsoft Graph 5.0 on your system. In this case, the layout of your final chart will be different and it will have different colors. With the ChartWizard on your screen, follow these steps.

TO CREATE A CHART WITH MICROSOFT GRAPH 5.0 CHARTWIZARD ON THE SCREEN

Step 1: Choose the Finish button in the ChartWizard – Step 1 of 4 dialog box. Word then displays the selected table rows in a Datasheet window.

Step 2: Close the Datasheet window by double-clicking its Control-menu box. When the Datasheet window is closed, the chart displays in the Word document window with sizing handles, which are used to resize it. Although you are working on the Word screen, you are still in the Microsoft Graph 5.0 application. Notice the Standard toolbar is different, and the commands in the menus have changed.

Step 3: Resize the chart by dragging its sizing handles. It should resemble the chart in Figure 1-81.

Step 4: Click outside the chart to exit from Microsoft Graph 5.0 and return to Word. Notice the Standard and Formatting toolbars reappear on the screen. The chart remains selected in Word. You can also resize the selected chart in Word by dragging its sizing handles.

Creating a Caption for a Figure

Just as you add captions to tables, you can add captions to figures, as shown in the steps on the next page.

TO ADD A CAPTION TO A FIGURE ▼

STEP 1 ▶

Select the chart by clicking in it. With the mouse pointer in the selected chart, click the right mouse button. From the shortcut menu, choose the Caption command. In the Caption dialog box, click the Label box arrow and select Figure. Click the Position box arrow and point to Above Selected Item.

Word displays the Caption dialog box (Figure 1-82). The default placement for captions of figures is below the figure. You want the caption above the figure. The chart in the document is selected. Selected charts display sizing handles at the corner and center locations.

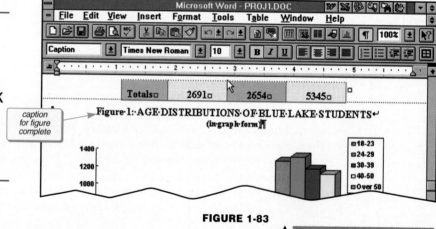

FIGURE 1-82

STEP 2 ▶

Select Above Selected Item in the Caption dialog box by clicking it. Click the Caption box and type
`: AGE DISTRIBUTIONS OF BLUE LAKE STUDENTS` **and choose the OK button. Follow the procedures in Steps 5 and 6 on page MSW40, substituting the word table with graph, to complete the caption.**

The caption for the figure is complete (Figure 1-83).

FIGURE 1-83

▶ ADDING FINISHING TOUCHES TO THE DOCUMENT

You decide to perform two more tasks to this document: add bullets to the list of Blue Lake conveniences and add a header to the document.

Adding Custom Bullets to a List

You can add the default bullets, small circles, to a list by selecting the list and clicking the Bullets button on the Formatting toolbar. In this project, you do not want the default bullets; instead you want the diamond-shaped bullets. To add bullets other than the default, use the Bullets and Numbering command from the Format menu.

Follow these steps to add diamond-shaped bullets to the list of conveniences at Blue Lake College. Because all of the paragraphs in the document are double-spaced and you want the list to be single-spaced, you must change the spacing to single and then add the bullets.

TO ADD CUSTOM BULLETS TO A LIST ▼

STEP 1 ►

Select the paragraphs in the list to be single-spaced, including the paragraph mark above the list. Press CTRL+1 to single space the list. Click the right mouse button in the selection to display a shortcut menu. Point to the Bullets and Numbering command in the shortcut menu.

The paragraphs are single-spaced and highlighted (Figure 1-84). The shortcut key combination, CTRL+1, single-spaces selected text.

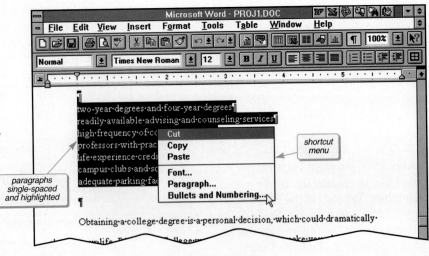

FIGURE 1-84

STEP 2 ►

Choose the Bullets and Numbering command. When the Bullets and Numbering dialog box displays, click the solid diamond-shaped bullets and point to the OK button.

Word displays the Bullets and Numbering dialog box (Figure 1-85). The diamond-shaped bulleted list sample has a box around it, indicating it is selected.

FIGURE 1-85

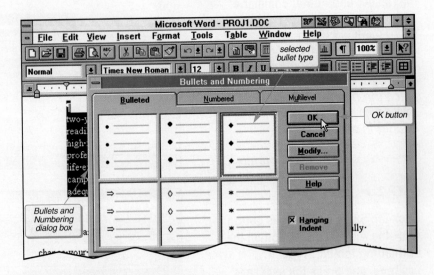

STEP 3 ►

Choose the OK button. Click outside the selection to remove the highlight.

Word places solid diamond-shaped bullets to the left of each paragraph (Figure 1-86).

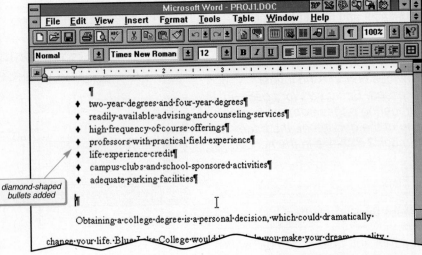

FIGURE 1-86

Adding a Header to the Sales Proposal

You want the college name and page number to display on the sales proposal; you do not, however, want the header on the title page. Recall that the title page and the body of the sales proposal are in separate sections. You do not want a header in section 1, but you do want one in section 2. When you initially create a header, Word assumes you want it in all sections. Thus, you must instruct Word not to place the header in section 1, as shown in these steps.

TO ADD A HEADER TO THE SALES PROPOSAL ▼

STEP 1 ▶

Double-click the word Page on the status bar to display the Go To dialog box. Type 2 in the Enter Page Number box and click the Go To button to move the insertion point to the top of Page 2. Click the Close button. From the View menu, choose the Header and Footer command.

Word displays the Header and Footer toolbar (Figure 1-87). The Same as Previous button (▤) is recessed, which instructs Word to place the header in the previous section. You do not want this header in section 1.

FIGURE 1-87

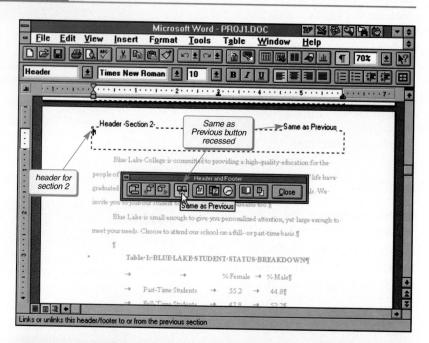

STEP 2 ▶

Click the Same as Previous button. Click the Align Right button on the Formatting toolbar. Type Blue Lake College and press the SPACEBAR. Click the Page Numbers button on the Header and Footer toolbar.

Word displays the header for section 2 (Figure 1-88). The Same as Previous button is no longer recessed. Because Word begins numbering pages from the beginning of the document, the page number 2 displays in the header.

STEP 3

Choose the Close button.

Headers and footers do not display on the screen in normal view.

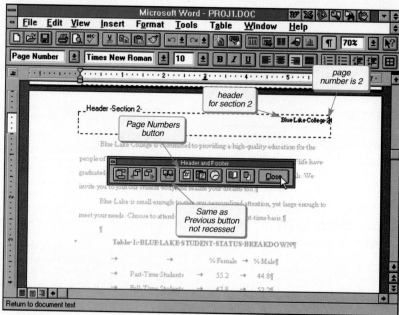

FIGURE 1-88

In Figure 1-88 the page number is a 2. You want to begin numbering the body of the sales proposal with a number 1. Thus, you need to instruct Word to begin numbering the pages in section 2 with the number 1, as shown below.

TO CHANGE THE STARTING PAGE NUMBER IN A SECTION ▼

STEP 1 ▶

Select the Insert menu and point to the Page Numbers command (Figure 1-89).

FIGURE 1-89

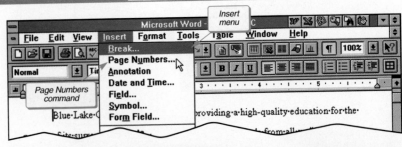

STEP 2 ▶

Choose the Page Numbers command. When the Page Numbers dialog box displays, point to the Format button (Format...).

Word displays the Page Numbers dialog box (Figure 1-90).

FIGURE 1-90

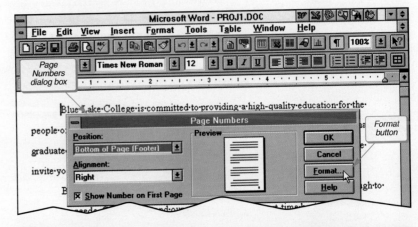

STEP 3 ▶

Choose the Format button. When the Page Number Format dialog box displays, select the Start At option in the Page Numbering area.

Word displays the Page Number Format dialog box (Figure 1-91). The number 1 displays in the Start At box by default.

STEP 4

Choose the OK button in the Page Number Format dialog box. Choose the Close button in the Page Numbers dialog box.

Word changes the starting page number for section 2 to the number 1.

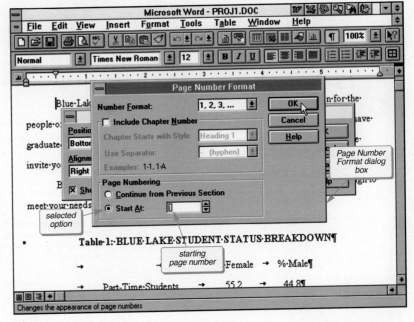

FIGURE 1-91

Check the spelling of the document. Save the document one final time and print the sales proposal. The printed document displays, as shown in Figure 1-92 on the next page.

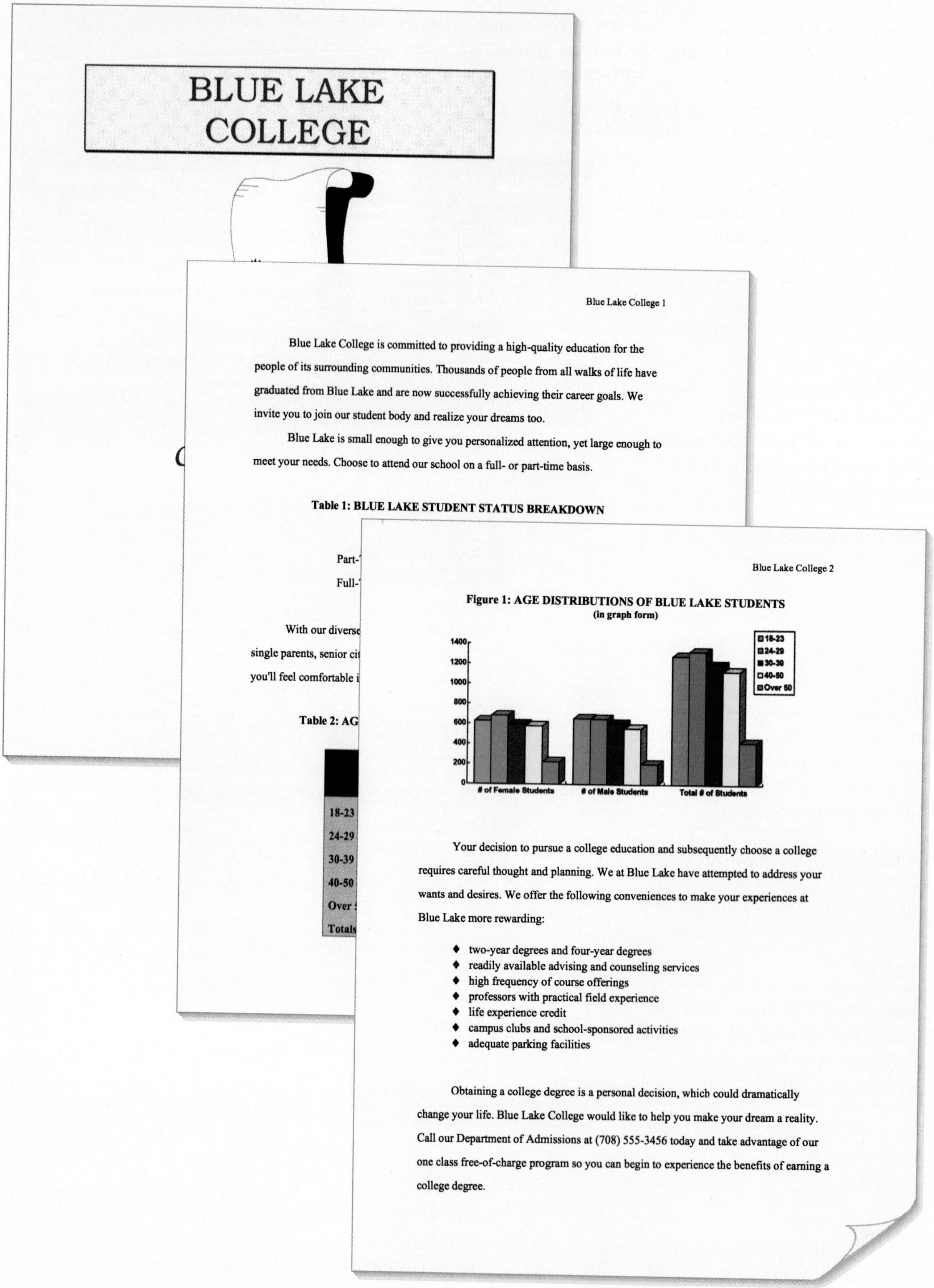

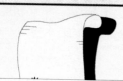

BLUE LAKE COLLEGE

Blue Lake College 1

Blue Lake College is committed to providing a high-quality education for the people of its surrounding communities. Thousands of people from all walks of life have graduated from Blue Lake and are now successfully achieving their career goals. We invite you to join our student body and realize your dreams too.

Blue Lake is small enough to give you personalized attention, yet large enough to meet your needs. Choose to attend our school on a full- or part-time basis.

Table 1: BLUE LAKE STUDENT STATUS BREAKDOWN

Part-

Full-

With our diverse

single parents, senior cit

you'll feel comfortable i

Table 2: AG

18-23
24-29
30-39
40-50
Over 5
Totals

Blue Lake College 2

Figure 1: AGE DISTRIBUTIONS OF BLUE LAKE STUDENTS
(in graph form)

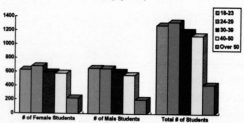

Your decision to pursue a college education and subsequently choose a college requires careful thought and planning. We at Blue Lake have attempted to address your wants and desires. We offer the following conveniences to make your experiences at Blue Lake more rewarding:

- two-year degrees and four-year degrees
- readily available advising and counseling services
- high frequency of course offerings
- professors with practical field experience
- life experience credit
- campus clubs and school-sponsored activities
- adequate parking facilities

Obtaining a college degree is a personal decision, which could dramatically change your life. Blue Lake College would like to help you make your dream a reality. Call our Department of Admissions at (708) 555-3456 today and take advantage of our one class free-of-charge program so you can begin to experience the benefits of earning a college degree.

FIGURE 1-92

▶ PROJECT SUMMARY

Project 1 introduced you to creating a proposal using tables and charts. First, you created a title page with a graphic, drop shadow, shading, color, and characters in a variety of font sizes. You learned how to insert an existing document into the active document. Then, you saved the active document with a new file-name. Next, you set custom tabs and used them to create a table. You used a caption to title the table. Then, you used the Insert Table button to create a second table. You formatted the table with a prede-fined Word table format. You opened Microsoft Graph to chart the second table. Finally, you added diamond-shaped bullets to a list of items and created a header for the second section of the document.

▶ KEY TERMS AND INDEX

caption (*MSW25*)
cell (*MSW26*)
cell selection bar (*MSW37*)
chart a table (*MSW41*)
Chart window (*MSW41*)
color characters (*MSW9*)
column boundary (*MSW34*)
column selection bar (*MSW37*)
CTRL+1 (*MSW45*)
CTRL+TAB (*MSW29*)
custom bullets (*MSW44*)
Datasheet window (*MSW41*)
dimension (*MSW27*)
end-of-cell mark (*MSW29*)

end-of-row mark (*MSW29*)
existing document (*MSW16*)
expanded (*MSW12*)
F9 (*MSW26*)
Font command (*MSW9*)
Formula command (*MSW30*)
gridlines (*MSW29*)
Insert Columns command (*MSW40*)
Insert Rows command (*MSW40*)
Microsoft Graph (*MSW41*)
open document (*MSW16*)
planning proposal (*MSW2*)
preview (*MSW16*)

research proposal (*MSW2*)
row selection bar (*MSW40*)
sales proposal (*MSW2*)
section break (*MSW15*)
sections (*MSW15*)
set custom tabs (*MSW21*)
shading (*MSW9*)
shadow box border (*MSW7*)
SHIFT+F5 (*MSW18*)
sizing handles (*MSW42*)
SUM (*MSW30*)
tab stops (*MSW21*)
table (MSW26)

Q U I C K   R E F E R E N C E

In Microsoft Word 6, you can accomplish a task in a number of ways. The following table provides a quick reference to each task presented in this project with its available options. The commands listed in the Menu column can be executed using either the keyboard or mouse. Some of the commands in the Menu column are also available in shortcut menus. If you have WordPerfect help activated, the key combinations listed in the Keyboard Shortcuts column will not work as shown.

Task	Mouse	Menu	Keyboard Shortcuts
Add a Caption to a Table or Figure		From Insert menu, choose Caption	
Add Color to Characters		From Format menu, choose Font	
Add Custom Bullets		From Format menu, choose Bullets and Numbering	
Add a Shadow Box Border		From Format menu, choose Borders and Shading	
Center a Selected Table		From Table menu, choose Cell Height and Width	
Change the Starting Page Number in a Section		From Insert menu, choose Page Numbers	
Change the Top Margin	Click Page Layout View button on scroll bar	From File menu, choose Page Setup	

(continued)

QUICK REFERENCE (continued)

Task	Mouse	Menu	Keyboard Shortcuts
Change the Space Between Characters		From Format menu, choose Font	
Clear a Custom Tab Stop	Drag tab stop marker down and out of ruler	From Format menu, choose Tabs	
Copy a Character Format	Click Format Painter button on Standard toolbar		
Delete a Selected Table Row or Column		From Table menu, choose Delete Rows or Delete Columns	
Find a File		From File menu, choose Find File	
Format a Table		From Table menu, choose Table AutoFormat	
Insert a Second Document into an Open Document		From Insert menu, choose File	
Insert an Empty Table	Click Insert Table button on Standard toolbar	From Table menu, choose Insert Table	
Insert a Section Break		From Insert menu, choose Break	
Insert a Tab Character into a Table Cell			Press CTRL+TAB
Insert a Table Column		From Table menu, choose Insert Column	
Insert a Table Row		From Table menu, choose Insert Rows	
Return to the Last Editing Location			Press SHIFT+F5
Save a Document with a New Filename		From File menu, choose Save As	Press F12
Select a Table		From Table menu, choose Select Table	Press ALT+5 on numeric keypad
Select a Table Cell	Click in cell selection bar		
Select a Table Column	Click in column selection bar	From Table menu, choose Select Column	Press ALT+click left mouse button
Select a Table Row	Click in row selection bar	From Table menu, choose Select Row	
Set Custom Tab Stops	Click desired location on ruler	From Format menu, choose Tabs	
Single-Space Paragraphs		From Format menu, choose Paragraph	Press CTRL+1
Sum Table Rows and Columns		From Table menu, choose Formula	
Update Caption Numbers			Select entire document; then press F9

STUDENT ASSIGNMENT 1
True/False

Instructions: Circle T if the statement is true or F if the statement is false.

T   F   1. A sales proposal offers a product or service to existing or potential customers.

T   F   2. To add a shadow box border around selected paragraphs, click the Borders button on the Formatting toolbar.

T   F   3. Color is added to characters using the Font dialog box.

T   F   4. All documents have at least one section.

T   F   5. A section break displays on the screen as a double dotted line separated by the words End of Section.

T   F   6. To expand the spacing between characters, click the Expand button on the Formatting toolbar.

T   F   7. In the Find File dialog box, you can preview the contents of files.

T   F   8. To save an active file with a new filename, click the Save As button on the Standard toolbar.

T   F   9. When you set a custom tab stop, Word clears all default tabs to the left of the custom tab stop.

T   F   10. To center text at a custom tab stop, click the Center button before entering the text.

T   F   11. To clear a custom tab stop, drag the tab stop down and out of the ruler.

T   F   12. A Word table is a collection of rows and columns.

T   F   13. The intersection of a table row and table column is called a cell.

T   F   14. You should turn off the gridlines before printing a table if you do not want the gridlines in your hardcopy.

T   F   15. To move from one table column to the next, press the TAB key.

T   F   16. To delete the contents of a cell, select the cell and press the DELETE key.

T   F   17. To sum the contents of a table row, select the row and click the AutoSum button on the Standard toolbar.

T   F   18. To delete a row from a table, select the row and choose the Delete Rows command from the Table menu or the shortcut menu.

T   F   19. Microsoft Graph is an embedded charting application that enables you to chart the data in a table.

T   F   20. To change the starting page number for a section, choose the Page Numbers command from the Insert menu.

STUDENT ASSIGNMENT 2
Multiple Choice

Instructions: Circle the correct response.

1. If, during the course of creating a document, you would like to change the _____, you must create a new section.
    a. margins   b. paper size   c. page number position   d. all of the above

2. To return the insertion point to your last editing location, press _____.
    a. F5   b. SHIFT+F5   c. CTRL+F5   d. ALT+F5

3. The Tab Alignment button is located on the _____.
    a. Standard toolbar   b. Formatting toolbar   c. ruler   d. status bar

(continued)

STUDENT ASSIGNMENT 2 (continued)

4. With Word, you can insert a second document _____.
   a. at the beginning of an active document
   b. in the middle of an active document
   c. at the end of an active document
   d. all of the above

5. To set a custom tab stop in Word, _____.
   a. click the Tab button on the Formatting toolbar
   b. click on the desired tab stop location on the ruler
   c. choose the Custom command from the Tab menu
   d. click the Set Tab button on the Standard toolbar

6. A table with 9 rows and 3 columns is referred to as a _____ table.
   a. 3×9 b. 9×3 c. 27   d. 12

7. To add a caption to a table, select the table and _____.
   a. click the Caption button on the Standard toolbar
   b. click the Caption button on the Formatting toolbar
   c. choose the Caption command from the Insert menu
   d. either a or c

8. In a table, the cell selection bar is located _____.
   a. at the left edge of a cell   b. at the right edge of a cell
   c. at the bottom edge of a cell   d. at the top edge of a cell

9. When in the column selection bar, the mouse pointer changes to a(n) _____.
   a. left-pointing arrow (↖)   b. right-pointing arrow (↗)
   c. up-pointing arrow (↑)   d. down-pointing arrow (↓)

10. To open the Microsoft Graph application, _____.
    a. click the Insert Chart button on the Standard toolbar
    b. choose the Microsoft Graph command from the Tools menu
    c. exit Word for Windows and double-click the Microsoft Graph program-item icon
    d. none of the above

STUDENT ASSIGNMENT 3
Understanding the Steps to Color Characters

Instructions: Fill in the Step numbers below to correctly order the process of coloring characters.

Step _____: In the Font dialog box, click the Color box arrow to display the list of available colors.

Step _____: Click the right mouse button in the selection to display a shortcut menu.

Step _____: Click outside the selection to remove the highlight.

Step _____: Select the characters to be colored.

Step _____: Choose the Font command from the shortcut menu.

Step _____: Choose the OK button in the Font dialog box.

Step _____: Select the desired color from the list.

STUDENT ASSIGNMENT 4
Understanding Custom Tab Stops

Instructions: Answer the questions below regarding Figure SA1-4. The numbers in the figure correspond to question numbers.

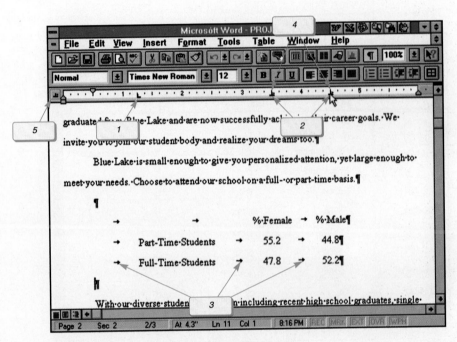

FIGURE SA1-4

1. What is the alignment of the tab stop at the 1.25" mark? _____

2. What is the alignment of the tab stops at the 3.5" and 4.5" marks? _____

3. Why do the right-pointing arrows appear between the tab stops? _____

4. What do the small dots at the 3.5" and 4.5" marks indicate? _____

5. What is this button used for? _____

STUDENT ASSIGNMENT 5
Understanding Tables

Instructions: In Figure SA1-5, arrows point to several items on the table. In the spaces provided, briefly identify each area. Then answer the questions concerning the table.

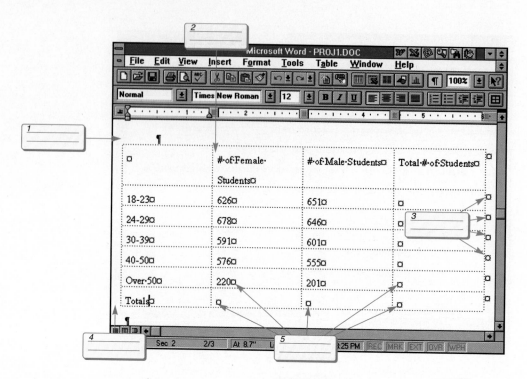

FIGURE SA1-5

1. How many rows and columns does this table have? _____

2. How do you advance from one table cell to the next? _____

3. How do you insert a tab character into a cell? _____

STUDENT ASSIGNMENT 6
Understanding the Microsoft Graph Window

Instructions: In Figure SA1-6, arrows point to several areas of the Microsoft Graph window. In the spaces provided, briefly identify each area.

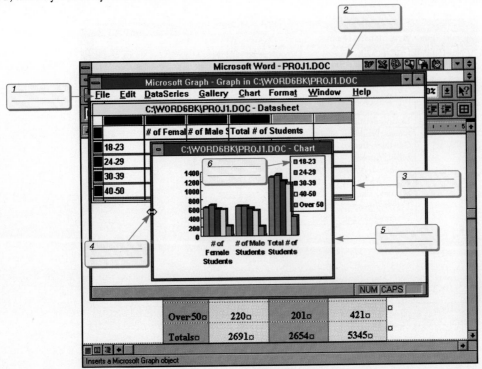

FIGURE SA1-6

COMPUTER LABORATORY EXERCISES

COMPUTER LABORATORY EXERCISE 1
Using the Help Menu to Learn About Tabs and Tables

1. From the Help menu, choose the Search for Help on command. Type `tabs` and press the ENTER key. Select Setting tab stops. Choose the Go To button. Read and print the information.
2. Choose the Close button. Choose the Search button. Choose the Show Topics button. Select Tab stops tips. Choose the Go To button. Read and print the information.
3. Choose the Search button. Choose the Show Topics button. Select Clearing or moving tab stops. Choose the Go To button. Read and print the information.
4. Choose the Close button. Choose the Search button. Choose the Show Topics button. Select Inserting a tab character in a cell. Choose the Go To button. Read and print the information.
5. Choose the Close button. Choose the Search button. Type `tables, creating` and press the ENTER key. Select Overview of Working with Tables. Choose the Go To button. Read and print the information.
6. Choose the Search button. Choose the Show Topics button. Choose the Go To button. Read and print the information.
7. Choose the Close button. Close the Word Help window.

COMPUTER LABORATORY EXERCISE 2
Adding Formulas and a Caption to a Table

Instructions: Start Word. Open the document CLE1-2 from the Word subdirectory on the Student Diskette that accompanies this book. The document is shown in Figure CLE1-2.

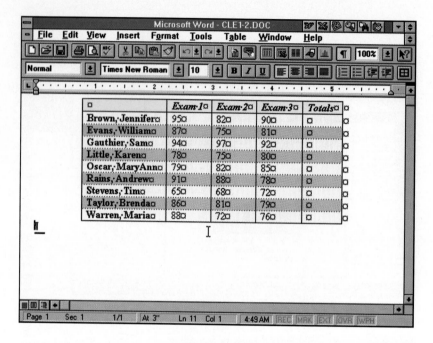

FIGURE CLE1-2

Perform the following tasks:

1. Position the mouse pointer in the fifth column of the second row.
2. From the Table menu, choose the Formula command.
3. Choose the OK button in the Formula dialog box.
4. Position the mouse pointer in the fifth column of the third row.
5. From the Table menu, choose the Formula command.
6. Select the word ABOVE in the proposed formula. Type left and choose the OK button in the Formula dialog box.
7. Repeat the procedure in Step 4 through Step 6 for the next seven rows.
8. From the Table menu, choose the Select Table command.
9. With the mouse pointer in the selected table, click the right mouse button to display a shortcut menu. From the shortcut menu, choose the Caption command.
10. In the Caption dialog box, change the label to Table by clicking the Label box arrow and selecting Table. Click in the Caption box and type : Student Exam Grades and choose the OK button.
11. Select the caption by clicking in the selection bar to its left. Center the caption by clicking the Center button on the Formatting toolbar. Change the font size to 12.
12. Save the revised document with the filename CLE1-2A.
13. Print the document.
14. From the File menu, choose the Close command.

COMPUTER LABORATORY EXERCISE 3
Adding a Shadow Box Border and Color to Paragraphs and Characters

Instructions: Start Word. Open the document CLE1-3 from the Word subdirectory on the Student Diskette that accompanies this book. The document is shown in Figure CLE1-3. The document resembles the college name on the title page of the sales proposal created in Project 1.

FIGURE CLE1-3

Perform the following tasks:

1. Select the paragraphs containing the college name by dragging the mouse through the selection bar to the left of lines 1 and 2.
2. From the Format menu, choose the Borders and Shading command.
3. If the Borders options do not display, click the Borders tab. In the Paragraph Borders and Shading dialog box, click the Shadow option in the Presets area; click 2 1/4 pt in the Style area; click the Color box arrow and select Red.
4. Click the Shading tab in the Paragraph Borders and Shading dialog box. Click 10% in the Shading list and choose the OK button.
5. With the mouse pointer still in the selected college name, click the right mouse button to display a shortcut menu.
6. Choose the Font command from the shortcut menu.
7. If the Font options do not display, click the Font tab. In the Font dialog box, click the Color box arrow and select Red. Choose the OK button.
8. Click outside the selection to remove the highlight.
9. Save the revised document with the filename CLE1-3A using the Save As command on the File menu.
10. Print the document by clicking the Print button on the Standard toolbar.
11. From the File menu, choose the Close command to close the document.

COMPUTER LABORATORY ASSIGNMENT 1
Creating a Proposal Using Tabs

Purpose: To become familiar with adding a shadow box border with shading and color, adding diamond-shaped bullets to a list, and using tabs to create a table.

Problem: You are on the town board of Clifton Heights. The board has recently funded the construction of a new public library. As a recent graduate in the field of creative arts, you have been asked to write an informal sales proposal (Figures CLA1-1a and CLA1-1b) to be sent to all community residents, announcing the new public library and explaining its benefits.

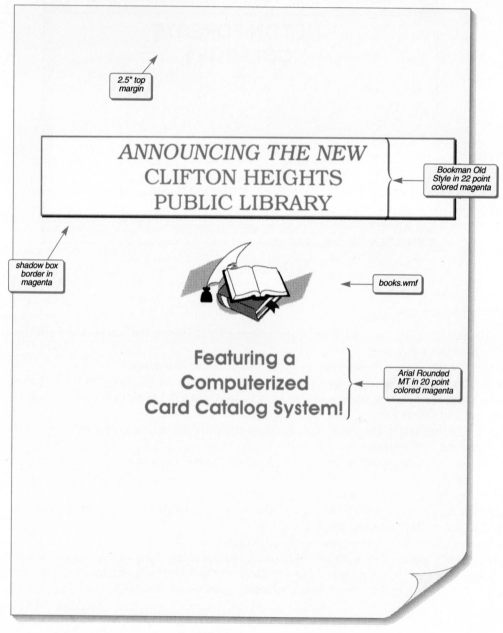

FIGURE CLA1-1a

Clifton Heights Public Library is conveniently located near you and has been designed to provide the community with a variety of information.

Our shelves are stocked with materials for your reading pleasure, as well as for your reference. We have a huge selection of each of the following:

- non-fiction books
- fiction books
- reference materials
- periodicals
- newspapers
- pamphlets
- video tapes
- compact discs and cassettes
- children's books, magazines, and tapes

You may check availability, as well as check out any, of these items directly through our computerized card catalog system. For demonstrations of how to use our computerized card catalog system, stop by the library at any of the times listed below:

bold and underlined →

COMPUTERIZED CARD CATALOG DEMONSTRATIONS

When?	Where?	A.M. Times?	P.M. Times?
Weekdays	Room A	9, 10, 11	2, 3, 4, 6, 7
Weekends	Room B	8, 9, 10, 11	1, 2, 3, 4

We also have four personal computers and six typewriters in our library for your use at any time.

We are open on weekdays from 8:30 a.m. to 8:30 p.m. and on weekends from 7:30 a.m. to 5:30 p.m. We are located at 1029 South Western Boulevard in Clifton Heights. Our telephone number is 989-555-1234.

centered and expanded by 3 points →

VISIT YOUR SOURCE FOR INFORMATION TODAY!

FIGURE CLA1-1b

(continued)

COMPUTER LABORATORY ASSIGNMENT 1 (continued)

Instructions: Perform the following tasks:

1. If it is not already recessed, click the Show/Hide ¶ button on the Standard toolbar.
2. Create the title page (as shown in Figure CLA1-1a on page MSW58).
3. Insert a section break. Return to the normal style. Adjust line spacing to double.
4. Create the body of the proposal (as shown in Figure CLA1-1b on the previous page). The body of the proposal has a single-spaced list with diamond-shaped bullets and a table created with tabs. The tabs are set at .875", 2", 3.125", and 4.375". The table title is a caption. Once you have inserted the caption, you will need to select it, change its font size to 12, underline it, and bold it.
5. Spell check the document.
6. Save the document with the filename CLA1-1.
7. View the document in print preview.
8. Print the document from within print preview.

COMPUTER LABORATORY ASSIGNMENT 2
Creating a Proposal Using the Insert Table and Insert Chart Buttons

Purpose: To become familiar with adding a shadow box border with shading and color, creating a table, and charting the table.

Problem: You are director of the Placement Office at The Computer Institute (TCI). You are currently on a campaign to recruit new students. Your major theme is guaranteed job placement for all graduates. You have been assigned the task of developing the proposal in Figures CLA1-2a and 1-2b on the following pages for prospective students.

Instructions: Perform the following tasks:

1. If it is not already recessed, click the Show/Hide ¶ button on the Standard toolbar.
2. Create the title page (as shown in Figure CLA1-2a).
3. Insert a section break. Return to the normal style. Adjust line spacing to double.
4. Create the body of the proposal (as shown in Figure CLA1-2b on page MSW62). The body of the proposal has a table created with the Insert Table button. The first four rows of the table are charted with the Insert Chart button. The table and chart have titles created with the Caption command.
5. Spell check the document.
6. Save the document with the filename CLA1-2.
7. View the document in print preview.
8. Print the document from within print preview.

FIGURE CLA1-2a

(continued)

COMPUTER LABORATORY ASSIGNMENT 2 (continued)

We at The Computer Institute (TCI) are so confident in our educational process that we <u>guarantee</u> job placement when you acquire your degree. We have placed thousands of graduates in computer programming, office automation, and systems analysis and design jobs. Our placement reputation speaks for itself.

Table 1: JOB PLACEMENT STATISTICS (in table form)

	Number of Graduates	Number of Placements
Computer Programming	1438	1429
Office Automation	954	954
Systems Analysis & Design	1276	1273
Totals	3668	3656

Grid 8 table format →

Figure 1: JOB PLACEMENT STATISTICS (in graph form)

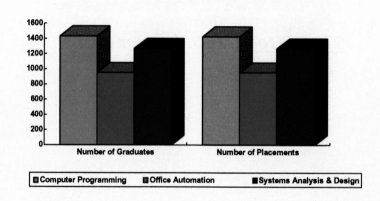

As you can see, we have a nearly **<u>100%</u>** success rate in placement of our graduates!

10 point bold → **CONTACT OUR ADMISSIONS OFFICE AT 555-2020 FOR DETAILS ON OUR PROGRAMS**

FIGURE CLA1-2b

COMPUTER LABORATORY ASSIGNMENT 3
Enhancing a Draft of a Proposal

Purpose: To become familiar with adding a shadow box border with shading and color, inserting an existing document into an active document, saving an active document with a new filename, creating a table with tabs, creating a table with the Insert Table button and charting the table, and adding a single-spaced bulleted list.

Problem: You are the owner of Star Realty. One of your employees has drafted an informal sales proposal to be sent to prospective clients in the downtown area. You decide to add pizzazz to the proposal by creating a title page. You also add a couple of tables and a chart to the body of the proposal.

Instructions: Perform the following tasks:

1. If it is not already recessed, click the Show/Hide ¶ button on the Standard toolbar.
2. Create the title page (as shown in Figure CLA1-3a on the next page).
3. Insert the draft of the body of the proposal beneath the title page using the File command from the Insert menu. The draft is called CLA1-3DR in the Word subdirectory on the Student Diskette that accompanies this book. The draft of the body of the proposal is shown in Figure CLA1-3b on page MSW65.
4. Add the following table, created with tabs, below the first paragraph in the proposal. Double-space the table and set custom tabs at 1", 2.5", and 4". Above the table as a caption, center, bold, and underline the title STAR REALTY CONDOMINIUM SALES.

	# of Prospects	# of Units Sold
This Year	2230	2039
Last Year	2098	1892

5. Use the Insert Table button to create the following table below the second paragraph in the proposal. Double-space the table. Above the table as a caption, center and bold the first line of the title AVERAGE CONDOMINIUM PRICES. Type (in table form) in 10 point, single-spaced below the first title line.

	Lower Floors of Building	Upper Floors of Building
2 Rooms	$100,000	$175,000
3 Rooms	$120,000	$235,000
4 Rooms	$135,000	$265,000
5 Rooms	$155,000	$300,000
6 Rooms	$195,000	$345,000
7 Rooms	$210,000	$365,000

6. Select all rows in the table and chart the table using the Insert Chart button. In the Microsoft Graph application, resize the chart so it is easy to read. Use the same caption as for the table, except change the word table to graph.
7. Single-space and add diamond-shaped bullets to the list of items beneath the third paragraph.
8. Save the active document with the filename CLA1-3 using the Save As command in the File menu.
9. View the document in print preview.
10. Print the document from within print preview.

(continued)

COMPUTER LABORATORY ASSIGNMENT 3 (continued)

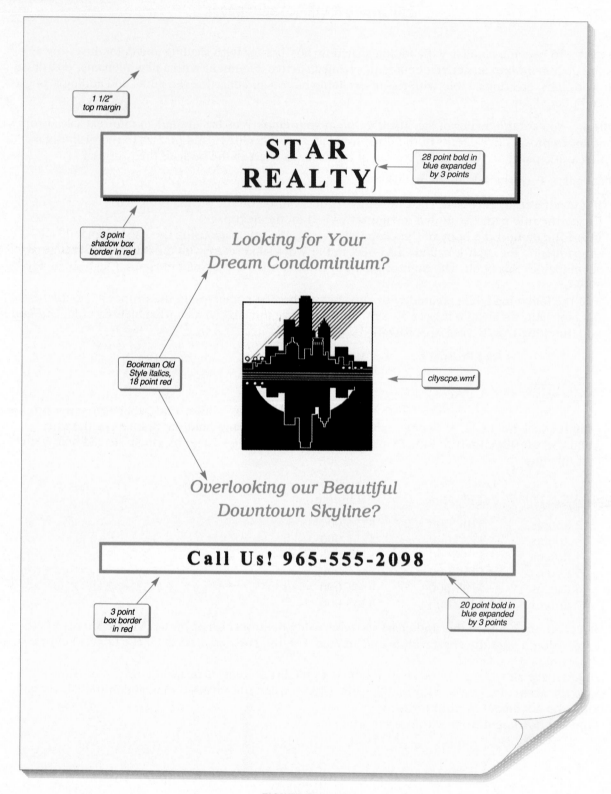

FIGURE CLA1-3a

At Star Realty we take pride in our record of serving satisfied customers. We specialize in locating prime condominiums in the downtown area. We have successfully located thousands of prime units for prospective clients. If you are in the market for a condominium, then Star Realty is the real estate office for you.

add table with tabs here

With our long history and reputation, we are able to negotiate the most affordable prices for our clients and seek loan arrangements that are best suited to their needs. Depending on the placement of the condominium in the building and the number of rooms, prices vary as shown below.

add table with Insert Table button here; then chart table

At Star Realty, we offer a wide variety of services to make your condominium search a pleasant and rewarding experience. Star Realty is committed to giving you red carpet treatment:

prime condominiums in beautiful downtown

well-trained, friendly real estate agents

no-hassle pre-purchase qualification

single-space and add diamond-shaped bullets

flexible hours

24-hour paging service

Star Realty would like to help you find the condominium of your dreams. Our office is conveniently located at 12 Michigan Avenue in Suite 44A. Stop by at your convenience or call us at 965-555-2098 for an appointment.

WE LOOK FORWARD TO SERVING YOU

FIGURE CLA1-3b

COMPUTER LABORATORY ASSIGNMENT 4
Creating a Sales Proposal

Purpose: To become familiar with designing a title page and preparing a proposal including tables and a chart.

Problem: You are to scan through the list of available Windows metafiles in the CLIPART subdirectory and select an area of interest to you. Assume you are the owner of a company that sells your selected product or service. Next, research the area by obtaining prices and other pertinent information to enhance your sale.

Instructions: Create a title page with one of the Windows metafiles. On the title page, use a drop shadow box with shading; color the characters, use a variety of font sizes; add spacing between some characters; italicize, bold, and underline some characters. Be creative. Then, enter the sales proposal. Include one table created with tabs and another created with the Insert Table button. Chart the table created with the Insert Table button. Be sure to check the spelling of your sales proposal before printing it. Save your proposal with the filename CLA1-4.

MICROSOFT WORD 6 FOR WINDOWS

PROJECT TWO

▼

GENERATING FORM LETTERS, MAILING LABELS, AND ENVELOPES

OBJECTIVES You will have mastered the material in this project when you can:

▶ Explain the merging process
▶ Explain the terms data field and data record
▶ Create a data source
▶ Switch from a data source to the main document
▶ Insert merge fields into the main document

▶ Use an IF field in the main document
▶ Merge and print form letters
▶ Selectively merge and print form letters
▶ Sort the data source
▶ Create and print mailing labels
▶ Create and print envelopes

▶ INTRODUCTION

Form letters are used regularly in both business and personal correspondence. The basic contents of a group of form letters are similar; however, items like name and address change from one letter to the next. Thus, form letters are personalized to the addressee. An individual is more likely to open and read a personalized letter than a standard Dear Sir or Dear Madam letter. Business form letters include announcements of sales to customers or introduction of company benefits to employees. Personal form letters include letters of application for a job or invitations to participate in a sweepstakes giveaway.

▶ PROJECT TWO — FORM LETTERS, MAILING LABELS, AND ENVELOPES

Project 2 illustrates the generation of a business form letter and corresponding mailing labels and envelopes. The form letter is sent to all new customers at Peripherals Plus, thanking them for their recent order and informing them of their customer service representative's name. The customer service representative's name varies, depending on the location of the customer. As shown in Figure 2-1 on the next page, the process of generating form letters involves creating a main document for the form letter and a data source, and merging, or *blending*, the two together into a series of individual letters.

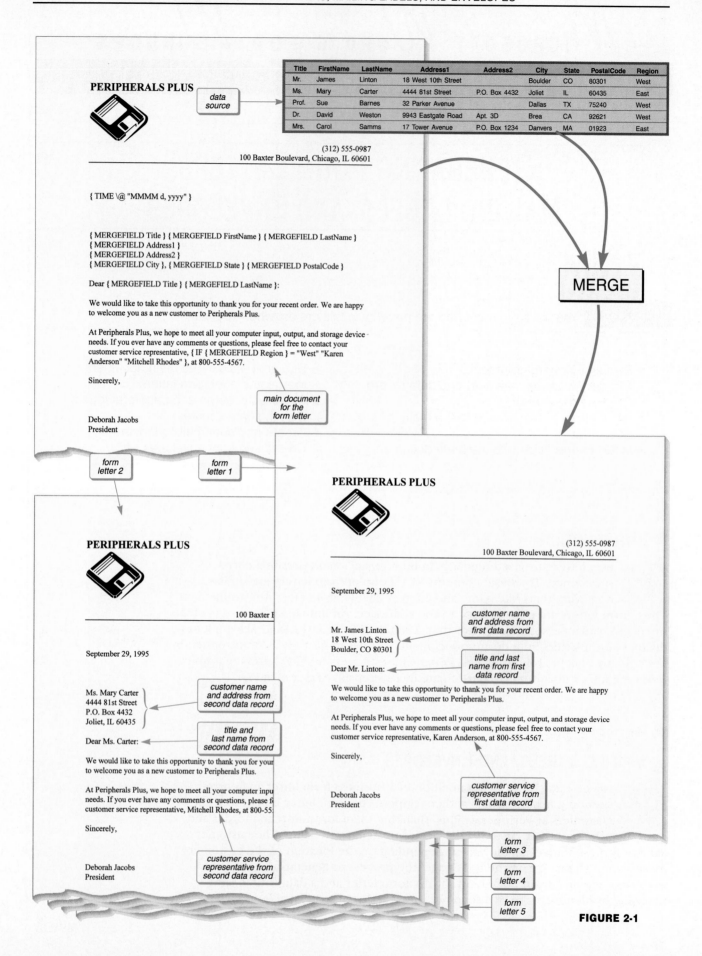

FIGURE 2-1

Merging

Merging is the process of combining the contents of a data source with a main document. The **main document** contains the constant, or unchanging, text, punctuation, spaces, and graphics. In Figure 2-1, the main document represents the portion of the form letters that is identical from one merged letter to the next. Conversely, the **data source** contains the variable, or changing, values in each letter. In Figure 2-1, the data source contains five different customers. One form letter is generated for each customer listed in the data source.

Document Preparation Steps

The following document preparation steps give you an overview of how the main document, data source, and form letters in Figure 2-1 and corresponding mailing labels and envelopes will be developed in this project. If you are preparing the documents in this project on a personal computer, read these steps without doing them.

1. Create a letterhead for Peripherals Plus correspondence.
2. Create a data source.
3. Create the main document for the form letter.
4. Merge and print the form letters.
5. Create and print mailing labels.
6. Create and print envelopes.

Displaying Nonprinting Characters

As discussed in earlier projects, it is helpful to display nonprinting characters that indicate where in the document you pressed the ENTER key, SPACEBAR, or TAB key. Thus, you should display the nonprinting characters by clicking the Show/Hide ¶ button on the Standard toolbar.

▶ CREATING COMPANY LETTERHEAD

I n large businesses, letterhead is preprinted on stationery used by everyone throughout the organization. In smaller organizations, however, preprinted letterhead may not be purchased because of its expense. An alternative for smaller businesses is to create their own letterhead and save it in a file. Then, company employees can open the letterhead file when they begin a document, create their document on the letterhead file, and save their document with a new name — to preserve the original letterhead file.

In Project 2, the letterhead at the top of the main document is created with a header, as shown in the steps on the next page.

TO CREATE COMPANY LETTERHEAD

Step 1: From the View menu, choose the Header and Footer command. Change the font size to 16 by clicking the Font Size box arrow and selecting 16. Click the Bold button on the Formatting toolbar. Type PERIPHERALS PLUS and press the ENTER key.

Step 2: From the Insert menu, choose the Picture command. Select the Windows metafile called disk.wmf by clicking it. Choose the OK button in the Insert Picture dialog box to insert the graphic into the header.

Step 3: Press the ENTER key. Change the point size to 12. Click the Bold button to turn off the bold format. Click the Align Right button on the Formatting toolbar. Type (312) 555-0987 and press the ENTER key. Type 100 Baxter Boulevard, Chicago, IL 60601 and press the ENTER key three times.

Step 4: Position the insertion point in the address line of the header. Click the Borders button on the Formatting toolbar to display the Borders toolbar. Click the Bottom Border button on the Borders toolbar to add a border beneath the address line paragraph. Click the Borders button on the Formatting toolbar to remove the Borders toolbar from the screen (Figure 2-2).

Step 5: Choose the Close button on the Header and Footer toolbar to return to the document window. Recall that a header does not display on the screen in normal view.

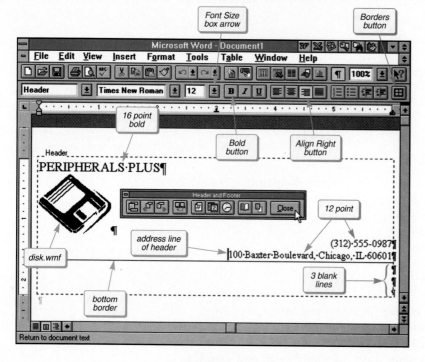

FIGURE 2-2

Once you have completed Step 4, the header area displays, as shown in Figure 2-2.

Now that you have created the company letterhead, the next step is to save it in a file.

TO SAVE THE COMPANY LETTERHEAD IN A FILE

Step 1: Insert your data disk into drive A.

Step 2: Click the Save button on the Standard toolbar.

Step 3: Type the filename ppltrhd in the File Name box. Do not press the ENTER key.

Step 4: If necessary, click the Drives box arrow and select drive A.

Step 5: Choose the OK button in the Save As dialog box.

The letterhead is saved with the filename PPLTRHD.DOC.

▶ IDENTIFYING THE MAIN DOCUMENT AND CREATING THE DATA SOURCE

C reating form letters requires merging a main document with a data source. To create form letters using Word's mail merge, you first identify the main document and create or specify the data source; then you create the main document; and finally you merge the data source with the main document to generate the form letters.

Identifying the Main Document

The first step in the mail merge process is to open the document you will use as the main document. If it is a new document, simply click the New button on the Standard toolbar. Because the main document in this project is to contain the company letterhead, you should leave the file PPLTRHD.DOC open in your document window. Once the main document file is open, you must identify it as such to Word's mail merge, as shown in these steps.

TO IDENTIFY THE MAIN DOCUMENT ▼

STEP 1 ▶

Select the Tools menu and point to the Mail Merge command (Figure 2-3).

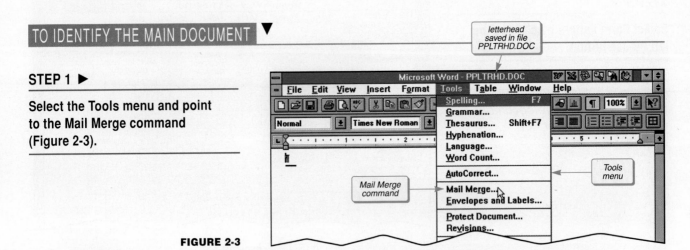

FIGURE 2-3

STEP 2 ▶

Choose the Mail Merge command. When the Mail Merge Helper dialog box displays, point to the Create button (Create ▼).

Word displays the Mail Merge Helper dialog box (Figure 2-4). Through this dialog box, you identify the main document and create the data source.

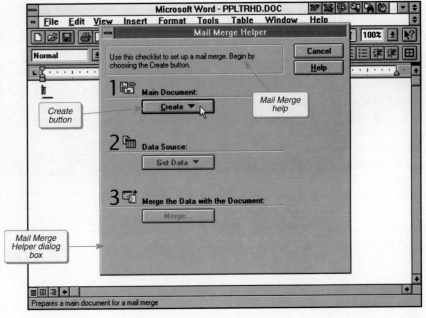

FIGURE 2-4

STEP 3 ►

Choose the Create button. Point to Form Letters in the list.

A list of main document types displays (Figure 2-5).

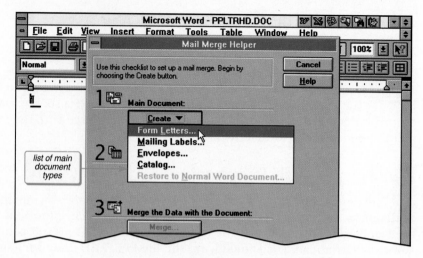

FIGURE 2-5

STEP 4 ►

Select Form Letters by clicking the left mouse button.

Word displays a Microsoft Word dialog box asking whether you want to use the active document for the form letters or not (Figure 2-6).

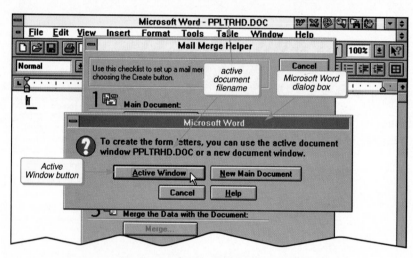

FIGURE 2-6

STEP 5 ►

Choose the Active Window button (Active Window).

Word returns you to the Mail Merge Helper dialog box (Figure 2-7). The merge document type is identified as form letters and the main document is A:\PPLTRHD.DOC, the company letterhead. An Edit button (Edit ▼) now displays in the Mail Merge Helper dialog box so you can modify the contents of the main document.

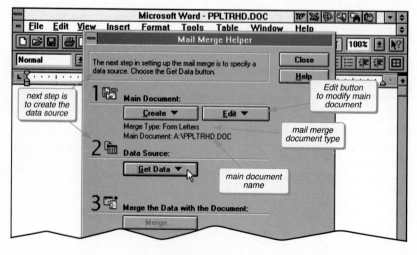

FIGURE 2-7

At this point, you do not create the main document; you simply identify it. As indicated in the Mail Merge Helper dialog box, the next step is to create the data source. After you create the data source, you will enter the main document text.

Creating the Data Source

A data source is a Word table (Figure 2-8). Recall from Project 1 that a Word table is a series of rows and columns. The top row of the data source is called the **header row.** Each row beneath the header row is called a **data record**. Data records contain the text that varies from one merged document to the next. The data source for this project contains five data records. In this project, each data record identifies a different customer. Thus, five form letters will be generated from this data source.

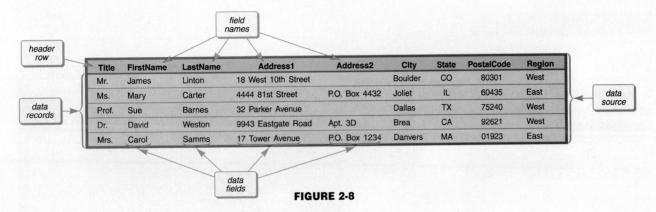

FIGURE 2-8

Each column in the data source is called a **data field**. A data field represents a group of similar data. In this project, the data source contains nine data fields: Title, FirstName, LastName, Address1, Address2, City, State, PostalCode, and Region.

In a data source, each data field must be uniquely identified with a name, called a **field name**. For example, the name FirstName represents the field (column) containing the first names of the customers. Field names are placed in the header row of the data source to identify the name of each column.

Field Name Conventions

The first step in creating a data source is to decide which fields it will contain. That is, you must identify the information varying from one merged document to the next. In Project 2, each record contains up to nine different fields for each customer: a courtesy title (e.g., Mrs.), first name, last name, first line of street address, second line of street address (optional), city, state, zip code, and region. Regions are divided into East and West, depending on the customer's state. The customer service representative is determined based on the customer's region.

For each field, you must decide on a field name. Field names must be unique. That is, no two field names may be the same. Field names cannot exceed 40 characters. The first character of a field name must be a letter; the remaining 39 characters can be either letters, numbers, or the underscore (_) character. Because spaces are not allowed in field names, use the underscore character or a mixture of upper- and lowercase letters to separate words in field names.

Because data sources often contain the same fields, Word provides you with a list of thirteen commonly used field names. You will use eight of the thirteen field names supplied by Word: Title, FirstName, LastName, Address1, Address2, City, State, and PostalCode. You will need to delete the other five field names from the list supplied by Word. That is, you will delete JobTitle, Company, Country, HomePhone, and WorkPhone. In this project, the only field that Word does not supply is the Region field. Thus, you will add a field name for the Region field.

Notice the first letter of each word in the field names is capitalized to make them easier to read. Fields and related field names may be listed in any order in the data source. The order of fields has no effect on the order they will print in the main document.

The following steps illustrate how to create a new data source.

TO CREATE A DATA SOURCE ▼

STEP 1 ▶

In the Mail Merge Helper dialog box, choose the Get Data button (Get Data ▼).

A list of data source options displays (Figure 2-9).

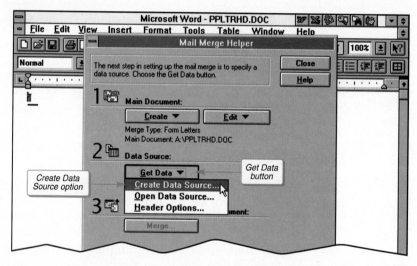

FIGURE 2-9

STEP 2 ▶

Select Create Data Source by clicking it.

Word displays the Create Data Source dialog box (Figure 2-10). In the Field Names in Header Row list box, Word displays a list of commonly used field names. You select field names to remove from the header row of the data source.

STEP 3

Point to JobTitle in the Field Names in Header Row list box.

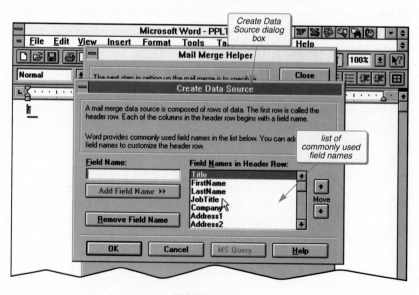

FIGURE 2-10

STEP 4 ▶

Select JobTitle by clicking it and point to the Remove Field Name button (Remove Field Name).

Word highlights JobTitle in the Field Names in Header Row list box (Figure 2-11).

STEP 5

Choose the Remove Field Name button.

Word removes the field name JobTitle from the list.

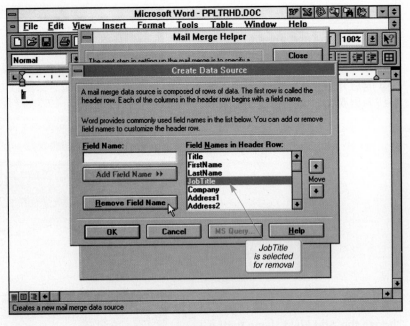

FIGURE 2-11

STEP 6 ▶

Select Company in the Field Names in Header Row list box. Choose the Remove Field Name button. Click the down arrow on the Field Names in Header Row vertical scroll bar until the scroll box is at the bottom of the scroll bar. Select Country in the Field Names in Header Row list box. Choose the Remove Field Name button. Select HomePhone in the Field Names in Header Row list box. Choose the Remove Field Name button. Select WorkPhone in the Field Names in Header Row list box. Choose the Remove Field Name button.

The remaining fields in the Field Names in Header Row list box are to be included in the data source (Figure 2-12). The last field name that was removed, WorkPhone, displays in the Field Name box. The next step is to add the Region field name to the list.

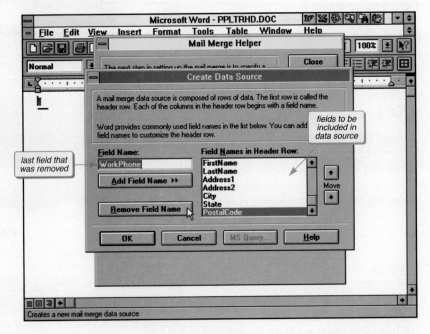

FIGURE 2-12

STEP 7 ▶

Type Region **and point to the Add Field Name button (** Add Field Name ▸▸ **).**

The field name, Region, displays in the Field Name box (Figure 2-13).

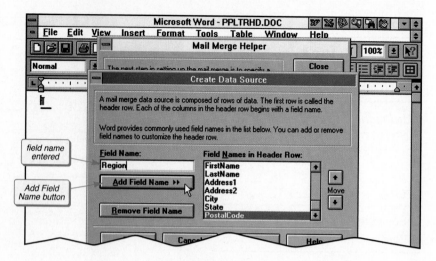

FIGURE 2-13

STEP 8 ▶

Choose the Add Field Name button. Point to the OK button in the Create Data Source dialog box.

Word adds the Region field name to the Field Names in Header Row list box (Figure 2-14).

STEP 9

Choose the OK button.

Word displays a Save Data Source dialog box. You assign the data source a filename in this dialog box.

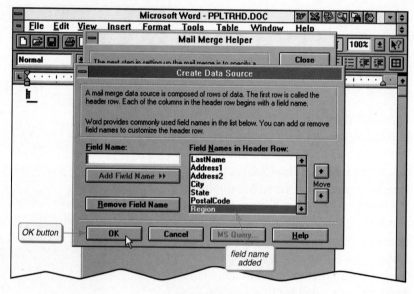

FIGURE 2-14

STEP 10 ▶

Type proj2ds **and, if necessary, change the drive to a:. Point to the OK button in the Save Data Source dialog box.**

Word displays the filename proj2ds in the File Name box (Figure 2-15). The data source for Project 2 will be saved with the filename PROJ2DS.DOC.

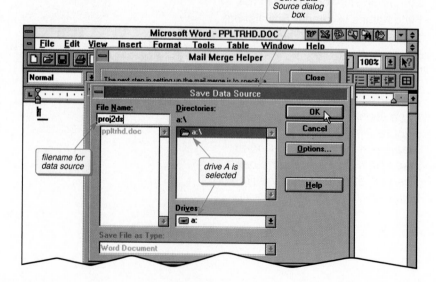

FIGURE 2-15

STEP 11 ►

Choose the OK button.

Word displays a Microsoft Word dialog box asking if you would like to edit the data source or the main document at this point (Figure 2-16). Because you want to add data records to the data source, you will edit the data source now.

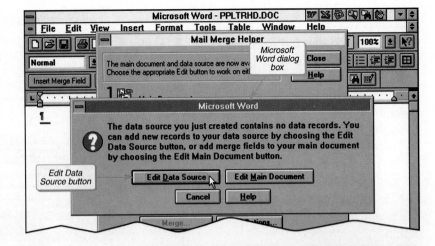

FIGURE 2-16

STEP 12 ►

Choose the Edit Data Source button (**) in the Microsoft Word dialog box.**

Word displays a Data Form dialog box (Figure 2-17). You use this dialog box to enter the data records into the data source. Notice the field names in the header row are displayed along the left edge of the dialog box with an empty text box to the right of each field name. The insertion point is in the first text box.

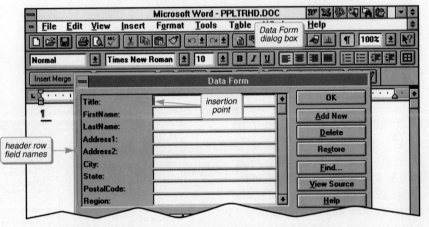

FIGURE 2-17

STEP 13 ►

Type `Mr.` **and press the TAB key. Type** `James` **and press the TAB key. Type** `Linton` **and press the TAB key. Type** `18 West 10th Street` **and press the TAB key twice. Type** `Boulder` **and press the TAB key. Type** `CO` **and press the TAB key. Type** `80301` **and press the TAB key. Type** `West` **and point to the Add New button (** **).**

The first data record values are entered into the Data Form dialog box (Figure 2-18). Notice you press the TAB key to advance from one text box to the next. If you notice an error in a text box, click in the text box and correct the error as you would in a document. The Add New button allows you to add another data record.

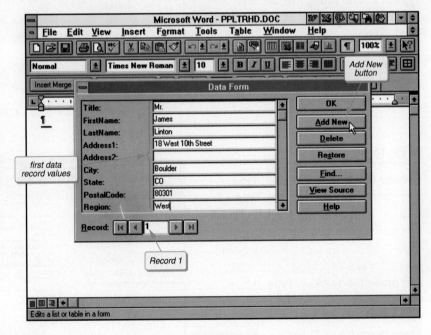

FIGURE 2-18

STEP 14 ▶

Choose the Add New button. Type `Ms.` and press the TAB key. Type `Mary` and press the TAB key. Type `Carter` and press the TAB key. Type `4444 81st Street` and press the TAB key. Type `P.O. Box 4432` and press the TAB key. Type `Joliet` and press the TAB key. Type `IL` and press the TAB key. Type `60435` and press the TAB key. Type `East` and point to the Add New button.

The second data record is entered (Figure 2-19).

FIGURE 2-19

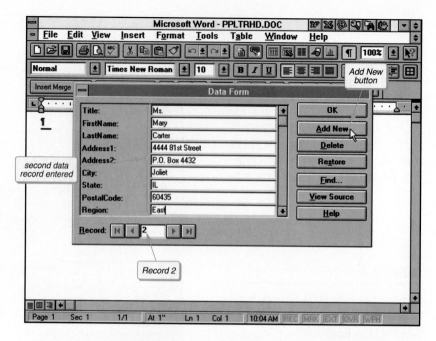

STEP 15 ▶

Choose the Add New button. Type `Prof.` and press the TAB key. Type `Sue` and press the TAB key. Type `Barnes` and press the TAB key. Type `32 Parker Avenue` and press the TAB key twice. Type `Dallas` and press the TAB key. Type `TX` and press the TAB key. Type `75240` and press the TAB key. Type `West`

The third data record is entered (Figure 2-20).

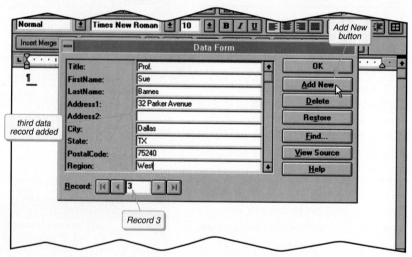

FIGURE 2-20

STEP 16 ▶

Choose the Add New button. Type `Dr.` and press the TAB key. Type `David` and press the TAB key. Type `Weston` and press the TAB key. Type `9943 Eastgate Road` and press the TAB key. Type `Apt. 3D` and press the TAB key. Type `Brea` and press the TAB key. Type `CA` and press the TAB key. Type `92621` and press the TAB key. Type `West`

The fourth data record is entered (Figure 2-21).

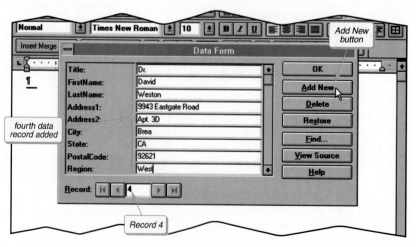

FIGURE 2-21

STEP 17 ►

Choose the Add New button. Type `Mrs.` and press the TAB key. Type `Carol` and press the TAB key. Type `Samms` and press the TAB key. Type `17 Tower Avenue` and press the TAB key. Type `P.O. Box 1234` and press the TAB key. Type `Danvers` and press the TAB key. Type `MA` and press the TAB key. Type `01923` and press the TAB key. Type `East` and point to the View Source button (View Source).

The fifth, and last, data record is entered (Figure 2-22). All of the data records have been entered into the data source, but Word has not saved the records in the file PROJ2DS.DOC yet.

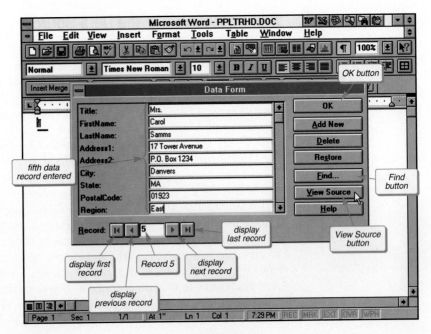

FIGURE 2-22

STEP 18 ►

Choose the View Source button. Choose the Save button on the Standard toolbar.

*Word displays the data records in table form (Figure 2-23). Because the data records are not saved in the data source file when you fill in the Data Source dialog box, you must save them here. A **Database toolbar** displays beneath the Formatting toolbar.*

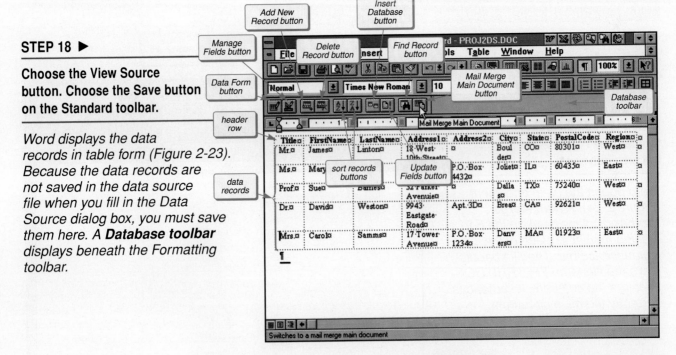

FIGURE 2-23

All of the data records have been entered into the data source and saved with the filename PROJ2DS.DOC. If, when you are entering your data records into the Data Form dialog box, you accidentally click the OK button instead of the Add New button, you will be returned to the main document. To return to the Data Form dialog box and continue adding data records, click the Edit Data Source button (⬛) on the Mail Merge toolbar, as shown in Figure 2-25 on page MSW82.

Editing Records in the Data Source

In the Data Form dialog box, you can add, change, or delete data records. To add a new record, click the Add New button, as shown in the previous steps. To change an existing record, display it in the Data Form dialog box by clicking the appropriate Record button(s) or by using the Find button to locate a particular data item (see Figure 2-22 on the previous page). For example, to find David Weston, you could click the Find button, enter Dr. in the Find What box and choose the OK button. Once you have changed an existing record's data, choose the OK button. To delete a record, display it in the Data Form dialog box, and choose the Delete button (Delete). If you accidentally delete a data record you want, click the Restore button to bring it back.

You can also add, change, and delete data records when you are viewing the source in table form, as shown in Figure 2-23. You can use the buttons on the Database toolbar to add and delete records in the table. Because the data source is a Word table, you can also add and delete records the same way you add and delete rows in a Word table, which was discussed in Project 1.

The data file is now complete. If you wish, you can print the data file by clicking the Print button on the Standard toolbar. The next step is to switch from the data source to the main document.

TO SWITCH FROM THE DATA SOURCE TO THE MAIN DOCUMENT ▼

STEP 1 ▶

Click the Mail Merge Main Document button (🖻) on the Database toolbar (see Figure 2-23 on the previous page).

*Word opens the main document (Figure 2-24). A **Mail Merge toolbar** displays beneath the Formatting toolbar in place of the Database toolbar. The title bar displays the filename PPLTRHD.DOC because the company letterhead is currently the main document.*

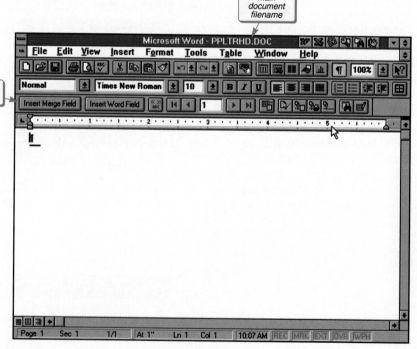

FIGURE 2-24

▶ CREATING THE MAIN DOCUMENT FOR THE FORM LETTER

The next step is to create the main document, which is a form letter (see Figure 2-1 on page MSW68). The form letter is based on a block style letter. That is, all paragraphs are left-justified. The current date displays in the left corner of the form letter below the letterhead. Recall that you created the letterhead earlier as a header and saved in a file called PPLTRHD.DOC.

All business letters have common elements, such as a date line, inside address, message, complimentary close, and signature block. The form letter in this project is a business letter that follows these guidelines:

▶ inside address is three blank lines below the date line
▶ salutation is one blank line below the inside address
▶ letter message is one blank line below the salutation
▶ paragraphs within the message are separated by one blank line
▶ complimentary close is one blank line below the message
▶ signature block is three blank lines below the complimentary close

The steps on the following pages illustrate how to create the main document for the form letter.

Saving the Main Document with a New Filename

The main document has the name PPLTRHD.DOC, the name of the company letterhead for Peripherals Plus. Because you want the letterhead to remain unchanged, you should save the main document with a new filename.

TO SAVE THE MAIN DOCUMENT WITH A NEW FILENAME

Step 1: Insert your data disk into drive A.
Step 2: From the File menu, choose the Save As command.
Step 3: Type the filename `proj2md` in the File Name box. Do not press the ENTER key.
Step 4: If necessary, click the Drives box arrow and select drive A.
Step 5: Choose the OK button in the Save As dialog box.

The main document is saved with the filename PROJ2MD.DOC.

Redefining the Normal Style

When you enter a document, it is based on the normal style. The normal style is defined as single-spaced, left-aligned paragraphs containing characters in 10 point Times New Roman. You can change the point size of all paragraph characters from 10 to 12 by selecting the paragraph mark at the upper left corner of the document window, clicking the Font Size box arrow, and selecting 12 from the list. In this project, you again want all of the characters to be in 12 point. However, to do this, you have to redefine the normal style to be 12 point because when you define the sales representative condition, Word enters the sales representative's name into the document using the normal style point size, which is 10.

To redefine the normal style, select the paragraph, change the formatting of the paragraph to the desired settings, and then redefine the normal style based on the selection, as shown in the steps on the next page.

TO REDEFINE THE NORMAL STYLE ▼

STEP 1 ▶

Select the paragraph mark in the upper left corner of the document window by clicking in the selection bar to its left. Click the Font Size box arrow and select 12. Click the word Normal in the Style box on the Formatting toolbar. Move the mouse pointer into the document window.

The paragraph mark in the upper left corner of the document window is selected (Figure 2-25). The font size for the selected paragraph mark is changed to 12 and the word Normal is selected in the Style box.

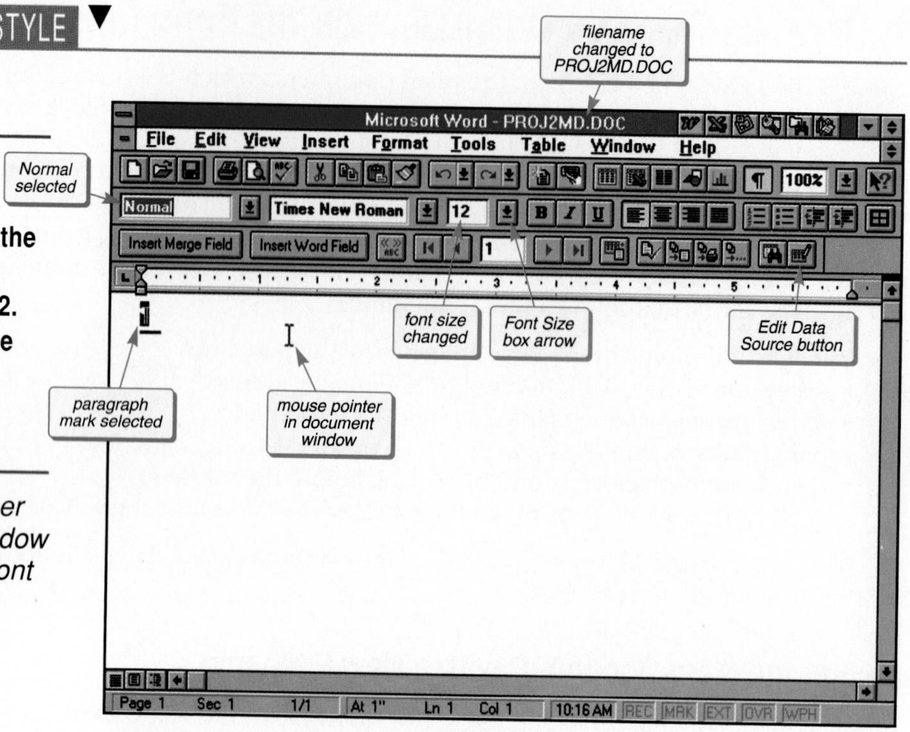

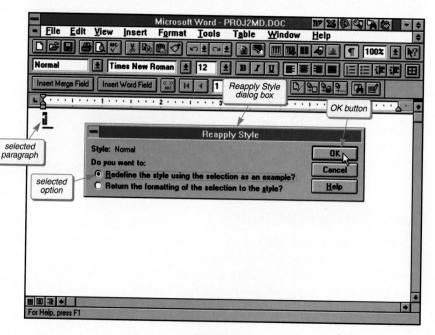

FIGURE 2-25

STEP 2 ▶

With the mouse pointer in the document window, click the left mouse button. If it is not selected, click the Redefine the style using the selection as an example? option in the Reapply Style dialog box.

Word displays a Reapply Style dialog box (Figure 2-26). The Redefine the style using the selection as an example? option is selected.

STEP 3

Choose the OK button. Click outside the selection to remove the highlight.

Word redefines the normal style to 12 point and returns you to the document window.

FIGURE 2-26

Adding the Current Date to the Form Letter

When sending letters to customers, you want the current date to print at the top of the letter. Word provides a method of inserting the computer's system date into a document. In this way, if you type the letter today and print it at a later date, it will print the current date. Follow these steps to insert the current date at the top of the main document.

TO INSERT THE CURRENT DATE IN A DOCUMENT ▼

STEP 1 ▶

Select the Insert menu and point to the Date and Time command (Figure 2-27).

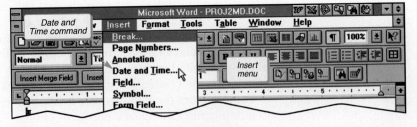

FIGURE 2-27

STEP 2 ▶

Choose the Date and Time command. When the Date and Time dialog box displays, select the format September 29, 1995 (the current date on your screen) by clicking it. If it is not selected, click the Insert as Field check box.

Word displays the Date and Time dialog box (Figure 2-28). A list of available formats for displaying the current date and time appear. Your screen will not show September 29, 1995; rather, it will display the current system date stored in your computer. The current date displays in the main document according to the selected format.

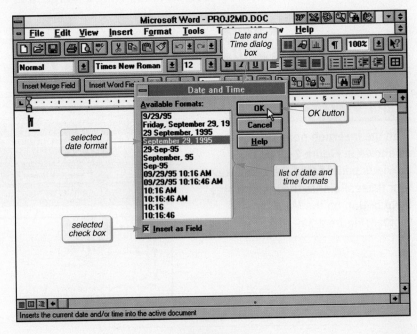

FIGURE 2-28

STEP 3 ▶

Choose the OK button.

Word displays the current date in the main document (Figure 2-29).

FIGURE 2-29

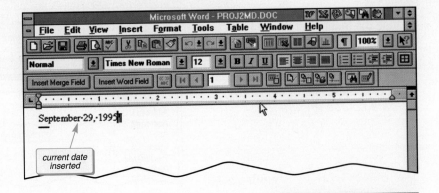

The current date is actually a field that Word updates when it prints the document. If you would like to update the field on the screen, position the insertion point in the date and press the function key F9. If, for some reason, you need to delete the date field from the main document, select it and press the DELETE key.

The next step is to enter the inside address on the letter. The contents of the inside address are located in the data source. Thus, you insert fields from the data source into the main document.

Inserting Merge Fields into the Main Document

Earlier in this project, you created the data source for the form letter. The first record in the data source, the header row, contains the field names of each field in the data source. To link the data source to the main document, you must insert these field names into the main document. In the main document, these field names are called **merge fields** because they merge, or combine, the main document with the contents of the data source. When a field is inserted into the main document from the data source, it is surrounded by **chevrons**. Chevrons mark the beginning and ending of a merge field (see Figure 2-32). The chevrons are not on the keyboard; therefore, you cannot type them directly into the document. They appear as a result of inserting a merge field with the Insert Merge Field button (Insert Merge Field) on the Mail Merge toolbar.

TO INSERT MERGE FIELDS INTO THE MAIN DOCUMENT ▼

STEP 1 ▶

With the insertion point positioned as shown in Figure 2-29 on the previous page, press the ENTER key four times. Point to the Insert Merge Field button on the Mail Merge toolbar (Figure 2-30).

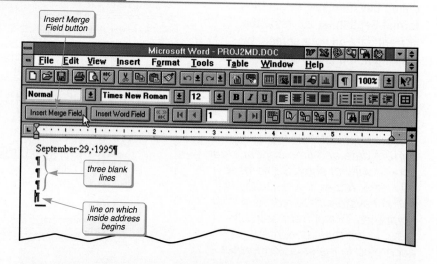

FIGURE 2-30

STEP 2 ▶

Choose the Insert Merge Field button. In the list of fields, point to Title.

Word displays a list of fields from the data source (Figure 2-31).

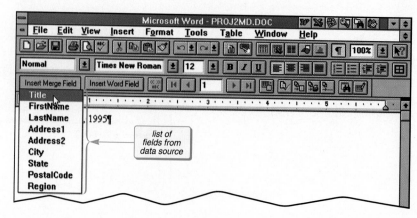

FIGURE 2-31

STEP 3 ▶

Select Title by clicking the left mouse button. When the list of fields disappears from the screen, press the SPACEBAR once.

Word displays the field name Title enclosed in chevrons in the main document (Figure 2-32). When you merge the data source with the main document, the customer's title will print in the location of the merge field Title. One space follows the ending chevron in the Title merge field.

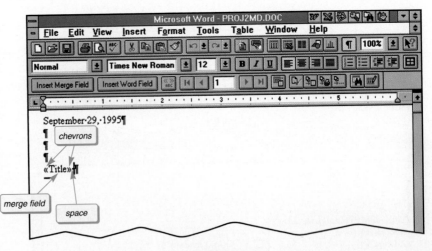

FIGURE 2-32

STEP 4 ▶

Choose the Insert Merge Field button. In the list of fields, point to FirstName (Figure 2-33).

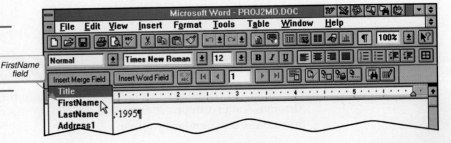

FIGURE 2-33

STEP 5 ▶

Click the left mouse button. When the list disappears from the screen, press the SPACEBAR once. Choose the Insert Merge Field button. In the list of fields, select LastName.

The first line of the inside address is complete (Figure 2-34).

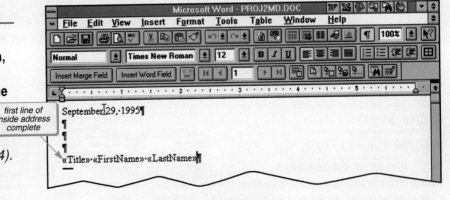

FIGURE 2-34

Completing the Inside Address Lines

The next step is to enter the remaining merge fields in the inside address lines as shown on the next page.

TO COMPLETE THE INSIDE ADDRESS

Step 1: Press the ENTER key. Choose the Insert Merge Field button. In the list of fields, select Address1.

Step 2: Press the ENTER key. Choose the Insert Merge Field button. In the list of fields, select Address2.

FIGURE 2-35

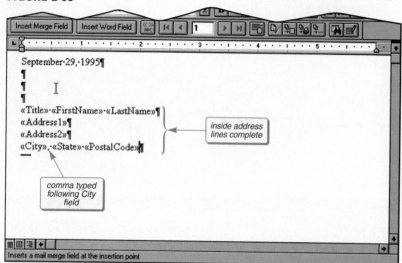

Step 3: Press the ENTER key. Choose the Insert Merge Field button. In the list of fields, select City. Type , (a comma) and press the SPACEBAR. Choose the Insert Merge Field button. In the list of fields, select State. Press the SPACEBAR once. Choose the Insert Merge Field button. In the list of fields, select PostalCode.

The inside address lines are complete (Figure 2-35).

If you accidentally insert the wrong merge field, drag the mouse pointer through the erroneous merge field, including the chevrons, and click the Cut button on the Standard toolbar.

Entering Merge Fields in the Salutation Line

The salutation in Project 2 begins with the word Dear placed at the left margin, followed by the customer's title and last name. You are to insert the appropriate merge fields after the word Dear, as shown in the following steps.

TO ENTER MERGE FIELDS IN THE SALUTATION ▼

STEP 1 ▶

Press the ENTER key twice. Type Dear and press the SPACEBAR. Choose the Insert Merge Field button. In the list of fields, point to Title.

Word displays the list of fields from the data source (Figure 2-36). The field you select will be added at the location of the insertion point in the document.

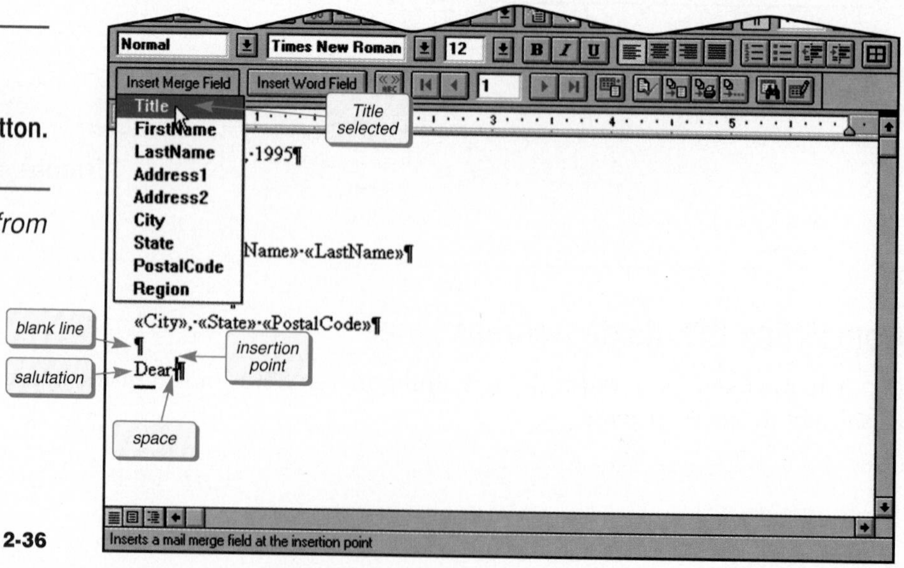

FIGURE 2-36

STEP 2 ▶

Click the left mouse button. Press the SPACEBAR. Choose the Insert Merge Field button. In the list of fields, select LastName. Type a colon (:).

The salutation is complete (Figure 2-37).

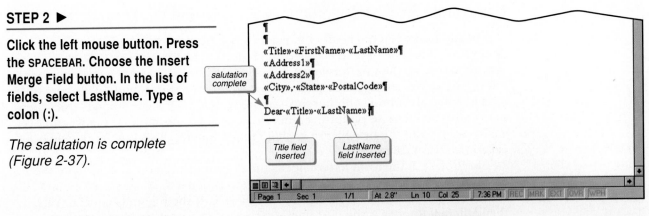

FIGURE 2-37

Entering the Body of the Form Letter

The next step is to enter the text in the body of the form letter. The entire first paragraph and the beginning of the second paragraph contain constant, or unchanging, text to be printed in each form letter.

TO BEGIN ENTERING THE BODY OF THE FORM LETTER

Step 1: Press the ENTER key twice. Type `We would like to take this opportunity to thank you for your recent order. We are happy to welcome you as a new customer to Peripherals Plus.`

Step 2: Press the ENTER key twice. Type `At Peripherals Plus, we hope to meet all your computer input, output, and storage device needs. If you ever have any comments or questions, please feel free to contact your customer service representative,` and press the SPACEBAR.

The body of the form letter displays, as shown in Figure 2-38. (Depending on your printer driver, your word-wrap may occur in different locations.)

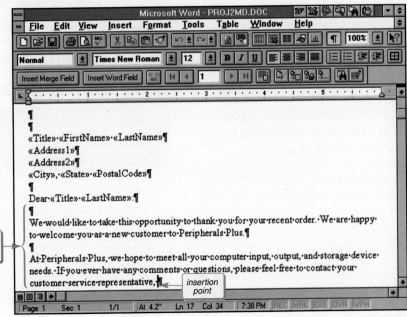

FIGURE 2-38

Using an IF Field to Conditionally Print Text in the Form Letter

In addition to merge fields, you can insert other types of fields in your main document. One type of field is called an **IF field**. One form of the IF field is: If a condition is true, then perform an action. For example, If Mary is a student, then inform her of the good student discount program for car insurance. This type of IF field is called **If...Then**. Another form of the IF field is: If a condition is true, then perform an action; else perform a different action. For example, If the weather is sunny, we'll go to the beach; else we'll go to the movies. This type of IF field is called **If...Then...Else**.

In Project 2, the form letter checks the customer's region to determine the customer's service representative. If the region is equal to West, then Karen Anderson is the customer's service representative. If the region is equal to East, then Mitchell Rhodes is the customer's service representative. To determine the customer's service representative, use the If...Then...Else: If the region is equal to West, then print Karen Anderson's name, else print Mitchell Rhodes' name.

The phrase that appears after the word If is called a **condition**. A condition is composed of an expression, followed by a mathematical operator, followed by a final expression.

EXPRESSIONS The **expression** in a condition can be either a merge field, a number, or a string of characters. Word surrounds the string of characters by quotation marks ("). Place two double quotation marks together (" ") to indicate an empty, or **null**, expression.

MATHEMATICAL OPERATORS The **mathematical operator** in a condition must be one of eight characters: = (equal to or matches the text), < (less than), <= (less than or equal to), > (greater than), >= (greater than or equal to),<> (not equal to or does not match text). ="" (is blank), or <>"" (is not blank).

In Project 2, the first expression is a merge field (Region); the operator is an equal sign (=); and the second expression is the text "West". If the condition is true, print Karen Anderson, else print Mitchell Rhodes. That is, If Region="West" "Karen Anderson" "Mitchell Rhodes".

Follow these steps to insert the IF field into the form letter.

TO INSERT AN IF FIELD INTO THE MAIN DOCUMENT ▼

STEP 1 ▶

Choose the Insert Word Field button on the Mail Merge toolbar. When Word displays the list of Word fields, point to If...Then...Else.

Word displays a list of Word fields that may be inserted into the main document (Figure 2-39).

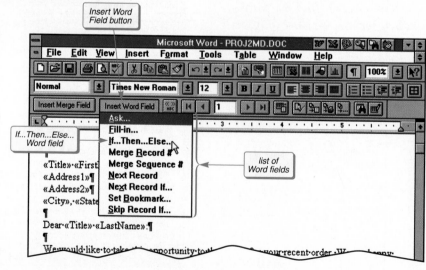

FIGURE 2-39

STEP 2 ▶

Click the left mouse button. When the Insert Word Field: IF dialog box displays, point to the Field Name box arrow.

Word displays an Insert Word Field: IF dialog box (Figure 2-40). The condition is identified in the IF area.

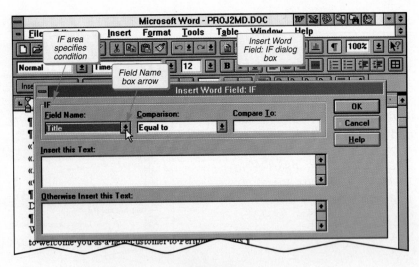

FIGURE 2-40

STEP 3 ▶

Click the Field Name box arrow to display a list of fields in the data source. Drag the scroll box to the bottom of the Field Name scroll bar and point to Region.

Word displays a list of fields in the data source (Figure 2-41).

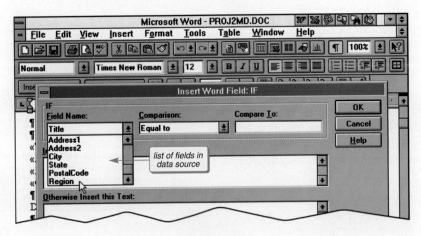

FIGURE 2-41

STEP 4 ▶

Select Region by clicking it. Click in the Compare To box.

Word displays Region in the Field Name box (Figure 2-42). The insertion point is in the Compare To box.

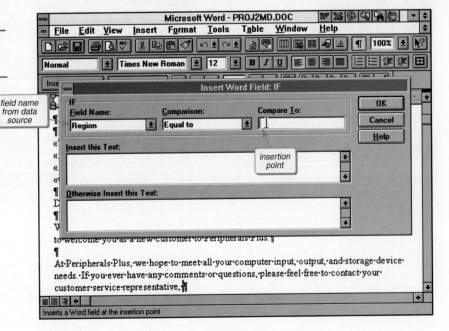

FIGURE 2-42

STEP 5 ▶

Type West **and press the TAB key. In the Insert this Text box, type** Karen Anderson **and press the TAB key. In the Otherwise Insert this Text box, type** Mitchell Rhodes **and point to the OK button.**

The entries in the Insert Word Field: IF dialog box are complete (Figure 2-43).

Microsoft Word - PROJ2MD.DOC
Insert Word Field: IF
Field Name:
Region
Comparison:
Equal to
Compare To:
West
OK
Cancel
Help
Insert this Text:
Karen Anderson
Otherwise Insert this Text:
Mitchell Rhodes
IF field entries complete

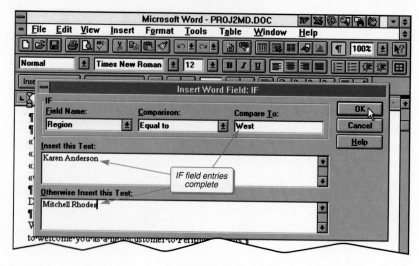

FIGURE 2-43

STEP 6 ▶

Choose the OK button.

Word returns you to the document (Figure 2-44). The name Karen Anderson displays at the location of the insertion point because she is the sales representative for the first record in the data source.

«Title»·«FirstName»·«LastName»¶
«Address1»¶
«Address2»¶
«City»,·«State»·«PostalCode»¶
Dear·«Title»·«LastName»:¶
We·would·like·to·take·this·opportunity·to·thank·you·for·your·recent·order.·We·are·happy·to·welcome·you·as·a·new·customer·to·Peripherals·Plus.¶
At·Peripherals·Plus,·we·hope·to·meet·all·your·computer·input,·output,·and·storage·device·needs.·If·you·ever·have·any·comments·or·questions,·please·feel·free·to·contact·your·customer·service·representative,·Karen·Anderson¶
sales representative name displays, instead of IF field
Page 1 Sec 1 1/1 At 4.2" Ln 17 Col 34 7:40 PM

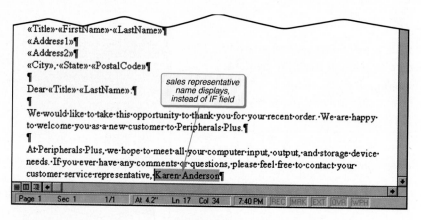

FIGURE 2-44

STEP 7 ▶

Press the END key to move to the insertion point to the end of the line and type , at 800-555-4567. **Press the ENTER key twice. Type** Sincerely, **and press the ENTER key four times. Type** Deborah Jacobs **and press the ENTER key. Type** President

The form letter is complete (Figure 2-45).

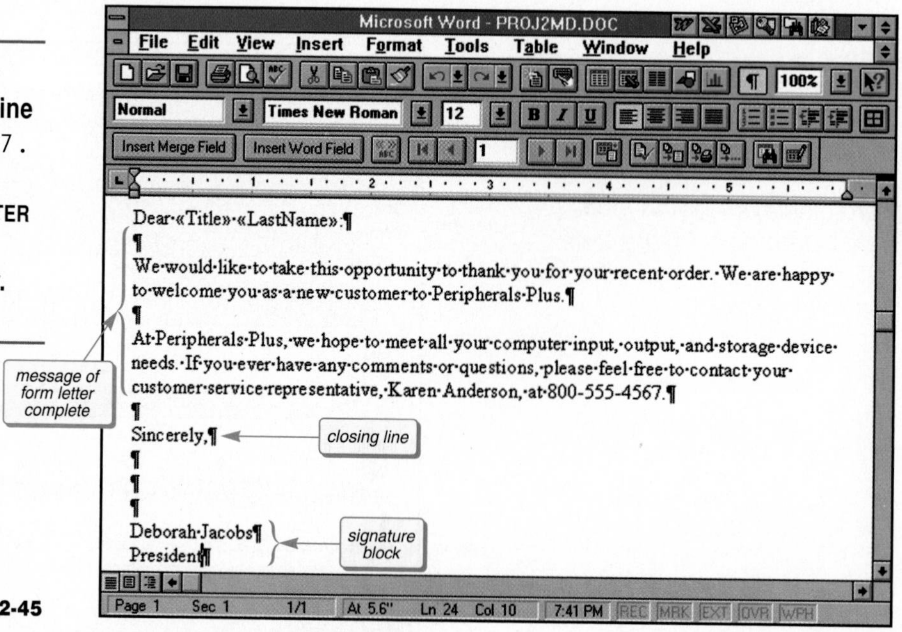

Microsoft Word - PROJ2MD.DOC
Insert Merge Field
Insert Word Field
Dear·«Title»·«LastName»:¶
We·would·like·to·take·this·opportunity·to·thank·you·for·your·recent·order.·We·are·happy·to·welcome·you·as·a·new·customer·to·Peripherals·Plus.¶
At·Peripherals·Plus,·we·hope·to·meet·all·your·computer·input,·output,·and·storage·device·needs.·If·you·ever·have·any·comments·or·questions,·please·feel·free·to·contact·your·customer·service·representative,·Karen·Anderson,·at·800-555-4567.¶
message of form letter complete
Sincerely,¶
closing line
Deborah·Jacobs¶
President¶
signature block
Page 1 Sec 1 1/1 At 5.6" Ln 24 Col 10 7:41 PM

FIGURE 2-45

The main document for the form letter is now complete, and you should save it again by clicking the Save button on the Standard toolbar.

Displaying Field Codes

Notice that the IF field does not display in the document window; instead, the value of the IF field displays. That is, Karen Anderson displays because she is the sales representative for the first data record.

The IF field is referred to as a **field code**, and the default mode for Microsoft Word is field codes off. Thus, field codes will not print or display unless you turn them on. You use one procedure to display field codes on the screen and a different procedure to print them on a hardcopy. Whether field codes are on or off on your screen has no effect on the print merge process. The following steps illustrate how to turn on field codes so you may see them on the screen. Most Word users only turn on field codes to verify their accuracy. Because field codes tend to clutter the screen, you may want to turn them off after checking their accuracy.

TO TURN FIELD CODES ON OR OFF FOR DISPLAY ▼

STEP 1 ▶

Select the Tools menu and point to the Options command (Figure 2-46).

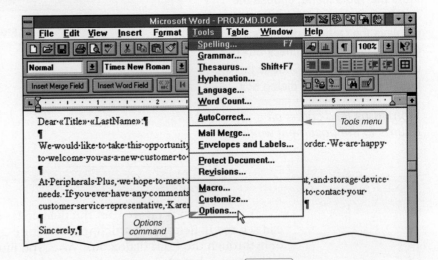

FIGURE 2-46

STEP 2 ▶

Choose the Options command. When Word displays the Options dialog box, select the Field Codes check box in the Show area of the View tab.

Word displays the Options dialog box (Figure 2-47). The Field Codes check box is selected. (If the options in the View tab do not display in your Options dialog box, click the View tab.)

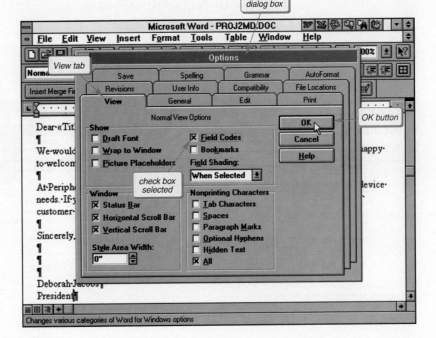

FIGURE 2-47

STEP 3 ▶

Choose the OK button. When Word returns to the document window, click the up arrow on the vertical scroll bar 5 times.

Word displays the main document with field codes on (Figure 2-48). With field codes on, the word MERGEFIELD appears before each merge field in the main document and the IF field displays. Also, braces replace the chevrons around merge fields.

STEP 4

From the Tools menu, choose the Options command. When Word displays the Options dialog box, click the Field Codes check box to deselect field codes. Choose the OK button in the Options dialog box.

Word turns field codes off and returns to the document window.

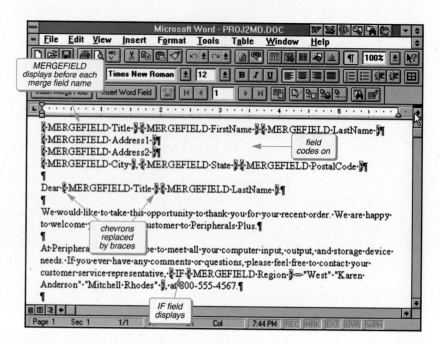

FIGURE 2-48

You may also want to print the field-codes-on version of the form letter so you can see the IF field on a hardcopy (see Figure 2-52). Field codes can be printed only through the Print dialog box. Also, you must remember to turn off the field codes option before merging the form letters; otherwise, all of your form letters will display field codes instead of data.

TO PRINT FIELD CODES IN THE MAIN DOCUMENT ▼

STEP 1 ▶

Select the File menu and point to the Print command (Figure 2-49).

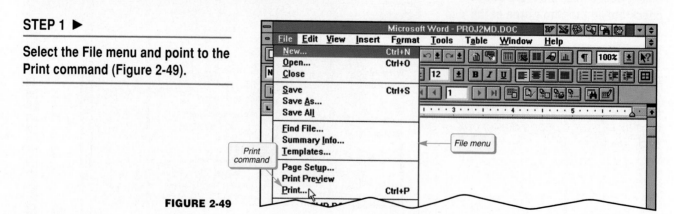

FIGURE 2-49

STEP 2 ▶

Choose the Print command. When the Print dialog box displays, point to the Options button (Options...).

Word displays the Print dialog box (Figure 2-50).

FIGURE 2-50

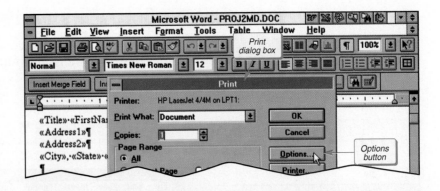

STEP 3 ▶

Choose the Options button. Select the Field Codes check box in the Include with Document area by clicking it. Point to the OK button.

Word displays the Options dialog box (Figure 2-51). The Field Codes check box is selected.

FIGURE 2-51

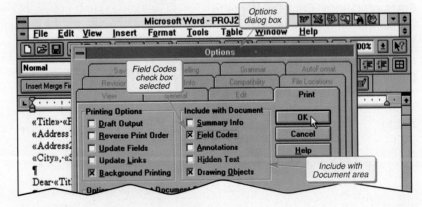

STEP 4

Choose the OK button. When Word displays the Print dialog box, choose the OK button.

Word sends the main document with field codes to the printer.

STEP 5

From the File menu, choose the Print command. Choose the Options button in the Print dialog box. Turn off field codes by clicking the Field Codes check box. Choose the OK button in the Options dialog box. Choose the Close button in the Print dialog box.

The field codes have been turned off. No future documents will print field codes.

STEP 6 ▶

Remove the document from the printer.

The main document hardcopy shows field codes on (Figure 2-52).

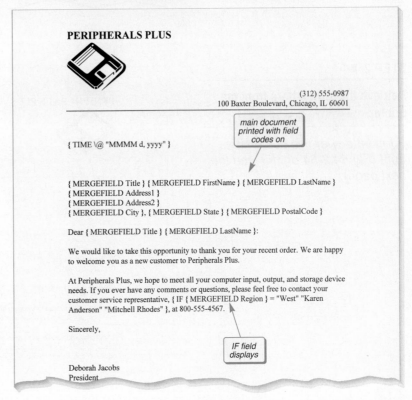

FIGURE 2-52

▶ MERGING THE DOCUMENTS AND PRINTING THE LETTERS

 he data source and form letter are complete. The next step is to merge them together to generate the individual form letters, as shown in the following steps.

TO MERGE THE DOCUMENTS AND PRINT THE FORM LETTERS ▼

STEP 1 ▶

Press CTRL+HOME. Click the Merge to Printer button (▨) on the Mail Merge toolbar (Figure 2-53). When the Print dialog box displays, choose the OK button.

Word sends the form letters to the printer.

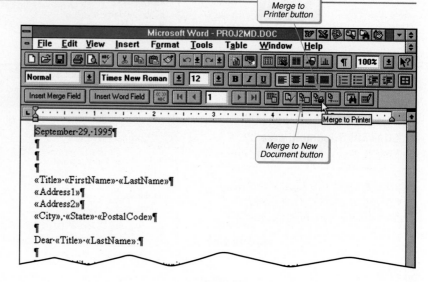

FIGURE 2-53

STEP 2 ▶

Retrieve the form letters from the printer.

Form letters for five customers print (Figure 2-54 on this and the next page).

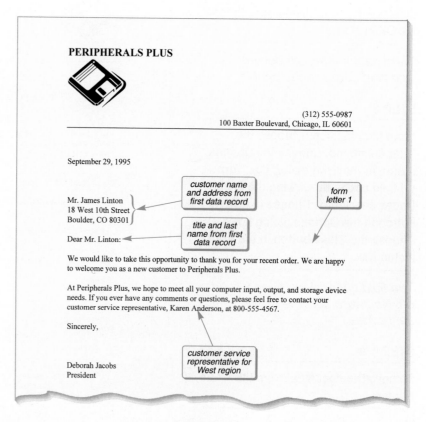

FIGURE 2-54

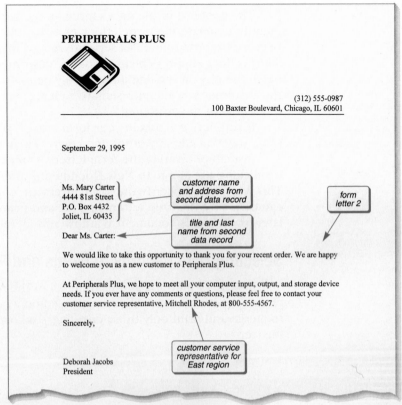

PERIPHERALS PLUS

(312) 555-0987
100 Baxter Boulevard, Chicago, IL 60601

September 29, 1995

Ms. Mary Carter
4444 81st Street
P.O. Box 4432
Joliet, IL 60435

customer name
and address from
second data record

form
letter 2

Dear Ms. Carter:

title and last
name from second
data record

We would like to take this opportunity to thank you for your recent order. We are happy to welcome you as a new customer to Peripherals Plus.

At Peripherals Plus, we hope to meet all your computer input, output, and storage device needs. If you ever have any comments or questions, please feel free to contact your customer service representative, Mitchell Rhodes, at 800-555-4567.

Sincerely,

Deborah Jacobs
President

customer service
representative for
East region

FIGURE 2-54 (continued)

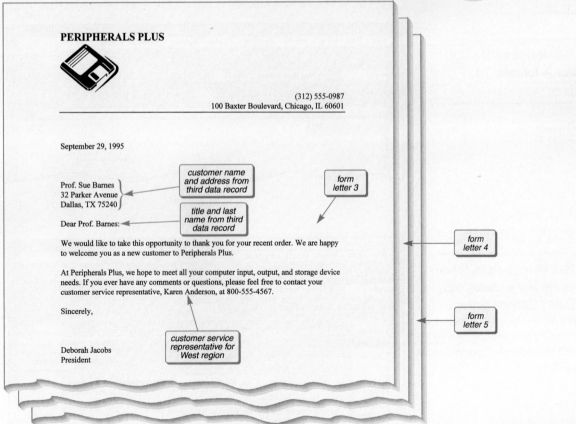

PERIPHERALS PLUS

(312) 555-0987
100 Baxter Boulevard, Chicago, IL 60601

September 29, 1995

Prof. Sue Barnes
32 Parker Avenue
Dallas, TX 75240

customer name
and address from
third data record

form
letter 3

Dear Prof. Barnes:

title and last
name from third
data record

form
letter 4

We would like to take this opportunity to thank you for your recent order. We are happy to welcome you as a new customer to Peripherals Plus.

At Peripherals Plus, we hope to meet all your computer input, output, and storage device needs. If you ever have any comments or questions, please feel free to contact your customer service representative, Karen Anderson, at 800-555-4567.

Sincerely,

form
letter 5

Deborah Jacobs
President

customer service
representative for
West region

The contents of the data source merge with the merge fields in the main document to generate the form letters. One form letter for each customer is generated because each customer is a separate record in the data source. Notice that the address lines suppress blanks. That is, customers without a second address line begin the city on the line immediately below the first address line. Also notice that the customer service representative changes from one letter to the next, based on the region of the customer.

If you notice errors in your form letters, you can edit your main document the same way you edit any other document. Then, save your changes and merge again.

Instead of printing the form letters, you can send them into a new document by clicking the Merge to New Document button (▣) on the Mail Merge toolbar. This way, you can verify the form letters are correct before you print them. You can then save the form letters in a file and print the file containing the form letters later or close this document window and merge as descibed in the previous steps.

Selecting Data Records to Merge and Print

Instead of merging and printing all of the records in the data source, you can choose which records will merge, based on a condition you specify. For example, to merge and print only those customers whose region is East, perform the following steps.

TO SELECTIVELY MERGE AND PRINT RECORDS ▼

STEP 1 ▶

Point to the Mail Merge button (▣) on the Mail Merge toolbar (Figure 2-55).

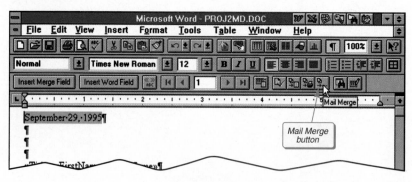

FIGURE 2-55

STEP 2 ▶

Choose the Mail Merge button. When Word displays the Merge dialog box, point to the Query Options button (Query Options...).

Word displays the Merge dialog box (Figure 2-56).

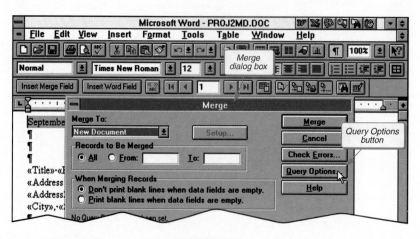

FIGURE 2-56

STEP 3 ►

Choose the Query Options button in the Merge dialog box. When the Query Options dialog box displays, be sure the Filter Records tab options display. Point to the Field box arrow in the Query Options dialog box.

Word displays the Query Options dialog box (Figure 2-57).

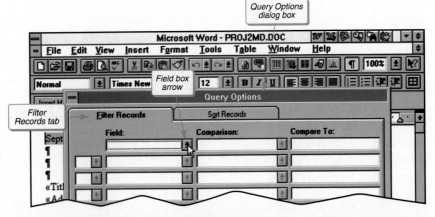

FIGURE 2-57

STEP 4 ►

Click the Field box arrow to display a list of fields in the data source. Scroll to the bottom of the list with the scroll box on the Field box vertical scroll bar. Point to Region.

Word displays a list of fields in the data source (Figure 2-58).

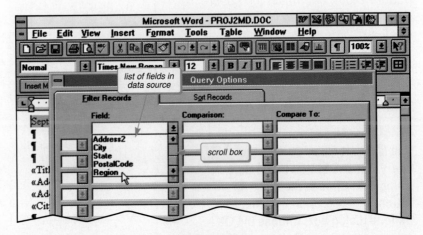

FIGURE 2-58

STEP 5 ►

Select Region by clicking it. In the Compare To text box, type `East` and point to the OK button.

Word displays Region in the Field box, Equal to in the Comparison box, and East in the Compare To box (Figure 2-59).

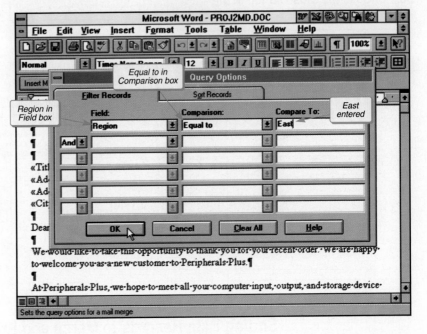

FIGURE 2-59

STEP 6 ▶

Choose the OK button in the Query Options dialog box. Choose the Close button in the Merge dialog box. When Word returns to the document window, click the Merge to Printer button on the Mail Merge toolbar. When Word displays the Print dialog box, choose the OK button.

Word prints the form letters (Figure 2-60) that match the specified condition: Region is Equal to East. Two form letters print because two customers are in the East region.

STEP 7

Choose the Mail Merge button on the Mail Merge toolbar. Choose the Query Options button in the Merge dialog box. Choose the Clear All button (Clear All) in the Query Options dialog box. Choose the OK button in the Query Options dialog box. Choose the Close button in the Merge dialog box.

Word removes the specified condition.

FIGURE 2-60

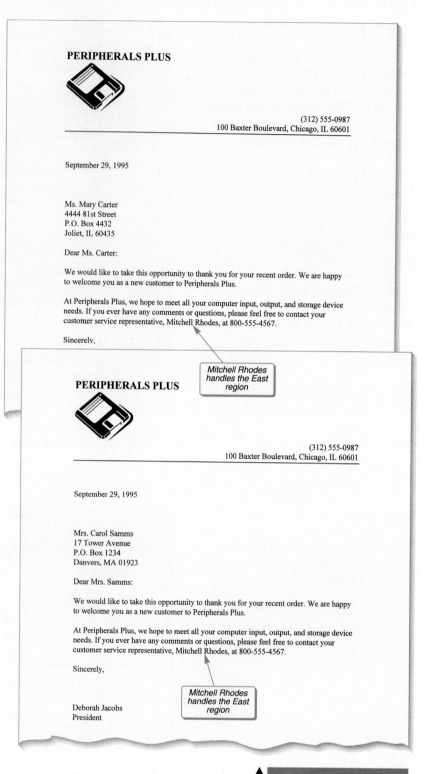

Sorting Data Records to Merge and Print

If you mail your form letters using the U.S. Postal Service's bulk rate mailing service, the post office requires you to sort and group the form letters by zip code. Recall from Project 1 that sorting is the process of ordering records on a field(s). Thus, follow these steps to sort the data records by the zip code field.

TO SORT THE DATA RECORDS ▼

STEP 1 ▶

Choose the Mail Merge button on the Mail Merge toolbar. When Word displays the Merge dialog box, choose the Query Options button. When the Query Options dialog box displays, point to the Sort Records tab.

Word displays the Query Options dialog box (Figure 2-61).

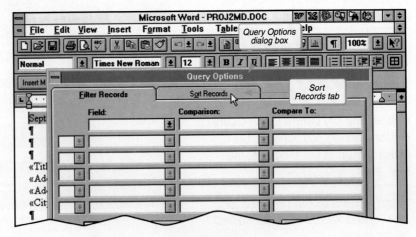

FIGURE 2-61

STEP 2 ▶

Click the Sort Records tab. When the Sort Records tab options display, point to the Sort By box arrow (Figure 2-62).

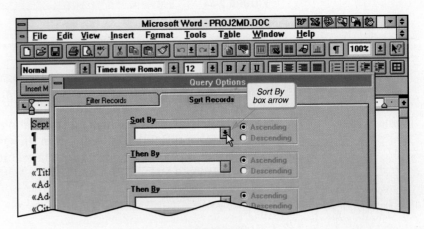

FIGURE 2-62

STEP 3 ▶

Click the Sort By box arrow to display a list of fields in the data source. Scroll to the bottom of the list with the scroll box on the Sort By box vertical scroll bar. Point to PostalCode.

Word displays a list of fields in the data source (Figure 2-63).

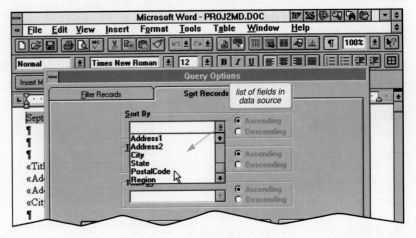

FIGURE 2-63

STEP 4 ▶

Select PostalCode by clicking it.
Point to the OK button.

*Word displays PostalCode in the
Sort By box (Figure 2-64).*

STEP 5

Choose the OK button in the Query
Options dialog box. Choose the
Close button in the Merge dialog
box.

*Word returns to the Merge dialog
box. The data records are sorted
by zip code.*

FIGURE 2-64

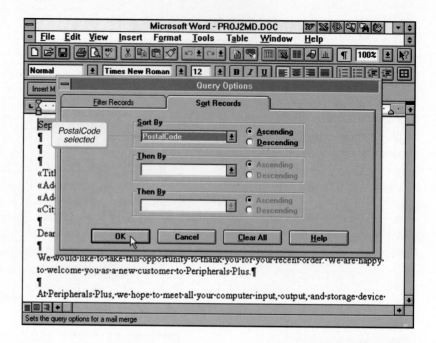

If you chose to merge the form letters again at this point, Word would print
them in order of zip code; that is, Carol Samms' letter would print first and David
Weston's letter would print last.

Because you want the mailing labels and envelopes also to print in order of
zip code, leave the sort condition set in the Query Options dialog box.

You can verify the order of the data records without printing them by using
the View Merged Data button on the Mail Merge toolbar, as shown below.

TO VIEW MERGED DATA IN THE MAIN DOCUMENT ▼

STEP 1 ▶

Click the View Merged Data button
(⊞) on the Mail Merge toolbar.

*Word displays the contents of the
first data record in the main document, instead of the merge fields
(Figure 2-65).*

STEP 2

Click the View Merged Data button
again.

*Word displays the merge fields in
the main document.*

FIGURE 2-65

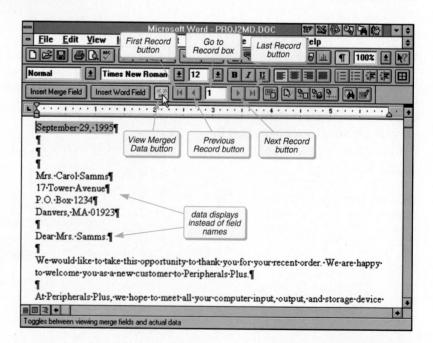

When you are viewing merged data in the main document, you can click the Last Record button (▐▶) to display the values in the last record in the data source; Next Record button (▶) to display the values in the next consecutive record number; Previous Record button (◀) to display the values in the previous record number; or First Record button (◀▌) to display the values in record one. You can also click in the Go to Record box and enter the record number you would like to display in the main document.

▶ CREATING AND PRINTING MAILING LABELS

Now that you have printed the form letters, the next step is to create mailing labels for the envelopes of the form letters. The mailing labels will use the same data source as the form letter, PROJ2DS.DOC. The format and content of the mailing labels will be exactly the same as the inside address in the form letter. That is, the first line will contain the customer's title, followed by the first name, followed by the last name. The second line will contain the customer's street address, and so on.

If your printer can print graphics, you can add a **POSTNET delivery-point bar code**, usually referred to simply as a **bar code**, above the address on each mailing label. Using a bar code speeds up the delivery service by the U.S. Postal Service. A bar code represents the addressee's zip code and first street address.

Follow the same basic steps as you did to create the form letters when you create mailing labels with bar codes, as shown on the following pages.

TO CREATE MAILING LABELS FROM AN EXISTING DATA SOURCE ▼

STEP 1 ▶

Point to the New button (▢) on the Standard toolbar (Figure 2-66).

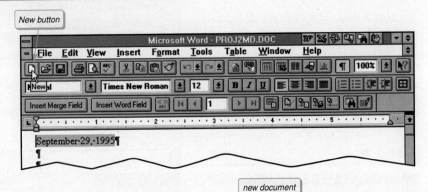

FIGURE 2-66

STEP 2 ▶

Click the New button. From the Tools menu, choose the Mail Merge command. When the Mail Merge Helper dialog box displays, click the Create button. Point to Mailing Labels.

Word displays a new document window for the mailing labels (Figure 2-67).

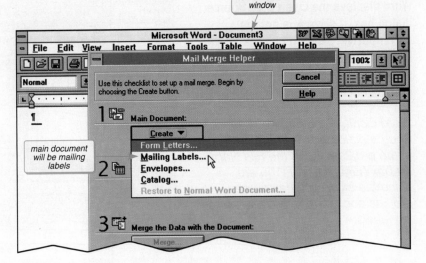

FIGURE 2-67

STEP 3 ▶

Select Mailing Labels.

Word displays a Microsoft Word dialog box asking whether you want to use the active document for the mailing labels or not (Figure 2-68).

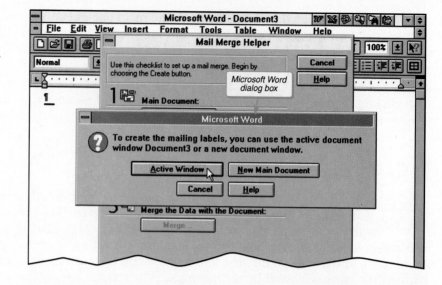

FIGURE 2-68

STEP 4 ▶

In the Microsoft Word dialog box, choose the Active Window button. When the Mail Merge Helper dialog box displays, click the Get Data button and point to Open Data Source.

Word returns you to the Mail Merge Helper dialog box (Figure 2-69). The document type is identified as mailing labels for the main document. Because you will use the same data source as you did for the form letters, you will open a data source instead of creating one.

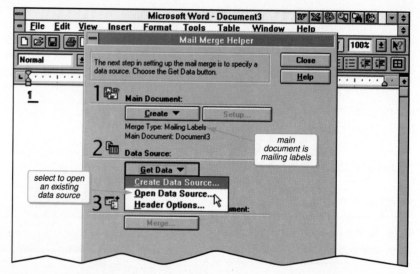

FIGURE 2-69

STEP 5 ▶

Select Open Data Source. When Word displays the Open Data Source dialog box, if drive A is not the current drive, select it by clicking the Drives drop-down box arrow and selecting a:. Then click the filename proj2ds.doc in the File Name list box.

Word displays the Open Data Source dialog box with the filename proj2ds.doc in the File Name list box (Figure 2-70). You are using the existing data source, proj2ds.doc, to generate the mailing labels.

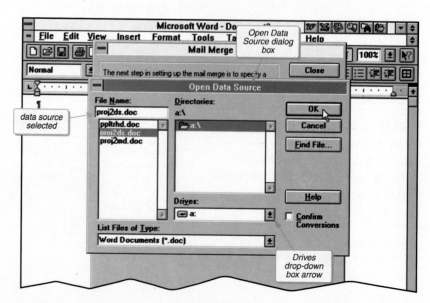

FIGURE 2-70

STEP 6 ▶

Choose the OK button in the Open Data Source dialog box.

Word displays a Microsoft Word dialog box asking if you want to set up the main document, the mailing labels (Figure 2-71).

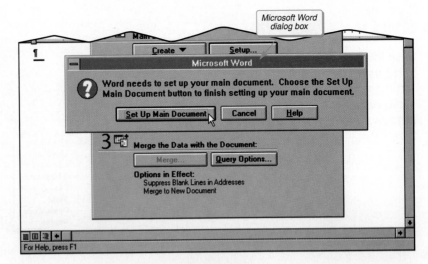

FIGURE 2-71

STEP 7 ▶

Choose the Set Up Main Document button (Set Up Main Document).

Word displays a Label Options dialog box (Figure 2-72). (If you have a dot matrix printer, your printer information will differ from Figure 2-72.) The Product Number list displays the product numbers for all possible Avery mailing label sheets compatible with your printer. The Label Information area displays details about the selected Avery product number. In this dialog box, you select the desired label type.

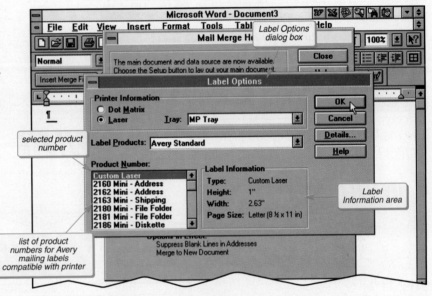

FIGURE 2-72

STEP 8 ▶

Click the OK button in the Label Options dialog box.

Word displays the Create Labels dialog box (Figure 2-73). You insert merge fields into the Sample Label area of the Create Labels dialog box the same way you inserted merge fields into the form letter main document.

FIGURE 2-73

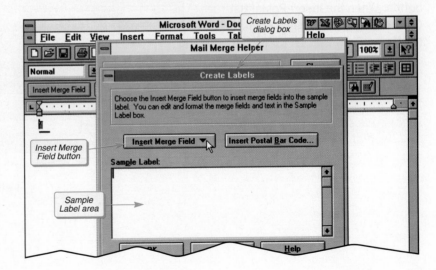

STEP 9 ▶

Click the Insert Merge Field button. In the list of fields, point to Title.

Word displays a list of fields in the data source (Figure 2-74).

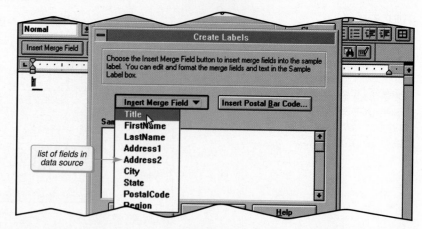

FIGURE 2-74

STEP 10 ▶

Follow Steps 3 through 5 on page MSW85 and then Steps 1 through 3 on page MSW86 to address the mailing label. Point to the Insert Postal Bar Code button (⌷ Insert Postal **B**ar Code... ⌷).

The mailing label layout is complete (Figure 2-75).

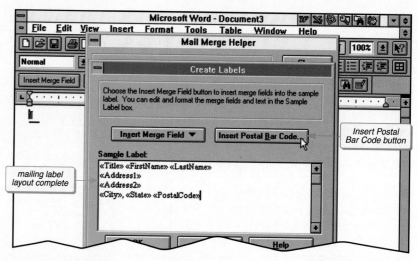

FIGURE 2-75

STEP 11 ▶

Choose the Insert Postal Bar Code button. When the Insert Postal Bar Code dialog box displays, point to the Merge Field with ZIP Code box arrow.

Word displays the Insert Postal Bar Code dialog box (Figure 2-76). A bar code contains the zip code and the first address line.

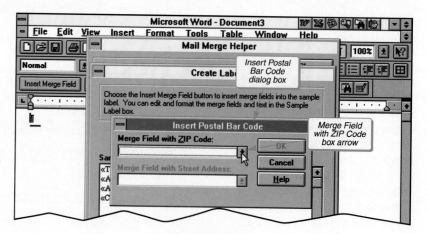

FIGURE 2-76

STEP 12 ▶

Click the Merge Field with ZIP Code box arrow. When Word displays the drop-down list of fields, scroll through the list and point to PostalCode.

Word displays a list of fields in the data source (Figure 2-77).

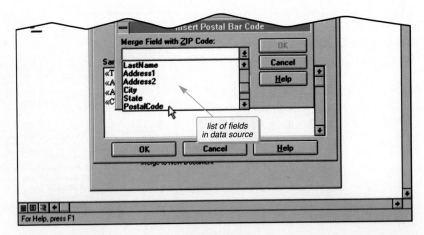

FIGURE 2-77

STEP 13 ▶

Select PostalCode from the list by clicking it. Click the Merge Field with Street Address box arrow and point to Address1.

Word displays PostalCode in the Merge Field with ZIP Code box (Figure 2-78).

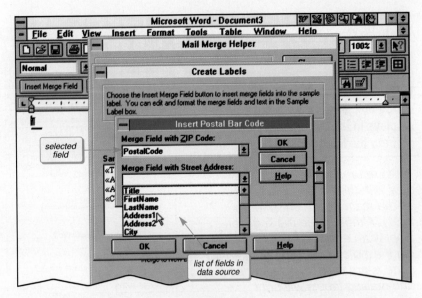

FIGURE 2-78

STEP 14 ▶

Select Address1 by clicking it and point to the OK button.

Word displays Address1 in the Merge Field with Street Address box (Figure 2-79).

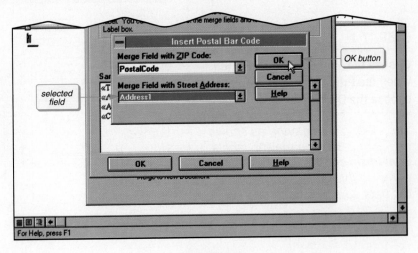

FIGURE 2-79

STEP 15 ▶

Choose the OK button in the Insert Postal Bar Code dialog box.

Word returns to the Create Labels dialog box, which indicates where the bar code will print (Figure 2-80).

FIGURE 2-80

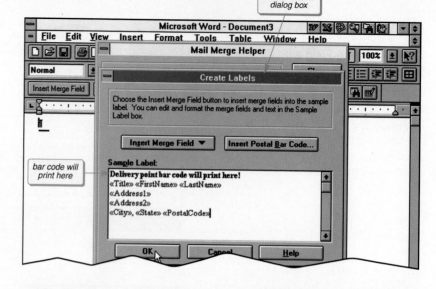

STEP 16 ▶

Choose the OK button in the Create Labels dialog box. Choose the Close button in the Mail Merge Helper dialog box. When the main document displays in the document window, point to the Merge to Printer button.

Word returns to the document window with the mailing label layout as the main document (Figure 2-81). Although the mailing labels display an error message, indicating the zip code portion of the bar code is not valid, the bar codes and mailing labels will print correctly.

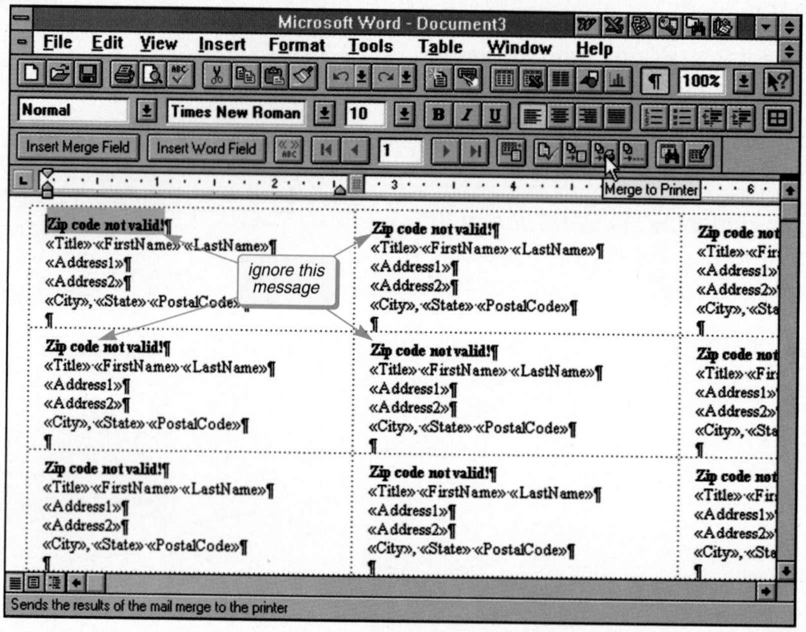

FIGURE 2-81

STEP 17 ▶

Choose the Merge to Printer button. When the Print dialog box displays, choose the OK button.

The mailing labels print, as shown in Figure 2-82. The mailing labels print in zip code order because earlier in this project you sorted the data source by zip code.

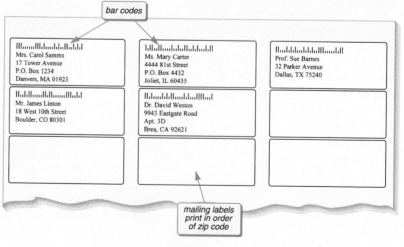

FIGURE 2-82

Save the mailing label main document by clicking the Save button on the
Standard toolbar. Use the filename PROJ2LBL.

► CREATING AND PRINTING ENVELOPES

I nstead of generating mailing labels to affix to envelopes, your printer may
have the capability of printing directly onto the envelopes. To print the
label information directly on the envelopes, follow the same basic steps
as you did to generate the mailing labels, as shown in these steps.

TO CREATE ENVELOPES FROM AN EXISTING DATA SOURCE ▼

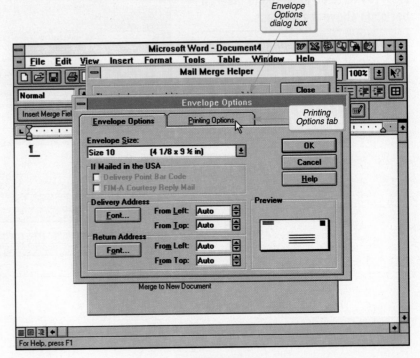

STEP 1 ►

Click the New button on the
Standard toolbar. From the Tools
menu, choose the Mail Merge
command. When the Mail Merge
Helper dialog box displays, click the
Create button. Point to Envelopes.

*Word displays a new document
window for the envelopes
(Figure 2-83).*

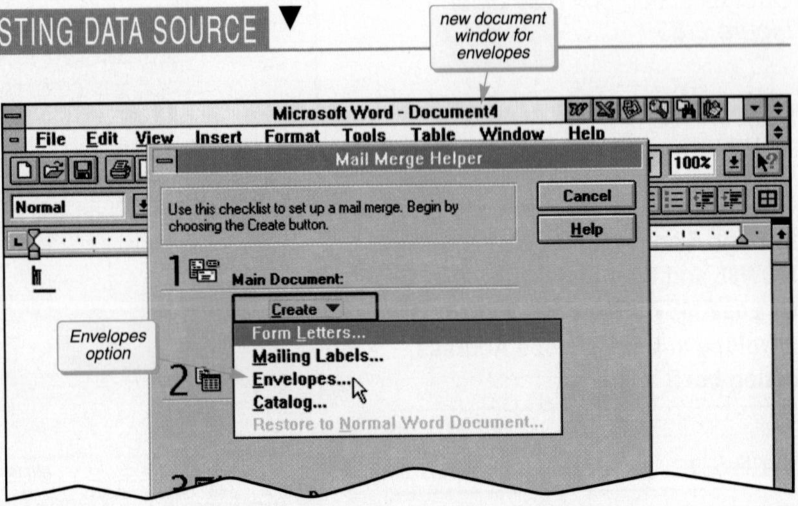

FIGURE 2-83

STEP 2 ►

Select Envelopes. In this Microsoft
Word dialog box, choose the Active
Window button. When the Mail Merge
Helper dialog box displays, click the
Get Data button and select Open
Data Source. When Word displays
the Open Data Source dialog box, if
drive A is not the current drive,
select it by clicking the Drives drop-
down box arrow and selecting a:.
Then click the filename proj2ds.doc
in the File Name list box. Choose the
OK button in the Open Data Source
dialog box. In the Microsoft Word
dialog box, choose the Set Up Main
Document button.

*Word displays the Envelope
Options dialog box (Figure 2-84).
(Depending on your printer, your
Envelope Options dialog box may
differ from Figure 2-84.)*

FIGURE 2-84

STEP 3 ▶

Click the Printing Options tab in the Envelope Options dialog box.

Word displays the options in the Printing Options tab (Figure 2-85). In the Feed Method area of this dialog box, you indicate how the envelopes sit in the printer. Depending on your printer driver, the options in your Printing Options dialog box may differ from Figure 2-85.

STEP 4

Click the OK button in the Envelope Options dialog box. Follow Steps 2 through 5 on pages MSW84 and MSW85 and then Steps 1 through 3 on page MSW86 to address the envelope in the Envelope Address dialog box.

STEP 5 ▶

Follow Steps 11 through 15 on pages MSW104 through MSW106 to insert a bar code above the address.

Word displays the completed envelope layout (Figure 2-86).

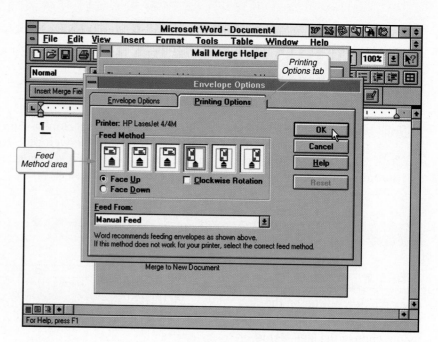

FIGURE 2-85

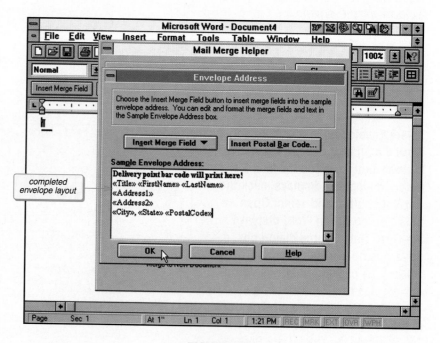

FIGURE 2-86

STEP 6 ▶

Choose the OK button in the Envelope Address dialog box. When the Mail Merge Helper dialog box displays, choose the Close button. When the main document displays in the document window, point to the Merge to Printer button on the Mail Merge toolbar.

Word returns to the document window with the envelope layout as the main document (Figure 2-87). Although an error message indicating the zip code portion of the bar code is not valid, the bar codes will print correctly.) The return address that prints in the upper left corner of the envelope is the user name and company name specified when you installed Word. Thus, your return address may be different from Figure 2-87.

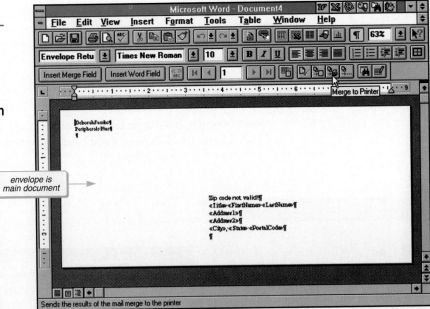

FIGURE 2-87

STEP 7 ▶

Choose the Merge to Printer button. When the Print dialog box displays, choose the OK button.

The envelopes print, as shown in Figure 2-88. The envelopes print in zip code order because earlier in this project, you sorted the data source by zip code.

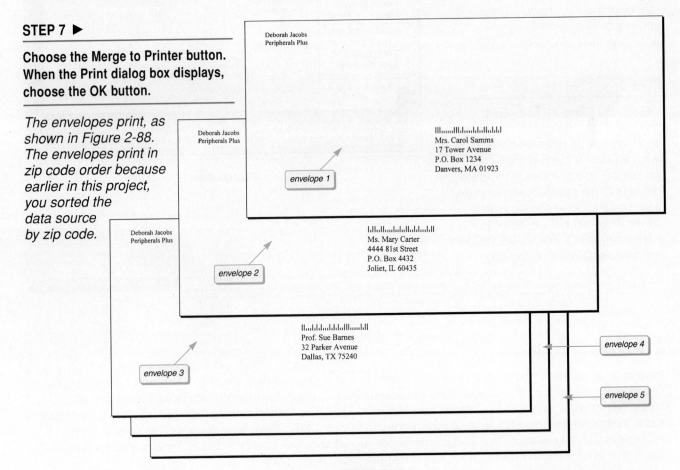

FIGURE 2-88

Save the envelope main document by clicking the Save button on the Standard toolbar. Use the filename PROJ2ENV.

You can change the return address lines on the envelope by selecting them and making the necessary corrections.

Closing All Open Files

You currently have four files open: PROJ2DS, PROJ2MD, PROJ2LBL, and PROJ2ENV. Instead of closing each one individually, you can close all open files at once, as shown in these steps.

TO CLOSE ALL OPEN DOCUMENTS ▼

STEP 1 ▶

Press and hold the SHIFT key. While holding the SHIFT key, select the File menu. Release the SHIFT key. Point to the Close All command.

Word displays a Close All command, instead of a Close command, in the File menu because you used the SHIFT key when selecting the menu (Figure 2-89).

STEP 2

Choose the Close All command.

Word closes all open documents and displays a blank document window. If you don't want the data records to be saved in sorted order, you would choose the No button when Word asks if you want to save changes to PROJ2DS.DOC in the Microsoft Word dialog box.

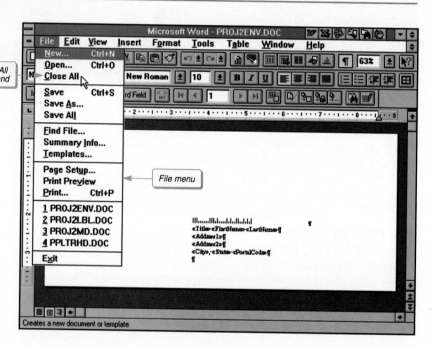

FIGURE 2-89

▶ PROJECT SUMMARY

Project 2 introduced you to generating form letters and corresponding mailing labels and envelopes. First, you created a company letterhead, then you identified the main document and created a data source. Next, you created the main document for the form letter. The form letter included merge fields and the IF field. In this project, you learned how to merge and print all the form letters, as well as only certain records in the data source. You also learned how to sort the data source records. Finally, you created and printed mailing labels and envelopes to correspond with the form letters.

▶ KEY TERMS AND INDEX

Q U I C K   R E F E R E N C E

In Microsoft Word 6, you can accomplish a task in a number of ways. The following table provides a quick reference to each task presented in this project with its available options. The commands listed in the Menu column can be executed using either the keyboard or the mouse. Some of the commands in the Menu column are also available in shortcut menus. If you have WordPerfect help activated, the key combinations listed in the Keyboard Shortcuts column will not work as shown.

Task	Mouse	Menu	Keyboard Shortcuts
Change Normal Style	Select text and click Style box	From Format menu, choose style	
Close All Open Documents		Press and hold SHIFT; select File menu; release SHIFT key; choose Close All	
Create Data Source		From Tools menu, choose Mail Merge	
Create Mailing Labels		From Tools menu, choose Mail Merge	
Insert Current Date		From Insert menu, choose Date and Time	Press ALT+SHIFT+D
Insert Merge Field	Click Insert Merge Field button on Mail Merge toolbar	From Insert menu, choose Field	
Merging and Printing	Clicking Merge to Printer button on Mail Merge toolbar	From Tools menu, choose Mail Merge	
Merging to a File	Click Merge to New Document button on Mail Merge toolbar	From Tools menu, choose Print Merge	
Print Document with Fields Codes		From File menu, choose Print	Press CTRL+P
Switch from Data Source to Main Document	Click Mail Merge Main Document button on Database toolbar	From Window menu, choose main document name	
Turn On/Off Field Code Display		From Tools menu, choose Options	

STUDENT ASSIGNMENT 1
True/False

Instructions: Circle T if the statement is true or F if the statement is false.

T F 1. Merging is the process of blending a data source into a main document.

T F 2. A data source contains the constant, or unchanging, text in a form letter.

T F 3. Each row in a data source is called a field.

T F 4. Data records begin in the first row of the data source.

T F 5. The header row contains the field names.

T F 6. A data source is actually a Word table.

T F 7. When your data source is the current active document, the buttons on the Standard toolbar change.

T F 8. To switch from the data source to the main document, click the Mail Merge Main Document button on the Database toolbar.

T F 9. Click the Current Date button on the Formatting toolbar to place the current date at the top of a document.

T F 10. To insert a merge field into the main document, type the beginning chevron, followed by the field name, followed by the ending chevron.

T F 11. A null expression is indicated by the text "NULL".

T F 12. A bar code consists of a zip code and the first street address line.

T F 13. The View Merged Data button on the Mail Merge toolbar displays all merged documents in the document window at the same time.

T F 14. When field codes are off, the IF field displays on the screen.

T F 15. To merge and print, click the Merge to Printer button on the Mail Merge toolbar.

T F 16. You can add a condition when merging and printing so only certain fields print from the data source.

T F 17. You cannot sort the data source.

T F 18. To create mailing labels, choose the Mail Merge command from the Tools menu.

T F 19. When field codes are on, the word MERGEFIELD displays in front of every merge field in the main document.

T F 20. When merging a data source to a main document, Word by default suppresses empty fields in the data source.

STUDENT ASSIGNMENT 2
Multiple Choice

Instructions: Circle the correct response.

1. Each column in a data source is called a _____.
   - a. character
   - b. field
   - c. record
   - d. file

2. The first row in a data source is called the _____.
   - a. initial row
   - b. data row
   - c. header row
   - d. start row

3. In a data source, field names _____.
   - a. can be duplicated
   - b. have a maximum length of 50 characters
   - c. must begin with a letter
   - d. all of the above

4. Which of the following is a valid field name?
   - a. FirstName
   - b. 1st-Name
   - c. First Name
   - d. both b and c

5. The Database toolbar allows you to _____.
   - a. add a new record
   - b. sort the data records
   - c. find a record
   - d. all of the above

6. In the main document, the Mail Merge toolbar is located between the _____ and the _____.
   - a. title bar, menu bar
   - b. menu bar, Standard toolbar
   - c. Standard toolbar, Formatting toolbar
   - d. Formatting toolbar, ruler

7. Which of the following mathematical operators stands for not equal to or does not match?
   - a. !=
   - b. <=
   - c. >=
   - d. <>

8. Text expressions in an IF field must be surrounded by _____.
   - a. equal signs (=)
   - b. apostrophes (')
   - c. quotation marks (")
   - d. hyphens (-)

9. The POSTNET bar code contains the _____ and _____.
   - a. first name, last name
   - b. zip code, first street address line
   - c. last name, first street address line
   - d. zip code, city

10. Merge fields in the main document are surrounded by _____.
   - a. chevrons
   - b. quotation marks
   - c. parentheses
   - d. brackets

STUDENT ASSIGNMENT 3
Understanding the Database Toolbar

Instructions: In Figure SA2-3, arrows point to various buttons on the Database toolbar when a data source is the active document. In the spaces provided, identify each button. Then, answer the questions below about the data source.

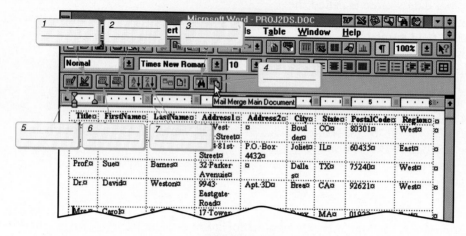

FIGURE SA2-3

1. What is the first row in the data source called? _____

2. What are the remaining rows in the data source called? _____

STUDENT ASSIGNMENT 4
Understanding the Mail Merge Toolbar

Instructions: In Figure SA2-4, arrows point to various buttons on the Mail Merge toolbar. In the spaces provided, identify each button.

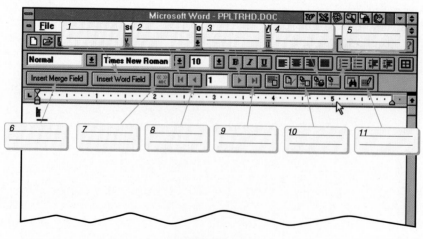

FIGURE SA2-4

STUDENT ASSIGNMENT 5
Understanding Field Name Rules

Instructions: Each field name listed below is invalid. In the spaces provided, briefly explain why each field name is invalid.

FIELD NAME   **EXPLANATION WHY FIELD NAME IS INVALID**

1. Street Address   _____

2. CustomerServiceRepresentativeStreetAddress   _____

3. 1st_Name   _____

4. P.O.Box   _____

5. Middle-Initial   _____

STUDENT ASSIGNMENT 6
Understanding IF Fields

Instructions: Below is the criteria for IF fields to be placed in main documents. In the spaces provided, write the IF field that meets the criteria.

Criteria: If Balance is equal to 0, then print No Balance Due; otherwise print Balance Due.

Completed IF Field: _____

Criteria: If GrossPay is greater than $2500, then print Over Budget; otherwise print Under Budget.

Completed IF Field: _____

C O M P U T E R   L A B O R A T O R Y   E X E R C I S E S

COMPUTER LABORATORY EXERCISE 1
Using the Help Menu to Learn About Form Letters, Mailing Labels, and Envelopes

Instructions: Start Word and perform the following tasks:

1. From the Help menu, choose the Search for Help on command. Type `form letters` and press the ENTER key. Select Setting up a merged main document, such as a form letter. Choose the Go To button. Read and print the information.
2. Choose the Close button. Choose the Search button. Choose the Show Topics button. Choose the Go To button. Read and print the information.
3. Choose the Search button. Choose the Show Topics button. Select Mail Merge: Step by Step. Choose the Go To button. Select Setting up and printing mailing labels by using Mail Merge. Read and print the information.
4. Choose the Close button. Select Setting up and printing envelopes by using Mail Merge. Read and print the information. Choose the Close button. Close the Help window.

COMPUTER LABORATORY EXERCISE 2
Printing the Main Document With and Without Field Codes

Instructions: Start Word. Open the document CLE2-2MD from the Word subdirectory on the Student Diskette that accompanies this book. A portion of the document is shown in Figure CLE2-2. By following the steps below, you are to print the document both with and without field codes.

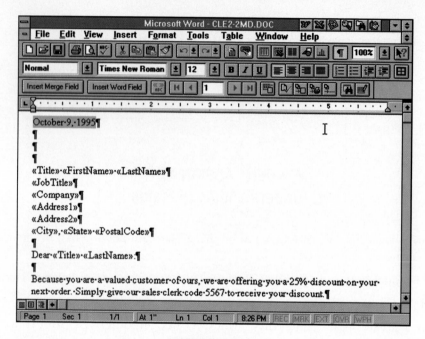

FIGURE CLE2-2

Perform the following tasks:

1. Click the Print button on the Standard toolbar.
2. Retrieve the printout from the printer.
3. From the File menu, choose the Print command.
4. Choose the Options button in the Print dialog box.
5. Turn on field codes by clicking the Field Codes check box in the Options dialog box.
6. Choose the OK button in the Options dialog box.
7. Choose the OK button in the Print dialog box. Retrieve the printout from the printer.
8. From the File menu, choose the Print command.
9. Choose the Options button in the Print dialog box.
10. Turn off the field codes by clicking the Field Codes check box in the Options dialog box.
11. Choose the OK button in the Options dialog box.
12. Choose the Close button in the Print dialog box.
13. Choose the Close command from the File menu.

COMPUTER LABORATORY EXERCISE 3
Selecting Data Records to Merge

Instructions: Start Word. Open the document CLE2-3MD from the Word subdirectory on the Student Diskette that accompanies this book. A portion of the document is shown in Figure CLE2-3.

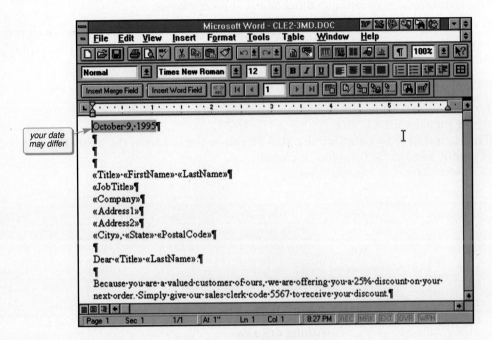

FIGURE CLE2-3

Perform the following tasks:

1. Choose the Mail Merge button on the Mail Merge toolbar.
2. Choose the Query Options button in the Merge dialog box.
3. Click the Field box arrow to display a list of fields. Scroll to the bottom of the list and select Balance.
4. Select Equal to in the Comparison list box.
5. Click in the Compared To text box and type 0 (the number zero).
6. Choose the OK button in the Query Options dialog box.
7. Choose the Close button in the Merge dialog box.
8. Choose the Merge to Printer button on the Mail Merge toolbar.
9. Choose the OK button in the Print dialog box. Retrieve the printouts from the printer.
10. Choose the Mail Merge button on the Mail Merge toolbar.
11. Choose the Query Options button in the Merge dialog box.
12. Choose the Clear All button in the Query Options dialog box.
13. Choose the OK button in the Query Options dialog box.
14. Choose the Close button in the Merge dialog box.
15. Press the SHIFT key and choose the Close All command from the File menu.

COMPUTER LABORATORY ASSIGNMENT 1
Creating a Data Source, Form Letter, and Mailing Labels

Purpose: To become familiar with creating a data source and a main document for a form letter, merging and printing the form letters, and generating mailing labels and envelopes.

Problem: Riverton University is holding its annual theatrical club fund raiser. As a president of the Theatrical Club, you have been assigned the task of recruiting local theatrical merchants to participate in the event. You decide to send a form letter to all merchants that participated last year.

Instructions: Perform the following tasks:

1. Create the letterhead shown at the top of Figure CLA2-1b on the next page using a header. Save the letterhead with the filename CLA2-1HD.
2. Begin the mail merge process by choosing the Mail Merge command from the Tools menu. Specify the current document window as the main document.
3. Create the data source shown in Figure CLA2-1a.

Title	FirstName	LastName	Company	Address1	Address2	City	State	PostalCode
Ms.	Jane	Sperry	Costumes R Us	70 River Road	P.O. Box 1234	Hammond	IN	46323
Mr.	Al	Krammer	Props N Things	P.O. Box 4567		Munster	IN	46321
Mr.	Jerry	Jones	The Makeup House	P.O. Box 9807		Highland	IN	46322
Mrs.	Karen	Clark	Stages, Inc.	5555 East Avenue		Hobart	IN	46342
Ms.	Betty	Vaughn	MJ Supplies	4321 81st Street	P.O. Box 8102	Highland	IN	46322

FIGURE CLA2-1a

4. Choose the View Data Source button from the Data Form dialog box to view the data source in table form. Save the data source with the name CLA2-1DS.
5. Print the data source.
6. Switch to the main document. Save the main document with the new filename CLA2-1MD. Create the main document for the form letter shown in Figure CLA2-1b. The current date should print at the top of the form letter. Change the normal style to a point size of 12 for the main document.

RIVERTON UNIVERSITY

theatre.wmf

(219) 555-7543
2213 - 154th Street, Hammond, IN 46323

October 9, 1995

«Title» «FirstName» «LastName»
«Company»
«Address1»
«Address2»
«City», «State» «PostalCode»

Dear «Title» «LastName»:

It's that time of year again! Our annual Theatrical Club Fund Raiser will be held on
Friday, December 8, 1995.

Last year, your company contributed to our fund raiser, and we'd like to ask for your
participation again this year. You helped to make our fund raiser a great success. If you
are available again this year, please contact me at 219-555-7543. We look forward to
hearing from you.

Sincerely,

Berry Thornton
Theatrical Club President

FIGURE CLA2-1b

7. Save the main document for the form letter again.
8. Print the main document.
9. Merge and print the form letters.
10. Click the New button on the Standard toolbar and create mailing labels using the same data source you used for the form letters. Put bar codes on the mailing labels.
11. Save the mailing labels with the filename CLA2-1LB.
12. Print the mailing labels.
13. If your printer allows, create envelopes using the same data source you used for the form letters. Put bar codes on the envelopes. Save the envelopes with the filename CLA2-1EN. Print the envelopes.

COMPUTER LABORATORY ASSIGNMENT 2
Creating a Data Source and a Form Letter with an IF Field

Purpose: To become familiar with creating a data source and a main document for the form letter, inserting an IF field in the main document, and merging and printing the form letters.

Problem: You are block coordinator for the annual block parties in your neighborhood. You have decided to use a form letter to announce this year's block party. For those people who have a spouse, you want the inside address and salutation to print both the husband's and wife's names. You decide to use an IF field for this task.

Instructions: Perform the following tasks:

1. Create the letterhead shown at the top of Figure CLA2-2b using a header. Save the letterhead with the filename CLA2-2HD.
2. Begin the mail merge process by choosing the Mail Merge command from the Tools menu. Specify the current document window as the main document.
3. Create the data source shown in Figure CLA2-2a.

FirstName	LastName	SpouseName	Address1	City	State	PostalCode
Ken	Bennings	Dawn	12 Western Avenue	Brea	CA	92622
Ellen	Reiter		15 Western Avenue	Brea	CA	92622
Mary	Fielder	Kevin	22 Western Avenue	Brea	CA	92622
John	Mason	Tammy	34 Western Avenue	Brea	CA	92622
Adam	Johnson		27 Western Avenue	Brea	CA	92622

FIGURE CLA2-2a

4. Choose the View Data Source button from the Data Form dialog box to view the data source in table form. Save the data source with the filename CLA2-2DS.
5. Print the data source.
6. Switch to the main document. Save the main document with the new filename CLA2-2MD. Create the main document for the form letter shown in Figure CLA2-2b. The current date should print at the top of the form letter. Change the normal style to a point size of 12 for the main document. In this assignment, the IF field text if true contains a merge field, the SpouseName. To make a merge field the text if true, fill in the dialog box except for the SpouseName field. When you return to the main document, turn field codes on, select inside the text if true quotation marks, and insert the SpouseName merge field. You will also need to adjust spaces in this address line.

ANNUAL BLOCK PARTY

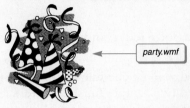

party.wmf

(714) 555-5678
70 Western Avenue, Brea, CA 92622

{ TIME \@ "MMMM d, yyyy" }

{ MERGEFIELD FirstName } { IF { MERGEFIELD SpouseName } <> "" "and {
MERGEFIELD SpouseName } '}{ MERGEFIELD LastName }
{ MERGEFIELD Address1 }
{ MERGEFIELD City }, { MERGEFIELD State } { MERGEFIELD PostalCode }

Dear { MERGEFIELD FirstName }{ IF { MERGEFIELD SpouseName } <> "" " and {
MERGEFIELD SpouseName } "}:

As block coordinator, I am announcing that our fifth annual block party will be held the
weekend of October 21 and 22, 1995. We will begin at 9:00 a.m. Saturday morning and
finish up at 5:00 p.m. Sunday afternoon.

Please contact me at 714-555-5678 to coordinate events, refreshments, and games. It
should be a fun-filled weekend!

Sincerely,

Vicki Barnes

FIGURE CLA2-2b

7. Save the main document for the form letter again.
8. Print the main document with field codes on. Don't forget to turn the field codes off.
9. Merge and print the form letters.

COMPUTER LABORATORY ASSIGNMENT 3
Designing a Data Source, Form Letter, Mailing Labels, and Envelopes from Sample Letters

Purpose: To become familiar with designing a data source, form letter, and mailing labels from sample drafted letters.

Problem: As staff benefits coordinator, your boss has asked you to schedule a meeting with all company employees to discuss the new benefits package. She drafted two sample finished letters for you and suggested you design a data source and form letter to generate similar letters for all company employees. The sample drafted letters are shown in Figure CLA2-3.

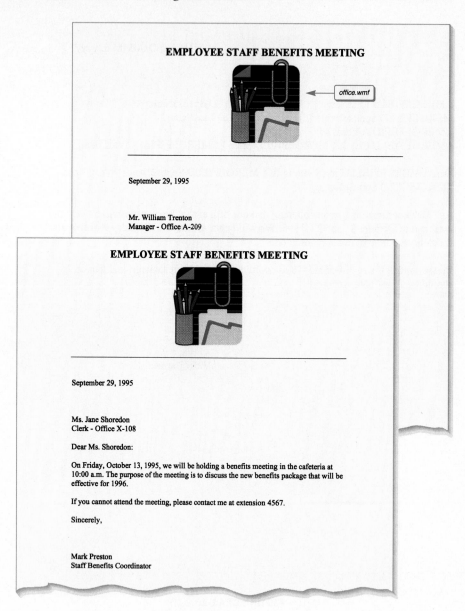

FIGURE CLA2-3

Instructions: Perform the following tasks:

1. Create the letterhead shown at the top of Figure CLA2-3 using a header. Save the letterhead with the filename CLA2-3HD.
2. Begin the mail merge process by choosing the Mail Merge command from the Tools menu. Specify the current document window as the main document.
3. Decide on field names to be used in the data source. Create a data source with five sample employees.
4. Choose the View Data Source button from the Data Form dialog box to view the data source in table form. Save the data source with the filename CLA2-3DS.
5. Print the data source.
6. Switch to the main document. Save the main document with the new filename CLA2-3MD. Create the main document for the form letter shown in Figure CLA2-3. Design the layout of the form letter from the sample letters. The current date should print at the top of the form letter. Change the normal style to a point size of 12 for the main document.
7. Save the main document for the form letter again.
8. Print the main document.
9. Merge and print the form letters.
10. Click the New button on the Standard toolbar and create mailing labels using the same data source you used for the form letters. Put bar codes on the mailing labels.
11. Save the mailing labels with the filename CLA2-3LB.
12. Print the mailing labels.
13. If your printer allows, create envelopes using the same data source you used for the form letters. Put bar codes on the envelopes. Save the envelopes with the filename CLA2-3EN. Print the envelopes.

COMPUTER LABORATORY ASSIGNMENT 4
Designing and Creating a Cover Letter

Purpose: To provide practice in planning, designing, and creating a data source, form letters, mailing labels, and envelopes.

Problem: You are currently seeking a full-time employment position in your area of expertise. You have already prepared a resume and would like to send it to a large group of potential employers. You decide to design a cover letter to send along with the resume.

Instructions: Design a cover letter for your resume. Create a data source with potential employers' names, addresses, and so forth. Design and create a letterhead for your cover letter using a header. Create the form letter and corresponding mailing labels. If your printer allows, also create envelopes.

*M*ICROSOFT *W*ORD 6 FOR *W*INDOWS

P R O J E C T   T H R E E

▼

CREATING A PROFESSIONAL NEWSLETTER

OBJECTIVES You will have mastered the material in this project when you can:

▶ Define desktop publishing terminology
▶ Add ruling lines above and below paragraphs
▶ Adjust shading margins in a paragraph
▶ Insert special characters in a document
▶ Format a document into multiple columns
▶ Format a drop capital letter in a paragraph

▶ Use a frame to position a graphic
▶ Insert a column break
▶ Insert a vertical rule between columns
▶ Add a box border around paragraphs
▶ Insert a pull-quote
▶ Change the color in a graphic

▶ INTRODUCTION

Professional-looking documents, such as newsletters and brochures, are often created using desktop publishing software. With **desktop publishing software**, you can divide a document into multiple columns, insert pictures and wrap text around them, change fonts and font sizes, add color and lines, and so on, to make the document more professional and attractive. A traditional viewpoint of desktop publishing software, such as PageMaker or Ventura, is that it enables you to load an existing word processing document and enhance it through formatting not provided in your word processor. Word for Windows, however, provides you with many of the formatting features that you would find in a desktop publishing package. Thus, you can create professional newsletters and brochures directly within Word for Windows.

▶ PROJECT THREE — NEWSLETTER

Project 3 uses Word to produce the monthly newsletter shown in Figure 3-1 on the next two pages. The newsletter is a monthly publication for members of the Home Buyers' Club. Notice that it incorporates the desktop publishing features of Word for Windows. The newsletter is divided into three columns; includes a graphic of houses and a pull-quote, both with text wrapped around them; has both horizontal and vertical lines to separate distinct areas; and uses different fonts, font sizes, shading, and color for various characters and the graphic.

MSW124

nameplate

HOME BUYERS' CLUB

ruling lines

BUYING OLD HOMES: Tips and Tricks - Part 1

headline

Monthly Newsletter   Vol. I • No. 8 • Aug. 9, 1995

subhead

issue information line

vertical rule

drop cap

BUYER BEWARE

When purchasing an old home with the intent of saving money, you must be aware of several potential hidden costs. Many items, if left unchecked, can lead to huge unexpected costs after you have closed a sale. Once you have located a potential house for purchase, be sure to check its location, foundation, crawl space, roof, exterior, garage, electric, heating, plumbing, kitchen, baths, living areas, bedrooms, and attic.

LOCATION

A home's location is an important point to note for resale value. Look at the neighborhood. Items that tend to lower a property's value are messy neighbors or nearby businesses. Look for access to stores and recreation areas to increase a property's value. Trees, fences, and patios are also a plus.

FOUNDATION

Stand away from the house and check that it is square and straight. Look at the roof line and walls for sagging, settling, and leaning. These problems could be caused from a bad foundation or poor drainage or a poorly built house.

One problem you may encounter with a foundation is cracks. Straight cracks are common and can be repaired easily. V'd cracks are usually an indication of a very costly problem, caused because cement was not poured properly. A second problem with foundations is termites. Termite extermination is costly, and damage can be costly to repair.

With poor drainage, especially on hillside houses, moisture penetrates the soil and makes it slippery - actually making the house slide. To check for proper drainage, examine the tile around the basement exterior and interior for cracks, and verify all sump pumps work properly. Improper drainage is a costly problem to fix.

CRAWL SPACE

Crawl spaces should be well vented to prevent moisture buildup and dry rot of wood. The crawl space foundation should be checked for cracks.

Continued next page...

MONTHLY MEETING

The Home Buyers' Club meeting will be held this month on Saturday, August 26 in the Region Room at Cary's Steak House in Harris. Dinner will be served at 6:00 p.m.; the meeting will begin at 7:00 p.m.; and our presentation will begin at 8:00 p.m. Our guest speaker, Mary Evans, will address contracts: What You Should Know Before Signing A Contract.

EVENTS

On Sunday, September 3, The Convention Center in Elmwood is hosting a Gardeners Show from 1:00 p.m. to 5:00 p.m. Hundreds of retailers will have exhibits. Many experts will be on hand to answer consumer questions. In the past, the Gardeners Show has proved to be an extremely worthwhile event for our members.

REMINDER

The Home Buyers' Club Second Annual Picnic is on Saturday, August 19 at Hughes Park in Romeoville. It is sure to be a fun-filled event for all family members. Bring your swimsuit and a dish to pass. See you at 1:00 p.m.!

FIGURE 3-1a

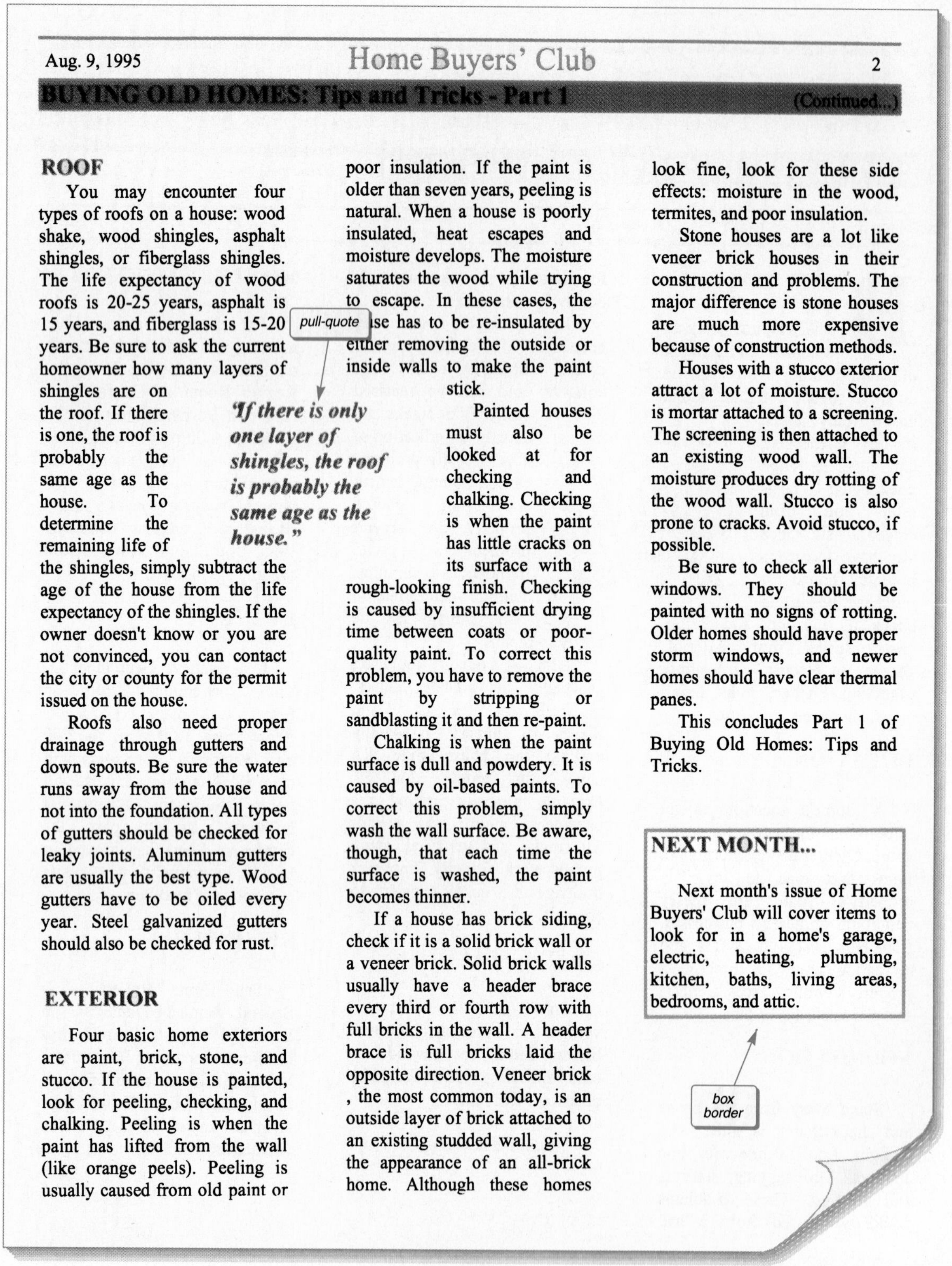

Aug. 9, 1995   Home Buyers' Club   2

BUYING OLD HOMES: Tips and Tricks - Part 1   (Continued...)

ROOF

You may encounter four types of roofs on a house: wood shake, wood shingles, asphalt shingles, or fiberglass shingles. The life expectancy of wood roofs is 20-25 years, asphalt is 15 years, and fiberglass is 15-20 years. Be sure to ask the current homeowner how many layers of shingles are on the roof. If there is one, the roof is probably the same age as the house. To determine the remaining life of the shingles, simply subtract the age of the house from the life expectancy of the shingles. If the owner doesn't know or you are not convinced, you can contact the city or county for the permit issued on the house.

pull-quote

'If there is only one layer of shingles, the roof is probably the same age as the house."

Roofs also need proper drainage through gutters and down spouts. Be sure the water runs away from the house and not into the foundation. All types of gutters should be checked for leaky joints. Aluminum gutters are usually the best type. Wood gutters have to be oiled every year. Steel galvanized gutters should also be checked for rust.

EXTERIOR

Four basic home exteriors are paint, brick, stone, and stucco. If the house is painted, look for peeling, checking, and chalking. Peeling is when the paint has lifted from the wall (like orange peels). Peeling is usually caused from old paint or poor insulation. If the paint is older than seven years, peeling is natural. When a house is poorly insulated, heat escapes and moisture develops. The moisture saturates the wood while trying to escape. In these cases, the house has to be re-insulated by either removing the outside or inside walls to make the paint stick.

Painted houses must also be looked at for checking and chalking. Checking is when the paint has little cracks on its surface with a rough-looking finish. Checking is caused by insufficient drying time between coats or poor-quality paint. To correct this problem, you have to remove the paint by stripping or sandblasting it and then re-paint.

Chalking is when the paint surface is dull and powdery. It is caused by oil-based paints. To correct this problem, simply wash the wall surface. Be aware, though, that each time the surface is washed, the paint becomes thinner.

If a house has brick siding, check if it is a solid brick wall or a veneer brick. Solid brick walls usually have a header brace every third or fourth row with full bricks in the wall. A header brace is full bricks laid the opposite direction. Veneer brick , the most common today, is an outside layer of brick attached to an existing studded wall, giving the appearance of an all-brick home. Although these homes look fine, look for these side effects: moisture in the wood, termites, and poor insulation.

Stone houses are a lot like veneer brick houses in their construction and problems. The major difference is stone houses are much more expensive because of construction methods.

Houses with a stucco exterior attract a lot of moisture. Stucco is mortar attached to a screening. The screening is then attached to an existing wood wall. The moisture produces dry rotting of the wood wall. Stucco is also prone to cracks. Avoid stucco, if possible.

Be sure to check all exterior windows. They should be painted with no signs of rotting. Older homes should have proper storm windows, and newer homes should have clear thermal panes.

This concludes Part 1 of Buying Old Homes: Tips and Tricks.

NEXT MONTH...

Next month's issue of Home Buyers' Club will cover items to look for in a home's garage, electric, heating, plumbing, kitchen, baths, living areas, bedrooms, and attic.

box border

FIGURE 3-1b

Desktop Publishing Terminology

As you create professional-looking newsletters and brochures, you should be aware of several desktop publishing terms. In Project 3 (Figure 3-1 on the previous two pages), the **nameplate**, or **banner**, is the top portion of the newsletter above the three columns. It contains the name of the newsletter; the **headline**, or subject, of the newsletter; and the **issue information line**. The horizontal lines in the nameplate are called **rules**, or **ruling lines**.

Within the body of the newsletter, a heading, such as BUYER BEWARE, is called a **subhead**. The vertical line dividing the second and third columns is a **vertical rule**. The text that wraps around the houses graphic is referred to as **wrap-around text**, and the space between the house and the words is called the **run-around**. The NEXT MONTH notice in the lower right corner of the second page has a **box border** around it.

Document Preparation Steps

The following document preparation steps give you an overview of how the document in Figure 3-1 on the previous two pages will be developed in this project. If you are preparing the document in this project on a personal computer, read these steps without doing them.

1. Create the nameplate.
2. Format the first page of the body of the newsletter.
3. Format the second page of the newsletter.
4. Add color to the newsletter.

Because this project involves several steps requiring you to drag the mouse, you may want to cancel an action if you drag to the wrong location. Remember that you can always click the Undo button on the Standard toolbar to cancel your most recent action.

Redefining the Normal Style

Recall from Project 2 that your desired document settings may differ from Word's default settings. In these cases, it is good practice to define your document settings and save these settings in the normal style to ensure that the entire document follows the same style. Much of the text in the newsletter in Project 3 has a font size of 12. Desktop publishers recommend this font size because people of all ages can easily read it.

Perform the steps on the next page to redefine the normal style to be a font size of 12.

TO REDEFINE THE NORMAL STYLE

Step 1: If it is not already recessed, click the Show/Hide ¶ button on the Standard toolbar.

Step 2: Select the paragraph mark in the top left corner of the document window by clicking in the selection bar to its left.

Step 3: Click the Font Size box arrow on the Formatting toolbar and select 12.

Step 4: Select the word Normal in the Style box on the Formatting toolbar by clicking it.

Step 5: Move the mouse pointer into the document window. Click the left mouse button.

Step 6: If it is not already selected, click the Redefine the style using the selection as an example option in the Reapply Style dialog box. Choose the OK button.

Step 7: Click anywhere outside the highlighted paragraph mark to remove the selection.

Word redefines the normal style to 12 point.

Changing all Margin Settings

Word is preset to use standard 8.5 by 11-inch paper, with 1.25-inch left and right margins and 1-inch top and bottom margins. For the newsletter in this project, you want all margins to be at .4-inch. Thus, you want to change the top, bottom, left, and right margin settings.

You can change the top and left margins using the rulers in page layout view. When you want to change all margins, it is more efficient to use the Page Setup command on the File menu, instead of the rulers, as shown in these steps.

TO CHANGE ALL MARGIN SETTINGS ▼

STEP 1 ►

Select the File menu and point to the Page Setup command (Figure 3-2).

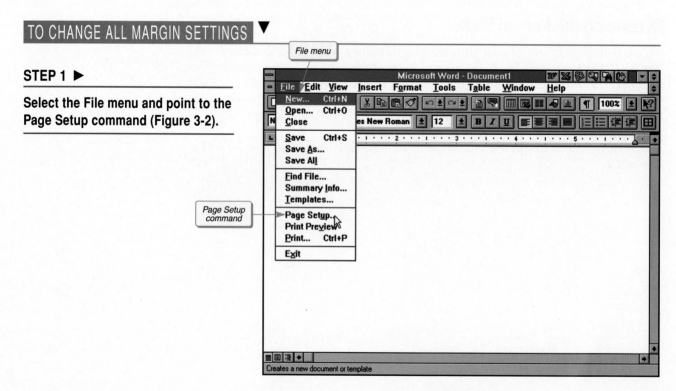

FIGURE 3-2

STEP 2 ▶

Choose the Page Setup command. When Word displays the Page Setup dialog box, point to the down arrow next to the Top text box.

Word displays the Page Setup dialog box (Figure 3-3). If the options in the Margins tab do not display in your Page Setup dialog box, click the Margins tab. Word lists the current margin settings in the text boxes and displays them graphically in the Preview area.

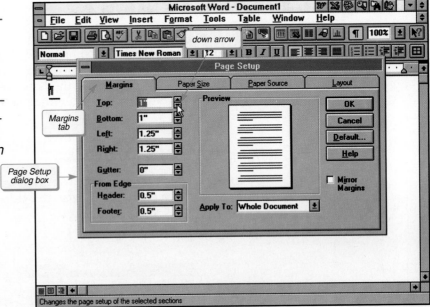

FIGURE 3-3

STEP 3 ▶

Repeatedly click the down arrow next to the Top text box, the Bottom text box, the Left text box, and the Right text box until each text box reads 0.4". Point to the OK button.

The top, bottom, left, and right margin settings decrease to 0.4" (Figure 3-4). Depending on the printer you are using, you may need to set the margins differently for this project. For example, if you are using a dot matrix printer, you may need to set the top, bottom, left, and right margins to .5".

STEP 4

Choose the OK button.

Word adjusts the margin settings for the current document.

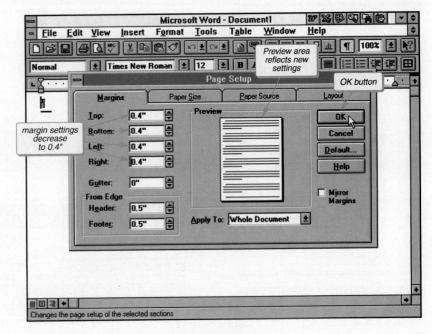

FIGURE 3-4

▶ CREATING THE NAMEPLATE

T he nameplate in Project 3 consists of all the text above the multiple columns (see Figure 3-1a on page MSW125). The nameplate consists of the newsletter title, HOME BUYERS' CLUB; the headline, BUYING OLD HOMES: Tips and Tricks - Part 1; and the issue information line. The steps on the following pages illustrate how to create the nameplate for the first page of the newsletter in Project 3.

Changing the Font and Font Size

In Project 3, the newsletter title uses the Arial font with a font size of 50. Perform these steps to create the newsletter title.

TO CHANGE THE FONT AND FONT SIZE ▼

STEP 1 ▶

Click the Font box arrow on the Formatting toolbar. Scroll through the list of available fonts until Arial appears. Select Arial by clicking it. Click 12 in the Font Size box.

Word selects 12 in the Font Size box (Figure 3-5). Arial displays in the Font box. Because 50 is not in the list of font sizes for Arial, you must type 50 into the Font Size box.

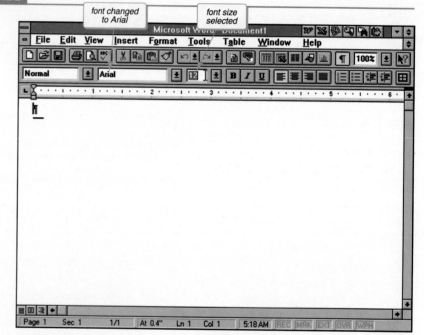

FIGURE 3-5

STEP 2 ▶

Type 50 and press the ENTER key.

Word displays 50 in the Font Size box (Figure 3-6).

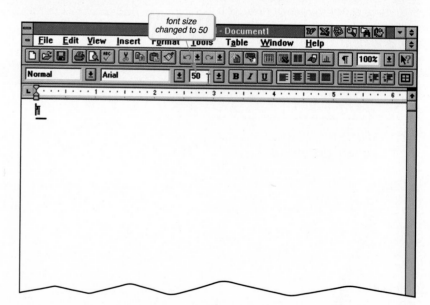

FIGURE 3-6

STEP 3 ▶

Click the Bold button on the Formatting toolbar. Type HOME BUYERS' CLUB **and press the ENTER key.**

Word displays the entered text in the Arial font with a font size of 50 (Figure 3-7).

current font

current font size

text entered in Arial font with font size of 50

right margin extends beyond document window

HOME·BUYERS'·CL

FIGURE 3-7

Makes the selection bold (toggle)

When you changed the margin settings earlier in this project, the right margin moved beyond the right edge of the document window. Thus, part of the newsletter title does not display in the document window.

If both your left and right margins do not display in the document window, perform the following steps to zoom page width.

TO ZOOM PAGE WIDTH

Step 1: Click the Zoom Control box arrow on the Standard toolbar.

Step 2: In the list of zoom controls, select Page Width by clicking it.

Word brings both the left and right margins into view in the document window (Figure 3-8).

The next step is to add rules, or ruling lines, above and below the newsletter title.

Zoom Control box arrow

HOME·BUYERS'·CLUB¶

both the left and right margins are in view

FIGURE 3-8

Adding Ruling Lines to Divide Text

In Word, you use borders to create ruling lines. Ruling lines generally display both above and below a paragraph. Perform the steps on the next page to add ruling lines above and below the newsletter title.

TO ADD RULING LINES TO A DOCUMENT ▼

STEP 1 ▶

Select the newsletter title by clicking in the selection bar to its left. Click the Borders button on the Formatting toolbar. On the Borders toolbar, click the Line Style box arrow. In the list of available line styles, point to 4 1/2 pt.

Word displays the Borders toolbar (Figure 3-9).

FIGURE 3-9

STEP 2 ▶

Select 4 1/2 pt by clicking it. Click both the Top Border and Bottom Border buttons on the Borders toolbar. Point to the Borders button on the Formatting toolbar.

The Top Border and Bottom Border buttons on the Borders toolbar are recessed (Figure 3-10).

FIGURE 3-10

STEP 3 ▶

Click the Borders button on the Formatting toolbar. Click the paragraph mark in line 2 to remove the selection from line 1.

Word places 4 1/2 point ruling lines both above and below the newsletter title (Figure 3-11).

FIGURE 3-11

Borders are part of paragraph formatting. If you press the ENTER key in a bordered paragraph, the border will carry forward to the next paragraph. To avoid this, move the insertion point outside of the bordered paragraph before pressing the ENTER key.

Adding the Headline with Shading

Shading is often used by desktop publishers to emphasize text. Because shading tends to reduce the legibility of text, the characters in the shading should have a larger font size and should be bold. One way to shade is by using the Borders and Shading command on the Format menu. You can also shade using the Borders toolbar.

By default, the shading begins at the left margin and extends to the right margin. You can adjust the shading area by reducing or lengthening the indent markers on the ruler.

In this project, the headline, BUYING OLD HOMES: Tips and Tricks - Part 1, is shaded. Only the headline is shaded; that is, the shading does not extend to the right margin. Perform these steps to shade the headline paragraph.

TO SHADE A HEADLINE PARAGRAPH ▼

STEP 1 ▶

Change the font size to 16. Click the Bold button. Type BUYING OLD HOMES: Tips and Tricks - Part 1 **and press ENTER. Select the entered text by clicking in the selection bar to its left. Click the Borders button on the Formatting toolbar. On the Borders toolbar, click the Shading box arrow.**

Word highlights the selected text and displays a list of available shading percentages (Figure 3-12).

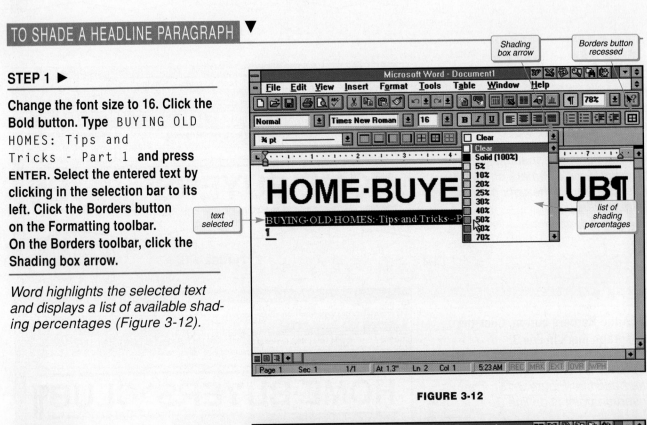

FIGURE 3-12

STEP 2 ▶

Select 50% by clicking it. Point to the right indent marker on the ruler.

Word shades the selected text (Figure 3-13).

FIGURE 3-13

STEP 3 ▶

Drag the right indent marker to the 4.75" mark on the ruler.

As you drag the mouse, Word displays a vertical dotted line in the document window, indicating the new location of the right indent marker (Figure 3-14).

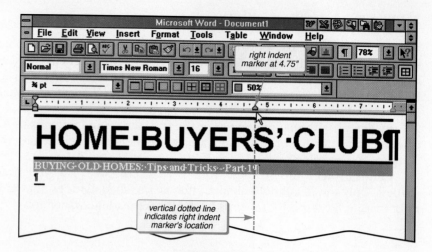

FIGURE 3-14

STEP 4 ▶

Release the mouse. Point to the Borders button on the Formatting toolbar.

Word adjusts the shading so it stops at the 4.75" mark on the ruler, instead of the right margin (Figure 3-15).

FIGURE 3-15

STEP 5 ▶

Click the Borders button. Click the paragraph mark in line 3.

Word removes the highlight from the headline (Figure 3-16). The insertion point is on line 3.

FIGURE 3-16

Entering the Issue Information Line

The issue information line in this project contains the volume, number, and date of the newsletter. It also displays a large round dot between the volume, number, and date. This special symbol, called a **bullet**, is not on the keyboard. You insert bullets and other special symbols, such as the Greek alphabet and mathematical characters, through the Symbol command.

Perform these steps to add a bullet in the issue information line.

TO ADD A BULLET TO TEXT ▼

STEP 1 ►

Press the ENTER key. Change the font size to 14. Type `Monthly Newsletter` and change the font size to 12. Click the 5.625" mark on the ruler to add a custom tab at that location. Press the TAB key. Type `Vol. I` followed by a space.

The first part of the issue information line is entered (Figure 3-17).

FIGURE 3-17

STEP 2 ►

Select the Insert menu and point to the Symbol command (Figure 3-18).

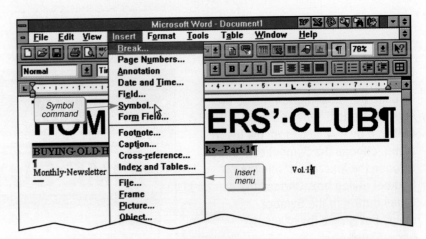

FIGURE 3-18

STEP 3 ►

Choose the Symbol command. If it is not already selected, click the bullet symbol in the Symbol dialog box. Point to the Insert button (Insert...).

Word displays the Symbol dialog box (Figure 3-19). If the Symbols options do not display in your Symbol dialog box, click the Symbols tab. If the Font box does not display Symbol, click the Font box arrow and select Symbol. A selected symbol is highlighted.

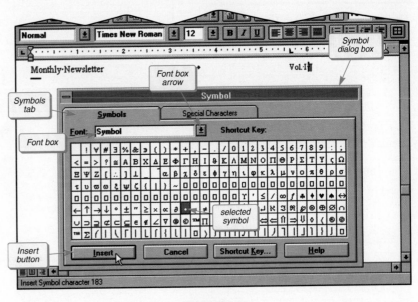

FIGURE 3-19

STEP 4 ►

Choose the Insert button. Point to the Close button (Close).

Word inserts the bullet character to the left of the insertion point in the document window (Figure 3-20). At this point, you can add additional symbols or close the Symbol dialog box.

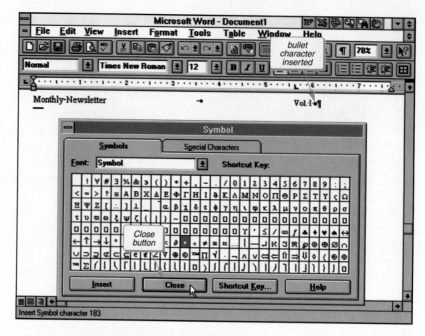

FIGURE 3-20

STEP 5 ►

Choose the Close button. Press the SPACEBAR once. Type No. 8 followed by a space. From the Insert menu, choose the Symbol command. Choose the Insert button in the Symbol dialog box. Choose the Close button in the Symbol dialog box. Press the SPACEBAR once. Type Aug. 9, 1995 and press the ENTER key.

The issue information line displays, as shown in Figure 3-21.

FIGURE 3-21

STEP 6 ▶

Select the issue information line by clicking in the selection bar to its left. Click the Borders button on the Formatting toolbar. On the Borders toolbar, click the Line Style box arrow. In the list of available line styles, select 2 1/4 pt. Click both the Top Border and Bottom Border buttons on the Borders toolbar. Click the Borders button on the Formatting toolbar. Click the paragraph mark in line 5.

The issue information line is complete (Figure 3-22).

FIGURE 3-22

You can also insert ANSI characters into a document by entering the ANSI code directly into the document. The **ANSI characters** are a predefined set of characters, including both characters on the keyboard and special characters, such as the bullet character. To enter the ANSI code, make sure the NUM LOCK key is on. Then, hold down the ALT key and type 0 (a zero), followed by the ANSI code for the character. You *must* use the numeric keypad when entering the ANSI code. For a complete list of ANSI codes, see your Microsoft Windows documentation.

The nameplate is now complete. Because you have completed a significant portion of work, you should save the newsletter by clicking the Save button on the Standard toolbar. Use the filename PROJ3.DOC. It is also a good idea to save this portion of the document, the nameplate, under a different name, such as NAMEPLAT, so you can load just the nameplate for future issues of the newsletter.

The next step is to enter the body of the newsletter.

▶ FORMATTING THE FIRST PAGE OF THE BODY OF THE NEWSLETTER

The body of the newsletter in this project is divided into three columns (see Figure 3-1a on page MSW125). The houses graphic displays between the first and second columns on page 1. A vertical rule separates the second and third columns on page 1. The steps on the following pages illustrate how to format the first page of the body of the newsletter with these desktop publishing features.

Formatting a Document into Multiple Columns

With Word, you can create two types of columns: parallel columns and snaking columns. **Parallel columns**, or table columns, are created with the Insert Table button. You created parallel columns in Project 1. The text in **snaking columns**, or newspaper-style columns, flows from the bottom of one column to the top of the next. The body of the newsletter in Project 3 uses snaking columns.

When you begin a document in Word, it has one column. You can divide a section of a document or the entire document into multiple columns. Within each column, you can type, modify, or format text.

To divide a section of a document into multiple columns, you must first create a section break. Recall from Project 1 that whenever you change margins, headers, footers, or columns in a document that Word requires you to insert a section break before the formatting change. In this project, the nameplate is one column and the body of the newsletter is three columns. Thus, you must insert a section break beneath the nameplate. Perform the following steps to divide the body of the newsletter into three columns.

TO CREATE MULTIPLE COLUMNS IN A SECTION OF A DOCUMENT ▼

STEP 1 ►

With the insertion point on line 5, press the ENTER key. From the Insert menu, choose the Break command. In the Break dialog box, click the Continuous option in the Section Breaks area. Point to the OK button.

Word displays the Break dialog box (Figure 3-23). The Continuous option instructs Word not to do a page break with the section break.

STEP 2

Choose the OK button.

Word inserts a section break above the insertion point, which is now in section 2.

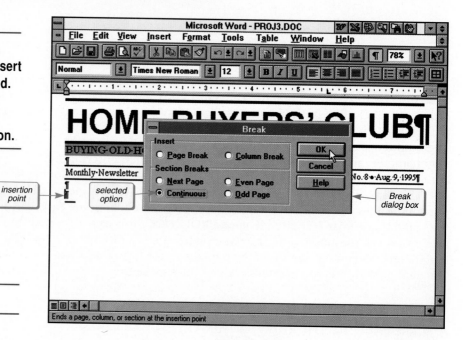

FIGURE 3-23

STEP 3 ▶

Click the Columns button on the Standard toolbar. Move the mouse pointer into the left-most column in the columns graphic beneath the Columns button.

Word displays a columns graphic beneath the Columns button (Figure 3-24). Drag the mouse through the number of columns you want in the section.

FIGURE 3-24

STEP 4 ▶

Drag the mouse pointer through the first three columns of the graphic (Figure 3-25).

FIGURE 3-25

STEP 5 ▶

Release the mouse button.

Word divides the section containing the insertion point into three columns (Figure 3-26). Notice that the ruler indicates the size of the three columns.

FIGURE 3-26

When you use the Columns button to create columns, Word creates columns with equal width. You can create columns of unequal width by choosing the Columns command from the Format menu.

Entering a Subhead and Associated Text

Subheads are headings placed throughout the body of the newsletter, such as BUYER BEWARE. In this project, the subheads are bold and have a point size of 14. The text beneath the subheads is justified. **Justified** means that the left and right margins are aligned, like newspaper columns. The first line of each paragraph is indented .25 inch. Perform the following steps to enter the first subhead and its associated text.

When purchasing an old home with the intent of saving money, you must be aware of several potential hidden costs. Many items, if left unchecked, can lead to huge unexpected costs after you have closed a sale. Once you have located a potential house for purchase, be sure to check its location, foundation, crawl space, roof, exterior, garage, electric, heating, plumbing, kitchen, baths, living areas, bedrooms, and attic.

FIGURE 3-27

TO ENTER SUBHEADS AND ASSOCIATED TEXT ▼

STEP 1 ▶

Change the font size to 14. Click the Bold button. Type BUYER BEWARE and click the Bold button. Change the font size back to 12 and press the ENTER key twice. Drag the first-line indent marker on the ruler to the .25" mark.

The first subhead is entered and the insertion point is indented .25-inch (Figure 3-28).

FIGURE 3-28

STEP 2 ▶

Click the Justify button (▤) on the Formatting toolbar. Type the paragraph beneath the BUYER BEWARE subhead. The paragraph text is shown in Figure 3-27 on the previous page.

Word automatically aligns both the left and right edges of the paragraph like newspaper columns (Figure 3-29). Notice that extra space is placed between some words when you justify text.

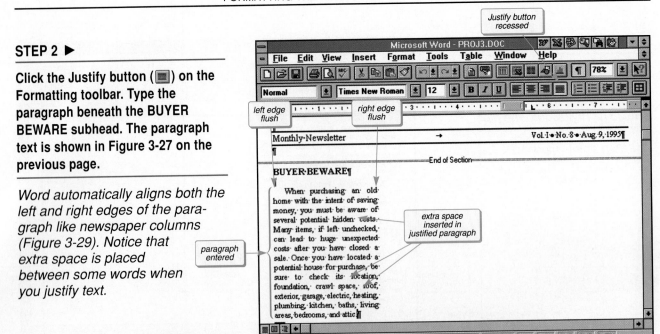

FIGURE 3-29

Inserting the Remainder of the Newsletter Text

Instead of entering the rest of the newsletter in this project, you can insert the file PROJ3TXT.DOC on the Student Diskette that accompanies this book into the newsletter. This file contains the remainder of the newsletter text. Perform these steps to insert PROJ3TXT.DOC into the newsletter.

TO INSERT A FILE INTO A COLUMN OF THE NEWSLETTER ▼

STEP 1 ▶

Press the ENTER key twice. Drag the first-line indent marker back to the 0-inch mark on the ruler. Insert into drive A the Student Diskette that accompanies this book. From the Insert menu, choose the File command. If necessary, click the Drives box arrow and select a:. Double-click the Word subdirectory in the Directories list box. Select proj3txt.doc by clicking it. Point to the OK button.

Word displays the File dialog box (Figure 3-30). The file proj3txt.doc is selected. The file will be inserted at the location of the insertion point in the document.

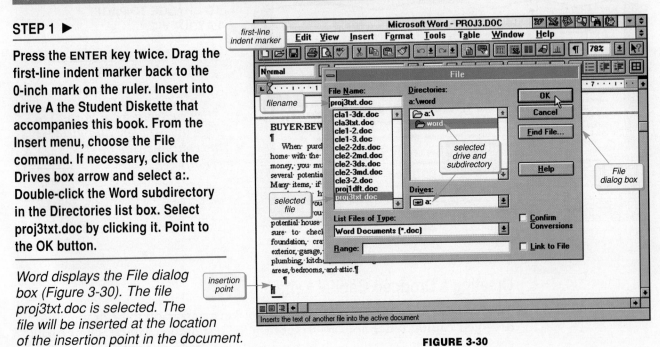

FIGURE 3-30

STEP 2 ▶

Choose the OK button.

Word inserts the file PROJ3TXT.DOC into the file PROJ3.DOC at the location of the insertion point (Figure 3-31).

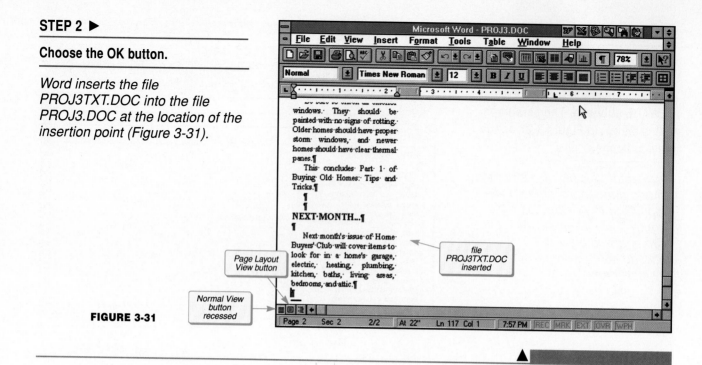

FIGURE 3-31

Notice in Figure 3-31 that the insertion point is on line 117 in this section. Depending on the printer you are using, your insertion point may be on a different line. Because a page is only 66 lines long, some of this column should actually be in the second and third columns. In normal view, the columns do not display side by side; instead, they display in one long column at the left margin. To see the columns side by side, switch to page layout view or display the document in print preview as shown.

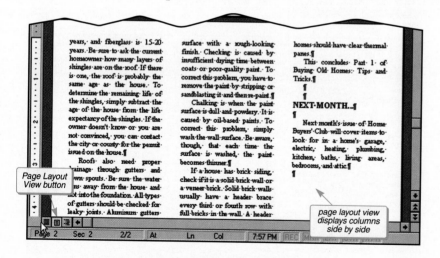

FIGURE 3-32

TO CHANGE TO PAGE LAYOUT VIEW

Step 1: Click the Page Layout View button on the horizontal scroll bar.

Word switches from normal to page layout view and displays the columns side by side (Figure 3-32).

Creating a Dropped Capital Letter

You can format the first character or word in a paragraph to be dropped. A **dropped capital letter** appears larger than the rest of the characters in the paragraph. The text in the paragraph wraps around the dropped capital letter. Perform these steps to create a dropped capital letter for the BUYER BEWARE subhead in the newsletter (see Figure 3-36 on page MSW144).

TO CREATE A DROPPED CAPITAL LETTER ▼

STEP 1 ▶

Press CTRL+HOME. Click anywhere in the BUYER BEWARE paragraph. Select the Format menu and point to the Drop Cap command.

The insertion point is in the BUYER BEWARE paragraph (Figure 3-33).

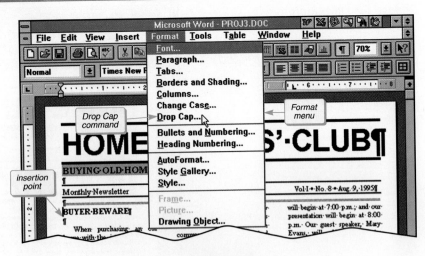

FIGURE 3-33

STEP 2 ▶

Choose the Drop Cap command. In the Drop Cap dialog box, point to the Dropped option.

Word displays the Drop Cap dialog box (Figure 3-34).

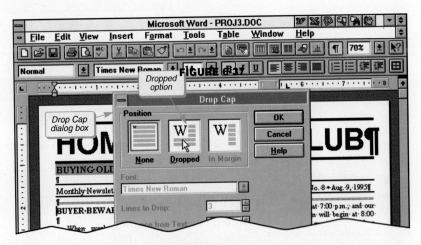

FIGURE 3-34

STEP 3 ▶

Select the Dropped option in the Position area by clicking it. Point to the OK button.

The Dropped option is selected (Figure 3-35).

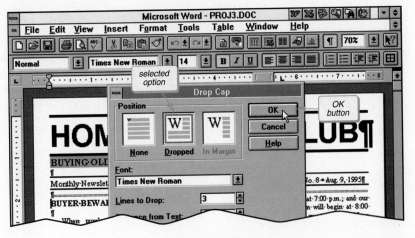

FIGURE 3-35

STEP 4 ▶

Choose the OK button.

Word drops the letter B in the BUYER BEWARE paragraph and wraps subsequent text around the dropped capital letter B (Figure 3-36).

FIGURE 3-36

When you drop a letter, Word places a frame around it. Frames are discussed in the next section.

The next step is to insert the houses graphic and position it between the first and second columns.

Positioning Graphics on the Page

When you use the Picture command to insert a graphic in a multi-column document, the graphic displays in the column that contains the insertion point. If you select the graphic and move it, it can only be moved into another column, not between columns. To move the graphic *between* columns, you must first enclose it in a **frame**. When you position a graphic in a frame, everything in the frame moves as one unit. Like an unframed graphic, you can resize a frame by dragging its sizing handles and position it anywhere on the page by dragging the frame itself. When you move the frame, its contents also move.

In this project, you insert the houses graphic, resize it, frame it, and finally, move it. Perform the following steps to position the houses graphic between the first and second columns of page 1 in the newsletter (see Figure 3-42 on page MSW146).

TO POSITION A GRAPHIC ON THE PAGE ▼

STEP 1 ▶

Scroll through the document and position the insertion point on the paragraph mark beneath the subhead LOCATION. Select the Insert menu and point to the Picture command (Figure 3-37).

STEP 2

Choose the Picture command. Select the metafile houses.wmf by scrolling through the File Name list box and clicking houses.wmf. Choose the OK button in the Insert Picture dialog box.

Word inserts the houses graphic at the location of the insertion point (see Figure 3-38).

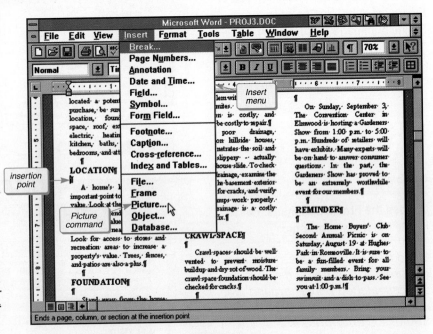

FIGURE 3-37

STEP 3 ▶

Click the houses graphic.

Word selects the houses graphic (Figure 3-38). Selected graphics display surrounded by a box with small rectangles, called sizing handles, at each corner and middle location, and you resize a graphic by dragging its sizing handles.

FIGURE 3-38

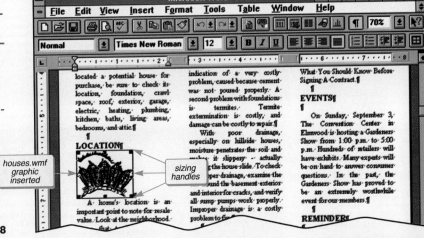

STEP 4 ▶

Drag the bottom middle sizing handle until the status bar reads Scaling: 140% High. Drag the right middle sizing handle until the status bar reads Scaling: 130% Wide. Depending on the printer you are using, you may need to resize the graphic to different percentages.

The graphic is resized (Figure 3-39).

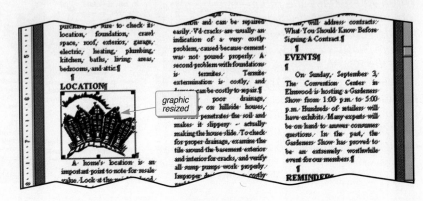

FIGURE 3-39

STEP 5 ▶

With the graphic still selected, select the Insert menu and point to the Frame command (Figure 3-40).

FIGURE 3-40

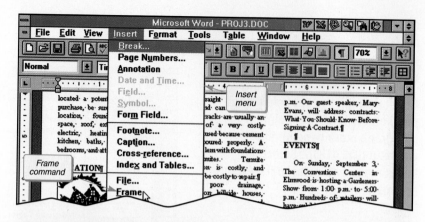

STEP 6 ▶

Choose the Frame command. Point inside the houses graphic.

*Word frames the houses graphic (Figure 3-41). A frame displays as a crosshatched border around the selection. When you insert a frame, it is **anchored** to the closest paragraph, which is marked with the anchor symbol (⚓). As you move the frame, the anchor also moves. When on a side of the frame, the mouse pointer changes to a left-pointing arrow with a four-headed arrow beneath it (⬍), called the **positioning pointer**.*

FIGURE 3-41

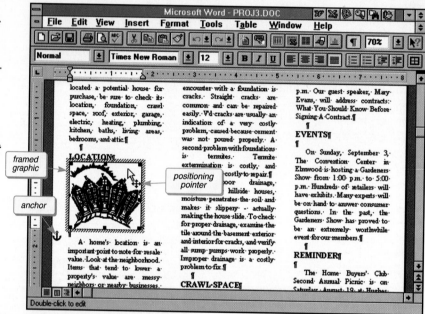

STEP 7 ▶

Drag the frame to the desired location. Click outside the graphic to remove the selection.

As you drag the frame, a dotted border indicates its new location. When you release the mouse button, the graphic is positioned at the location of the moved frame (Figure 3-42). (You may have to drag the house a couple of times to position it properly.) Try to position the graphic as close as possible to Figure 3-42. Depending on your printer, the wordwrap will occur in different locations.

FIGURE 3-42

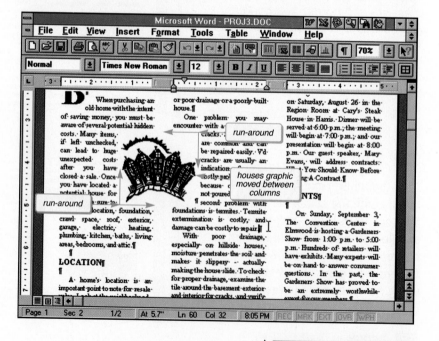

Notice in Figure 3-42 that the text in columns one and two wrap around the houses graphic. Thus, it is called wrap-around text. The space between the houses graphic and the wrap-around text is called the run-around.

The next step is to insert a column break.

Inserting a Column Break

Notice in Figure 3-1a on page MSW125 that the third column is not a continuation of the article. The third column contains several announcements. The Buying Old Homes article is actually continued on the second page of the newsletter. You want the announcements to be separated into the third column. Thus, you must force a **column break** at the bottom of the second column. Word inserts column breaks at the location of the insertion point.

TO INSERT A COLUMN BREAK ▼

STEP 1 ►

Scroll through the document to display the bottom of the second column in the document window. Click on the paragraph mark immediately above the subhead MONTHLY MEETING.

The insertion point is on line 80 (Figure 3-43).

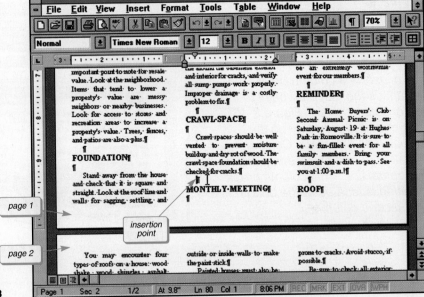

FIGURE 3-43

STEP 2 ►

Press the ENTER key. Click the Italic button on the Formatting toolbar. **Type** Continued next page... **and click the Italic button again. Press the** RIGHT ARROW **key.**

The insertion point is immediately to the left of the letter M in MONTHLY MEETING (Figure 3-44). The continued message displays at the bottom of the second column.

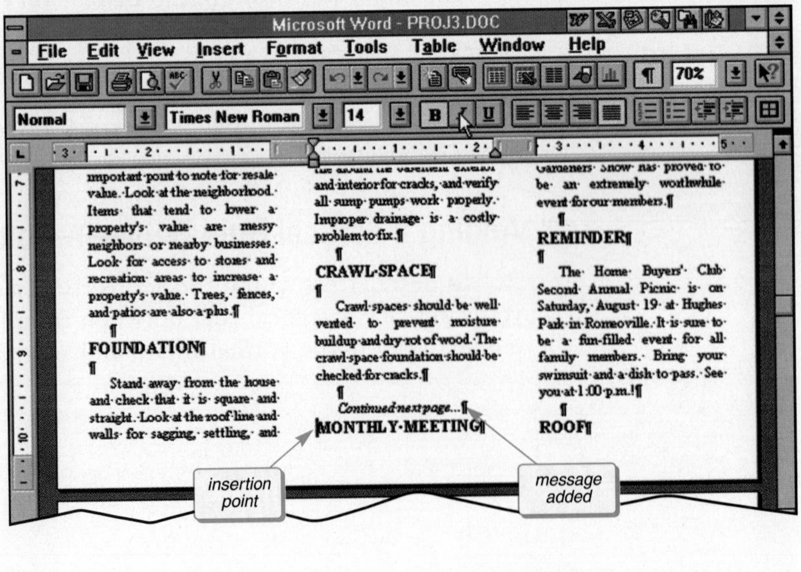

FIGURE 3-44

STEP 3 ▶

From the Insert menu, choose the Break command. When the Break dialog box displays, select the Column Break option by clicking it. Point to the OK button.

Word displays the Break dialog box (Figure 3-45). The Column Break option is selected.

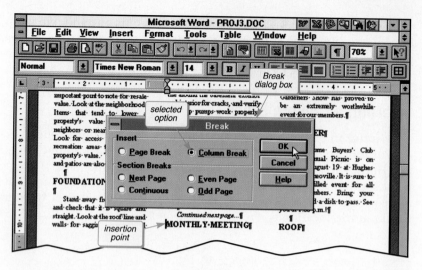

FIGURE 3-45

STEP 4 ▶

Choose the OK button in the Break dialog box.

Word inserts a column break and advances the insertion point to the top of column three (Figure 3-46). Column breaks display on the screen with the words Column Break separated by a thinly dotted horizontal line. This column break notation is located at the bottom of the second column.

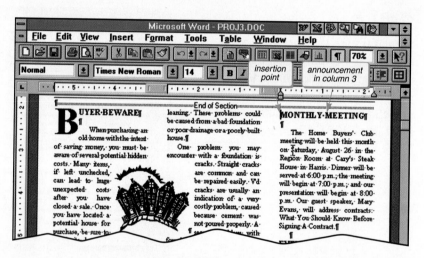

FIGURE 3-46

The subhead ROOF should display on the top of page 2. If it does not, you will insert a section page break later in this project. Or, you can try changing the margins for the document by selecting the entire document and choosing the Page Setup command from the File menu.

The next step is to place a vertical rule between the second and third columns in the newsletter.

Adding a Vertical Rule Between Columns

In newsletters, you often see vertical rules separating columns. With Word, you can place a vertical rule between all columns by choosing the Columns command from the Format menu and selecting the Line Between check box.

In this project, you want a vertical rule *only* between the second and third columns. To do this, you add a left border placed several points from the text. Recall that a point is approximately 1/72 of an inch. Perform these steps to add a vertical rule between the second and third columns in the newsletter (see Figure 3-52 on page MSW151).

TO ADD A VERTICAL RULE BETWEEN THE SECOND AND THIRD COLUMNS ▼

STEP 1 ▶

Position the mouse pointer in the selection bar to the left of the third column (Figure 3-47).

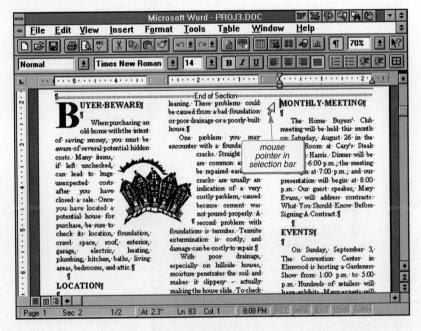

FIGURE 3-47

STEP 2 ▶

Drag the mouse down to highlight all of the third column (Figure 3-48).

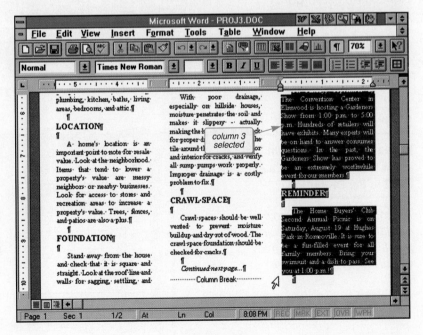

FIGURE 3-48

STEP 3 ▶

From the Format menu, choose the Borders and Shading command. When the Paragraph Borders and Shading dialog box displays, point to the left side of the model in the Border area.

Word displays the Paragraph Borders and Shading dialog box (Figure 3-49). Click the sides of the model in the Border area to apply borders to the selected paragraph.

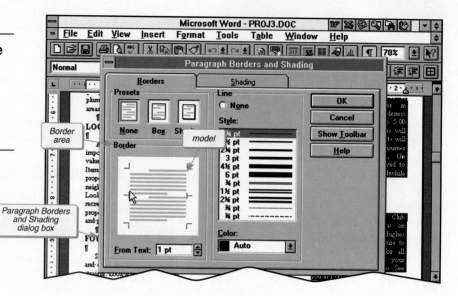

FIGURE 3-49

STEP 4 ▶

Click the left side of the model in the Border area. Point to the up arrow next to the From Text box.

Word draws a line along the left edge of the model in the Border area (Figure 3-50). Triangles mark the selected side. The From Text box indicates the number of points that the border is positioned from the text.

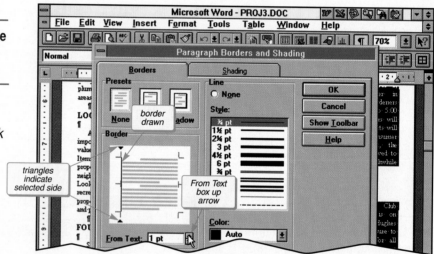

FIGURE 3-50

STEP 5 ▶

Repeatedly click the From Text up arrow until the text box reads 15 pt. Point to the OK button.

As you click the up arrow, the model represents the border position relative to the text (Figure 3-51).

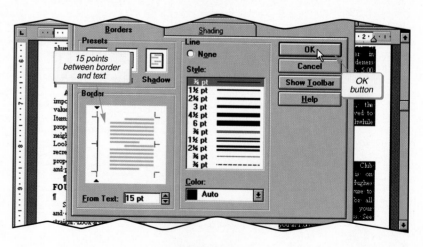

FIGURE 3-51

STEP 6 ▶

Choose the OK button. Click in the selection to remove the highlight.

Word draws a border positioned 15 points from the left edge of the text (Figure 3-52). A vertical rule displays between the second and third columns of the newsletter.

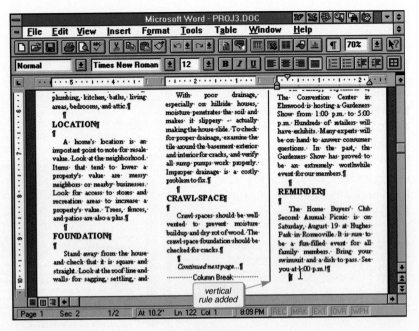

FIGURE 3-52

The first page of the newsletter is completely formatted.

▶ FORMATTING THE SECOND PAGE OF THE NEWSLETTER

The second page of the newsletter continues the article that began in the first two columns of page 1 (see Figure 3-1b on page MSW126). The nameplate on the second page is much more brief than on page 1. In addition to the text in the article, page 2 contains a pull-quote and a box border around the NEXT MONTH notice. The following pages illustrate how to create and format the second page of the newsletter in this project.

Creating the Nameplate on the Second Page

Because the document is currently formatted into three columns and the nameplate is a single column, the next step is to change the number of columns to one. Recall that each time you change the number of columns in a document, you must create a new section. To ensure that the ROOF subhead always displays at the top of the second page, you will first insert a page section break. Then, you will insert a continuous section break. Between the page and continuous section breaks, you will enter the nameplate in one column for the second page, as shown in the steps on the next page.

TO FORMAT THE SECOND PAGE NAMEPLATE ▼

STEP 1 ▶

Scroll through the document and position the mouse pointer to the left of the letter R in the ROOF subhead. From the Insert menu, choose the Break command. When the Break dialog box displays, click the Next Page option button in the Section Breaks area. Point to the OK button.

Word displays the Break dialog box (Figure 3-53). This section break ensures that the ROOF subhead will always begin at the top of the second page.

STEP 2

Choose the OK button.

Word inserts a section break above the insertion point.

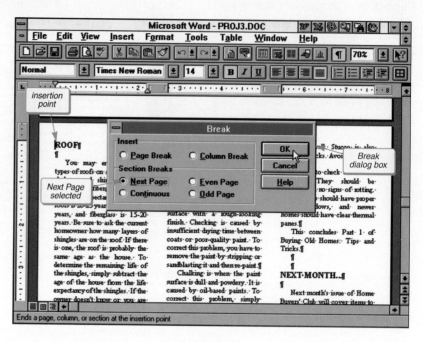

FIGURE 3-53

STEP 3 ▶

From the Insert menu, choose the Break command. When the Break dialog box displays, click the Continuous option button in the Section Breaks area. Point to the OK button.

Word displays the Break dialog box (Figure 3-54). The Continuous option is selected.

STEP 4

Choose the OK button.

Word creates a new section at the location of the insertion point.

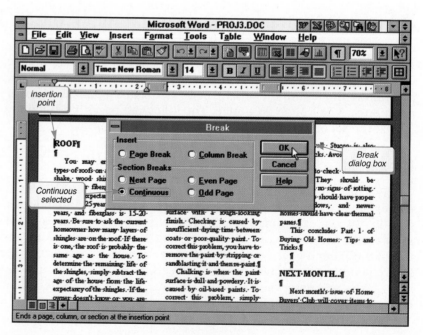

FIGURE 3-54

STEP 5 ▶

Press the UP ARROW key to position the insertion point in section three. Click the Columns button on the Standard toolbar. Press and hold the left mouse button in the left column of the column graphic.

Word highlights the left column in the column graphic and displays 1 Column beneath the graphic (Figure 3-55). The current section, for the nameplate, will be formatted to one column.

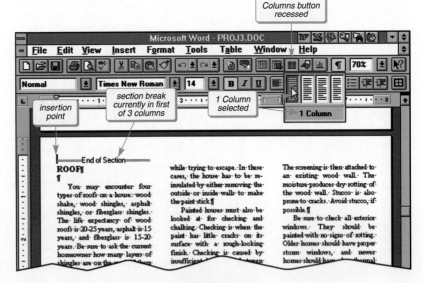

FIGURE 3-55

STEP 6 ▶

Release the mouse button.

Word formats the current section to one column (Figure 3-56).

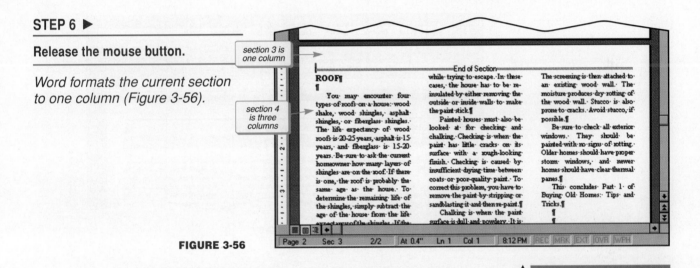

FIGURE 3-56

The next step is the enter the nameplate for the second page of the newsletter.

TO ENTER THE NAMEPLATE ON THE SECOND PAGE

Step 1: Press the ENTER key twice. Return the characters in this section to the normal style by selecting the paragraph mark on line 1 and the paragraph mark and section break on line 2. Then, click the word Normal in the Style box. Move the mouse pointer into the document window and click the left mouse button. In the Reapply Style dialog box, select Return the formatting of the selection to the style. Choose the OK button.

Step 2: Move the insertion point to the paragraph mark above the section break and type Aug. 9, 1995 and click the 2.75" mark on the ruler to set a custom tab stop. Press the TAB key. Change the font size to 20. Type Home Buyers' Club and change the font size back to 12. Click the 7.5" mark (or a close mark) on the ruler and press the TAB key. Type 2 and press the ENTER key.

Step 3: Select the line typed in Step 2 by clicking in the selection bar to its left. Click the Borders button on the Formatting toolbar. On the Borders toolbar, click the Line Style box arrow. In the list of available line styles, select 2 1/4 pt and click both the Top Border and Bottom Border buttons on the Borders toolbar. Click the Borders button on the Formatting toolbar. Click the paragraph mark in line 2.

Step 4: Change the font size to 16. Click the Bold button. Type `BUYING OLD HOMES: Tips and Tricks - Part 1` and click the Bold button. Change the font size back to 12. Click the 6.75" mark (or a close mark) on the ruler. Press the TAB key. Type `(Continued...)` and press the ENTER key.

Step 5: Select the line typed in Step 4. Click the Borders button on the Formatting toolbar. On the Borders toolbar, click the Shading box arrow and select 50%. Click the Borders button on the Formatting toolbar. Click the paragraph mark on line 3 to remove the selection.

The nameplate for page 2 is complete (Figure 3-57).

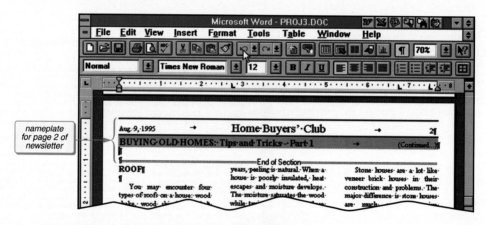

FIGURE 3-57

The next step is to insert a pull-quote between the first and second columns on page 2 of the newsletter.

Inserting a Pull-Quote

A **pull-quote** is a quotation pulled from the text of the document and given graphic emphasis so it stands apart and grasps the attention of the reader. Because of their bold emphasis, pull-quotes should be used sparingly in documents. The newsletter in this project has a pull-quote on the second page between the first and second columns (see Figure 3-1b on page MSW126).

To create a pull-quote, you first type the quotation with the rest of the text or you could copy the quotation from the text. To position it between columns, you frame it and move it to the desired location. Perform these steps to create the pull-quote in Project 3 (see Figure 3-65 on page MSW158).

TO CREATE A PULL-QUOTE ▼

STEP 1 ►

Position the insertion point on the paragraph mark below the ROOF subhead on page two of the newsletter (Figure 3-58).

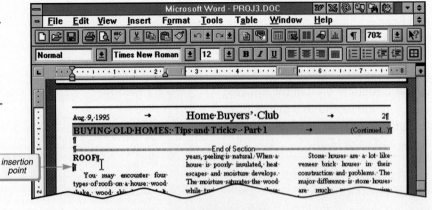

FIGURE 3-58

STEP 2 ►

Press the ENTER key. Change the font size to 14. Click the Bold and Italic buttons on the Formatting toolbar. Type "If there is only one layer of shingles, the roof is probably the same age as the house." Click the Bold and Italic buttons on the Formatting toolbar. Select the pull-quote by positioning the mouse pointer in the selection bar to the left of the pull-quote and double-clicking.

The pull-quote is highlighted (Figure 3-59).

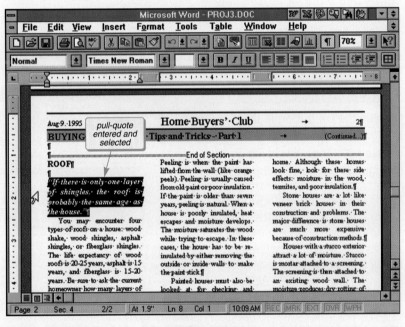

FIGURE 3-59

STEP 3 ►

From the Insert menu, choose the Frame command.

Word places a frame around the selected text (Figure 3-60). As discussed earlier, the frame can be moved or resized.

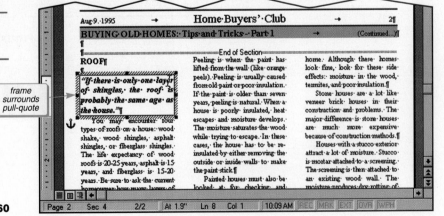

FIGURE 3-60

STEP 4 ▶

From the Format menu, choose the Paragraph command. If the Indents and Spacing options do not display in the Paragraph dialog box, click the Indents and Spacing tab. In the Indentation area, change Left to 0.4" and Right to 0.4". In the Spacing area, change Before to 6 pt and After to 6 pt. Click the Alignment box arrow and select Left.

Word displays the Paragraph dialog box (Figure 3-61). The pull-quote will be left-aligned with a 0.4-inch space on the left and right edges and 6 pts, approximately one blank line, above and below it.

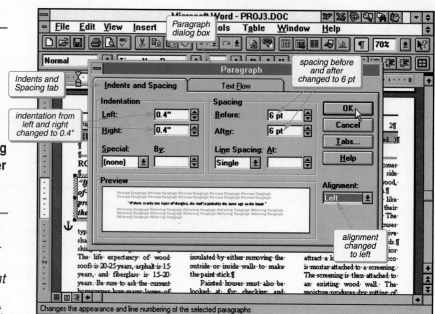

FIGURE 3-61

STEP 5 ▶

Choose the OK button in the Paragraph dialog box. Position the mouse pointer on the frame so it changes to the positioning pointer.

Word displays the pull-quote left-aligned with a 0.4" space between it and the frame on the left and right sides. Approximately one blank line displays above and below it (Figure 3-62). Notice that Word places a border around the pull-quote. When you add a frame to a paragraph, Word automatically places a border around it.

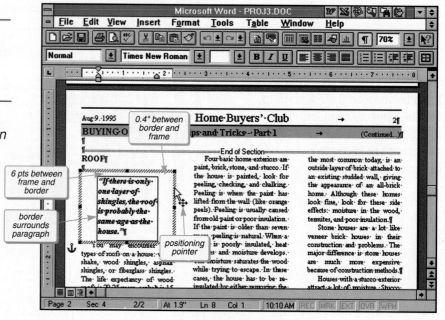

FIGURE 3-62

STEP 6 ►

Drag the frame to its new position (Figure 3-63). You may need to drag it a couple of times to position it similar to Figure 3-63. Try to position it as close to Figure 3-63 as possible. Depending on your printer, your wordwrap may occur in different locations.

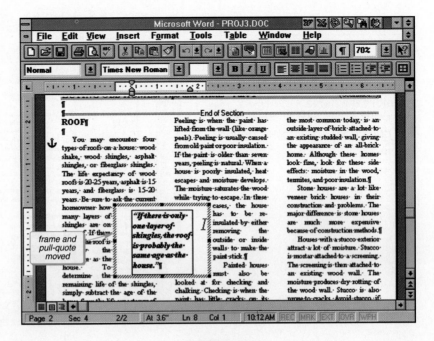

FIGURE 3-63

STEP 7 ►

Click the Borders button on the Formatting toolbar. On the Borders toolbar, point to the No Border button (▦).

Word displays the Borders toolbar (Figure 3-64).

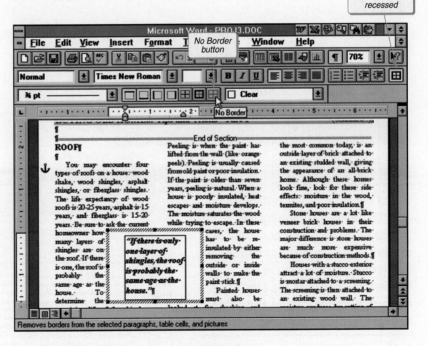

FIGURE 3-64

STEP 8 ▶

Click the No Border button. Click the Borders button on the Formatting toolbar. Click outside the pull-quote to remove the frame.

The pull-quote is complete (Figure 3-65).

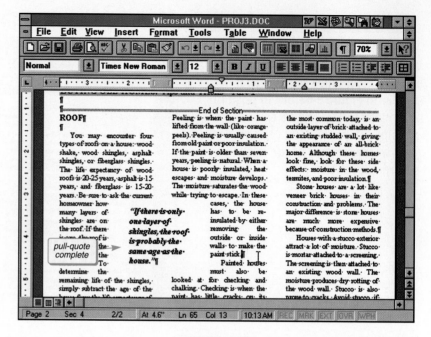

FIGURE 3-65

Adding a Box Border Around Paragraphs

The NEXT MONTH notice at the bottom of the third column on page 2 has a box border around it (Figure 3-67). Use the Borders toolbar to add a box border, as shown in these steps.

TO ADD A BOX BORDER AROUND PARAGRAPHS ▼

STEP 1 ▶

Select the paragraphs in the NEXT MONTH notice by dragging the mouse in the selection bar to the left of them. Click the Borders button on the Formatting toolbar. On the Borders toolbar, click the Line Style box arrow. Select 2 1/4 pt and point to the Outside Border button.

Word displays the Borders toolbar (Figure 3-66).

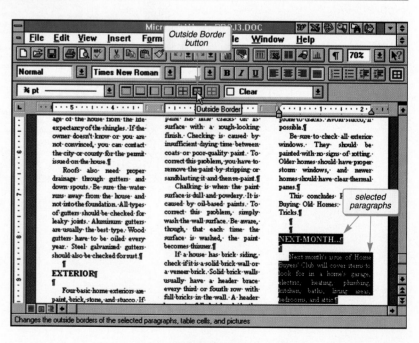

FIGURE 3-66

STEP 2 ▶

Click the Outside Border button. Click inside the box border to remove the selection.

Word recesses the Top Border, Bottom Border, Left Border, and Right Border buttons on the Borders toolbar and a box border appears around the NEXT MONTH notice (Figure 3-67).

STEP 3

Click the Borders button on the Formatting toolbar to remove the Borders toolbar.

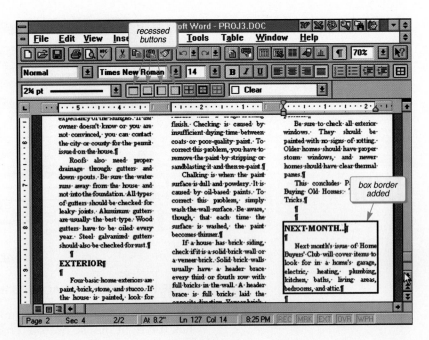

FIGURE 3-67

The second page of the newsletter is complete. Save this project again by clicking the Save button on the Standard toolbar.

The next step is to add color to the characters, lines, and graphics in the newsletter.

▶ ENHANCING THE NEWSLETTER WITH COLOR

Many of the characters and lines in the newsletter in Project 3 are colored (see Figures 3-1a and 3-1b on pages MSW125 and MSW126). The houses graphic is also colored. As you learned in Project 1, you color characters through the Font dialog box and lines through the Borders and Shading dialog box. Perform these steps to change the color of the characters and borders in the newsletter.

TO CHANGE COLORS OF THE TITLE

Step 1: Press CTRL+HOME. Select the title by clicking in the selection bar to its left. Move the mouse pointer into the selection and click the right mouse button. From the shortcut menu, choose the Font command.

Step 2: When the Font dialog box displays, click the Color box arrow and select Red. Choose the OK button.

Step 3: From the Format menu, choose the Borders and Shading command. If the Borders options do not display in the Paragraph Borders and Shading dialog box, click the Borders tab. Click the Color box arrow and select Cyan. Choose the OK button. Click outside the selection to remove the highlight.

The title characters are colored in red with cyan ruling lines (Figure 3-68 on the next page).

FIGURE 3-68

TO COLOR THE HEADLINE CHARACTERS IN WHITE

Step 1: Select the headline. Move the mouse pointer into the selection and click the right mouse button. From the shortcut menu, choose the Font command.

Step 2: When the Font dialog box displays, click the Color box arrow and select White. Choose the OK button. Click outside the selection to remove the highlight.

TO COLOR THE ISSUE INFORMATION LINE

Step 1: Select the issue information line. Move the mouse pointer into the selection and click the right mouse button. From the shortcut menu, choose the Font command.

Step 2: When the Font dialog box displays, click the Color box arrow and select Red. Choose the OK button.

Step 3: From the Format menu, choose the Borders and Shading command. When the Paragraph Borders and Shading dialog box displays, click the Color box arrow and select Cyan. Choose the OK button. Click outside the selection to remove the highlight.

TO COLOR THE SUBHEADS

Step 1: Select the first subhead, BUYER BEWARE, by dragging the mouse through it. Move the mouse pointer into the selection and click the right mouse button. From the shortcut menu, choose the Font command.

Step 2: When the Font dialog box displays, click the Color box arrow and select Dk Green. Choose the OK button.

Step 3: Repeat the procedure in Steps 1 and 2 for each of these subheads: LOCATION, FOUNDATION, CRAWL SPACE, MONTHLY MEETING, EVENTS, REMINDER, ROOF, EXTERIOR, and NEXT MONTH... .

TO COLOR THE BOX BORDER

Step 1: Select the NEXT MONTH box by dragging the mouse through the text in the box. From the Format menu, choose the Borders and Shading command.

Step 2: When the Paragraph Borders and Shading dialog box displays, click the Color box arrow and select Red. Choose the OK button. Click outside the selection to remove the highlight.

TO COLOR THE PULL-QUOTE

Step 1: Select the pull-quote by dragging the mouse from the left quotation mark through the right quotation mark. Move the mouse pointer into the selection and click the right mouse button. From the shortcut menu, choose the Font command.

Step 2: When the Font dialog box displays, click the Color box arrow and select Dk Magenta. Choose the OK button. Click outside the selection to remove the highlight.

TO COLOR THE TITLE ON PAGE 2

Step 1: Select the title. Move the mouse pointer into the selection and click the right mouse button. From the shortcut menu, choose the Font command.

Step 2: When the Font dialog box displays, click the Color box arrow and select Red. Choose the OK button.

Step 3: From the Format menu, choose the Borders and Shading command. When the Paragraph Borders and Shading dialog box displays, click the Color box arrow and select Cyan. Choose the OK button. Click outside the selection to remove the highlight.

TO COLOR THE HEADLINE ON PAGE 2

Step 1: Select the headline. Move the mouse pointer into the selection and click the right mouse button. From the shortcut menu, choose the Font command.

Step 2: When the Font dialog box displays, click the Color box arrow and select White. Choose the OK button. Click outside the selection to remove the highlight.

Use the Save As command on the File menu to save the colored newsletter with the filename PROJ3A.DOC. The characters and lines of the newsletter are now colored (Figure 3-69).

FIGURE 3-69

The next step is to change the color of the houses graphic.

Changing the Color of a Graphic

The houses graphic in the newsletter is colored in black and white. To change its color, you use the **Drawing toolbar**. Through the Drawing toolbar, you can create **drawing objects** such as rectangles, squares, polygons, ellipses, and lines. You can also change the line and background color of a graphic as shown below.

TO CHANGE THE COLOR OF A GRAPHIC ▼

STEP 1 ▶

Scroll through the document and point to the houses graphic.

Word changes the mouse pointer to the positioning pointer in the graphic (Figure 3-70).

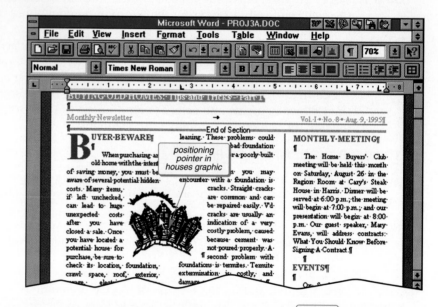

FIGURE 3-70

STEP 2 ▶

Double-click the houses graphic.

Word displays the Drawing toolbar at the bottom of the screen above the status bar and places the selected graphic in a new document window titled, Picture in PROJ3A.DOC (Figure 3-71).

STEP 3

Point to the Select Drawing Objects button ( ) on the Drawing toolbar.

Because you want all of the houses in the graphic, or drawing objects, to be colored the same color, you should select all of the drawing objects in the graphic at once.

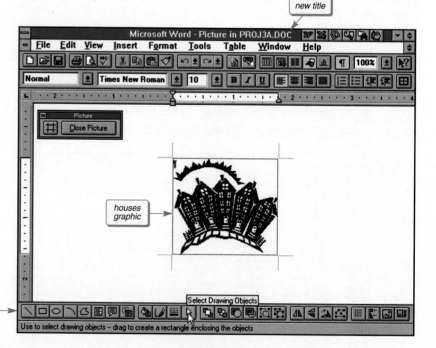

FIGURE 3-71

STEP 4 ▶

Click the Select Drawing Objects button. Point outside the upper-left corner of the graphic.

Word recesses the Select Drawing Objects button (Figure 3-72).

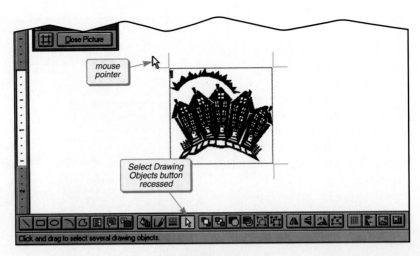

FIGURE 3-72

STEP 5 ▶

Drag the mouse to outside the lower-right corner of the graphic.

The dotted border completely surrounds the graphic (Figure 3-73).

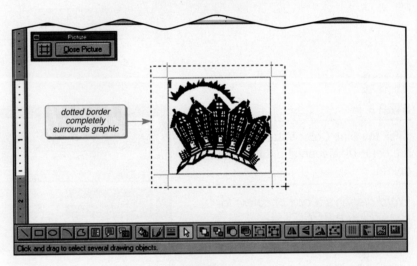

FIGURE 3-73

STEP 6 ▶

Release the mouse button. Point to the Group button (⊞) on the Drawing toolbar.

Word selects every drawing object in the houses graphic (Figure 3-74). Selected drawing objects display with sizing handles around them. Because you want all of the drawing objects colored the same, you want to group all of the drawing objects into one single unit. Word displays groups faster than individual drawing objects.

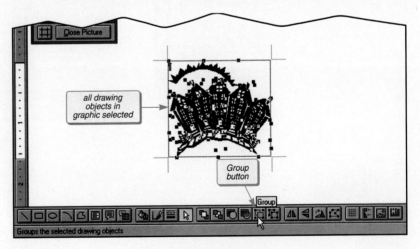

FIGURE 3-74

STEP 7 ▶

Click the Group button. Point to the Line Color button (▨) on the Drawing toolbar.

Word groups all of the drawing objects into a single unit (Figure 3-75). Sizing handles only display around the perimeter of the entire graphic.

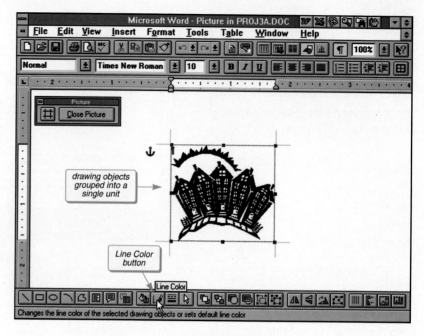

FIGURE 3-75

STEP 8 ▶

Click the Line Color button. Point to the color Dk Magenta in the box of colors.

Word displays a box of colors for lines (Figure 3-76).

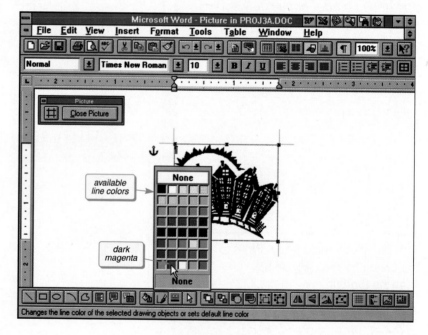

FIGURE 3-76

STEP 9 ▶

Select Dk Magenta by clicking it. Point to the Fill Color button (⬚) on the Drawing toolbar.

Word changes the line colors in the graphic to dark magenta (Figure 3-77).

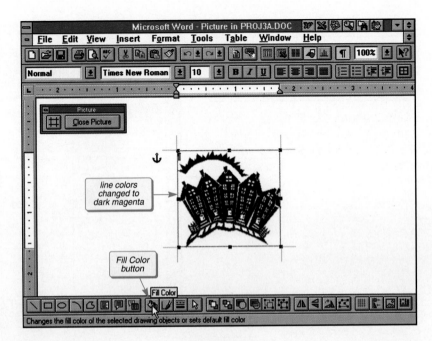

FIGURE 3-77

STEP 10 ▶

Click the Fill Color button. Point to the color Yellow in the box of colors.

Word displays a box of colors for fill color (Figure 3-78).

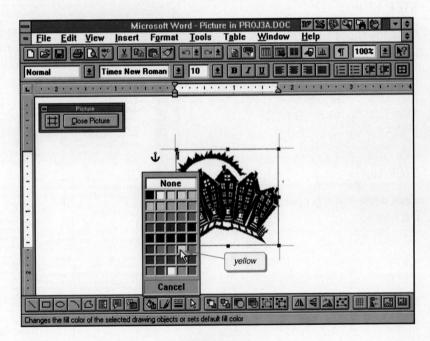

FIGURE 3-78

STEP 11 ▶

Select Yellow by clicking it. Point to the Close Picture button on the Picture toolbar.

Word changes the fill color in the graphic to yellow (Figure 3-79). The graphic colors are now complete.

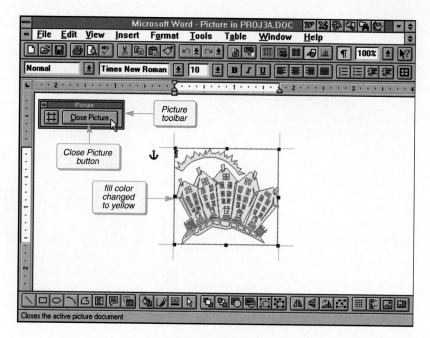

FIGURE 3-79

STEP 12 ▶

Click the Close Picture button.

Word returns to the PROJ3A.DOC document window and changes the color of the houses graphic to yellow on dark magenta (Figure 3-80).

STEP 13

Click outside the graphic to remove the frame.

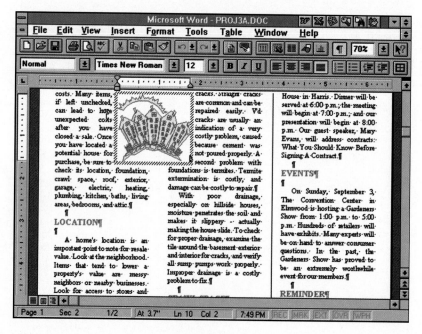

FIGURE 3-80

The newsletter is now complete. Use the Save As command on the File menu to save the newsletter with the colored house with the filename PROJ3B.DOC. Then, print the newsletter by clicking the Print button. If you have a color printer, it will print in color, as shown in Figures 3-1a and 3-1b on pages MSW125 and MSW126. If your printer stops in the middle of the printout, it may not have enough memory to print the colored graphic. In this case, open PROJ3A.DOC and print the newsletter with the black and white graphic.

▶ PROJECT SUMMARY

Project 3 introduced you to creating a professional-looking newsletter with desktop publishing features. You created nameplates with ruling lines and shading. You formatted the body of the newsletter into three columns and added a vertical rule between the second and third columns. You learned how to frame both graphics and a pull-quote and move them between columns. In the newsletter, you added a box border around paragraphs. Finally, you colored a variety of characters and lines in the document and changed the colors of the houses graphic.

▶ KEY TERMS AND INDEX

anchored (*MSW146*)
ANSI characters (*MSW137*)
banner (*MSW127*)
Borders and Shading command
  (*MSW159*)
box border (*MSW127*)
Break command (*MSW138*)
bullet (*MSW134*)
column break (*MSW147*)
Columns button (*MSW139*)
Columns command (*MSW140*)

desktop publishing software
  (*MSW124*)
Drawing toolbar (*MSW162*)
drawing objects (*MSW162*)
dropped capital letter (*MSW142*)
frame (*MSW144*)
headline (*MSW127*)
issue information line (*MSW127*)
justified (*MSW140*)
Justify button (*MSW141*)
nameplate (*MSW127*)
Paragraph command (*MSW156*)

parallel columns (*MSW138*)
positioning pointer (*MSW146*)
pull-quote (*MSW154*)
rules (*MSW127*)
ruling line (*MSW127*)
run-around (*MSW127*)
snaking columns (*MSW138*)
subhead (*MSW127*)
Symbol command (*MSW135*)
vertical rule (*MSW127*)
wrap-around text (*MSW127*)

Q U I C K   R E F E R E N C E

In Microsoft Word 6, you can accomplish a task in a number of ways. The following table provides a quick reference to each task presented in this project with its available options. The commands listed in the Menu column can be executed using either the keyboard or mouse. Some of the commands in the Menu column are also available in shortcut menus. If you have WordPerfect help activated, the key combinations listed in the Keyboard Shortcuts column will not work as shown.

Task	Mouse	Menu	Keyboard Shortcuts
Add Box Border to Selected Paragraphs	Click Borders button on Formatting toolbar	From Format menu, choose Borders and Shading	
Add Color to Ruling Lines		From Format menu, choose Borders and Shading	
Add Ruling Lines	Click Borders button on Formatting toolbar	From Format menu, choose Borders and Shading	
Add Vertical Rule Between All Columns		From Format menu, choose Columns	
Add Vertical Rule Between Some Columns		From Format menu, choose Borders and Shading	
Change a Graphic's Colors	Click Drawing button on Standard toolbar	From Format menu, choose Drawing Object	

(continued)

QUICK REFERENCE (continued)

Task	Mouse	Menu	Keyboard Shortcuts
Create Multiple Columns	Click Columns button on Standard toolbar	From Format menu, choose Columns	
Drop a Capital Letter		From Format menu, choose Drop Cap	
Insert a Frame		From Insert menu, choose Frame	
Insert Bullet Symbol		From Insert menu, choose Symbol	
Insert Column Break		From Insert menu, choose Break	Press CTRL+SHIFT+ENTER
Justify Text	Click Justify button on Formatting toolbar	From Format menu, choose Paragraph	Press CTRL+J
Remove Selected Section Break	Click Cut button on Standard toolbar		Press DELETE

S T U D E N T   A S S I G N M E N T S

STUDENT ASSIGNMENT 1
True/False

Instructions: Circle T if the statement is true or F if the statement is false.

T F 1. Word for Windows provides you with many of the desktop publishing features you would find in a specialized package.

T F 2. The space between a framed object and the text that wraps around the framed object is called wrap-around text.

T F 3. The default font in Word is Arial.

T F 4. In the desktop publishing field, ruling lines, or rules, are vertical lines that separate columns.

T F 5. To format the first character of a paragraph as a dropped capital letter, click the Drop Cap button on the Formatting toolbar.

T F 6. When inserting special characters by typing their ANSI code, you must use the numeric keypad to type the code.

T F 7. Snaking columns are created with the Insert Table button on the Standard toolbar.

T F 8. To change the color of a graphic, click the Fill Color and Line Color buttons on the Drawing toolbar.

T F 9. Columns display side by side in the document window in normal view.

T F 10. To move a graphic between columns, you must first enclose it in a frame.

T F 11. To insert a column break, click the Columns button on the Standard toolbar.

T F 12. When you frame a graphic, Word places a box border around it.

T F 13. A pull-quote is a quotation mark displayed in a font size larger than 40 points.

T F 14. The Drawing toolbar displays beneath the Formatting toolbar.

T F 15. Use the Justify button on the Formatting toolbar to make text in a paragraph flush at both margins, like newspaper columns.

T   F   16. To insert a bullet character into a document, choose the Symbol command from the Insert menu.
T   F   17. When shading a paragraph, the shading begins at the left margin and stops at the paragraph mark.
T   F   18. The default number of columns in a document is three.
T   F   19. When you frame a graphic, Word anchors it to the nearest paragraph.
T   F   20. The positioning pointer is used to move a frame.

STUDENT ASSIGNMENT 2
Multiple Choice

Instructions: Circle the correct response.

1. In the desktop publishing field, the _____ is located at the top of a newsletter.
    a. box border   b. nameplate   c. wrap-around text   d. pull-quote

2. To add ruling lines to a selected paragraph, _____.
    a. click the Borders button on the Formatting toolbar
    b. choose the Ruling Lines command from the Format menu
    c. click the ruler
    d. click the Ruler button on the Standard toolbar

3. To insert special characters and symbols into a document, _____.
    a. choose the Symbol command from the Insert menu
    b. hold down the ALT key and type 0 (a zero), followed by the ANSI character code
    c. either a or b
    d. neither a nor b

4. Each section in a document can have its own _____.
    a. number of columns   b. margin settings   c. headers   d. all of the above

5. To enclose a selected graphic or paragraph in a frame, _____.
    a. choose the Frame command from the Tools menu
    b. choose the Frame command from the Insert menu
    c. choose the Borders and Shading command from the Format menu
    d. none of the above

6. To display paragraphs so the left and right margins are flush, like newspaper columns, click the
    _____ button on the Formatting toolbar.
    a. Align Left   b. Center   c. Align Right   d. Justify

7. To change the color of the lines in a graphic, click the _____ button on the Drawing toolbar.
    a. Line Color   b. Color   c. Line   d. none of the above

8. To group multiple selected drawing objects into a single unit, click the _____ button on the
    Drawing toolbar.
    a. Multiple Objects   b. Group   c. Box   d. Select

9. When the first letter in a paragraph is larger than the rest of the characters in the paragraph, the
    letter is called a(n) _____.
    a. large cap   b. big cap   c. drop cap   d. enlarged cap

10. To add color to a selected paragraph's ruling lines, _____.
    a. choose the Color command from the Format menu
    b. choose the Borders and Shading command from the Format menu
    c. choose the Ruling Lines command from the Format menu
    d. none of the above

STUDENT ASSIGNMENT 3
Understanding Toolbar Buttons

Instructions: In Figure SA3-3, arrows point to several of the buttons on the Standard toolbar, Formatting toolbar, Borders toolbar, and Drawing toolbar. In the spaces provided, briefly explain the purpose of each button.

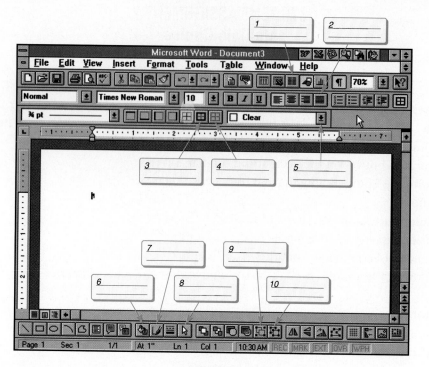

FIGURE SA3-3

STUDENT ASSIGNMENT 4
Understanding Desktop Publishing Terminology

Instructions: In the spaces provided, briefly define each of the desktop publishing terms listed.

TERM	DEFINITION
1. nameplate	
2. ruling line	
3. vertical rule	
4. issue information line	
5. subhead	
6. wrap-around text	
7. run-around	
8. box border	
9. pull-quote	

STUDENT ASSIGNMENT 5
Understanding the Steps to Shade a Paragraph

Instructions: Fill in the step numbers below to correctly order the process of shading a paragraph.

Step _____: Click the Borders button on the Formatting toolbar.

Step _____: Select the paragraph.

Step _____: Click the Shading box arrow on the Borders toolbar.

Step _____: Click the Borders button on the Formatting toolbar.

Step _____: Select a pattern in the Shading list.

STUDENT ASSIGNMENT 6
Understanding Commands in Menus

Instructions: Write the appropriate command name to accomplish each task and the menu name in which each command is located.

TASK	COMMAND NAME	MENU NAME
Add Drop Cap	_____	_____
Add Color to Ruling Lines	_____	_____
Add Ruling Lines	_____	_____
Add Vertical Rule Between Certain Columns	_____	_____
Insert Bullet Symbol	_____	_____
Insert Column Break	_____	_____

C O M P U T E R   L A B O R A T O R Y   E X E R C I S E S

COMPUTER LABORATORY EXERCISE 1
Using the Help Menu to Learn About Word's Desktop Publishing Features

Instructions: Start Word and perform the following tasks:

1. Choose the Index command from the Help menu. Choose the Search button. Type `columns` and press the ENTER key. Select Newspaper-Style Columns. Choose the Go To button. Select Creating columns of equal width. Read and print the information.
2. Choose the Close button. Choose the Search button. Type `drop caps` and press the ENTER key. Choose the Go To button. Read and print the information.
3. Choose the Close button. Choose the Search button. Type `frames` and press the ENTER key. Choose the Go To button. Select Inserting a frame around selected items. Read and print the information. Choose the Close button. Select Positioning a frame by dragging. Read and print the information.
4. Choose the Close button. Choose the Search button. Type `drawing objects` and press the ENTER key. Select More drawing tips. Choose the Go To button. Read and print the information. Close the Help window.

COMPUTER LABORATORY EXERCISE 2
Adding Ruling Lines and Shading to Paragraphs

Instructions: Start Word. Open the document CLE3-2 from the Word subdirectory on the Student Diskette that accompanies this book. The document is shown in Figure CLE3-2. The document is a nameplate for a newsletter. Following the steps below, you are to add ruling lines to the title of the newsletter and print it.

FIGURE CLE3-2

Perform the following tasks:

1. Select the newsletter title by clicking in the selection bar to its left.
2. Click the Borders button on the Formatting toolbar.
3. Click the Line Style box arrow on the Borders toolbar and select 4 1/2 pt.
4. Click the Top Border button on the Borders toolbar.
5. Click the Bottom Border button on the Borders toolbar.
6. Select the newsletter headline by clicking in the selection bar to its left.
7. Click the Shading box arrow on the Borders toolbar and select 50%.
8. Click the Borders button on the Formatting toolbar.
9. Drag the right indent marker left until the shading stops at the paragraph mark immediately after the headline.
10. Click outside the selection to remove the highlight.
11. Save the revised nameplate with the filename CLE3-2A.
12. Print the revised nameplate.

COMPUTER LABORATORY EXERCISE 3
Adding Color to a Graphic

Instructions: Start Word. Performing the steps below, you are to add color to a graphic. The colored graphic is shown in Figure CLE3-3.

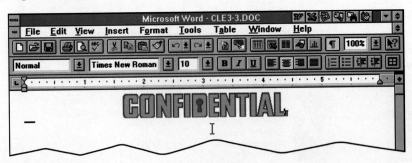

FIGURE CLE3-3

Perform the following tasks:

1. From the Insert menu, choose the Picture command.
2. Scroll through the list of Windows metafiles and select confiden.wmf.
3. Choose the OK button in the Insert Picture dialog box.
4. Double-click the graphic.
5. Click the Select Drawing Objects button on the Drawing toolbar.
6. Position the mouse outside the upper-left border of the graphic and drag the mouse to outside the lower-right corner so a dotted border completely surrounds the graphic.
7. Click the Group button on the Drawing toolbar.
8. Click the Fill Color button and select Cyan.
9. Click the Line Color button and select Dk Blue.
10. Click the Ungroup button, which is the button to the right of the Group button, on the Drawing toolbar.
11. Select the keyhole in the graphic by clicking it.
12. Click the Fill Color button and select Dk Magenta.
13. Click the Close Picture button on the Picture toolbar.
14. Click the Center button on the Formatting toolbar.
15. Save the colored graphic with the filename CLE3-3.
16. Print the graphic.

COMPUTER LABORATORY ASSIGNMENTS

COMPUTER LABORATORY ASSIGNMENT 1
Formatting the First Page of a Newsletter

Purpose: To become familiar with creating a newsletter with desktop publishing features, such as multiple columns, graphics, fonts, ruling lines, and vertical rules.

Problem: You are an associate editor of the Home Buyers' Club monthly newsletter. The September edition is due out in three weeks. You have been assigned the task of preparing the first page of the newsletter (Figure CLA3-1 on the next page).

(continued)

COMPUTER LABORATORY ASSIGNMENT 1 (continued)

Instructions: Perform the following tasks:

1. Change the margins to 0.4 inch on all sides. (Depending on your printer, you may need different margin settings.)
2. Redefine the normal style to a font size of 12.
3. Create the nameplate. Use the following formats: a) title - Arial font, 50 point bold; b) headline - 15 point bold and shaded 50%; c) all other text is 12 point.
4. Insert the body page 1 into column 1 beneath the nameplate. The body of page 1 is in a file called CLA3TXT.DOC in the Word subdirectory on the Student Diskette that accompanies this book.
5. Format the first page of the newsletter according to Figure CLA3-1. The graphic is called checkmark.wmf, which is framed, resized, and colored. To change its colors, select each drawing object individually and change the fill color of each drawing object.
6. Save the document with the filename CLA3-1.
7. Print the document.

HOME BUYERS' CLUB

BUYING OLD HOMES: Tips and Tricks - Part 2

Monthly Newsletter · Vol. I • No. 9 • Sep. 14, 1995

 Last month's Home Buyers' Club discussed how to check a home's location, foundation, crawl space, roof, and exterior before making a purchase. This month's issue discusses the garage, electric, plumbing, heating, kitchen, baths, living areas, bedrooms, and attic.

GARAGE

If the house has a garage, check its exterior, foundation, and roof as discussed in last month's newsletter. In addition, check the door operation.

ELECTRIC

Ask the current owner the amount of voltage and ampere service coming into the house - 240 volts and 200 amp are desirable. If the owner is unsure, you may be able to check yourself. In an older house, look at the number of wires coming into the house from above. Two wires means 120 volts and three wires means 240 volts, which is usually 200 amp service. Newer houses are wired with 240 volts.

Check in the basement for fuses or circuit breakers. Check the condition of Romex wiring or conduit. Look upstairs for the number of outlets on one circuit breaker, number of outlets in the rooms, size of the wires, condition of wires inside the walls, and so on.

PLUMBING

Plumbing can be very costly, especially in older houses. Look in the basement at whether the pipes are copper, cast-iron, or old lead. Newer homes almost always have copper.

Check all sinks for dripping (cold and hot) and leaking below cabinets. Check the toilets for leaking around the floor board. These are not costly repairs.

Check the bathtub and showers for leaking (cold and hot). Usually these have hidden leaks, which can be found under the floor below. In the room below, check the dry wall for signs of leaks, like water stains.

Check the water pressure. In older houses, cast iron pipes tend to rust and restrict flow. Copper pipe does not have this problem. Turn all faucets on at once, and flush the toilets. Then take note of the pressure. Low pressure could be a costly problem. Be aware that in some cases city water is restricted before coming into the house.

Continued next page...

MONTHLY MEETING

The Home Buyers' Club meeting will be held this month on Saturday, September 23 in the Banquet Room at Geeno's Surf & Turf in Bellview. Dinner will be served at 6:00 p.m.; the meeting will begin at 7:00 p.m.; and our presentation will begin at 8:00 p.m. Our guest speaker, Tim Zimmerman, will address plumbing: Does Your Water Pressure Measure Up?

ELECTIONS

During our November meeting, we will be electing new officers for our Home Buyers' Club. Officer terms run for one year. Officers meet twice a month. Member dues are waived for officers during their term. If you are interested in serving as either President, Vice President, Secretary, or Treasurer, contact Joe Deevers at (737) 555-9623 by the end of September.

NEXT MONTH...

Next month's issue of Home Buyers' Club will cover renting houses for profit. Topics covered will include taxes, insurance, tenants, landlord responsibilities, revenues and expenses, and maintenance.

FIGURE CLA3-1

COMPUTER LABORATORY ASSIGNMENT 2
Creating the Second Page of a Newsletter

Purpose: To become familiar with creating a newsletter with desktop publishing features, such as multiple columns, graphics, fonts, ruling lines, and vertical rules.

Problem: You are an associate editor of the Home Buyers' Club monthly newsletter. The September edition is due out in three weeks. You have been assigned the task of preparing the second page of the newsletter.

Instructions: Perform the following tasks:

1. Open the file CLA3-1 from your data disk.
2. Save it with the file-name CLA3-2.
3. Create page 2 of the newsletter shown in Figure CLA3-2. Use the following formats:
   a) Home Buyers' Club in nameplate –19 point;
   b) headline –15 point bold; c) subheads –14 point bold; d) all other text is 12 point.
4. Save the document again.
5. Print the document.

FIGURE CLA3-2

Sep. 14, 1995   Home Buyers' Club   2

BUYING OLD HOMES: Tips and Tricks - Part 2   (Continued...)

PLUMBING (Cont'd)

Check the hot water heater by turning on the hot water in the kitchen. Note the time it takes to turn hot and its temperature. Ask the owner the age of the hot water heater. Life expectancy of hot water heaters is 15 years; copper lined tanks last 20 years.

If you are looking at a country home, check the type of well and pump. Older homes have old wells. Have the water checked and the condition of the well. New wells are costly.

HEATING

Gas and electric forced air heat are the most common and are very good. Check for their age, duct work, and the number of supplies throughout the house. Turn the unit on and check its operation. These units are also good for central air conditioning because they adapt directly to it.

Hot water baseboard heat is another good, clean way to heat a home; but it can cause water leaks, takes up space along walls, is slow for recovery, and cannot accommodate central air conditioning. Stay away from old gravity-fed furnaces. In older houses, count on replacing this type of furnace.

Floor electric heaters and electric baseboard heaters are usually found in additions and are dangerous. They are not recommended and could be costly to add on to the regular heating system.

KITCHEN

In a kitchen, you should check the cabinets for door operation, space, etc. Count the number of outlets. See if there is enough light from the light fixtures. If appliances are included, be sure they work. Check if exhaust fan is vented outside. Check if the sink is chipped, scratched, or cracked. If the sink has a garbage disposal, be sure it works.

"If appliances are included, be sure they work."

BATHROOM

Bathrooms can be very costly to redo and/or recondition. Check if fixtures are modern or are chipped and cracked. Check if walls are solid, not rotted. If tiled, check the condition of the grout. Bad grout can be expensive to repair.

LIVING AREAS & BEDROOM

Check for insulation in walls by taking a light switch cover off of an inside wall. Look at the insulation with a flashlight. If no sign of insulation, the outside wall usually must be removed, which is costly.

Check all doors for operation, not sticking or scraping the floor. These are easy and inexpensive to repair.

Jump up and down on the floors. They will squeak if loose. If joists are properly built, squeaking is caused from the house settling and can be easily fixed. If the walls shake and the floor acts like a spring, floor joists are poorly built; this house should be avoided.

Look for moisture, especially in the ceiling area. It could be caused from a leaking roof or a bathroom above.

Check hardwood floors for scratching. This can be costly to repair. Check walls for paint, paper, or paneling condition.

Make sure all switches and lights work. Check for lights in closets.

ATTIC

Check that the attic is insulated properly with at least 10 inches thick of insulation. Check for water leaks with a flashlight. When dry, you will see where water has been running down. Check for proper ventilation: vents at soffit (where the roof meets the house) and the top roof ridge. Rafters should be contructed in this area with 2 x 6 boards 16 inches apart and cross braced. Older homes and some pre-fab houses are usually not cross braced.

The checks presented in this article are designed to save you time and money before your purchase. If you are in doubt, have your chosen house checked by a professional before you sign a contract.

COMPUTER LABORATORY ASSIGNMENT 3
Creating a Newsletter

Purpose: To become familiar with creating a newsletter with desktop publishing features, such as multiple columns, graphics, fonts, ruling lines, and vertical rules.

Problem: As senior marketing representative for All-Aboard Cruiselines, you send a monthly newsletter to all people signed up for a cruise with your organization. These newsletters are designed to inform the upcoming passengers of ship procedures, policies, and so on. The subject of this month's newsletter is What To Pack.

(continued)

COMPUTER LABORATORY ASSIGNMENT 3 (continued)

Instructions:

1. Change the margins to 0.4-inch on all sides. (Depending on your printer, you may need different margin settings.)
2. Redefine the Normal style to a point size of 12.
3. Create the newsletter shown in Figure CLA3-3. Use the following formats: a) title – Arial font, 39 point bold; b) text at left margin of issue information line – 14 point; c) headlines – bold; d) subheads – 14 point bold; e) graphic – luggage.wmf; f) pull-quote – 16 point bold; g) all other text is 12 point.
4. Save the document with the filename CLA3-3.
5. Print the document.

ALL-ABOARD CRUISELINES

GUEST NEWSLETTER   Vol. I • No. 10 • Oct. 3, 1995

WHAT TO PACK

In this issue...

Each month, from now until your cruiseship departs, you will receive a newsletter like this giving you tips and guidelines for your cruise. We want your cruise to be as enjoyable an experience as possible. In this month's issue of All-Aboard Cruiselines, our newsletter topic is shipboard attire.

Shipboard Day Attire

On the ship during the day, you will want to be as comfortable as possible. For poolside activities, be sure to bring your swimsuit. We also recommend a cover-up for walking from the pool into the air-conditioned rooms in the ship. Because the deck can be slippery, bring crepe-soled shoes. And pack sunhat or visor to protect your face from the bright sunshine.

When not by the pool, you might wear walking shorts, lightweight slacks or skirts, short-sleeved blouses or shirts, knit tops or polo shirts. If you enjoy exercising, bring your jogging or workout suit and join our crew for daily workouts. For relaxing in your cabin, a comfortable robe and slippers is a must. Because cabin space is limited, try to limit suitcases to one per person.

Attire for Excursions Ashore

Because many of the islands require conservative attire, be sure to bring appropriate clothing for excursions ashore. Acceptable clothes include casual dress or skirt and blouse, casual light summer pants, walking shorts, and polo shirts. You will do a lot of walking ashore, so be sure to bring comfortable walking shoes.

Shipboard Evening Attire

On board dinners will include both formal and informal nights. On formal nights, men are expected to wear either a tuxedo or dark suit and women should wear either a cocktail dress or gown. On informal nights, men can wear slacks, a jacket, shirt, and tie. Women may wear a dress or pants outfit on informal dinner nights.

Other Gear

In addition to clothing, you should remember such poolside essentials as sunscreen lotion, a beach towel, sunglasses, and reading material. Don't forget your camera and film and a tote bag. Other gear you may need includes sporting equipment, prescriptions or medication (including those for motion sickness), extra eyeglasses or contact lenses.

> "Don't forget your camera and film."

CAPTAIN'S NOTES

Cabin voltage is 110 volts AC. Be sure your hair dryer and other electrical appliances are compatible with this current.

When boarding our ships, you must bring a passport, certified birth certificate, or certified naturalization certificate.

We recommend you insure all baggage and items of value prior to boarding our ships. We are not responsible for stolen goods.

WE'RE DELIGHTED YOU'RE PLANNING ON CRUISING WITH US!

FIGURE CLA3-3

COMPUTER LABORATORY ASSIGNMENT 4
Designing and Creating a Newsletter

Purpose: To provide practice in planning, designing, and creating a newsletter.

Problem: You work in the Media Services department for your school. You have been assigned the task of designing a newsletter to be sent to all houses in a 30-mile radius of the school. The newsletter is to inform the community of the campus, its people, and its events.

Instructions: Design a two-page newsletter for your school. Use all of the desktop publishing features presented in this project. Be sure the colors and graphics work well together.

S P R E A D S H E E T S

USING MICROSOFT EXCEL 5 FOR WINDOWS

MICROSOFT EXCEL 5 FOR WINDOWS

PROJECT ONE

▼

WORKING WITH TEMPLATES AND MULTIPLE WORKSHEETS IN A WORKBOOK

OBJECTIVES You will have mastered the material in this project when you can:

▶ Create and use a template
▶ Copy data between worksheets
▶ Utilize custom formats
▶ Create formulas that reference cells in different sheets in a workbook
▶ Change chart types
▶ Enhance embedded charts
▶ Summarize data using consolidation

▶ Add comments to cells
▶ Add a header or footer to a workbook
▶ Change the margins
▶ Drag a column in a chart to change the corresponding number in a worksheet
▶ Find text in the workbook
▶ Replace text in the workbook

▶ INTRODUCTION

There are business applications that require data from several worksheets to be summarized onto one worksheet. For example, many businesses maintain daily sales data on separate worksheets. At the end of the week, these businesses have seven worksheets of data, one for each day of the week, which is then summarized onto one worksheet for the entire week.

Excel's three-dimensional capabilities make it easy for you to complete this type of application. For example, the sales for each day would be maintained on a separate sheet in a workbook. The eighth sheet in the workbook would contain a summary of the seven daily sheets. You use the tabs at the bottom of the Excel window to move from sheet to sheet. Furthermore, Excel has the capability to reference cells found on different sheets, which allows you to easily summarize the daily sales data. You could even extend the application to summarize the weekly worksheets onto a monthly sheet and the monthly sheets onto a yearly sheet. The process of summarizing information found on multiple sheets is called **consolidation**.

Another important concept you will be introduced to in this project is the use of a template. A **template** is a special workbook you can use as a pattern to create new workbooks that are similar. A template usually consists of a **general format** (worksheet title, column and row titles, numeric format) and formulas that are common to all the worksheets. For example, with the daily sales application, the seven daily worksheets and the weekly worksheet would be identical, except for the numbers. For such an application, it is to your advantage to create a template, save it, and then copy it eight times to a workbook, once for each day of the week and once for the end-of-the-week summary.

Finally, this project introduces you to using the Find and Replace commands.

E2

▶ PROJECT ONE — BEAVISTON PUBLIC SAFETY DIVISION BUDGET PROPOSAL

In June of each year, the controller for the town of Beaviston, Florida, tenders to the town board a preliminary Public Safety Division budget for the next year. The Public Safety Division is made up of the Fire, Police, and Streets and Sanitation departments. Each of the three departments develops its own budget proposal for the upcoming year, which also includes the current year's budget and the variance between the two years. The individual department budget proposals are submitted to the controller and consolidated onto one budget proposal for the Public Safety Division. An example of the consolidation process is shown in Figure 1-1. Graphs that compare the next year's budget proposal to the current year's budget are included to illustrate the variances.

FIGURE 1-1

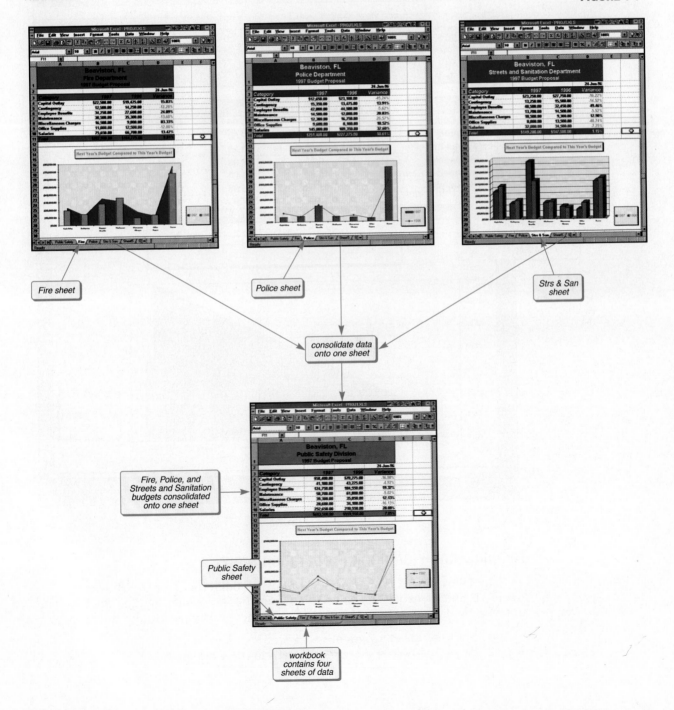

Because the three departments and division worksheets are similar, a template (Figure 1-2) is first created and then copied four times into the Public Safety Division Budget Proposal workbook. Thus, the objective of Project 1 is to create the template and use it to build the workbook made up of four sheets, one for each department and one for the division.

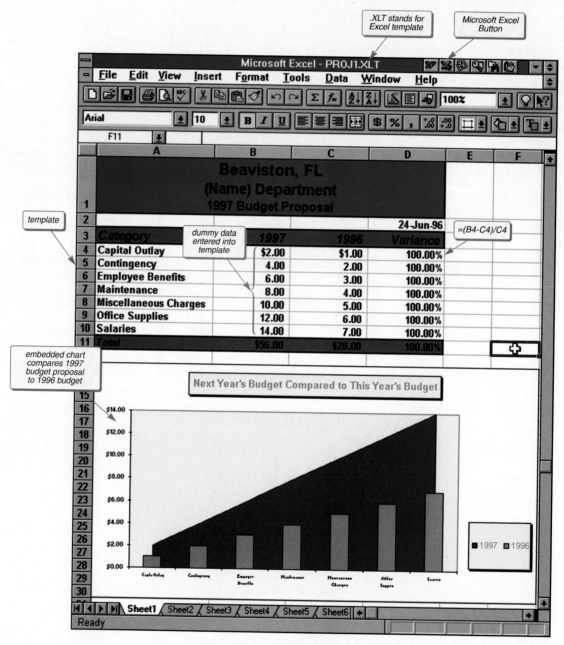

FIGURE 1-2

Template and Workbook Preparation Steps

The following list is an overview of how to build the template shown in Figure 1-2 and the workbook shown in Figure 1-1. If you are building the template and workbook on a personal computer, read these 14 steps without doing them.

1. Start the Excel program.
2. Apply the bold style to all the cells in the worksheet.

3. Increase the width of columns A through D, enter the worksheet titles, row titles, column titles, and system date.
4. Use the fill handle to enter dummy data for the 1996 budget and 1997 proposed budget. Next, determine department totals and enter the variance formulas in column D.
5. Save the workbook as a template using the filename PROJ1.XLT.
6. Format the template.
7. Create an embedded combination area and column chart as part of the template that compares the next year's proposed budget to the current year's budget. Format the chart.
8. Check spelling, save the template a second time, and then close it.
9. Open the template. Copy Sheet1 to Sheet2, Sheet3, and Sheet4. Save the workbook as PROJ1.XLS.
10. Modify the worksheet title, enter the data, and change the chart type on each of the sheets that represent the three departments.
11. Modify the worksheet title of the division sheet. Enter the SUM function and copy it to consolidate the data found on the three department sheets. Change the chart type.
12. Add workbook documentation to a cell on the division sheet.
13. Add a header to the four sheets and change the margins.
14. Save, preview, and print the workbook.

The following sections contain a detailed explanation of these steps.

Starting Excel

To start Excel, follow the steps summarized below.

TO START EXCEL

Step 1: If the Office Manager toolbar displays, use the mouse to point to the Microsoft Excel button ( ) (Figure 1-2). If the Office Manager toolbar does not display at the top right of your screen, then point to the Microsoft Excel program-item icon ( ) in the Microsoft Office group window.

Step 2: If the Office Manager toolbar displays, then with the mouse pointer pointing to the Microsoft Excel button, click the left mouse button. If the Office Manager toolbar does not display at the top right of your screen, then double-click the Microsoft Excel program-item icon in the Microsoft Office group window.

▶ CREATING THE TEMPLATE

Learning how to use templates is important if you plan to use a similar worksheet design in your workbooks. In the case of Project 1, there are four sheets (Figure 1-1) that are nearly identical. Thus, the first step in building the Public Safety Division Budget Proposal workbook is to create a template (Figure 1-2) that contains the labels, formulas, and formats that are found on each of the sheets. Once the template is saved to disk, it can be used as often as required to initiate a new workbook. Many worksheet users create a template for each application on which they work. The templates can be as simple as containing a special font you want to use in an application or more complex as is the case in the template for Project 1.

You create and modify a template the same as a worksheet. The only difference between a worksheet and a template is in the way in which it is saved.

Bolding the Font and Changing Column Widths of the Template

The first step in this project is to change the font of the entire template to bold so all entries are emphasized and change the column widths as follows: A = 22.00 and B through D = 14.00.

TO BOLD THE FONT IN THE TEMPLATE AND CHANGE COLUMN WIDTHS

Step 1: Click the Select All button immediately above row heading 1 and to the left of column heading A.

Step 2: Click the Bold button on the Standard toolbar. Select cell A1.

Step 3: Move the mouse pointer to the border between column heading A and column heading B so the mouse pointer shape changes to a split double arrow. Drag the mouse pointer to the right until the width displayed in the reference area in the formula bar is equal to 22.00 and then release the left mouse button.

Step 4: Select columns B through D by pointing to column heading B and dragging though column heading D. Move the mouse pointer to the borderline between column headings D and E and drag the mouse to the right until the width displayed in the reference area is 14.00. Release the left mouse button.

Column A has a width of 22.00 and columns B through D have a width of 14.00.

Entering the Template Title and Row Titles

There are three lines of text in the template title in cell A1. To enter the three lines of text in one cell, press ALT+ENTER after each of the first two lines. After the third line, press the ENTER key; or click the check box in the formula bar; or press an arrow key to complete a cell entry. Enter the row titles using the following steps.

TO ENTER THE TEMPLATE TITLE AND ROW TITLES

Step 1: Select cell A1. Type `Beaviston, FL` and press ALT+ENTER. Type `(Name) Department` and press ALT+ENTER. Type `1997 Budget Proposal` and press the DOWN ARROW key twice.

Step 2: With cell A3 selected, type `Category` and press the DOWN ARROW key.

Step 3: Enter the remaining row titles in column A as shown in Figure 1-3 on the next page.

Pressing ALT+ENTER after each line in the template title in cell A1 causes the insertion point to move down one line in the cell. This procedure allows you to control the width of each line of text entered into a cell.

Excel will **wrap text** to the next line when a word will not fit on a line in a cell instead of overflowing it into the cell to the right. However, you have to first select the Wrap Text check box on the Alignment tab. To display the Alignment tab, choose the Format Cells command on the shortcut menu and click the Alignment tab.

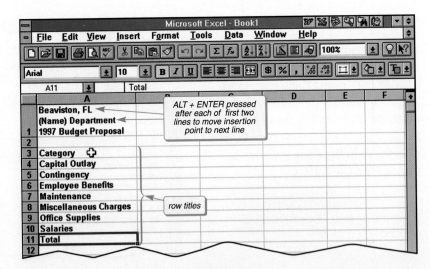

FIGURE 1-3

Entering the Template Column Titles and System Date

The next step is to enter the column titles in row 3 and the system date in cell D2. If a cell entry contains only digits, such as 1997, then Excel considers it to be numeric. Because of the method this project presents to determine the sums in columns B and C and the chart range that will be selected later, enter the two numeric entries in row 3 as text. To enter a number as text, begin it with an apostrophe (') as shown in the following steps. The apostrophe (') is found on the key with the quotation marks (").

TO ENTER THE TEMPLATE COLUMN TITLES AND SYSTEM DATE ▼

STEP 1 ▶

Select cell B3. Type '1997 and press the RIGHT ARROW key. Type '1996 and press the RIGHT ARROW key. Type Variance and press the ENTER key.

STEP 2 ▶

Select the range B3:D3 and click the Align Right button on the Formatting toolbar.

STEP 3 ▶

Select cell D2. Type =now() and click the enter box or press the ENTER key.

The column titles and system date display as shown in Figure 1-4.

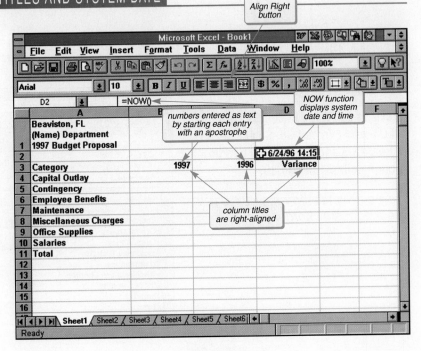

FIGURE 1-4

STEP 4 ▶

With the mouse pointer in cell D2, click the right mouse button and choose the Format Cells command. When the Format Cells dialog box displays, click the Number tab. Select Date in the Category box and d-mmm-yy in the Format Codes box. Choose the OK button.

The system date displays using the new format (Figure 1-5).

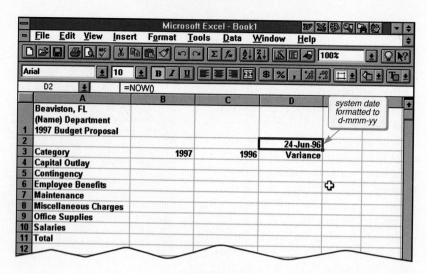

FIGURE 1-5

Entering Dummy Numbers and Summing Them in the Template

Dummy numbers are used in place of actual data in a template to verify the formulas. Usually, you select numbers that allow you to quickly check if the formulas are generating the proper results. In Project 1, the budget category dollar amounts are entered into the range B4:C10. The following steps use the fill handle to create a series of numbers in column B that begins with 2 and increments by 2 and a series of numbers in column C that begins with 1 and increments by 1. To create a series, you must enter the first two numbers so Excel can determine the increment amount.

TO ENTER DUMMY NUMBERS AND SUM THEM IN THE TEMPLATE ▼

STEP 1 ▶

Enter 2 in cell B4, 4 in cell B5, 1 in cell C4, and 2 in cell C5. Select the range B4:C5 and drag the fill handle through cells B10 and C10.

Excel surrounds the range B4:C10 with a dark grey border (Figure 1-6).

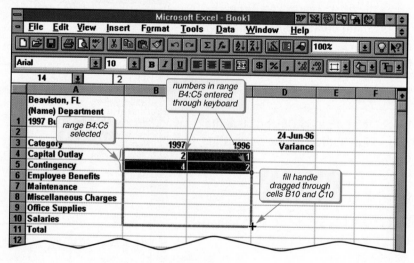

FIGURE 1-6

STEP 2 ▶

Release the left mouse button. Select the range B11:C11, and click the AutoSum button on the Standard toolbar.

Excel assigns the sum of the values in the range B4:B10 to cell B11 and the sum of the values in the range C4:C10 to cell C11 (Figure 1-7).

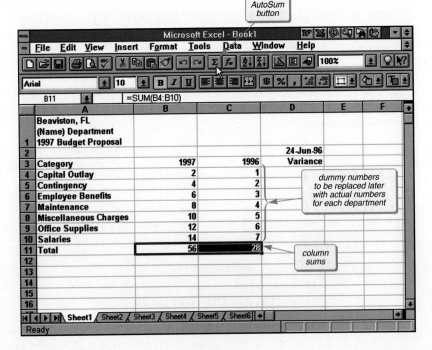

FIGURE 1-7

Notice, if 1997 in cell B3 and 1996 in cell C3 had been entered as numbers, then Excel would have included them in the sums. Because they were entered with an initial apostrophe, Excel considers them to be text, and therefore, does not include them in the ranges to sum in cells B11 and C11.

Entering the Variance Formula in the Template

The variances in column D (see Figure 1-1 on page E3) are equal to the corresponding 1997 budget amount less the 1996 budget amount divided by the 1996 budget amount. For example, the formula to enter in cell D4 is =(B4-C4)/C4. This formula displays a decimal result that indicates the percent increase or decrease in the 1997 budget amount when compared to the 1996 budget amount. Once the formula is entered into cell D4, it can be copied to the range D5:D11.

TO ENTER THE VARIANCE FORMULA IN THE TEMPLATE

Step 1: Select cell D4 and enter =(B4-C4)/C4
Step 2: With cell D4 selected, drag the fill handle down through cell D11, and then release the left mouse button. Select cell F11.

The formula is entered into cell D4 and copied to the range D5:D11 (Figure 1-8 on the next page).

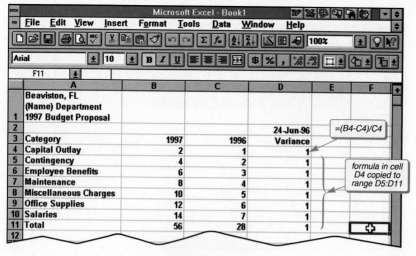

FIGURE 1-8

Excel displays a 1 in each cell in the range D4:D11 because the numbers in column B are twice the corresponding numbers in column C. Thus, the 1s in column D represent 100% proposed budget increases between 1996 and 1997. Later, when the actual budget numbers replace the dummy numbers in columns B and C, these percent values will be different. Shortly, column D will be formatted so the numbers display as percents instead of whole numbers.

Saving the Template

Saving a template is accomplished by selecting Template in the Save File as Type box in the Save As dialog box. Excel saves the template with an extension of **.XLT,** which stands for Excel Template.

TO SAVE A TEMPLATE ▼

STEP 1 ▶

Click the Save button on the Standard toolbar. When the Save As dialog box displays, type `proj1` in the File Name box. Select drive A in the Drives drop-down list box.

STEP 2 ▶

Select Template from the Save File as Type drop-down list box.

The Save As dialog box displays as shown in Figure 1-9.

STEP 3 ▶

Choose the OK button. You may optionally enter summary information in the Summary Information dialog box. Choose the OK button.

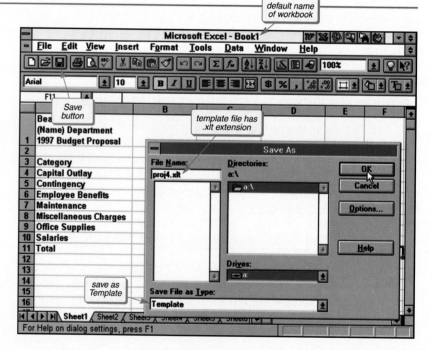

FIGURE 1-9

Excel saves the template proj1.xlt to the disk in drive A. The filename PROJ1.XLT displays in the title bar as shown in Figure 1-10.

The **Save File as Type box** allows you to save an Excel workbook in many different forms. For example, you can save a workbook (only the active sheet) as an ASCII file. A file stored in **ASCII file format** can be read by any software package. You can also save workbooks so other spreadsheet software such as Lotus 1-2-3 and Quattro Pro can read them.

▶ FORMATTING THE TEMPLATE

The next step is to format the template so it displays as shown in Figure 1-10. Keep in mind that the formats selected will show up in each of the sheets for which the template is used. The following list summarizes the sequence of formatting to be applied.

1. Change the font size of the template title in cell A1. Center cell A1 across columns A through D.
2. Italicize and change the font size of the column titles in row 3. Italicize the row title Total in cell A11.
3. Assign the background color teal and a heavy border to the nonadjacent ranges A1:D1, A3:D3, and A11:D11.
4. Apply a Currency format to the nonadjacent ranges B4:C4 and B11:D11. Apply a Comma format to the range B5:C10.
5. Apply a Percent format to the range D4:D11.

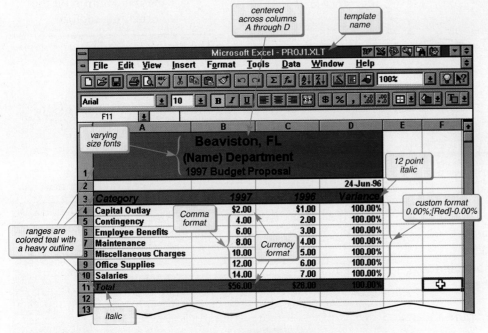

FIGURE 1-10

Applying Formats to the Template Title

To emphasize the template title in cell A1, the font size will be changed to the following: line 1 = 16 point; line 2 = 14 point; and line 3 = 12 point. Font sizes can be assigned to individual characters or groups of characters in a cell. The following steps change the font size and center the template title across columns A through D. After the font size of the text in cell A1 is changed, but before it is centered, the text will wrap on several lines. As soon as cell A1 is centered across columns A through D, the text will wrap on three lines.

TO APPLY FORMATS TO THE TEMPLATE TITLES

Step 1: Double-click cell A1 to activate in-cell editing. Drag across the first line of text. Click the Font Size arrow on the Formatting toolbar and choose 16 point.

Step 2: With in-cell editing still active in cell A1, use the techniques described in Step 1 to change the font size of line 2 to 14 point and line 3 to 12 point. Click the check box in the formula bar or press the ENTER key.

Step 3: With cell A1 selected, drag through cell D1. Click the Center Across Columns button on the Formatting toolbar.

Step 4: Select the range A3:D3. Click the Font Size arrow on the Formatting toolbar and choose 12 point. Click the Italic button on the Formatting toolbar.

Step 5: Select cell A11 and click the Italic button on the Formatting toolbar.

The template displays as shown in Figure 1-11.

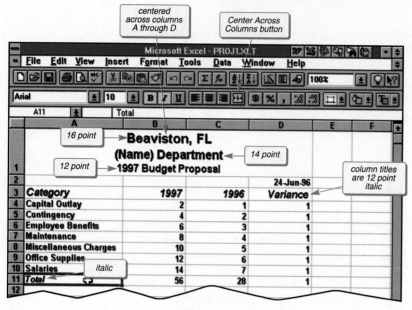

FIGURE 1-11

To help make the titles stand out even more, the background colors will be changed and a heavy outline will be drawn around these three areas.

TO CHANGE THE BACKGROUND COLOR AND ADD AN OUTLINE ▼

STEP 1 ▶

Hold down the CTRL key and drag through the ranges A1:D1, A3:D3, and A11:D11. Click the Color button arrow on the Formatting toolbar.

The Color palette displays (Figure 1-12).

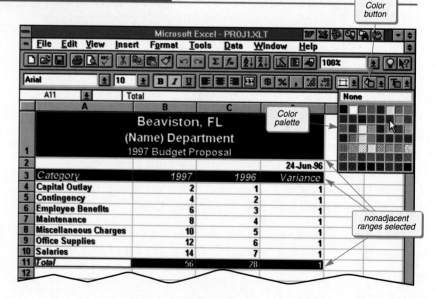

FIGURE 1-12

STEP 2 ▶

Choose teal (column 6, row 2) on the Color palette.

STEP 3 ▶

Click the Borders button arrow on the Formatting toolbar.

The Borders palette displays (Figure 1-13).

FIGURE 1-13

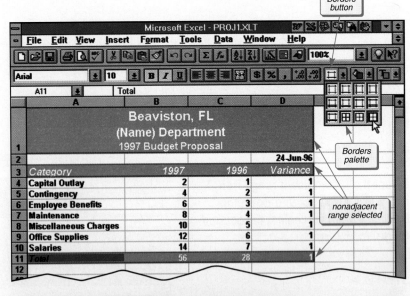

STEP 4 ▶

Choose the heavy border (column 4, row 3) on the Borders palette.

The template title, column titles, and total row display as shown in Figure 1-14.

FIGURE 1-14

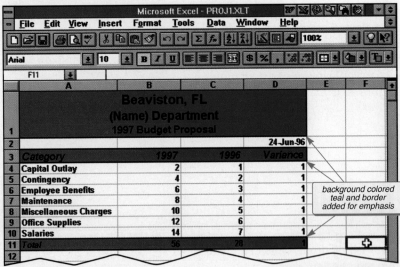

Applying Number Formats from the Format Cells Dialog Box

For most spreadsheet applications the buttons on the Formatting toolbar will suffice for applying format codes to the numbers in cells. These buttons offer limited formatting choices. Using the Format Cells dialog box, you can select from a larger number of format codes. A **format code** is a series of format symbols that define a format. For example, earlier in this project you formatted the system date in cell D2 using the format code d-mmm-yy.

The template in this project (see Figure 1-2 on page E4) calls for following the standard accounting convention for a table of numbers by adding dollar signs to the first row of numbers (row 3) and the totals row (row 11). To accomplish this task, you could select the range and click the Currency style button on the Formatting toolbar. However, the format code applied to the selected cells would result in applying a fixed dollar sign. A **fixed dollar sign** always displays in the same position in a cell regardless of the number of digits in the number. The alternative to a fixed dollar sign is a floating dollar sign. A **floating dollar sign** always displays immediately to the left of the first significant digit. Because this project uses a floating dollar sign, a format code must be selected in the Format Cells dialog box, instead of using the Currency Style button.

The following steps apply a format code to the ranges B4:C4 and B11:C11 using the Format Cells command on the shortcut menu. The steps then use the Comma Style button on the Formatting toolbar to format the range B5:C10.

TO APPLY A FORMAT CODE FROM THE FORMAT DIALOG BOX ▼

STEP 1 ▶

Select the nonadjacent range B4:C4 and B11:C11 by holding down the CTRL key when you select the second range.

STEP 2 ▶

With the mouse pointer in one of the two selected areas, click the right mouse button.

Excel displays the shortcut menu (Figure 1-15).

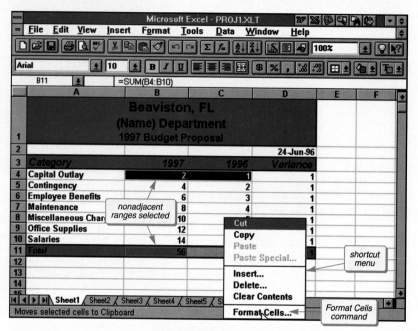

FIGURE 1-15

STEP 3 ▶

Choose the Format Cells command from the shortcut menu.

Excel displays the Format cells dialog box.

STEP 4 ▶

Click the Number tab. Select Currency in the Category box and the format code $#,##0.00_);($#,##0.00) in the Format Codes box.

The Format Cells dialog box displays as shown in Figure 1-16.

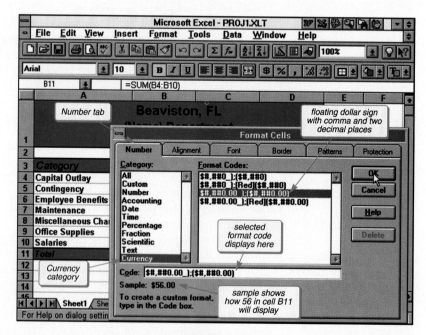

FIGURE 1-16

STEP 5 ▶

Choose the OK button in the Format Cells dialog box.

The selected ranges display as shown in Figure 1-17.

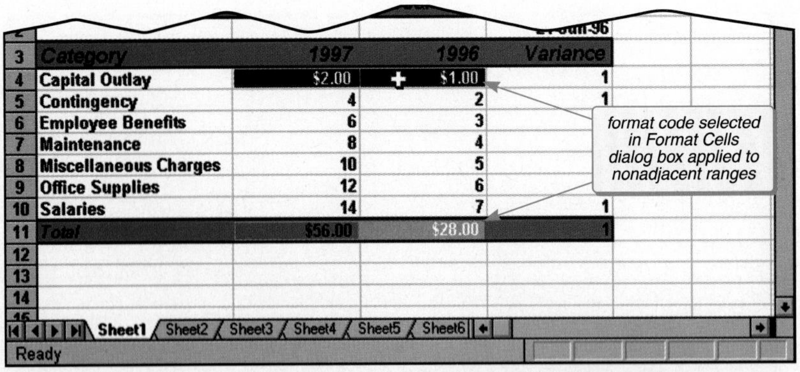

FIGURE 1-17

STEP 6 ▶

Select the range B5:C10 and click the Comma Style button on the Formatting toolbar.

Excel displays the numbers in the range B5:C10 using the Comma format (Figure 1-18). Later, when larger numbers are entered into the worksheets that are based on the template, these numbers will include a comma.

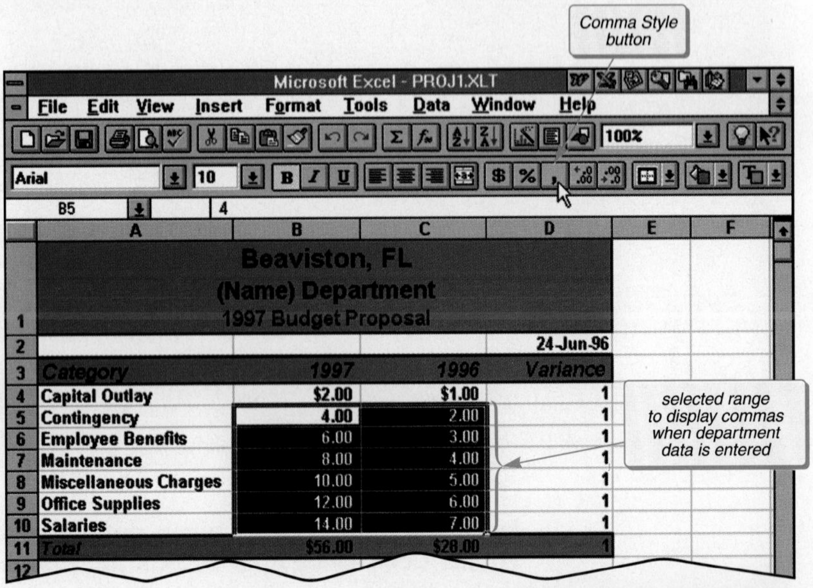

FIGURE 1-18

Each format symbol within the format code $#,##0.00_);($#,##0.00) selected in Step 4 has special meaning. Table 1-1 on the next page summarizes the most frequently used format symbols and their meanings. For a complete listing of the format symbols, choose the Search for Help on command from the Help menu. Next, type format codes in the top box, and click the Show Topics button. When Number Format Codes displays in the lower box, choose the Go To button. Excel displays a table consisting of all the format symbols.

A format code can have up to four sections: positive numbers, negative numbers, zeros, and text as shown below. Each section is divided by a semicolon.

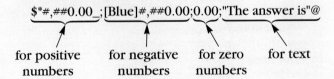

$*#,##0.00_;[Blue]#,##0.00;0.00;"The answer is"@

for positive numbers | for negative numbers | for zero numbers | for text

For most applications, a format code will only have a positive section and, possibly, a negative section.

Creating a Customized Format Code

The next step is to format the variances in the range D4:D11. This project requires that positive numbers in this range display using the format code 0.00%. Negative numbers display in red using a format code of 0.00% with a leading minus sign. The required format code is 0.00%;[Red]-0.00%. As shown in

▶ **TABLE 1-1**

FORMAT SYMBOL	EXAMPLE OF SYMBOL	DESCRIPTION
General	General	Displays the number in General format, which means no dollar signs, no commas, no decimal point unless required, or no trailing zeros to the right of the decimal point.
#	###.##	Digit placeholder. If there are more digits to the right than there are number signs, Excel rounds the number. Extra digits to the left are displayed.
0 (zero)	#,##0.00	Same as number sign (#), except that if the number is less than one, Excel displays a zero in place of the one.
. (period)	#0.00	Ensures a decimal point will display in the number. Determines how many digits display to left and right of decimal point.
%	0.00%	Excel multiplies the value of the cell by 100 and displays a percent sign following the number.
, (comma)	#,##0.00	Displays the thousands separator.
$ or - or +	$#,##0.00;($#,##0.00)	Displays a floating dollar sign.
* (asterisk)	$* ##0.00	Displays a fixed sign ($, +, or -) to the left in cell followed by spaces until the first significant digit.
[color]	#.##;[Red]#.##	Displays the characters in the cell in the designated color. In the example, positive numbers display in the default color and negative numbers display in red.
_	#,##0.00_	Skips the width of the character that follows the underline.
()	#0.00;(#0.00)	Displays negative numbers surrounded by parentheses.

Figure 1-19, this format code is not available in the Percentage category in the Format Cells dialog box. Thus, it must be created by entering the format code in the Code box in the Format Cells dialog box. A format code that you create in the Code box is called a **custom format code**.

TO CREATE A CUSTOM FORMAT CODE ▼

FIGURE 1-19

STEP 1 ▶

Select the range D4:D11. With the mouse pointer in the selected range, click the right mouse button. Choose the Format Cells command. When the Format Cells dialog box displays, select Percentage in the Category box to see if the required format code is available.

STEP 2 ▶

Because the format code is not available, click in the Code box and type `0.00%;[Red]-0.00%`

The Format Cells dialog box displays as shown in Figure 1-19. Make sure you type zeros and not the letter O in the code box.

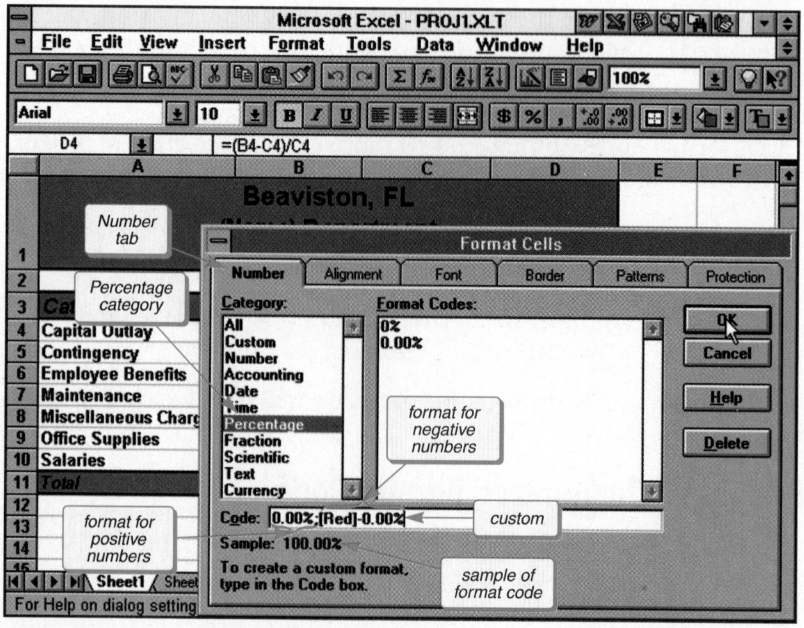

STEP 3 ►

Choose the OK button.

The percents in the range D4:D11 display as shown in Figure 1-20.

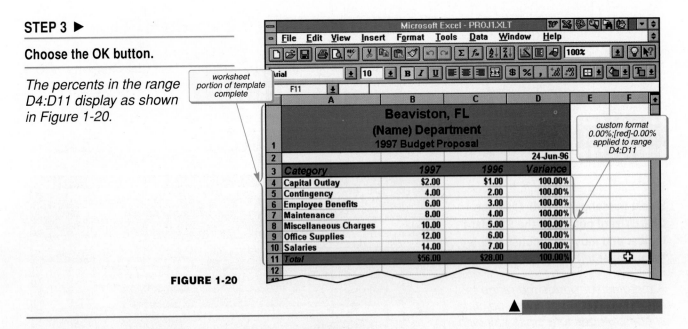

FIGURE 1-20

When you create a custom format code, Excel displays it in the Format Codes box to make it available for other cells in the workbook.

The worksheet portion of the template is complete. Save the template to disk as PROJ1.XLT before continuing with this project.

► ADDING A CHART TO THE TEMPLATE

The next step is to add an embedded combination area and column chart to the template in the range A13:F30 using the ChartWizard button on the Standard toolbar. The **combination area and column chart** allows you to compare two sets of numbers in one chart. In the proposed budget template, the chart compares next year's proposed budget (area) to the current year budget (column) as shown in Figure 1-21.

After creating the chart in this section, formats will be applied to the chart title, legends, and font along the axis. Techniques are then presented to resize and change the color of the chart.

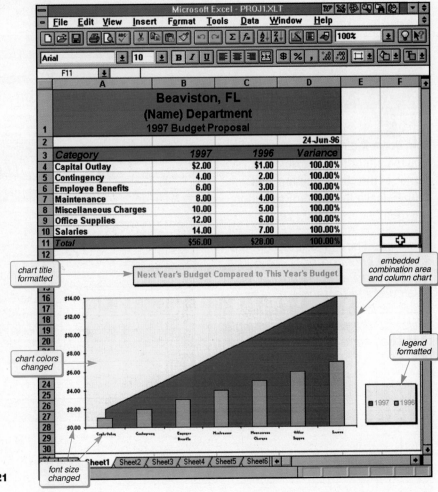

FIGURE 1-21

Creating an Embedded Chart Using the ChartWizard Button

An embedded chart is one that resides on the same sheet as the numbers being charted. To create a combination area and column chart that compares next year's proposed budget to this year's budget, perform the following steps.

TO DRAW AN EMBEDDED COMBINATION AREA AND COLUMN CHART ▼

STEP 1 ►

Select the range A3:C10. Click the ChartWizard button on the Standard toolbar and move the mouse pointer to the upper left corner of cell A13.

A marquis surrounds the range to chart, A3:C10. The mouse pointer shape changes to a cross hair with a chart symbol (Figure 1-22).

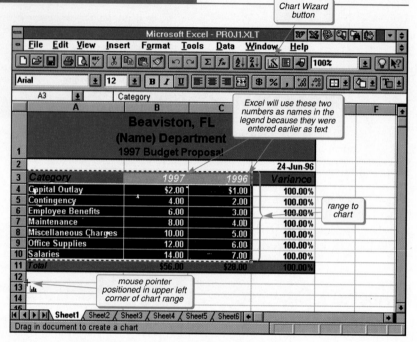

FIGURE 1-22

STEP 2 ►

Hold down the ALT key and drag the mouse pointer to the lower right corner of the chart location (cell F30). Release the left mouse button and then release the ALT key.

The mouse pointer is positioned at the lower right corner of cell F30, and the chart area is surrounded by a solid line rectangle (Figure 1-23). Holding down the ALT key while you drag snaps the rectangle to the cell edge nearest the mouse pointer.

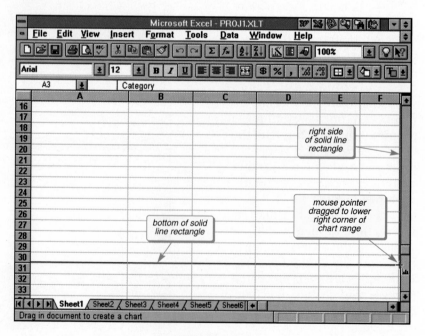

FIGURE 1-23

STEP 3 ▶

Release the left mouse button.

Excel responds by displaying the ChartWizard - Step 1 of 5 dialog box (Figure 1-24).The Range box contains the chart range. In this dialog box, you can change the range by typing a new one or dragging on a new range in the template.

FIGURE 1-24

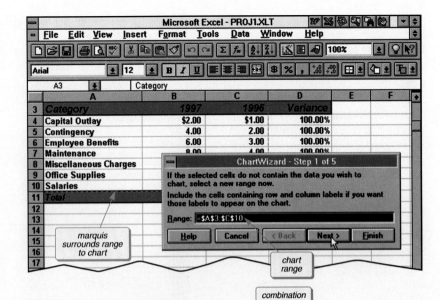

STEP 4 ▶

Choose the Next button in the ChartWizard – Step 1 of 5 dialog box.

The ChartWizard – Step 2 of 5 dialog box displays with fifteen charts from which to choose.

STEP 5 ▶

Select Combination (column 4, row 2).

Excel highlights the Combination chart type (Figure 1-25).

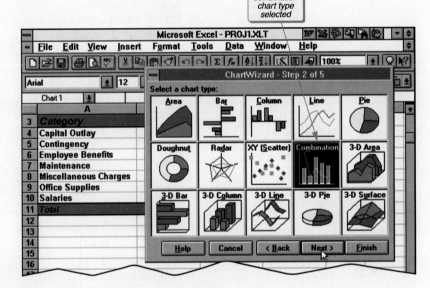

FIGURE 1-25

STEP 6 ▶

Choose the Next button in the ChartWizard – Step 2 of 5 dialog box.

The ChartWizard – Step 3 of 5 dialog box displays with six different built-in combination chart formats from which to choose.

STEP 7 ▶

Select box 4, the one with the area and column charts.

Excel highlights the selected combination chart format (Figure 1-26).

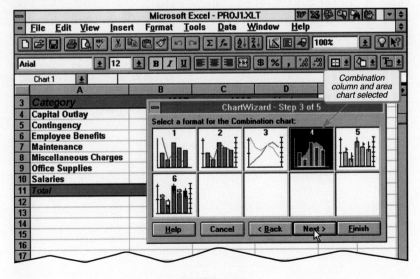

FIGURE 1-26

STEP 8 ▶

Choose the Next button in the ChartWizard – Step 3 of 5 dialog box.

The ChartWizard – Step 4 of 5 dialog box displays showing a sample of the combination chart (Figure 1-27).

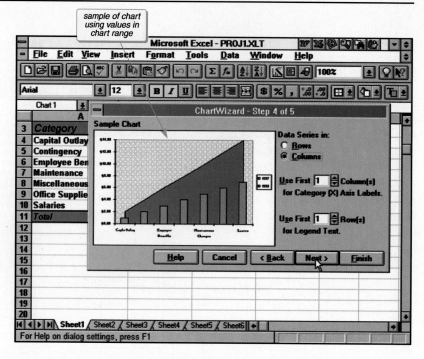

FIGURE 1-27

STEP 9 ▶

Choose the Next button in the ChartWizard – Step 4 of 5 dialog box.

The ChartWizard — Step 5 of 5 dialog box displays. In this dialog box, you can add a chart title.

STEP 10 ▶

In the Chart Title box, type Next Year's Budget Compared to This Year's Budget **as shown in Figure 1-28.**

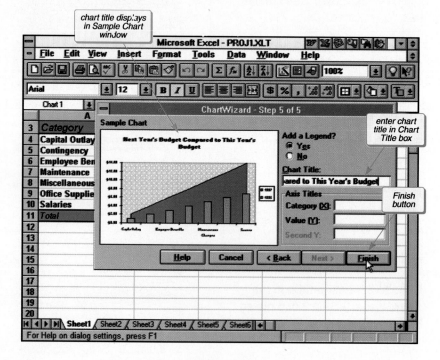

FIGURE 1-28

STEP 11 ►

Choose the Finish button on the ChartWizard – Step 5 of 5 dialog box.

Excel draws the combination chart in the range A13:F30, selects it, and displays it (Figure 1-29). Notice that not all category names display along the horizontal axis. This problem will be resolved shortly.

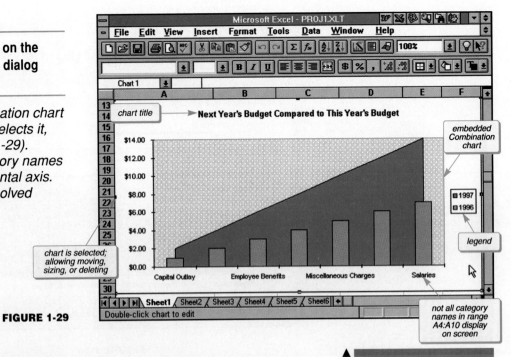

FIGURE 1-29

The embedded column chart in Figure 1-29 compares the six budget categories proposed for next year (range B4:B10) to the six budget categories for this year (range C4:C10). The legend on the right side contains the two labels (1997 and 1996) in cells B3 and C3. Because the dummy numbers increase in a linear fashion in the worksheet portion of the template, the area and column charts also increase in a linear fashion from left to right.

Formatting the Chart Title

Before you can format a chart item in an embedded chart, the chart must be active. Activate a chart by double-clicking anywhere within the chart area. An active chart has a heavy gray border surrounding it. An **active chart** is different from a selected chart. A **selected chart** has a thin border with handles surrounding it. You *select* a chart to resize it or move it to another area on the sheet. You *activate* a chart to format it. Perform the following steps to activate the chart and format the chart title.

TO FORMAT THE CHART TITLE

Step 1: Double-click the embedded chart. Click the chart title. The embedded chart is surrounded by a heavy gray border. The chart title is surrounded by a heavy dark border.

Step 2: Click the Color button arrow and choose pale yellow (column 4, row 5) on the Color palette.

Step 3: Click the Font Color button arrow and choose red (column 3, row 1) on the Font Color palette.

Step 4: Click the Drawing button on the Standard toolbar. Dock the Drawing toolbar at the bottom of the window.

Step 5: Click the Drop Shadow button on the Drawing toolbar. Click outside the chart title.

The chart title displays as shown in Figure 1-30 on the next page.

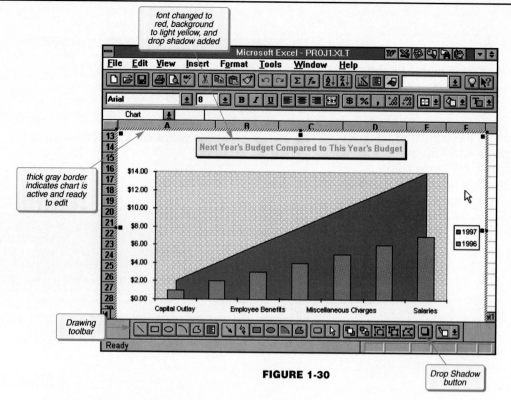

FIGURE 1-30

Resizing the Plot Area

The **plot area** is the rectangle (gray background in Figure 1-30) formed by the two axes in the chart area. The following steps show how to resize the plot area so the legend can be enlarged.

TO RESIZE THE PLOT AREA ▼

STEP 1 ▶

With the embedded chart active, click the gray colored background portion of the plot area. Point to the right center handle. Drag to the left approximately one inch.

The plot area is reduced in size (Figure 1-31).

STEP 2 ▶

Release the left mouse button.

The plot area is resized.

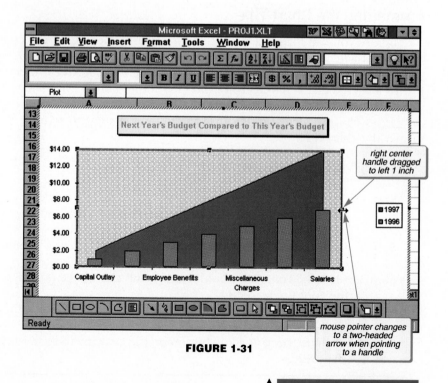

FIGURE 1-31

Formatting, Moving, and Resizing the Legend

The next step is to format, move, and resize the legend on the right side of the plot area. Perform the following steps.

TO FORMAT, MOVE, AND RESIZE THE LEGEND

Step 1: With the embedded chart active, select the legend by clicking on it. With the mouse pointer pointing to the center of the legend, drag it down to its new location (Figure 1-32).

Step 2: Increase the size of the legend by dragging the handles so it is the same size as the legend in Figure 1-32.

Step 3: Click the Color button on the Formatting toolbar to change the background color to pale yellow.

Step 4: Click the Font Color button on the formatting toolbar to change the font color to red.

Step 5: Click the Drop Shadow button on the Drawing toolbar.

The legend displays as shown in Figure 1-32.

You can move the legend to any location in the chart area, including inside the plot area.

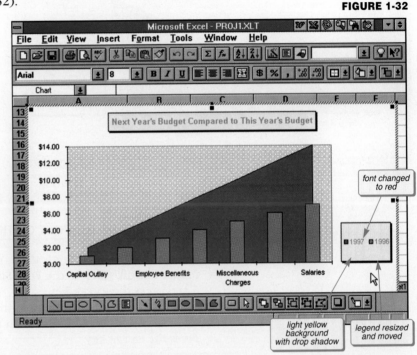

FIGURE 1-32

Changing the Colors of the Plot Area and Data Markers

The next step is to change the colors of the plot area and data markers. The **data markers** are the columns and purple area within the plot area.

TO CHANGE THE COLORS OF THE PLOT AREA AND DATA MARKERS

Step 1: With the chart area active, select the plot area by clicking it. Click the Color button on the Formatting toolbar to assign the color on the face of the Color button.

Step 2: Select all the columns by clicking one of them. Click the Color button arrow on the Formatting toolbar. Choose red (column 3, row 1) on the Color palette.

Step 3: Select the area chart by clicking it. Click the Color button arrow on the Formatting toolbar. Choose blue (column 1, row 4) on the Color palette.

The combination area and column chart appears as shown in Figure 1-33 on the next page.

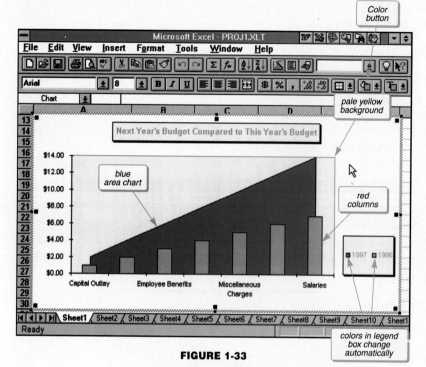

FIGURE 1-33

Notice that when you change the colors of the data markers, Excel also changes the colors of the identifiers within the legend.

Changing the Size of the Font on the Axes

The **category axis** (x-axis) is the horizontal line below the plot area in Figure 1-33. The **value axis** (y-axis) series is the vertical line to the left of the plot area. With the current size of the font (8 point) on the category axis, not all the labels display. Thus, the font size on the category axis must be reduced from 8 point to 4 point. To maintain a reasonable proportion between the labels on the axes, the font on the value axis will be changed to 6 point.

TO CHANGE THE SIZE OF THE FONT ON THE AXES

Step 1: Select the value axis (vertical axis) by pointing to it and clicking the left mouse button. Click in the Font Size box on the Formatting toolbar, type 6 and press the ENTER key.

Step 2: Select the category axis by pointing to it and clicking the left mouse button. Click in the Font Size box on the Formatting toolbar, type 4 and press the ENTER key.

The fonts along the axes display as shown in Figure 1-34.

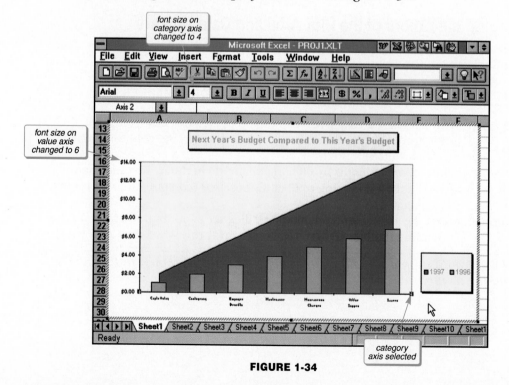

FIGURE 1-34

With the new font size (Figure 1-34), all seven category names display, instead of only four (Figure 1-33).

Checking Spelling, Saving, and Closing the Template

The template is complete (Figure 1-35). The next steps are to check spelling, save the template, and then close it.

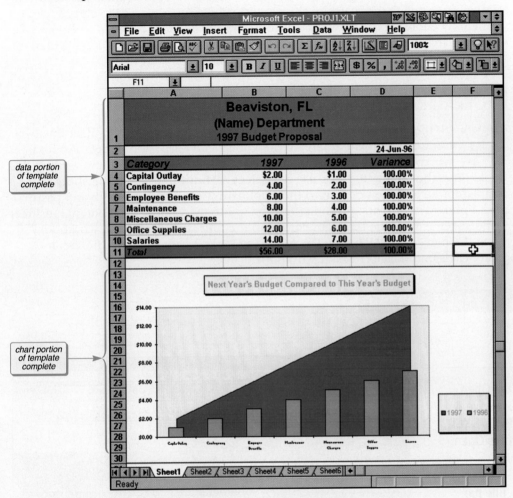

FIGURE 1-35

TO CHECK SPELLING, SAVE, AND CLOSE THE TEMPLATE

Step 1: Select cell A1. Click the Spelling button on the Standard toolbar. Change any misspelled words.

Step 2: Click the Save button on the Standard toolbar.

Step 3: Select the File menu and choose the Close command.

The template is saved using the filename PROJ1.XLT. The template is removed from the Excel window.

▶ ALTERNATIVE USES OF TEMPLATES

Before continuing the use of templates to create the Public Safety Division Budget Proposal workbook, be aware that Excel provides additional uses of templates. You can specify font, formatting, column widths, or any other defaults by creating templates with the desired formats and saving them to the XLSTART subdirectory. The **XLSTART subdirectory** is called the **startup directory**. Templates stored in the XLSTART subdirectory are called **autotemplates**. After saving templates to this special subdirectory, you can select any one of them by choosing the **New command** from the File menu. If you store one of the templates in the XLSTART subdirectory using the filename BOOK.XLT, then Excel uses the formats you assigned to it every time you start Excel.

▶ CREATING A WORKBOOK FROM A TEMPLATE

With the template stored on disk, the second phase of this project involves using the template to create the Public Safety Division Budget Proposal workbook shown in Figure 1-1 on page E3. To create the new workbook, open the template. Next, use the Select All button to select the sheet the template is on and then copy it to the Clipboard. Click the Sheet2 tab and paste the Clipboard's contents. In similar fashion, paste the Clipboard's contents to sheet 3 and sheet 4. With the template copied to the four sheets, save the workbook using the filename PROJ1.XLS. The following steps create and save the Public Safety Division Budget Proposal workbook.

TO CREATE A WORKBOOK FROM A TEMPLATE ▼

STEP 1 ▶

Click the Open button on the Standard toolbar. When the Open dialog box displays, select drive A and select the template PROJ1.XLT. Choose the OK button in the Open dialog box. Excel opens the template PROJ1.XLT and changes the name in the title bar to Proj11.

Excel changes the name in the title bar to ensure that the workbook will not be mistakenly saved in place of the template PROJ1.XLT.

STEP 2 ▶

Click the Select All button and click the Copy button on the Standard toolbar.

The template is selected as shown in Figure 1-36. The template is also on the Clipboard.

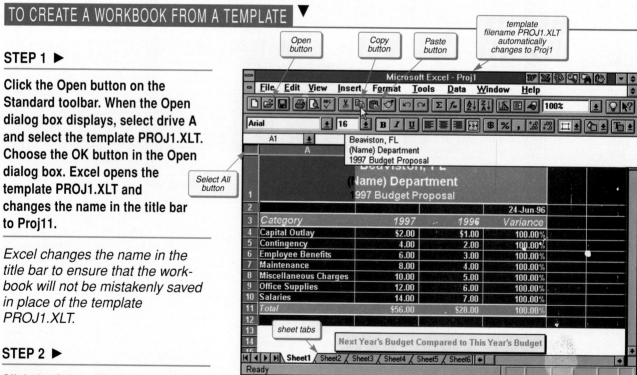

FIGURE 1-36

STEP 3 ▶

Click the Sheet2 tab. Click the Paste button on the Standard toolbar. Click the Sheet3 tab. Click the Paste button on the Standard toolbar. Click the Sheet4 tab. Click the Paste button on the Standard toolbar.

STEP 4 ▶

With Sheet4 tab active, hold down the SHIFT key and click the Sheet1 tab to select all four sheets. Click cell F11 so it is the active cell on all sheets. Hold down the SHIFT key and click the Sheet4 tab to deselect Sheet 1 through Sheet 3.

Excel removes the highlight from the four sheets and displays Sheet4 with cell F11 selected.

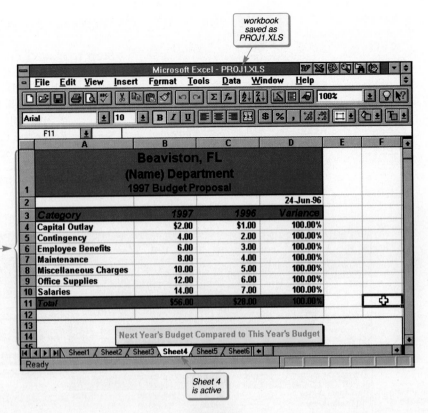

FIGURE 1-37

STEP 5 ▶

Select the File menu and choose the Save As command. When the Save As dialog box displays, type `PROJ1` in the File Name box. Select drive A. Choose the OK button.

Excel saves the Public Safety Division Budget Proposal workbook with four identical sheets to drive A using the filename PROJ1.XLS (Figure 1-37).

Modifying the Fire Sheet

With the skeleton of the Public Safety Division Budget Proposal workbook created, the next step is to modify the individual sheets. The following steps change the title of the Fire sheet and enter the Fire Department's proposed budget numbers.

▶ **TABLE 1-2**

CELL	VALUE	CELL	VALUE
B4	22500	C4	19425
B5	12500	C5	14250
B6	34250	C6	27600
B7	30500	C7	35300
B8	16500	C8	9000
B9	11000	C9	12500
B10	75650	C10	66700

TO MODIFY THE FIRE SHEET

Step 1: Double-click the Sheet1 tab. When the Rename dialog box displays, type Fire in the Name box. Choose the OK button.

Step 2: Double-click cell A1, double-click (Name) in line 2, and type Fire

Step 3: Enter the data in Table 1-2 in the range B4:C10.

Step 4: Click the Save button on the Standard toolbar.

The Fire sheet displays as shown in Figure 1-38.

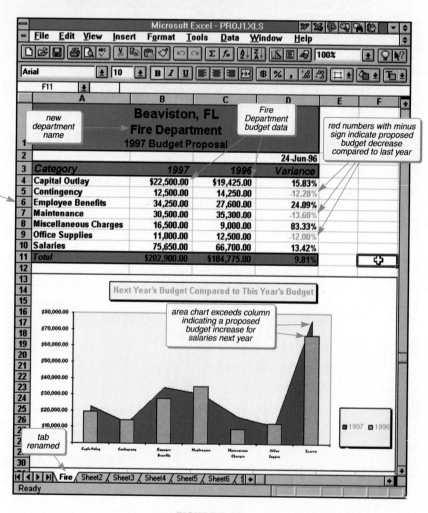

FIGURE 1-38

Notice as you enter the new data, Excel immediately updates the variances, displaying negative variances in red. In addition, Excel redraws the combination area and column chart found below the worksheet each time you enter a new value.

Modifying the Police Sheet

Three additional items that were not a problem with Fire sheet must be modified in the remaining three sheets as follows:

1. To differentiate between the four sheets in the workbook, the titles and total row are formatted with different colors. For example, the Police sheet uses white characters on a blue background.

2. Because of the way the sheets were created (copy and paste), the charts on the second, third, and fourth sheets all refer to the range A3:C10 on the Fire sheet. Thus, the charts will not be linked to the worksheet on the same sheet, unless the chart range is changed.

3. Each sheet has a different combination chart (see Figure 1-1 on page E3). Therefore, the chart type must be changed on the last three sheets.

The following steps modify the worksheet portion of the Police sheet.

TO MODIFY THE SPREADSHEET PORTION OF THE POLICE SHEET

Step 1: Double-click the Sheet2 tab. When the Rename dialog box displays, type `Police` in the Name box. Choose the OK button.

Step 2: Double-click cell A1 and replace (Name) in line 2 with `Police`

Step 3: Select the range A1:D1. Hold down the CTRL key and select the nonadjacent ranges A3:D3 and A11:D11. Click the Color button arrow on the Formatting toolbar. Choose blue (column 1, row 4) on the Color palette. Click the Font Color button arrow on the Formatting toolbar. Choose white (column 2, row 1) on the Font Color palette.

Step 4: Enter the data in Table 1-3 in the range B4:C10.

Step 5: Click the Save button on the Standard toolbar.

The Police sheet displays as shown in Figure 1-39.

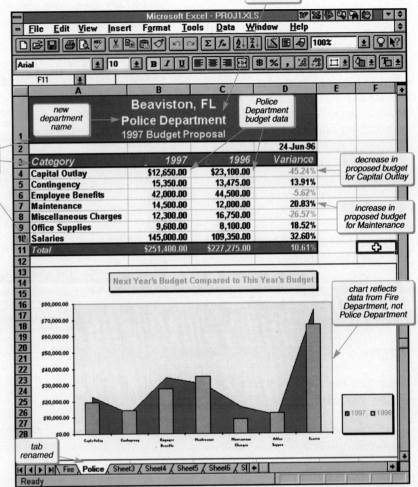

FIGURE 1-39

Notice in Figure 1-39, that although new data was entered into the Police sheet, its chart has not changed. In fact, the chart in Figure 1-39 is identical to the chart in Figure 1-38. This is because the Police sheet was created by copying the Fire sheet. The following steps change the chart range so it corresponds to the worksheet on the Police sheet.

▸ **TABLE 1-3**

CELL	VALUE	CELL	VALUE
B4	12650	C4	23100
B5	15350	C5	13475
B6	42000	C6	44500
B7	14500	C7	12000
B8	12300	C8	16750
B9	9600	C9	8100
B10	145000	C10	109350

TO CHANGE THE CHART RANGE ▼

STEP 1 ▶

Activate the chart on the Police sheet by double-clicking it.

A heavy gray border surrounds the chart. You may end up with the chart displaying in its own window. If this happens, click any cell in the worksheet and reduce the size of the chart so it fits in the window. Then double-click the chart again.

STEP 2 ▶

Click the ChartWizard button on the Standard toolbar.

Excel displays the ChartWizard – Step 1 of 2 dialog box which contains the Range box.

STEP 3 ▶

Drag over the sheet reference Fire! in the Range box.

The sheet reference is highlighted in the Range box (Figure 1-40).

STEP 4 ▶

Press the DELETE key. Point to the Finish button in the ChartWizard – Step 1 of 2 dialog box.

The sheet reference Fire! disappears from the range box (Figure 1-41). When there is no sheet reference in the Range box, the range refers to the sheet the embedded chart is on.

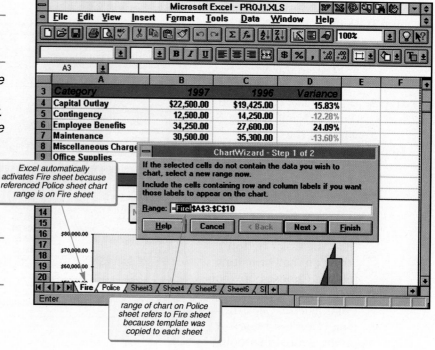

Excel automatically activates Fire sheet because referenced Police sheet chart range is on Fire sheet

range of chart on Police sheet refers to Fire sheet because template was copied to each sheet

FIGURE 1-40

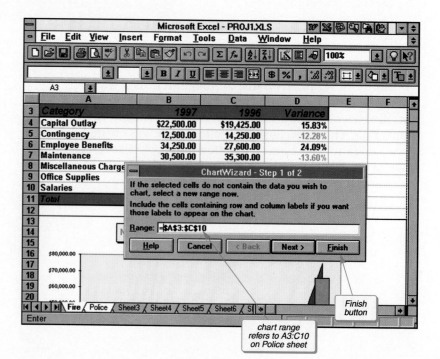

chart range refers to A3:C10 on Police sheet

Finish button

FIGURE 1-41

STEP 5 ▶

Choose the Finish button in the ChartWizard – Step 1 of 2 dialog box.

The combination area and column chart on the Police sheet reflect the data in the range A3:C10 of the Police sheet (Figure 1-42).

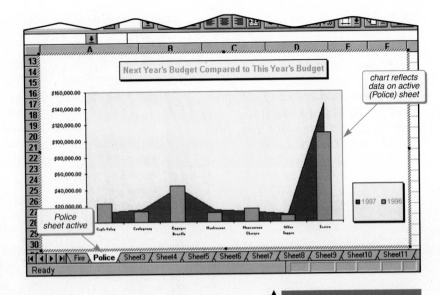

FIGURE 1-42

The next step is to change the chart type from a combination area and column chart to a combination line and column chart.

TO CHANGE THE CHART TYPE ▼

STEP 1 ▶

If the embedded chart on the Police sheet is not active, double-click it.

A heavy gray border surrounds the chart.

STEP 2 ▶

With the mouse within the chart area, click the right mouse button.

Excel displays a shortcut menu.

STEP 3 ▶

Choose the AutoFormat command. When the AutoFormat dialog box displays, select the combination line and column chart (format number 1) in the Formats box.

The AutoFormat dialog box displays with the combination line and column chart selected (Figure 1-43).

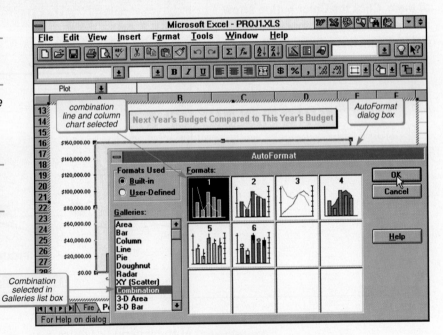

FIGURE 1-43

STEP 4 ▶

Choose the OK button on the AutoFormat dialog box.

The combination area and column chart on the Police sheet is changed to a combination line and column chart (Figure 1-44).

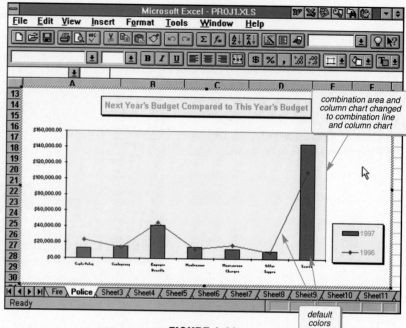

FIGURE 1-44

STEP 5 ▶

Select the columns by clicking one of them. Click the Color button arrow on the Formatting toolbar. Choose red (column 1, row 2) on the Color palette.

The columns in the chart display in red (Figure 1-45).

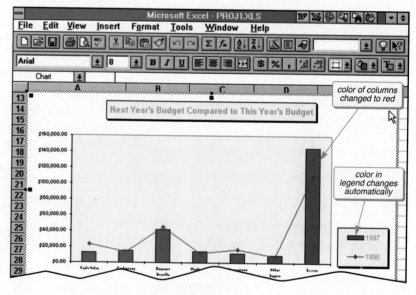

FIGURE 1-45

As indicated in the legend in Figure 1-45, the columns represent the 1997 proposed budget for the Police Department. The line represents the 1996 budget for the Police Department. You can see from the Salaries column in the chart that the Police Department is requesting a significant increase in its salary budget for 1997. The completed Police sheet displays as shown in Figure 1-46.

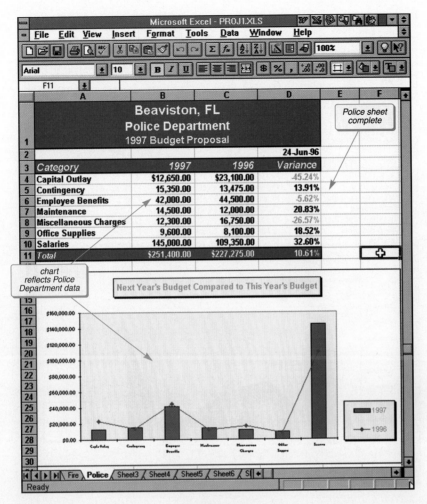

FIGURE 1-46

Modifying the Streets and Sanitation Sheet

As was done on the Police sheet, the data, color, chart range, and chart type must be changed on the Streets and Sanitation sheet. The following steps modify the worksheet portion of the Streets and Sanitation sheet.

TO MODIFY THE WORKSHEET PORTION OF THE STREETS AND SANITATION SHEET

Step 1: Double-click the Sheet3 tab. When the Rename dialog box displays, type `Strs & San` in the Name box. Choose the OK button.

Step 2: Double-click cell A1 and replace (Name) in line 2 with Streets and Sanitation

Step 3: Select the range A1:D1. Hold down the CTRL key and select the nonadjacent ranges A3:D3 and A11:D11. Click the Color button arrow on the Formatting toolbar. Choose green (column 2, row 2) on the Color palette. Click the Font Color button arrow on the Formatting toolbar. Choose white (column 2, row 1) on the Font Color palette.

Step 4: Enter the data in Table 1-4 on the next page in the range B4:B10.

Step 5: Click the Save button on the Standard toolbar.

The Streets and Sanitation sheet displays as shown in Figure 1-47 on the next page.

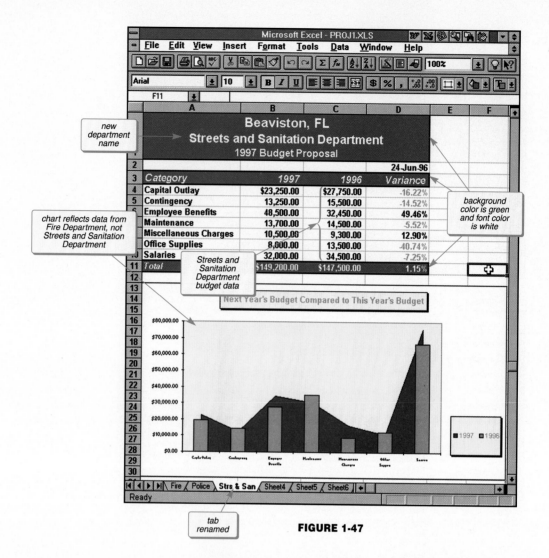

FIGURE 1-47

▸ **TABLE 1-4**

CELL	VALUE	CELL	VALUE
B4	23250	C4	27750
B5	13250	C5	15500
B6	48500	C6	32450
B7	13700	C7	14500
B8	10500	C8	9300
B9	8000	C9	13500
B10	32000	C10	34500

Here again, the new data is not reflected in the chart (Figure 1-47). The chart is identical to the one in Figure 1-38 on page E28 because it was created by copying the Fire sheet. The following steps change the chart range.

TO CHANGE THE CHART RANGE

Step 1: Activate the chart on the Strs & San sheet by clicking it. A heavy gray border surrounds the chart.

Step 2: Click the ChartWizard tool on the Standard toolbar. Excel displays the ChartWizard – Step 1 of 2 dialog box which contains the Range box.

Step 3: Drag over the sheet reference Fire! in the Range box. Press the DELETE key.

The chart range refers to the Streets and Sanitation sheet (Figure 1-48).

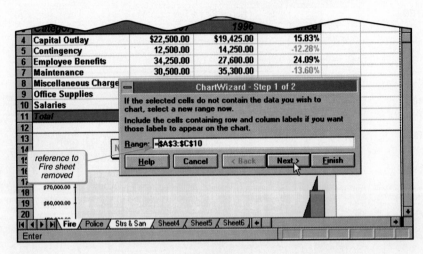

FIGURE 1-48

Step 4: Choose the Finish button in the ChartWizard – Step 1 of 2 dialog box.

The combination area and column chart reflect the data in the range A3:C10 of the Strs and San sheet (Figure 1-49).

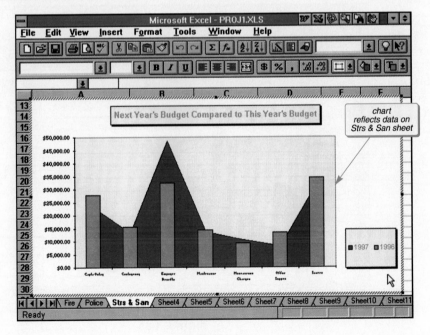

FIGURE 1-49

The next step is to change the Strs & San sheet's chart type from a combination area and column chart to a 3-D column chart.

TO CHANGE THE CHART TYPE ▼

STEP 1 ▶

With the chart area active and the mouse pointer within the chart area, click the right mouse button.

STEP 2 ▶

Choose the AutoFormat command. When the AutoFormat dialog box displays, select 3-D Column in the Galleries box. Select the column chart with gridlines (format number 4) in the Formats box.

The AutoFormat dialog box displays with the three-dimensional column chart selected (Figure 1-50).

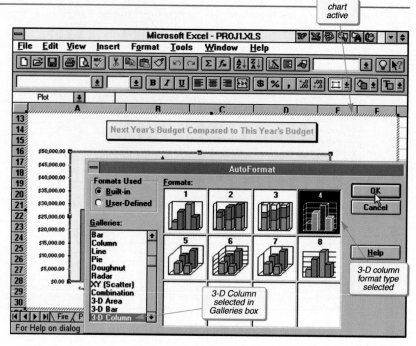

FIGURE 1-50

STEP 3 ▶

Choose the OK button in the AutoFormat dialog box.

The combination area and column chart on the Strs & San sheet is changed to a 3-D column chart (Figure 1-51).

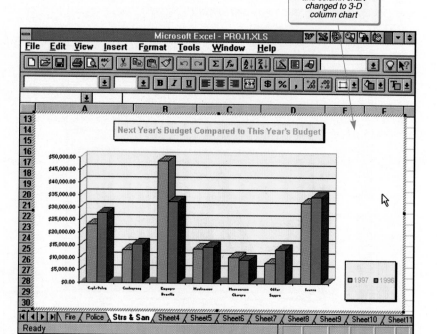

FIGURE 1-51

STEP 4 ▶

Select the blue columns (leftmost) by clicking one of them. Click the Color button arrow on the Formatting toolbar. Choose green (column 2, row 2) on the Color palette.

STEP 5 ▶

Select the purple columns (rightmost) by clicking one of them. Click the Color button arrow on the Formatting toolbar. Choose brown (column 4, row 2) on the Color palette.

The Streets and Sanitation sheet is complete as shown in Figure 1-52.

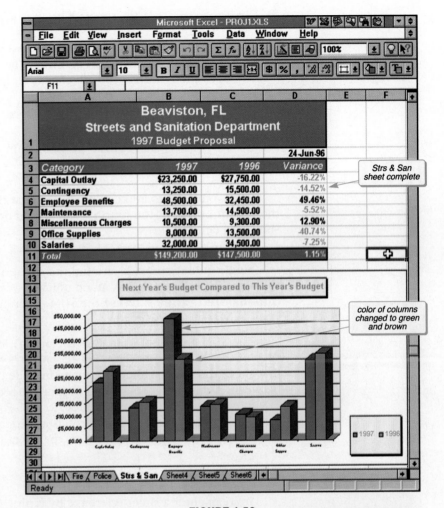

FIGURE 1-52

With the three department sheets complete, the next step is to modify the Public Safety Division sheet (Sheet4). However, before modifying Sheet4, it is important that you understand how to reference cells in other sheets in a workbook, because this sheet contains the totals of the first three sheets.

▶ REFERENCING CELLS IN OTHER SHEETS IN A WORKBOOK

To reference cells in other sheets in a workbook, you use the sheet name, also called the **sheet reference**. For example, you refer to cell B4 on the Fire sheet in the following fashion:

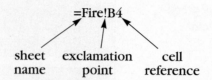

Thus, one way to add cell B4 on the first three sheets in this project and place the sum in cell B4 of the fourth sheet would be to select cell B4 on the fourth sheet and enter:

=Fire!B4+Police!B4+'Strs & San'!B4

Single quotation marks around the sheet name Strs & San are required because the name includes spaces. A much quicker way to find the sum of the **three-dimensional range** is to use the SUM function as follows:

=SUM('Fire:Strs & San'!B4)

The SUM argument ('Fire:Strs & San'!B4) instructs Excel to sum cell B4 on each of the three sheets (Fire, Police, and Strs & San). The colon (:) between the first sheet and the last sheet means to include these sheets and all sheets in between. A range that spans two or more sheets in a workbook, such as Fire!:'Strs & San'!B4, is called a **3-D reference**.

A sheet reference, such as Fire!, is always absolute. Thus, unlike a relative cell reference, when you copy formulas, the sheet reference will remain constant.

Entering a Sheet Reference

You can enter a sheet reference by typing it or by clicking the sheet tab to activate it. When you click the sheet tab, Excel automatically adds the name followed by an exclamation point at the insertion point in the formula bar and activates the sheet. Next, click or drag through the cells you want to reference on the sheet.

If you are spanning sheets, click the first sheet, select the cell or range of cells, and then hold down the SHIFT key and click the last sheet. Excel will include the cell or range on the two sheets and all the sheets between. It will also add the colon between the first sheet and the last sheet referenced.

Modifying the Public Safety Sheet

The following paragraphs include steps that modify the Public Safety sheet so it summarizes the budget amounts for each category for the three departments and appears as shown in Figure 1-53.

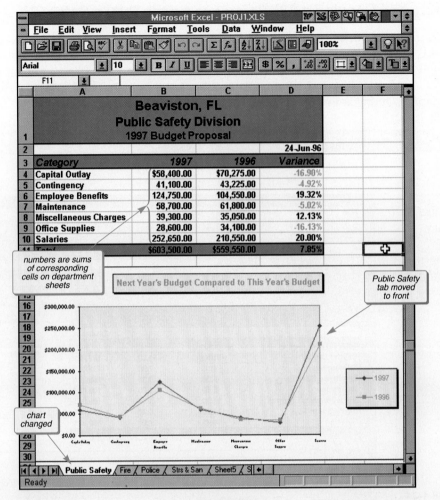

FIGURE 1-53

TO CHANGE THE BACKGROUND COLORS OF THE PUBLIC SAFETY SHEET

Step 1: Double-click the Sheet4 tab. When the Rename dialog box displays, type Public Safety in the Name box. Choose the OK button.

Step 2: Double-click cell A1 and replace (Name) Department in line 2 with Public Safety Division

Step 3: Select the range A1:D1. Hold down the CTRL key and select the nonadjacent ranges A3:D3 and A11:D11. Click the Color button arrow on the Formatting toolbar. Choose brown (column 4, row 2) on the Color palette.

The worksheet title, column titles, and total row display as shown in Figure 1-53.

Entering and Copying a 3-D Reference on the Public Safety Sheet

The next step in changing Sheet4 so it displays as shown in Figure 1-53 is to enter the SUM function in each of the cells in the range B4:C10. The SUM functions will determine the sums of the budget values for the three departments by category. Thus, cell B4 on the Public Safety sheet will be equal to the sum of the 1997 Capital Outlay amounts in cells Fire!B4, Police!B4, and Strs & San!B4.

TO ENTER AND COPY 3-D REFERENCES ON THE PUBLIC SAFETY SHEET ▼

STEP 1 ▶

With the Public Safety sheet active, select cell B4. Click the AutoSum button on the Standard toolbar.

The SUM function displays without a range (Figure 1-54).

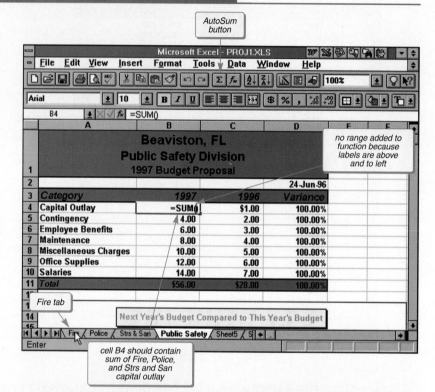

FIGURE 1-54

STEP 2 ▶

Click the Fire tab and select cell B4. Hold down the SHIFT key and click the Strs & San tab.

A marquis surrounds cell Fire!B4 (Figure 1-55). All four sheet tabs are highlighted. The Fire tab displays in bold because it is the active sheet. The SUM function displays in the formula bar.

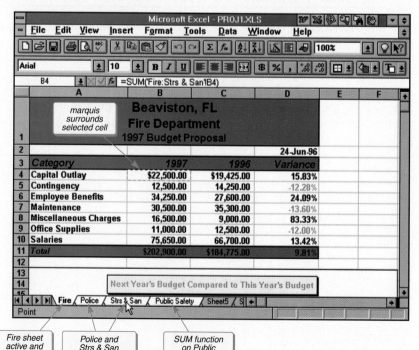

FIGURE 1-55

STEP 3 ▶

Click the enter box in the formula bar or press the ENTER key.

The Public Safety sheet becomes the active sheet. The sum of the cells Fire!B4, Police!B4, and Strs & San!B4 displays in cell B4 of the Public Safety sheet (Figure 1-56). The SUM function assigned to cell B4 displays in the formula bar.

FIGURE 1-56

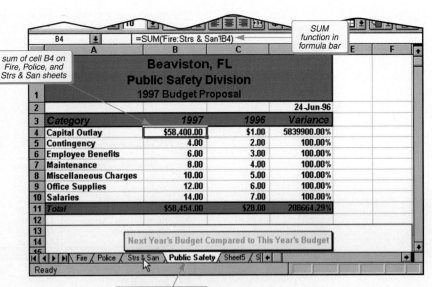

STEP 4 ▶

With cell B4 active, drag the fill handle through cell C4. Release the left mouse button.

Excel copies the formula in cell B4 to cell C4 (Figure 1-57). The cell reference in the SUM function in cell C4 references cell C4 on each of the three sheets.

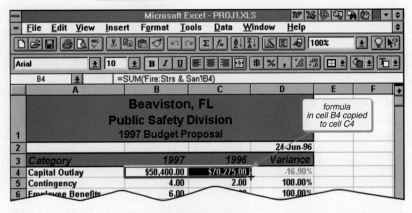

FIGURE 1-57

STEP 5 ▶

Select the range B4:C4 on the Public Safety sheet. Drag the fill handle down through cell C10.

Excel shades the border of the paste area (Figure 1-58).

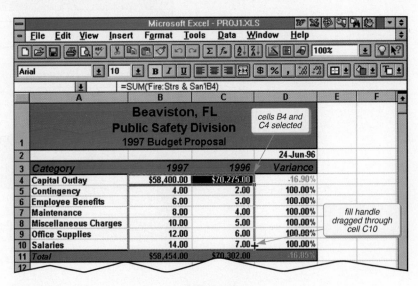

FIGURE 1-58

STEP 6 ▶

Release the left mouse button.

Excel copies the formulas in cells B4 and C4 to the range B5:C10 (Figure 1-59).

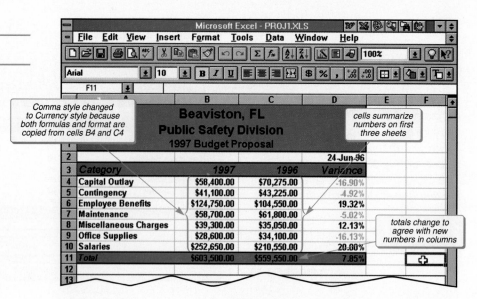

FIGURE 1-59

STEP 7 ▶

Select the range B5:C10 and click the Comma Style button on the Formatting toolbar.

The worksheet portion of the Public Safety sheet is complete (Figure 1-60).

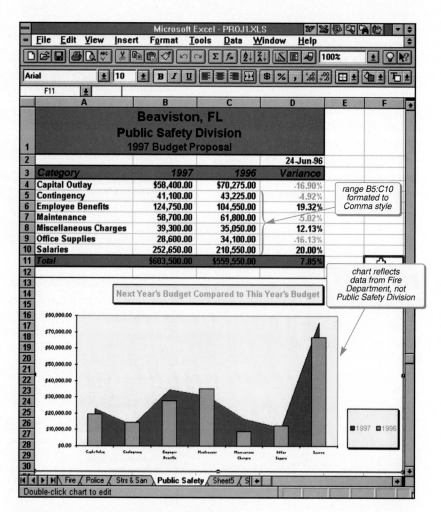

FIGURE 1-60

The reason for reformatting the range B5:C10 is that when you copy a cell, the format is also copied. Thus, the Currency style assigned to cell B4 earlier was copied to cell C4 and then to the range B5:C10.

A close look at Figure 1-60 reveals that the embedded chart is using the range Fire!A3:C10 instead of Public Safety!A3:C10. Hence, the next step is to change the chart range.

TO CHANGE THE CHART RANGE

Step 1: Activate the chart on the Public Safety sheet by double-clicking it.

Step 2: Click the ChartWizard tool on the Standard toolbar. Excel displays the ChartWizard – Step 1 of 2 dialog box which contains the Range box.

Step 3: Drag over the sheet reference Fire! in the Range box. Press the DELETE key. Choose the Finish button in the ChartWizard – Step 1 of 2 dialog box.

The combination area and column chart reflects the data in the range A3:C10 of the Public Safety sheet (Figure 1-61).

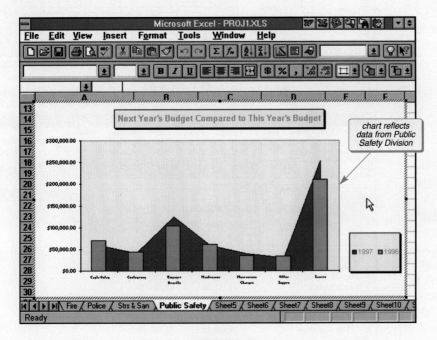

FIGURE 1-61

The next step is to change the chart type from a combination area and column chart to a line chart. A **line chart** is usually used to show a trend, but it also can be used to compare multiple series of numbers on the same chart.

TO CHANGE THE CHART TYPE ▼

STEP 1 ▶

With the chart area active and the mouse pointer within the chart area, click the right mouse button.

STEP 2 ▶

Choose the AutoFormat command. When the AutoFormat dialog box displays, select Line in the Galleries box. Select the line chart with data point markers (format number 1) in the Formats box.

The AutoFormat dialog box displays with the line chart with data point markers chart selected (Figure 1-62).

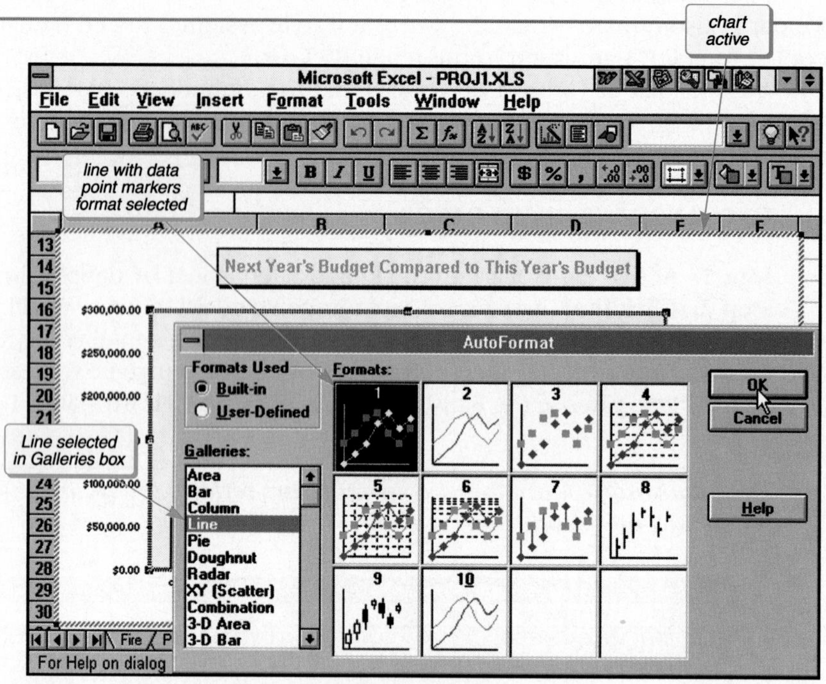

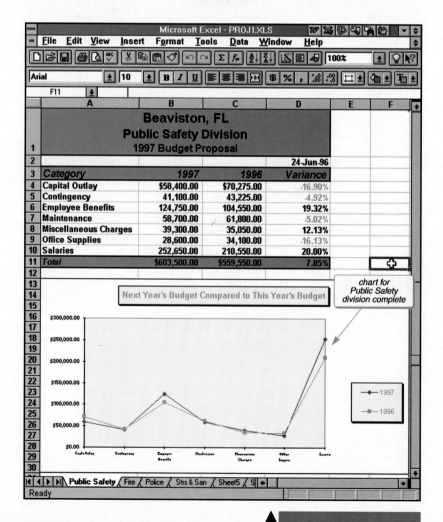

FIGURE 1-62

STEP 3 ▶

Choose the OK button in the AutoFormat dialog box. Select cell F11 (or any other cell) to deactivate the chart area. Drag the Public Safety tab to the left of the Fire tab so it displays first in the workbook.

The combination area and column chart on the Public Safety sheet is changed to a line chart with data point markers (Figure 1-63). The Public Safety sheet is positioned first in the workbook.

STEP 4 ▶

Click the Save button on the Standard toolbar to save the workbook.

FIGURE 1-63

The workbook is complete. The next section introduces you to adding comments to a workbook.

▶ ADDING COMMENTS TO A WORKBOOK

C omments, or **notes,** in a workbook are used to describe the function of a cell, a range of cells, a sheet, or the entire workbook. Comments are used to identify workbooks and clarify entries that would otherwise be difficult to understand.

In Excel, you can assign comments to any cell in the workbook using the **Note command** on the Insert menu. Overall workbook comments should include the following:

1. Worksheet title
2. Author's name
3. Date created
4. Date last modified (use N/A if it has not been modified)
5. A short description of the purpose of the worksheet

The following steps add workbook comments to cell F1 on the Public Safety sheet.

TO ADD A NOTE TO A CELL ▼

STEP 1 ▶

Select cell F1 on the Public Safety sheet. Select the Insert menu.

The Insert menu displays (Figure 1-64).

STEP 2 ▶

Choose the Note command.

Excel displays the Cell Note dialog box. The Cell box identifies the active cell (F1). The Notes in Sheet box lists the cell locations of all notes in the active sheet.

STEP 3 ▶

Enter the note in the Text Note box as shown in Figure 1-65. Press the ENTER key after each line.

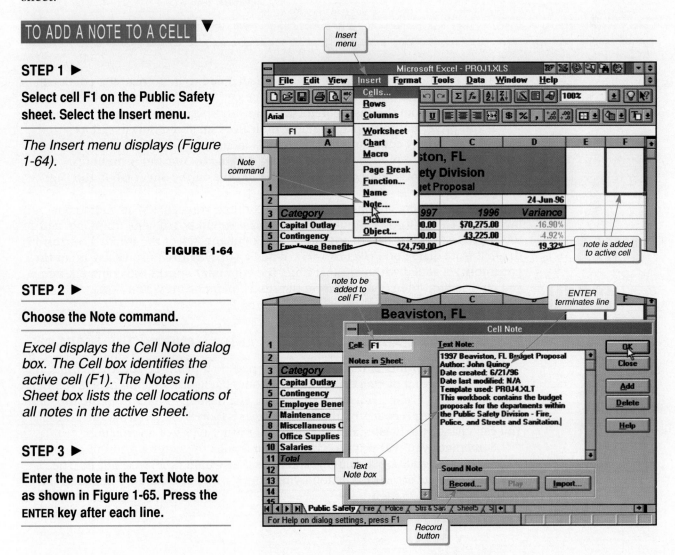

FIGURE 1-64

FIGURE 1-65

STEP 4 ▶

Choose the OK button in the Cell Note dialog box.

*Excel adds a small red dot, called a **note indicator**, in the upper right corner of cell F1 to indicate a note has been added to it (Figure 1-66). If a red dot does not appear in the cell, choose the Options command from the Tools menu. Click the View tab and click Note Indicator.*

STEP 5 ▶

Click the Save button on the Standard toolbar to save the workbook.

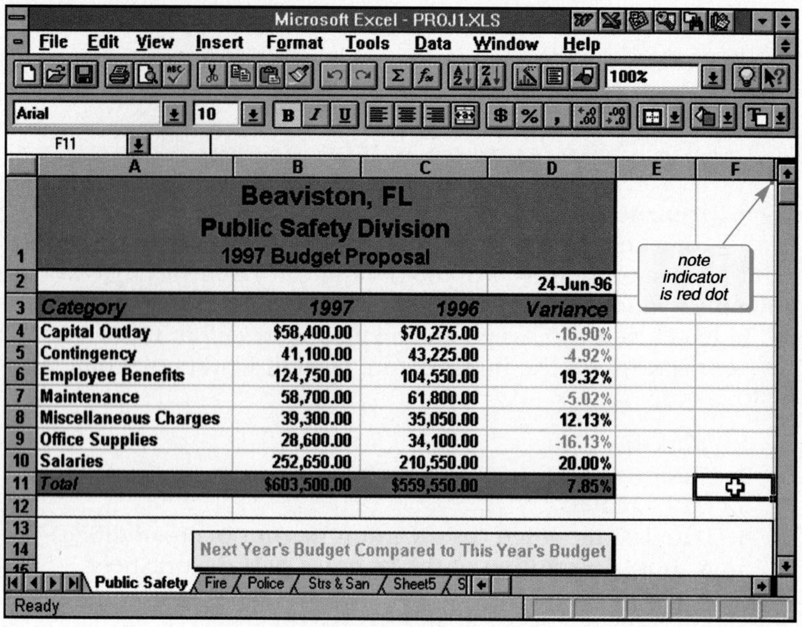

FIGURE 1-66

A red dot indicates that a cell has a note attached to it. To read the comment, or note, any time the sheet is active, select the cell with the note and choose the Note command from the Insert menu or press SHIFT+F2.

If you prefer not to display the note indicator (small red dot) in cell A1, choose the Options command from the Tools menu; and on the View tab, remove the x from the Note Indicator check box by clicking it. You can print notes attached to cells by selecting the **Notes check box** on the Sheet tab in the Page Setup dialog box.

Besides entering comments in the form of text, you can add an audio comment to a cell (up to two minutes) if you have a sound board, a microphone, and the appropriate software. To add the audio comment, select the **Record button** in the Cell Note dialog box (Figure 1-65). When a **sound note** (also called an **audio comment**) is added without a text note, the computer speaks the comment when you choose the Note command from the Insert menu or press SHIFT+F2.

▶ ADDING A HEADER AND FOOTER AND CHANGING THE MARGINS

A **header** prints at the top of a every page in a printout. A **footer** prints at the bottom of every page in a printout (see Figure 1-74 on page E51). By default, Excel prints the tab name as the header, .5 inch from the top, and the page number preceded by the word Page as a footer, .5 inch from the bottom. You can change the header and footer to print other types of information.

Sometimes you will want to change the margins to center a printout on the page or include additional columns and rows that would otherwise not fit. The **margins** in Excel are set to the following: top = 1 inch; bottom = 1 inch, left = .75 inch; and right = .75 inch.

Changing the header and footer, turning gridlines off, and changing the margins are all part of the function called **page setup**. You use the Page Setup command on the shortcut menu or File menu to carry out the page setup function. The following procedure shows you how to step through page setup. Be sure you select all the sheets that contain information before you change the header, footer, or margin, or some of the page setup characteristics will occur only on the selected sheet.

You should also be aware that Excel does not copy page setup characteristics when one sheet is copied to another. Thus, applying page setup characteristics to the template before copying it to the Public Safety Division Budget Proposal workbook would not work.

TO CHANGE THE HEADER AND FOOTER ▼

STEP 1 ▶

With the Public Safety sheet active, hold down the SHIFT key and click the Strs & San tab. Point to the menu bar and click the right mouse button.

Excel displays a shortcut menu (Figure 1-67). The first four tabs at the bottom of the window are highlighted.

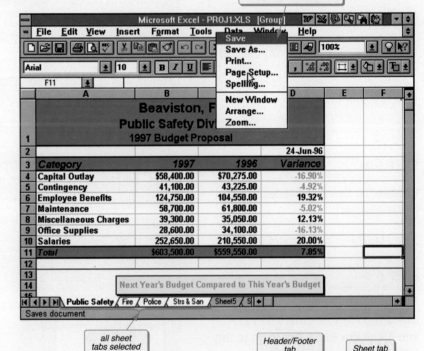

FIGURE 1-67

STEP 2 ▶

Choose the Page Setup command.

The Page Setup dialog box displays.

STEP 3 ▶

If necessary, click the Sheet tab in the Page Setup dialog box. In the Print box, click the Gridlines check box to remove the x. Point to the Header/Footer tab.

The Sheet tab on the Page Setup dialog box displays (Figure 1-68). The Gridlines check box is cleared.

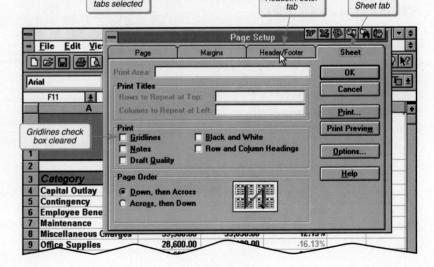

FIGURE 1-68

STEP 4 ▶

Click the Header/Footer tab.

Samples of the current header and footer display (Figure 1-69).

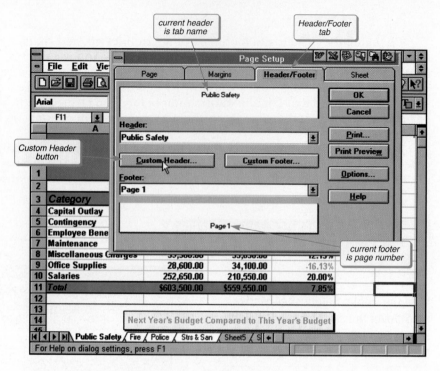

FIGURE 1-69

STEP 5 ▶

Choose the Custom Header button (Custom Header...).

The Header dialog box displays.

STEP 6 ▶

Click the Left Section box. Type John Quincy, Controller **and press the ENTER key to go to the next line. Type** Preliminary Budget Proposal **and click the Center Section box. Click the Sheet Name button (▣) in the Header dialog box. Click the Right Section box. Type** Page **followed by a space and click the Page Number button (▣) in the Header dialog box. Type** of **followed by a space. Click the Total Pages button (▣).**

The Header dialog box displays with the new header as shown in Figure 1-70.

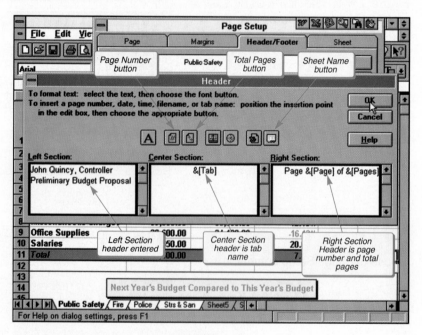

FIGURE 1-70

STEP 7 ▶

Choose the OK button in the Header dialog box. Choose the Custom Footer button (Custom Footer...). Drag across the footer Page &[Page] and press the DELETE key to remove it. Choose the OK button in the Footer dialog box.

The Header/Footer tab in the Page Setup dialog box displays as shown in Figure 1-71.

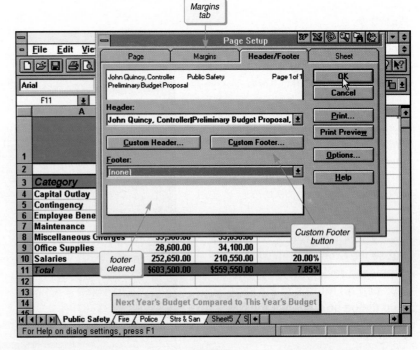

FIGURE 1-71

STEP 8 ▶

Click the Margins tab in the Page Setup dialog box. Click the top box and change the top margin to 1.5. Click the Header box and change the distance from the top of the page to .75.

The Margins tab in the Page dialog box displays as shown in Figure 1-72.

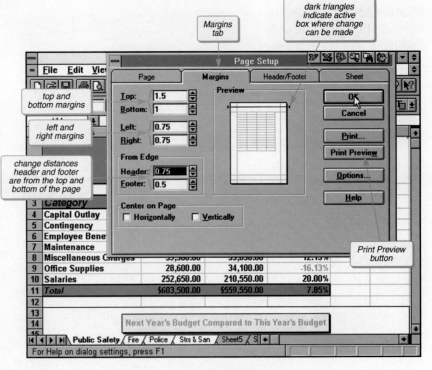

FIGURE 1-72

STEP 9 ▶

Choose the Print Preview button in the Page Setup dialog box to preview the workbook.

The Public Safety sheet displays as shown in Figure 1-73. Although difficult to read, the header displays at the top of the page. You can choose the Zoom button to get a better view of the page.

STEP 10 ▶

Choose the Close button when you are finished reviewing the preview. When control returns to the Page Setup dialog box, choose the OK button.

STEP 11 ▶

Click the Save button on the Standard toolbar to save the workbook with the new print settings.

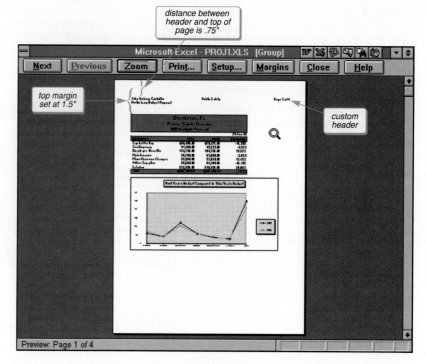

FIGURE 1-73

Notice when you click one of the buttons in the Header dialog box (Figure 1-70), Excel enters a code into the active section. A **code** such as &[Page] means insert the page number. Table 1-5 summarizes the buttons, their codes, and functions in the Header or Footer dialog box.

▶ **TABLE 1-5**

BUTTON	NAME	CODE	FUNCTION
A	Font		Displays the Font dialog box
	Page Number	&[Page]	Inserts a page number
	Total Pages	&[Pages]	Insert the total number of pages
	Date	&[Date]	Inserts the system date
	Time	&[Time]	Inserts the system time
	Filename	&[File]	Inserts the filename of the workbook
	Sheet Name	&[Tab]	Inserts the tab name

Printing the Workbook

The following steps print the workbook.

TO PRINT THE WORKBOOK

Step 1: Ready the printer.
Step 2: If the four sheets in the workbook are not selected, click the Public Safety tab and then hold down the SHIFT key and click the Strs & San tab.
Step 3: Click the Print button on the Standard toolbar.

The workbook prints as shown in Figure 1-74.

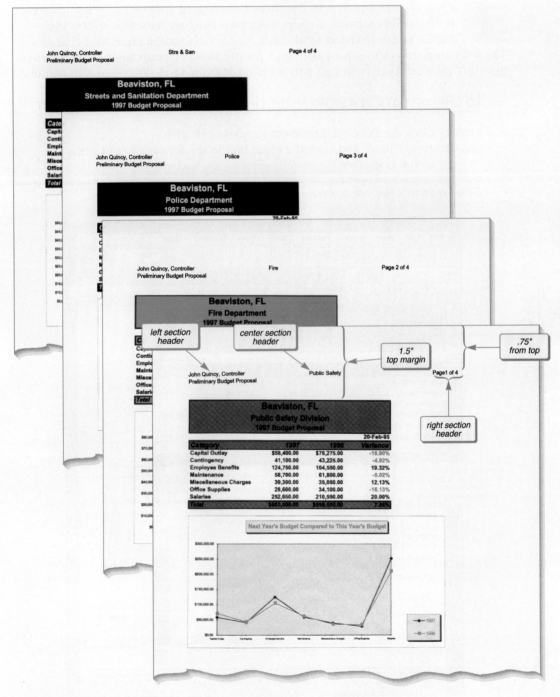

FIGURE 1-74

An alternative to using the SHIFT key and mouse to select the sheets in Step 2 is to point to one of the tabs and click the right mouse button. The **sheet tab shortcut menu** displays. Choose the **Select All Sheets command**. Other commands available on this shortcut menu include Insert, Delete, Rename, and Move or Copy. All these commands relate to manipulating sheets in a workbook. For example, you can use this menu to insert a new sheet, delete the active sheet, rename the active sheet, or move or copy the active sheet.

► CHANGING DATA IN THE WORKBOOK

If you change any data in the three department sheets, Excel immediately redraws the embedded chart. Because changing data also affects the Public Safety Division worksheet, its corresponding chart also changes. The following steps show how the chart for the Police Department changes when the 1997 proposed salary in cell B10 is changed from $145,000.00 to $90,000.00.

TO CHANGE DATA IN A WORKSHEET THAT AFFECTS THE EMBEDDED CHART

Step 1: Click the Police tab to select it. Select cell B10.
Step 2: Type 90000 and click the enter box in the formula bar or press the ENTER key.

Excel redraws the embedded chart (Figure 1-75).

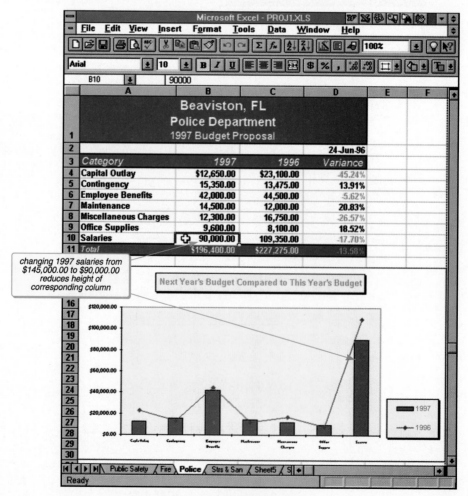

FIGURE 1-75

Compare the chart in Figure 1-75 to Figure 1-46 on page E33. You can see that the Salaries column is much shorter after changing the 1997 proposed salary from $145,000.00 to $90,000.00.

Changing Data in a Worksheet by Resizing a Column in the Chart

You can resize a column in the embedded chart, and Excel will change the corresponding data in the cell as shown in the following steps.

TO CHANGE DATA IN A WORKSHEET BY RESIZING A COLUMN IN A CHART ▼

STEP 1 ▶

Hold down the SHIFT key and click the Police tab, and then double-click within the embedded chart.

STEP 2 ▶

Select the Employee Benefits column. Point to the top center handle.

The column is surrounded by black handles which indicate the column can be resized (Figure 1-76).

FIGURE 1-76

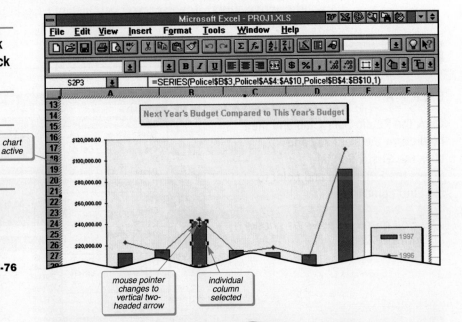

STEP 3 ▶

Drag the handle down to approximately $14,400. Notice the moving marker on the value axis as you drag down. Release the left mouse button. Select cell F11.

The Employee Benefits column in the embedded chart is shorter than it was before, and the value in the corresponding cell (B6) changes from $42,000.00 (Figure 1-75) to $14,400.00 (Figure 1-77).

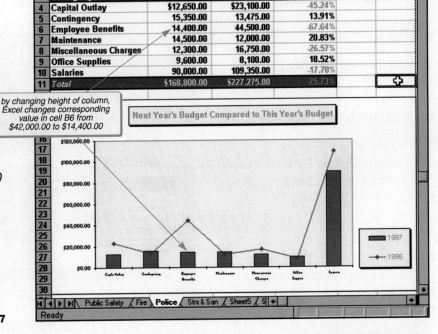

FIGURE 1-77

► FINDING AND REPLACING TEXT OR NUMBERS

T o find cells that contain specific characters, choose the **Find command** on the Edit menu. To find and replace characters in cells, choose the **Replace command** on the Edit menu.

Finding Text or Numbers

The following steps show you how to find the text *Misc* in *Miscellaneous Charges* (cell A8) in the workbook. If you select a range before invoking the Find command, Excel searches the range on the active sheet. If you select a cell, Excel searches all selected sheets. Excel searches row by row, beginning with row 1 of the active sheet. However, you can instruct Excel to search column by column selecting a check box in the Find dialog box.

TO FIND TEXT OR NUMBERS ▼

STEP 1 ►

Click the Public Safety tab and then hold down the SHIFT key and click the Strs & San tab. Select the Edit menu and point to the Find command.

The Edit menu displays as shown in Figure 1-78.

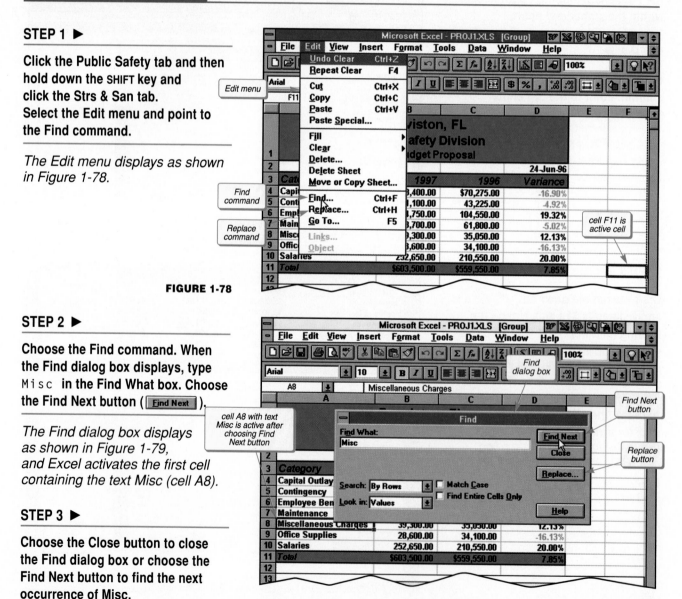

FIGURE 1-78

STEP 2 ►

Choose the Find command. When the Find dialog box displays, type `Misc` in the Find What box. Choose the Find Next button (Find Next).

The Find dialog box displays as shown in Figure 1-79, and Excel activates the first cell containing the text Misc (cell A8).

STEP 3 ►

Choose the Close button to close the Find dialog box or choose the Find Next button to find the next occurrence of Misc.

FIGURE 1-79

Using **wildcard characters** (*, or ?), you can find variations of the sequence of characters you type into the Find What box. The asterisk (*) represents any number of characters in that same position. The question mark (?) represents any character in that same position. For example, if you type *ies in the Find What dialog box, Excel will stop on any cell containing text that ends with ies. If you type S?1 in the Find What box, Excel will stop on any cell containing text that includes a sequence of characters with the letter S, followed by any character, followed by letter l. Table 1-6 summarizes the options found in the Find dialog box.

If you hold down the SHIFT key when you choose the Find Next button, Excel finds the previous occurrence.

▶ **TABLE 1-6**

OPTION	FUNCTION
Find Next button	Finds next occurrence
Close button	Closes Find dialog box
Replace button	Displays the Replace dialog box where occurrence can be replaced
Search box	Instructs Excel to search across rows or down columns
Look in box notes	Instructs Excel to search in cell formulas, cell values, or cell notes
Match Case check box	Instructs Excel to be case sensitive
Find Entire Cells Only check box	Instructs Excel to find only exact and complete matches

Replacing Text or Numbers

The following steps show you how to replace the first occurrence in the workbook of the word Salaries with Salary.

TO REPLACE TEXT OR NUMBERS ▼

STEP 1 ▶

Click the Public Safety tab and then hold down the SHIFT key and click the Strs & San tab. Select the Edit menu and point to the Replace command.

The Edit menu displays as shown earlier in Figure 1-78.

STEP 2 ▶

Choose the Replace command. When the Replace dialog box displays, type Salaries in the Find What box and type Salary in the Replace with box. Choose the Find Next button.

The Replace dialog box displays and Excel finds the first cell containing the word Salaries (cell A10) on the Public Safety sheet (Figure 1-80).

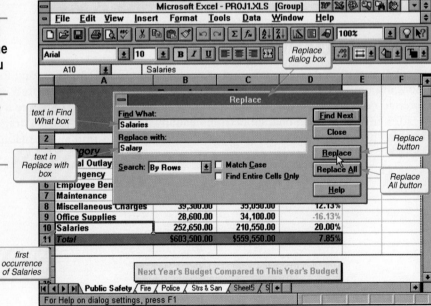

FIGURE 1-80

STEP 3 ▶

Choose the Replace button
(Replace).

Excel replaces the word Salaries with the word Salary in cell A10 (Figure 1-81) and finds the next occurrence of Salaries.

STEP 4 ▶

Choose the Close button to close the Replace dialog box without making the replacement and then click the Public Safety tab.

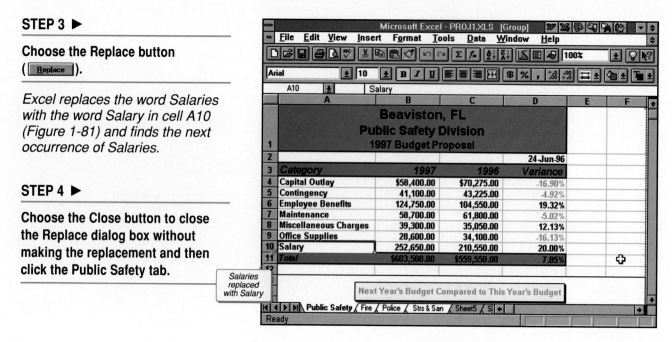

FIGURE 1-81

The **Replace All button** (Replace All) in the Replace dialog box (Figure 1-80) causes Excel to replace all occurrences of the text in the selected sheets. The remaining options in the Replace dialog box are the same as in the Find dialog box described in Table 1-6.

▶ PROJECT SUMMARY

Project 1 introduced you to creating and using a template, customizing formats, changing chart types, and enhancing embedded charts. Using the steps and techniques presented in the project, you learned how to reference cells in other sheets and add comments to a cell. To enhance a printout, you learned how to add a header and footer and change margins. Finally, you learned how to drag a column in a chart to change the corresponding number in the worksheet and how to find and replace text and numbers.

▶ KEY TERMS AND INDEX

Q U I C K   R E F E R E N C E

In Microsoft Excel, you can accomplish a task in a number of ways. The following table provides a quick reference to each task presented in this project with its available options. The commands listed in the Menu column can be executed using either the keyboard or mouse. Many of the commands in the Menu column are also available on the shortcut menu.

Task	Mouse	Menu	Keyboard Shortcuts
Add a Note		From Insert menu, choose Note	Press SHIFT+F2
Apply Custom Formats		From Format menu, choose Cells; click Number tab, then enter format code in Code box	
Change a Header/Footer		From File menu, choose Page Setup	
Change Margins		From File menu, choose Page Setup	
Copy a Sheet to Another Sheet	Click Select All button; click Copy button on Standard toolbar; click Sheet tab; click Paste button on Standard toolbar		Press CTRL+A to select sheet; press CTRL+C; click sheet tab; press CTRL+V

QUICK REFERENCE (continued)

Task	Mouse	Menu	Keyboard Shortcuts
Display a Note		From Insert menu, choose Note	Press SHIFT+F2
Find Text		From Edit menu, choose Find	Press CTRL+F
Move to the Next or Previous Tab in a Workbook or Dialog Box			Press CTRL+PAGE DOWN (next sheet); press CTRL+PAGE UP (previous sheet)
Print a Note		From File menu, choose Page Setup	
Replace Text		From Edit menu, choose Replace	Press CTRL+H
Save a Template		From File menu, choose Save As; select Template in Save File As Type box	
Select a Grouping of Sheets	Click first sheet tab, hold down SHIFT key, then click last sheet tab	From sheet tab shortcut menu, choose Select All Sheets	
Select Nonadjacent Sheets	Click first sheet tab, hold down CTRL key, then click other sheet tabs		

S T U D E N T   A S S I G N M E N T S

STUDENT ASSIGNMENTS
STUDENT ASSIGNMENT 1 True/False

Instructions: Circle T if the statement is true or F if the statement is false.

T F 1. In Excel, formulas can reference cells found on different sheets of a workbook.

T F 2. Templates are not used to create new workbooks that are similar.

T F 3. Summarizing information that appears on multiple sheets of a workbook is referred to as consolidation.

T F 4. A template is saved with the same extension as a workbook.

T F 5. The purpose of dummy numbers is to fill in cells in a template.

T F 6. A fixed dollar sign will appear in the same position in a cell no matter how many digits there are in the number that follows it.

T F 7. Combination area and column charts show one set of numbers from a worksheet in two different formats on one chart.

T F 8. The value axis series is the horizontal line to the left of the plot area of a chart.

T F 9. A template may be copied to the clipboard and pasted to one or more sheets in a workbook.

T F 10. When a template is used to create a worksheet and embedded chart, the worksheet can be modified but the embedded chart cannot be modified.

T F 11. A three-dimensional range is indicated in Excel functions by sheet references that reference cells in other sheets of a workbook.

T F 12. Line charts are not used to show trends and are the same as area charts.

T F 13. A note indicator appears in the upper right corner of a cell to indicate a note has been attached to that particular cell.

T   F   14. If you have the appropriate hardware, an audio comment can be added to a cell.

T   F   15. Workbook headers and footers appear only on the first page of a printout.

T   F   16. Workbook margins including top, bottom, left, and right cannot be changed.

T   F   17. The codes used in headers and footers will insert page numbers, system date, system time, the filename of the workbook, or the tab name.

T   F   18. To display the shortcut menu with commands for manipulating sheets in a workbook, point to the title bar and click the right mouse button.

T   F   19. You can resize a column in a chart to change data in its associated worksheet.

T   F   20. A custom format code cannot be created in Excel.

STUDENT ASSIGNMENT 2
Multiple Choice

Instructions: Circle the correct response.

1. The Wrap Text check box is found on the _____ tab of the Format Cells dialog box.
   a. Number
   b. Alignment
   c. Fonts
   d. Protection

2. To enter numeric data as text, the number must begin with _____.
   a. a letter
   b. a quotation mark
   c. an apostrophe
   d. an exclamation point

3. Templates are saved with an extension of _____.
   a. .xlw
   b. .xls
   c. .tpt
   d. .xlt

4. Format codes are used to define formats for _____.
   a. numbers
   b. dates
   c. text
   d. all of the above

5. _____ around the chart indicates if a chart is active.
   a. A heavy gray border
   b. A turquoise border
   c. A thin border with handles
   d. A heavy border with handles

6. _____ around the chart indicates the chart is selected.
   a. A heavy gray border
   b. A turquoise border
   c. A thin border with handles
   d. A heavy border with handles

7. Comments are added to a workbook through the use of the _____ command on the Insert menu.
   a. Name
   b. Note
   c. Function
   d. Object

(continued)

STUDENT ASSIGNMENT 1 (continued)

8. Excel automatically places a _____ at the bottom of each page in a printout.
   a. tab name
   b. filename
   c. page number
   d. date

9. The Excel function called page setup allows you to _____.
   a. copy pages of a workbook
   b. check the spelling of a workbook
   c. change the margins of a workbook
   d. select all the sheets of a workbook

10. Templates, called _____ are stored in the XLSTART subdirectory.
   a. autotemplates
   b. startup templates
   c. new templates
   d. format templates

STUDENT ASSIGNMENT 3
Understanding Dialog Boxes and Tabs

Instructions: Identify the command and tab that cause the dialog box and tab to display and allow you to make the indicated changes. Enter N/A in the Tab column if it does not apply.

CHANGE/TASK	COMMAND	TAB
1. Assign a note to a cell	_____	_____
2. Change the margins	_____	_____
3. Change the header	_____	_____
4. Remove gridlines	_____	_____
5. Change to a new chart type	_____	_____
6. Select all sheets	_____	_____
7. Rename a sheet	_____	_____
8. Insert a sheet	_____	_____
9. Find text	_____	_____
10. Replace text	_____	_____

STUDENT ASSIGNMENT 4
Understanding 3-D References

Instructions: The workbook in Figure SA1-4 is made up of five sheets labeled Dept1, Dept2, Dept3, Dept4, and Division. On the next page write the formula or function that accomplishes each of the specified tasks. Assume cell F2 is active on the Division sheet. Each of the five tasks is independent of the others.

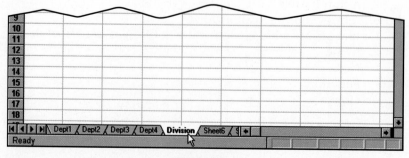

FIGURE SA1-4

1. Assign Division!F2 the sum of cell B10 on each of the department's sheets.

   Function: _____

2. Assign to cell Division!F2 the product of cell A1 on the Dept1 sheet and cell D5 on the Dept3 sheet.

   Formula: _____

3. Assign to cell Division!F2 cell H1 on the Division sheet times the quantity of cell R3 on the Dept2 sheet minus cell A6 on the Dept1 sheet.

   Formula: _____

4. Assign to cell Division!F2 the expression (D ^ 3 - 4 * F * H) / (4 - H) where the value of D is cell A8 on the Dept1 sheet, F is cell D3 on the Dept2 sheet, and H is cell B2 on the Dept3 sheet.

   Formula: _____

5. Assign to cell Division!F2 the value of cell B6 on the Dept3 sheet.

   Formula: _____

STUDENT ASSIGNMENT 5
Working with Customized Formats

Instructions:

Using Table 1-1 on page E16, determine the results that will display in the RESULTS IN and COLOR columns of Table SA1-5. Assume the column width of the cell that will display the value can hold 10 characters (including special characters). If the column width is not big enough, enter a series of 10 asterisks in the RESULTS IN column. Use the letter b to indicate positions containing blank characters.

You may want to enter the numbers in cells (column width = 10.00) in a blank sheet and apply the formats to determine the answers. As examples, the first two problems in the table are complete. If the number displays in a color other than black, indicate the color in the color column, otherwise enter N/A.

PROBLEM	CELL CONTENTS	FORMAT APPLIED	RESULTS IN	COLOR
1	25	###.00	bbbbb25.00	N/A
2	-297.34	##0.00;[Red]-##0.00	bbb-297.34	Red
3	14.816	###.##	[ ]	[ ]
4	-3841.92	#,##0.00;[Green]#,##0.00	[ ]	[ ]
5	5281.42	$ #,##0.00	[ ]	[ ]
6	214.76	$##,##0.00	[ ]	[ ]
7	32	#,##0.00;[Red](#,##0.00)	[ ]	[ ]
8	7	+##0.00	[ ]	[ ]
9	0	#,###	[ ]	[ ]
10	.14363	##.####	[ ]	[ ]
11	99567.768	$##,##0.00	[ ]	[ ]
12	.129	##0.00%	[ ]	[ ]
13	.8	$#,##0.00	[ ]	[ ]
14	412999351	$#,###,###	[ ]	[ ]
15	7	+#,##0.00	[ ]	[ ]

STUDENT ASSIGNMENT 6
Understanding the Header and Footer Buttons

Instructions: Using the Header dialog box in Figure SA1-6, match the numbered bubbles to the codes labeled with letters.

LETTER	NUMBER
A	_____
B	_____
C	_____
D	_____
E	_____
F	_____

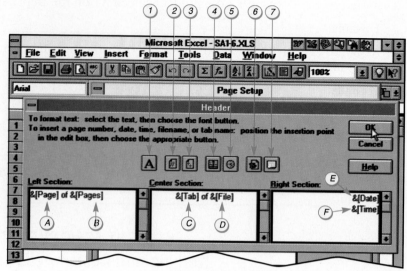

FIGURE SA1-6

COMPUTER LABORATORY EXERCISES

COMPUTER LABORATORY EXERCISE 1
Using the Help Menu to Understand 3-D References

Instructions: Start Excel and perform the following tasks using a computer.

1. Choose the Search for help on command from the Help menu. Type format in the top box of the Search dialog box. Choose the Show Topics button. With Number Format Codes selected in the lower box in the Search dialog box, choose the Go To button. When the information displays, read it, and then choose the Print Topic command from the File menu in the Help window. Double-click the Control-menu box in the Help window.

2. Choose the Search for help on command from the Help menu. Type template in the top box of the Search dialog box. Choose the Show Topics button. One at a time, select each topic in the lower box and choose the Go To button. Read and print each topic. When you are finished with the last one, double-click the Control-menu box in the Help window.

3. Choose the Search for help on command from the Help menu. Type cell reference in the top box of the Search dialog box. Select cell reference to other sheets in the upper list box. Choose the Show Topics button. Choose the Go To button. When the information displays, choose the Print button in the How To window. Close the Help menu.

COMPUTER LABORATORY EXERCISE 2
Enhancing a Chart

Instructions: Follow the steps below to modify the chart in the workbook CLE1-2.XLS so it displays as shown in Figure CLE1-2.

1. Open the workbook CLE1-2 from the subdirectory Excel5 on the Student Diskette.
2. Activate the chart by double-clicking it. Use the AutoFormat command on the shortcut menu to change the column chart to the 3-D area chart (Galleries box = 3-D Area and Formats box = 6). Change the color of the area chart to dark red (column 1, row 2) on the Color palette. Adjust the size and perspective of the chart by selecting it and dragging the handles.
3. Activate the Drawing toolbar to use the Drop Shadow and Arrow buttons. Format the chart title. Add and format the text box and arrow as shown in Figure CLE1-2.
4. Save the workbook using the filename CLE1-2A.
5. Add a header that includes your name and course number on two lines in the Left Section box, the computer laboratory exercise number (CLE1-2) in the Center Section box, and the system date and your instructor name on two lines in the Right Section box. Remove the footer.
6. Print the workbook without cell gridlines.
7. Save the workbook with the printsettings by clicking the Save button on the Standard toolbar.

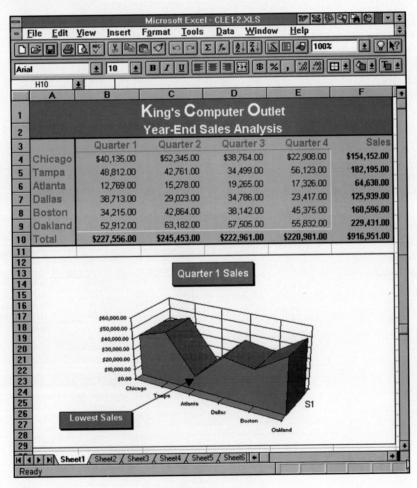

FIGURE CLE1-2

COMPUTER LABORATORY EXERCISE 3
Consolidating Data in a Workbook

Instructions: Perform the following steps to consolidate the four weekly payroll sheets into the monthly payroll sheet chart in the workbook CLE1-3.XLS. The Month Totals sheet should display as shown in the lower screen in Figure CLE1-3.

1. Open the workbook CLE1-3 from the subdirectory EXCEL5 on the Student Diskette.
2. One at a time, click the first four tabs and review the weekly totals. Click on the Month Totals tab to activate it.
3. Use the SUM function and 3-D references to sum the hours worked and gross pay for each employee to determine the monthly totals. See pages E40 through E42.
4. Save the workbook using the filename CLE1-3A.
5. Add a header that includes your name and course number on two lines in the Left Section box, the computer laboratory exercise number (CLE1-3) in the Center Section box, and the system date and your instructor name on two lines in the Right Section.
6. Print the workbook without cell gridlines.
7. Save the workbook with the print settings by clicking the Save button on the Standard toolbar.

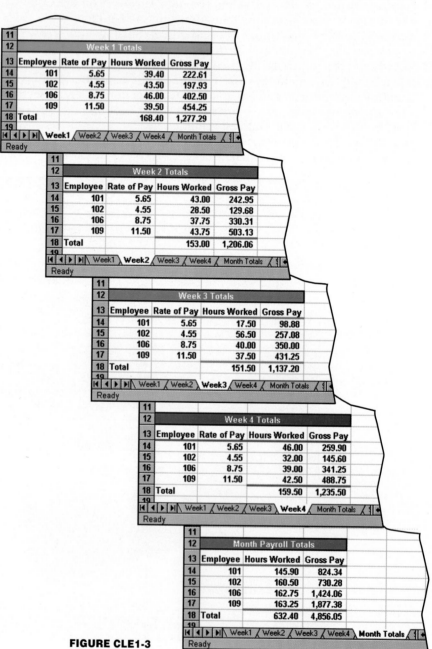

FIGURE CLE1-3

COMPUTER LABORATORY ASSIGNMENT 1
Creating a Company Template

Purpose: To become familiar with creating, saving, and opening a template that changes Excel's defaults.

Problem: You are a summer intern in the Information Systems department at Southeast Airlines. Your specialty is designing worksheets. The company uses a product that allows people to share information across a computer network. Your supervisor has instructed you to create a company-specific template for employees to open when they use Excel (Figure CLA1-1a).

Instructions: The template should include the following:

1. Apply the comma format to all cells. Change the font of all cells to 12 point CG Times. Increase all column widths to 12. (**Hint**: Click the Select All button to make these changes).

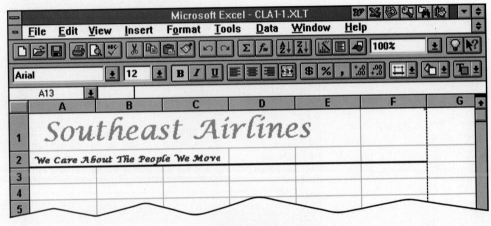

FIGURE CLA1-1a

2. Add a note to cell F1 identifying the template and its purpose (see page E45 for the type of information to include in the note). Include your name as the author.
3. Enter the titles in cells A1 and A2 as shown in Figure CLA1-1a. Change the font in cells A1 and A2 to Lucida Calligraphy (or something similar). In cell A1, change the font size and color to 26 point red. In cell A2, change the font size and color to 8 point blue. Draw a heavy bottom border across the range A2:F2.
4. Enter your name, course, computer laboratory assignment (CLA1-1), date, and instructor name in the range A8:A12.
5. Save the template using the filename CLA1-1. Remember, you must select Template in the Save File as Type box in the Save As dialog box when you save the template.
6. Print the template and note. To print the note, click the Note check box in the Sheet tab in the Page Setup dialog box. Your printout of page 2 should resemble Figure CLA1-1b. After the note prints, click the Note check box to toggle off printing the note.
7. Close the template. Open the template. Save the template as a regular workbook using the filename CLA1-1.

Note: Template for Southeast Airlines
Author: John Quincy
Date created: 6/24/96
Date last modified: N/A
This template changes the Excel defaults to those recommended by Southeast Airlines. To use this template, open it and then save it using a new filename.

FIGURE CLA1-1b

COMPUTER LABORATORY ASSIGNMENT 2
Using a Template to Create a Multiple-Sheet Sales Analysis Workbook

Purpose: To become familiar with using a template to create a multiple-sheet workbook.

Problem: Unified Audio Center has outlets in Maui, Sanibel, and Bali. Each outlet sells products by telephone, by mail, by fax or to walk-in customers. The Information Systems department generates a year-end sales analysis workbook from a template. The workbook contains four sheets, one for each of the three outlets and one for the company. The Company Totals sheet displays as shown in Figure CLA1-2.

The template is stored in the subdirectory Excel5 on the Student Diskette. You have been assigned the task of creating the year-end sales analysis workbook from the template.

Instructions: Perform the following tasks:

1. Open the template CLA1-2.XLT from the subdirectory Excel5 on the Student Diskette. Click the Select All button and copy the template to the Clipboard. One at a time, paste the contents of the Clipboard to Sheet2, Sheet3, and Sheet4. Save the workbook using the filename CLA1-2.XLS.

2. Enter the data in Table CLA1-2 onto the three outlet sheets. Before entering the data on each sheet, rename the sheet tabs (Maui, Sanibel, Bali, and Company Totals). Change the title in cell A1 on each sheet. Change the chart range for the second and third sheets so it refers to the data on the same sheet the chart is on. Change the chart type and colors on these two sheets. Click the Save button on the Standard toolbar to save the workbook.

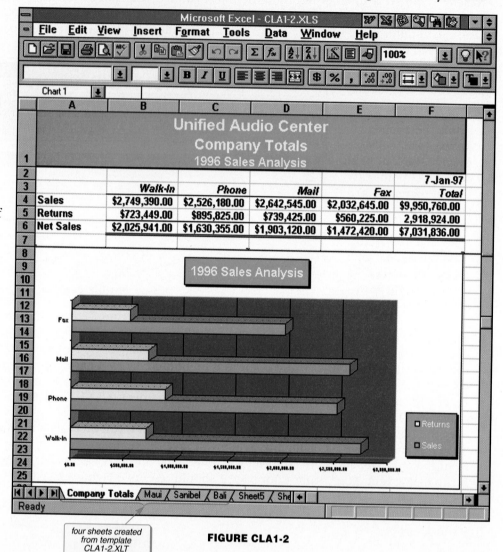

four sheets created from template CLA1-2.XLT

FIGURE CLA1-2

		MAUI	SANIBEL	BALI
Walk-In	Sales	$957,890	$879,150	$912,350
	Returns	325,450	123,675	274,324
Phone	Sales	792,800	754,730	978,650
	Returns	425,900	123,150	346,775
Mail	Sales	954,235	753,210	935,100
	Returns	123,000	211,675	404,750
Fax	Sales	786,400	592,345	653,900
	Returns	132,650	235,125	192,450

3. On the Company Totals sheet, use the SUM function, 3-D references, and the fill handle to total the corresponding cells on the three outlet sheets. Change the chart range and colors. The Company Totals sheet should resemble the one in Figure CLA1- 2. Save the workbook by clicking the Save button on the Standard toolbar.

4. Select all four sheets. Change the header to include your name, course, computer laboratory exercise (CLA1-2.XLT), date, and instructor name. Change the footer to include the page number and total pages. Print the workbook without gridlines.

5. Save the workbook with the print settings.

COMPUTER LABORATORY ASSIGNMENT 3
Creating a Template and Consolidated Profit Forecast Sheet

Purpose: To become familiar with creating, saving, and opening a template and creating a multiple-sheet workbook.

Problem: The consulting firm you work for has assigned you to be the lead spreadsheet specialist on its account with Jewels and Denim Ltd. to create a Profit Forecast workbook. Jewels and Denim Ltd. has outlets in two major cities, Chicago and New York. The workbook is to include a worksheet and pie chart for each outlet and a summary worksheet with a pie chart for the company.

Instructions: Perform the following tasks:

1. Create the template in Figure CLA1-3. The column widths are as follows: A = 19.00; B through E = 12.00; and F = 13.00. Bold all cells. Change the font in the template title to Old Bookman (or something similar). The font in the first line of the title is 26 point. The font in the second line is 16 point. Draw a bottom border and italicize the column titles. Italicize the label Profit in cell A6 and draw a single top border and a double bottom border on row 6.

2. Enter the dummy data shown in Figure CLA1-3 into the Assumptions table in the range A8:E12. Format the text in the Assumptions section as shown in Figure CLA1-3. Enter all percents with a trailing percent sign (%). Format cell B9 to a Currency style with a floating dollar sign and two decimal places. Format the range B10:E12 to a Percentage style with two decimal places. Add the colors shown in Figure CLA1-3.

3. All the values that display in rows 4 through 6 are based on the assumptions in rows 8 through 12. A surcharge is added to the expenses whenever the Qtr Growth Rate is negative. Use the following formulas:
   a. Sales in cell B4: =B9
   b. Sales in cell C4: =B4 * (1 + C10)
   c. Copy cell C4 to the range D4:E4
   d. Expenses in cell B5: =IF(B10 < 0, B4 * (B11 + B12), B4 * B11)
   e. Profit in cell B6: =B4 - B5
   f. Copy the range B5:B6 to the range C5:E6
   g. Use the SUM function to determine totals in column F.

4. Create the 3-D pie chart that shows the contribution of each quarter to the total profit as shown in Figure CLA1-3. Use the chart ranges B3:E3 and B6:E6.

5. Save the template using the filename CLA1-3.XLT. Make sure the Save as File Type box is set to Template. Close the template.

6. Open the template. Copy the template to Sheet2., and Sheet3. Save the workbook using the filename CLA1-3.

(continued)

COMPUTER LABORATORY ASSIGNMENT 3 (continued)

7. Rename the tabs appropriately. Change the assumptions for Chicago to the following: Qtr1 Sales Amount = $598,000; Qtr2 Growth Rate = 3%; Qtr3 Growth Rate = -2.5%; Qtr4 Growth Rate = 1.5%; Qtr Expense Rate = 52%, 54.5%, 48.75%, and 54%; Surcharge = 2%, 1.75%, 3.5%, and 2.25%. Change the assumptions for New York to the following: Qtr1 Sales Amount = $675,000; Qtr2 Growth Rate = -3%; Qtr3 Growth Rate = 2%; Qtr4 Growth Rate = 4.75%; Qtr Expense Rate = 51%, 49.5%, 51%, and 57%; Surcharge = 1%, 2.25%, 1.75%, and 2%.

8. Delete the Assumptions table from the Summary sheet. Use 3-D references and the fill handle to determine totals on the Summary sheet. You should end up with the following totals in column F on the Summary sheet: Sales = $5,121,193.76; Expenses = $2,712,024.66; and Profit = $2,409,169.10.

9. Change the chart range so each pie chart refers to the data on the same sheet.

10. Save the workbook by clicking the Save button on the Standard toolbar.

11. Select all three sheets. Change the header to include your name, course, computer laboratory exercise (CLA1-3.XLT), date, and instructor name. Change the footer to include the page number and total pages. Print the workbook without gridlines.

12. Save the workbook by clicking the Save button on the Standard toolbar.

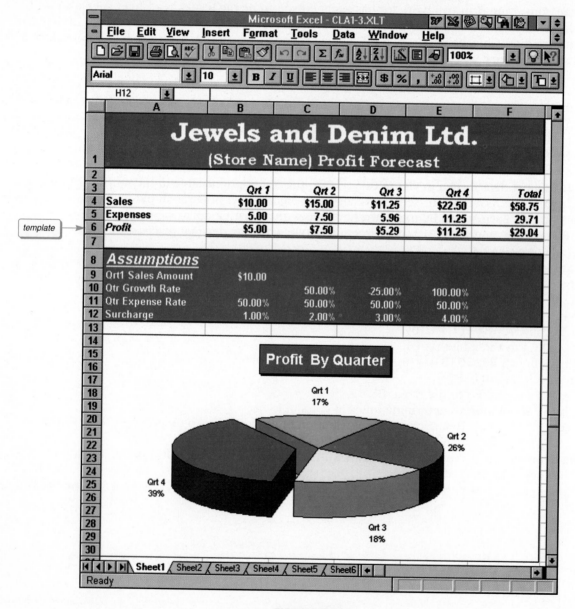

FIGURE CLA1-3

COMPUTER LABORATORY ASSIGNMENT 4
Creating a Template and Consolidated Balance Sheet

Purpose: To provide experience using Excel to create a template and consolidated balance sheet.

Problem: Some businesses are divided into smaller companies for the purpose of better organization. Tri-Quality International, by whom you are employed as an analyst is a parent to two companies — Modern Elek Avenue and Analog Haven. Create a template for the consolidated balance sheet workbook similar to the one in Figure CLA1-4. Save the template using the filename CLA1-4. Close the template and then open it. Copy it to three sheets and then enter the data shown in Table CLA1-4 on the next page. Use 3-D references to consolidate the data on the first two sheets into one sheet that represents Tri-Quality International. Draw on a separate sheet in the workbook a 3-D pie chart that shows the consolidated contributions of each asset category to the total. Format the pie chart appropriately. Select all three sheets and enter your name, course, computer laboratory assignment number (CLA1-4), date, and instructor name as a header.

Save the workbook using the filename CLA1-4.

Submit the following:

1. A description of the problem. Include the purpose of the template and consolidated Balance Sheet workbook, a statement outlining the results, the required data, and calculations.

2. A printed copy of the template and workbook without gridlines.

3. A printed copy of the formulas in the summary sheet.

4. A short description explaining how to use the workbook.

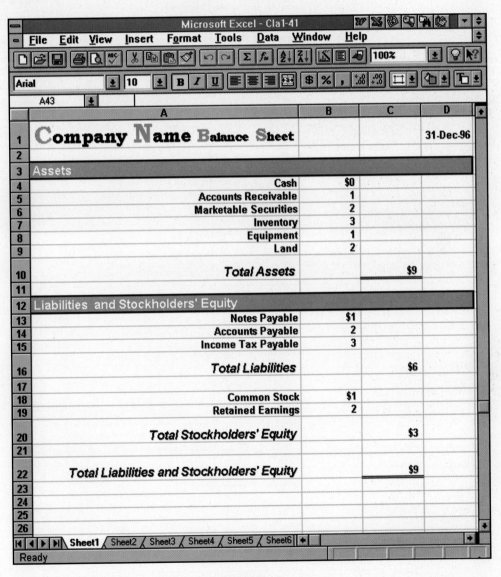

FIGURE CLA1-4

(continued)

COMPUTER LABORATORY ASSIGNMENT 4 (continued)

	MODERN ELK AVENUE	ANALOG HAVEN
Assets		
Cash	$211,000	$123,000
Accounts Receivable	72,500	63,500
Marketable Securities	179,150	213,500
Inventory	459,000	357,000
Equipment	213,000	114,000
Land	579,000	362,000
Liabilites and Stockholders' Equity		
Notes Payable	$62,500	$51,500
Accounts Payable	212,850	179,150
Income Tax Payable	73,000	49,500
Common Stock	585,200	625,100
Retained Earnings	780,100	327,750

MICROSOFT EXCEL 5 FOR WINDOWS

PROJECT TWO

▼

DATA TABLES, MACROS USING VISUAL BASIC, AND SCENARIO MANAGER

OBJECTIVES You will have mastered the material in this project when you can:

- Assign a name to a cell and refer to the cell in a formula by using the assigned name
- Determine the monthly payment of a loan using the financial function PMT
- State the purpose of the FV and PV functions
- Enter a series of percents using the fill handle
- Build a data table to analyze data in a worksheet

- Write a macro in Visual Basic to automate data entry into a worksheet
- Analyze worksheet data by changing values and goal seeking
- Use Excel's Scenario Manager to record and save different sets of what-if assumptions and the corresponding results of formulas
- Protect and unprotect cells

▶ INTRODUCTION

O ne of the more powerful aspects of Excel is its capability to analyze worksheet data or answer what-if questions. A what-if question regarding a loan might be, "What if the interest rate for a loan increases by 1% — how would the increase affect the monthly payment?" Or, "What if you know the result you want a formula in a worksheet to return, but you do not know the data required to attain that value?" Excel has the capability to quickly answer these types of questions and save you the time of performing trial-and-error analysis. You learned earlier how to analyze data by using Excel's recalculation feature and goal seeking. This project uses these two methods of analyzing data and describes two additional ones — data tables and Scenario Manager.

This project also introduces you to the use of macros and cell protection. Use a macro to reduce a series of actions to the click of a button or a keystroke. Cell protection ensures that you do not accidentally change values that are critical to the worksheet.

▶ PROJECT TWO — WESAVU MONEY LOAN ANALYSIS WORKBOOK

Project 2 creates the WeSavU Money Loan Analysis workbook. The workbook is made up of three worksheets: (1) a worksheet that determines the monthly payment, total interest, and total cost for a loan; (2) a macro that instructs Excel to accept new loan data from the worksheet user; and (3) a worksheet that summarizes what-if questions. The latter is called a **Scenario Summary worksheet.**

The Loan Analysis worksheet (Figure 2-1) includes three distinct sections: (1) a loan analysis section in the range A1:B11; (2) a button titled New Loan in the range A13:A14 that, when clicked, executes the macro shown in Figure 2-2; and (3) a data table in the range D1:G16 that can be used to show the effect of different interest rates on the monthly payment, total interest, and total cost of the loan. The Scenario Summary worksheet will be shown and discussed later in this project.

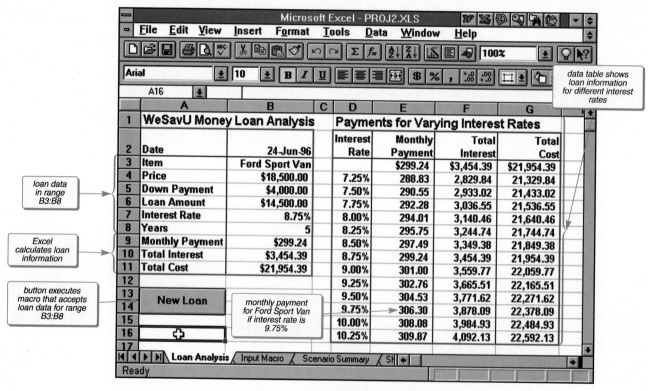

FIGURE 2-1

The loan analysis section on the left in Figure 2-1 answers the following question: What is the monthly payment (cell B9), total interest (cell B10), and total cost (cell B11) for a Ford Sport Van (cell B3) that costs $18,500.00 (cell B4), if the down payment is $4,000.00 (cell B5), the interest rate is 8.75% (cell B7), and the term of the loan is 5 years (cell B8)? As shown in Figure 2-1, the monthly payment is $299.24 (cell B9), the total interest is $3,454.39 (cell B10), and the total cost of the Ford Sport Van is $21,954.39 (cell B11). Excel determines the monthly payment in cell B9 using the PMT function. Formulas are used to calculate the total interest and total cost in cells B10 and B11. The loan analysis section of the worksheet can determine the answers to loan questions for the WeSavU Money Loan Company as fast as you can enter the new loan data in the range B3:B8.

The function of the button titled New Loan in the range A13:A14 (Figure 2-1) is to automate the entry of loan data. The button executes the macro in Figure 2-2 that simplifies the loan data entry into cells B3 through B8. Using a button that executes a macro to enter the loan data is especially helpful for users who know little about computers and worksheets.

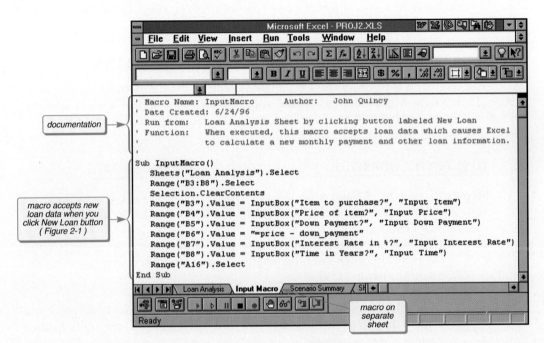

FIGURE 2-2

The third section of the worksheet in Figure 2-1 is the data table on the right side of the screen. Each time you enter new loan data into the worksheet, the data table recalculates new values for the monthly payment, total interest, and total cost for the different interest rates in column D. A **data table** is a powerful what-if tool because it can automate your data analyzes and organize the answers returned by Excel. The data table in Figure 2-1 answers thirteen different what-if questions. The questions pertain to the effect the thirteen different interest rates in column D have on the monthly payment, total interest, and total cost. For example, what will be the monthly payment for the Ford Sport Van if the interest rate is 9.75%, instead of 8.75%? The answer, $306.30, is in cell E14.

The macro in Figure 2-2 is made up of a series of Visual Basic statements that are executed when you click the New Loan button (Figure 2-1). Visual Basic statements tell Excel to carry out an operation, such as select a range or clear the selection. Creating a macro is a form of **programming.** The programming language you use with Excel 5 is called **Visual Basic for Applications**, or **VBA**.

Changing the Font of the Entire Worksheet

After you start Excel, the first step in this project is to change the font of the entire worksheet to bold. By bolding the font, the characters in the worksheet stand out.

TO CHANGE THE FONT OF THE ENTIRE WORKSHEET

Step 1: Click the Select All button immediately above row heading 1 and to the left of column heading A (see Figure 2-3).

Step 2: Click the Bold button on the Formatting toolbar.

As you enter text and numbers onto the worksheet, they will display in Arial bold.

Entering the Worksheet Title, Row Titles, and System Date

The next step is to enter the loan analysis section title, row titles, and system date. To make the worksheet easier to read, the width of columns A and B and the height of rows 1 and 2 will be increased. The font size of the worksheet title will also be changed from 10 point to 12 point.

TO ENTER THE WORKSHEET TITLE, ROW TITLES, AND SYSTEM DATE

Step 1: Select cell A1 and enter `WeSavU Money Loan Analysis`

Step 2: With cell A1 active, click the Font Size arrow on the Formatting toolbar and choose 12.

Step 3: Position the mouse pointer on the border between row headings 1 and 2 and drag down until the height of row 1 in the reference area in the formula bar is 21.00.

Step 4: Select cell A2 and enter the row title `Date`

Step 5: Position the mouse pointer on the border between row headings 2 and 3 and drag until the height of row 2 in the reference area in the formula bar is 27.00.

Step 6: Enter the following row titles:

CELL	ENTRY	CELL	ENTRY	CELL	ENTRY
A3	Item	A6	Loan Amount	A9	Monthly Payment
A4	Price	A7	Interest Rate	A10	Total Interest
A5	Down Payment	A8	Years	A11	Total Cost

Step 7: Select columns A and B. Position the mouse pointer on the border between column headings B and C and drag until the width of column B in the reference area in the formula bar is 16.00.

Step 8: Select cell B2. Enter `=now()`

Step 9: With the mouse pointer in cell B2, click the right mouse button and choose the Format Cells command. When the Format Cells dialog box displays, click the Number tab if necessary, select Date in the Category box, and select d-mmm-yy in the Format Codes box. Choose the OK button.

Step 10: Click the Save button on the Standard toolbar. Save the workbook using the filename PROJ2.XLS.

The worksheet title, row titles, and system date display as shown in Figure 2-3.

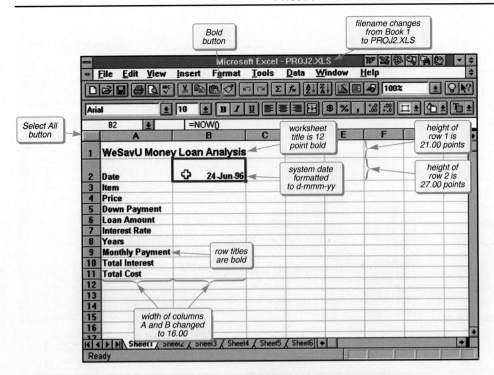

FIGURE 2-3

Outlining and Adding Borders to the Loan Analysis Section of the Worksheet

An **outline** is used to box-in an area of the worksheet so it stands out. In this case, the outline is used to separate the loan analysis section in the range A1:B11 from the data table in the range D1:G16. Light borders are also used within the outline to further subdivide the loan analysis text and numbers as shown in Figure 2-1 on page E72.

TO DRAW AN OUTLINE AND BORDERS ▼

STEP 1 ▶

Select the range A2:B11. With the mouse pointer in the selected range, click the right mouse button to display the shortcut menu.

The shortcut menu displays (Figure 2-4).

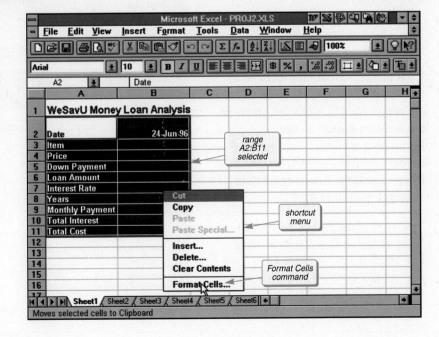

FIGURE 2-4

STEP 2 ▶

Choose the Format Cells command. When the Format Cells dialog box displays, select the Border tab. Click the Color box arrow. Select red (column 1, row 2 on the palette). Select the regular border in the Style area (column 1, row 3). Click the Outline box in the Border area.

*The **Border tab** in the Format Cells dialog box displays as shown in Figure 2-5.*

FIGURE 2-5

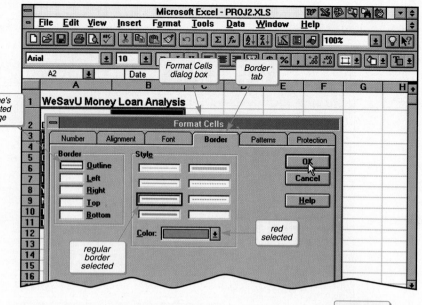

STEP 3 ▶

Choose the OK button in the Format Cells dialog box. Select the range A2:B2. Click the arrow on the Borders button on the Formatting toolbar.

The loan analysis section of the worksheet displays along with the Border palette as shown in Figure 2-6.

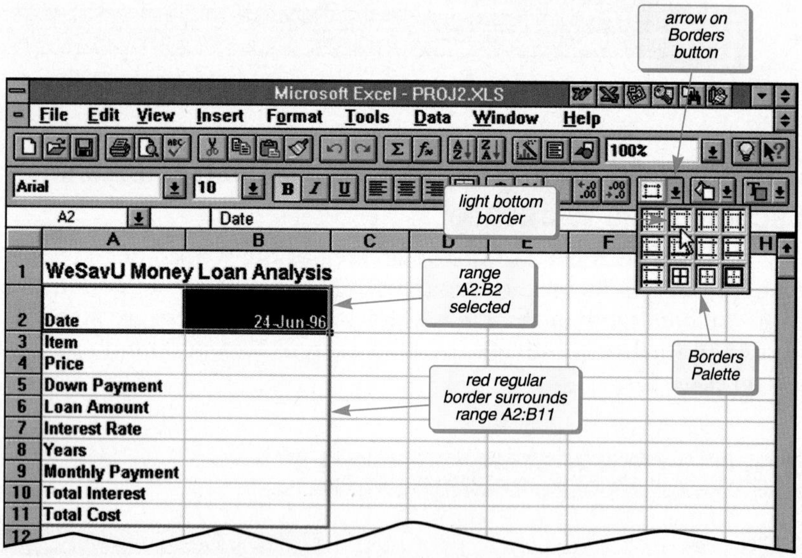

FIGURE 2-6

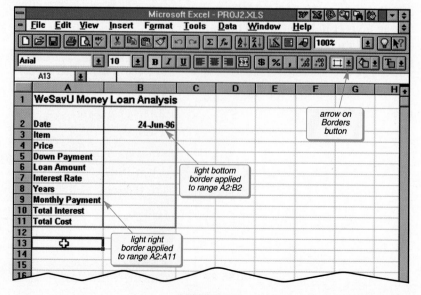

STEP 4 ▶

Click the bottom border (column 2, row 1) on the Borders palette. Select the range A2:A11. Click the arrow on the Borders button on the Formatting toolbar. Click the right border (column 4, row 1) on the Borders palette. Select cell B13 to deselect the range A2:A11.

The loan analysis section is outlined in red. It has a border dividing row 2 from the rest of the rows and a right border dividing the two columns (Figure 2-7).

FIGURE 2-7

Entering the Loan Data

According to the worksheet in Figure 2-1 on page E72, the item to be purchased, the price of the item, the down payment, the interest rate, and the number of years until the loan is paid back are entered into cells B3 through B5 and cells B7 and B8. These five values make up the loan data.

TO ENTER THE LOAN DATA

Step 1: Select cell B3. Enter `Ford Sport Van` and click the Align Right button on the Formatting toolbar. Select cell B4 and enter `18500`. Select cell B5 and enter `4000`.

Step 2: Skip cell B6 and select cell B7. Enter `8.75%`. Select cell B8 and enter `5`.

The loan data displays in the worksheet as shown in Figure 2-8. The interest rate is formatted to the 0.00% Percent style because the percent sign (%) was typed as part of the entry in cell B7.

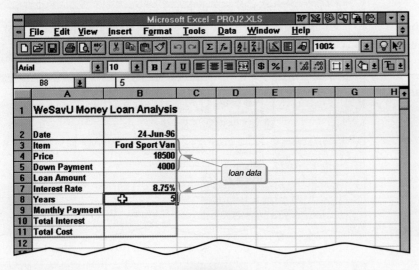

FIGURE 2-8

The four remaining entries in the loan analysis section of the worksheet, loan amount (cell B6), monthly payment (cell B9), total interest (cell B10), and total cost (cell B11), require formulas that reference cells B4, B5, B7, and B8. The formulas will be entered referencing names assigned to cells instead of cell references because names are easier to remember than cell references.

▶ CREATING NAMES BASED ON ROW TITLES

Naming a cell that you plan to reference in a formula helps make the formula easier to read and remember. For example, the loan amount in cell B6 is equal to the price in cell B4 less the down payment in cell B5. Therefore, according to what you learned in the earlier project, you can write the loan amount formula in cell B6 as =B4 - B5. However, by assigning the corresponding row titles in column A as the names of cells B4 and B5, you can write the loan amount formula as =Price – Down_Payment, which is clearer and easier to remember than =B4 - B5.

To name cells, you first select the range encompassing the row titles that include the names and the cells to be named (range A4:B11). Next, you use the **Name command** on the Insert menu, then choose the **Create command** on the cascading menu. In the **Create Names dialog box**, you select Top Row, Left Column, Bottom Row, or Right Row depending on where the names are located in relation to the cells to be named. In this case, the names are the row titles in column A. Therefore, you select Left Columns. On the basis of the range you select prior to invoking the command, Excel will make a selection of its own, which you can change in the Create Names dialog box.

In the following steps, each row title in the range A4:A11 is assigned to the adjacent cell in column B. Because the data in cell B2 and the item in cell B3 will not be referenced in formulas, there is no need to include them in the range.

TO CREATE NAMES ▼

STEP 1 ▶

Select the range A4:B11. Select the Insert menu and choose the Name command.

The range A4:B11 is selected and Excel displays the Name command cascading menu (Figure 2-9).

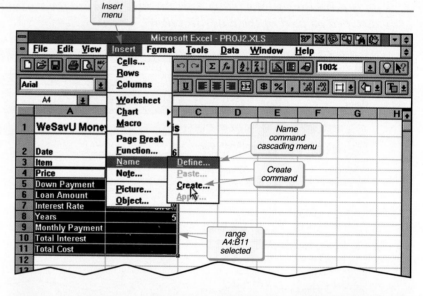

FIGURE 2-9

STEP 2 ▶

Choose the Create command from the cascading menu.

Excel displays the Create names dialog box (Figure 2-10). Excel automatically selects the Left Column box because the general direction of the range in Step 1 is downward.

STEP 3 ▶

Choose the OK button in the Create Names dialog box.

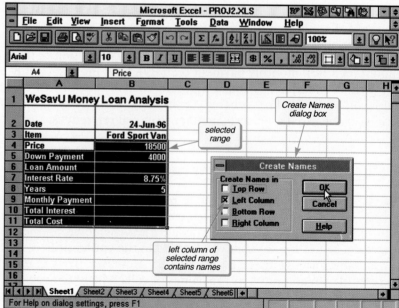

FIGURE 2-10

After Step 3, you can use the names in the range A4:A11 in formulas to reference the adjacent cells in the range B4:B11. Excel is not case-sensitive with respect to names of cells. Hence, you can enter the names of cells in formulas in uppercase or lowercase. Some names, such as Down Payment in cell A5, include a space because they are made up of two words. To use a name in a formula that is made up of two or more words, replace any space with the underscore character (_). For example, Down Payment is written as down_payment when you want to reference the adjacent cell B5. Consider these three additional details regarding the assignment of names to cells:

1. A name can be a minimum of one character or a maximum of 255 characters.
2. If you want to assign a name that is not a text item in an adjacent cell, use the Define command on the cascading menu shown in Figure 2-9 or select the cell or range and type the name in the reference area in the formula bar.
3. The worksheet names display in alphabetical order in the Name box when you click the Name box arrow (Figure 2-11).

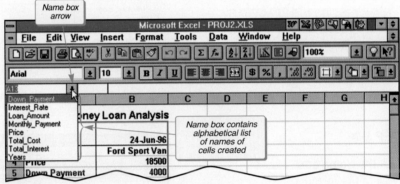

FIGURE 2-11

Using the Name Box and Point Mode to Enter a Formula

The next step is to enter in cell B6 the formula =Price – Down_Payment. You can enter the formula as you have in the previous project by using the keyboard and the Point mode. However, the Name box offers an alternative to the Point mode that allows you to point to the names of cells, instead of to the cells themselves. The following steps show how to use the Point mode and the Name box to enter the formula =Price – Down_Payment in cell B6.

TO ENTER THE LOAN AMOUNT FORMULA USING THE NAME BOX ▼

STEP 1 ▶

Select cell B6. Type = and click the Name box arrow in the formula bar.

The Name box displays with Loan_Amount selected because the cell it names (cell B6) is the active one (Figure 2-12).

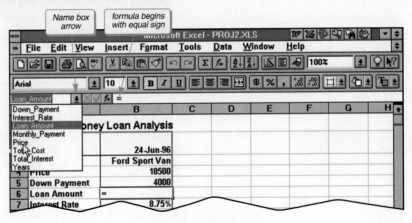

FIGURE 2-12

STEP 2 ▶

Click the name Price in the Name drop-down list box. Press the SPACEBAR, type a minus sign (-), and press the SPACEBAR.

The first term in the formula displays in the formula bar and in cell B6 (Figure 2-13). Pressing the SPACEBAR inserts spaces before and after the minus sign for readability.

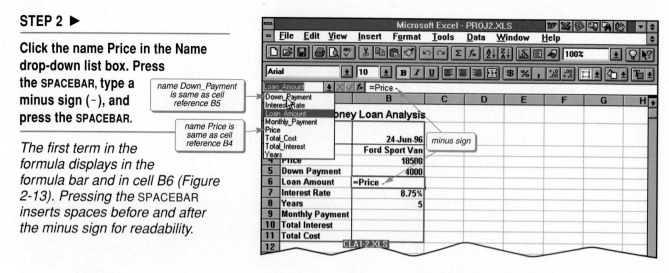

FIGURE 2-13

STEP 3 ▶

Click the Name box arrow in the formula bar. Click the name Down_Payment in the Name drop-down list box. Click the enter box or press the ENTER key.

Excel assigns the formula =Price – Down_Payment to cell B6 and displays the result of the formula (14500) in cell B6 (Figure 2-14).

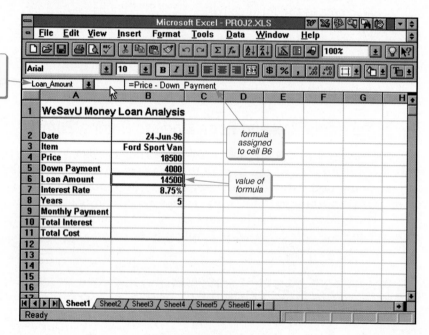

FIGURE 2-14

Notice that when cell B6 is selected, Excel displays the name of the cell (Loan_Amount) in the reference area in the formula bar instead of the cell reference B6. Besides using the Name box to assign names in formulas, you can click a name in the Name drop-down list box to select the cell it names. For example, to select cell B9, click on Monthly_Payment in the Name drop-down list box.

Formatting to Currency Style with a Floating Dollar Sign

After entering the loan amount formula, the next step is to format the non-adjacent ranges B4:B6 and B9:B11 to the Currency style with a floating dollar sign.

TO FORMAT TO CURRENCY STYLE WITH A FLOATING DOLLAR SIGN ▼

STEP 1 ▶

Select the range B4:B6. Hold down the CTRL key and select the range B9:B11. With the mouse pointer in one of the selected ranges, click the right mouse button to display the shortcut menu. Choose the Format Cells command. When the Format Cells dialog box displays, click the Number tab. Select Currency in the Category box and $#,##0.00_);[Red]($#,##0.00) in the Format Codes box.

The Format Cells dialog box displays as shown in Figure 2-15.

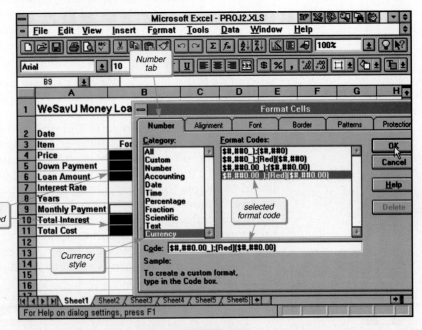

FIGURE 2-15

STEP 2 ▶

Choose the OK button in the Format Cells dialog box.

The price, down payment, and loan amount in the range B4:B6 have been formatted to Currency style and display as shown in Figure 2-16. Later when numbers display in the range B9:B11, they will display using the Currency style.

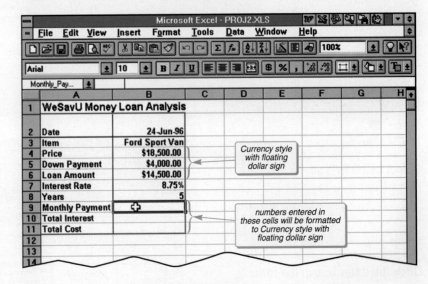

FIGURE 2-16

An alternative to formatting the numbers to the Currency style, as described in the previous steps, is to enter the numbers in the desired format. For example, the number 18500 could have been entered earlier as $18,500.00 and the Currency style with a floating dollar sign would have been automatically assigned to the cell. The same can be said for the remaining dollar amounts entered earlier. A third alternative is to enter the dollar amount in cell B4 and then use the Format Painter button on the Standard toolbar to format the remaining cells containing dollar amounts.

▶ DETERMINING THE MONTHLY PAYMENT

Using Excel's PMT function, you can determine the monthly payment (cell B9) on the basis of the loan amount (cell B6), the interest rate (cell B7), and the term of the loan (cell B8). The general form of the **PMT function** is

=PMT(rate, payments, loan amount)

where rate is the interest rate per payment period, payments is the number of payments, and loan amount is the amount of the loan. Rate, payments, and loan amount are called **arguments.**

In the worksheet shown in Figure 2-16 on the previous page, cell B7 is equal to the annual interest rate. However, loan institutions calculate the interest, which is their profit, on a monthly basis. Thus, the first value in the PMT function is Interest_Rate / 12 (cell B7 divided by 12) instead of Interest_Rate (cell B7). The number of payments (or periods) is equal to 12 * Years (12 times cell B8) because there are twelve months, or twelve payments, per year.

Excel considers the value returned by the PMT function to be a debit and therefore, returns a negative number as the monthly payment. To display the monthly payment as a positive number precede the loan amount with a negative sign. Thus, the loan amount is equal to -Loan_Amount. The PMT function for cell B9 becomes the following:

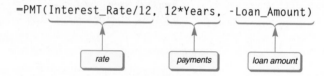

The following steps use the PMT function to determine the monthly payment in cell B7.

TO ENTER THE PMT FUNCTION ▼

STEP 1 ▶

Select cell B9. Type
=pmt(interest_rate / 12,
12 * years, -loan_amount)

STEP 2 ▶

Click the enter box in the formula bar or press the ENTER key.

Excel displays the monthly payment of $299.24 in cell B9 (Figure 2-17) for a loan amount of $14,500.00 (cell B6) with an annual interest rate of 8.75% (cell B7) for five years (cell B8). Notice that with cell B9 selected, the PMT function displays in the formula bar.

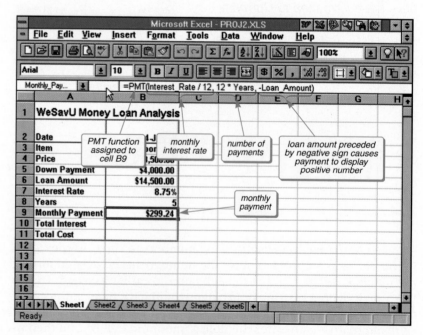

FIGURE 2-17

An alternative way to enter the PMT function is by using the Function Wizard button on the Standard toolbar. In addition, using the Point mode along with the Name box arrow in the formula bar, you can select the cells representing the rate, payment, and loan amount.

Besides the PMT function, Excel has fifty-two additional **financial functions** to help you solve the most complex financial problems. These functions save you from entering long, complicated formulas to obtain the results you require. Table 2-1 summarizes three of the most often used financial functions.

▶ **TABLE 2-1**

FUNCTION	DESCRIPTION
FV(rate, periods, payment)	Returns the future value of an investment based on periodic, constant payments and constant interest rate.
PMT(rate, periods, loan amount)	Returns the periodic payment of a loan.
PV(rate, periods, payment)	Returns the present value of an investment made up of a series of payments.

To view a complete list of Excel's financial functions, select the Help menu and choose the Search for Help on command. When the Search dialog box displays, type financial functions in the top box. Choose the Show Topic button. Select Financial Functions in the lower box and choose the Go To button. Excel responds by displaying a list of all the financial functions. An alternative to using the Help menu to learn about the financial functions is to click the Function Wizard button on the Standard toolbar as described in the following steps.

TO OBTAIN INFORMATION ON FINANCIAL FUNCTIONS USING THE FUNCTION WIZARD BUTTON

Step 1: Select any empty cell in the worksheet. Click the Function Wizard button on the Standard toolbar.

Step 2: Select Financial in the Function Category box when the Function Wizard – Step 1 of 2 dialog box displays.

Step 3: One by one, select the functions in the Function Name box and read the description below the Function Category box.

Step 4: When you are finished, choose the Cancel button in the Function Wizard – Step 1 of 2 dialog box.

▶ DETERMINING THE TOTAL INTEREST AND TOTAL COST

The next step is to determine the total interest (the loan institution's profit) and the borrower's total cost of the item being purchased. The total interest (cell B10) is equal to:

12 * Years * Monthly_Payment – Loan_Amount

The total cost of the item to be purchased (cell B11) is equal to:

12 * Years * Monthly_Payment + Down_Payment

To enter the total interest and total cost formulas, perform the steps on the following page.

TO DETERMINE THE TOTAL INTEREST, TOTAL COST, AND SAVE THE WORKBOOK

Step 1: Select cell B10. Enter the formula:
```
=12 * years * monthly_payment - loan_amount
```
Step 2: Select cell B11. Enter the formula:
```
=12 * years * monthly_payment + down_payment
```
Step 3: Click the Save button on the Standard toolbar to save the workbook using the filename PROJ2.XLS.

Excel displays the total interest, $3,454.39, in cell B10 and the total cost of the Ford Sport Van to be purchased, $21,954.39, in cell B11 (Figure 2-18).

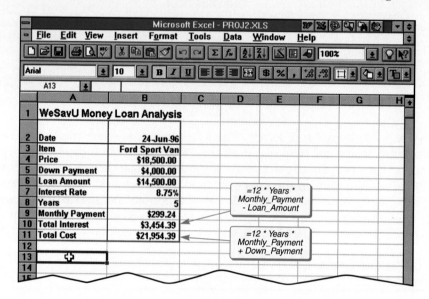

FIGURE 2-18

With the loan analysis section of the worksheet complete, you can determine the monthly payment, total interest, and total cost for any reasonable loan data. After entering the data table in the next section, alternative loan data will be entered to illustrate Excel's recalculation feature.

▶ USING A DATA TABLE TO ANALYZE WORKSHEET DATA

The next step is to build the data table section of the worksheet in the range D1:G16 (right side of Figure 2-19). A **data table** is a range of cells that shows the answers to formulas in which different values have been substituted.

You have already seen that if a value is changed in a cell referenced elsewhere in a formula in the worksheet, Excel immediately recalculates and stores the new value in the cell assigned the formula. What if you want to compare the results of the formula for several different values? It would be unwieldy to write down or remember all the answers to the what-if questions. This is where a data table becomes useful because it will organize the answers in the worksheet for you automatically.

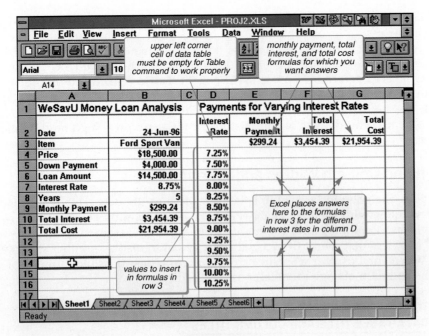

FIGURE 2-19

Data tables are built in an unused area of the worksheet. You may vary one or two values and display the results of the specified formulas in table form. The right side of Figure 2-19 illustrates the makeup of a one-input data table. With a **one-input data table**, you vary one cell reference (in this project, cell B7, the interest rate) and Excel fills the table with the results of one or more formulas. In this project, they are the monthly payment, total interest, and total cost.

The interest rates that will be used to analyze the loan formulas in this project range from 7.25% to 10.25% in increments of 0.25%. The data table (Figure 2-20) illustrates the impact of varying the interest rate on three formulas: the monthly payment (cell B9), total interest paid (cell B10), and the total cost of the item to be purchased (cell B11).

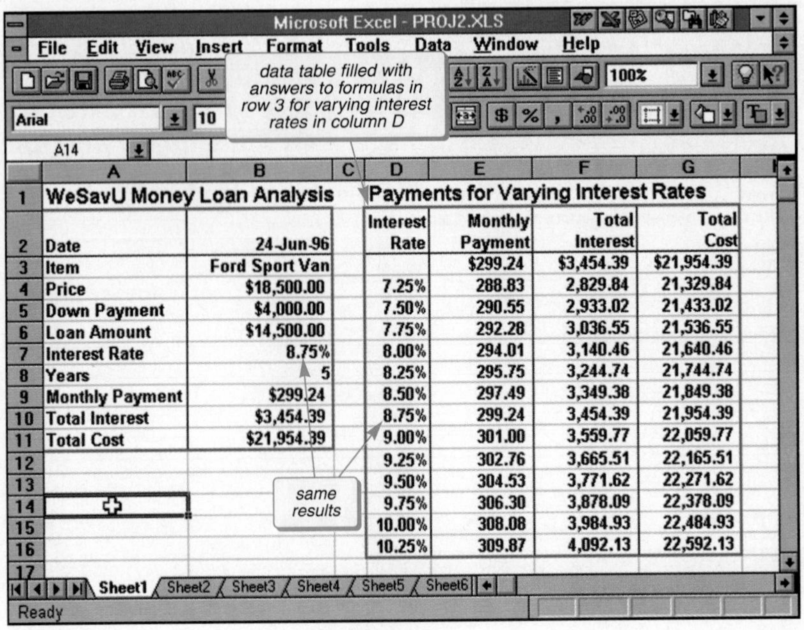

FIGURE 2-20

The steps that follow are used to construct the data table in Figure 2-20: (1) adjust the widths of columns C through G; (2) enter the data table title and column titles in the range D1:G2; (3) use the data fill handle to enter the varying interest rates in column D; (4) enter the formulas in the range E3:G3 for which the data table is to determine answers; (5) use the **Table command** on the **Data menu** to define the range D3:G16 as a data table and identify the interest rate in cell B7 as the **input cell**, the cell to vary; and (6) outline the data table to highlight it. The techniques to accomplish these tasks are presented on the following pages.

Changing Column Widths and Entering Titles

First, the columns are set to specific widths so the data table will fit in the same window with the loan analysis section. Keep in mind you may have to adjust the widths of columns after the numbers and text are assigned to the cells because large numbers that won't fit in a cell cause Excel to display number signs (#) in the cell. When you design a worksheet, you make the best possible estimate of column widths and then change them later as required.

TO CHANGE COLUMN WIDTHS AND ENTER THE
DATA TABLE TITLE AND COLUMN TITLES

Step 1: Use the mouse to change the widths of columns C through G as follows: C = 3.00; D = 6. 71; and E, F, and G = 11. 29.

Step 2: Select cell D1 and enter Payments for Varying Interest Rates

Step 3: Click the Font Size arrow on the Formatting toolbar and choose 12.

Step 4: Enter the following in the range D2:G2:

CELL	ENTRY
D2	Interest ALT+ENTER Rate
E2	Monthly ALT+ENTER Payment
F2	Total ALT+ENTER Interest
G2	Total ALT+ENTER Cost

Step 5: Select the range D2:G2. Click the Align Right button on the Formatting toolbar.

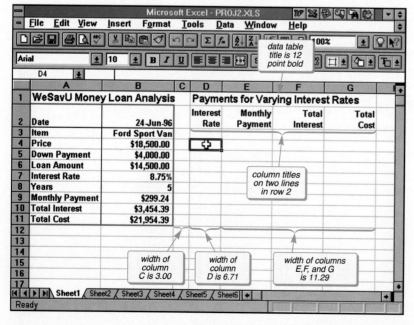

The data table title and column headings display as shown in Figure 2-21. Pressing ALT + ENTER *in Step 4 instructs Excel to continue the entry on the next line of the cell.*

FIGURE 2-21

Creating a Percent Series Using the Fill Handle

After changing the column widths and entering the titles, the next step is to create the percent series in column D using the fill handle.

TO CREATE A PERCENT SERIES USING THE FILL HANDLE ▼

STEP 1 ▶

Enter 7.25% in cell D4 and 7.50% in cell D5.

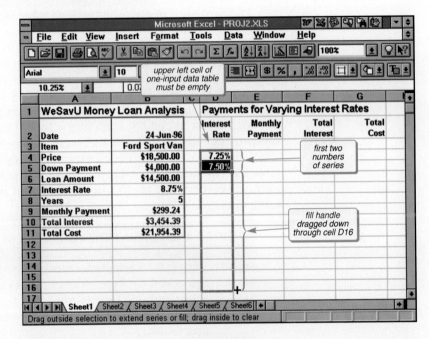

FIGURE 2-22

STEP 2 ▶

Select the range D4:D5 and point to the fill handle. Drag the fill handle down through cell D16.

Excel shades the border of the paste area (Figure 2-22).

STEP 3 ▶

Release the mouse button. Select cell E3.

Excel generates the series of numbers, 7.25% to 10.25% in increments of 0.25%, in the range D4:D16 (Figure 2-23).

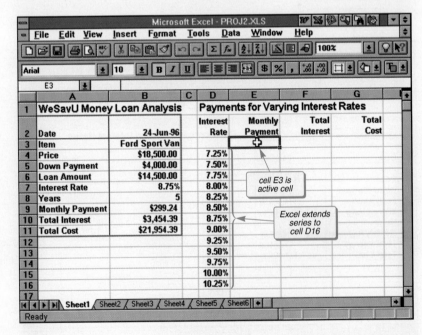

FIGURE 2-23

The percents in column D are the values Excel uses to compute the formulas entered at the top of the data table in row 3. Notice that the series beginning with 7.25% in column D was not started in cell D3 because the cell immediately above the series and to the left of the formulas in the data table (Figure 2-22 on the previous page) must be empty for a one-input data table.

Entering the Formulas in the Data Table

The next step in creating the data table is to enter the three formulas in row 3 in cells E3, F3, and G3. The three formulas are the same as the monthly payment formula in cell B9, the total interest formula in cell B10, and the total cost formula in cell B11.

Excel provides three ways to enter these formulas in the data table: (1) retype the formulas in cells E3, F3, and G3; (2) copy cells B9, B10, and B11 to cells E3, F3, and G3, respectively; or (3) enter the formulas =Monthly_Payment in cell E3, =Total_Interest in cell F3, and enter =Total_Cost in cell G3. Recall that earlier in this project cells B9 through B11 were assigned names.

Using the names preceded by an equal sign to define the formulas in the data table has two advantages: (1) it is more efficient; and (2) if you change any of the formulas in the range B9:B11, the formulas at the top of the data table are automatically updated.

TO ENTER AND FORMAT THE FORMULAS IN THE DATA TABLE

Step 1: With cell E3 selected, enter =Monthly_Payment

Step 2: Select cell F3. Type =Total_Interest

Step 3: Select cell G3. Type =Total_Cost

Step 4: Select the range E3:G3. Click the Currency Style button on the Formatting toolbar.

The results of the formulas display in the range E3:G3 (Figure 2-24).

Here again, the formulas could have been entered using the Point mode and the Name box arrow in the formula bar.

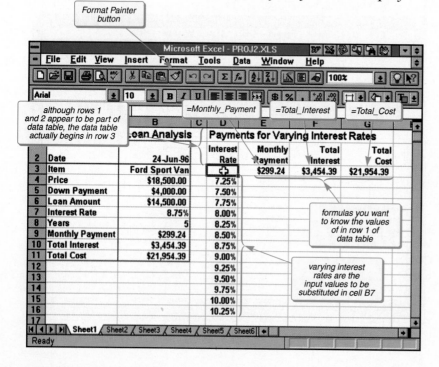

FIGURE 2-24

Defining the Data Table

After creating the interest rates in column D and assigning the formulas in row 3, the next step is to define the range D3:G16 as a data table.

TO DEFINE A RANGE AS A DATA TABLE   ▼

STEP 1 ▶

Select the range D3:G16. Select the Data menu.

*Excel displays the Data menu (Figure 2-25). Notice in the worksheet that the range D3:G16 does not include the data table title in row 1 and column headings in row 2. The column headings are **NOT** part of the data table even though they identify the columns in the table.*

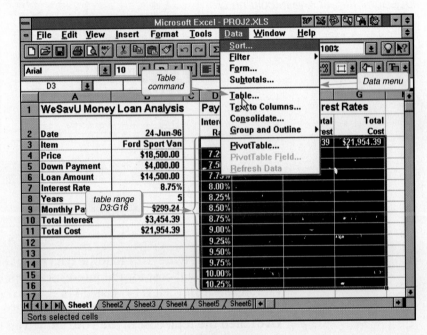

FIGURE 2-25

STEP 2 ▶

Choose the Table command from the Data menu. When the Table dialog box displays, select the Column Input Cell box in the Table dialog box. Click cell B7 or type $B$7, the input cell.

*A marquis surrounds the selected input cell B7 and Excel assigns cell B7 to the Column Input Cell box in the **Table dialog box** (Figure 2-26).*

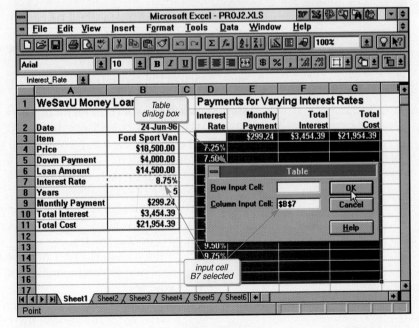

FIGURE 2-26

STEP 3 ▶

Choose the OK button in the Table dialog box.

Excel immediately fills the data table by calculating the three formulas at the top of the data table for each interest rate in column D (Figure 2-27).

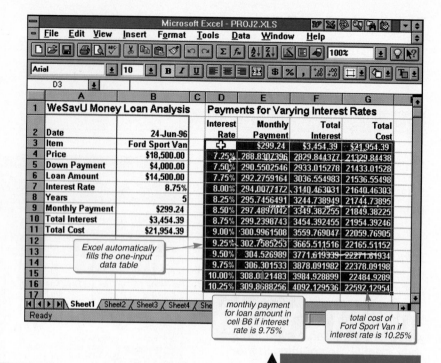

FIGURE 2-27

Notice in Figure 2-27 that the data table displays the monthly payment, total interest, and total cost for the interest rates in column D. For example, if the interest rate is 9.75% (cell D14) instead of 8.75% (cell B7), the monthly payment is $306.30 (cell E14) instead of $299.24 (cell B9). If the interest rate is 10.25% (cell D16) then the total cost of the Ford Sport Van is approximately $22,592.13 (cell G16) instead of $21,954.39 (cell B11). Thus, a 1.5% increase in the interest rate results in a $637.74 increase in the total cost of the Ford Sport Van.

TO OUTLINE AND FORMAT THE DATA TABLE AND SAVE THE WORKBOOK

Step 1: Select the range E4:G16. Click the Comma Style button on the Formatting toolbar.

Step 2: Select the range D2:G16. With the mouse pointer in the selected range, click the right mouse button.

Step 3: When the shortcut menu displays, choose the Format Cells command. When the Format Cells dialog box displays, click the Border tab.

Step 4: Click the Color box arrow on the Border tab. Select red (column 1, row 2 on the palette). Select Outline in the Border box. Select the regular border in the Style box (column 1, row 3). Choose the OK button in the Format Cells dialog box.

Step 5: Select the range D2:G2. Click the arrow on the Borders button on the Formatting toolbar. Choose the light bottom border (column 2, row 1) on the Borders palette.

Step 6: Select the range D2:F16. Click the Borders button arrow on the Formatting toolbar. Choose the light right border (column 4, row 1) on the Borders palette.

Step 7: Double-click the Sheet1 tab. When the Rename dialog box displays, type `Loan Analysis` and choose the OK button.

Step 8: Click the Save button on the Standard toolbar to save the workbook using the filename PROJ2.XLS.

The worksheet displays as shown in Figure 2-28.

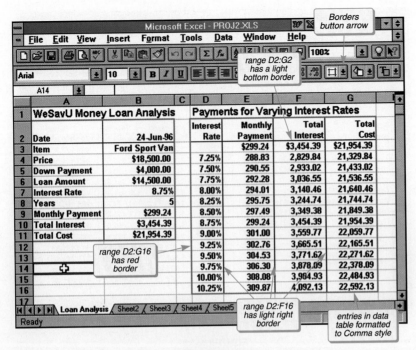

FIGURE 2-28

The following list details important points you should know about data tables:

1. The input cell must be a cell reference in the formula(s) you are analyzing.
2. You can have as many active data tables in a worksheet as you want.
3. You delete a data table as you would any other item on a worksheet. That is, select the data table and press the DELETE key.
4. For a data table with one varying value, the cell in the upper left corner of the table (cell D3 in Figure 2-28) must be empty.
5. To add additional formulas to a one-input data table, enter them in adjacent cells in the same row as the current formulas and define the entire range as a data table by using the Table command on the Data menu.
6. A one-input data table can vary only one value, but can analyze as many formulas as you want.

▶ ENTERING NEW LOAN DATA

With the loan analysis and data table sections of the worksheet complete, you can use them to generate new loan information. For example, assume you want to purchase a $178,500.00 house. You have $36,500.00 for a down payment and want the loan for 15 years. The loan company is currently charging 8.75% interest for a 15-year loan. The following steps show how to enter the new loan data.

TO ENTER NEW LOAN DATA

Step 1: Select cell B3. Enter the item to be purchased, House
Step 2: Select cell B4. Enter the price of the house, 178500
Step 3: Select cell B5. Enter the down payment, 36500
Step 4: Leave the interest rate at 8.75% in cell B7.
Step 5: Select cell B8. Enter the number of years, 15

Excel automatically recalculates the loan information in cells B6, B9, B10, B11, and the data table (Figure 2-29 on the following page). Do not save the workbook with the changes.

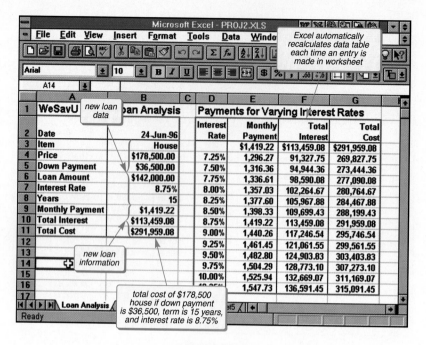

FIGURE 2-29

You can use the worksheet to calculate the loan information for any reasonable loan data. As you can see from Figure 2-29, the monthly payment for the house is $1,419.22. The total interest (loan institution's profit) is $113,459.08. The total cost of the house is $291,959.08.

▶ CREATING A MACRO TO AUTOMATE LOAN DATA ENTRY

A **macro** is made up of a series of Visual Basic statements that tell Excel how to complete a task. A macro like the one shown in Figure 2-30 is used to automate routine workbook tasks such as entering new data into a worksheet. Macros are almost a necessity for worksheets that are built to be used by people who know little or nothing about computers and worksheets.

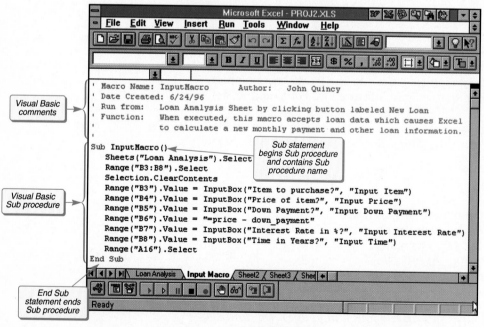

For example, in the previous section new loan data was entered to calculate new loan information. However, the user who enters the data must know what cells to select and how much loan data is required to obtain the desired results. To facilitate entering the loan data, a worksheet and macro can be set up so the user simply clicks a button to execute the macro. The instructions that make up the macro (Figure 2-30) then guide the user through entering the required loan data in the range B3:B8.

FIGURE 2-30

Visual Basic Statements

Visual Basic for Applications is a powerful programming language available with Excel that you can use to carry out most of the workbook activities. Visual Basic statements (or **Visual Basic code**) are entered on a **module sheet**. **Visual Basic statements** are instructions to Excel. In the case of Project 2, all the statements are entered into a single **Sub procedure**. A Sub procedure begins with a **Sub statement** and ends with an **End Sub statement** (Figure 2-30).

The Sub statement includes the name of the Sub procedure. This Sub procedure name is important because it is used later to run the macro. In Project 2, the Sub procedure name used is InputMacro, but it could be any name with fewer than 40 characters.

Remark statements begin with the word **Rem** or an apostrophe ('). In Figure 2-30, there are six remark lines prior to the Sub statement. These remarks contain overall Sub procedure documentation, and therefore, are optionally placed above the Sub statement. Rem statements have no effect on the execution of a macro.

This project is concerned with using the seven Visual Basic statements and one Visual Basic function listed in Table 2-2. **InputBox** is a **function**, instead of a statement because it returns a value to the Sub procedure.

▶ **TABLE 2-2**

VISUAL BASIC STATMENTS*	DESCRIPTION
Rem or '	Initiates a comment for human consumption
Sub name ()	Begins a Sub procedure
Sheets("sheet name").Select	Selects the worksheet to affect
Range("range").Select	Selects a range
Selection.ClearContents	Clears the selected range
Range("cell").Value	Assigns the value following the equal sign to the cell
Inputbox("Message", "Title of Dialog Box)	Displays *Message* in a dialog box with the title *Title of Dialog Box*
End Sub	Ends the Sub procedure

Planning a Macro

When you execute a macro, Excel steps through the Visual Basic statements one at a time beginning at the top of the Sub procedure. Excel bypasses any statements that begin with Remark, Rem, or an apostrophe ('). Thus, when you plan a macro you should remember that the order in which you place the statements in the Sub procedure determines the sequence of execution.

Once you know what you want the macro to do, write it out on paper. Before entering the macro into the computer, desk-check it. Put yourself in the position of Excel and step through the instructions and see how it affects the worksheet. Testing a macro before entering it is an important part of the development process and is called **desk-checking.**

You should add comments before each Sub procedure because they help you remember the purpose of the macro at a later date.

Inserting a Module Sheet

You write a macro on a module sheet, which is a blank sheet with no cells. You insert a module sheet by choosing the **Macro command** on the Insert menu. The following steps show how to insert a module sheet.

TO INSERT A MODULE SHEET ▼

STEP 1 ►

With the Loan Analysis worksheet on the screen choose the Macro command from the Insert menu.

Excel displays a cascading menu (Figure 2-31).

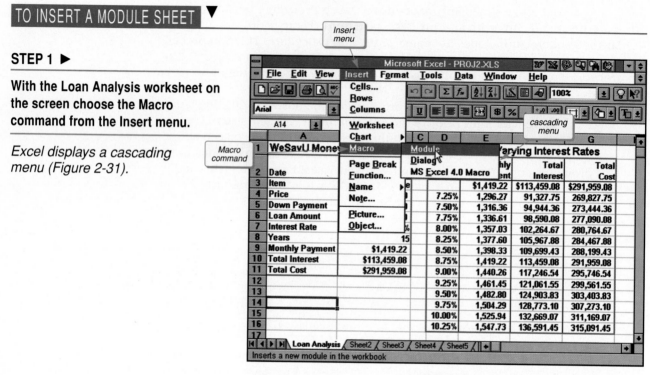

FIGURE 2-31

STEP 2 ►

Choose the Module command from the cascading menu.

*Excel inserts a module sheet with the name Module1 on its tab (Figure 2-32). The insertion point is in column 1 of the first line. The **Visual Basic toolbar** displays. If the Visual Basic toolbar does not display, point to any toolbar, click the right mouse button, and choose Visual Basic from the shortcut menu. If necessary, drag the Visual Basic toolbar below the tabs.*

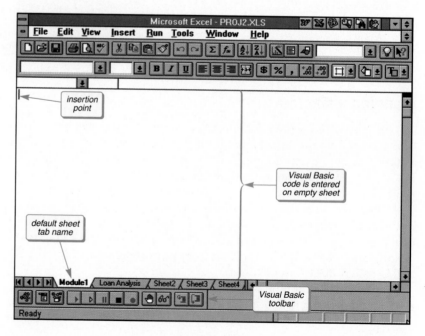

FIGURE 2-32

Entering the Macro on the Module Sheet

You enter a macro by typing the lines of Visual Basic code (statements) the same way you would if you were using word processing software. The macro editor is a full-screen editor. Thus, you can move the insertion point to previous lines to make corrections. At the end of a line, press the ENTER key or use the DOWN ARROW key to move to the next line. If you make a mistake in a statement and notice it, use the arrow keys and the DELETE or BACKSPACE key to correct it.

Each time you type a line and move the insertion point to the next line, Excel checks the syntax of the statement. If you overlook an error, such as a missing parenthesis, Excel displays the line in red and also displays a dialog box to alert you that the previous statement is in error. When you are finished entering the macro, move to another sheet by clicking a sheet tab.

TO ENTER A MACRO ON A MODULE SHEET ▼

STEP 1 ▶

Type the six Rem statements as shown in Figure 2-33.

Excel automatically displays the remark lines in green after you press the ENTER key or DOWN ARROW key.

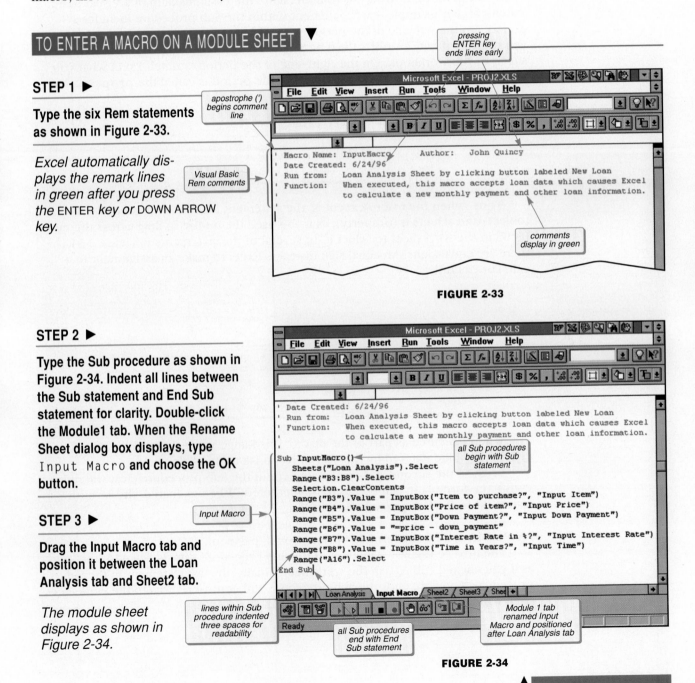

FIGURE 2-33

STEP 2 ▶

Type the Sub procedure as shown in Figure 2-34. Indent all lines between the Sub statement and End Sub statement for clarity. Double-click the Module1 tab. When the Rename Sheet dialog box displays, type Input Macro and choose the OK button.

STEP 3 ▶

Drag the Input Macro tab and position it between the Loan Analysis tab and Sheet2 tab.

The module sheet displays as shown in Figure 2-34.

FIGURE 2-34

More About Macros and Visual Basic Statements

When the module sheet is active, Excel displays a Visual Basic toolbar docked at the bottom of the screen. Figure 2-35 describes the function of each button. Once you begin writing macros on your own, you will find these buttons to be handy, especially for testing macros.

For more information on the Visual Basic toolbar, choose the Search for Help on command from the Help menu. When the Search dialog box displays, type `Visual Basic toolbar` in the top box. Choose the Show Topic button. Select Visual Basic Toolbar in the bottom box and choose the Go To button. Close the Help window when you are finished.

There is a much more to Visual Basic for Applications than is presented here. Your central focus, however, is to understand the basic makeup of a Visual Basic statement. For example, each statement within the Sub procedure includes a period. On the left side of the period you tell Excel the object on the worksheet you want to affect. An **object** can be a cell, a range, a chart, a button, the worksheet, or the workbook. On the right side of the period, you tell Excel what you want to do to the object. The right side of the period is called the **property**. For example,

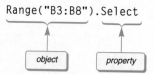

Thus, when the macro executes, the statement identifies the range B3:B8 (object) and selects it (property), as if you used the mouse to drag across the range B3:B8 in the worksheet to select it. In several of the statements in Figure 2-34, there are equal signs. An equal sign instructs Excel to make an assignment to a cell. For example,

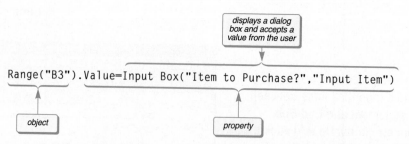

When executed as part of the macro, this Range.Value statement assigns to cell B3 the value entered by the user in response to the dialog box.

Because the second and third statement in the Sub procedure clear the range B3:B8, the formula in cell B6 has to be reentered. When executed, the seventh statement in the Sub procedure:

```
Range("B6").Value = "=price - down_payment"
```

reenters in cell B6 the formula =price - down_payment.

The next to the last statement in the Sub procedure selects cell A16, the same as if you clicked cell A16 in the worksheet. Finally, the last statement in the Sub procedure, End Sub, ends the Sub procedure and control returns to the worksheet from which the Sub procedure was executed.

For additional information on Visual Basic statements, select the Help menu and choose the Contents command. Choose Programming with Visual Basic by clicking it. You can also choose the Examples and Demos command on the Help menu, and then choose Using Visual Basic.

Using a macro is a two-step process. First, you enter the macro on a module sheet as was done earlier in this project. Next, you execute it. There are several ways to execute a macro. For example, you can click the **Run Macro button** on the Visual Basic toolbar (Figure 2-35). Another way is to create a button on the worksheet or on a toolbar, assign the macro to it, and then click the button. This project details the steps to assign a macro to a button on the worksheet.

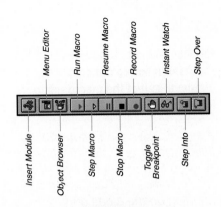

FIGURE 2-35

▶ ADDING A BUTTON TO THE WORKSHEET TO EXECUTE A MACRO

To create a button, you use the **Create Button button** on the Drawing toolbar. You size and locate a button in the same way you would a chart. You then assign the macro to it by using the name in the Sub statement (InputMacro). Finally, you change the name on the button by editing it. The following steps show how to create a button and assign to it the macro InputMacro. Recall, that InputMacro was the name placed earlier in the Sub statement.

TO ADD A BUTTON TO THE WORKSHEET AND ASSIGN A MACRO TO IT ▼

STEP 1 ▶

Click the Loan Analysis tab to activate the worksheet. Click the Drawing button on the Standard toolbar. Dock the Drawing toolbar at the bottom of the screen.

STEP 2 ▶

Click the Create Button button on the Drawing toolbar. Drag the mouse pointer from the top left corner of cell A13 to the lower right corner of cell A14.

Excel draws a light border around the button area (Figure 2-36).

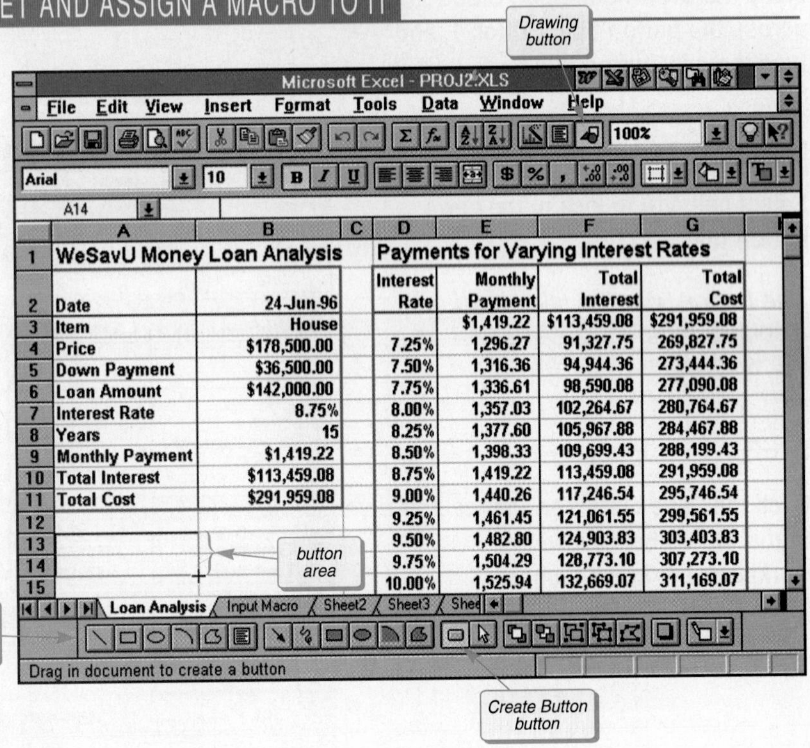

FIGURE 2-36

STEP 3 ▶

Release the left mouse button. When the Assign Macro dialog box displays, select the macro name InputMacro.

*Excel displays the button with the title Button 1 and also displays the **Assign Macro dialog box** (Figure 2-37). Notice that the button has handles on the sides and a shaded border. The handles and shaded border indicate you can resize and relocate the button on the worksheet after the Assign Macro dialog box is closed.*

STEP 4 ▶

Choose the OK button in the Assign Macro dialog box. Click the Drawing button on the Standard toolbar to close the Drawing toolbar. Drag across the button title, Button 1, and type the new button title New Loan

STEP 5 ▶

Select cell A16 to lock in the new button title.

The button with the title New Loan displays in the range A13:A14 on the worksheet (Figure 2-38).

STEP 6 ▶

Click the Save button on the Standard toolbar to save the workbook using the filename PROJ2.XLS.

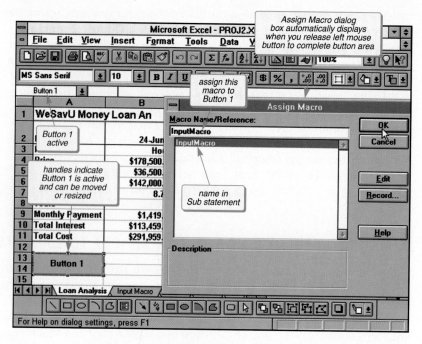

FIGURE 2-37

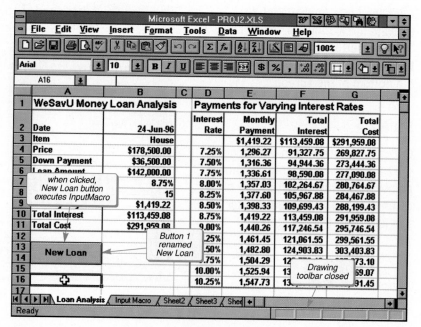

FIGURE 2-38

If you want to resize, relocate, or change the name of the button any time after Step 6, hold down the CTRL key and click the button. Once the button is surrounded by the shaded border and handles, you can modify it. You can also choose the **Assign Macro command** from the Tools menu or shortcut menu to assign a different macro to the button. When you finish editing the button, select any cell to deselect it.

EXECUTING THE MACRO

Follow the steps below to enter the loan data: Item — 25' Cabin Cruiser; Price — $32,550.00; Down Payment — $8,250.00; Interest Rate — 10.25%; Years — 7. You should be aware that when the macro executes, the second and third statements clear the range. Thus, any formula in the worksheet that includes the operation of division may result in the display of the diagnostic message **#DIV/0!** in the cell.

TO EXECUTE THE MACRO AND ENTER NEW LOAN DATA ▼

STEP 1 ▶

Click the New Loan button. When Excel displays the Input Item dialog box with the prompt message, Item to purchase?, type 25' Cabin Cruiser (Figure 2-39).

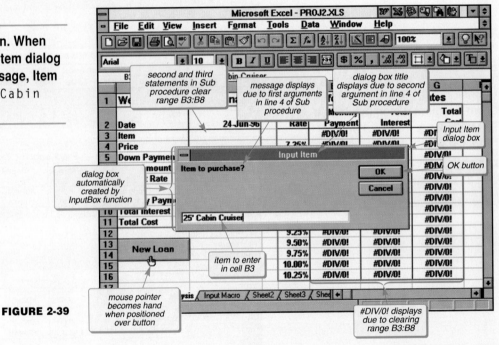

FIGURE 2-39

STEP 2 ▶

Choose the OK button in the Input Item dialog box or press the ENTER key. When Excel displays the Input Price dialog box with the prompt message, Price of item?, type 32550 (Figure 2-40).

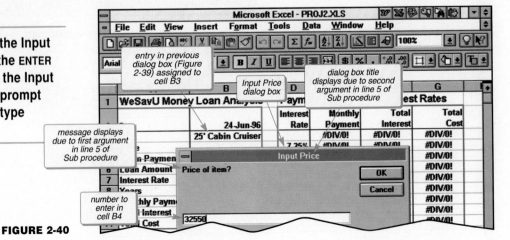

FIGURE 2-40

STEP 3 ▶

Choose the OK button in the Input Price dialog box. When Excel displays the Input Down Payment dialog box with the prompt message, Down Payment?, type 8250 (Figure 2-41).

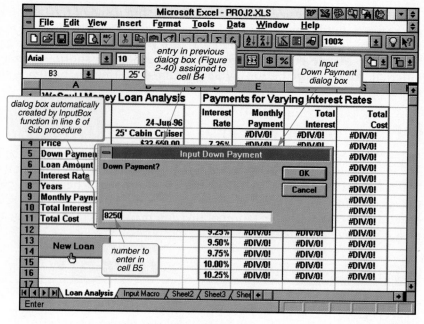

FIGURE 2-41

STEP 4 ▶

Choose the OK button in the Input Down Payment dialog box. When Excel displays the Input Interest Rate dialog box with the prompt message, Interest Rate in %?, type 10.25% (Figure 2-42).

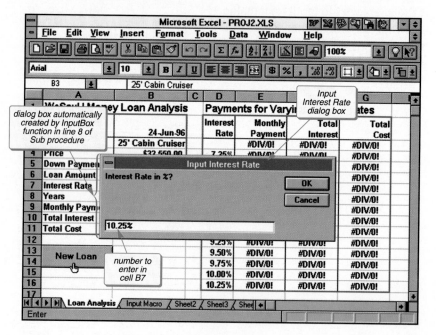

FIGURE 2-42

STEP 5 ►

Choose the OK button in the Input Interest Rate dialog box. When Excel displays the Input Time dialog box with the prompt message, Time in Years?, type 7 (Figure 2-43).

STEP 6 ►

Choose the OK button in the Input Time dialog box.

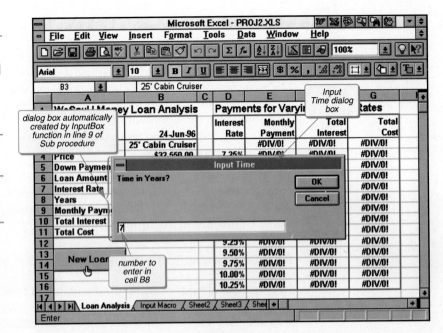

FIGURE 2-43

Excel recalculates the loan information for the new loan data, and cell A16 is the active cell (Figure 2-44). Figure 2-44 shows that the monthly payment is $406.55 (cell B9), the total interest is $9,850.59 (cell B10), and the total cost is $42,400.59 (cell B11) for the 25' Cabin Cruiser. In addition, Excel automatically recalculates new results in the data table (range D3:G16) for the new loan data.

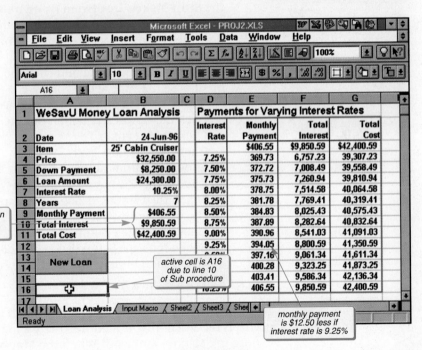

FIGURE 2-44

► RECORDING A MACRO

Excel has a **Macro Recorder** that creates a macro automatically from the actions you perform and commands you choose. The MacroRecorder can be turned on, during which time it records your activities, and then turned off to terminate the recording. What you do during the time it is turned on can be **played back** (executed) as often as you want. Thus, the Macro Recorder is like a tape recorder in that it records everything you do to a workbook over a period of time. Once the macro is recorded, you can do one of the following to play it back.

1. Assign the macro to a button on the worksheet as was done earlier in this project and click the button.
2. Assign the macro to a custom button on a toolbar and click the button.
3. Choose the **Macro command** on the Tools menu.
4. Click the Run Macro button (▶) on the Visual Basic toolbar.
5. Add a command to the Tools menu that plays back the macro and then choose the command.
6. Assign the macro to a graphic, such as a chart, so when you click it, the macro plays back.

The following series of steps shows you how to record a macro to print the Loan Analysis worksheet in landscape orientation and then return the orientation to portrait. To guard against macro catastrophes, the workbook is saved before invoking the Macro Recorder.

TO RECORD A MACRO TO PRINT THE LOAN ANALYSIS WORKSHEET IN LANDSCAPE

Step 1: Click the Save button on the Standard toolbar to save the workbook using the filename PROJ2.XLS.

Step 2: From the Tools menu, choose Record Macro, and then choose Record New Macro from the cascading menu.

Step 3: When the Record New Macro dialog box displays, type the macro name PrintLandscape in the Macro Name box.

Step 4: Choose the OK button in the Record New Macro dialog box. Excel displays the **Stop Macro button** in its own toolbar and displays the message "Recording" on the status bar at the bottom of the screen. The Macro Recorder is on. Whatever actions you do are recorded.

Step 5: Complete the following actions:
   a. Point to the menu bar and click the right mouse button.
   b. Choose the Page Setup command.
   c. When the Page Setup dialog box displays, click the Page tab.
   d. Click the Landscape option button.
   e. Click the Sheet tab.
   f. Click the Gridlines box.
   g. Choose the Print button.
   h. Choose the OK button in the Print dialog box.
   i. When the Printing dialog box disappears, point to the menu bar and click the right mouse button.
   j. Choose the Page Setup command
   k. When the Page Setup dialog box displays, click the Page tab, click the Portrait option button, and then choose the OK button.

Step 6: Click the Stop Macro button.

Notice that you are able to step through the actions and see the results as the macro is recorded. If you recorded the wrong actions, select the Tools menu, and choose the Macro command. When the **Macro dialog box** displays, select the name of the macro (PrintLandscape) and choose the Delete button and then start recording again.

Playing Back a Recorded Macro

The following steps show you how to play back the recorded macro Print-Landscape by choosing the Macro command on the Tools menu.

TO PLAY BACK A RECORDED MACRO

Step 1: From the Tools menu, choose the Macro command.

Step 2: When the Macro dialog box displays, select the macro name PrintLandscape in the Macro Name/Reference box.

Step 3: Choose the Run button (▶) in the Macro dialog box.

Step 4: Click the Save button to save the workbook using the filename PROJ2.XLS.

The Excel window blinks as the macro is executed. The report prints as shown in Figure 2-45.

Loan Analysis

WeSavU Money Loan Analysis	
Date	20-Feb-95
Item	25' Cabin Cruiser
Price	$32,550.00
Down Payment	$8,250.00
Loan Amount	$24,300.00
Interest Rate	10.25%
Years	7
Monthly Payment	$406.55
Total Interest	$9,850.59
Total Cost	$42,400.59

Payments for Varying Interest Rates

Interest Rate	Monthly Payment	Total Interest	Total Cost
	$406.55	$9,850.59	$42,400.59
7.25%	369.73	6,757.23	39,307.23
7.50%	372.72	7,008.49	39,558.49
7.75%	375.73	7,260.94	39,810.94
8.00%	378.75	7,514.58	40,064.58
8.25%	381.78	7,769.41	40,319.41
8.50%	384.83	8,025.43	40,575.43
8.75%	387.89	8,282.64	40,832.64
9.00%	390.96	8,541.03	41,091.03
9.25%	394.05	8,800.59	41,350.59
9.50%	397.16	9,061.34	41,611.34
9.75%	400.28	9,323.25	41,873.25
10.00%	403.41	9,586.34	42,136.34
10.25%	406.55	9,850.59	42,400.59

FIGURE 2-45

You can view the macro that the Macro Recorder created by clicking the right tab scrolling button, and when the Module1 tab appears, click it. As you can see from the Module 1 sheet, the PrintLandscape macro is 70 Visual Basic statements long. Also notice when the Module1 sheet is active, the Visual Basic toolbar appears at the bottom of the screen. Click the Loan Analysis tab if it is not active.

For more information on using the Macro Recorder, choose the Search for Help on command from the Help menu. Type `macro recorder` in the top box and choose the Show Topics button. Select Overview of Writing and Editing a Macro in the lower box and choose the Go To button.

▶ GOAL SEEKING TO DETERMINE THE DOWN PAYMENT FOR A SPECIFIC MONTHLY PAYMENT

If you know the result you want a formula to produce, you can use **goal seeking** to determine the value of a cell on which the formula depends. The example on the following page uses the Goal Seek command to determine the down payment so the monthly payment for the 25' Cabin Cruiser will be exactly $300.00.

TO DETERMINE THE DOWN PAYMENT FOR A SPECIFIC MONTHLY PAYMENT ▼

STEP 1 ▶

Select cell B9, the cell with the monthly payment amount. From the Tools menu, choose the Goal Seek command. When the Goal Seek dialog box displays, enter 300 in the To value box. Select the By changing cell box. In the worksheet, use the mouse pointer to select cell B5.

The Goal Seek dialog box displays as shown in Figure 2-46. Notice in the dialog box that the first entry indicates the cell you want to seek a goal on (cell B9), the second box indicates the specific value you are seeking ($300.00), and the third box indicates the cell to vary (cell B5).

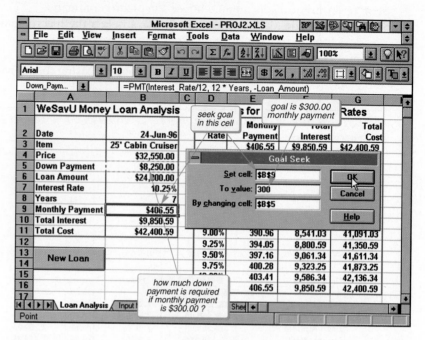

FIGURE 2-46

STEP 2 ▶

Choose the OK button in the Goal Seek dialog box.

Excel displays the Goal Seek Status dialog box indicating it has found an answer. Excel also changes the monthly payment in cell B9 to the goal ($300.00) and changes the down payment in cell B5 to $14,618.83 (Figure 2-47).

STEP 3 ▶

Choose the OK button in the Goal Seek Status dialog box.

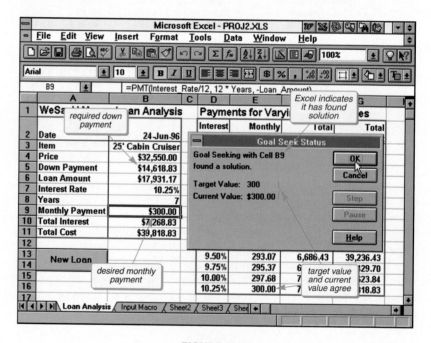

FIGURE 2-47

Thus, according to Figure 2-47, if the 25' Cabin Cruiser costs $32,550.00, the interest rate is 10.25%, the term is 7 years, and you want to pay exactly $300.00 a month, then you must pay a down payment of $14,618.83.

Notice in this goal seeking example, it is not required that the cell to vary be directly referenced in the formula or function. For example, the monthly payment formula in cell B9 is =PMT(interest_rate / 12, 12 * years, loan_amount). There is no mention of the down payment in the PMT function. However, because the loan amount, which is referenced in the PMT function, is based on the down payment, Excel is able to goal seek on the monthly payment by varying the down payment.

You can reset the worksheet to the values displayed prior to goal seeking by choosing the Cancel button while the Goal Seek Status dialog box is on the screen. If the dialog box is no longer on the screen, you can reset the worksheet by clicking the Undo button on the Standard toolbar or selecting the Edit menu and choosing the Undo Goal Seek command. The Undo Goal Seek command is only available until a new entry is made into the worksheet.

▶ USING SCENARIO MANAGER TO ANALYZE DATA

An alternative to using a data table to analyze worksheet data is to use Excel's Scenario Manager. The **Scenario Manager** allows you to record and save different sets of what-if assumptions (data values) called **scenarios**. For example, earlier in this project (Figure 2-29 on page E92), a monthly payment of $1,419.22 was determined for the following loan data: Item — House; Price —$178,500.00; Down Payment — $36,500.00; Interest Rate — 8.75%; and Years —15. One scenario for the house loan might be, "What is the monthly payment, total interest, and total cost if the interest rate is the same (8. 75%) but the number of years changes from 15 to 30?" Another scenario might be: "What is the monthly payment, total interest, and total cost if the interest rate is increased by 1% to 9.75% and the number of years remains at 15?" Each set of values represents a what-if assumption. The primary uses of Scenario Manager are to:

1. Create different scenarios with multiple sets of changing cells.
2. Build a summary worksheet that contains the different scenarios.
3. View the results of each scenario on your worksheet.

The following sections show how to use the Scenario Manager for each of the procedures just listed. Once you create the scenarios, you can instruct Excel to build the summary worksheet. The summary worksheet the Scenario Manager generates is actually an outlined worksheet (Figure 2-48) you can print and manipulate like any other worksheet. An **outlined worksheet** is one that contains symbols (buttons) above and to the left that allow you to collapse and expand rows and columns.

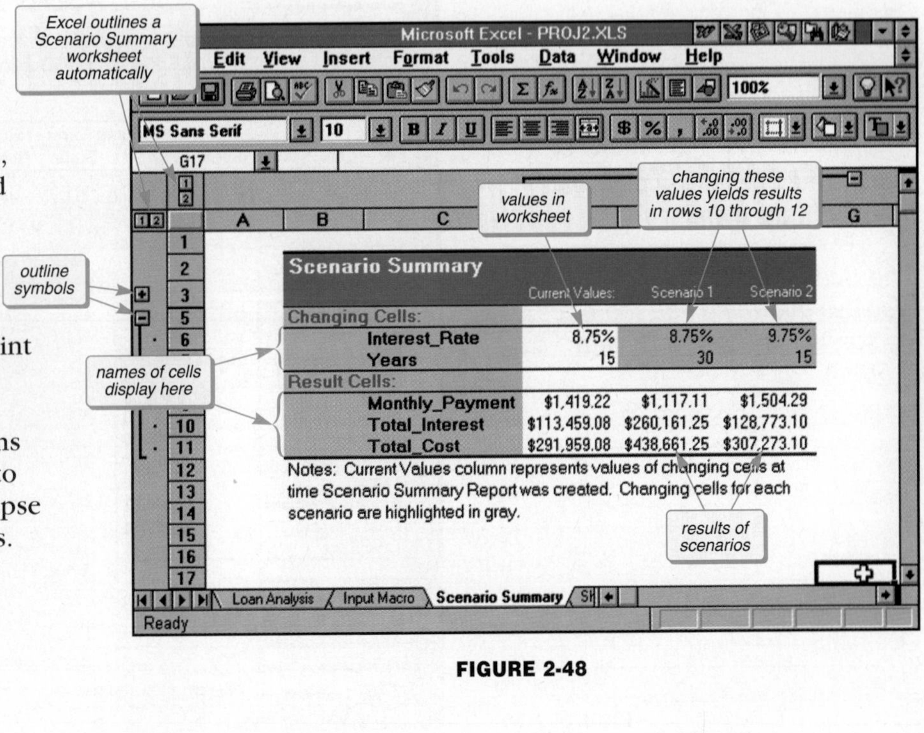

FIGURE 2-48

Before illustrating the Scenario Manager, click the New Loan button and enter the loan data for the house as shown in Figure 2-29 on page E92.

The following steps create the two scenarios and the Scenario Summary worksheet shown in Figure 2-48 on the previous page by using the **Scenarios command** on the Tools menu. The worksheet illustrates the monthly payment, total interest, and total cost for two scenarios and for the current values in the Loan Analysis worksheet. The current interest rate equals 8.75% and the current years equal 15 (Figure 2-29). The first scenario sets the interest rate to 8.75% and the number of years to 30. The second scenario sets the interest rate to 9.75% and the number of years to 15.

TO CREATE SCENARIOS AND A SCENARIO SUMMARY WORKSHEET ▼

STEP 1 ▶

With the loan data for the house in Figure 2-29 entered, select the Tools menu (Figure 2-49).

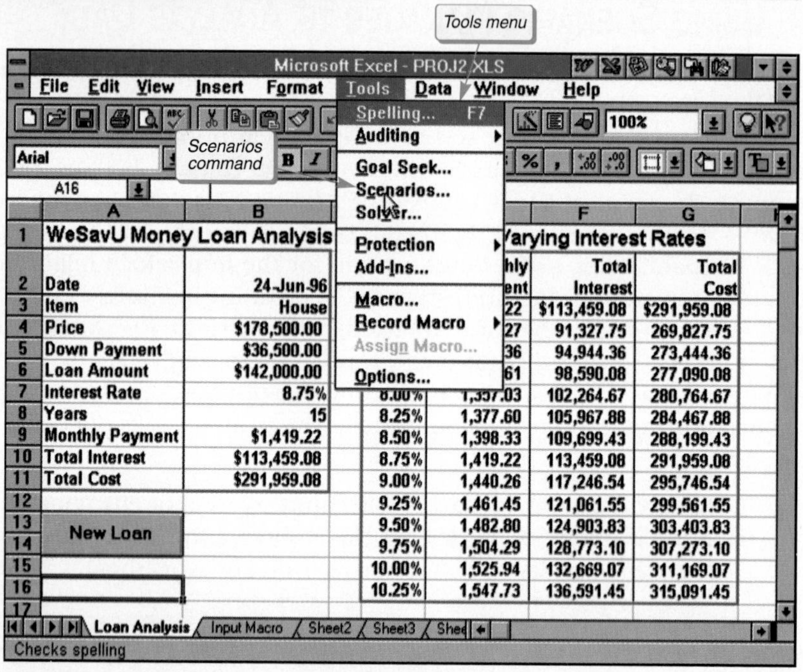

FIGURE 2-49

STEP 2 ▶

Choose the Scenarios command from the Tools menu.

The Scenario Manager dialog box displays informing you there are no scenarios defined (Figure 2-50).

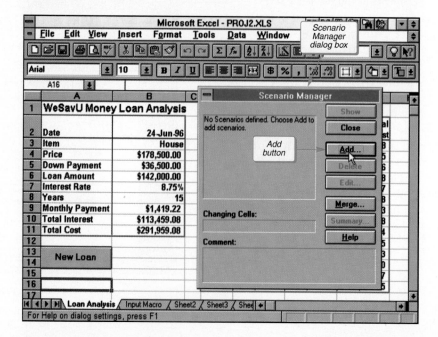

FIGURE 2-50

STEP 3 ▶

Choose the Add button to add a scenario. When the Add Scenario dialog box displays, type `Scenario 1` in the Scenario Name box, click in the Changing Cells box, and drag over the range B7:B8 in the worksheet.

Excel displays a marquis around the cells in the worksheet to change (interest rate in cell B7 and years in cell B8) and assigns the range B7:B8 to the Changing Cells box in the Add Scenario dialog box (Figure 2-51).

FIGURE 2-51

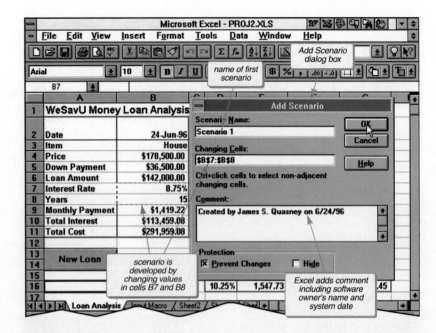

STEP 4 ▶

Choose the OK button in the Add Scenario dialog box. When the Scenario Values dialog box displays, select the Years box and type `30`

*The **Scenario Values dialog box** displays as shown in Figure 2-52.*

FIGURE 2-52

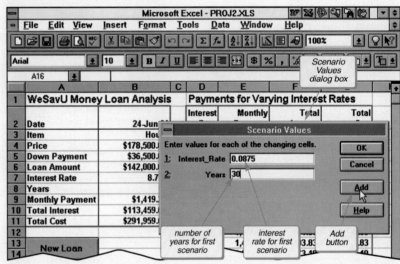

STEP 5 ▶

Choose the Add button in the Scenario Values dialog box to add the second scenario. When the Add Scenario dialog box displays, type `Scenario 2` in the Scenario Name box.

The Add Scenario dialog box displays as shown in Figure 2-53. Notice that Excel automatically assigns the range $B$7:$B$8 to the Changing Cells box because this range is used in the prior scenario.

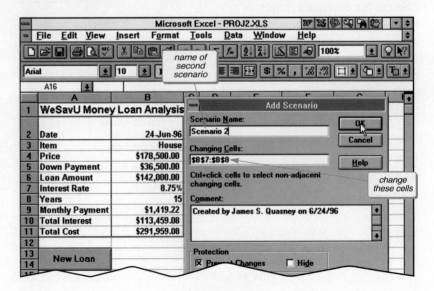

FIGURE 2-53

STEP 6 ►

Choose the OK button in the Add Scenario dialog box. When the Scenario Values dialog box displays, enter 9.75% in the Interest_Rate box and 15 in the Years box.

The Scenario Values dialog box displays as shown in Figure 2-54.

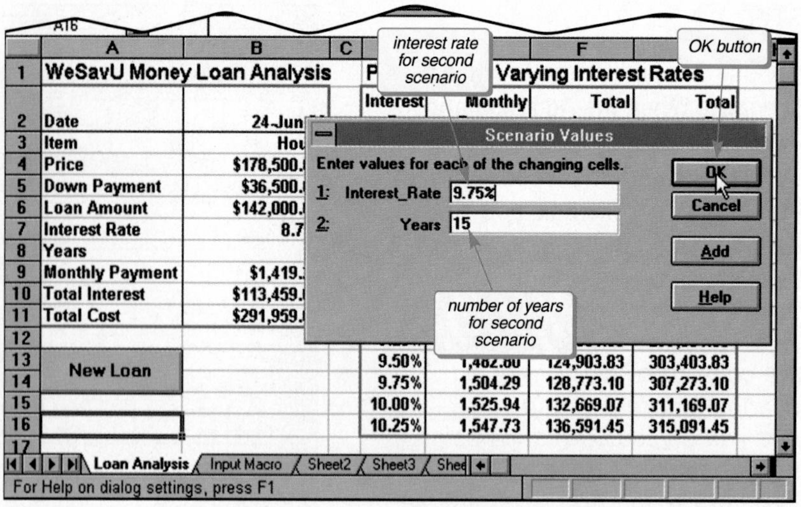

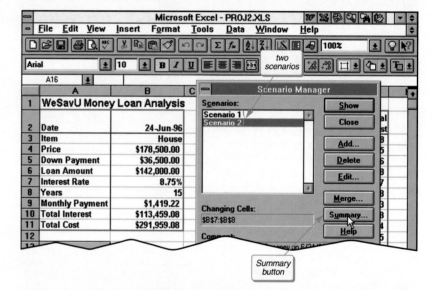

FIGURE 2-54

STEP 7 ►

Because this is the last scenario to create, choose the OK button in the Scenario Values dialog box.

The Scenario Manager dialog box displays with the two named scenarios (Figure 2-55).

FIGURE 2-55

STEP 8 ►

Choose the Summary button (Summary...) in the Scenario Manager dialog box. When the Scenario Summary dialog box displays, click in the Result Cells box and drag over the range B9:B11 to indicate the cells you want results for.

*The **Scenario Summary dialog box** displays as shown in Figure 2-56.*

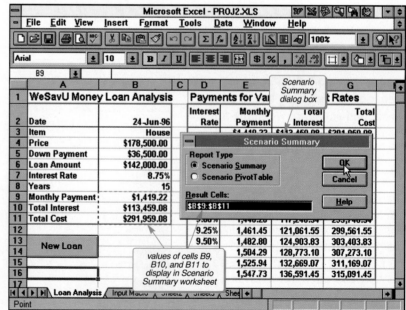

FIGURE 2-56

STEP 9 ▶

Choose the OK button in the Scenario Summary dialog box. Drag the Scenario Summary tab to the immediate right of the Input Macro tab.

The Scenario Summary worksheet displays as shown in Figure 2-57.

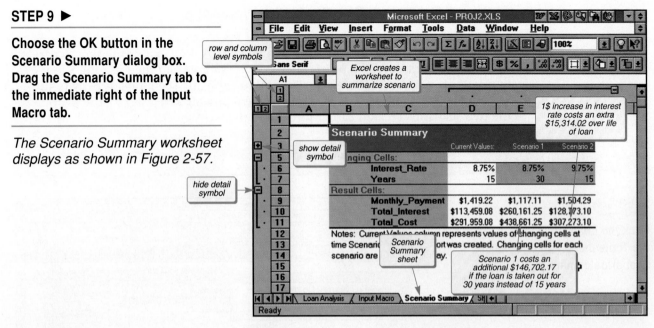

FIGURE 2-57

The Scenario Summary worksheet in Figure 2-57 shows the results of the current values (column D) in the Loan Analysis worksheet and two scenarios in columns E and F. Compare the Scenario 1 column to the Current Values column. In the Scenario 1 column, the interest rate is the same as in the Current Values column, but the length of time is 30 years instead of 15 years. Because the loan is for twice the length of time, the monthly payment decreases by $302.11 per month, but the total cost of the loan increases by $146,702.17 to $438,661.25. In the Scenario 2 column, the number of years is the same as the Current Values column, but the interest rate is 1% greater. The 1% change increases the monthly payment by $85.07 per month and the total cost of the house to $307,273.10 or $15,314.02 more than the loan data in the Current Values column.

Working with an Outlined Worksheet

Excel automatically outlines the Scenario Summary worksheet. The **outline symbols** display above the worksheet and to the left (Figure 2-57). You click the outline symbols to expand or collapse the worksheet. For example, if you click the **show detail symbol** (▣) Excel displays additional rows or columns that are summarized on the displayed row or column. If you click a **hide detail symbol** (▤), Excel hides any detail rows that extend through the length of the corresponding **row level bar** (▭) or **column level bar** (▯). You can also expand or collapse a worksheet by clicking the **row level symbol** (▨) or **column level symbol** (▨) above and to the left of row title 1. An outline is especially useful when working with large worksheets. To remove an outline, choose the **Group and Outline command** on the Data menu, then choose the **Clear Outline command** from the cascading menu.

Applying Scenarios Directly to the Worksheet

When you work with scenarios, it is not necessary to create the Scenario Summary worksheet shown in Figure 2-57 on page E109. You can create the scenarios following the first seven steps of the previous example and then use the Show button in the Scenario Manager dialog box to apply the scenarios directly to the worksheet for which they were created. The following steps show how to apply the two scenarios created earlier directly to the worksheet.

TO APPLY SCENARIOS DIRECTLY TO THE WORKSHEET ▼

STEP 1 ▶

Click the Loan Analysis tab. Select the Tools menu and choose the Scenarios command.

The Scenario Manager dialog box displays (Figure 2-58).

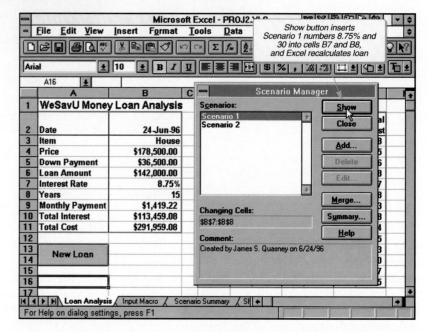

FIGURE 2-58

STEP 2 ▶

With Scenario 1 selected in the Scenarios box, choose the Show button (⬛ Show ⬛).

Excel inserts the numbers from Scenario 1 into the worksheet and recalculates all formulas (Figure 2-59). Notice that the entries in the range B7:B11 have changed so they agree with the results in column E of the Scenario Summary Report worksheet shown in Figure 2-57 on the previous page.

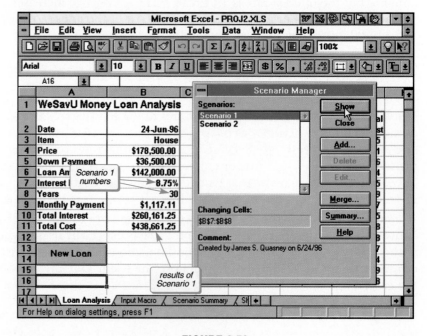

FIGURE 2-59

STEP 3 ▶

Select Scenario 2 in the Scenarios box in the Scenario Manager dialog box. Choose the Show button.

Excel inserts the numbers from Scenario 2 into the worksheet and recalculates all formulas (Figure 2-60). Here again, the results in the worksheet agree exactly with column F of the Scenario Summary worksheet shown in Figure 2-57 on page E109.

STEP 4 ▶

Choose the Close button in the Scenario Manager dialog box. Click the Save button on the Standard toolbar.

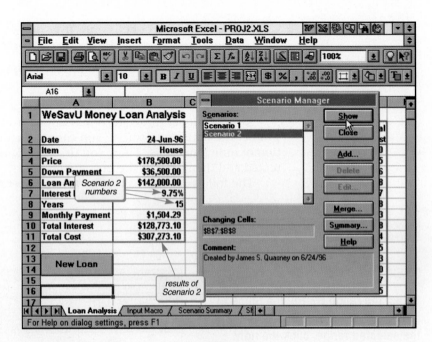

FIGURE 2-60

You can undo the scenario results by clicking the Undo button on the Standard toolbar or choosing the Undo Show command on the Edit menu. If you want, you can then choose the Redo Show command on the Edit menu to change the worksheet back to the results of the scenario.

Scenario Manager is an important what-if tool for organizing your assumptions. Using Scenario Manager, you can define different scenarios with up to 32 changing cells per scenario. Once you have entered the scenarios, you can show them one by one as illustrated in the previous example or you can create the Scenario Summary worksheet.

Before moving on to the next section, change the value in cell B7 to 8.75% and the value in cell B8 to 15. The worksheet should generate the results shown in Figure 2-58.

▶ PROTECTING THE WORKSHEET

When you build a worksheet that will be used by people who know little or nothing about computers and worksheets, it is important to protect the cells in the worksheet that you don't want changed, such as cells that contain text and formulas. In the Loan Analysis worksheet (see Figure 2-61 on the next page), there are only five cells that the user should be allowed to change: the item in cell B3; the price in cell B4; the down payment in cell B5; the interest rate in cell B7; and the years in cell B8. Also, because of the way the macro assigned to the New Loan button works, cell B6 should be unprotected. The remaining cells in the worksheet should be protected so that they cannot be changed by the user.

When you create a new worksheet, all the cells are unprotected. **Unprotected cells**, or **unlocked cells**, are cells with values you can change at any time while **protected cells**, or **locked cells**, are cells that you cannot change. If a cell is protected and the user attempts to change its value, Excel displays a dialog box with a message indicating the cells are protected.

You should protect cells only after the worksheet has been fully tested and displays the correct results. Protecting a worksheet is a two-step process:

1. Select the cells you want to leave unprotected and change their cell protection settings to unprotected.
2. Protect the entire worksheet.

At first glance, these steps may appear to be backwards. However, once you protect the entire worksheet, you cannot change anything including the protection of individual cells. Thus, you first deal with the cells you want to leave unprotected and then protect the entire worksheet.

The following steps show how to protect the Loan Analysis worksheet.

TO PROTECT A WORKSHEET ▼

STEP 1 ▶

Select the range B3:B8, the range to unprotect. With the mouse pointer in the selected range, click the right mouse button.

Excel displays the shortcut menu (Figure 2-61).

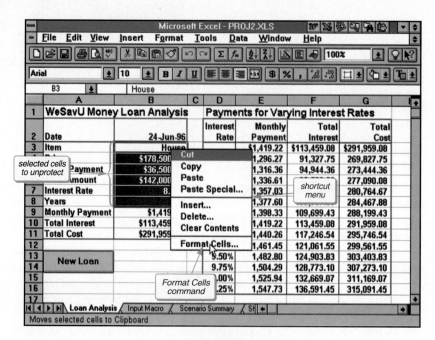

FIGURE 2-61

STEP 2 ▶

Choose the Format Cells command. When the Format Cells dialog box displays, click the Protection tab. Click the Locked check box.

*The **Protection tab** in the Format Cells dialog box displays with the x removed from the **Locked check box** (Figure 2-62).*

STEP 3 ▶

Choose the OK button in the Format Cells dialog box.

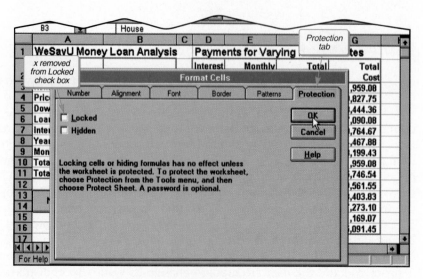

FIGURE 2-62

STEP 4 ▶

Select the Tools menu. Choose the Protection command.

Excel displays the Tools menu and cascading menu (Figure 2-63).

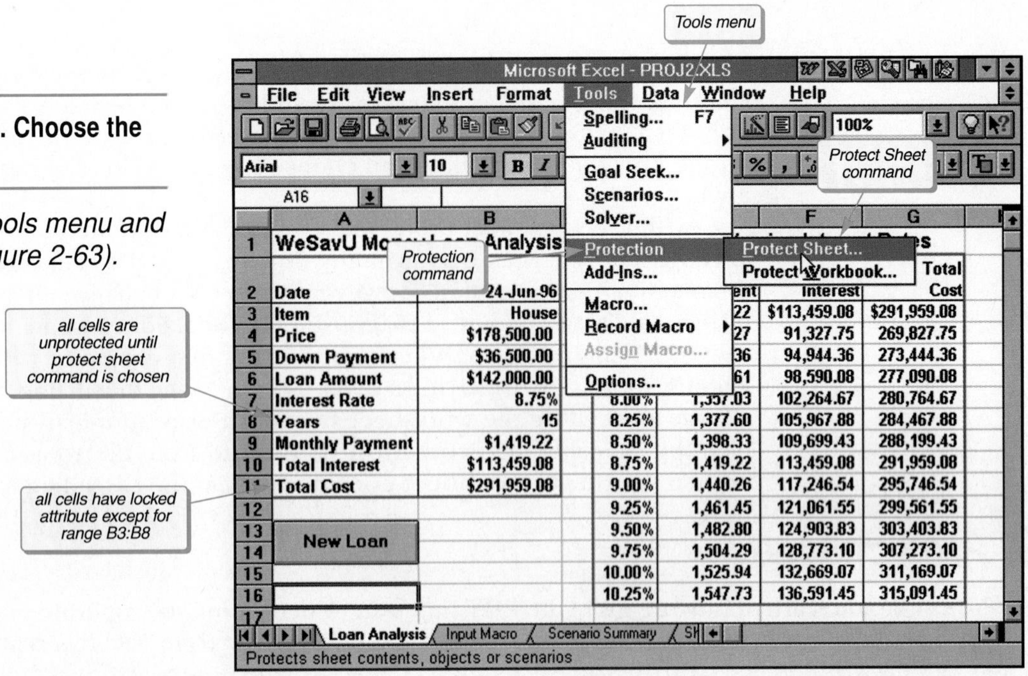

all cells are unprotected until protect sheet command is chosen

all cells have locked attribute except for range B3:B8

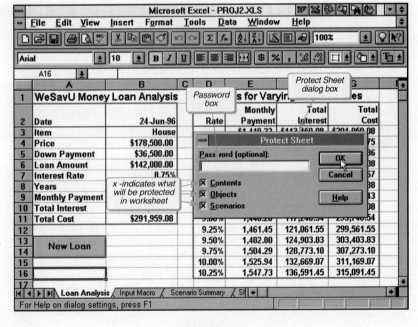

FIGURE 2-63

STEP 5 ▶

Choose the Protect Sheet command from the cascading menu.

*Excel displays the **Protect Sheet dialog box** (Figure 2-64).*

STEP 6 ▶

Choose the OK button in the Protect Sheet dialog box. Click the Save button on the Standard toolbar to save the protected workbook.

All the cells in the worksheet are protected, except for the range B3:B8. The range B3:B8 includes the cells in which you enter new loan data.

FIGURE 2-64

Notice in the Protect Sheet dialog box in Figure 2-64 that you can add a password. You add a **password** when you want to keep others from changing the worksheet from protected to unprotected. You can also click any of the three check boxes (Contents, Objects, and Scenarios) shown in Figure 2-64 to unprotect them. Contents refers to the entries in the worksheet. Objects are charts and buttons. Scenarios refer to those scenarios associated with the worksheet being protected.

The protection only pertains to the active worksheet. If you want to protect additional sheets, select them before you begin the protection process or use the **Protect Workbook command** on the cascading menu that displays (Figure 2-63 on the previous page) when you choose the Protection command from the Tools menu.

With the worksheet protected, you can still execute the macro InputMacro by clicking the New Loan button at any time because the cells referenced (B3:B8) by the macro are unprotected. However, if you try to change any protected cell, Excel displays a dialog box with a diagnostic message. For example, try to change the row title Item in cell A3. When you type the first character with cell A3 selected, Excel responds by displaying a diagnostic message in a dialog box. If you want to change any cells in the worksheet such as titles or formulas, unprotect the document by choosing the **Protection command** from the Tools menu, and then choose the **Unprotect Sheet command** from the cascading menu.

▶ PROJECT SUMMARY

In Project 2, you learned how to apply the PMT function to determine the monthly payment of a loan. The project presented steps and techniques showing you how to analyze data by creating a data table and working with the Scenario Manager. This project also explained how macros are used to automate worksheet tasks. You learned how to build a macro that accepts loan data. Once the macro was built, you used the Create Button button to assign the macro to a button in the worksheet. Using the button, you executed the macro. You also learned how to record a macro and play it back. Finally, you learned how to protect a document so a user can change only the contents of cells that you left unprotected.

▶ KEY TERMS AND INDEX

In Microsoft Excel, you can accomplish a task in a number of ways. The following table provides a quick reference to each task presented in this project with its available options. The commands listed in the Menu column can be executed using either the keyboard or mouse. Many of the commands in the Menu column are also available on the shortcut menu.

Task	Mouse	Menu	Keyboard Shortcuts
Borders	Click Borders button arrow on Formatting toolbar	From Format menu, choose Cells	Press CTRL+1
Create a Button	Click Create Button button on Drawing toolbar		
Create a Data Table		From Data menu, choose Table	
Create a Macro	Click Insert Module button on Visual Basic toolbar		
Create a Scenario Summary Worksheet		From Tools menu, choose Scenarios	
Display the Visual Basic toolbar	Point to any toolbar and click right mouse button, then choose Visual Basic	From Insert menu, choose Macro, then choose Module	
Edit a Button	CTRL+click button to edit		
Name Cells	Click in reference area in formula bar and type name	From Insert menu, choose Name, then choose Create	Press CTRL+SHIFT+F3
Outline a Range	Click Borders button arrow on Formatting toolbar	From Format menu, choose Cells	Press CTRL+SHIFT+&
Protect a Worksheet		From Tools menu, choose Protection, then choose Protect Sheet	
Record a Macro	Click Record Macro button on Visual Basic toolbar	From Tools menu, choose Record Macro, then choose Record New Macro	
Run (or Execute or Play Back) a Macro	Click Run Macro button on Visual Basic toolbar	From Tools menu, choose Macro	
Select a Named Range	Click name in name box in formula bar	From Edit menu, choose Go To	Press F5
Stop Recording a Macro	Click Stop Macro button on Visual Basic toolbar		
Unprotect a Worksheet		From Tools menu, choose Protection, then choose Unprotect Sheet	
Unprotect Cells		From Format menu, choose Cells	

STUDENT ASSIGNMENT 1
True/False

Instructions: Circle T if the statement is true or F if the statement is false.

T F 1. A Visual Basic statement in a macro tells Excel to carry out an activity such as select a cell or clear a selection.
T F 2. You can click a name in the Name box to append the name to a formula you are creating.
T F 3. To efficiently assign a label (such as a row title) in the worksheet to an adjacent cell, select the Insert command, choose the Name command, and then choose the Define command.
T F 4. If cell B4 is named Balance and cell B5 is named Payment, then the formula =B4 - B5 can be written as =Balance - Payment.
T F 5. A data table is a cell that answers what-if questions.
T F 6. The cell you vary in a one-input data table is called the input cell.
T F 7. Use the Open command from the File menu to create a module sheet.
T F 8. A macro is made up of a series of Visual Basic statements.
T F 9. The Visual Basic statement, Selection.ClearContents, is used to clear the selected cell or range of cells.
T F 10. You end a Sub procedure with the End Sub statement.
T F 11. In a Visual Basic Sub procedure, to specify a range in the active worksheet, use the object Range("range").
T F 12. A module sheet has cells similar to a worksheet.
T F 13. Desk-checking refers to checking the Windows desktop.
T F 14. The Create Button button is on the Standard toolbar.
T F 15. To edit a button on the worksheet, hold down the CTRL key and click the button to edit.
T F 16. When executed, the macro function InputBox causes a dialog box to display.
T F 17. The Scenario Manager can be used to organize answers to what-if questions in a worksheet.
T F 18. When you open a new workbook it is unprotected.
T F 19. Select the cells to unprotect after you protect the entire worksheet.
T F 20. If you attempt to change the value of a protected cell, Excel immediately returns control to Windows.

STUDENT ASSIGNMENT 2
Multiple Choice

Instructions: Circle the correct response.

1. A worksheet that summarizes what-if questions is called a _____.
   a. scenario
   b. outlined worksheet
   c. Report worksheet
   d. Scenario Summary worksheet
2. To name a cell, use the _____ command on the Insert menu.
   a. Name
   b. Paste Function
   c. Apply Names
   d. Paste Name
3. When the name of a cell is made up of two or more words, replace the spaces between the words with _____ when you use the name in a formula.
   a. minus signs (-)
   b. number signs (#)
   c. circumflexes (^)
   d. underscores (_)

4. Use the _____ function to determine a monthly payment on a loan.
   a. FV
   b. PMT
   c. PV
   d. NOW

5. If payments are to be made on a monthly basis and the length of the loan is given in years, then _____ for the periods argument in the PMT function.
   a. multiply years by 12
   b. divide years by 12
   c. enter years
   d. multiply years by 365

6. Data tables are usually created _____.
   a. in an unused area of the worksheet
   b. on a toolbar
   c. in a cell
   d. on a chart sheet

7. In a one-input data table, the input cell _____.
   a. must be referenced directly or indirectly in the formula(s) at the top of the data table
   b. is the upper left corner cell of the worksheet
   c. is a range of cells
   d. must be defined on the module sheet

8. In a macro, use the _____ property to assign a value to a cell.
   a. Assign
   b. Clear
   c. Select
   d. Value

9. For a one-input data table to work properly, _____.
   a. the upper left cell must be empty
   b. the input cell must be on another worksheet
   c. the input cell must be blank
   d. the input cell must be defined as the upper left cell in the data table

10. After creating a module sheet, return to the worksheet by _____.
    a. selecting the Window menu
    b. clicking the worksheet tab
    c. choosing the Open command on the File menu
    d. entering the End Sub statement

STUDENT ASSIGNMENT 3
Understanding Functions, Data Analysis, and Worksheet Protection

Instructions: Fill in the correct answers.

1. Write a function to determine the monthly payment (PMT function) on a loan of $75,000.00, over a period of 20 years, at an annual interest rate of 8.4%. Make sure the function returns the monthly payment as a positive number.

   Function: _____

2. Write a function to determine the future value (FV function) of a $100.00 a month investment for 10 years if the interest rate is fixed at 6% and compounded monthly.

   Function: _____

(continued)

STUDENT ASSIGNMENT 3 (continued)

3.   Write a function to determine the present value (PV function) or how much it would cost, for an annuity that pays $500.00 a month for 20 years and pays 8% compounded monthly. Display the cost of the annuity as a positive number by placing a minus sign before the monthly payment.

Function: _____

4.   Explain the purpose of a data table.

_____

_____

_____

5.   Describe what Scenario Manager is used for.

_____

_____

_____

6.   Explain the difference between a protected cell and an unprotected cell. How do you change the contents of a cell that is protected?

_____

_____

_____

STUDENT ASSIGNMENT 4
Understanding Excel Menus and Commands

Instructions: Identify the menu and initial command (command on cascading menu not required) that displays the dialog box that allows you to make the indicated change.

	MENU	COMMAND
1. Name cells	_____	_____
2. Create a data table	_____	_____
3. Create a macro sheet	_____	_____
4. Record a macro	_____	_____
5. Change the macro assigned to a button	_____	_____
6. Protect a worksheet	_____	_____
7. Unprotect cells	_____	_____
8. Draw a color outline	_____	_____
9. Seek a goal for a cell assigned a formula	_____	_____
10. Create a Scenario Summary worksheet	_____	_____

STUDENT ASSIGNMENT 5
Understanding Macro Functions

Instructions: Assume a module sheet is open. In the space provided, write the Visual Basic statement that completes the specified task.

1. Select the range A1:D23 on the worksheet: _____

2. Clear the selected range: _____

3. Assign the formula =B6 - B7 to cell A10 in the worksheet: _____

4. Accept a value from the user and assign it to cell G25 in the worksheet: _____

_____

5. End the Sub procedure: _____

STUDENT ASSIGNMENT 6
Understanding Worksheet Entries

Instructions: Indicate how you would make the suggested corrections.

Part 1: In the worksheet in Figure SA2-6a the monthly payment, total interest, total cost, and data table results display in red within parentheses. The red color and parentheses indicate negative numbers. What would you do to display the results as positive numbers? (**Hint:** Review the formula in the formula bar.)

Change the formula in cell: _____ to _____

FIGURE SA2-6a

(continued)

STUDENT ASSIGNMENT 6 (continued)

Part 2: In the worksheet in Figure SA2-6b, some or all of the loan data in the range B3:B8 was entered incorrectly. The loan data should be as follows: Item — House; Price — $178,500.00; Down Payment — $36,500.00; Interest Rate — 10.75%; and Years — 15. Explain the error and method of correction.

Error: _____

Method of correction: _____

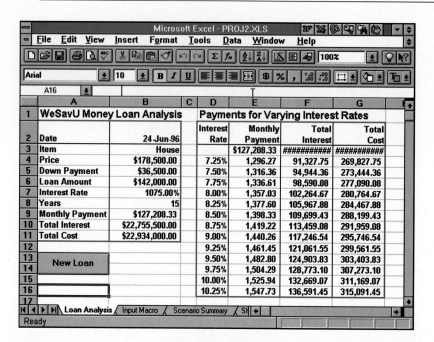

FIGURE SA2-6b

COMPUTER LABORATORY EXERCISES

COMPUTER LABORATORY EXERCISE 1
Using the Help Menu to Learn About Data Tables and Macros

Instructions: Start Excel and perform the following tasks.

1. Choose the Contents command from the Help menu. Choose Using Microsoft Excel. Choose Solving Problems by Analyzing Data. Choose Solving What-If Problems. One at a time, choose the eight items in the list, read them, and print them. Close the Help window.

2. Select the Help menu and choose the Examples and Demos command. When the Examples and Demos window displays, choose Performing What-If Analysis. When you finish with the first tutorial, choose Using Visual Basic.

3. Select the Help menu and choose the Search for Help on command. In the top box, type Visual Basic and choose the Show Topic button. One at a time, read and print the help information on each of the following topics:
   a. Overview of Writing and Editing a Macro
   b. Recording code into an existing macro
   c. Writing a macro

COMPUTER LABORATORY EXERCISE 2
Creating a One-Input Data Table

Instructions: Start Excel. Open the worksheet CLE2-2 from the sub-directory Excel5 on the Student Diskette that accompanies this book. As shown in Figure CLE2-2a, the worksheet computes the proposed annual salary (cell B4) from the proposed percent salary increase (cell B2) and the current annual salary (cell B3).

Perform the following tasks to create the one-input data table shown in Figure CLE2-2b.

1. Select the range A4:B4. Choose the Name command from the Insert menu, then choose the Create command to assign the name in cell A4 to cell B4.
2. Enter and format the data table title and column titles in the range A6:B7 as shown in Figure CLE2-2b. Use the fill handle to create the series of numbers in the range A9:A14.
3. Assign cell B8 the formula =proposed_salary.
4. Create a data table in the range A8:B14. Use cell B2 as the column input cell.
5. Draw borders around the data table as shown in Figure CLE2-2b.
6. Save the worksheet using the filename CLE2-2A. Print the worksheet without cell gridlines.
7. Use the goal seeking capabilities of Excel to determine the proposed percent increase in cell B2 if the proposed salary in cell B4 is set to $25,500,000. Your final result should be 0.59% in cell B2. Print the worksheet.

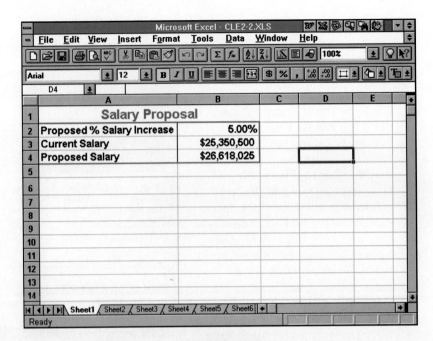

FIGURE CLE2-2a

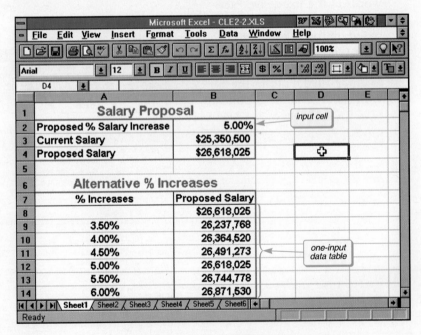

FIGURE CLE2-2b

COMPUTER LABORATORY EXERCISE 3
Assigning a Command Macro to a Button

Instructions: Start Excel and perform the following tasks.

1. Open the worksheet CLE2-3 from the subdirectory Excel5 on the Student Diskette that accompanies this book.
2. Click the Input Macro tab and print the macro. Click the Inventory Listing tab. Click the Drawing button on the Standard toolbar to display the Drawing toolbar. Add the button shown in Figure CLE2-3a. Assign the macro titled InputMacro (Figure CLE2-3b) to the button. Change the title of the button to Acceptable Total Parts.
3. Unprotect cell D9 and then protect the worksheet.
4. Click the Acceptable Total Parts button and enter 100000. The words in the Excessive Parts column (column F) change based on the value entered. Print the worksheet without cell gridlines. Use the button to enter 79000. Print the worksheet without gridlines.
5. Save the worksheet as CLE2-3A.

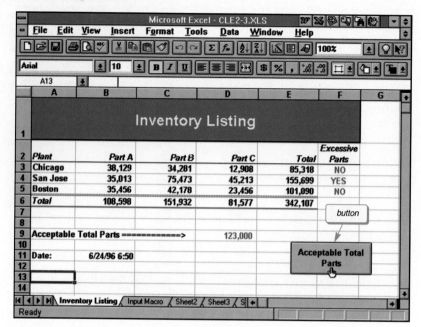

FIGURE CLE2-3a

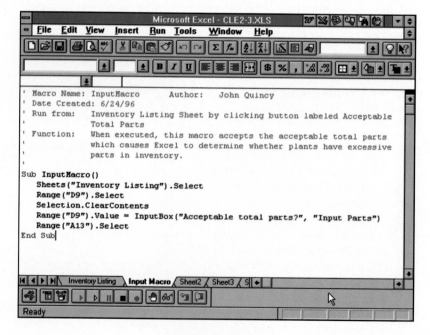

FIGURE CLE2-3b

COMPUTER LABORATORY ASSIGNMENT 1
Determining the Monthly Mortgage Payment

Purpose: To become familiar with using the PMT function, names, one-input data tables, macros, and buttons.

Problem: You are a part-time consultant for the Crown Loan Company. You have been asked to build a worksheet (Figure CLA2-1a) that determines the monthly mortgage payment and includes a one-input data table that shows the monthly payment, total interest, and total cost of a mortgage for varying years. The worksheet will be used by loan officers who know little about computers and worksheets. Thus, create a macro (Figure CLA2-1b on the following page) that will guide the user through entering the mortgage data. Assign the macro to a button on the worksheet.

FIGURE CLA2-1a

Instructions: Perform the following tasks:

1. Bold the entire worksheet.
2. Enter the Mortgage Payment section of the worksheet. Assign cell B2 the NOW function so it displays the system date and time. It is not necessary that you display the exact date shown in Figure CLA2-1a. Create names for the range B3:B6 using the Name command on the Insert menu. Assign cell B6 the following formula using the Point mode and the name box in the formula bar:
   =PMT(Interest_Rate / 12, 12 * Years, -Principal)
3. Enter the following mortgage data: Principal = $100,000; Interest Rate = 9.50%; Years = 30. Format the range B3:B6 as shown in Figure CLA2-1a.

(continued)

COMPUTER LABORATORY ASSIGNMENT 1 (continued)

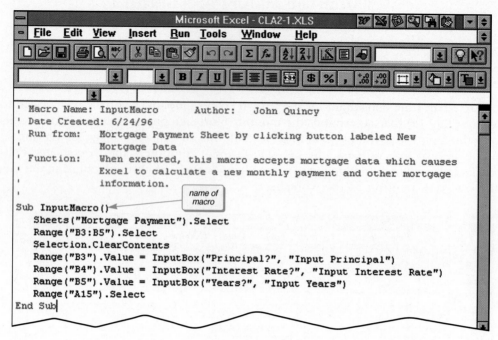

FIGURE CLA 2-1b

4. Enter the Payments for Varying Years section of the worksheet. Assign cell E3 the formula, =Monthly_Payment, cell G3 the formula, =12 * Years * Monthly_Payment, and cell F3 the formula, =G3 - Principal. Use the fill handle to create the series in the range D4:D15. Create a data table in the range D3:G15 using the Table command on the Data menu. Use cell B5 as the input cell.

5. Color the worksheet and add drop shadows as shown in Figure CLA2-1a.

6. Add your name, course, computer laboratory assignment number (CLA2-1), date, and instructor name in column A beginning in cell A14. Save the worksheet using the filename CLA2-1. Print the worksheet without cell gridlines. Rename the tab for the worksheet Mortgage Payment.

7. Use the Macro command on the Insert menu to create the macro in Figure CLA2-1b. Rename the tab for the macro Input Mortgage Data.

8. Click the Mortgage Payment tab. Display the Drawing toolbar. Create the button shown below the Mortgage Payment section in Figure CLA2-1a on the previous page. Assign the macro InputMacro to the button. Hide the Drawing toolbar. Unprotect the range B3:B5. Protect the worksheet. Click the Save button on the Standard toolbar to save the worksheet.

9. Use the button to determine the mortgage payment for the following mortgage data and print the worksheet for each data set: (a) Principal — $63,500, Interest Rate — 7.75%, and Years —15; (b) Principal — $343,250, Interest Rate — 8.25%, and Years — 30. The Mortgage Payment for (a) is $597.71 and for (b) $2,578.72.

COMPUTER LABORATORY ASSIGNMENT 2
Determining the Future Value of an Investment

Purpose: To become familiar with using the FV function, names, two-input data tables, macros, and buttons.

Problem: The insurance company you work for is in need of a Future Value worksheet that its agents can use with a portable computer when they visit clients. A future value computation tells the user what a constant monthly payment is worth after a period of time if the insurance company pays a fixed interest rate.

An agent survey indicates they want a worksheet similar to the one in Figure CLA2-2a that includes not only a future value computation, but also a **two-input data table** that determines future values for varying interest rates and monthly payments. The survey indicates that the agents know little about computers and worksheets. Thus, you must create a macro (Figure CLA2-2b on the following page) that will guide the agent through entering the future value data. Assign the macro to a button.

Instructions: Perform the following tasks:

1. Bold the entire worksheet.
2. Enter the Future Value Computations section of the worksheet. Assign cell B2 the NOW function so it displays the system date. Format the system date so it appears as shown in Figure CLA2-2a. Enter the data in cells B3, B4, and B5 as shown in Figure CLA2-2a. Create names for the range B3:B6. Assign cell B6 the following formula:
=FV(Interest_Rate / 12, 12 * Years, -Monthly_Payment)
Assign cell B7 the following formula:
=12 * Years * Monthly_Payment

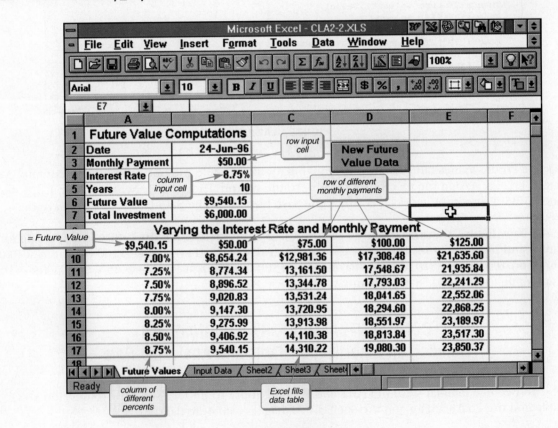

FIGURE CLA2-2a

3. Enter the Varying the Interest Rate and Monthly Payment data table. Assign cell A9 the formula, =Future_Value. Assign cells B9, C9, D9, and E9 the following monthly payments, $50.00, $75.00, $100.00, and $125.00, respectively. Use the fill handle to create the series in the range A10:A17. Create a data table in the range A9:E17 using the Table command from the Data menu. Use cell B3 as the row input cell and cell B4 as the column input cell. Rename the Sheet1 tab Future Values.
4. Add your name, course, computer laboratory assignment number (CLA2-2), date, and instructor name in column A beginning in cell A19. Save the workbook using the filename CLA2-2. Print the worksheet without cell gridlines with the future value data shown in Figure CLA2-2a.
5. Use the Macro command from the Insert menu to create the macro in Figure CLA2-2b on the following page. Rename the tab Input Data. Print the macro.

(continued)

COMPUTER LABORATORY ASSIGNMENT 2 (continued)

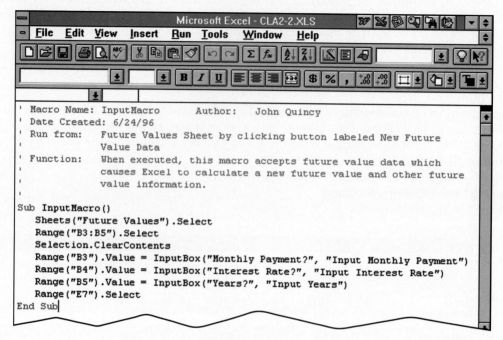

FIGURE CLA2-2b

6. Click the Future Values tab. Display the Drawing toolbar. Create the button shown in column D in Figure CLA2-2a. Assign the macro InputMacro to the button. Hide the Drawing toolbar. Unprotect the range B3:B5. Protect the worksheet. Click the Save button on the Standard toolbar to save the workbook.

7. Use the New Future Value Data button (Figure CLA2-2a) to determine the future value for the following data and print the worksheet for each data set: (a) Monthly Payment — $100.00, Interest Rate — 7.25%, and Years — 30; (b) Monthly Payment — $300.00, Interest Rate — 9.25%, and Years —10. The Future Value for (a) is $128,189.33 and for (b) is $58,881.96.

COMPUTER LABORATORY ASSIGNMENT 3
Building an Amortization Table and Analyzing Data

Purpose: To become familiar with the PMT and PV functions. To understand how to develop an amortization table and use goal seeking and the Scenario Manager to analyze data.

Problem: Each student in your Office Automation course is assigned a *live project* with a local company. You have been assigned to the Crown Loan Company to generate the loan information worksheet in Figure CLA2-3a and the Scenario Summary worksheet in Figure CLA2-3b. The president also wants you to demonstrate the goal seeking capabilities of Excel.

Instructions: Perform the following tasks to create the two worksheets:

1. Enter the worksheet title in cell A1. Enter the text in the ranges A2:A4 and D2:D4. Enter 13500 in cell B2, 2300 in cell B3, 7.75% in cell E2, and 5 in cell E3 (Figure CLA2-3a). Create names for the cells in the range B2:B4 and E2:E4 by using the names in the adjacent cells. In cell B4, enter the formula:

   =Price - Down_Pymt. In cell E4, enter the PMT function:

   =PMT(Rate / 12, 12 * Years, -Loan_Amount)

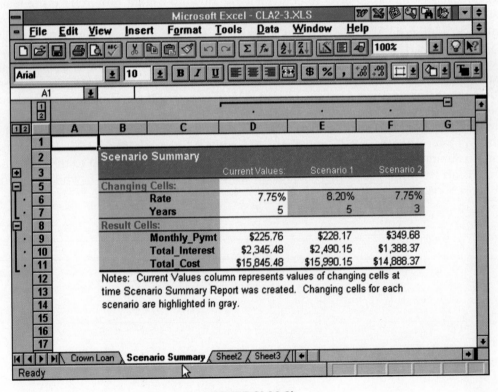

FIGURE CLA2-3a

FIGURE CLA2-3b

(continued)

COMPUTER LABORATORY ASSIGNMENT 3 (continued)

2. Enter the column titles for the amortization schedule in the range A5:E13. Use the fill handle to generate the years in the range A6:A10.
3. Assign the formulas and functions to the cells indicated in the table below:

CELL	FORMULA OR FUNCTION
B6	=Loan_Amount
C6	=IF(A6 <= Years, PV(Rate / 12, 12 * (Years - A6), -Monthly_Pymt), 0)
D6	=B6 - C6
E6	=IF(B6 > 0, 12 * Montly_Pymt - D6, 0)
B7	=C6
D11	=SUM(D6:D10)
E11	=SUM(E6:E10)
E12	=Down_Pymt
E13	=D11 + E11 + E12

4. Copy cell B7 to the range B8:B10. Copy the range C6:E6 to the range C7:E10. Draw the borders shown in Figure CLA2-3a. Rename the tab Crown Loan.
5. Save the workbook using the file name CLA2-3. Print the worksheet without cell gridlines with the loan data and loan information in Figure CLA2-3a.
6. Unprotect the ranges B2:B4 and E2:E3. Protect the worksheet. Save the worksheet.
7. Use Excel's goal seeking capabilities to determine the down payment required for the loan data in Figure CLA2-3a if the monthly payment is set to $200.00. The down payment that results for a monthly payment of $200.00 is $3,577. 87. Print the worksheet. Change the down payment in cell B3 back to $2,300.00.
8. Unprotect the worksheet. Name cell E11 Total_Interest by choosing the Name command from the Insert menu, and then choosing the Define command from the cascading menu. Use the same command to assign the name Total_Cost to cell E13. These names will show up in the Scenario Summary worksheet in the next step. Protect the worksheet.
9. Use Scenario Manager to create a Scenario Summary worksheet (Figure CLA2-3b) for the following scenarios: (1) Interest Rate — 8.2% and Years — 5 and (2) Interest rate — 7.75% and Years — 3. After the Scenario Summary worksheet displays, move the Scenario Summary tab to the immediate right of the Crown Loan tab. Print the Scenario Manager worksheet. Activate the Crown Loan worksheet and save the workbook.

COMPUTER LABORATORY ASSIGNMENT 4
Planning a Mortgage Payment Worksheet

Purpose: To become familiar with planning a worksheet.

Problem: You are a consultant working for Fair Loan Company. You have been assigned to create a worksheet similar to the one in Figure CLA2-3a and a Scenario Summary worksheet similar to the one in Figure CLA2-3b. In the worksheet you are to create, the amortization table should be extended to 30 years. See Computer Laboratory Assignment 3 for the formulas to use.

Create a macro to accept the loan data. Assign the macro to a button in the worksheet. Create a Scenario Summary worksheet that shows the monthly mortgage payment, total interest, and total cost for a 30-year loan with three different interest rates. Add a one-input data table to the worksheet that analyzes the monthly mortgage payment, total interest, and total cost for varying interest rates between 5.00% and 10.00% in increments of .25%.

Record a macro that saves and prints the workbook by clicking one button on the worksheet.

Instructions: Design and create the Mortgage Payment worksheet. Develop your own test data. Enter your name, course, computer laboratory assignment number (CLA2-4), date, and instructor name in column A in separate but adjacent cells. Save the workbook using the filename CLA2-4. Submit the following:

1. A description of the problem. Include the purpose of the worksheet, a statement outlining the results, the required data, and calculations.
2. A handwritten design of the worksheet.
3. A printed copy of the worksheet, macro, and Scenario Summary worksheet.
4. A printed copy of the formulas in the worksheet.
5. A short description explaining how to use the worksheet.

Microsoft Excel 5 for Windows

Sorting and Filtering a Worksheet Database

OBJECTIVES You will have mastered the material in this project when you can:

▸ Create a database
▸ Use a data form to display records, add records, delete records, and change field values in a database
▸ Sort a database on one field or multiple fields
▸ Display automatic subtotals
▸ Use a data form to find records that meet comparison criteria

▸ Filter data to display records in a database that meet comparison criteria
▸ Use the advanced filtering features to display records in a database that meet comparison criteria
▸ Apply database functions to generate information about the database
▸ Analyze a database using a pivot table

▸ INTRODUCTION

n this project, you will learn about the database capabilities of Excel. A **worksheet database**, also called a **database** or **list**, is an organized collection of data. For example, telephone books, grade books, and lists of company employees are databases. In these cases, the data related to a person is called a **record**, and the data items that make up a record are called **fields**. In a list of company employees, some of the fields would be name, hire date, and age.

A worksheet's row and column structure can easily be used to organize and store a database (Figure 3-1). Each row of a worksheet can be used to store a record and each column can store a field. In addition, a row of column titles at the top of the worksheet is used as **field names** to identify each field.

Once you create a database in Excel, you can do the following:

1. Add and delete records.
2. Change the values of fields in records.
3. Sort the records so they appear in a different order.
4. Determine subtotals for numeric fields.
5. Display records that meet comparison criteria.
6. Analyze data using database functions.
7. Summarize information about the database using a pivot table.

This project illustrates all seven of these database capabilities.

▶ PROJECT THREE — N-VIRO PERSONNEL DATABASE

N-Viro is an environmental consulting firm with 15 employees. The personnel data maintained by N-Viro is shown in Figure 3-1. The field names, columns, types of data, and column widths are described in Table 3-1. Because the N-Viro Personnel Database is visible on the screen, it is important that it be readable. Therefore, some of the column widths in Table 3-1 are determined from the field names and not the maximum length of the data.

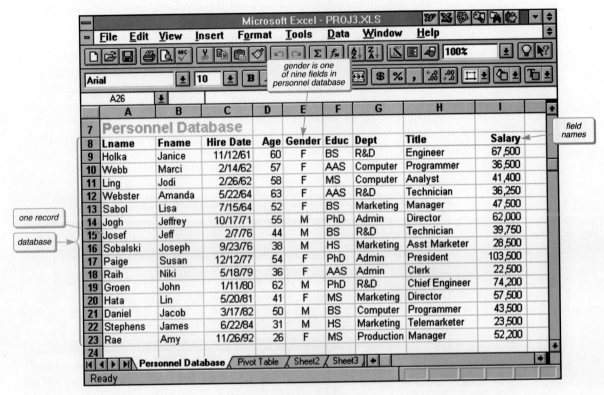

FIGURE 3-1

▶ **TABLE 3-1**

COLUMN TITLES (FIELD NAMES)	COLUMN	TYPE OF DATA	COLUMN WIDTH
Lname	A	Text	10.00
Fname	B	Text	8.00
Hire Date	C	Date	9.00
Age	D	Numeric	5.00
Gender	E	Text	7.00
Educ	F	Text	5.00
Dept	G	Text	9.00
Title	H	Text	13.00
Salary	I	Numeric	9.00

As you will see when creating a database, the column titles (field names) play an important role in the commands you issue to manipulate the data in the database. These column titles must be text and can contain a maximum of 255 characters. However, it's best to keep them short, as shown in row 8 of Figure 3-1 on the previous page.

One difference between the N-Viro Personnel Database in Figure 3-1 and the worksheets discussed in previous projects is the location of the data on the worksheet. In all of the previous worksheets, you began the entries in row 1. When you enter a database onto a worksheet, you usually leave several rows empty above it for adding entries that are used to analyze the data.

Once the N-Viro personnel database is entered onto the worksheet, it will be sorted and manipulated to illustrate how you can quickly generate information. One way to generate database information is to create a pivot table. A **pivot table** gives you the capability to summarize data in the database and then rotate the table's row and column titles to give you different views of the summarized data. Figure 3-2 illustrates two views of the same pivot table. In this pivot table, the salary of the employees is summarized by department and gender. Compare the top worksheet in Figure 3-2 to the bottom one. Notice how the row and column titles have been interchanged to give you different views of the same data.

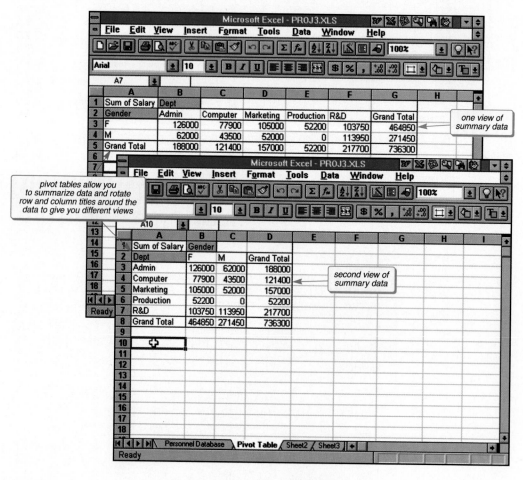

FIGURE 3-2

Project Steps

The following list is an overview of this project. If you are building this project on a personal computer, read these 13 steps without doing them.

1. Start the Excel program.
2. Enter and format the database title and column titles.
3. Assign the column titles in row 8 and the row immediately below it the name Database. Save the workbook.
4. Enter the employee records into the database using a data form.
5. Display employee records using a data form.
6. Sort the employee records in the database.
7. Determine salary subtotals.
8. Use a data form to display employee records that meet a comparison criteria in the database one at a time.
9. Filter the database using the AutoFilter command.
10. Filter the database using the Advanced Filter command.
11. Extract employee records from the database that meet comparison criteria.
12. Apply database functions to the database to generate information.
13. Create and manipulate a pivot table.

The following pages contain a detailed explanation of these steps.

Starting Excel and Setting Up the Database

Start Excel in the same manner described in project 1. Once a blank worksheet displays, follow these steps to change the column widths to those specified in Table 3-1 on page E131; change the height of row 7 to 18 points; and enter and format the database title and column titles. Although Excel does not require the database title in cell A7, it is a good practice to include one on the worksheet to show where the database begins.

TO SET UP THE DATABASE

Step 1: Use the mouse to change the column widths as follows: A = 10.00, B = 8.00, C = 9.00, D = 5.00, E = 7.00, F = 5.00, G = 9.00, H = 13.00, and I = 9.00.

Step 2: Select cell A7 and enter `Personnel Database`

Step 3: Click the Font Size button on the Formatting toolbar and choose 14. Position the mouse pointer on the border between row heading 7 and row heading 8. When the mouse pointer changes to a split double arrow, drag down until 18.00 displays in the reference area.

Step 4: Enter the column titles in row 8 as shown in Figure 3-1 on page E131. Hold down the CTRL key and select the range A8:I8. Click the Bold button on the Formatting toolbar. Click the Font color button on the Formatting toolbar and choose red (column 1, row 2).

Step 5: With the mouse pointer in the selected range (A8:I8), click the right mouse button. Choose the Format Cells command. Click the Border tab. Click the Color box arrow in the Style area and choose dark red (column 1, row 2). Click the regular border in the Style area (column 1, row 2). Click the Bottom box in the Border area. Choose the OK button.

Step 6: Click column heading E to select the column. Click the Center button on the Formatting toolbar so all entries in column E will be centered. Click column title I to select the column. Click the Comma Style button on the Formatting toolbar. Click the Decrease Decimal button on the Formatting toolbar twice so all entries in column I will display using the Comma style with zero decimal places. Select cell A10.

The worksheet displays as shown in Figure 3-3.

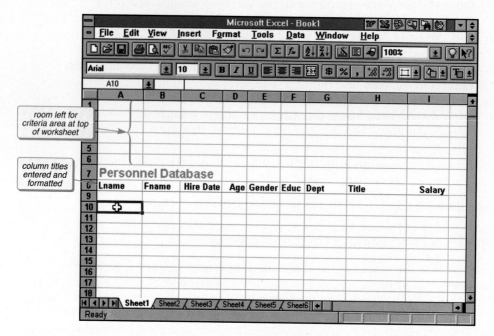

FIGURE 3-3

▶ CREATING A DATABASE

Although Excel can usually identify a **database range** on a worksheet without any qualifications, it is best to give it the name Database. Using the name Database eliminates any confusion when commands are entered to manipulate the database. Thus, to create the N-Viro Personnel Database shown in Figure 3-1 on page E131, you define the name Database to be the range A8:I9 by selecting the range and typing Database in the reference area in the formula bar. The range assigned to the name Database encompasses the column titles (row 8) and one blank row (row 9) below the column titles. The blank row is for expansion of the database. As records are added using a data form, Excel automatically expands the range of the name Database to encompass the last record. The following steps also rename the Sheet1 tab as Personnel Database and save the workbook using the filename PROJ3.XLS.

TO NAME THE DATABASE AND SAVE THE WORKBOOK ▼

STEP 1 ▶

Select the range A8:I9. Click in the reference area in the formula bar and type Database

STEP 2 ▶

Press the ENTER key.

The worksheet displays as shown in Figure 3-4.

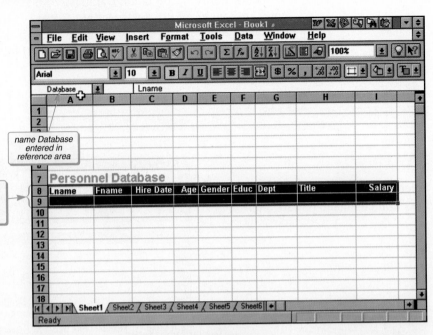

FIGURE 3-4

STEP 3 ▶

Select cell A9. Double-click the Sheet1 tab at the bottom of the screen. When the Rename Sheet dialog box displays, type Personnel Database and choose the OK button.

STEP 4 ▶

Select any cell in the worksheet. Click the Save button on the Standard toolbar. When the Save As dialog box displays, type proj3 in the File name box. Select drive A in the Drives box, and then choose the OK button. If the Summary Info dialog box displays, enter any appropriate information and then choose the OK button.

The worksheet displays as shown in Figure 3-5.

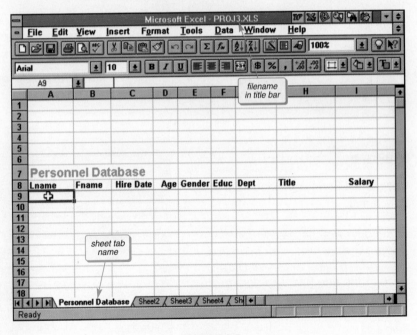

FIGURE 3-5

Entering Records into the Database Using a Data Form

After defining the name Database to be two rows long, a data form is used to enter the personnel records. A **data form** is a dialog box in which Excel includes the field names in the database and corresponding boxes in which you enter the field values. The following steps add the employee records to the N-Viro Personnel Database as shown in Figure 3-1 on page E131.

TO ENTER RECORDS INTO A DATABASE USING A DATA FORM ▼

STEP 1 ▶

Select the Data menu and point to the Form command (Figure 3-6).

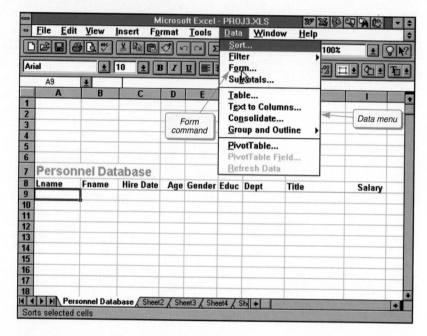

FIGURE 3-6

STEP 2 ▶

Choose the Form command from the Data menu.

Excel displays the data form (Figure 3-7), which is a dialog box, with the tab title Personnel Database in the title bar. The data form includes the field names and corresponding boxes for entering the field values.

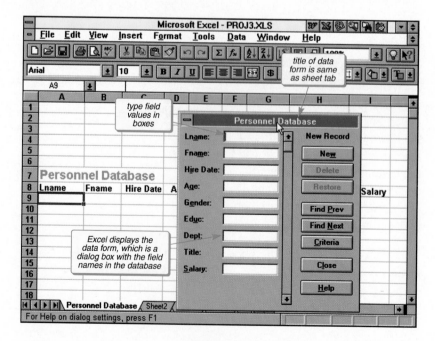

FIGURE 3-7

STEP 3 ▶

Enter the first personnel record into the data form as shown in Figure 3-8. Use the mouse or the TAB key to move the insertion point down to the next box and the SHIFT+TAB keys to move the insertion point to the previous box in the data form.

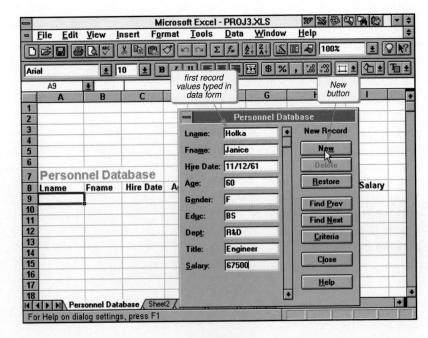

FIGURE 3-8

STEP 4 ▶

Choose the New button (New) in the data form or press the ENTER key. Type the second personnel record into the data form as shown in Figure 3-9.

Excel adds the first personnel record to row 9 in the database range on the worksheet, and the second record displays in the data form (Figure 3-9).

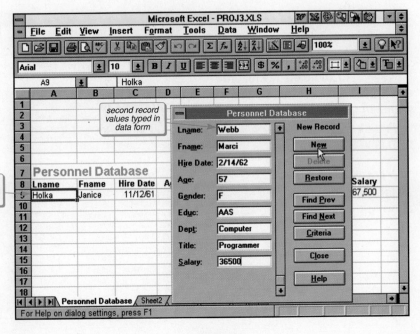

FIGURE 3-9

STEP 5 ▶

Choose the New button in the data form or press the ENTER key to enter the second personnel record. Enter the next twelve personnel records in rows 11 through 22 of Figure 3-1 on page E131 using the data form. Type the last personnel record in row 23 of Figure 3-1.

Excel enters the records into the database range as shown in Figure 3-10. The last record displays in the data form.

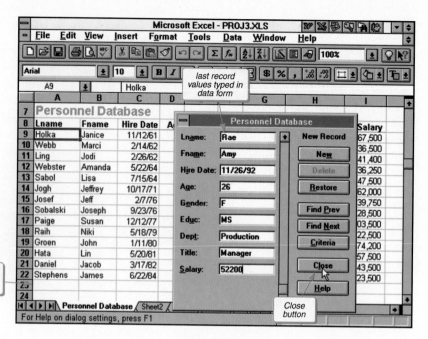

FIGURE 3-10

STEP 6 ▶

With the last record typed in the data form, choose the Close button (Close) to complete the record entry. Click the Save button on the Standard toolbar to save the workbook using the filename PROJ3.XLS.

The N-Viro Personnel Database displays as shown in Figure 3-11.

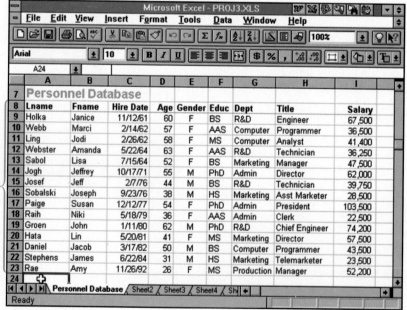

FIGURE 3-11

In addition to using a data form to build a database, you can enter the records in the same fashion as you entered data onto previous worksheets and then define the name Database to be all the columns and rows (A8:I23). This project presents the data form because it is considered to be a more accurate and reliable method of data entry, and it automatically extends the range of the name Database.

Moving from Field to Field on a Data Form

To move from field to field on a data form, you can use the TAB key as described earlier in Step 3 or you can hold down the ALT key and press the key that corresponds to the underlined letter in the name of the field to which you want to move. An underlined letter in a field name is called an **access key**. Thus, to select the field titled Fname in Figure 3-11 you can hold down the ALT key and press the M key (ALT+M) because m is the access key for the field name Fname.

Reviewing the Appearance of the N-Viro Personnel Database

Refering to the data shown in Figure 3-11, notice the following:

1. In column C, the dates are right-justified because Excel treats dates as numbers.
2. Excel formats the dates in the data form (Figure 3-12 on the following page) to the m/d/yyyy style when you enter them in the form mm/dd/yy.
3. The Gender codes in column E are centered because Step 6 on page E134 applied the center format to column E, which means all entries in column E will be centered.
4. The salary entries in column I display using the Comma style with no decimal places because Step 6 on page E134 applied this format to column I.

Guidelines to Follow When Creating a Database

Listed in Table 3-2 are some guidelines to use when creating a database in Excel.

▶ **TABLE 3-2**

Database Size and Location on Worksheet
1. Do not enter more than one database per worksheet.
2. Maintain at least one blank row between a database and other worksheet entries.
3. Do not store other worksheet entries in the same rows as your database.
4. Define the name Database to be the database range.
5. A database can have a maximum of 256 fields and 16,384 records on a worksheet.
Column Titles (Field Names)
1. Place column titles in the first row of the database.
2. Do not use blank rows or rows with dashes to separate the column titles from the data.
3. Apply a different format to the column titles and data. For example, bold the column titles and display the data below the column titles using a regular style. Varying the format between the column titles and data is necessary only if you do not assign the name Database to the database range.
4. Column titles (field names) can be up to 255 characters in length.
Contents of Database
1. Each column should have similar data. For example, employee gender should be in the same column for all employees.
2. Do not use spaces in data to improve readability.
3. Format the data to improve readability, but do not vary the format in a column.

▶ USING A DATA FORM TO VIEW RECORDS AND CHANGE DATA

At any time while the worksheet is active, you can use the Form command on the Data menu to display records, add new records, delete records, and change the data in records. When a data form is initially opened, Excel displays the first record in the database. To display the sixth record as shown in Figure 3-12, you choose the Find Next button (Find Next) until the sixth record displays. Each time you choose the Find Next button, Excel advances to the next record in the database. If necessary, you can use the Find Prev button (Find Prev) to back up to a previous record. You can also use the UP ARROW key and DOWN ARROW key or the vertical scroll bar to the left of the buttons to move among records.

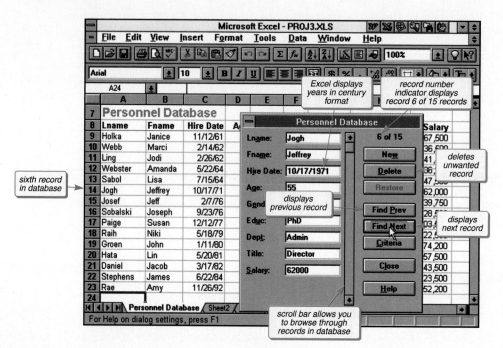

FIGURE 3-12

To change data in a record, you first display it in a data form. Next, you select the fields to change, one at a time. Finally, you use the DOWN ARROW key or the ENTER key to confirm the field changes. If you change field values in a data form and then select the Find Next button to move to the next record, the field changes will not be made.

To add a new record, you choose the New button. A data form always adds the new record to the bottom of the database. To delete a record, you first display it in a data form and then choose the Delete button (Delete). Excel automatically moves all records below the deleted record up one row.

Printing a Database

Printing the database is accomplished using the same procedures you followed in earlier projects. If there is data on the worksheet that is not part of the database you want to print, then follow these steps to print only the database.

TO PRINT A DATABASE

Step 1: Point to the menu bar and click the right mouse button.

Step 2: Choose the Page Setup command from the shortcut menu. Click the Sheet tab. Turn off gridlines. Type `Database` in the Print Area box.

Step 3: Choose the OK button.

Step 4: Ready the printer and click the Print button on the Standard toolbar.

Later, if you want to print the entire worksheet, remove the name Database from the Print Area box on the Sheet tab in the Page Setup dialog box.

▶ SORTING A DATABASE

The data in a database is easier to work with and more meaningful if the records are arranged in sequence on the basis of one or more fields. Arranging records in sequence is called **sorting**. Data is in **ascending sequence** if it is in order from lowest to highest, earliest to most recent, or in alphabetical order. For example, the records were entered into the N-Viro Personnel Database beginning with the earliest hire date to the most recent hire date. Thus, the database in Figure 3-12 is sorted in ascending sequence by hire date. Data that is in sequence from highest to lowest in value is in **descending sequence**.

Sort by clicking the **Sort Ascending button** (⏬) or **Sort Descending button** (⏫) on the Standard toolbar or by choosing the **Sort command** on the Data menu. If you're sorting on a single field (column), use one of the Sort buttons on the Standard toolbar. If you're sorting on multiple fields, use the Sort command on the Data menu. Make sure you select a cell in the field to sort on before you click the button. The field you select to sort the records on is called the **sort key**. The first sort example reorders the records by last name.

Sorting the Database by Last Name in Ascending Sequence

To sort the records by last name in ascending sequence, select a cell in column A and click the Sort Ascending button on the Standard toolbar as shown in the following steps.

TO SORT A DATABASE BY LAST NAME IN ASCENDING SEQUENCE ▼

STEP 1 ►

Select cell A9 and point to the Sort Ascending button on the Standard toolbar (Figure 3-13).

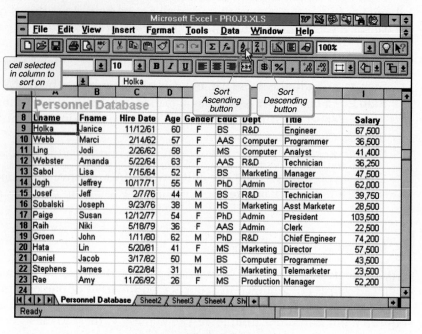

FIGURE 3-13

STEP 2 ►

Click the Sort Ascending button.

Excel sorts the database by last name in ascending sequence (Figure 3-14).

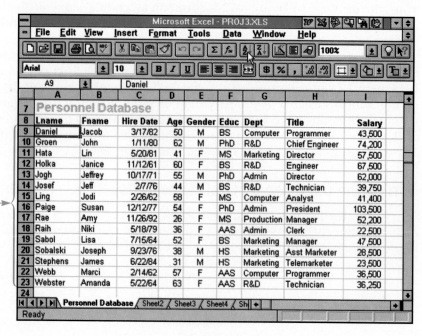

FIGURE 3-14

Sorting the Database by Last Name in Descending Sequence

To sort the records by last name in descending sequence, select a cell in column A and click the Sort Descending button on the Standard toolbar as shown in the following steps.

TO SORT A DATABASE BY LAST NAME IN DESCENDING SEQUENCE

Step 1: Select cell A9.
Step 2: Click the Sort Descending button on the Standard toolbar.

Excel sorts the database by last name in descending sequence (Figure 3-15).

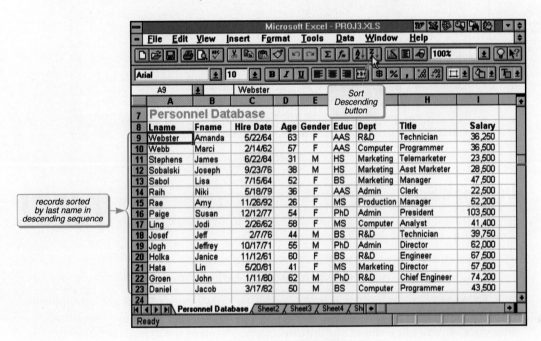

records sorted by last name in descending sequence

FIGURE 3-15

Returning the Database to Its Original Order

Follow these steps to change the sequence of the records back to their original order by hire date in ascending sequence.

TO RETURN THE DATABASE TO ITS ORIGINAL ORDER

Step 1: Select cell C9.
Step 2: Click the Sort Ascending button on the Standard toolbar.

Excel reorders the records in their original sequence by hire date (Figure 3-16 on the next page).

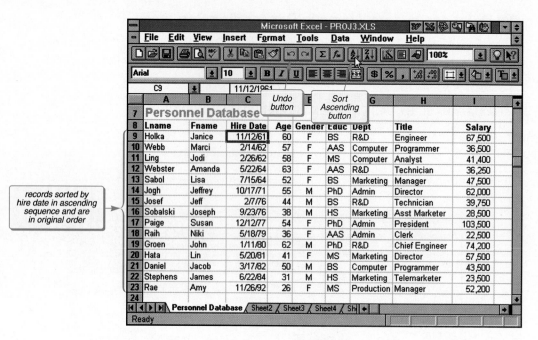

records sorted by
hire date in ascending
sequence and are
in original order

FIGURE 3-16

Undoing a Sort

If you are not satisfied with the results of a sort, you can undo it by immediately using one of the following procedures:

1. Click the **Undo button** on the Standard toolbar.
2. Choose the **Undo Sort command** from the Edit menu.

These two procedures will only work if you have not entered any commands since the sort operation. For example, after sorting by last name in descending sequence, if you click the Undo button on the Standard toolbar, Excel displays the records in their most recent order — by last name in ascending sequence. If you click the Undo button a second time, Excel displays the records by last name in descending sequence. Thus, the Undo button does not allow you to revert back to an original order once multiple sorts have taken place. For this reason, it is a good idea to enter records into a database in sequence on one of the fields so you can display the database in its original order when necessary. Some Excel users use the fill handle to create a series in an additional field in the database that is used only to reorder the records into their original sequence.

Sorting the Database on Multiple Fields

Excel allows you to sort a maximum of three fields at a time. The sort example that follows uses the Sort command on the Data menu to sort the N-Viro Personnel Database by salary (column I) within education (column F) within gender (column E). In this case, gender is the **major sort key** (Sort By field), education is the **intermediate sort key** (First Then By field), and salary is the **minor sort key** (Second Then By field). The first two keys will be sorted in ascending sequence. The salary field will be sorted in descending sequence.

The phrase *sort by salary within education within gender* means that the records are arranged in sequence by gender code. Within gender, the records are arranged in sequence by education code. Within education, the records are arranged in sequence by salary.

TO SORT A DATABASE ON MULTIPLE COLUMNS ▼

STEP 1 ▶

With a cell in the database selected, select the Data menu.

The Data menu displays (Figure 3-17).

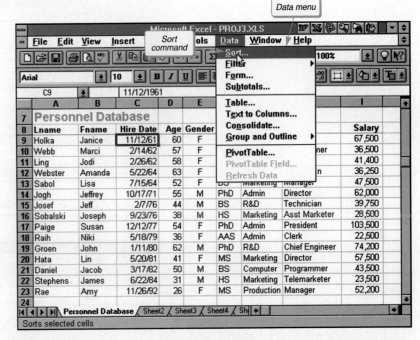

FIGURE 3-17

STEP 2 ▶

Choose the Sort command. When the Sort dialog box displays, click the Sort By arrow.

The Sort By drop-down list shows the field names in the database (Figure 3-18).

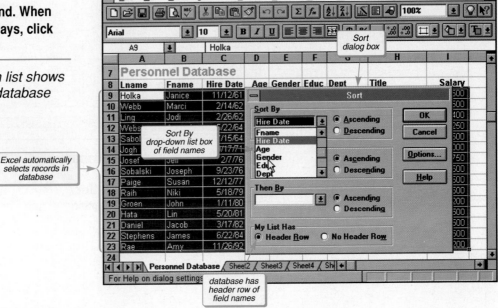

FIGURE 3-18

STEP 3 ▶

Select Gender in the Sort By drop-down list. Click the first Then By box arrow and select Educ. Click the second Then By arrow and then select Salary. Click the Descending option button in the second Then By area.

The Sort dialog box displays as shown in Figure 3-19.

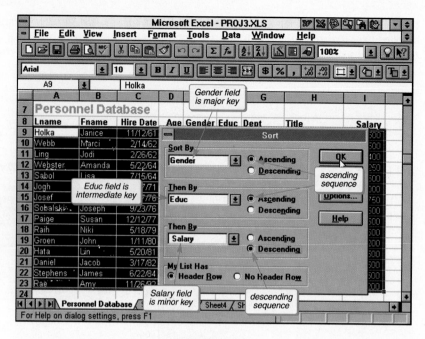

FIGURE 3-19

STEP 4 ▶

Choose the OK button in the Sort dialog box.

Excel sorts the personnel data-base by salary within education within gender as shown in Figure 3-20.

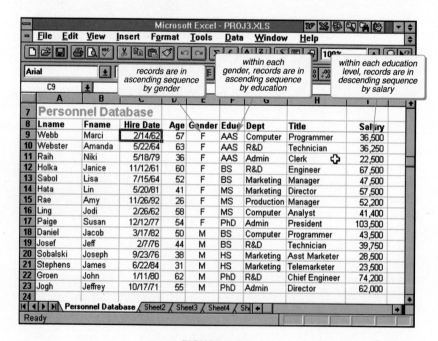

FIGURE 3-20

In Figure 3-20, the records are in ascending sequence by the gender codes (F or M) in column E. Within each gender code, the records are in ascending sequence by the education codes (AAS, BS, HS, MS, PhD) in column F. Finally, within the education codes, the salaries are in descending sequence in column I. Remember, if you make a mistake in a sort operation, you can reorder the records into their original sequence by immediately clicking the Undo button on the Standard toolbar.

Because Excel sorts the database using the current order of the records, the previous example could have been completed by sorting on one field at a time, beginning with the least important one.

Sorting with More than Three Fields

Excel allows you to sort on more than three fields by sorting two or more times. The most recent sort takes precedence. Hence, if you plan to sort on four fields, you sort on the three least important keys first and then sort on the major key. If you want to sort on fields, Lname within Title within Dept within Gender, you first sort on Lname (Second Then By column) within Title (first Then By column) within Dept (Sort By column). After the first sort operation is complete, you finally sort on the Gender field by selecting one of the Gender field cells and clicking the Sort Ascending button on the Standard toolbar.

▶ DISPLAYING AUTOMATIC SUBTOTALS IN A DATABASE

Displaying **automatic subtotals** is a powerful tool for summarizing data in a database. Excel only requires that you sort the database on the field for which you want subtotals to be based and then use the **Subtotals command** on the Data menu. The field you sort on, prior to choosing the Subtotals command, is called the **control field**. When the control field changes, Excel displays a subtotal for the numeric fields you select in the Subtotal dialog box. For example, if you sort on the Dept field and request subtotals on the Salary field, then Excel displays a salary subtotal every time the Dept field changes, and a salary grand total for the entire database.

In the Subtotal dialog box, you select the subtotal function you want to use. The most often used subtotal functions are listed in Table 3-3.

▶ TABLE 3-3

SUBTOTAL FUNCTIONS	DESCRIPTION
Sum	Sums a column
Count	Counts the number of entries in a column
Average	Determines the average of numbers in a column
Max	Determines the maximum value in a column
Min	Determines the minimum value in a column

Besides displaying subtotals, Excel also creates an outline for the database. The following example shows you how to display salary subtotals by department. Because the insertion of subtotals increases the number of rows, the Zoom Control box on the Standard toolbar is used to display the entire database.

TO DISPLAY SALARY SUBTOTALS BY DEPARTMENT ▼

STEP 1 ▶

Select cell G9. Click the Sort Ascending button on the Standard toolbar.

The N-Viro Personnel Database displays by department in ascending sequence as shown in Figure 3-21.

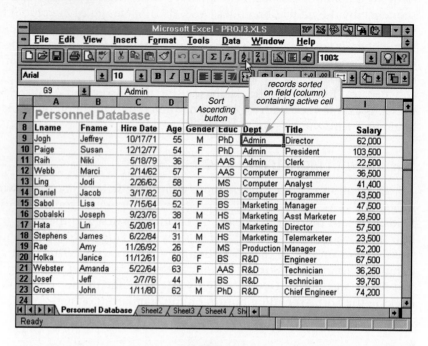

FIGURE 3-21

STEP 2 ▶

Select the Data menu.

The Data menu displays (Figure 3-22).

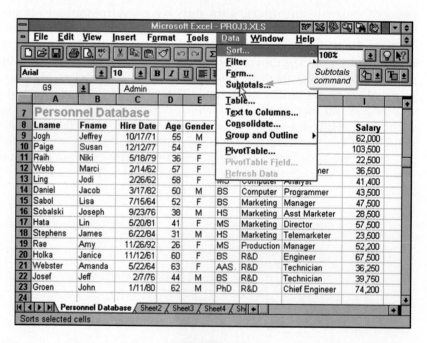

FIGURE 3-22

STEP 3 ►

Choose the Subtotals command. When the Subtotals dialog box displays, click the At Each Change in box arrow and select Dept. Select Salary in the Add Subtotal to box.

The Subtotal dialog box displays as shown in Figure 3-23. The At Each Change in box contains the Dept field. The Use Function box contains Sum by default. In the Add Subtotal to box, the Salary field is selected.

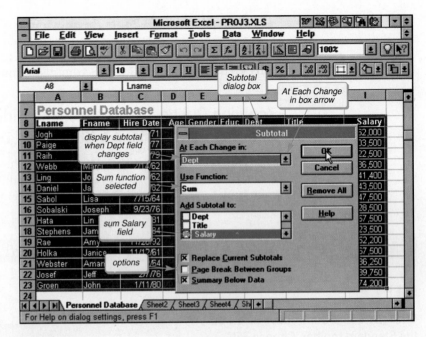

FIGURE 3-23

STEP 4 ►

Choose the OK button.

Excel inserts new rows in the N-Viro Personnel Database. Each new row contains salary subtotals for each department (Figure 3-24). The database is also outlined and extends beyond the window.

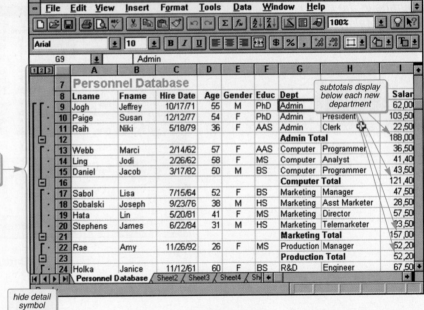

FIGURE 3-24

Notice in Figure 3-24 on the previous page that Excel has added subtotal rows in the middle of the database. Names for each subtotal row are derived from the department names. Thus, in row 12, the text *Admin Total* precedes the actual total salary of $188,000 for the Administration department.

Zooming Out on a Worksheet and Hiding and Showing Detail Data in a Subtotaled Database

The following steps show how to use the Zoom Control box on the Standard toolbar to reduce the size of the display so all records show. The steps also illustrate how to use the outline features of Excel to display only the total rows.

TO ZOOM OUT ON A WORKSHEET AND HIDE AND SHOW DETAIL IN A SUBTOTALED DATABASE ▼

STEP 1 ►

Click the Zoom Control box arrow on the Standard toolbar. Choose 75%.

Excel displays the worksheet in reduced form so all the rows and columns in the database, including the subtotals and grand total, display (Figure 3-25).

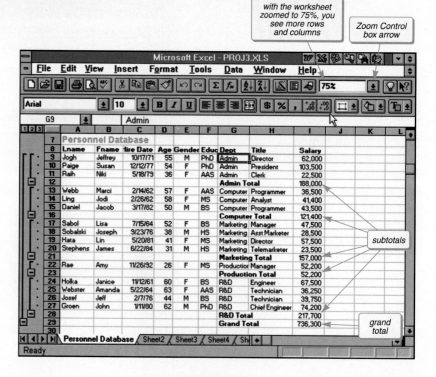

FIGURE 3-25

STEP 2 ▶

Click the row level 2 symbol in the group next to the Select All button to hide all detail rows.

Excel displays only the subtotal and grand total rows (Figure 3-26).

STEP 3 ▶

Click the row level 3 symbol next to the Select All button to display hidden detail rows. Click the Zoom Control box and choose 100%.

Excel displays the worksheet in normal size (Figure 3-24 on page E149).

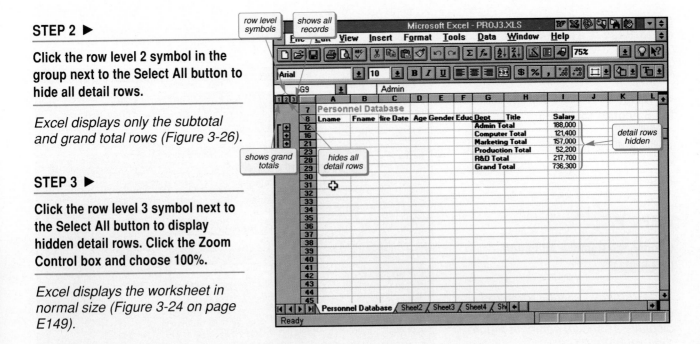

FIGURE 3-26

By utilizing the outlining features of Excel, you can quickly hide and show detail data. You should be aware that when you hide data, you can chart the resulting rows and columns as if they are adjacent to one another. Thus, in Figure 3-26 you can chart the salary subtotals as an adjacent range even though they are not in adjacent rows when the worksheet displays in normal form.

Removing Subtotals from the Database

Excel provides two ways to remove subtotals and the accompanying outline from a database. First, you can click the Undo button on the Standard toolbar or use the Undo Subtotals command on the Edit menu if you have not entered any commands since creating the subtotals. Second, you can choose the Remove All button in the Subtotal dialog box. The following steps show how to use the Remove All button.

TO REMOVE SUBTOTALS FROM A DATABASE ▼

STEP 1 ▶

Select the Data menu and choose the Subtotals command.

Excel selects the database and displays the Subtotal dialog box (Figure 3-27).

STEP 2 ▶

Choose the Remove All button (Remove All).

Excel removes all total rows and the outline from the database so it displays as shown earlier in Figure 3-21 on page E148.

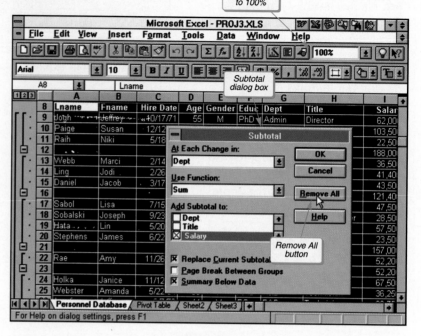

FIGURE 3-27

From the previous sections, you can see how easy it is to add and remove subtotals from a database. This allows you to quickly generate the type of information that database users require to help them make decisions about products or company direction.

Before moving on to the next section, follow these steps to sort the N-Viro Personnel Database into its original order by hire date in ascending sequence.

TO SORT THE DATABASE BY HIRE DATE

Step 1: Select cell C9.
Step 2: Click the Sort Ascending button on the Standard toolbar.

The records in the N-Viro Personnel Database are sorted by hire date in ascending sequence (Figure 3-16 on page E144).

▶ FINDING RECORDS USING A DATA FORM

o find records in the database that pass a test made up of comparison criteria, you can use the Find Prev and Find Next buttons together with the Criteria button ( ) in the data form. **Comparison criteria** are one or more conditions that include the field names and entries in the corresponding boxes in a data form. For example, you can instruct Excel to find and display only those records that pass the test:

Hire Date < 1/1/80 **AND** Gender = F **AND** Age < 40

For a record to display in the data form, it has to pass **All** three parts of the test. Finding records that pass a test is useful for maintaining the database. When a record that passes the test displays in the data form, you can change the field values or delete it from the database.

Use the relational operators (=, <, >, >=, ≥ <=, ≤ and <>) to form the comparison criteria in a data form.The following steps illustrate how to use a data form to find records that pass the following test:

Age ≥ 40 **AND** Gender = M **AND** Education <>AAS **AND** Salary > $40,000.

TO FIND RECORDS USING A DATA FORM ▼

STEP 1 ▶

From the Data menu, choose the Form command.

The first record in the N-Viro Personnel Database displays in the data form (Figure 3-28).

STEP 2 ▶

Choose the Criteria button in the data form.

Excel displays the data form with blank boxes.

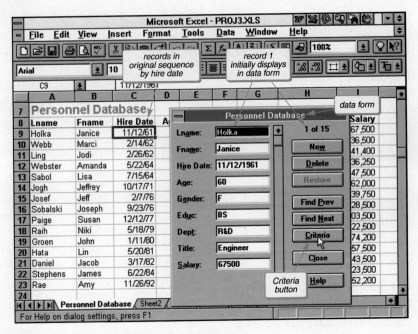

FIGURE 3-28

STEP 3 ▶

Type >=40 in the Age box, =M in the Gender box, <>AAS in the Educ box, and >40000 in the Salary box.

The data form displays with the comparison criteria as shown in Figure 3-29. The comparison criteria are 40 years or older, any degree other than AAS and earning a salary greater than $40,000.

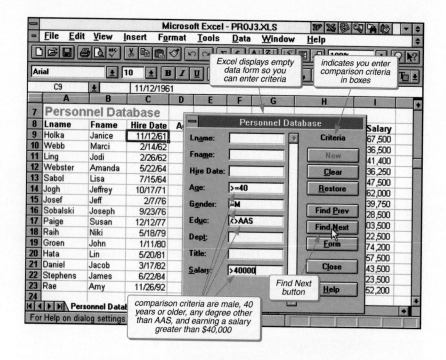

FIGURE 3-29

STEP 4 ▶

Choose the Find Next button in the data form.

Excel immediately displays the first record in the database (record 6) that passes the test (Figure 3-30). Mr. Jeffrey Jogh is a 55 year old male with a PhD who earns $62,000. The first 5 records in the database failed the test.

STEP 5 ▶

Use the Find Next and Find Prev buttons to display other records in the database that pass the test. When you have finished displaying records, select the Close button in the data form.

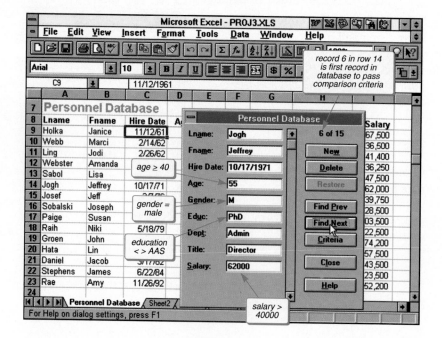

FIGURE 3-30

Three records in the personnel database pass the test: record 6 (Mr. Jeffrey Jogh), record 11 (Mr. John Groen), and record 13 (Mr. Jacob Daniel). Each time you choose the Find Next button, Excel displays the next record that passes the test. You can also use the Find Prev button to display the previous record that passed the test.

Notice in the comparison criteria established in Figure 3-29, no blank characters appear between the relational operators and the values. Leading or trailing blank characters have a significant impact on text comparisons. For example, there is a big difference between =M and = M.

Excel is not **case-sensitive**. That is, Excel considers uppercase and lowercase characters in a criteria comparison to be the same. For example, =m is the same as =M.

Using Wildcard Characters in Comparison Criteria

For text fields, you can use **wildcard characters** to find records that share certain characters in a field. Excel has two wildcard characters, the question mark (?) and the asterisk (*). The **question mark** (?) represents any single character in the same position as the question mark. For example, if the comparison criteria for Lname (last name) is =We?b, then any last name passes the test that has the following: We as the first two characters, any third character, and the letter b as the fourth character. Webb (record 2 in row 10) passes the test.

Use the **asterisk** (*) in a comparison criteria to represent any number of characters in the same position as the asterisk. Jo*, *e, Web*r, are examples of valid text with the asterisk wildcard character. Jo* means all text that begins with the letters Jo. Jogh (record 6 in row 14) and Josef (record 7, row 15) pass the test. The second example, *e, means all text that ends with the letter e. Paige (record 9 in row 17) and Rae (record 15 in row 23) pass the test. The third example, Web*r, means all text that begins with the letters Web and ends with the letter r. Only Webster (record 4 in row 12) passes the test.

If the comparison criteria calls for searching for a question mark (?) or asterisk (*), then precede either one with a tilde (~). For example, to search for the text What?, enter What~? in the comparison criteria.

Using Computed Criteria

A **computed criteria** involves using a formula in a comparison criteria. For example, the computed criterion formula =Age > Salary / 1000 in the Age field on a data form finds all records whose Age field is less than the corresponding Salary field divided by 1000.

▶ FILTERING A DATABASE USING AUTOFILTER

An alternative to using a data form to find records that pass a test is to use AutoFilter. Whereas the data form displays one record at a time, **Auto Filter** enables you to display all the records that meet a criteria as a subset of the database. AutoFilter hides records that do not pass the test, thus displaying only those that pass the test.

You apply AutoFilter to a database by choosing the **Filter command** on the Data menu, and then choosing AutoFilter from the cascading menu. Excel responds by adding drop-down arrows directly on the field names at the top of the database in row 8. Clicking an arrow displays a list of the unique items in the field (column). If you select an item from the list, Excel immediately hides records that do not contain the item. The item you select from the drop-down list is called the **filter criterion**. If you select an item from a second field, Excel displays a subset of the first subset.

The following steps show how to use AutoFilter to display those records in the N-Viro Personnel Database that pass the following test:

Gender =M **AND** Educ =PhD

TO APPLY AUTOFILTER TO A DATABASE ▼

STEP 1 ►

Select any cell in the database. Select the Data menu and choose the Filter command.

Excel displays a cascading menu (Figure 3-31).

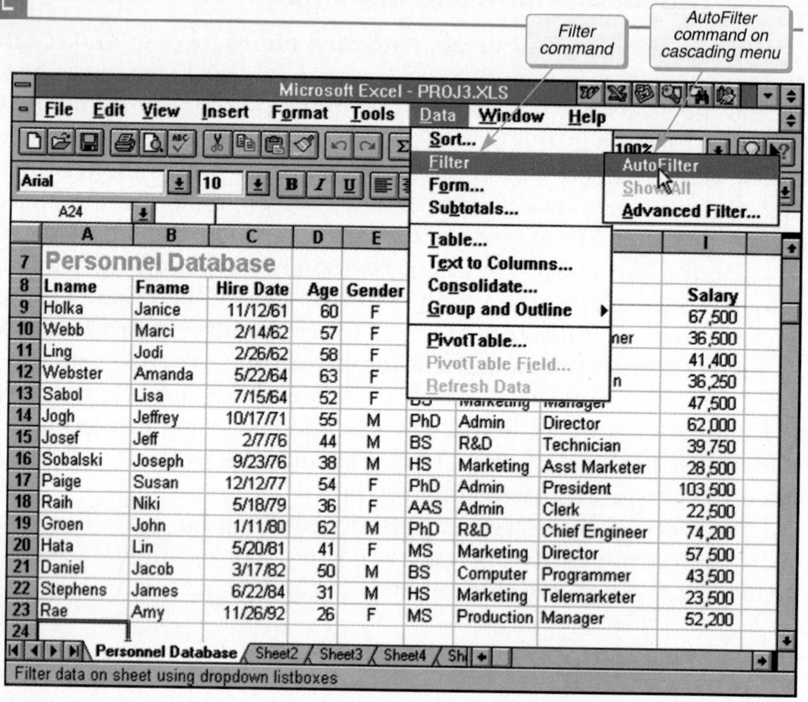

FIGURE 3-31

STEP 2 ►

Choose the AutoFilter command.

Drop-down arrows appear on each field name in row 8 (Figure 3-32).

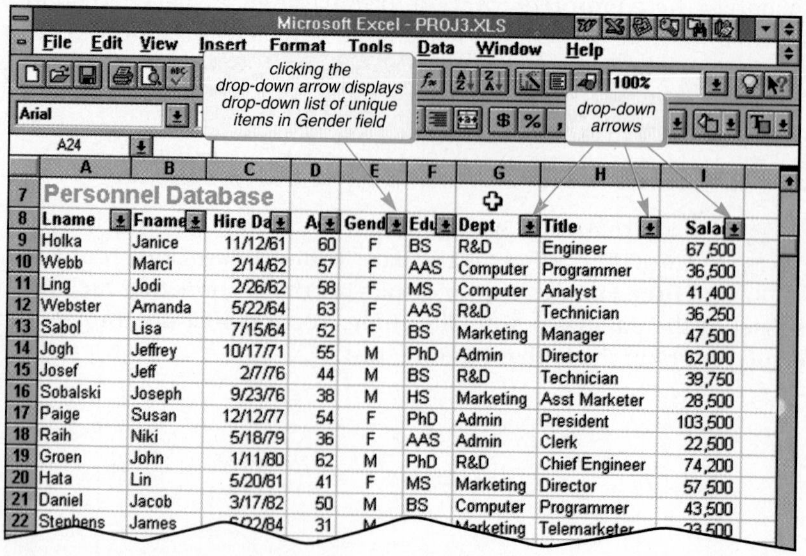

FIGURE 3-32

STEP 3 ▶

Click the Gender drop-down arrow.

A list of the entries F and M in the Gender field displays (Figure 3-33). (All), (Custom...), (Blanks), and (NonBlanks) are found in every AutoFilter drop-down list. When you first choose the AutoFilter command, the filter criterion for each field in the database is set to All. Thus, all records display.

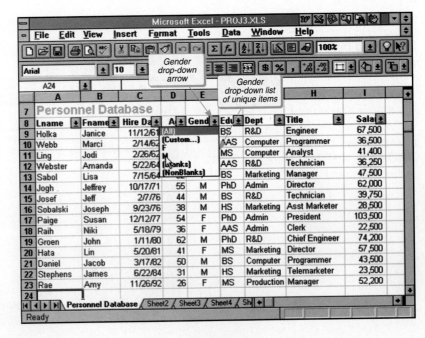

FIGURE 3-33

STEP 4 ▶

Select M from the Gender drop-down list. Click the Educ arrow.

Excel hides all records representing females. Thus, only records representing males display (Figure 3-34). The Educ drop-down list of entries displays.

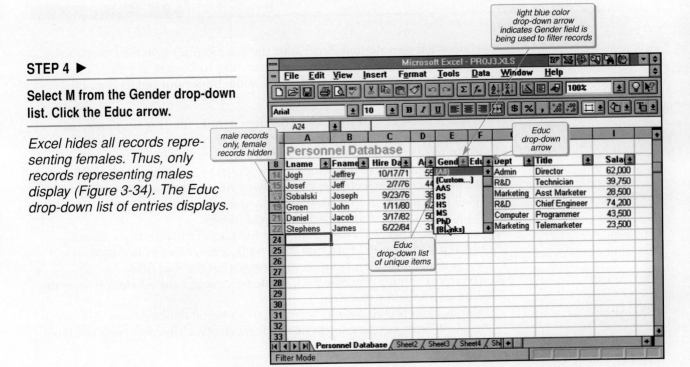

FIGURE 3-34

STEP 5 ▶

Select PhD from the Educ drop-down list.

*Excel hides all records representing males that do not have a PhD. Only two records pass the filter criterion Gender = M **AND** Educ = PhD (Figure 3-35).*

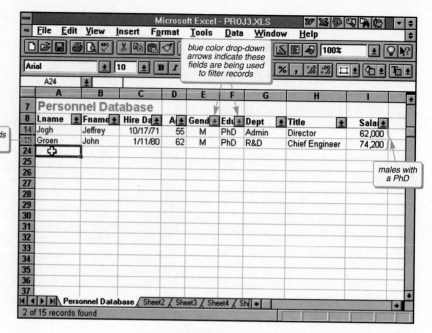

FIGURE 3-35

It is important to note that Excel adds the second filter criterion to the first. Thus, there are two tests that each record must pass to display as part of the final subset of the database. Listed below are some important points regarding AutoFilter.

1. When AutoFilter is active, Excel displays in blue the row headings and drop-down arrows used to establish the filter.
2. If you have multiple lists (other columns of data) on the worksheet, select a cell within the database prior to choosing the AutoFilter command.
3. If a single cell is selected before applying AutoFilter, Excel assigns arrows to all field names in the database. If you select certain field names, Excel assigns arrows to only the selected field names.
4. To find the rows with blank cells in a field, select Blanks from the drop-down list for that field. To find rows with nonblank cells in a field, select the NonBlanks option from the drop-down list for that field.
5. To remove a filter criterion for a single field, select the All option from the drop-down list for that field.
6. Automatic subtotals should be added to a filtered database only after applying AutoFilter, because Excel does not recalculate after selecting the filter criterion.

Removing AutoFilter

To display all records and remove the drop-down arrows, choose the Filter command from the Data menu, then choose the AutoFilter command. To display all records and keep the drop-down arrows on the field names, choose the **Show All command** on the Filter cascading menu. The following steps illustrate how to display all records and remove the drop-down arrows.

TO REMOVE AUTOFILTER ▼

STEP 1 ►

Select a cell in the database. Select the Data menu and choose the Filter command.

The Data menu and cascading menu display as shown in Figure 3-36.

STEP 2 ►

Choose the AutoFilter command.

All the records in the N-Viro Personnel Database display as shown in Figure 3-31 on page E156. The AutoFilter command is like a toggle switch. Choose it once and the drop-down arrows are added to the field names. Choose it again, and the drop-down arrows are removed and any hidden records display.

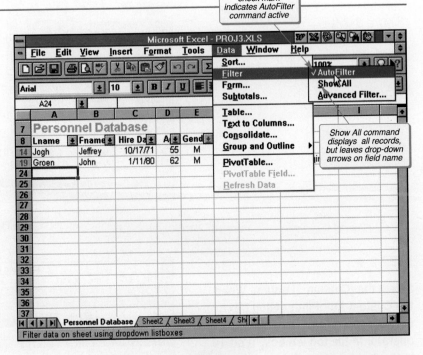

FIGURE 3-36

Entering Custom Criteria with AutoFilter

One of the options available in all the drop-down lists is (Custom...). The **(Custom...) option** allows you to enter custom criteria, such as multiple options in a drop-down list and ranges of numbers. The following steps show how to display records in the N-Viro Personnel Database that represent employees whose ages are in the range 40 to 50 inclusive ($40 \geq Age \leq 50$).

TO ENTER CUSTOM CRITERIA ▼

STEP 1 ▶

Select the Data menu and choose the Filter command, then choose the AutoFilter command. Click the Age drop-down arrow.

The Age drop-down list displays (Figure 3-37).

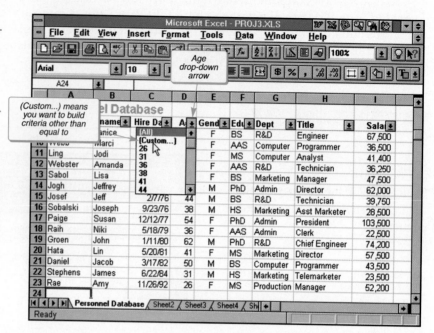

FIGURE 3-37

STEP 2 ▶

Select the (Custom...) option. When the Custom AutoFilter dialog box displays, select the >= relational operator in the top left box. Type 40 in the top right box. Select the <= relational operator in the bottom left box. Type 50 in the bottom right box.

The Custom AutoFilter dialog box displays as shown in Figure 3-38.

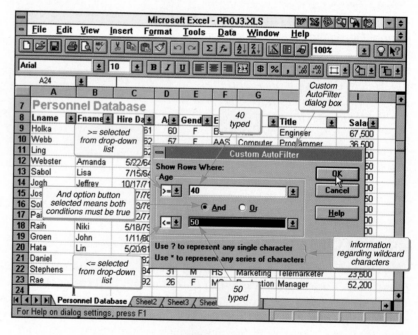

FIGURE 3-38

STEP 3 ▶

Choose the OK button in the Custom AutoFilter dialog box.

The records in the N-Viro Personnel Database that represent employees whose ages are between 40 and 50 inclusive display (Figure 3-39). Records that represent employees whose age are not between 40 and 50 inclusive are hidden.

STEP 4 ▶

Select the Data menu and choose the Filter command. Choose the AutoFilter command from the cascading menu.

All records in the N-Viro Personnal Database display as shown in Figure 3-31 on page E156.

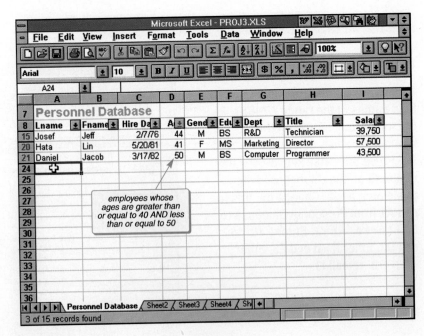

FIGURE 3-39

Notice in the Custom AutoFilter dialog box in Figure 3-38 that you can select the And or the Or operator to indicate whether both parts of the criteria must be true (And) or only one of the two must be true (Or). Use the And operator when the custom criteria is continuous over a range of values, such as Age between 40 **AND** 50 inclusive ($40 \leq Age \leq 50$). Use the Or operator when the custom criteria is not continuous, such as Age less than or equal to 40 **OR** greater than or equal to 50 ($40 \geq Age \geq 50$).

As with data forms, you can use wildcard characters to build the custom criteria as described at the bottom of the Custom AutoFilter dialog box in Figure 3-38.

▶ CREATING A CRITERIA RANGE ON THE WORKSHEET

Instead of using a data form or AutoFilter to establish criteria, you can set up a **criteria range** on the worksheet and use it to manipulate records that pass the comparison criteria. To set up a criteria range, you copy the database field names to another area of the worksheet, preferably above the database in case, it is expanded downward or to the right in the future. Next, you enter the comparison criteria in the row immediately below the field names in the criteria range. Then you name the criteria range Criteria. After naming the criteria range, use the **Advanced Filter command** on the Filter cascading menu. The following steps show how to set up criteria in the range A2:I3 to find records that pass the test: Gender =M **AND** Age >40 **AND** Salary >50000.

TO SET UP A CRITERIA RANGE ON THE WORKSHEET ▼

STEP 1 ►

Select the database title and field names in the range A7:I8. Click the Copy button on the Standard toolbar. Select cell A1. Press the ENTER key to copy the contents on the Clipboard to the paste area A1:I2. Change the title in cell A1 from Personnel Database to Criteria Area. Enter >40 in cell D3. Enter M in cell E3. Enter >50000 in cell I3.

The worksheet in Figure 3-40 displays.

STEP 2 ►

Select the range A2:I3. In the reference area in the formula bar, type Criteria and press the ENTER key.

The name Criteria is defined to be the range A2:I3. The Advanced AutoFilter command will automatically recognize the range named Criteria as the criteria range.

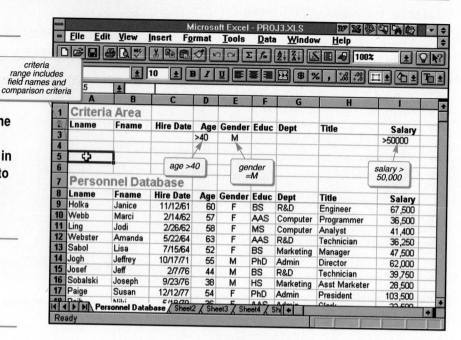

FIGURE 3-40

Remember these important points about setting up a criteria range:

1. Do not begin a test for equality involving text (Gender =M) with an equal sign because Excel will assume the text (M) is a range name rather than text.
2. If you include a blank row in the criteria range (for example, rows 2 and 3 and the blank row 4), all records will pass the test.
3. To ensure the field names in the criteria range are spelled exactly the same as in the database, use the Copy command to copy the database field names to the criteria range as illustrated in the previous steps.
4. The criteria range is independent of the criteria set up in a data form.
5. You can print the criteria range by entering the name Criteria in the Print Area box on the Sheet tab in the Page Setup dialog box as discussed earlier for printing a database range (see page E141).

▶ DISPLAYING RECORDS THAT MEET A CRITERIA USING THE ADVANCED FILTER COMMAND

The Advanced Filter command is similar to the AutoFilter command, except that it does not add drop-down arrows to the field names. Instead, it uses the comparison criteria set up on the worksheet in a criteria range (A2:I3). Follow these steps to display the records in the database that pass the test (Gender = M **AND** Age > 40 **AND** Salary > 50000) defined in the previous set of steps and shown in Figure 3-40.

TO DISPLAY RECORDS USING THE ADVANCED FILTER ▼

STEP 1 ▶

Select the Data menu and choose the Filter command.

The Data menu and a cascading menu display (Figure 3-41).

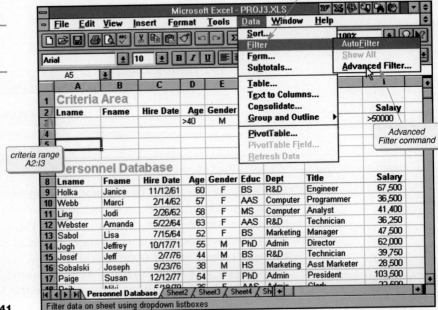

FIGURE 3-41

STEP 2 ▶

Choose the Advanced Filter command.

The Advanced Filter dialog box displays (Figure 3-42). In the Action area, the Filter the List, in-place option button is selected automatically. Excel selects the database (range A8:I23) in the List Range box, because it is assigned the name Database. Excel also selects the criteria range (A2:I3) in the Criteria Range box, because it is assigned the name Criteria.

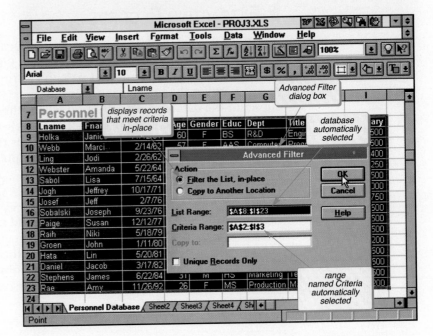

FIGURE 3-42

STEP 3 ►

Choose the OK button.

Excel hides all records that do not meet the comparison criteria, leaving only two records on the worksheet (Figure 3-43). Jeffrey Jogh (row 14) and John Groen (row 19) are the only two in the personnel database that are older than 40, male, and earn a salary greater than $50,000.

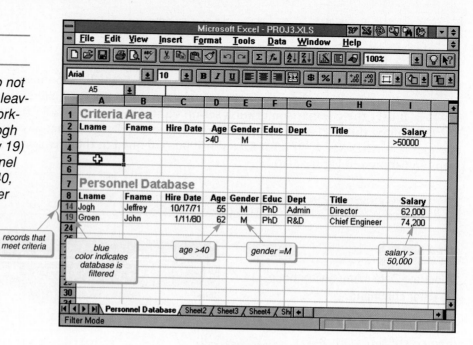

FIGURE 3-43

Notice the Advanced Filter command displays a subset of the database in the same fashion as the AutoFilter command. The primary difference between the two is that the Advanced Filter command allows you to create more complex comparison criteria, because the criteria range can be as many rows long as necessary, allowing for many sets of comparison criteria.

To display all records in the N-Viro Personnel Database, select the Data menu and choose the Filter command, then choose the Show All command.

▶ EXTRACTING RECORDS

I f you select the Copy to Another Location in the Action area of the Advanced Filter dialog box (Figure 3-42 on the previous page), Excel copies the records that pass the test to another part of the worksheet, rather than displaying a subset of the database. The location where the records are copied to is called the **extract range.** The way the extract range is set up is similar to the way the criteria range was set up earlier. Once the records that pass the test in the criteria range are **extracted** (copied), you can manipulate and print them as a group.

Creating the Extract Range

To create an extract range, copy the field names of the database to an area on the worksheet, preferably well below the database range. Next, name the range containing the field names Extract by using the reference area. Finally, use the Advanced Filter command to extract the records. The following steps show how to set up an extract range below the N-Viro Personnel Database.

TO CREATE AN EXTRACT RANGE ON THE WORKSHEET ▼

STEP 1 ▶

Select the database title and field names in the range A7:I8. Click the Copy button on the Standard toolbar. Select cell A27. Press the ENTER key to copy the contents on the Clipboard to the paste area A27:I28. Change the title in cell A27 from Personnel Database to Extract Area. Select the range A28:I28. Type the name Extract in the reference area in the formula bar and press the ENTER key. Select any cell on the worksheet. Select the Data menu and choose the Filter command.

The worksheet displays as shown in Figure 3-44. Notice that the name Extract is only assigned the field names in row 28. Excel will automatically copy the records to the rows below the range named Extract.

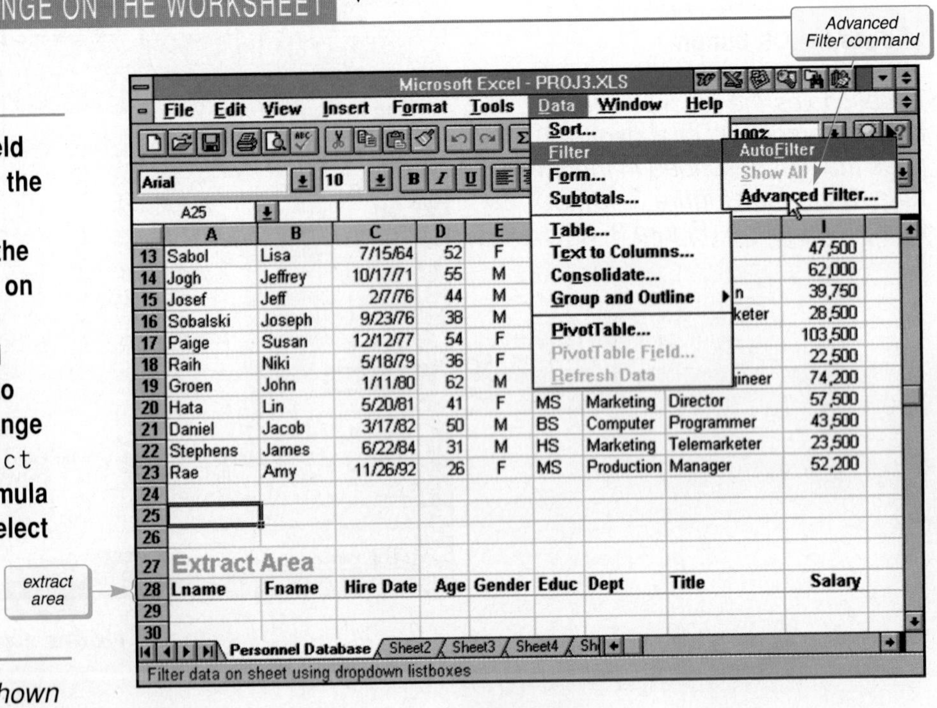

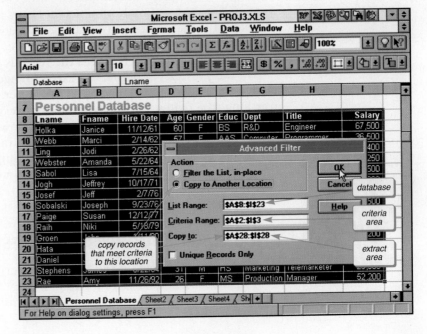

FIGURE 3-44

STEP 2 ▶

Choose the Advanced Filter command from the cascading menu. When the Advanced Filter dialog box displays, select the Copy to Another Location option button in the Action area.

Excel automatically assigns the range A8:I23 to the List Range box because the range A8:I23 is named Database (Figure 3-45). It also assigns the range named Criteria (A2:I3) to the Criteria Range box and the range named Extract (A28:I28) to the Copy to box.

FIGURE 3-45

STEP 3 ▶

Choose the OK button.

Excel copies the records from the N-Viro Personnel Database that pass the test described in the criteria range (see Figure 3-43) to the extract range (Figure 3-46).

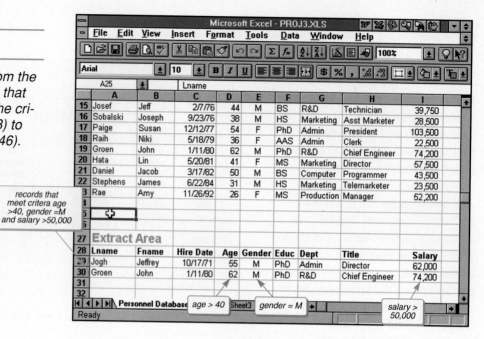

records that meet criteria age >40, gender =M and salary >50,000

FIGURE 3-46

When you set up the extract range, you do not have to copy all the field names in the database to the proposed extract range. Instead of using the copy command, you can copy only those field names you want and they can be in any order. You can also type the field names, but it is not recommended.

When you choose the Advanced Filter command and select the Copy to Another Location option button, Excel clears all the cells below the field names in the extract range. Hence, if you change the comparison criteria in the criteria range and choose the Extract command a second time, Excel clears the original extracted records before it copies the records that pass the new test.

In the previous example, the extract range was defined as a single row containing the field names (range A28:I28). When you define the extract range as one row long (the field names), any number of records can be extracted from the database because Excel will use all the rows below row 28 to the bottom of the worksheet. The alternative is to define an extract range with a fixed number of rows. However, if you define a fixed-size extract range, and if more records are extracted than there are rows available, Excel displays a dialog box with a diagnostic message indicating the extract range is full.

▶ MORE ABOUT COMPARISON CRITERIA

T he way you set up the comparison criteria in the criteria range determines the records that will pass the test when you use the Filter command. Different comparison criteria are described on the next page.

A Blank Row in the Criteria Range

If the criteria range contains a blank row, then all the records in the database pass the test. For example, the blank row in the criteria range in Figure 3-47 causes all records to pass the test.

FIGURE 3-47

Using Multiple Comparison Criteria with the Same Field

If the criteria range contains two or more entries under the same field name, then records that pass either comparison criterion pass the test. For example, the criteria range in Figure 3-48 causes all records that represent employees who have an AAS degree **OR** a BS degree to pass the test.

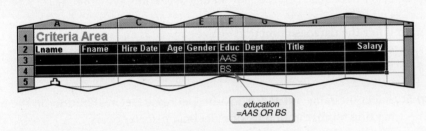

FIGURE 3-48

If an **AND** applies to the same field name (Age >50 **AND** Age <55), then you must duplicate the field name (Age) in the criteria range. That is, add the field name Age to the right of Salary in column I, delete the name Criteria by using the Name command on the Insert menu, and then define the name Criteria in the reference area to be equal to the new range that includes the second Age field.

Comparison Criteria in Different Rows and Under Different Fields

When the comparison criteria under different field names are in the same row, then records pass the test only if they pass all the comparison criteria. If the comparison criteria for the field names are in different rows, then the records must pass only one of the tests. For example, in the criteria range in Figure 3-49, all records that represent employees who are greater than 60 years old **OR** earn more than $70,000 pass the test.

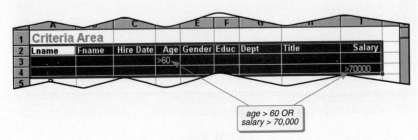

FIGURE 3-49

▶ USING DATABASE FUNCTIONS

Excel has twelve **database functions** that you can use to evaluate numeric data in a database. One of the functions is called the **DAVERAGE function**. As the name implies, you use the DAVERAGE function to find the average of numbers in a database field that pass a test. This function serves as an alternative to finding an average using the Subtotals command on the Data menu. The general form of the DAVERAGE function is

=DAVERAGE(database, "field name", criteria range)

where database is the name of the database, field name is the name of the field in the database, and criteria range is the comparison criteria or test to pass.

In the following steps, the DAVERAGE function is used to find the average age of the female employees and the average age of the male employees in the N-Viro Personnel Database.

TO USE THE DAVERAGE DATABASE FUNCTION

Step 1: Enter the field name Gender twice, once in cell K1 and again in cell L1. Enter the code for females F in cell K2. Enter the code for males M in cell L2.

Step 2: Enter Average Female Age in cell M1. Enter Average Male Age in cell M2.

Step 3: Enter the database function =daverage(database, "Age", K1:K2) in cell O1.

Step 4: Enter the database function =daverage(database, "Age", L1:L2) in cell O2.

Step 5: Select the range O1:O2. Click the Decrease Decimal button on the formatting toolbar until only one decimal place appears.

Excel computes and displays the average age of the females in the database (49.7) in cell O1 and the average age of the males in the database (46.7) in cell O2 (Figure 3-50).

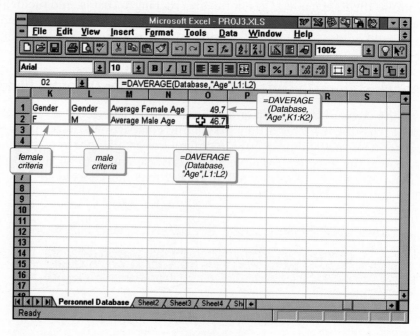

FIGURE 3-50

Notice in Figure 3-50 the first value (Database) in the function references the database defined earlier in this project (range A8:I23). The second value ("Age") identifies the field on which to compute the average. Excel requires that you surround the field name with quotation marks unless the field has been assigned a name through the reference area in the formula bar. The third value (K1:K2 for the female average) defines the criteria range.

Other database functions that are similar to the functions described in previous projects include the DCOUNT, DMAX, DMIN, and DSUM functions. For a complete list of the database functions, click the Function Wizard button on the Standard toolbar. When the FunctionWizard – Step 1 of 2 dialog box displays, select Database in the Function Category list box. The database functions display in the Function Name list box.

▶ CREATING A PIVOT TABLE TO ANALYZE DATA

A pivot table gives you the capability of summarizing data in the database and then rotating the table's row and column titles to give you different views of the summarized data. You usually create a pivot table on another page in the same workbook as the database you are analyzing, although you can create it on the same sheet as the worksheet.

The **PivotTable command** on the Data menu starts the PivotTable Wizard, which guides you through creating a pivot table. The **PivotTable Wizard** does not modify the database in any way. It uses the data in the database to generate information.

The pivot table to be created in this project is shown in Figure 3-51. The table summarizes salary information by gender and department for the N-Viro Personnel Database built earlier in this project.

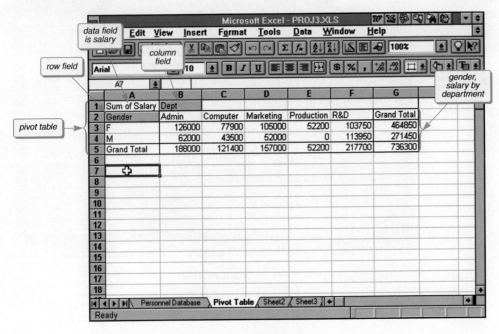

FIGURE 3-51

To create the pivot table in Figure 3-51, you need only select three fields from the database when requested by the PivotTable Wizard:

1. row field
2. column field
3. data field

In Figure 3-51 on the previous page, the row field is Gender — female (F) and male (M). The column field is the Dept — Admin, Computer, Marketing, Production, and R&D. The data field is Salary. Grand total salaries automatically display for the row and column fields in row 5 and in column G. For example, from the table in Figure 3-51, you can see in the Computer department, the female employees are paid a total salary of $77,900, while the male employees are paid a total salary of $43,500.

Column G shows that all females in the company are paid $464,850 and all males are paid $271,450. The total company salary, $736,300, displays in cell G5.

The data analysis power of pivot tables is found in its ability to allow you to view the data by interchanging or pairing up the row and column fields by dragging the buttons located over cells A2 and B1 in Figure 3-51. The process of rotating the field values around the data field will be discussed later in this project.

To create the pivot table shown in Figure 3-51, perform the following steps.

TO CREATE A PIVOT TABLE ▼

STEP 1 ►

Press CTRL+HOME, and then select cell A24 so the database displays on the screen. Select the Data menu and point to the PivotTable command.

The database displays on the screen, and then the Data menu displays. The mouse pointer points to the PivotTable command (Figure 3-52).

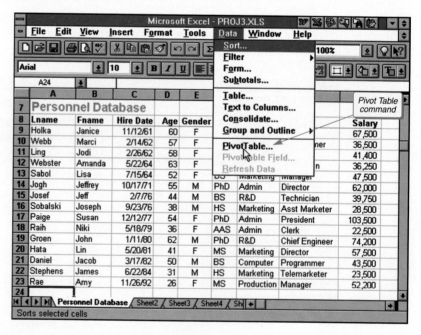

FIGURE 3-52

STEP 2 ▶

Choose the PivotTable command.

The PivotTable Wizard – Step 1 of 4 dialog box displays (Figure 3-53). The Microsoft Excel List or Database option button is selected automatically, because the default option is to use the database on the worksheet.

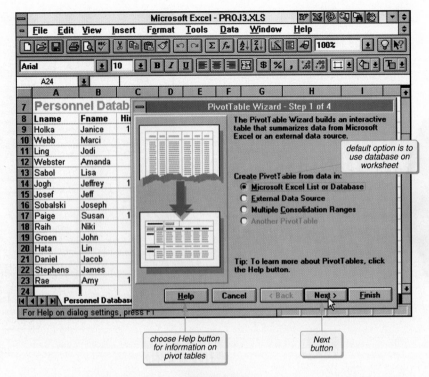

FIGURE 3-53

STEP 3 ▶

Choose the Next button.

Excel displays the PivotTable Wizard – Step 2 of 4 dialog box with the name Database automatically selected in the Range box (Figure 3-54). The database is surrounded by a marquis, which disappears in the next step.

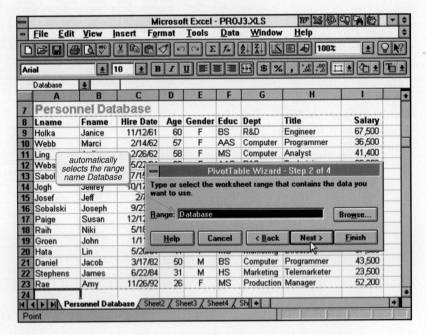

FIGURE 3-54

STEP 4 ▶

Choose the Next button.

Excel displays the PivotTable Wizard – Step 3 of 4 dialog box (Figure 3-55). At the top of the dialog box are instructions and definitions that help you create the pivot table. On the right side of the dialog box are buttons, one for each field in the N-Viro Personnel Database. You drag these buttons to locations (ROW, COLUMN, and DATA) in the middle of the dialog box.

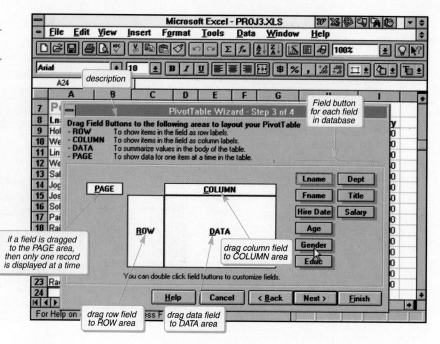

FIGURE 3-55

STEP 5 ▶

Drag the Gender button (Gender) to the ROW area. Drag the Dept button (Dept) to the COLUMN area. Drag the Salary button (Salary) to the DATA area.

The PivotTable Wizard – Step 3 of 4 dialog box displays as shown in Figure 3-56.

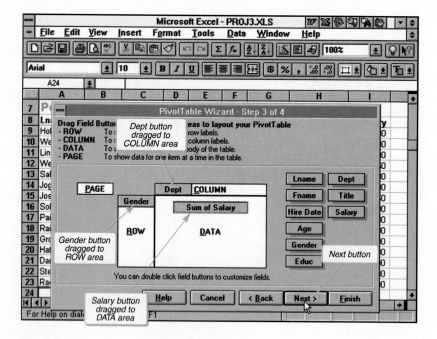

FIGURE 3-56

STEP 6 ►

Choose the Next button. With the PivotTable Starting Cell box selected, press the DELETE key. Point to the Finish button.

The PivotTable Wizard – Step 4 of 4 dialog box displays (Figure 3-57). At the top right corner of the dialog box, Excel's starting location for the pivot table is blank and the pivot table name is Pivot-Table1. When you leave the Pivot Table Starting Cell box blank, Excel automatically creates the pivot table on a new sheet. The mouse pointer points to the Finish button.

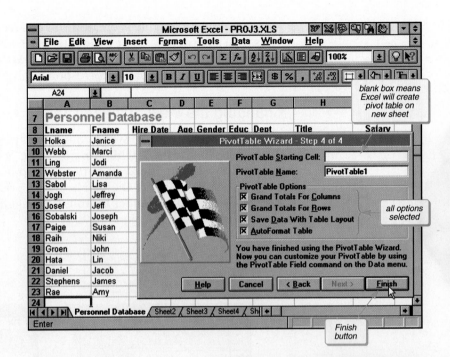

FIGURE 3-57

STEP 7 ►

Choose the Finish button. Double-click the Sheet17 tab and rename it Pivot Table. Drag the Pivot Table tab to the immediate right of the Personnel Database tab.

Excel creates and displays the pivot table on a new sheet as shown in Figure 3-58. The pivot table summarizes the salaries by gender and department.

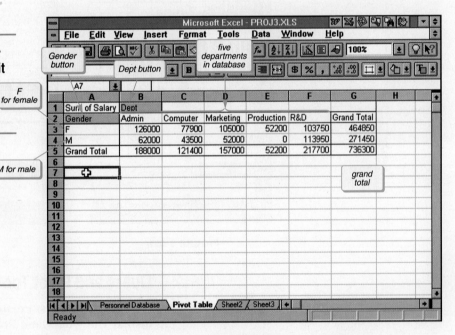

FIGURE 3-58

STEP 8 ►

Click the Save button on the Standard toolbar to save the workbook using the filename PROJ3.XLS.

Once the pivot table is created you can treat it like any other worksheet. Thus, you can print or chart a pivot table. If you update the data in the N-Viro Personnel Database, choose the **Refresh Data command** from the Data menu or shortcut menu to update the corresponding pivot table.

Changing the View of a Pivot Table

You can rotate the row and column fields around the data field by dragging the buttons on the pivot table from one side of the salary data to another. For example, if you drag the Dept button on top of the Gender button, you change the view of the pivot table to the one in Figure 3-59a. As you will note, if you interchange the Dept and Gender buttons by dragging them to their new locations, you get the view shown in Figure 3-59b.

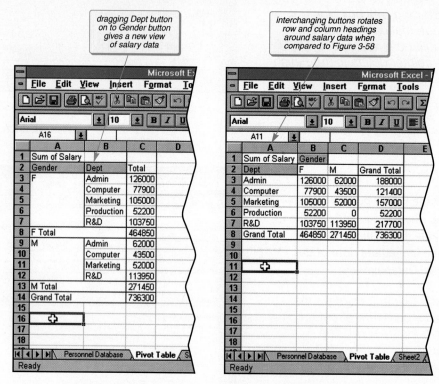

FIGURE 3-59a   **FIGURE 3-59b**

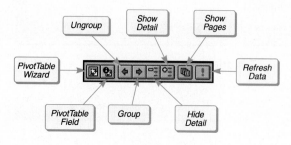

FIGURE 3-60

Query and Pivot Toolbar

When you first create a pivot table, Excel may display the Query and Pivot toolbar shown in Figure 3-60. The buttons allow you to quickly modify the appearance of the pivot table. You can also use the buttons to reenter the PivotTable Wizard and refresh the data after updating the database.

▶ PROJECT SUMMARY

In Project 3, you learned how to create, sort, and query a database. Creating a database involves naming a range in the worksheet Database. After naming the range, you can then add, change, and delete records in the database through a data form. Sorting a database is presented in steps using the Sort Ascending and Sort Descending buttons on the Standard toolbar or by using the Sort command on the Data menu. Once a database is sorted, you can use the Subtotals command on the Data menu to generate subtotals that display within the database range. Filtering a database involves displaying a subset of the database or copying (extracting) records that pass a test. Finally, you learned to use database functions and the pivot tables to analyze data in the database.

▶ KEY TERMS AND INDEX

(Custom...) option *(E159)*
access key *(E139)*
Advanced AutoFilter command *(E161)*
ascending sequence *(E141)*
asterisk (*) wildcard *(E151)*
AutoFilter *(E155)*
AutoFilter command *(E156)*
automatic subtotals *(E147)*
case-sensitive *(E155)*
comparison criteria *(E153)*
computed criteria *(E155)*
control field *(E147)*
criteria range *(E161)*
data form *(E136)*
Data menu *(E170)*
database *(E130)*
database function *(E168)*
database range *(E134)*

DAVERAGE function *(E168)*
descending sequence *(E141)*
extract range *(E164)*
extracted *(E164)*
field *(E130)*
field names *(E130)*
filtering a database *(E155)*
Filter command *(E156)*
filter criterion *(E156)*
Form command *(E136)*
intermediate sort key *(E144)*
list *(E130)*
major sort key *(E144)*
minor sort key *(E144)*
pivot table *(E132)*
PivotTable command *(E169)*
PivotTable Wizard *(E169)*
PivotTable Wizard dialog box *(E171)*

question mark (?) wildcard *(E155)*
record *(E130)*
Refresh Data command *(E174)*
Remove All button *(E152)*
Show All command *(E159)*
Sort Ascending button *(E141)*
Sort command *(E141)*
Sort Descending button *(E141)*
Sort dialog box *(E145)*
sort key *(E141)*
sorting *(E141)*
subtotal functions *(E147)*
Subtotals command *(E147)*
Undo button *(E144)*
Undo Sort command *(E144)*
wildcard characters *(E155)*
worksheet database *(E130)*

Q U I C K R E F E R E N C E

In Microsoft Excel, you can accomplish a task in a number of ways. The following table provides a quick reference to each task presented in this project with its available options. The commands listed in the Menu column can be executed using either the keyboard or mouse. Many of the commands in the Menu column are also available on the shortcut menu.

Task	Mouse	Menu	Keyboard Shortcuts
AutoFilter	Click AutoFilter button (custom)	From Data menu, choose Filter, then choose AutoFilter	
Advanced Filter		From Data menu, choose Filter, then choose Advanced Filter	

(continued)

QUICK REFERNCE (continued)

Task	Mouse	Menu	Keyboard Shortcuts
Data Form		From Data menu, choose Form	
Pivot Table	Click PivotTable Wizard on Query and Pivot toolbar	From Data menu, choose Pivot Table	
Refresh Data in Pivot Table	Click Refresh Data button on Query and Pivot toobar	From Data menu, choose Refresh Data	
Remove Subtotals		From Data menu, choose Subtotals, then choose Remove All button	
Sort	Click Sort Ascending button or Sort Descending button on Standard toolbar	From Data menu, choose Sort	
Subtotals		From Data menu, choose Subtotals	

S T U D E N T   A S S I G N M E N T S

STUDENT ASSIGNMENT 1
True/False

Instructions: Circle T if the statement is true or F if the statement is false.

T F 1. The series of numbers 1, 2, 3, 4, 5, 6 is in descending sequence.

T F 2. The column titles in a database are used as field names.

T F 3. When you name a database using the reference area in the formula bar, select only the row that contains the field names.

T F 4. A data form is not a dialog box.

T F 5. To add a new record to the database using a data form, select the New button.

T F 6. Excel treats dates as text.

T F 7. Excel allows you to sort on up to four fields at one time.

T F 8. A criteria range consisting of field names and empty cells below the field names will cause Excel to process all the records in the database.

T F 9. The wildcard character asterisk (*) can only be used at the end of text that is part of the comparison criteria.

T F   10. When you use the Subtotals command and apply the SUM function, Excel also displays grand totals.

T F   11. In the phrase "sort age within seniority within trade," age is the major key.

T F   12. To find records that pass a test using a data form, you first must set up a criteria range in the worksheet.

T F   13. To undo a sort operation, click the Undo button on the Standard toolbar before issuing any other commands.

T F   14. Excel is not case-sensitive when evaluating comparison criteria.

T F   15. Use the Refresh Data command on the Data menu to clear a worksheet.

T F   16. The DAVERAGE function is used to find the average of numbers in a database field that pass a test.

T F   17. A pivot table is used to summarize data and display different views of the data.

T F   18. Blank characters are significant in text-type comparison criteria.

T F   19. The criteria range in a worksheet is independent of the criteria set up in a data form.

T F   20. Each time you add a record using a data form to a range named Database, Excel expands the range of Database by one row.

STUDENT ASSIGNMENT 2
Multiple Choice

Instructions: Circle the correct response.

1. Which one of the following commands adds drop-down arrows to the field names at the top of the database?
   a. Subtotals
   b. AutoFilter
   c. Form
   d. Pivot Table

2. Which one of the following characters when used in comparison criteria represents any character in the same position?
   a. tilde (~)
   b. number sign (#)
   c. asterisk (*)
   d. question mark (?)

3. To copy all records that pass a test defined in a criteria range, use the _____ command on the Filter cascading menu.
   a. Filter
   b. Advanced Filter
   c. Subtotals
   d. Show All

(continued)

STUDENT ASSIGNMENT 2 (continued)

4. When a data form is first opened, Excel displays the _____ record in the database.
   a. first
   b. last
   c. blank
   d. second

5. If you make a mistake and sort a database on the wrong field, immediately select the _____ command from the Edit menu.
   a. Clear
   b. Replace
   c. Undo Sort
   d. Repeat Sort

6. To select a field in a database to sort on when the Sort dialog box displays, enter the _____ in the Sort By box.
   a. cell reference of the field (column) in the first record
   b. cell reference of the field (column) in the last record
   c. cell reference of any cell in the field (column)
   d. all of the above will work

7. With a data form active and criteria defined, use the _____ button to display the former record in the database that passes the test.
   a. Find Next
   b. Find Prev
   c. New
   d. Close

8. A database field name referenced in a database function must be surrounded by _____.
   a. quotation marks (")
   b. apostrophes (')
   c. brackets ({ })
   d. colons (:)

9. The Pivot Table command on the Data menu is used to create a _____.
   a. chart
   b. database
   c. summary table
   d. scenario

10. To set up a criteria range that will cause the Filter command to process all records, include a(n) _____ in the criteria range.
   a. blank cell under the first field name
   b. asterisk under all field names
   c. ="" under all field names
   d. blank row

STUDENT ASSIGNMENT 3
Understanding Sorting

Instructions: In the spaces below Figure SA3-3, write the sort order of the records in the Personnel Database in Figure SA3-3. Use the term *within* to describe the sort order. For example, minor field *within* intermediate field *within* major field. Also indicate the sequence (ascending or descending) of each field.

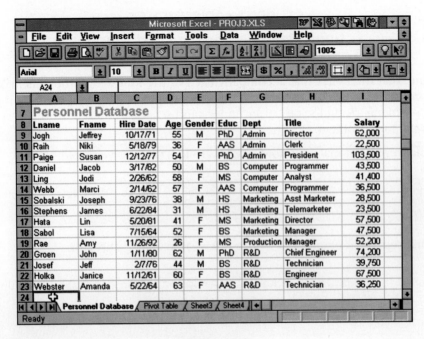

FIGURE SA3-3

Order: _____ within _____ within _____

Field(s) in ascending sequence: _____   Field(s) in descending sequence: _____

STUDENT ASSIGNMENT 4
Understanding Dialog Boxes and Commands

Instructions: Identify the menu and command that carry out the operation or cause the dialog box to display and allow you to make the indicated changes. Make an entry in the Cascading Menu column only if it applies.

	MENU	COMMAND	CASCADING MENU
1. Sort a database	_____	_____	_____
2. Undo a sort operation	_____	_____	_____
3. Add subtotals to a database	_____	_____	_____
4. Add drop-down arrows to the field names in a database	_____	_____	_____
5. Name a Database range	_____	_____	_____
6. Filter a database using a criteria range	_____	_____	_____
7. Create a pivot table	_____	_____	_____
8. Display a data form	_____	_____	_____

STUDENT ASSIGNMENT 5
Understanding Comparison Criteria

Instructions: Assume that the tables that accompany each of the following problems make up the criteria range. Fill in the comparison criteria to select records from the database in Figure 3-1 on page E131 according to these problems. To help you better understand what is required for this assignment, the answer is given for the first problem.

1. Select records that represent male employees who are less than 30 years old.

Lname	Fname	Hire Date	Age	Gender	Educ	Dept	Title	Salary
			<30	M				

2. Select records that represent employees whose title is Manager or Director.

Lname	Fname	Hire Date	Age	Gender	Educ	Dept	Title	Salary

3. Select records that represent employees whose last names begin with "Jo", education is BS, and are assigned to the R&D department.

Lname	Fname	Hire Date	Age	Gender	Educ	Dept	Title	Salary

4. Select records that represent employees who are at least 30 years old and were hired before 1/1/90.

Lname	Fname	Hire Date	Age	Gender	Educ	Dept	Title	Salary

5. Select records that represent male employees or employees who are at least 50 years old.

Lname	Fname	Hire Date	Age	Gender	Educ	Dept	Title	Salary

6. Select records that represent female engineer employees who are at least 40 years old and whose last names begin with the letter H.

Lname	Fname	Hire Date	Age	Gender	Educ	Dept	Title	Salary

STUDENT ASSIGNMENT 6
Understanding Filtering a Database

Instructions: Using Figure SA3-6, answer the following questions:

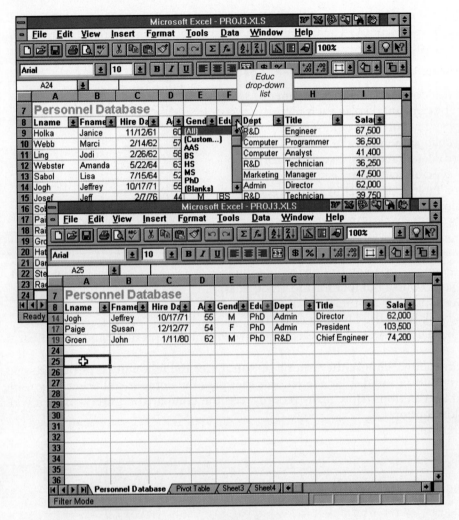

FIGURE SA3-6

1. Which menu name and command names display the drop-down arrows on the field names in row 8 of the top screen in Figure SA3-6? _____

2. How do you display the Educ drop-down list? _____

3. Which option in the Educ drop-down list would you select to generate the display in the bottom screen in Figure SA3-6?

COMPUTER LABORATORY EXERCISE 1
Using a Data Form to Maintain a Database

Instructions: Start Excel. Open the workbook CLE3-1 from the subdirectory Excel5 on the Student Diskette that accompanies this book. The first sheet in the workbook is shown in Figure CLE3-1. It contains a database of union employees.

Perform the following tasks:

1. Choose the Form command on the Data menu. Select the Find Next button and display each record.
2. The three types of maintenance performed on databases are: (a) change the values of fields, (b) add records, and (c) delete records. Use a data form to complete the type of maintenance specified in the first column of Table CLE3-1 below to the records identified by employee name in the Union Database shown in Figure CLE3-1.
3. Add your name as the last record in the database. If necessary, increase the width of column A so your name fits. Enter an age of 35 and a department number of 3. Use your course number for the Trade field. Use your division number for the Years of Seniority field.
4. Save the workbook using the filename CLE3-1A.
5. Print the database with gridlines off. Click the Save File button on the Standard toolbar to save the workbook.
6. With a data form active, choose the Criteria button. Enter the following criteria: Age <32, Dept = 3. Select the Form button and display the records that pass the comparison criteria by using the Find Next and Find Prev buttons. How many records pass the comparison criteria? When you are finished, choose the Close button.
7. Close the workbook.

5	Union Database					
6	Employee	Gender	Age	Dept	Trade	Years of Seniority
7	Jordon, David	M	48	1	Operator	7
8	Peat, Jeffrey	M	27	1	Machinist	5
9	Hill, Judith	F	36	2	Operator	12
10	Abram, Paul	M	30	2	Machinist	8
11	Jenings, Carl	M	35	1	Oiler	15
12	Lyndowe, Jodi	F	32	3	Oiler	13
13	Jean, Marcell	F	23	1	Operator	4
14	Lerner, Nicole	F	20	3	Machinist	1
15	Pylerski, Alex	M	45	2	Operator	23
16	Delford, James	M	25	3	Oiler	3

Union / Sheet2 / Sheet3 / Sheet4 / Sheet5 / Sheet6

Ready

FIGURE CLE3-1

TYPE OF MAINTENANCE	EMPLOYEE	GENDER	AGE	DEPT	TRADE	YEARS OF SENIORITY
Change	Peat, Jeffrey		32	3		
Change	Delford, James				Machinist	7
Delete	Lerner, Nicole					
Delete	Abram, Paul					
Add	Daniels, Jacob	M	48	1	Oiler	0
Add	Beet, Sharon	F	22	2	Operator	0

COMPUTER LABORATORY EXERCISE 2
Sorting a Database and Determining Subtotals

Part 1 Instructions: Start Excel. Open the workbook CLE3-2 (Figure CLE3-2a) from the subdirectory Excel5 on the Student Diskette that accompanies this book. Sort the database according to the six sort problems below. Print the database for each sort problem without gridlines. Save the workbook with each sort solution using the file name CLE3-2x, where x is the sort problem number. For each sort problem, open the original workbook CLE3-2.

1. Sort the database into descending sequence by division.
2. Sort the database by district within division. Both sort keys are to be in ascending sequence.
3. Sort the database by department within district within division. All three sort keys are to be in ascending sequence.
4. Sort the database into descending sequence by sales.
5. Sort the database by department within district within division. All three sort keys are to be in descending sequence.
6. Sort the database by salesperson within department within district within division. All four sort keys are to be in ascending sequence.

Part 2 Instructions: One at a time, close all the workbooks created in Part 1 by using the Close command on the File menu. Next, open the workbook CLE3-2 (Figure CLE3-2a) from the subdirectory Excel5 on the Student Diskette. Sort the database by department within district within division. Select ascending sequence for all three sort keys. Use the Subtotals command to generate subtotals by division.

Microsoft Excel - CLE3-2.XLS

| | File | Edit | View | Insert | Format | Tools | Data | Window |

Arial   10   B I U

A17

	A	B	C	D	E
1			Sales Report		
2	Division	District	Department	Salesperson	Sales
3	2	2	2	301	120,391.12
4	1	2	2	210	324,156.32
5	2	1	3	315	342,516.54
6	1	2	1	215	867,212.00
7	1	1	1	316	723,190.50
8	2	1	1	435	564,738.20
9	1	2	3	102	994,019.12
10	1	2	2	211	98,621.40
11	3	1	2	302	432,516.60
12	2	1	1	409	657,341.32
13	2	2	2	123	109,283.00
14	2	2	3	213	839,201.50
15	1	1	2	111	718,294.90
16					
17					
18					

Sales Report / Sheet2 / Sheet3 / Sheet4 / Sheet5 /

Ready

FIGURE CLE3-2a

(continued)

COMPUTER LABORATORY EXERCISE 2 (continued)

Type 90% in the Zoom Control box on the Standard toolbar so the worksheet appears as shown in Figure CLE3-2b. Print the database with the subtotals. Use the Subtotals command to remove the subtotals. Choose 100% from the Zoom box drop-down list box on the Standard toolbar. Close the workbook.

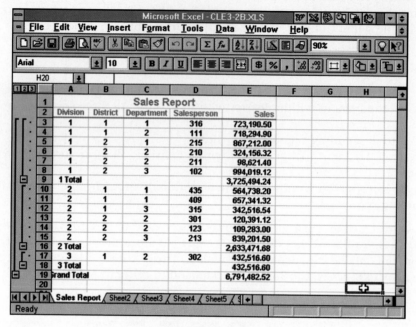

FIGURE CLE3-2b

COMPUTER LABORATORY EXERCISE 3
Filtering a Database

Instructions: Start Excel and perform the following tasks:

1. Open the workbook CLE3-3 from the subdirectory Excel 5 on the Student Diskette that accompanies this book. The workbook displays with the drop-down arrows as shown in Figure CLE3-3. Step through each filter exercise in Table CLE3-3 on the next page and print the results for each with gridlines off.

To complete a filter exercise, select the appropriate drop-down arrow and option. Use the (Custom...) option in filter exercises 3, 4, 5, 7, and 9. After you print the filtered list solution for each, choose the Show All command on the Filter cascading menu before you begin another filter exercise. When you are finished with the last filter exercise, remove the drop-down arrows by choosing the AutoFilter command on the Filter cascading menu. You should end up with the following number of records: 1 = 3; 2 = 3; 3 = 2; 4 = 1; 5 = 4; 6 = 2; 7 = 7; 8 = 2; 9 = 1; and 10 = 10.

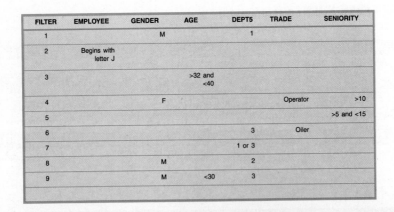

FILTER	EMPLOYEE	GENDER	AGE	DEPT5	TRADE	SENIORITY
1		M		1		
2	Begins with letter J					
3			>32 and <40			
4		F			Operator	>10
5						>5 and <15
6				3	Oiler	
7				1 or 3		
8		M		2		
9		M	<30	3		

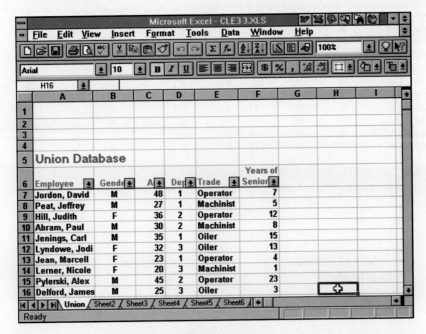

FIGURE CLE3-3

COMPUTER LABORATORY ASSIGNMENTS

COMPUTER LABORATORY ASSIGNMENT 1
Building and Sorting a Database of Prospective Programmers

Purpose: To become familiar with building a database using a data form and sorting a database.

Problem: You are an applications software specialist for Computer People, Inc. You have been assigned the task of building the Prospective Programmer Database shown in Figure CLA3-1. Create the database beginning in row 6 of the worksheet. Use the information in Table CLA3-1 on the following page.

(continued)

COMPUTER LABORATORY ASSIGNMENT 1 (continued)

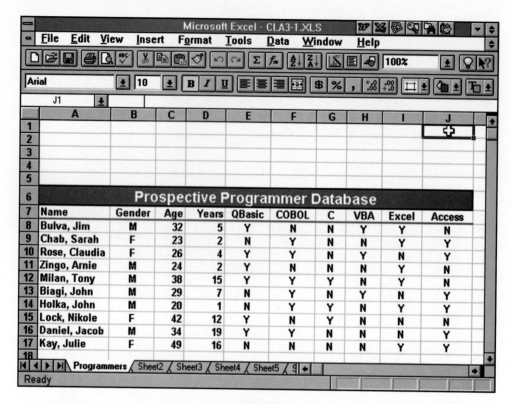

FIGURE CLA3-1

COLUMN HEADINGS (FIELD NAMES)	COLUMN	TYPE OF DATA	COLUMN WIDTH
Name	A	Text	13
Gender	B	Text	8
Age	C	Numeric	5
Years	D	Numeric	7
Qbasic	E	Text	8
COBOL	F	Text	8
C	G	Text	5
VBA	H	Text	6
Excel	I	Text	7
Access	J	Text	9

COMPUTER LABORATORY ASSIGNMENT 1 (continued)

Instructions: Perform the following tasks:

1. Bold the entire worksheet. Change the column widths as described in Table CLA3-1. Enter the database title and column titles (field names) as shown in Figure CLA3-1. Use the reference area in the formula bar to define the name Database as the range A7:J8. Use the Form command on the Data menu to display a data form to enter the ten records.

2. Enter your name, course, computer laboratory exercise (CLA3-1), date, and instructor name in the range A30:A34. Print the worksheet without gridlines. Save the workbook using the filename CLA3-1.

3. Sort the records in the database into ascending sequence by name. Print the sorted version.

4. Sort the records in the database by age within gender. Select ascending sequence for the gender code and ascending sequence for the age. Print the sorted version.

COMPUTER LABORATORY ASSIGNMENT 2
Filtering the Prospective Programmer Database

Purpose: To become familiar with finding records that pass a test using a data form, and to filter a database using the AutoFilter and Advanced Filter commands.

Problem: Complete the filtering operations on the Prospective Programmer Database described in Parts 1, 2, and 3 of this assignment. If you were not required to build the database in Computer Laboratory Assignment 1, ask your instructor for a copy of CLA3-1.

Part 1 Instructions: Open the workbook CLA3-1 (Figure CLA3-1). Save the workbook using the filename CLA3-2. Use the Criteria button on a data form to enter the comparison criteria for the following tasks. Use the Find Next button on the data form to find the records that pass the comparison criteria. Write down and submit the names of the prospective programmers who pass the comparison criteria for tasks a through d.

a. Find all records that represent prospective programmers who are male and can program in COBOL.

b. Find all records that represent prospective programmers who can program in QBasic and VBA and use Excel.

c. Find all records that represent prospective female programmers who are at least 29 years old and can use Access.

d. Find all records that represent prospective programmers who know Excel and Access.

e. All prospective programmers who did not know Access were sent to a seminar on the software package. Use the Find Next button to locate the records of these programmers and change the Access field entry on the data form from the letter N to the letter Y. Make sure you press the ENTER key or press the DOWN ARROW key after changing the letter. Save the database using the filename CLA3-2A. Print the worksheet without gridlines. Close CLA3-2A.

(continued)

COMPUTER LABORATORY ASSIGNMENT 2 (continued)

Part 2 Instructions: Open the workbook CLA3-2. Use the AutoFilter command on the Filter cascading menu and redo Part 1 a, b, c, and d. Use the Show All command on the Filter cascading menu before starting problems b, c, and d. Print the worksheet without gridlines for each problem. Change the laboratory assignment number in the range A30:A34 to CLA3-22x, where x is the problem letter. Choose the Auto Filter command on the Filter cascading menu to remove the drop-down arrows. Close CLA3-2 without saving it.

Part 3 Instructions: Open the workbook CLA3-2. Add a criteria range by copying the database title and field names (range A7:J8) to range A1:J2. Change cell A1 to Criteria Area. Use the reference area in the formula bar to name the criteria range (A1:J2) Criteria. Add an extract range by copying the database title and field names (range A7:J8) to range A21:J22. Change cell A21 to Extract Area. Use the reference area in the formula bar to name the extract range (A1:J2) Extract. Your worksheet should look similar to the screen in Figure CLA3-2a.

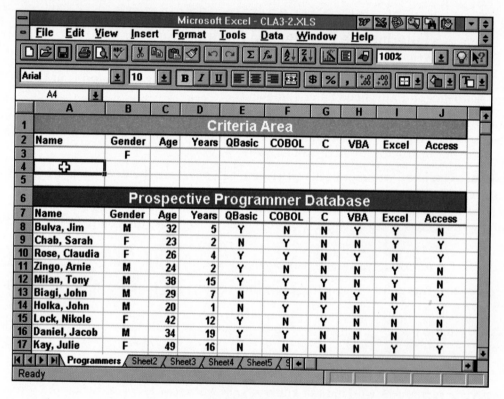

FIGURE CLA3-2a

Use the Advanced Filter command on the Filter cascading menu to extract records that pass the tests in tasks a through e below. Change the laboratory assignment number in the range A30:A34 to CLA3-23x, where x is the problem letter. Print the entire worksheet without gridlines after each extraction.

a. Extract the records that represent prospective programmers who are female (Figure CLA3-2b).

b. Extract the records that represent prospective programmers who can program in QBasic and cannot program in VBA.

c. Extract the records that represent prospective male programmers who are at least 30 years old and can use Excel.

d. Extract the records that represent prospective programmers who know VBA and Access.

e. Extract the records that represent prospective programmers who do not know how to use any programming language. Save the workbook using the filename CLA3-2B.

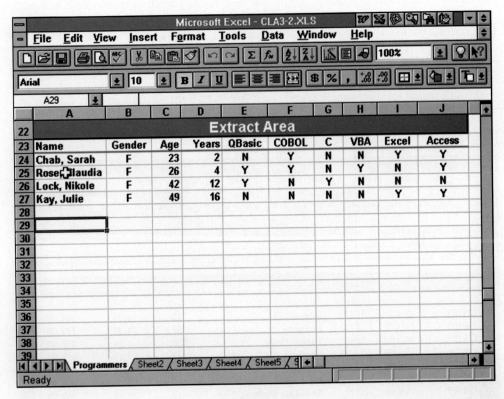

FIGURE CLA3-2b

COMPUTER LABORATORY ASSIGNMENT 3
Finding Subtotals and Creating a Pivot Table for an Order Entry Database

Purpose: To become familiar with building a database using a data form, displaying subtotals, zooming, and creating a pivot table.

Problem: You are employed as a spreadsheet specialist in the order entry department of JM Sports, Inc. You have been given the following assignments:

1. Develop an order entry database that keeps track of the outstanding orders (Figure CLA3-3a on the next page).
2. Display subtotals of the number ordered and amount (Figure CLA3-3b on page E191).
3. Create a pivot table for summarizing the amount (Figure CLA3-3c on page E191).

(continued)

COMPUTER LABORATORY ASSIGNMENT 3 (continued)

Part 1 Instructions: Perform the following tasks to create the database shown in the range A6:G18 in Figure CLA3-3a.

1. Change the font of the worksheet to bold. Change the column widths to the following: A = 9, B = 11, C = 8, D = 16, E = 12, F = 11, and G = 12. Enter and format the database title and field names in the range A5:G6. Center entries in column B. Align the field names as shown in row 6 in Figure CLA3-3a.
2. Enter the first record without using a data form. Enter the formula =E7 * F7 in cell G7. Define the name Database as the range A6:G7. Use a data form to enter the remaining order records.
3. Enter your name, course, computer laboratory assignment (CLA3-3a), date, and instructor name in the range A20:A24.
4. Save the workbook using the filename CLA3-3. Use the Page Setup command on the File menu or short-cut menu to change the left and right margins to 0.5 inch and turn off gridlines. Print the worksheet. Click the Save button on the Standard toolbar to save the workbook.

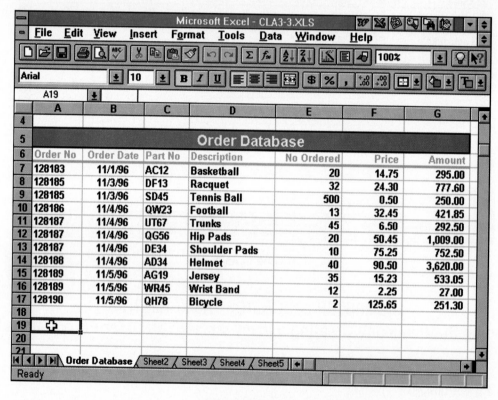

FIGURE CLA3-3a

Part 2 Instructions: Perform the following tasks to develop the subtotals shown in Figure CLA3-3b.

1. Select a cell within the range of Database. Choose the Subtotals command on the Data menu and determine totals for the No Ordered and Amount fields by the Order No field.
2. Change the magnification of the worksheet to 75% (Figure CLA3-3b).
3. Print the worksheet.
4. Hide detail records so only total rows display. Print the worksheet.
5. Change the magnification back to 100%. Use the Subtotals command on the Data menu to remove subtotals.

FIGURE CLA3-3b

Part 3 Instructions: Using the Order Database, create the pivot table shown in Figure CLA3-3c on a separate worksheet. The table summarizes dollar amount information by order number and order date (A7:G17). Use the Pivot Table command to create the pivot table. Print the pivot table without gridlines. Drag the Order No and Order Date buttons around on the pivot table to obtain different views of the information. Save the workbook using the filename CLA3-3A.

FIGURE CLA3-3c

COMPUTER LABORATORY ASSIGNMENT 4
Creating a Video Cassette Database

Purpose: To become familiar with planning, creating, and manipulating a database.

Problem: Obtain a list of at least fifteen movies from a nearby video store or library with the following information: movie title, year made, movie type (comedy, science fiction, suspense, drama, religious), director, producer, number of academy awards, and cost of the video. Create a video cassette database. Sort the database in alphabetical order by movie title. Create subtotals of the cost of videos by type. Using different combinations of comparison criteria, filter the database. For example, display movies that were produced prior to 1990 and have a movie type equal to comedy. Also, create a pivot table that summarizes the cost by type and director.

Enter your name, course, computer laboratory assignment number (CLA3-4), date, and instructor name well below the database in column A in separate but adjacent cells. Save the workbook using the filename CLA3-4.

Instructions: Submit the following:

1. A description of the problem. Include the purpose of the database, a statement outlining the required data, and calculations.
2. A handwritten design of the database.
3. A printed copy of the worksheet without gridlines.
4. A short description explaining how to use the worksheet.

DATABASE

USING MICROSOFT ACCESS 2 FOR WINDOWS

MICROSOFT ACCESS 2 FOR WINDOWS

PROJECT ONE

PRESENTING DATA: REPORTS AND FORMS

OBJECTIVES You will have mastered the material in this project when you can:

- ▸ Create a query for a report
- ▸ Use Report Wizards to create a report
- ▸ Use the Report window to modify a report design
- ▸ Understand sections in a report
- ▸ Save a report
- ▸ Close a report
- ▸ Print a report
- ▸ Create a report with grouping and subtotals
- ▸ Remove totals from a report
- ▸ Italicize letters in a report
- ▸ Center the title of a report
- ▸ Change properties of an item on a report

- ▸ Move between Design view, Print Preview, and Sample Preview
- ▸ Use FormWizards to create an initial form
- ▸ Use the Form window to modify a form design
- ▸ Move fields on a form
- ▸ Place a calculated field on a form
- ▸ Place a combo box on a form
- ▸ Place a rectangle on a form
- ▸ Change colors on a form
- ▸ Change the format of a field on a form
- ▸ View data using a form

▶ INTRODUCTION

P roject 1 introduces you to presenting the data in a database in a pleasing and useful way, either on paper or on the screen. Reports generated on a printer represent one way of presenting data. Figure 1-1 shows a report that lists the number, name, address, city, state, zip code, and available credit (credit limit minus current balance) of all customers. In addition, at the bottom of the report, the total of all the available credit amounts is listed. This report is similar to the one produced by clicking the Print button. It has two significant differences, however.

First, not all fields are included. The CUSTOMER table includes a Cust Type field, a Balance field, a Credit Limit field, and a Sales Rep Number field, none of which appears on this report. Second, this report contains a field, Available Credit, which does not appear in the CUSTOMER table. Available Credit is computed by subtracting the balance from the credit limit.

Available Credit Report

04-Oct-94

Customer Number	Name	Address	City	State	Zip Code	Available Credit
AN91	Atwater-Nelson	213 Watkins	Oakdale	IN	48101	$3,521.50
AW52	Alliance West	266 Ralston	Allanson	IN	48102	$4,507.80
BD22	Betodial	542 Prairie	Oakdale	IN	48101	$4,943.00
CE76	Carson Lanard Enterprise	96 Prospect	Bishop	IL	61354	$4,875.00
FC63	Forrest Eccles Co.	85 Stocking	Fergus	MI	48902	($822.00)
FY16	Fedder-Yansen	198 Pearl	Oakdale	IN	48101	$3,088.00
PA12	Paris Dev.	146 Dearhurst	Trent	MI	48252	$7,000.00
RO22	Robertson, Inc.	682 Maumee	Allanson	IN	48102	$6,663.75
RO92	Ronald A. Orten	872 Devonshire	Benson	MI	49246	$2,580.00

$36,357.05

FIGURE 1-1

The report shown in Figure 1-2 on the next page is similar to the one in Figure 1-1, but it contains an additional feature, grouping. **Grouping** means creating separate collections of records that share some common characteristic. In the report in Figure 1-2, for example, the records have been grouped by sales rep number. There are three separate groups: one for sales rep 04, one for sales rep 07, and one for sales rep 11. The appropriate sales rep number appears before each group, and the total of the balances for the customers in the group (called a **subtotal**) appears after, along with the percentage that this total represents of the overall total.

Another way of presenting data is through custom forms. You have already used a form to view records in a table, as well as to update records. The form was a standard form automatically created by the FormWizard. An alternative to simply using the form Microsoft Access creates is to design and use **custom forms**, whose characteristics you specify, like the one shown on the next page in Figure 1-3.

This project covers the design and creation of reports and forms.

▶ CREATING A REPORT

The simplest way to create a report design is to use Report Wizards. For some reports, Report Wizards can produce exactly the desired report. For others, however, first use Report Wizards to produce a report that is as close as possible to the desired report. Then, use the Report window to modify the report, transforming it into exactly the correct form. In either case, once the report is created and saved, you can print it at any time. Access will use the current data in the database for the report, formatting and arranging it in exactly the way specified when the report was created.

If a report uses only the fields in a single table, then use the table as a basis for the report. If the report uses extra fields (i.e., Available Credit) or uses multiple tables, however, the simplest way to create the report is first to create a query. The query should contain the exact fields and tables required for the report. This query forms the basis for the report.

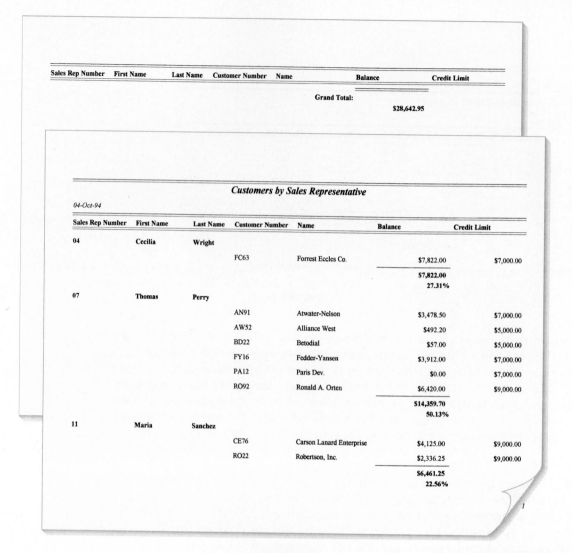

FIGURE 1-2

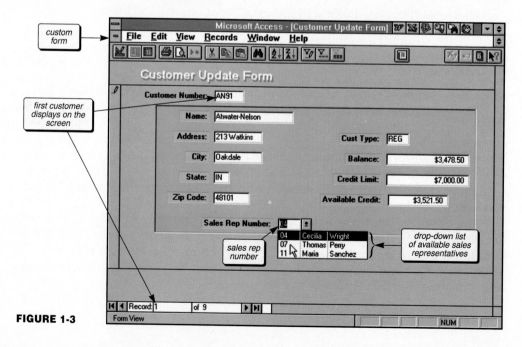

FIGURE 1-3

Creating the Query

The process for creating a query for a report is identical to the process for creating queries. Perform the following steps to create the query for the first report.

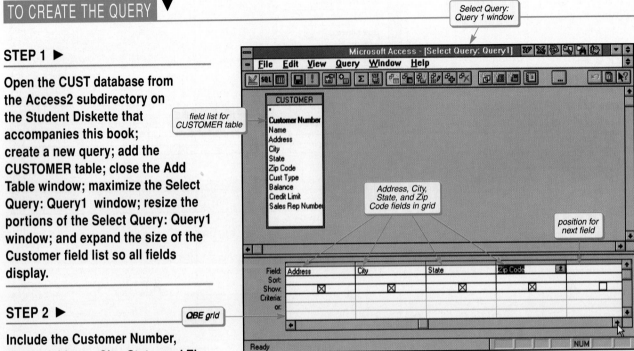

TO CREATE THE QUERY ▼

STEP 1 ▶

Open the CUST database from the Access2 subdirectory on the Student Diskette that accompanies this book; create a new query; add the CUSTOMER table; close the Add Table window; maximize the Select Query: Query1 window; resize the portions of the Select Query: Query1 window; and expand the size of the Customer field list so all fields display.

STEP 2 ▶

Include the Customer Number, Name, Address, City, State, and Zip Code fields in the QBE grid. To include a field, point to the field in the field list and double-click it.

FIGURE 1-4

STEP 3 ▶

Click the right scroll arrow twice to shift the fields to the left so space for an extra field is visible.

The fields have shifted to the left (Figure 1-4). The Address, City, State, and Zip Code fields display. The position for the next field also displays.

STEP 4 ▶

Point to the position for the next field and click the left mouse button. Press SHIFT+F2 to produce the Zoom dialog box. Type `Available Credit: [Credit Limit]-[Balance]` **(Figure 1-5)**.

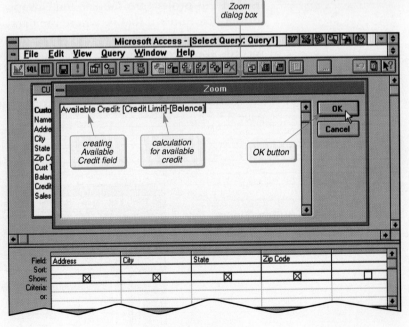

FIGURE 1-5

STEP 5 ▶

Choose the OK button. Select
the File menu.

*The Available Credit field displays
in the QBE grid (Figure 1-6). The
File menu displays.*

STEP 6 ▶

Choose the Save command. Type
`Available Credit Query` **as**
**the name of the query and choose
the OK button.**

The query is saved.

STEP 7 ▶

Close the query by double-clicking
its Control-menu box.

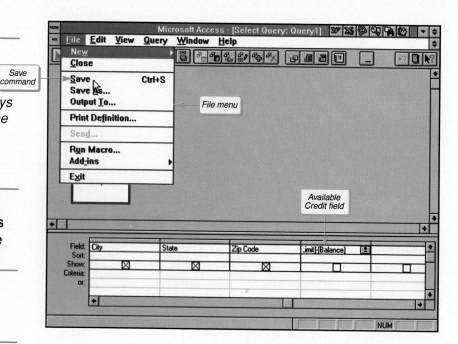

FIGURE 1-6

Creating a Report

To create a report, first choose the Report button (▣) and then choose the
New button. Next, use the Report Wizard to create the report. Access leads you
through a series of choices and questions. Access then creates the report
automatically.

The Report Wizard can create several different types of reports. The two types
used in this project are Tabular and Groups/Totals. **Tabular reports** present data
in a tabular fashion; that is, where the data appears in the form of a table. The
report in Figure 1-1 on page A3 is a tabular report. **Groups/Totals reports** group
records according to some criteria, such as having the same sales rep number, and
produce subtotals after each group. The report in Figure 1-2 on page A4 is an
example of such a report.

Perform the following steps to create the report shown in Figure 1-1 on
page A3.

TO CREATE A TABULAR REPORT ▼

STEP 1 ▶

Point to the Report button (Figure
1-7).

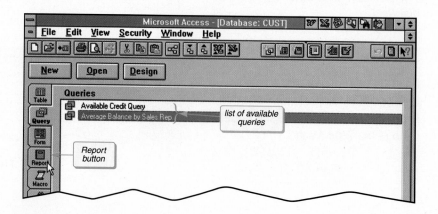

FIGURE 1-7

STEP 2 ▶

Choose the Report button and then choose the New button. Click the down arrow to display a list of available tables and queries and select the Available Credit Query.

The New Report dialog box displays (Figure 1-8) and Available Credit Query is selected.

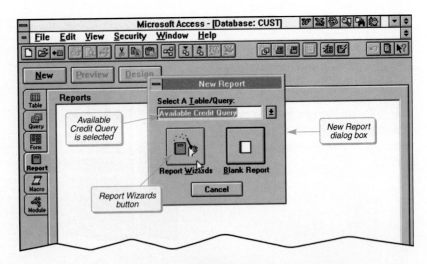

FIGURE 1-8

STEP 3 ▶

Choose the Report Wizards button (▣), select Tabular as the report type.

The Report Wizards dialog box displays (Figure 1-9). Tabular is selected as the report type.

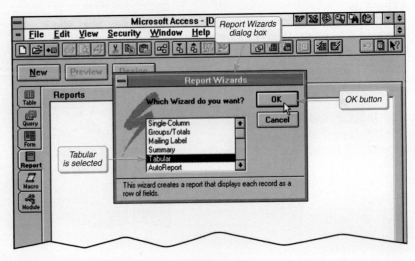

FIGURE 1-9

STEP 4 ▶

Choose the OK button and then point to the Add All Fields button (▣).

The Tabular Report Wizard dialog box displays (Figure 1-10), requesting the fields for the report. To add a selected field to the list of fields on the report, click the Add Field button. To add all fields, click the Add All Fields button.

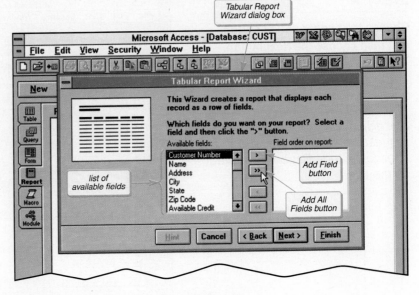

FIGURE 1-10

STEP 5 ▶

Click the Add All Fields button to add all the fields and then choose the Next button.

The Tabular Report Wizard dialog box displays (Figure 1-11), requesting the field or fields to sort by.

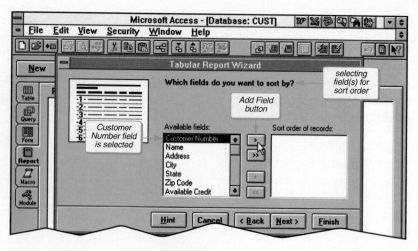

FIGURE 1-11

STEP 6 ▶

Because the correct field (Customer Number) is already selected, click the Add Field button. Choose the Next button.

The Tabular Report Wizard dialog box displays (Figure 1-12), requesting the style for the report.

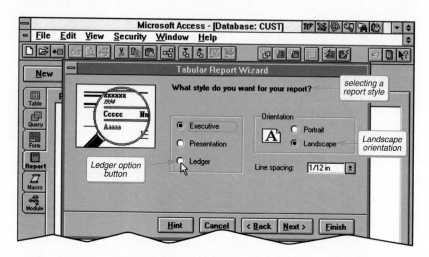

FIGURE 1-12

STEP 7 ▶

Choose the Ledger option button and then choose the Next button. **Type** Available Credit Report **as the report title.**

The Tabular Report Wizard dialog box displays (Figure 1-13), requesting a title for the report. Available Credit Report is entered as the title.

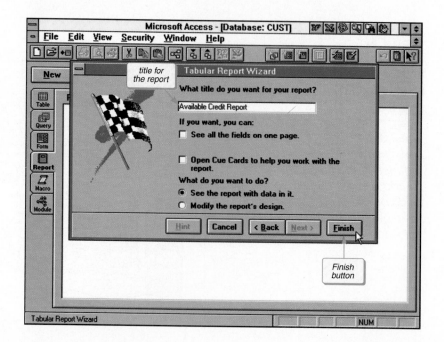

FIGURE 1-13

STEP 8 ▶

Choose the Finish button.

The report design is complete and displays in the Report window (Figure 1-14).

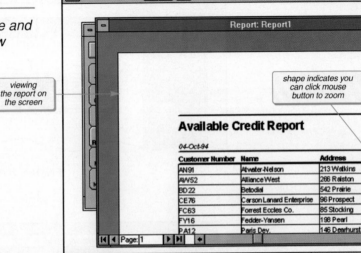

viewing
the report on
the screen

shape indicates you
can click mouse
button to zoom

mouse
pointer

Available Credit Report

04-Oct-94

Customer Number	Name	Address	City	St
AN91	Atwater-Nelson	213 Watkins	Oakdale	IN
AW52	Alliance West	266 Ralston	Allanson	IN
BD22	Betodial	542 Prairie	Oakdale	IN
CE76	Carson Lanard Enterprise	96 Prospect	Bishop	IL
FC63	Forrest Eccles Co.	85 Stocking	Fergus	M
FY16	Fedder-Yansen	198 Pearl	Oakdale	IN
PA12	Paris Dev.	146 Dearhurst	Trent	M

FIGURE 1-14

Using the Report Window

Within the Report Window, there are three different possible views: Design view, Sample Preview, and Print Preview. Use **Design view** to modify the design (layout) of the report. Use **Sample Preview** to see a small portion of the report with sample data. Use **Print Preview** to see the entire width of the report. To move from Design view to Print Preview or Sample Preview, click the Print Preview button or Sample Preview button () on the toolbar. To move from either Print Preview or Sample Preview to Design view, click the Close Window button on the toolbar. To transfer between Print Preview and Sample Preview, make sure the mouse pointer points somewhere within the report (it will look like a magnifying glass) and then click the left mouse button.

Perform the following steps first to change from Sample Preview to Print Preview. The next step changes to Design view by closing the window.

TO USE THE REPORT WINDOW ▼

STEP 1 ▶

With the mouse pointer within the report, click the left mouse button.

The Sample Preview (see Figure 1-14) is replaced by Print Preview (Figure 1-15).

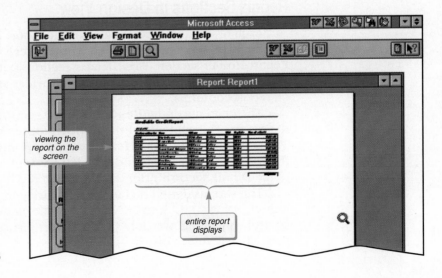

viewing the
report on the
screen

entire report
displays

FIGURE 1-15

STEP 2 ▶

Point to the Close Window button (Figure 1-16).

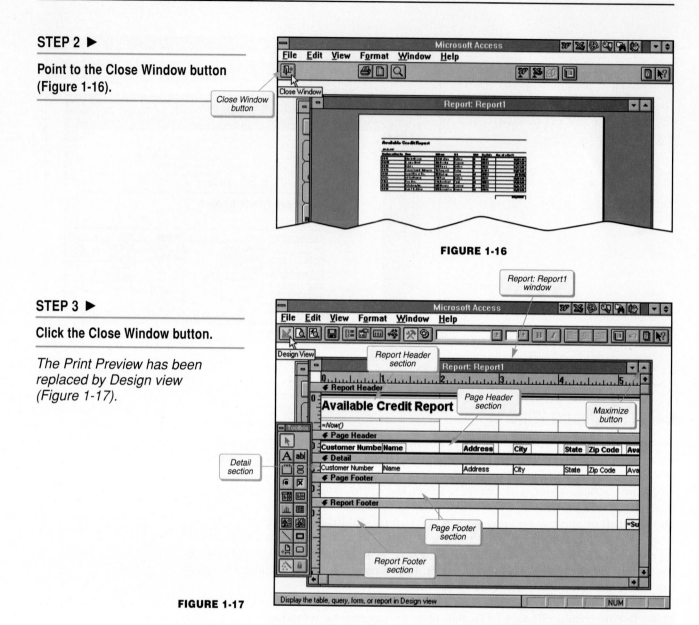

FIGURE 1-16

STEP 3 ▶

Click the Close Window button.

The Print Preview has been replaced by Design view (Figure 1-17).

FIGURE 1-17

Report Sections in Design View

Each of the different portions of the report is described in what is termed a **section**. The sections are labeled on the screen (see Figure 1-17). Notice the Report Header section, Page Header section, Detail section, Page Footer section, and Report Footer section. A toolbox provides assistance in placing various objects on reports or forms.

The contents of the **Report Header section** print once, at the beginning of the report. The contents of the **Report Footer section** print once, at the end. The contents of the **Page Header section** print once, at the top of each page, and the contents of the **Page Footer section** print once, at the bottom. The contents of the **Detail section** print once for each record in the table.

The various dotted rectangles, appearing in Figure 1-17, (Available Credit Report, =Now( ), Customer Number, Name, and so on) are called **controls**. The control containing Available Credit Report displays the report title. The control containing =Now( ) displays the date.

The controls in the Detail section display the contents of the corresponding fields. The control containing Customer Number, for example, displays the customer number. The controls in the Page Header section display exactly as they appear and serve as **captions** for the data. The Customer Number control in this section, for example, displays the words "Customer Number" immediately above the column of customers, thus making it clear to anyone reading the report that the items in the column are, in fact, customer numbers.

To move, resize, delete, or modify a control, select it by pointing to it and click the left mouse button. Small squares called **handles** appear around the border of the control. Drag the control to move it, drag one of the handles to resize it, or press the DELETE key to delete it. Clicking a second time produces an insertion point in the control in order to modify its contents.

Saving the Report

Use the Save command on the File menu to save the report, as in the following steps.

TO SAVE THE REPORT ▼

STEP 1 ▶

Select the File menu (Figure 1-18).

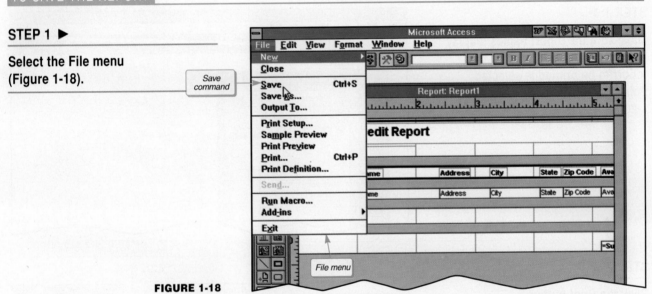

FIGURE 1-18

STEP 2 ▶

Choose the Save command and then type Available Credit Report as the report name.

The Save As dialog box displays (Figure 1-19). The report name is entered.

STEP 3 ▶

Choose the OK button.

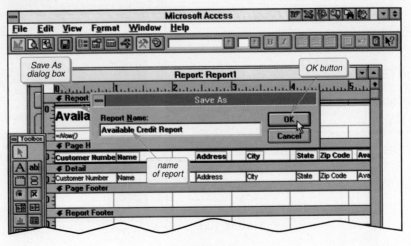

FIGURE 1-19

Closing a Report

Once the report is complete, close the report by closing the window containing the report design. Perform the following step to close the report.

TO CLOSE THE REPORT

Step 1: Make sure Design view displays. If Sample Preview or Print Preview displays, click the Close button on the toolbar to return to Design view. Then, close the window by double-clicking the Control-menu box.

Printing a Report

To print the report, select the report name in the Database window and then click the Print button, as in the following steps.

TO PRINT THE REPORT ▼

STEP 1 ▶

Make sure the report names display in the Database window and the report to be printed is selected. Point to the Print button (Figure 1-20).

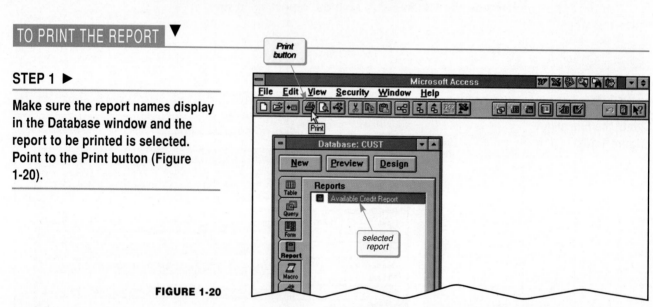

FIGURE 1-20

STEP 2 ▶

Click the Print button.

The Print dialog box displays (Figure 1-21).

STEP 3 ▶

Choose the OK button in the Print dialog box.

The report prints. It looks the same as the report that was shown in Figure 1-1 on page A3.

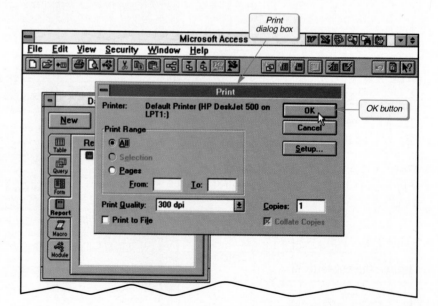

FIGURE 1-21

▶ GROUPING

S ometimes, you want to **group** records in a report; that is, to create separate collections of records sharing some common characteristic. In the report in Figure 1-2 on page A4, for example, the records were grouped by sales rep. There are three separate groups: one for each sales rep.

In grouping, reports typically include two other types of sections: a group header and a group footer. A **group header** is printed before the records in a particular group, and a **group footer** is printed after. In Figure 1-2, the group header indicates the sales rep. The group footer includes the total of the balances for the customers of that sales rep. Such a total is called a **subtotal**, because it is just a subset of the overall total of the balances.

To group records in Access, use Groups/Totals as the report style. Again, create an appropriate query before creating the report.

Creating the Query

Because the report involves data from two tables, the query needs to draw data from two tables. Perform the following steps to create an appropriate query for the report.

TO CREATE THE QUERY ▼

STEP 1 ▶

Create a new query by choosing the Query button in the Database window and then choosing the New button. Include both the CUSTOMER and SLSREP tables. Resize the two portions of the screen. Include the Sales Rep Number, the First Name, and Last Name fields from the SLSREP table. Include the Customer Number and Name fields from the CUSTOMER table in the query as well (Figure 1-22).

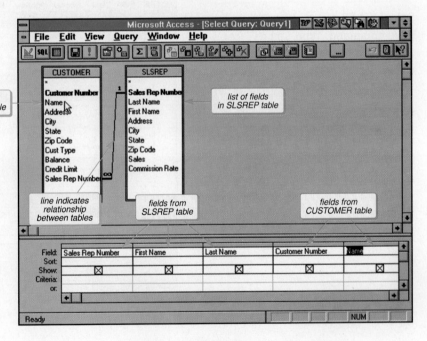

FIGURE 1-22

STEP 2 ▶

Include the Balance and Credit Limit fields from the CUSTOMER table. To verify that they have been included, click the right scroll arrow twice.

The Balance and Credit Limit fields display (Figure 1-23).

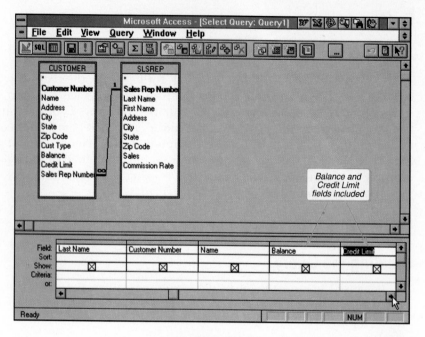

FIGURE 1-23

STEP 3 ▶

Select the File menu and choose the Save command. Type `Sales Reps and Customers` as the query name (Figure 1-24).

STEP 4 ▶

Choose the OK button to save the query. Close the query.

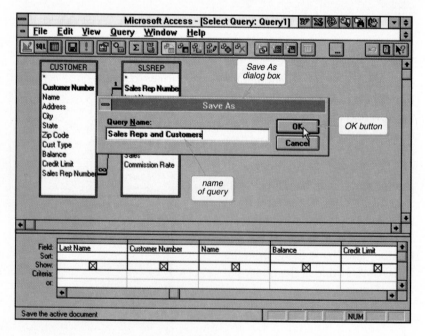

FIGURE 1-24

TO CREATE THE REPORT ▼

STEP 1 ▶

Choose the Report button and then choose the New button. Select the Sales Reps and Customers query.

STEP 2 ▶

Choose the Report Wizards button and select Groups/Totals as the report type.

The Report Wizards dialog box displays (Figure 1-25). Groups/ Totals is selected as the report type.

FIGURE 1-25

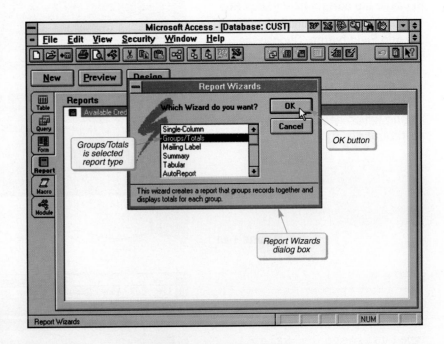

STEP 3 ▶

Choose the OK button (Figure 1-26).

FIGURE 1-26

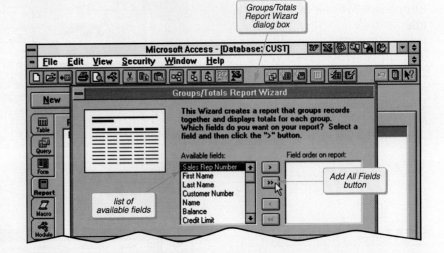

STEP 4 ▶

Click the Add All Fields button to add all the fields and then choose the Next button.

The Groups/Totals Report Wizard dialog box displays (Figure 1-27), requesting the field or fields to group by.

FIGURE 1-27

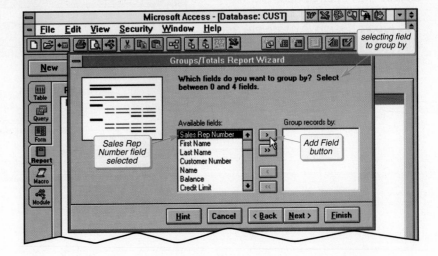

STEP 5 ▶

Because the correct field (Sales Rep Number) is already selected, click the Add Field button. Choose the Next button.

The Groups/Totals Report Wizard dialog box displays (Figure 1-28), asking which field should be used for grouping.

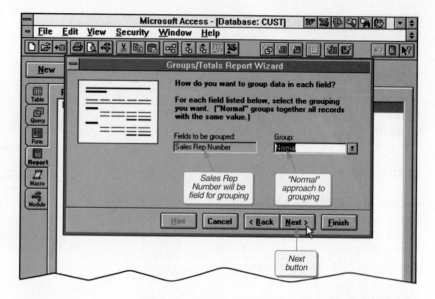

FIGURE 1-28

STEP 6 ▶

Choose the Next button until the screen in Figure 1-29 displays. **Type** Customers by Sales Representative **as the report title.**

The Groups/Totals Report Wizard dialog box displays (Figure 1-29), requesting a title for the report. Customers by Sales Representative is entered as the title.

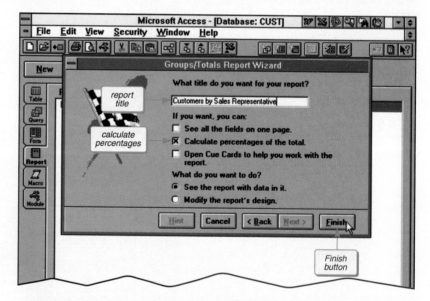

FIGURE 1-29

STEP 7 ▶

Choose the Finish button.

The report design is complete and displays in the Report: Report1 window (Figure 1-30).

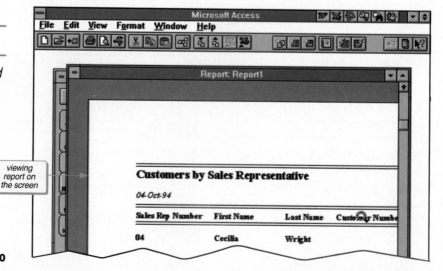

FIGURE 1-30

Changing from Sample Preview to Print Preview

To see the entire report, change from Sample Preview to Print Preview. To do so, point to a portion of the report so the pointer shape becomes a magnifying glass and then click the left mouse button, as in the following steps.

TO CHANGE FROM SAMPLE PREVIEW TO PRINT PREVIEW

STEP 1 ▶

While in Sample Preview (Figure 1-30), click the left mouse button.

The display changes to Print Preview so the entire width of the report displays (Figure 1-31).

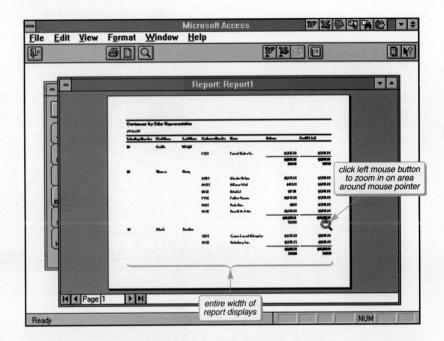

FIGURE 1-31

STEP 2 ▶

Move the mouse pointer to the approximate position shown in Figure 1-31 and then click the left mouse button.

The display changes again so only the portion around the mouse pointer displays (Figure 1-32).

STEP 3 ▶

Click the Close Window button to switch from Print Preview to Design view.

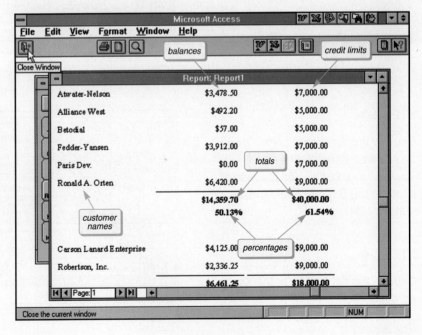

FIGURE 1-32

Saving the Report

You will need to make changes to the report design. Before making further changes, however, it's a good idea to save the report. That way, if you make mistakes as you are modifying the design, you can close the report without saving and then open it again. By doing so, you will have restored the report to its current state; that is, none of your changes will have been made.

To save the report, use the Save command on the File menu, as shown in the following steps.

TO SAVE THE REPORT ▼

STEP 1 ▶

Select the File menu (Figure 1-33).

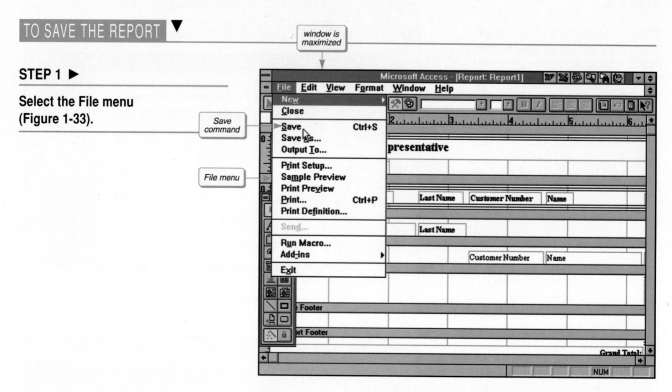

FIGURE 1-33

STEP 2 ▶

Choose the Save command. Type `Customers by Sales Representative` as the report name in the Save As dialog box (Figure 1-34).

STEP 3 ▶

Choose the OK button in the Save As dialog box.

The report is saved.

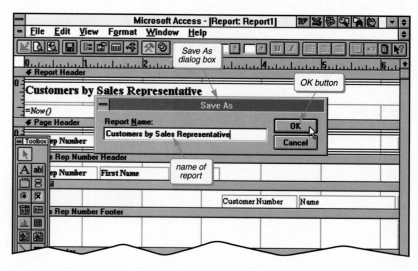

FIGURE 1-34

Removing Unwanted Totals

To remove a total or other field that should not be included in the final report, first select it by pointing to it and click the left mouse button. Then, press the DELETE key, as shown in the following steps.

STEP 1 ►

Maximize the window containing the report design. Point to the right scroll arrow (Figure 1-35).

STEP 2 ►

Click the right scroll arrow until the right-hand edge of the report displays and then click the down scroll arrow until the bottom of the report displays.

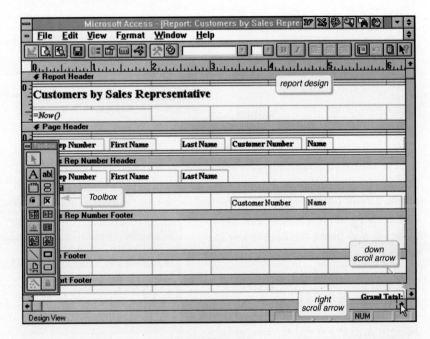

FIGURE 1-35

STEP 3 ►

Point to the entry that reads =Sum([Credit Limit]) in the Sales Rep Number Footer (Figure 1-36) and then click the left mouse button to select the field.

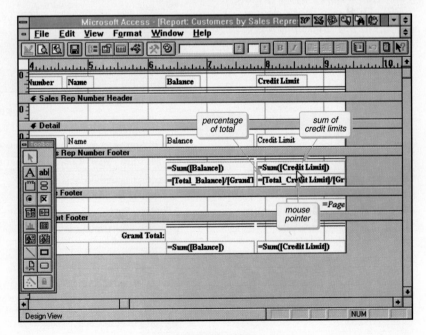

FIGURE 1-36

STEP 4 ▶

Press the DELETE key to remove the sum of credit limits and then point to the entry that reads, =[Total_Credit Limit]/[Gr. Click the left mouse button to select it and then press the DELETE key to remove it.

The entry for the sum of the credit limits has been removed (Figure 1-37).

FIGURE 1-37

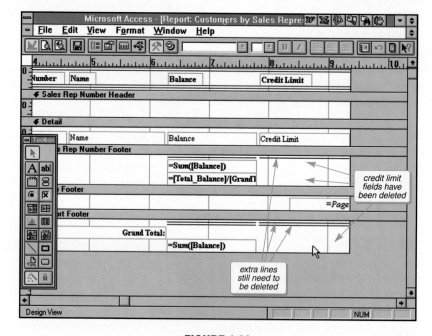

STEP 5 ▶

Point to the entry that reads, =Sum([Credit Limit]), in the Report Footer, click the left mouse button to select it, and press the DELETE key to remove it.

The entry for the percentage of credit limits has been removed from the Sales Rep Number Footer, and the entry for the total of credit limits has been removed from the Report Footer (Figure 1-38). The lines that Access placed in the design to emphasize the totals still need to be removed.

FIGURE 1-38

STEP 6 ▶

Point to the line in the Sales Rep Number Footer that is directly under the Credit Limit control (Figure 1-39).

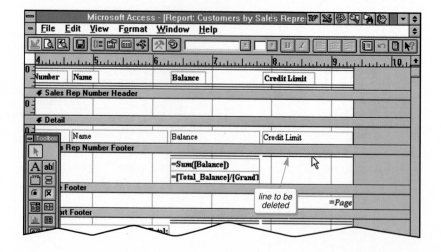

FIGURE 1-39

STEP 7 ►

Select the line by clicking the left mouse button.

Handles appear on the line, indicating that it is selected (Figure 1-40).

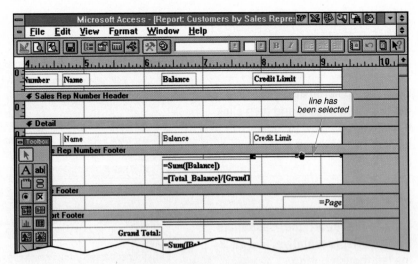

FIGURE 1-40

STEP 8 ►

Press the DELETE key to remove the line. Use the same technique to remove each of the two lines in the Report Footer that are under the Credit Limit control.

The lines under the Credit Limit control have been removed (Figure 1-41).

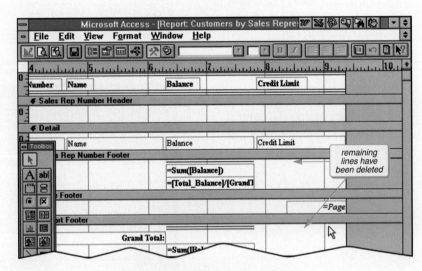

FIGURE 1-41

Changing the Report Header

To change the physical characteristics of any portion of a report, use the shortcut menu for the portion to be changed. To change the report title so the letters are italicized, for example, or so the title is centered, first select the control containing the title (the rectangle in which the title displays), then click the right mouse button to produce its shortcut menu. Choose the Properties command from the shortcut menu to produce a list of the properties that can be changed. To italicize the letters in the title, change the Font Italic property from No to Yes. To center the title, change the Text Align property from Left to Center.

In general, if you have a change you wish to make to a portion of a report or form, produce the shortcut menu, choose the Properties command, and then examine the list of properties for the property you wish to change. Once you have found it, you can make the change.

Perform the steps on the next page to use the Properties command to italicize and center the title.

TO CHANGE THE REPORT HEADER ▼

STEP 1 ▶

Click the up scroll arrow to move to the top of the report and then click the left scroll arrow to move back to the left-hand side of the report.

STEP 2 ▶

Point to the report title, Customers by Sales Representative, and click the left mouse button.

The control containing Customers by Sales Representative is selected (Figure 1-42).

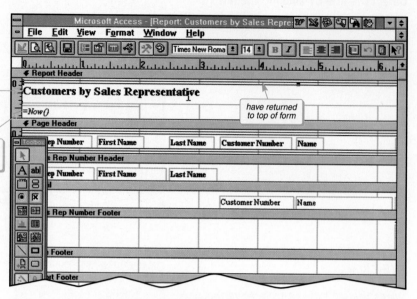

FIGURE 1-42

STEP 3 ▶

Point anywhere inside the control (the rectangle) containing the report title and click the right mouse button.

The shortcut menu for the control displays (Figure 1-43).

FIGURE 1-43

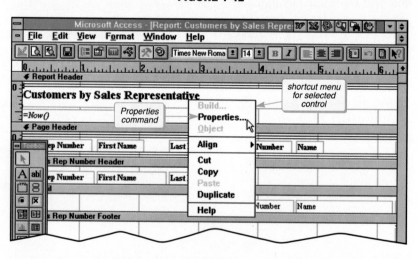

STEP 4 ▶

Choose the Properties command and then point to the text box for the Font Italic property (Figure 1-44).

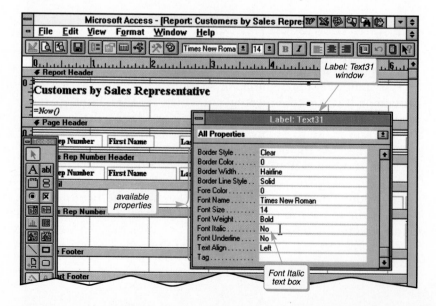

FIGURE 1-44

STEP 5 ▶

Click the left mouse button and then click the drop-down arrow that displays in the Font Italic text box.

The options for the Font Italic property display (Figure 1-45).

STEP 6 ▶

Select Yes as the option for the Font Italic property by pointing to it and clicking the left mouse button.

FIGURE 1-45

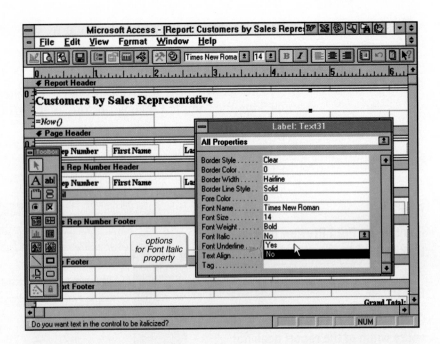

STEP 7 ▶

Point to the text box for the Text Align property, click the left mouse button, and then click the drop-down arrow that displays.

The options for the Text Align property display (Figure 1-46).

STEP 8 ▶

Select Center as the option for the Text Align property by pointing to it and clicking the left mouse button.

FIGURE 1-46

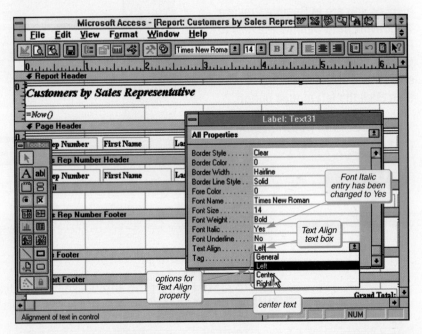

STEP 9 ▶

Close the Label: Text31 window by double-clicking its Control-menu box.

The report title appears in italics and is centered within the report (Figure 1-47).

FIGURE 1-47

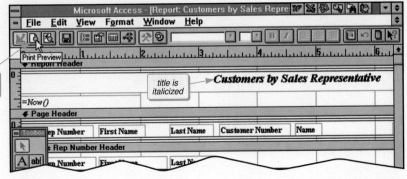

The changes to the header are now complete.

Previewing the Report

To see what the report looks like with sample data, preview the report by clicking the Sample Preview button, as shown in the following steps.

TO PREVIEW THE REPORT ▼

STEP 1 ►

Point to the Print Preview button (Figure 1-47 on the previous page).

STEP 2 ►

Click the Print Preview button. If the entire width of the report does not display, you are in Sample Preview. To convert from Sample Preview to Print Preview, move the mouse pointer (a magnifying glass) somewhere within the report and then click the left mouse button.

A preview of the report displays (Figure 1-48).

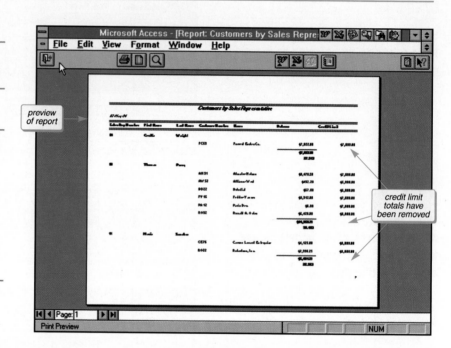

preview of report

credit limit totals have been removed

FIGURE 1-48

Closing the Report

To close a report, be sure Design view displays and then close the window. Perform the following step to close the report.

TO CLOSE THE REPORT

Step 1: If the Print Preview window displays, close it by clicking the Close Window button. Then, close the Report window by double-clicking the Control-menu box. Choose the Yes button to save the report.

Printing a Report

To print the report, select it in the Database window and then click the Print button, as shown in the following steps.

TO PRINT THE REPORT

Step 1: Make sure that the reports display in the Database window and that the Customers by Sales Representative report to be printed is selected. Point to the Print button.

Step 2: Click the Print button and then choose the OK button in the Print dialog box.

The report prints. It looks the same as the report that was shown in Figure 1-2 on page A4.

▶ REPORT DESIGN CONSIDERATIONS

hen designing and creating reports, keep in mind the following guidelines.

1. The purpose of any report is to provide certain information. Ask yourself if the report conveys this information effectively. Is the meaning of the rows and columns in the report clear? Are the column captions easily understood? Are there any abbreviations on the report that would not be clear to those looking at the report?
2. Be sure to allow sufficient white space between groups. To accomplish this, enlarge the group footer.
3. You can use different fonts and sizes, but do not overuse them. Using more than two or three different fonts and/or sizes often gives a cluttered and amateurish look to the report.
4. Be consistent when creating reports. Once you have decided on a general style, stick with it.

▶ CREATING AND USING CUSTOM FORMS

Y ou have already used a form to add new records to a table, as well as to change existing records. When you did, you created a basic form using the AutoForm button. Although the form did provide some assistance in the task, the form was not particularly pleasing. The standard form stacked fields on top of each other at the left side of the screen. This section covers custom forms that can be used in place of the basic form created by the wizards. To create such a form, first use the appropriate FormWizards to create a basic form. Then, modify the design of this form, transforming it into the correct one.

Beginning the Form Creation

To create a form, first choose the Form button and then choose the New button. Next, use the appropriate FormWizards to create the form. The FormWizards leads you through a series of choices and questions. Access will then create the form automatically.

Perform the steps on the next page to create an initial form that will be modified later to produce the form shown in Figure 1-3 on page A4.

TO BEGIN CREATING A FORM ▼

STEP 1 ▶

Make sure the CUST database is open and then choose the Form button.

The list of forms currently available displays (Figure 1-49).

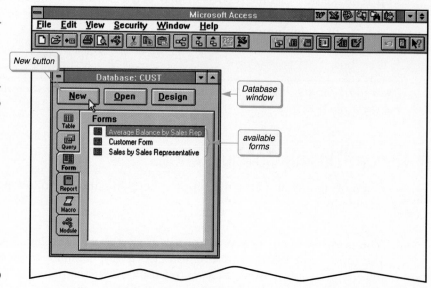

FIGURE 1-49

STEP 2 ▶

Choose the New button, click the drop-down arrow, and then select the CUSTOMER table.

The New Form dialog box displays (Figure 1-50). The CUSTOMER table is selected.

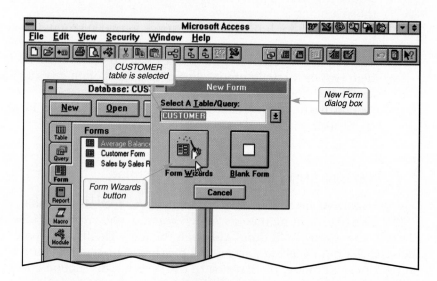

FIGURE 1-50

STEP 3 ▶

Click the Form Wizards button and then choose the OK button in the Form Wizard dialog box that displays. (The correct FormWizard, Single-Column, is already selected.)

The Single-Column Form Wizard dialog box displays (Figure 1-51). The Customer Number field is selected.

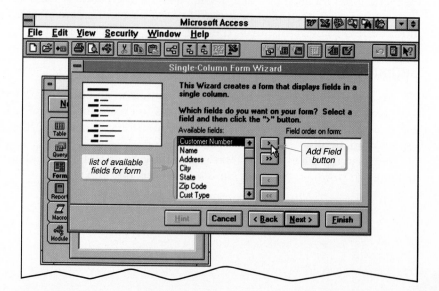

FIGURE 1-51

STEP 4 ▶

Add all fields except the Sales Rep Number field by repeatedly clicking the Add Field button.

All fields have been added to the form except the Sales Rep Number field (Figure 1-52).

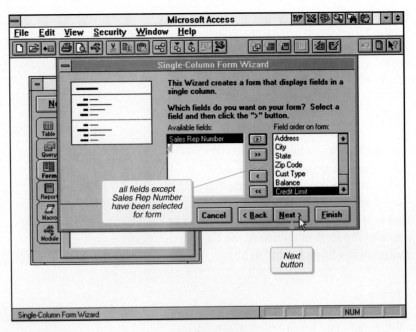

FIGURE 1-52

STEP 5 ▶

Choose the Next button.

The Single-Column Form Wizard dialog box displays, asking for a form style (Figure 1-53).

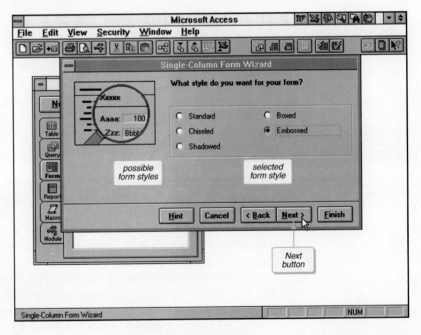

FIGURE 1-53

STEP 6 ▶

Choose the Next button and then type Customer Update Form as the title for the form (Figure 1-54).

STEP 7 ▶

Choose the Finish button to complete and display the form. Select the File menu and choose the Save Form command. Type Customer Update Form as the name of the form and choose the OK button in the Save As dialog box.

STEP 8 ▶

Double-click the Control-menu box for the Customer Update Form window to close the form.

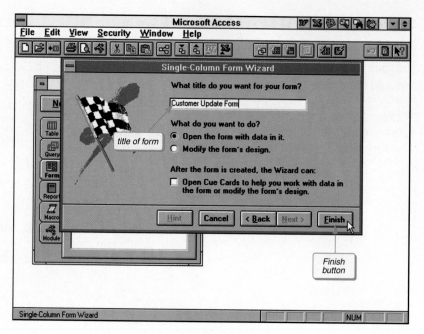

FIGURE 1-54

Modifying the Form Design

To modify the design of an existing form, select the form from the Database window and then choose the Design button. Then, modify the design. The modification can include moving fields, adding new fields, and changing field characteristics. It can also include adding special effects, such as rectangles and combo boxes. Colors can be changed as well.

Just as with reports, the various items on a form are called controls. There are three types. **Bound controls** are used to display data extracted from the database, such as the customer number and name. Bound controls have **attached labels** that typically display the name of the field that furnishes the data for the control. The words Customer Number that appear before the Customer Number control field are the attached label.

Unbound controls are not associated with data from the database and are used to display such things as the form's title. Finally, **calculated controls** are used to display data that is calculated from data in the database, such as available credit, which is calculated by subtracting the balance from the credit limit.

Some of the changes involve using the property sheet for the control to be changed. The **property sheet** is a list of properties for the control that can be modified. You can use the property sheet of the rectangle on the form, for example, to change the color of the rectangle, or you can use the property sheet of the Available Credit control to change the format that Access uses to display the contents of the control. To produce the property sheet, point to the desired control and then double-click the left mouse button. Finally, make the change and close the window containing the property sheet.

Perform the following steps to modify the design of the Customer Update Form created earlier.

TO MODIFY THE FORM DESIGN ▼

STEP 1 ▶

Make sure the CUST database is open and the Form button is selected.

STEP 2 ▶

Highlight the Customer Update Form, choose the Design button, maximize the window, and then point to the right-hand edge of the form.

The Customer Update Form displays in a maximized window (Figure 1-55). The pointer, which has changed to a dark heavy plus sign with two arrowheads points to the right-hand edge of the form.

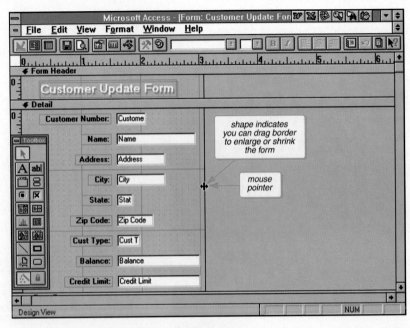

FIGURE 1-55

STEP 3 ▶

Drag the right-hand edge of the form to the 6" mark on the ruler and then point to the Cust Type field (Figure 1-56).

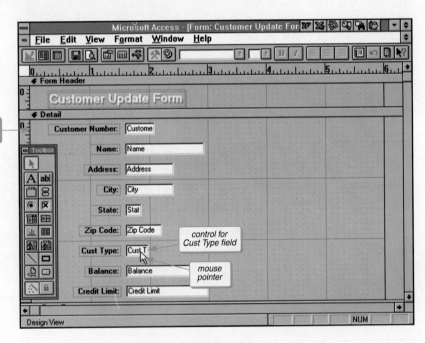

FIGURE 1-56

STEP 4 ▶

Click the left mouse button to select the Cust Type field and then move the pointer until the shape changes to a hand (✋).

Handles appear, indicating the field is selected (Figure 1-57). The pointer has changed to a hand.

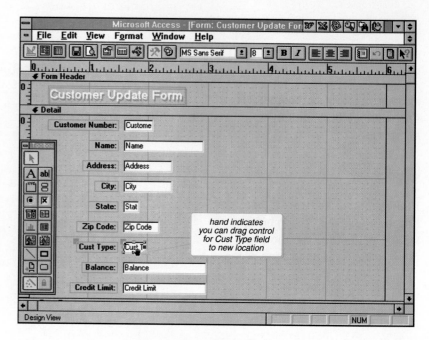

FIGURE 1-57

STEP 5 ▶

Drag the Cust Type field to the position shown in Figure 1-58. Use the same steps to move the other fields to the positions shown in Figure 1-58.

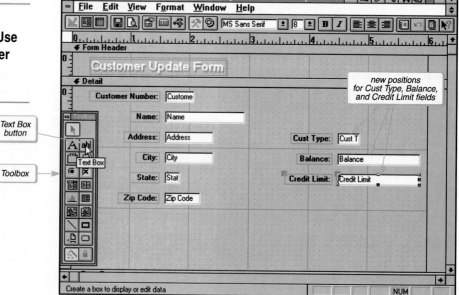

FIGURE 1-58

▲

Adding a New Field

To add a new field, use the Text Box button (⬛) in the Toolbox. (If the Toolbox does not display, select the View option and choose the Toolbox command.) Position the field on the form and then indicate the contents of the field. Perform the following steps to add the Available Credit field to the form.

TO ADD A NEW FIELD ▼

STEP 1 ▶

Point to the Text Box button (see Figure 1-58).

STEP 2 ▶

Click the Text Box button and then move the pointer, which has changed shape to a small plus sign together with a box containing the letters ab (+ab), to the position shown in Figure 1-59.

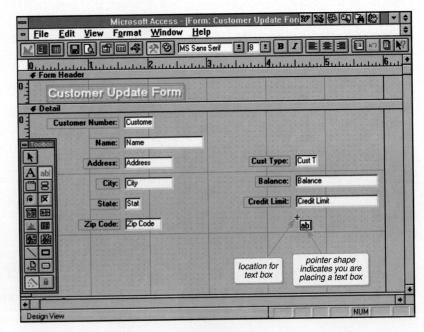

FIGURE 1-59

STEP 3 ▶

Click the left mouse button to place a text box. Type
`=[Credit Limit]-[Balance]`
as the expression in the text box.

A text box displays on the form (Figure 1-60). The expression for the text box, =[Credit Limit] –[Balance] displays in the text box.

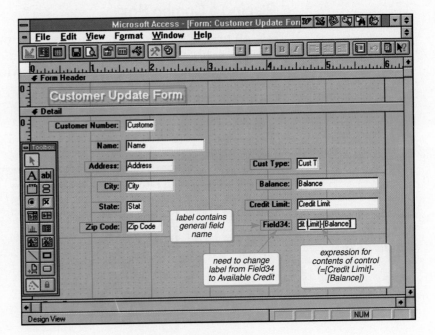

FIGURE 1-60

STEP 4 ▶

Point to the field label (the box that contains Field34) (your number might be different) and click the left mouse button twice to produce an insertion point in the label. Press the DELETE key to delete Field34, type `Available Credit:` and press the ENTER key.

The label has been changed to Available Credit: (Figure 1-61).

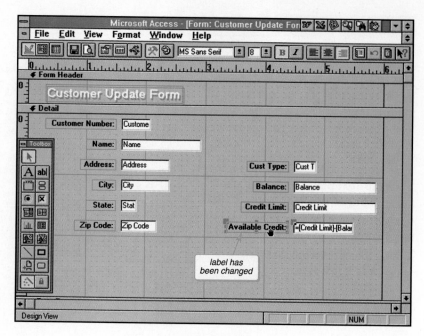

FIGURE 1-61

Placing a Combo Box

To place a **combo box**, which is a box that allows a user to select entries from a list, use the Combo Box button () in the Toolbox. A wizard will then lead you through the process. Perform the following steps to place a combo box for the Sales Rep Number on the form.

TO PLACE A COMBO BOX ▼

STEP 1 ▶

Make sure the Control Wizards button is selected. Point to the Combo Box button in the Toolbox (Figure 1-62).

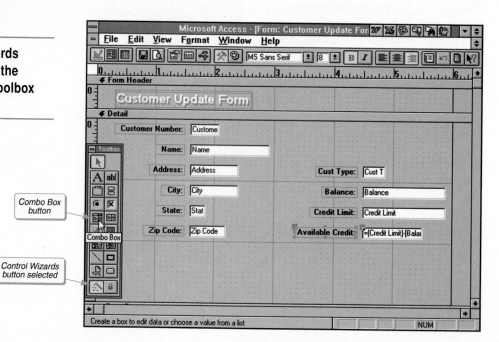

FIGURE 1-62

STEP 2 ▶

Click the Combo Box button and then move the pointer, whose shape has changed to a small plus sign with a combo box (⁺▤), to the position shown in Figure 1-63.

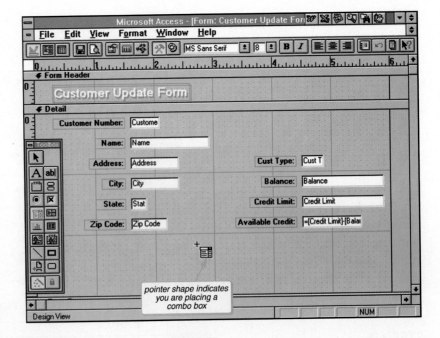

FIGURE 1-63

STEP 3 ▶

Click the left mouse button to place a combo box.

The Combo Box Wizard dialog box displays (Figure 1-64), instructing you to indicate how the combo box is to get values for the list.

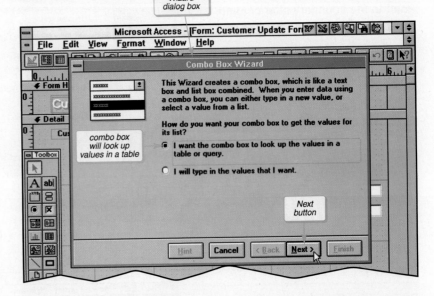

FIGURE 1-64

STEP 4 ▶

Choose the Next button in the Combo Box Wizard dialog box, select the SLSREP table, and then point to the Next button.

The SLSREP table is selected as the table to provide values for the combo box (Figure 1-65).

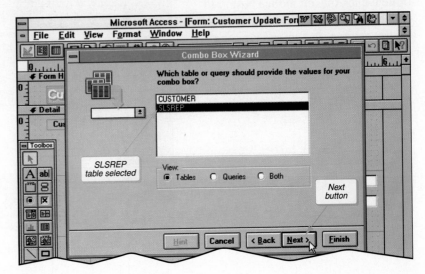

FIGURE 1-65

STEP 5 ▶

Choose the Next button.

The Sales Rep Number field is selected as a field whose values are to be listed in the combo box (Figure 1-66).

STEP 6 ▶

Click the Add Field button to add the Sales Rep Number as a field in the combo box. Select the First Name field and then click the Add Field button. Select the Last Name field and then click the Add Field button. Then, choose the Next button.

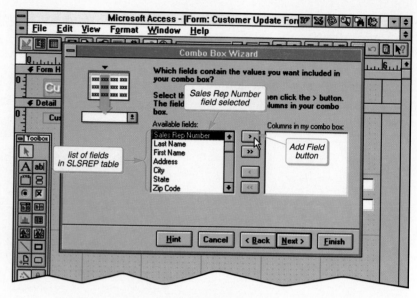

FIGURE 1-66

STEP 7 ▶

Point to the boundary after column 1 (Col1:).

The mouse pointer, whose shape has changed to a dark heavy plus sign with two arrowheads is positioned on the border between the first two columns (Figure 1-67).

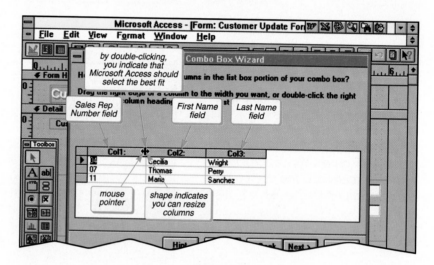

FIGURE 1-67

STEP 8 ▶

Double-click the left mouse button to cause Access to select the best fit for the column. Repeat the process for the second and third columns.

The columns have all been resized (Figure 1-68).

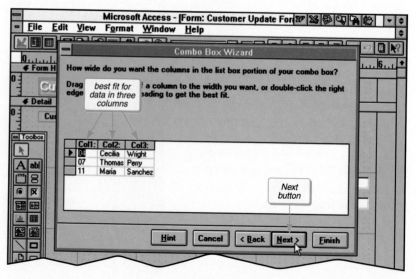

FIGURE 1-68

STEP 9 ▶

Choose the Next button.

The Sales Rep Number field is selected as the field that contains the value for the database (Figure 1-69).

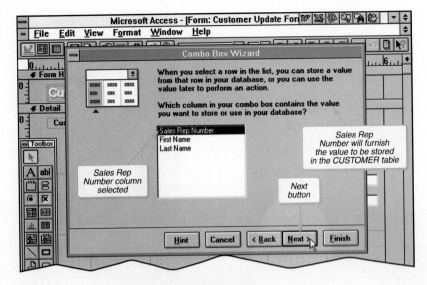

FIGURE 1-69

STEP 10 ▶

Choose the Next button. Then, click the Store that value in this field: option button. Click the drop-down arrow and then select the Sales Rep Number field.

The Store that value in this field: option button is selected and the Sales Rep Number field is selected (Figure 1-70).

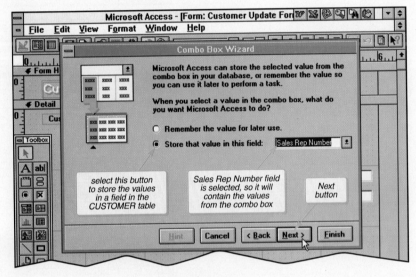

FIGURE 1-70

STEP 11 ▶

Choose the Next button. Enter `Sales Rep Number:` **as the label for the combo box (Figure 1-71).**

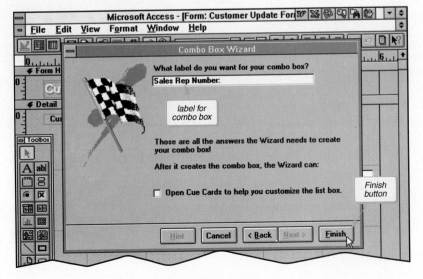

FIGURE 1-71

STEP 12 ▶

Choose the Finish button. Point to the handle on the left-hand edge of the combo box label.

The pointer changes to a double arrow, indicating you can drag the left-hand edge (Figure 1-72).

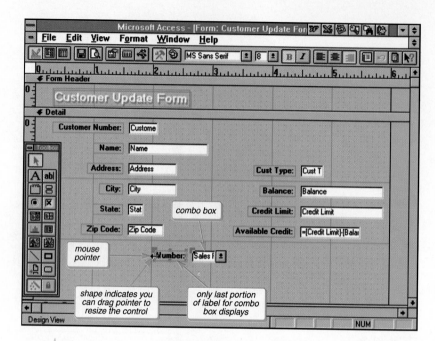

FIGURE 1-72

STEP 13 ▶

Double-click the left mouse button so the enter label (Sales Rep Number:) displays (Figure 1-73).

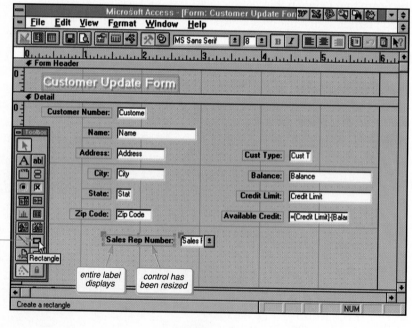

FIGURE 1-73

Placing a Rectangle on the Form

To place a rectangle on the form, use the Rectangle button (▣). The rectangle will cover any fields that are underneath it, so that the fields will not display. To correct this problem, choose the Send to Back command. This command will "send" the contents of the rectangle "to" the "back;" that is, it will be behind the fields.

Perform the following steps to place a rectangle on the form.

TO PLACE A RECTANGLE ON THE FORM ▼

STEP 1 ▶

Point to the Rectangle button (Figure 1-73).

STEP 2 ▶

Click the Rectangle button and move the pointer, whose shape has changed to a small plus sign with a rectangle ($^+_\square$), to the position shown in Figure 1-74.

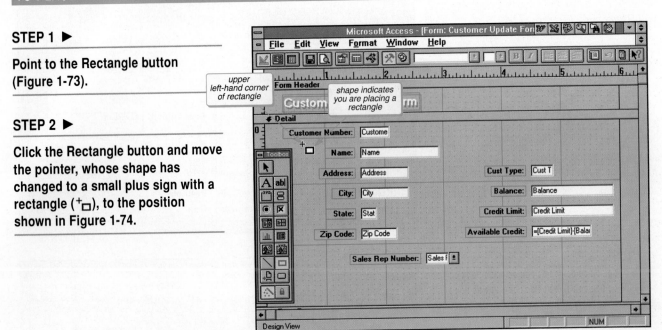

FIGURE 1-74

STEP 3 ▶

Press and hold down the left mouse button and then drag the pointer to form a rectangle containing all the fields except the Customer Number.

A rectangle displays in the form (Figure 1-75). The rectangle covers all the fields so they do not display.

STEP 4 ▶

Select the Format menu and choose the Send to Back command.

The fields display within the rectangle.

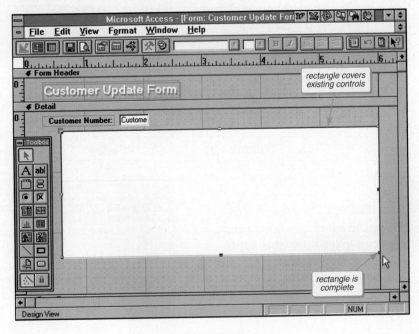

FIGURE 1-75

STEP 5 ▶

Point within the rectangle and click the right mouse button.

The shortcut menu for the rectangle displays (Figure 1-76).

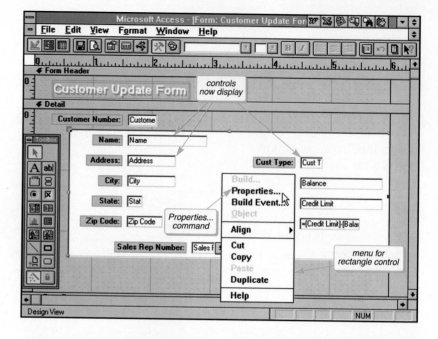

FIGURE 1-76

STEP 6 ▶

Choose the Properties command and point to the Back Color text box.

The Rectangle: Box42 dialog box displays (Figure 1-77). The mouse pointer, which points to the Back Color text box, has changed shape to an I-beam.

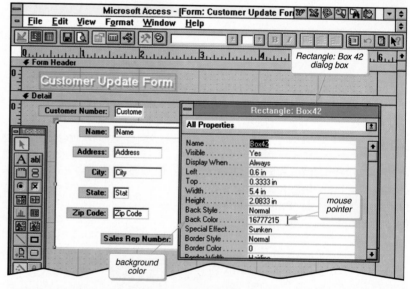

FIGURE 1-77

STEP 7 ▶

Select the Back Color text box by clicking the left mouse button and then point to the three dots button (⊡) that appears to the right of the text box (Figure 1-78).

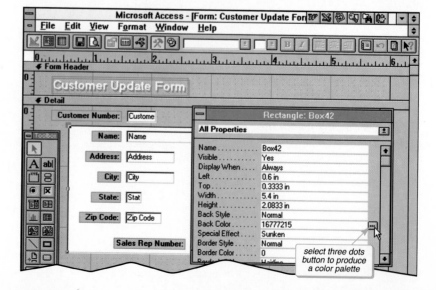

FIGURE 1-78

STEP 8 ▶

Select the three dots button to produce a color palette. Point to the color shown in Figure 1-79 (light blue).

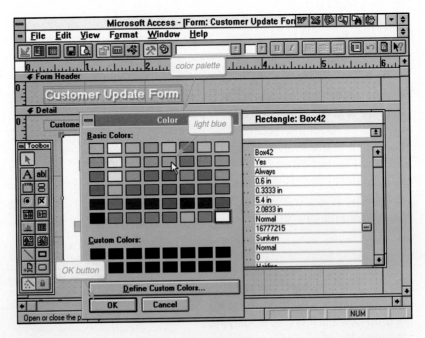

FIGURE 1-79

STEP 9 ▶

Click the left mouse button to select the color and then choose the OK button. Close the Rectangle: Box42 dialog box by double-clicking its Control-menu box.

The color of the rectangle has changed to light blue (Figure 1-80).

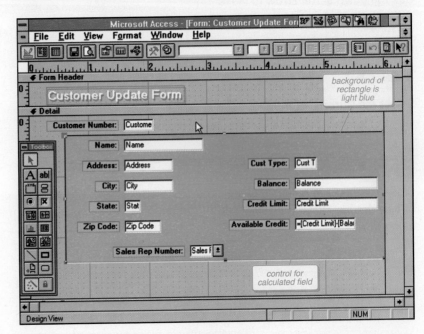

FIGURE 1-80

Changing the Format of a Field

Access automatically formats fields from the database appropriately because it knows their data types. Usually, you will find the formats assigned by Access to be acceptable. For calculated fields, such as Available Credit, however, Access will just assign a general format. To use a special format, such as currency, which displays the number with a dollar sign and two decimal places, requires special action.

Perform the steps on the next page to change the format for the Available Credit field to currency.

TO CHANGE THE FORMAT OF A FIELD ▼

STEP 1 ▶

Point somewhere outside the rectangle and click the left mouse button to deselect the rectangle. Then, point to the Available Credit field (see Figure 1-80 on the previous page) and double-click it to produce the property sheet for the Available Credit control.

STEP 2 ▶

Point to the Format text box and click the left mouse button. Point to the drop-down arrow that displays to produce a list of available formats. Use the down scroll arrow to move down to the Currency format (Figure 1-81).

STEP 3 ▶

Select the Currency format by clicking the left mouse button.

STEP 4 ▶

Close the Text Box: Field36 dialog box by double-clicking its Control-menu box.

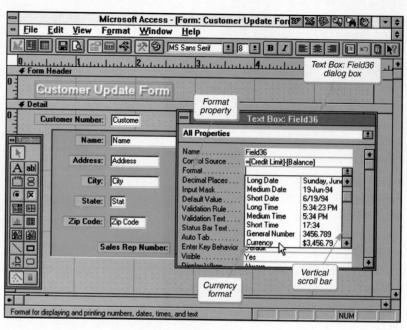

FIGURE 1-81

Saving a Form

To save a form from Design View, choose the Save command from the File menu. Perform the following step to save the form.

TO SAVE A FORM

Step 1: Select the File menu and choose the Save command.

Viewing the Form

To see how the form will appear with data in it, choose the Form View button (▦), as shown in the following steps.

TO VIEW THE FORM ▼

STEP 1 ▶

Point to the Form View button
(Figure 1-82).

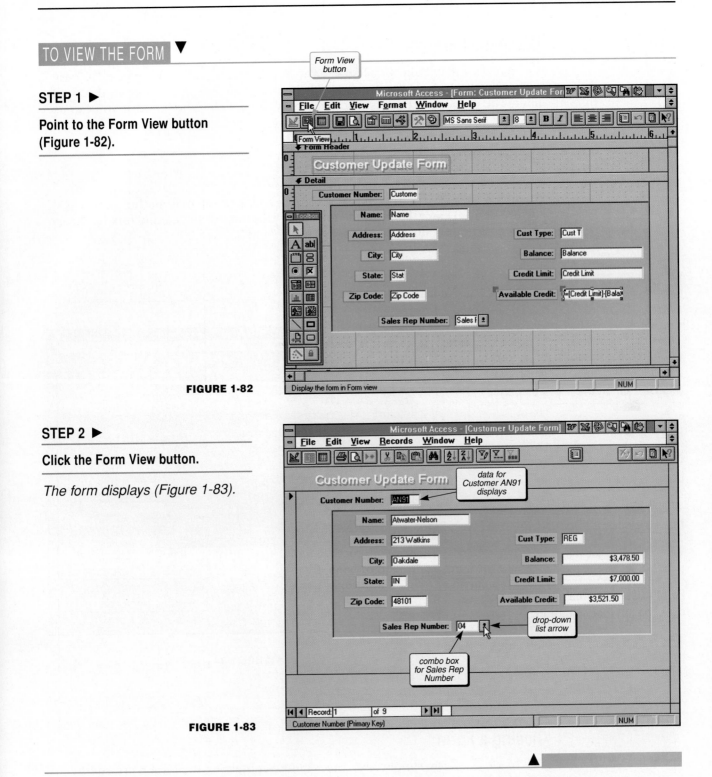

FIGURE 1-82

STEP 2 ▶

Click the Form View button.

The form displays (Figure 1-83).

FIGURE 1-83

Opening a Form

If you have just selected the Form View button, the form is currently open and
ready for use. In the future, however, you will need to open the form from the
Database window. To do so, choose the Form button, highlight the form, and then
choose the Open button.

Using the Form

Access will not allow changes to the available credit amount. Instead, Access will calculate this amount automatically by subtracting the balance from the credit limit. The other difference is that this form contains a combo box that you can use to select a sales rep number.

Using the Combo Box

To use a combo box, either type an entry or click the drop-down arrow to produce a drop-down list of possible entries and then select from the list by clicking the desired entry. Perform the following steps to use the combo box to change the sales representative for the first customer to 07.

TO USE THE COMBO BOX ▼

STEP 1 ▶

Point to the drop-down arrow next to the Sales Rep Number combo box (Figure 1-83 on the previous page).

STEP 2 ▶

Click the arrow next to the combo box.

A list of available sales representatives displays (Figure 1-84).

STEP 3 ▶

Point to sales representative 07 and click the left mouse button.

The Sales Rep Number changes to the selected number.

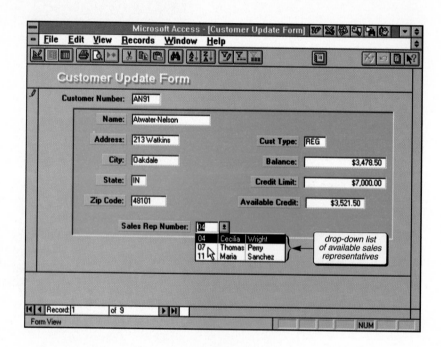

FIGURE 1-84

Closing a Form

To close a form, simply close the window containing the form. Perform the following step to close the form.

TO CLOSE A FORM

Step 1: Double-click the Control-menu box on the Form window. If you are asked if you want to save changes to the form, answer No, because you saved the design earlier.

▶ FORM DESIGN CONSIDERATIONS

s you design and create custom forms, keep in mind the following guidelines.

1. Remember that someone using your form may be looking at the form for several hours at a time. Forms that are excessively cluttered or that contain too many different effects (colors, fonts, frame styles, and so on) can become very difficult on the eyes.
2. Place the fields in logical groupings. Fields that relate to each other should be close to each other on the form. Consider using rectangles to emphasize the groupings of related fields.
3. If the data that a user will enter comes from a paper form, make the screen form resemble the paper form as closely as possible.

▶ PROJECT SUMMARY

Project 1 covered the issues involved in presenting the data in a database. You learned how to create and print reports. You learned the purpose of the various sections and how to modify their contents. You also learned how to group in a report. You learned how to create and use custom forms. You learned how to move controls, create new controls, add rectangles, add combo boxes, and change the characteristics of various objects in a form. You also learned how to use a form to view or update data. Finally, you learned some general principles to help you design effective reports and forms.

▶ KEY TERMS AND INDEX

attached labels *(A28)*
bound controls *(A28)*
calculated controls *(A28)*
captions *(A11)*
combo box *(A32)*
controls *(A10)*
custom forms *(A3)*
Design view *(A9)*
Detail section *(A10)*

group *(A13)*
group footer *(A13)*
group header *(A13)*
grouping *(A3)*
Groups/Totals reports *(A6)*
handles *(A11)*
Page Footer section *(A10)*
Page Header section *(A10)*
Print Preview *(A9)*

property sheet *(A28)*
Report Footer section *(A10)*
Report Header section *(A10)*
Sample Preview *(A9)*
section *(A10)*
subtotal *(A3, A13)*
Tabular reports *(A6)*
unbound controls *(A28)*

In Access, you can accomplish a task in a number of different ways. The following table provides a quick reference to each task presented in this project with its available options. The commands listed in the Menu column can be executed using either the keyboard or mouse.

Task	Mouse	Menu	Keyboard Shortcuts
Add a Control to a Report or Form	Click Text Box button in Toolbox	From View menu, choose Field List, drag desired field	
Add a Rectangle	Click Rectangle button in Toolbox		
Change the Attached Label for a Control	Click control twice to produce insertion point and type new value		
Change the Color of a Control	Double-click control and change Back Color	From View menu, choose Properties, change Back Color	
Change the Column Caption	Click caption until selected and make change		
Change the Column Caption Position	Drag caption	From View menu, choose Properties, change Left and Top entries	
Change the Column Caption Size	Select caption and drag appropriate handle	From View menu, choose Properties, change Width and Height entries	
Change from Design View to Print Preview	Click Print Preview button	From File menu, choose Print Preview	
Change from Design View to Sample Preview	Click Sample Preview button	From File menu, choose Sample Preview	
Change from Print Preview to Sample Preview	Point to body of report and click	From File menu, choose Sample Preview	
Change from Sample or Print Preview to Design View	Click Design View button		
Change from Sample Preview to Print Preview	Point to body of report and click	From File menu, choose Print Preview	
Close a Form or a Report	Double-click Control-menu box	From File menu, choose Close	
Create a Calculated Control	Click Text Box button in Toolbox, place control, and enter calculation		
Create a Combo Box	Double-click Combo Box button in Toolbox		
Create a Form or a Report	Choose Form or Report button and choose New button	From File menu, choose New, choose Form or Report	

Task	Mouse	Menu	Keyboard Shortcuts
Display a Toolbox	Click Toolbox button on toolbar	From View menu, choose Toolbox	
Display a Property Sheet	Double-click control	From View menu, choose Properties	
Group in a Report	Click Report Wizards button and select Groups/Totals		
Move a Control	Drag control	From View menu, choose Properties, change Left and Top entries	
Print a Report	Click Print button	From File menu, choose Print	
Remove a Control	Click control and press DELETE	From Edit menu, choose Delete	Press DELETE
Remove a Toolbox from the Screen	Click Toolbox button on toolbar	From View menu, choose Toolbox	
Resize a Section	Drag bottom of section	From View menu, choose Properties, change Height entry	
Save a Form or a Report		From File menu, choose Save	
Use a Combo Box	Click arrow		Press UP or DOWN ARROW
Use a FormWizard	Create new form and click Form Wizards button		
Use a Report Wizard	Create new report and click Report Wizards button		

S T U D E N T   A S S I G N M E N T S

STUDENT ASSIGNMENT 1
True/False

Instructions: Circle T if the statement is true or F if the statement is false.

T   F   1. To include a calculated field in a report, create a query and base the report on the query.

T   F   2. Only reports that do not need to be modified in any way can be created with Report Wizards.

T   F   3. To create a new report, choose the Report button, choose the New button, name the report, and then select the table or query to include in the report.

T   F   4. Within the Report window, Print Preview displays the entire width of the report.

T   F   5. The contents of a Report Footer will appear only once on a report.

T   F   6. The Report window uses small squares called handholds to indicate which portion of the report is currently selected.

T   F   7. The various entries appearing in a report, such as the report title and a column heading, are called controls.

(continued)

STUDENT ASSIGNMENT 1 (continued)

T   F   8. To remove a field from a report, select the field and press the DELETE key.

T   F   9. To center a report title, select the title control and choose Properties from the shortcut menu.

T   F   10. There are three types of controls on a form: bound controls, unbound controls, and tabulated controls.

T   F   11. On a form, bound controls are used to display the title.

T   F   12. Each control on a form has an associated property sheet that lists the properties that can be modified for the control.

T   F   13. To add a new field to a form, choose the Text Box button in the Toolbox.

T   F   14. A combo box is a box that allows you to select entries from a list.

T   F   15. To place a rectangle on a form and uncover the fields beneath the rectangle, choose the Rectangle button, draw the rectangle, and then choose the Uncover command from the Format menu.

T   F   16. On a report, controls in the Page Header display exactly as they are and serve as captions for the data.

T   F   17. A subtotal for a report appears in a group header.

T   F   18. To create a report that contains subtotals, select Groups/Totals as the report style in Report Wizards.

T   F   19. To view a report with sample data, click the Sample Preview button.

T   F   20. To save a form created with a FormWizard, choose the Save command from the File menu.

STUDENT ASSIGNMENT 2
Multiple Choice

Instructions: Circle the correct response.

1. The process of creating separate collections of records sharing some common characteristic is known as _____.
   a. collecting
   b. matching
   c. grouping
   d. categorizing

2. To create a new report using Report Wizards, choose the Report button, choose the New button, and then _____.
   a. choose the Report Wizard
   b. select the table or query to include in the report
   c. enter a name for the new report
   d. choose the Design button

3. To remove a field from a report, select the field and then _____.
   a. press the DELETE key
   b. press the CTRL+D keys
   c. press the CTRL+DELETE keys
   d. click the right mouse button

4. The portions of the Report window (i.e., Report Header, Page Header) are called _____.
   a. segments
   b. areas
   c. sections
   d. bands

5. The Report window uses small squares called _____ to indicate which portion of the report is currently selected.
   a. handholds
   b. handles
   c. braces
   d. grippers

6. To center a report title, select the title control and choose _____ from the shortcut menu.
   a. Alignment
   b. Center
   c. Title
   d. Properties
7. Controls that are used to display data in a database are called _____ on a custom form.
   a. bound controls
   b. unbound controls
   c. field controls
   d. data controls
8. On a form, _____ are used to display data that is calculated from data in the database.
   a. tabulated controls
   b. defined controls
   c. calculated controls
   d. extended controls
9. To place a rectangle on a form and uncover the fields beneath the rectangle, choose the Rectangle button, draw the rectangle, and then choose the _____ command from the Format menu.
   a. Uncover
   b. Move to Front
   c. Display Data
   d. Send to Back
10. To change characteristics, such as the color of a rectangle or the format of a control, use the _____ for the control.
   a. property sheet
   b. design sheet
   c. inspector sheet
   d. control sheet

STUDENT ASSIGNMENT 3
Understanding the Report Window

Instructions: In Figure SA1-3, arrows point to the major components of the Report window. Identify the various parts of the Report window in the spaces provided. Answer the following questions about the window.

1. How many times will the control with the label =Sum[On Hand Value] print?

   _____

2. What is the purpose of the control =Now( )?

   _____

3. What values will print once at the top of every page?

   _____

   _____

   _____

FIGURE SA1-3

STUDENT ASSIGNMENT 4
Understanding the Form Design Window

Instructions: In Figure SA1-4, arrows point to various items on the Form Design window. Identify these items in the spaces provided. Answer the following questions about the screen.

1. What control is currently selected?

   _____

2. Identify the unbound control(s) on the form.

   _____

3. Identify the bound control(s) on the form.

   _____

   _____

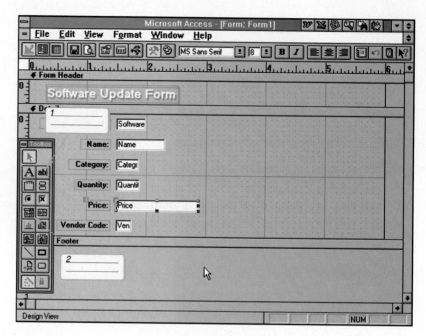

FIGURE SA1-4

STUDENT ASSIGNMENT 5
Using the Report Design Window

Instructions: Figure SA1-5 shows a Report window for the Software table. Use this figure to help explain how to perform the following tasks on the Report window.

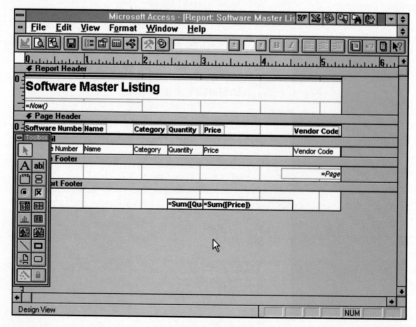

FIGURE SA1-5

1. Center the report title.

_____

_____

_____

2. View a sample of the report on the screen.

_____

_____

_____

3. Delete the controls for the sum of Quantity and Price.

_____

_____

_____

4. Preview the entire report.

_____

_____

_____

5. Expand the size of the Detail section.

_____

_____

_____

STUDENT ASSIGNMENT 6
Using the Form Design Window

Instructions: Figure SA1-6 shows the Form Design window for the Software table. Use this figure to help explain how to perform the tasks on the next page on the Form Design window.

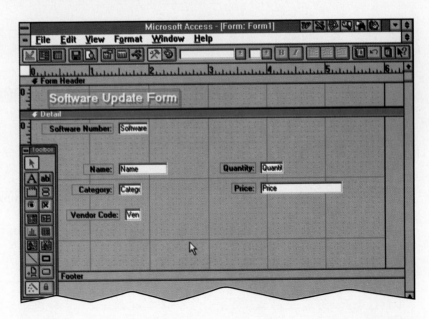

FIGURE SA1-6

(continued)

STUDENT ASSIGNMENT 6 (continued)

1. Move the Software Number control to the center of the form.

   _____

   _____

   _____

2. Add a control to display On Hand Value (Quantity*Price). The control should have the label, On Hand Value, and should be directly underneath Quantity and Price.

   _____

   _____

   _____

3. Display the On Hand Value control in Currency format.

   _____

   _____

   _____

4. Display the form with data on the screen.

   _____

   _____

   _____

5. Add a rectangle to the form that contains all fields except Software Number. The data should display in the foreground.

   _____

   _____

   _____

C O M P U T E R   L A B O R A T O R Y   E X E R C I S E S

COMPUTER LABORATORY EXERCISE 1
Using the Help Menu

Instructions: Perform the following tasks:

1. Start Access
2. Open the Soft database in the Access2 subdirectory on the Student Diskette that accompanies this book.
3. Select the Help menu, choose the Search command and type `reports totals` as shown in Figure CLE1-1. Select Calculating Totals in reports.

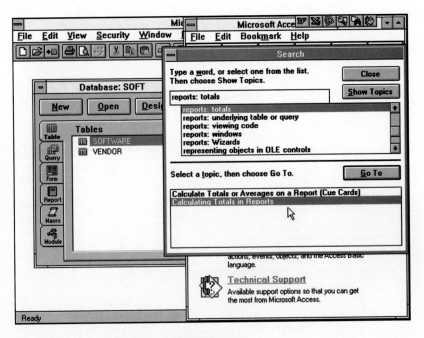

FIGURE CLE1-1

4. Read the information in the Help window and answer the following questions.
   a. How do you calculate a total for one record?

   _____

   _____

   _____

   b. When can you use the name of a calculated control in the Sum function?

   _____

   _____

   _____

5. Close the Help menu and then close the Soft database.
6. Exit Access.

COMPUTER LABORATORY EXERCISE 2
Creating a Report for the Soft Database

Instructions: Perform the following tasks:

1. Start Access and open the Soft database in the Access2 subdirectory on the Student Diskette that accompanies this book.
2. Create a query that includes both the Software and Vendor tables. Include the Vendor Code, Vendor Name, Software Number, Name, and a calculated field for On Hand Value (Quantity*Price). Save the query as Software by Vendor.
3. Using the query, create the report shown in Figure CLE1-2.
4. Print the report.
5. Save the report as Software by Vendor.
6. Close the report, close the database, and exit Access.

(continued)

COMPUTER LABORATORY EXERCISE 2 (continued)

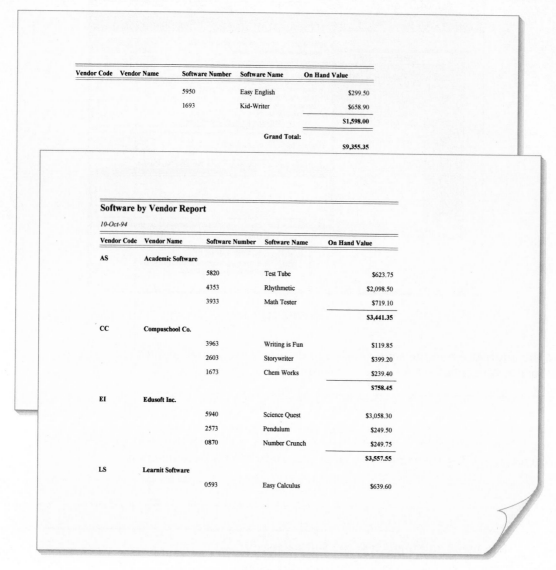

Vendor Code	Vendor Name	Software Number	Software Name	On Hand Value
		5950	Easy English	$299.50
		1693	Kid-Writer	$658.90
				$1,598.00
			Grand Total:	
				$9,355.35

Software by Vendor Report

10-Oct-94

Vendor Code	Vendor Name	Software Number	Software Name	On Hand Value
AS	Academic Software			
		5820	Test Tube	$623.75
		4353	Rhythmetic	$2,098.50
		3933	Math Tester	$719.10
				$3,441.35
CC	Compuschool Co.			
		3963	Writing is Fun	$119.85
		2603	Storywriter	$399.20
		1673	Chem Works	$239.40
				$758.45
EI	Edusoft Inc.			
		5940	Science Quest	$3,058.30
		2573	Pendulum	$249.50
		0870	Number Crunch	$249.75
				$3,557.55
LS	Learnit Software			
		0593	Easy Calculus	$639.60

FIGURE CLE1-2

COMPUTER LABORATORY EXERCISE 3
Creating a Form for the Soft Database

FIGURE CLE1-3

Instructions: Perform the following tasks:

1. Start Access and open the Soft database in the Access2 subdirectory on the Student Diskette that accompanies this book.
2. Using FormWizards, create a form for the Software table. Include all fields except Vendor Code on the form. Use Software Update Form as the title for the form.

3. Modify the form in the Form Design window to create the form shown in Figure CLE1-3. The form includes a combo box for Vendor Code and a calculated control for On Hand Value.
4. Print the form. To print the form, view the form with data, click the Print button, and choose Selection as the Print Range.
5. Save the form as Software Update Form.
6. Close the form, close the database, and exit Access.

COMPUTER LABORATORY ASSIGNMENTS

NOTE: The Computer Laboratory Assignments for Microsoft Access 2 require that you use database files stored on the Student Diskette. These database files are compressed and must be expanded before you can use them. Do the following to expand the database file you are instructed to open in the selected assignment:

1. Copy the required .EXE file from the Access2 subdirectory on the Student Diskette that accompanies this book to a blank diskette. For example, if you are doing Computer Laboratory Assignment 1, then copy ITEMS.EXE.

2. Exit Windows. At the DOS prompt, type A:.

3. At the A:\> prompt, type the name of the compressed file and press the ENTER key to expand it. For example, type ITEMS to expand the file and create the database file required for Computer Laboratory Assignment 1.

COMPUTER LABORATORY ASSIGNMENT 1
Presenting Data in the Items Database

Purpose: To provide practice in creating reports and forms.

Instructions: Use the Items database in the Access2 subdirectory of the Student Diskette that accompanies this book for this assignment. Execute each task on the computer and print the results.

1. Create the report shown in Figure CLA1-1a for the Product table. Include all fields except Warehouse Number in the report. Include a calculated field for the On Hand Value (Units on Hand*Price).

Product Master Report

10-Oct-94

Product Number	Product Description	Item Class	Units On Hand	Price	On Hand Value
AD29	Shaver	PC	104	$59.99	$6,238.96
AK13	Ice Cream Maker	HW	68	$39.96	$2,717.28
AY83	Hair Dryer	PC	112	$16.99	$1,902.88
BE24	Breadmaker	HW	34	$199.96	$6,798.64
BL07	Microwave Oven	AP	11	$149.99	$1,649.89
BX55	Electric Wok	HW	95	$39.99	$3,799.05
CBO3	Gas Dryer	AP	2	$299.99	$599.98
CC04	Makeup Mirror	PC	44	$29.99	$1,319.56
CX22	Luxury Spa & Whirlpool	PC	20	$109.96	$2,199.20
CZ91	Juice Extractor	HW	82	$49.96	$4,096.72
					$31,322.16

FIGURE CLA1-1a

(continued)

COMPUTER LABORATORY ASSIGNMENT 1 (continued)

2. Save the report as Product Master Report.
3. Print the report.
4. Create the form shown in Figure CLA1-1b on the next page for the Items database. Include a combo box for Item Class Code. Include a calculated control for the On Hand Value.

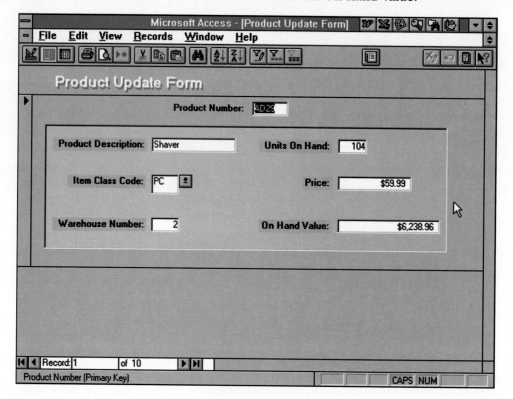

FIGURE CLA1-1b

5. Print the form. To print the form, view the form with data, click the Print button, and choose Selection as the Print Range.
6. Save the form as Product Update Form.
7. Close the form, close the database, and exit Access.

COMPUTER LABORATORY ASSIGNMENT 2
Presenting Data in the Employee Database

Purpose: To provide practice in creating reports and forms.

Instructions: Use the Emp database in the Access2 subdirectory of the Student Diskette that accompanies this book for this assignment. Execute each task on the computer and print the results.

1. Create the report shown in Figure CLA1-2a for the Employee database. The report groups employees by department and displays the average pay rate for each department. Note that the report is sorted by Employee Last Name within department and that Employee First Name appears before Employee Last Name. (Hint: To display the average, change SUM in the group footer to AVG.)
2. Print the report.
3. Save the report as Employees by Department.

Department Code	Department Name	Employee First Name	Employee Last Name	Pay Rate
		Andrew	Rodgers	$7.75
		Evelyn	Whitestone	$6.90
			Average Pay Rate	$7.69
04	Shipping			
		Luke	Fitzmeyer	$8.65
		Mark	McCall	$8.10
		Peter	Semple	$6.80
			Average Pay Rate	$7.85

Employees by Department

10-Oct-94

Department Code	Department Name	Employee First Name	Employee Last Name	Pay Rate
01	Accounting			
		Maria	Alvarez	$9.30
		David	Navarre	$11.00
		Anne	Radleman	$9.90
			Average Pay Rate	$10.07
02	Customer Service			
		Tanya	Chou	$8.00
		John	Evanston	$6.30
		Ella	Fisher	$9.30
		Alberto	Mendes	$8.90
		Kim	Pierce	$6.30
			Average Pay Rate	$7.76
03	Purchasing			
		Daniel	Lewiston	$9.00
		Tao	Ping	$7.10

1

FIGURE CLA1-2a

4. Create the form shown in Figure CLA1-2b on the next page for the Employee table. Include a combo box for Department Code.
5. Print the form. To print the form, view the form with data, click the Print button, and choose Selection as the Print Range.
6. Save the form as Employee Update Form.
7. Close the form, close the database, and exit Access..

(continued)

COMPUTER LABORATORY ASSIGNMENT 2 (continued)

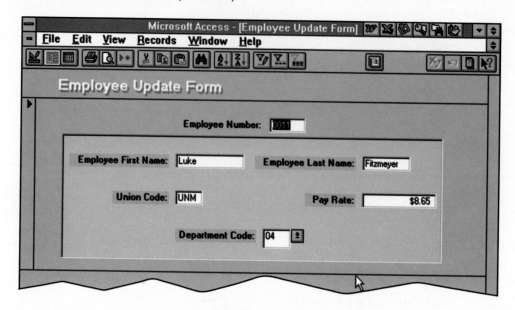

FIGURE CLA1-2b

COMPUTER LABORATORY ASSIGNMENT 3
Presenting Data in the Movie Database

Purpose: To provide practice in creating reports and forms.

Instructions: Use the Mov database in the Access2 subdirectory of the student diskette that accompanies this book for this assignment. Execute each task on the computer and print the results.

1. Create the report shown in Figure CLA1-3a for the Movie table. Include all fields except Length and Color Type in the report. Place the Movie Type field before the Year Made field. Sort the report by Movie Title within Movie Type. (Hint: To split a caption over two lines, place the insertion point at the position where you want to split the caption and then press SHIFT+ENTER).

Movie Report

10-Oct-94

Movie Number	Movie Title	Movie Type	Year Made	Nominations	Awards	Director Code
003	Dancing Duo	COMEDY	1972	3	1	04
010	Father Act Too	COMEDY	1979	3	1	01
001	Amy Mason	DRAMA	1978	5	4	01
017	My Brother Pete	DRAMA	1956	6	3	03
007	The Brass Ring	DRAMA	1949	0	0	03
015	House of Laughter	HORROR	1969	2	0	04
012	Last Resort	HORROR	1980	1	0	01
019	Caterpillars	SCI FI	1964	2	0	02
002	Breakdown	SUSPEN	1965	4	0	04
020	Missing Month	SUSPEN	1941	1	1	02
013	Strange Business	SUSPEN	1959	6	2	03
023	Mojave	WESTER	1937	0	0	02
004	The Dirty Horse	WESTER	1960	1	0	03
008	Wild Wild Willie	WESTER	1970	3	1	03

FIGURE CLA1-3a

2. Print the report.
3. Save the report as Movie Report 1.

4. Create the report shown in Figure CLA1-3b for the Movie table. This report groups movies by Director Code.

Director Code	Director Name	Movie Number	Movie Title	Year Made	Nominations	Awards
		004	The Dirty Horse	1960	1	0
		008	Wild Wild Willie	1970	3	1
					16	6
04	Lefever, F. X.					
		002	Breakdown	1965	4	0
		003	Dancing Duo	1972	3	1
		015	House of Laughter	1969	2	0
					9	1

Movies by Director

10-Oct-94

Director Code	Director Name	Movie Number	Movie Title	Year Made	Nominations	Awards
01	Harhuis, Stacy					
		001	Amy Mason	1978	5	4
		010	Father Act Too	1979	3	1
		012	Last Resort	1980	1	0
					9	5
02	Greiner, Kimberly					
		019	Caterpillars	1964	2	0
		020	Missing Month	1941	1	1
		023	Mojave	1937	0	0
					3	1
03	Valdez, Roberto					
		017	My Brother Pete	1956	6	3
		013	Strange Business	1959	6	2
		007	The Brass Ring	1949	0	0
						1

FIGURE CLA1-3b

5. Print the report.
6. Save the report as Movies by Director.

(continued)

COMPUTER LABORATORY ASSIGNMENT 3 (continued)

7. Create the form shown in Figure CLA1-3c for the Movie table. Include a combo box for Director Code.

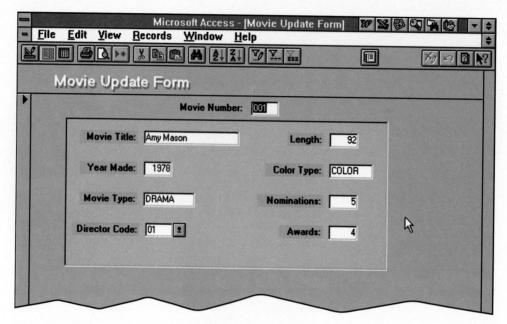

FIGURE CLA1-3c

8. Print the form. To print the form, view the form with data, click the Print button, and choose Selection as the Print Range.
9. Save the form as Movie Update Form.
10. Close the form, close the database, and exit Access.

COMPUTER LABORATORY ASSIGNMENT 4
Presenting Data in the Book Database

Purpose: To provide practice in creating reports and forms.

Problem: The bookstore owner has asked you to prepare the following reports:

1. A report of all books in the database. The report does not need to include Cover Type, but the owner would like to know the average price of all books in the database. (Hint: To display the average price, change SUM in the Report Footer to AVG.)
2. A report of all books grouped by Publisher and a report with books grouped by Book Type. She would like to know the average of all books in the database and the average by Publisher and Book Type.

The owner is impressed with the improved accuracy in data entry resulting from the validity checks you added to the database, but she would now like to make the data forms more attractive for her employees. She has also asked you to provide her with attractive data screens for both the Book and the Publisher tables.

Instructions: Use the Books database in the Access2 subdirectory of the Student Diskette that accompanies this book for this assignment. Execute each task on the computer and print the results.

$\mathcal{M}$ICROSOFT $\mathcal{A}$CCESS 2 FOR $\mathcal{W}$INDOWS

P R O J E C T   T W O

ADVANCED TOPICS

OBJECTIVES You will have mastered the material in this project when you can:

▸ Use date, memo, and OLE fields
▸ Enter data in date fields
▸ Enter data in memo fields
▸ Enter pictures into OLE fields
▸ Change row and column spacing in tables
▸ Save table properties

▸ Create a form with a subform
▸ Move and resize fields on a form
▸ Use a form that contains a subform
▸ Change border styles and colors of labels
▸ Use date and memo fields in a query

▶ INTRODUCTION

This project creates the form shown in Figure 2-1 on the next page. The form incorporates the following features previously not covered:

▸ Three new fields are added to the SLSREP table. The Start Date field gives the hire date of the sales representative. A Note field is used by the organization to store a note describing important characteristics of the sales representative. The note can be as long or as short as the organization desires. Finally, there is a Sales Rep Picture field that holds the sales rep picture.
▸ The form shows not only data concerning the sales representative, but also the representative's customers. The customers are displayed as a table on the form.

Before creating this form, the structure of the SLSREP table must be modified to incorporate the three new fields, each of which uses a new field type. Then, these new fields need to be filled in with appropriate data. The way you do this depends on the field type. Finally, you need to create the form, including the table of customer data and the scroll bars.

Once the table is modified and the form is created, you will learn how to use the new field types in queries.

FIGURE 2-1

▶ DATE, MEMO, OR OLE FIELDS

T he data shown in the table in Figure 2-1 incorporates the following field types:

1. **Date (D) field** — The field can contain only valid dates.
2. **Memo (M) field** — The field can contain text that is variable in length. The length of the text stored in memo fields is virtually unlimited.
3. **OLE (O) field** — The field can contain objects created by other applications that support **OLE (Object Linking and Embedding)** as a server. Object Linking and Embedding is a special feature of Microsoft Windows that creates a special relationship between Microsoft Access and the application that created the object. In this project, for example, the object will be created by the Microsoft Draw application, an application that is an OLE server and that allows the creation of pictures. When you edit the object, Microsoft Access returns automatically to the application that created the object.

► CHANGING THE STRUCTURE OF A TABLE

Perform the following steps to add the Start Date field, the Note field, and the Sales Rep Picture field to the SLSREP table.

TO CHANGE THE STRUCTURE OF A TABLE ▼

STEP 1 ►

Open the CUST database from the Access2 subdirectory on the Student Diskette that accompanies this book and highlight the SLSREP table (Figure 2-2).

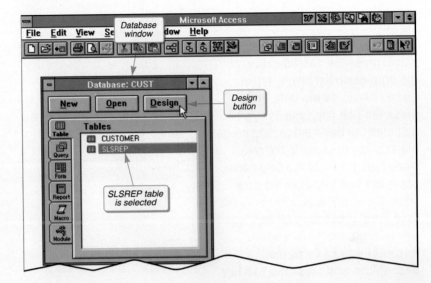

FIGURE 2-2

STEP 2 ►

Choose the Design button.

The Table: SLSREP window displays (Figure 2-3).

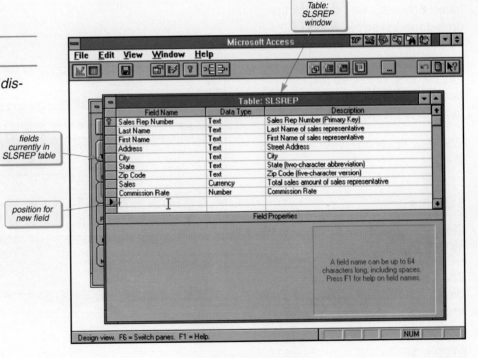

FIGURE 2-3

STEP 3 ▶

Point to the position for the new field (in the Field Name column in the row following Commission Rate) and click the left mouse button to select the field.

STEP 4 ▶

Type `Start Date` as the field name, press the TAB key, click the drop-down list arrow, select `Date/Time` as the Data Type, press the TAB key, type `Starting date` as the Description, and press the TAB key to move to the next field. Type `Note` as the field name, press the TAB key, click the drop-down list arrow, select `Memo` as the Data Type, press the TAB key, type `Note concerning sales representative` as the Description, and press the TAB key to move to the next field. Type `Sales Rep Picture` as the field name, press the TAB key, click the drop-down list arrow, select `OLE Object` as the Data Type, press the TAB key, type `Picture of sales representative` as the Description, and press the TAB key to move to the next field.

The new fields are entered (Figure 2-4).

STEP 5 ▶

Close the window by double-clicking its Control-menu box.

The Microsoft Access dialog box displays asking if you want to save the changes (Figure 2-5).

STEP 6 ▶

Choose the Yes button.

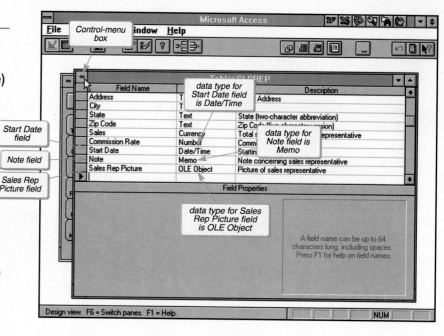

FIGURE 2-4

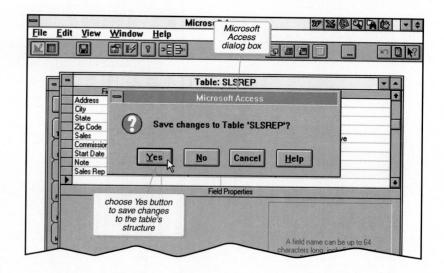

FIGURE 2-5

The new fields have been added to the structure.

▶ UPDATING THE NEW FIELDS

ow that the new fields have been added to the table, they need to be filled in. The way you do so depends on the field type. The following sections cover the methods for updating date fields, memo fields, and OLE fields.

Updating Date Fields

To enter date fields, simply type the dates, including slashes (/). Perform the following steps to add the start dates for all three sales representatives using Datasheet view.

TO ENTER DATA IN DATE FIELDS ▼

STEP 1 ▶

With the Database window on the screen, highlight the SLSREP table (Figure 2-6).

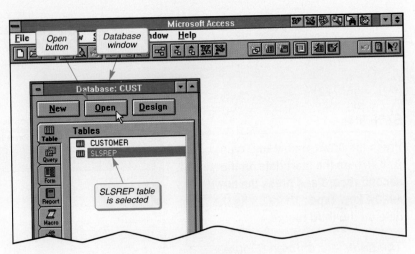

FIGURE 2-6

STEP 2 ▶

Choose the Open button and then maximize the window.

The SLSREP table displays in Datasheet view in a maximized window (Figure 2-7).

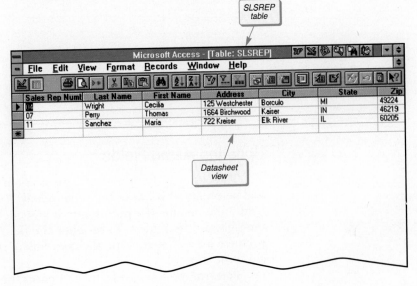

FIGURE 2-7

STEP 3 ▶

Repeatedly click the right scroll
arrow until the new fields display
(Figure 2-8).

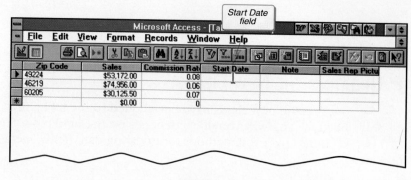

FIGURE 2-8

STEP 4 ▶

Select the Start Date field on the
first record by clicking it and then
type 6/8/89 (Figure 2-9).

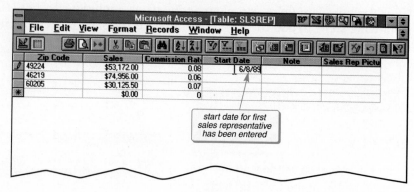

FIGURE 2-9

STEP 5 ▶

Press the DOWN ARROW key. Type
8/4/90 as the start date on the
second record and press the DOWN
ARROW key. Type 10/2/88 as the
date on the third record.

*The dates are entered (Figure
2-10).*

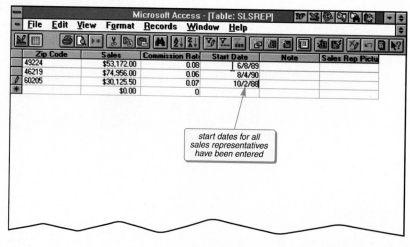

FIGURE 2-10

Updating Memo Fields

The easiest way to update a memo field is to use a Zoom box. This way, there
will be plenty of room to type the memo. To update a memo field, first select the
field to be updated by pointing to it and clicking the left mouse button. Next, click
the right mouse button to produce the field's shortcut menu and select Zoom to
produce a Zoom box. Type the contents of the memo in the box. When finished,
close the box.

Perform the following steps to enter the notes concerning each sales rep.

TO ENTER DATA IN MEMO FIELDS ▼

STEP 1 ▶

Point to the Note field for the first record (Figure 2-11).

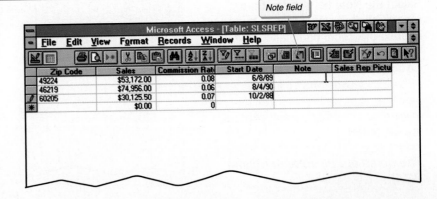

FIGURE 2-11

STEP 2 ▶

Select the Note field on the first record by clicking the left mouse button. Then, click the right mouse button to produce the Note field's shortcut menu.

The shortcut menu for the Note field displays (Figure 2-12).

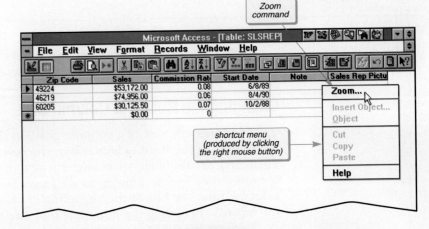

FIGURE 2-12

STEP 3 ▶

Choose the Zoom command and then type Fluent in French, German, and Spanish. Likes to travel. Technically strong. in the Zoom box (Figure 2-13).

STEP 4 ▶

Choose the OK button in the Zoom box to remove the box from the screen. Select the Note field on the second record, click the right mouse button, choose the Zoom command, type Somewhat fluent in Spanish. Willing to travel. Works well with new companies. Very innovative. and choose the OK button.

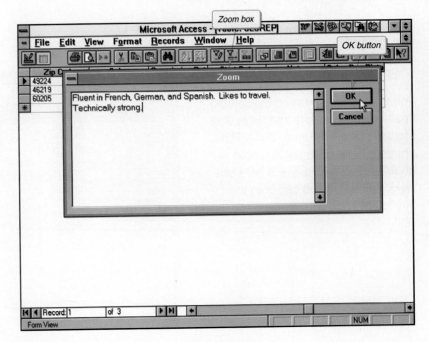

FIGURE 2-13

STEP 5 ▶

Select the Note field on the third record, click the right mouse button, choose the Zoom command, type Technically excellent. Good reputation among established customers. Advice is well-respected among customers. and choose the OK button.

The notes are all entered (Figure 2-14).

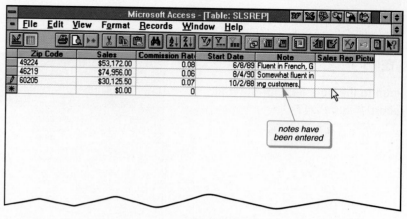

FIGURE 2-14

Only a small portion of the notes displays in the datasheet. To have more of the notes display, expand the size of the rows and the columns.

Changing the Row and Column Size

To change the size of a column, position the pointer on the right boundary of the column in the **field selector bar**, the row containing the list of field names. Then, drag the boundary to change the size of the column. To change the size of the rows, position the pointer on the lower boundary of any record's **record selector box**, the box at the beginning of each record that you can click to select the record. Then, drag the boundary to resize the rows.

Perform the following steps to resize the column containing the Note field and also to resize the rows of the table so a larger portion of the notes will display.

TO CHANGE THE ROW AND COLUMN SIZE ▼

STEP 1 ▶

Point to the line between the column headings for the Note and Sales Rep Picture columns (Figure 2-15). The pointer shape changes to a bold double-arrow with a line in between (✛), indicating you can drag the line to resize the column.

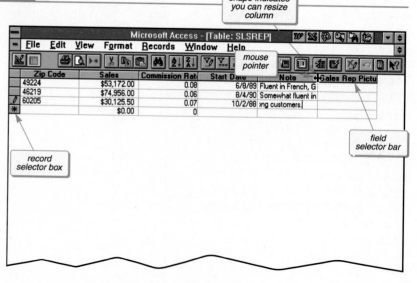

FIGURE 2-15

STEP 2 ▶

Drag the line to the position shown in Figure 2-16.

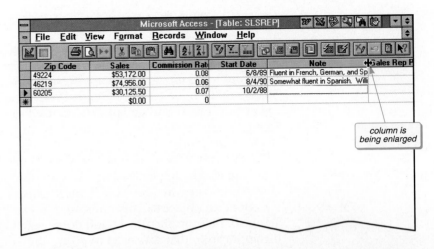

FIGURE 2-16

STEP 3 ▶

Point to the beginning of the line immediately below the first row (Figure 2-17). Again, the pointer changes to a bold arrow with a line in between (⬍), indicating you can drag the line to resize the row.

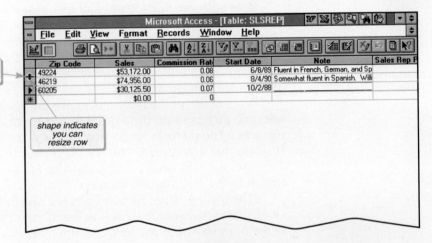

FIGURE 2-17

STEP 4 ▶

Drag the line to the position shown in Figure 2-18.

The entire note on each sales representative displays.

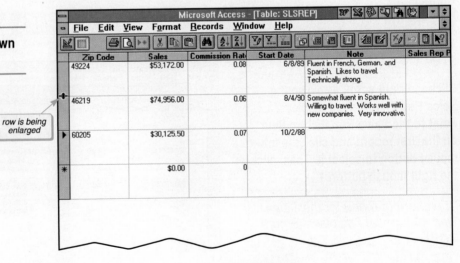

FIGURE 2-18

Updating OLE Fields

To insert data into an OLE field, select the field and then click the right mouse button to produce the shortcut menu. Choose the Insert Object command from the shortcut menu. You then are presented with a list of the various types of objects that can be inserted. Select the type of object to be inserted. Access then opens the corresponding application used to create the object. In this project, for example, the objects are Microsoft Drawings, so Access will open the Microsoft Draw application.

Microsoft Draw contains features that allow drawing of custom pictures. Pictures can also be imported from files on disk. In either case, exiting from Microsoft Draw and saving the picture will insert the picture in the database.

Once an object has been inserted, it can be updated at any point in the future. To do so, point to the object and double-click the left mouse button. Access opens the application that was used to create the object (for example, Microsoft Draw). You can then use that application to edit the object. Exiting the application and saving the changes will make the corresponding change to the database.

If, as with the Sales Reps' pictures, you will not be modifying the picture at a later date, you can conserve space in your database by converting the data from OLE data to what Access terms a "picture." You will no longer be able to double-click the left mouse button to use Microsoft Draw to modify the picture. You could, however, replace the picture with a new one using the same technique you used to add it in the first place.

Perform the following steps to use the Microsoft Draw application to enter sales rep pictures into the Sales Rep Picture field and then convert them to Access pictures. (The pictures are located in the ACCESS2 subdirectory on the Student Diskette that accompanies this book. If you are not using this diskette for your database, you will need to copy the files PICT1.PCX, PICT2.PCX, and PICT3.PCX from it to the disk you are using.)

(The quality of the pictures you see on your screen depends on the particular video driver that your system is using. If your pictures do not appear to be as sharp as the ones shown in the text, it simply means your system is using a different video driver. You did not do anything wrong.)

TO ENTER DATA IN OLE FIELDS AND CONVERT THE DATA TO PICTURES ▼

STEP 1 ▶

Click the right scroll arrow so the Sales Rep Picture field displays. Point to the Sales Rep Picture field on the first record and click the left mouse button to select it. Then, click the right mouse button.

The shortcut menu for the Sales Rep Picture field displays (Figure 2-19).

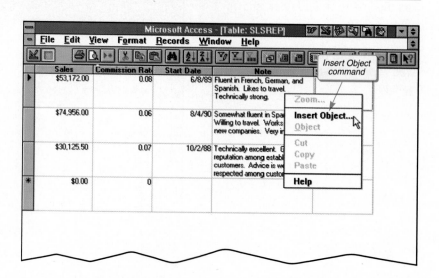

FIGURE 2-19

STEP 2 ▶

Choose the Insert Object command.

The Insert Object dialog box displays (Figure 2-20).

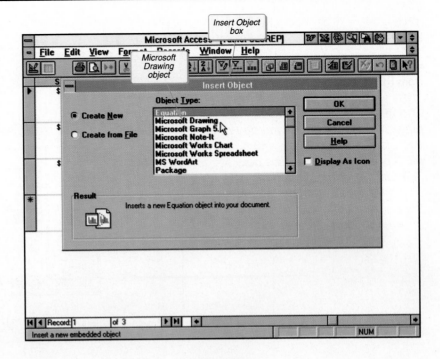

FIGURE 2-20

STEP 3 ▶

Select Microsoft Drawing by pointing to it and clicking the left mouse button and then choose the OK button. Select the File menu.

The Microsoft Draw – Drawing in Table: SLSREP dialog box displays (Figure 2-21). The File menu displays.

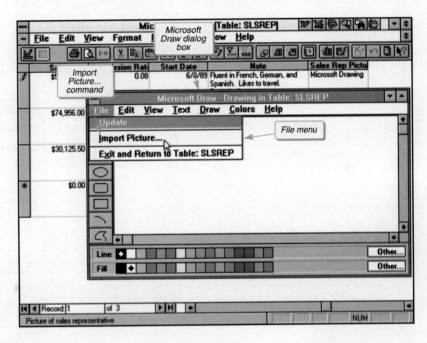

FIGURE 2-21

STEP 4 ▶

Choose the Import Picture command from the File menu.

The Import Picture dialog box displays (Figure 2-22a). If you do not see pict1.pcx, pict2.pcx, and pict3.pcx listed in the Files box, point to the access2subdirectory and double-click the left mouse button, producing the screen shown in Figure 2-22b.

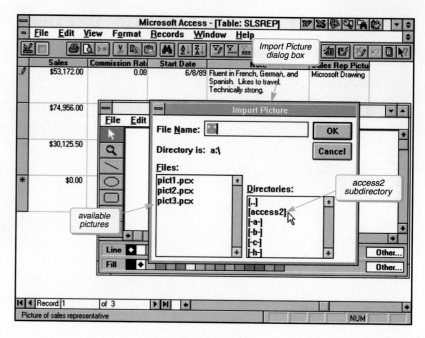

FIGURE 2-22a

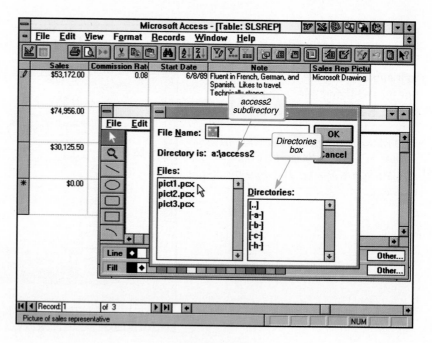

FIGURE 2-22b

STEP 5 ▶

Select pict1.pcx by pointing to it and clicking the left mouse button and then choose the OK button. Select the File menu.

The picture displays in the Microsoft Draw – Drawing in Table: SLSREP dialog box (Figure 2-23). The File menu displays.

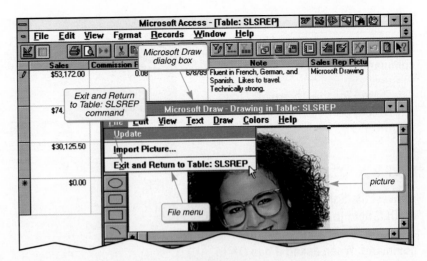

FIGURE 2-23

STEP 6 ▶

Choose the Exit and Return to Table: SLSREP command.

The Microsoft Draw dialog box displays (Figure 2-24).

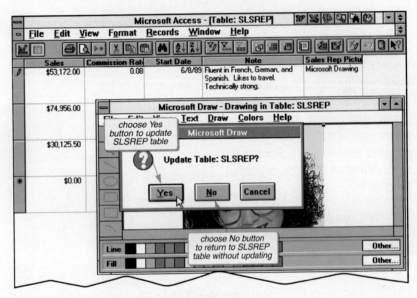

FIGURE 2-24

STEP 7 ▶

Choose the Yes button to update the SLSREP table. Then, point to the Sales Rep Picture field for the record you just updated and click the right mouse button.

The Sales Rep Picture field's shortcut menu displays (Figure 2-25).

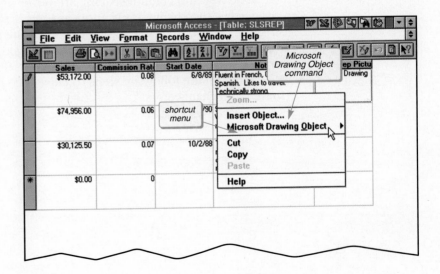

FIGURE 2-25

STEP 8 ▶

Select the Microsoft Drawing Object command.

The menu for the Microsoft Drawing Object command displays (Figure 2-26).

STEP 9 ▶

Convert the Sales Rep's picture from an OLE field to a picture by choosing the Change to Picture command. When asked if it is OK to make this change, choose the Yes button.

STEP 10 ▶

Insert the pictures in the second and third records using the techniques illustrated in Steps 2 through 9. For the second record, import the picture named pict2.pcx in the access2 subdirectory. For the third record, import the picture named pict3.pcx.

The pictures are now entered.

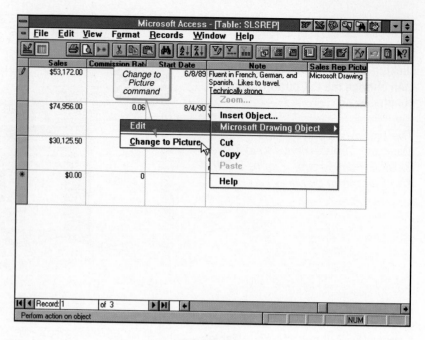

FIGURE 2-26

Saving the Table Properties

The row and column spacing are **table properties**. When changing any table properties, the changes only apply as long as the table is active *unless they are saved*. If saved, they will apply every time the table is open. To save them, simply close the table. If any properties have changed, Microsoft Access will ask if you want to save the changes. By answering Yes, the changes will be saved.

Perform the following steps to close the table and save the properties that have been changed.

TO CLOSE THE TABLE AND SAVE THE PROPERTIES ▼

STEP 1 ▶

Close the table by double-clicking its Control-menu box.

The Microsoft Access dialog box displays (Figure 2-27).

STEP 2 ▶

Choose the Yes button to save the table properties.

The properties are now saved.

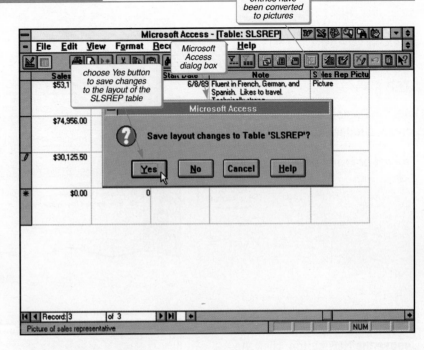

FIGURE 2-27

▶ ADVANCED FORM TECHNIQUES

T he form in this project includes data from both the SLSREP and CUSTOMER tables. The form will display data concerning one sales rep. It will also display data concerning the sales rep's many customers. Formally, the relationship between sales reps and customers is called a **one-to-many relationship** (*one* sales rep has *many* customers).

To include the data for the many customers of a sales rep on the form, the customer data must appear in a **subform**, which is a form that is contained in another form. The form in which the subform is contained is called the **main form**.

One of the wizards you can select when creating a form is the Main/Subform Form Wizard. This wizard will lead you through the steps necessary to create both the main form and the subform. Once the forms have been created, you can modify them.

Peform the following steps to create the form.

TO CREATE A FORM ▼

STEP 1 ▶

With the Database window on the screen, choose the Form button.

The list of forms displays (Figure 2-28).

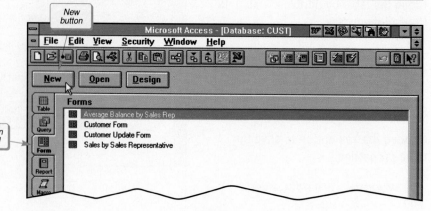

FIGURE 2-28

STEP 2 ▶

Choose the New button, click the down arrow in the New Form dialog box that displays and then select the SLSREP table.

The New Form dialog box displays (Figure 2-29). The SLSREP table is selected.

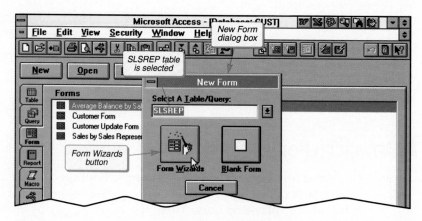

FIGURE 2-29

STEP 3 ▶

Choose the Form Wizards button.

The Form Wizards dialog box displays (Figure 2-30) asking you to select the appropriate Wizard.

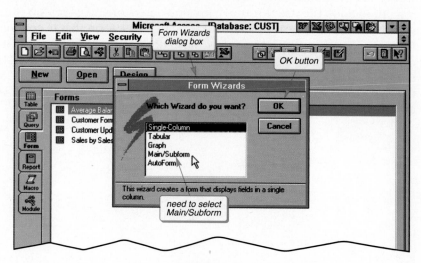

FIGURE 2-30

STEP 4 ►

Select Main/Subform by pointing to it and clicking the left mouse button. Then, choose the OK button.

The Main/Subform Wizard dialog box displays (Figure 2-31) requesting the table that contains data for the subform. The correct table (CUSTOMER) is already selected.

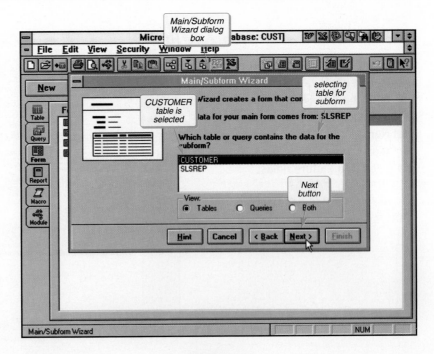

FIGURE 2-31

STEP 5 ►

Choose the Next button.

The Main/Subform Wizard dialog box displays (Figure 2-32) requesting the fields for the main form.

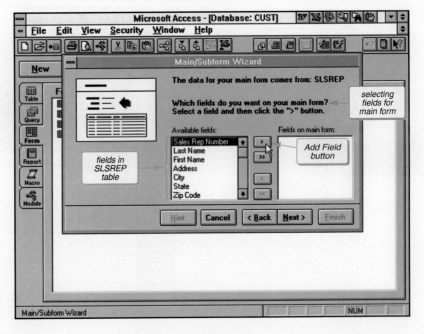

FIGURE 2-32

STEP 6 ▶

Include the Sales Rep Number field by making sure it is highlighted and then click the Add Field button. Use the same technique to select the First Name, Last Name, Sales, Commission Rate, Start Date, Note, and Sales Rep Picture fields.

The appropriate fields are selected (Figure 2-33).

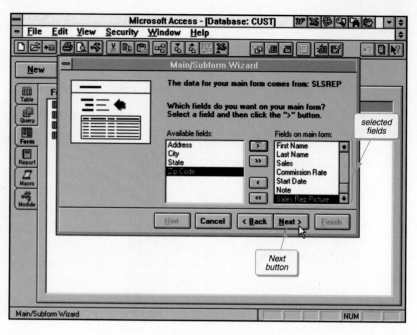

FIGURE 2-33

STEP 7 ▶

Choose the Next button.

The Main/Subform Wizard dialog box displays (Figure 2-34) requesting the fields for the subform.

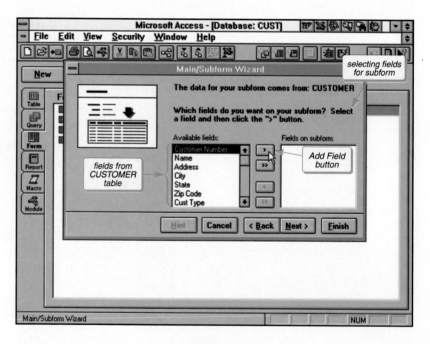

FIGURE 2-34

STEP 8 ▶

Select the Customer Number, Name, Balance, and Credit Limit fields (Figure 2-35).

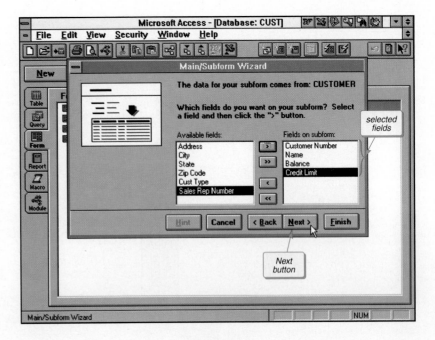

FIGURE 2-35

STEP 9 ▶

Choose the Next button.

The Main/Subform Wizard dialog box displays asking for a form style (Figure 2-36).

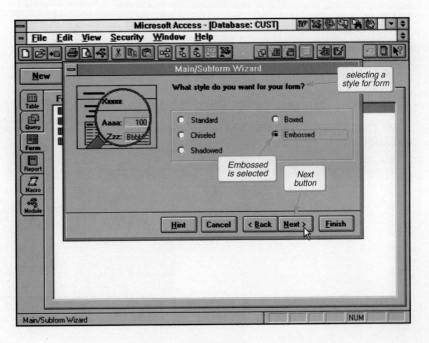

FIGURE 2-36

STEP 10 ▶

Choose the Next button and then
type Sales Representative
Form as the title for the form
(Figure 2-37).

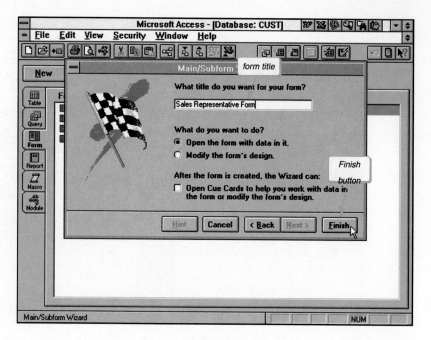

FIGURE 2-37

STEP 11 ▶

Choose the Finish button to
complete the form.

*The Microsoft Access dialog box
displays (Figure 2-38). The message indicates that you must save
the subform.*

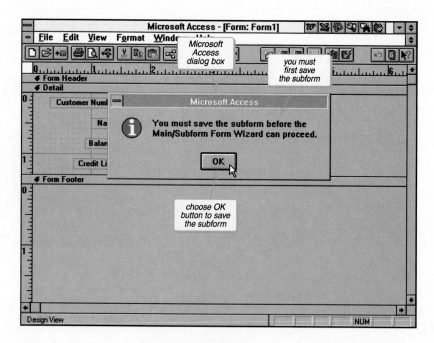

FIGURE 2-38

STEP 12 ▶

Choose the OK button.

STEP 13 ▶

Type Customer subform as the name of the subform (Figure 2-39).

STEP 14 ▶

Choose the OK button.

The form is created.

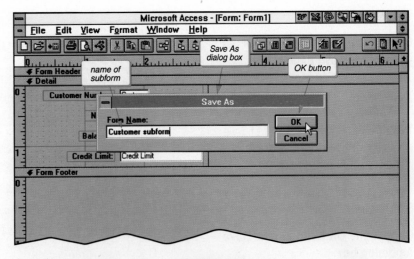

FIGURE 2-39

Saving the Form

To save a form and close it at the same time, simply close it. Access will ask if you want to save the changes. By answering Yes, the changes will be saved. Perform the following steps to close and save the form.

TO SAVE THE FORM ▼

STEP 1 ▶

Close the form by double-clicking the form's Control-menu box.

The Microsoft Access dialog box displays (Figure 2-40).

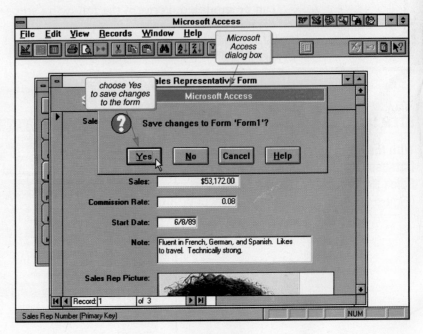

FIGURE 2-40

STEP 2 ▶

Choose the Yes button to indicate you want to save the form.

STEP 3 ▶

Type Sales Representative Master Form in the Save As dialog box (Figure 2-41).

STEP 4 ▶

Choose the OK button in the Save As dialog box.

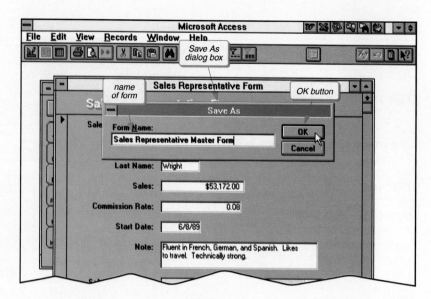

FIGURE 2-41

The form and subform have now been saved as part of the database and are available for future use.

Modifying the Form Design

To modify the form design, highlight the design in the Database window and choose the Design button. The design will then display in Design view where it can be modified. Perform the following steps to modify the design of the form just created by the wizard.

TO MODIFY THE FORM DESIGN ▼

STEP 1 ▶

With the Form button selected in the Database window, highlight the Sales Representative Master Form (Figure 2-42).

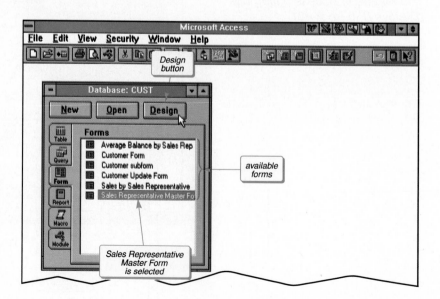

FIGURE 2-42

STEP 2 ▶

Choose the Design button and then maximize the window.

The form design displays in a maximized window (Figure 2-43).

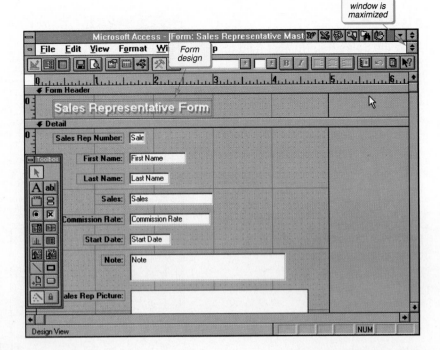

FIGURE 2-43

At this point, you can make modifications to the design.

Moving and Resizing Fields

Fields on this form can be moved and resized. First, select them by pointing to them and clicking the left mouse button. To move them, move the pointer to the boundary of the field so it becomes a hand and then drag the field. To resize a field, drag the appropriate handle. Perform the following steps to move the fields on the form and to appropriately resize some of the fields.

TO MOVE AND RESIZE FIELDS ▼

STEP 1 ▶

Point to the Sales Rep Number field, click the left mouse button to select the field, and then move the pointer until the shape changes to a hand.

Handles appear, indicating the field is selected (Figure 2-44). The pointer has changed to a hand.

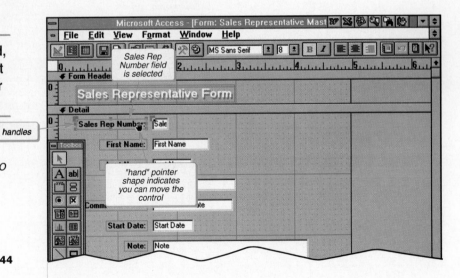

FIGURE 2-44

STEP 2 ▶

Drag the Sales Rep Number field to the position shown in Figure 2-45. Use the same steps to move the Last Name and Sales fields to the positions shown in Figure 2-45. Point to the handle at the right-hand edge of the control for the Sales field. (If the handles do not appear, point within the field portion of the control; that is, the white space, and click the left mouse button.) The pointer should change shape to a double-headed arrow.

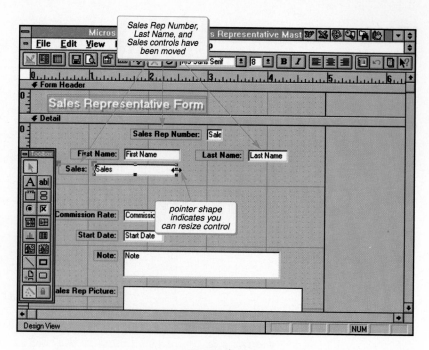

FIGURE 2-45

STEP 3 ▶

Drag the handle to change the size of the control to the one shown in Figure 2-46. Move the Commission Rate field to the position shown in Figure 2-46 and change the size of the control to the one shown. Move the Start Date field to the position shown in Figure 2-46. Move the Note field to the position shown in the figure and resize it to the size shown.

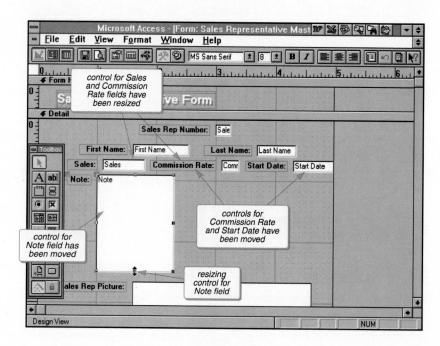

FIGURE 2-46

STEP 4 ▶

Move the Sales Rep Picture to the position shown in Figure 2-47. Click the right scroll arrow so the entire Sales Rep Picture field displays as shown in the figure. Point to the handle on the right-hand edge of the control.

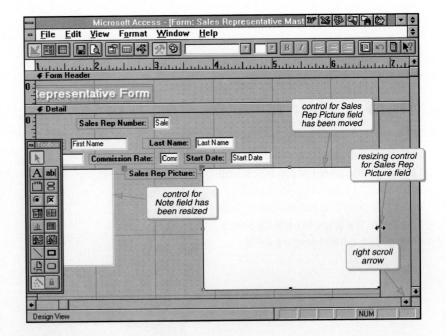

FIGURE 2-47

STEP 5 ▶

Resize the control for the Sales Rep Picture field to the one shown in Figure 2-48.

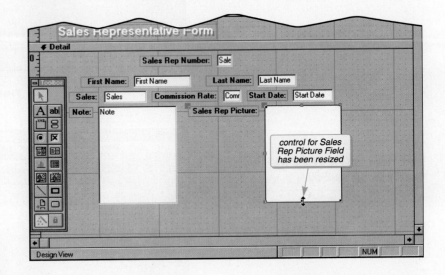

FIGURE 2-48

The changes have been made. The next step is to move the subform closer to the Note and Sales Rep Picture fields.

Moving the Subform

Now that the fields have been moved, the subform can be moved higher on the form. To do so, first use the down scroll arrow to shift the screen down so the portion of the form containing the subform displays. Then, move the subform to the correct location. Finally, use the up scroll arrow to shift the screen up to display the top portion of the form.

Perform the following steps to move the subform.

TO MOVE THE SUBFORM ▼

STEP 1 ▶

Click the left scroll arrow to move to the left-hand side of the form and then click the down scroll arrow until the subform displays. Point to the subform, click the left mouse button, and move the pointer until its shape changes to a hand (Figure 2-49).

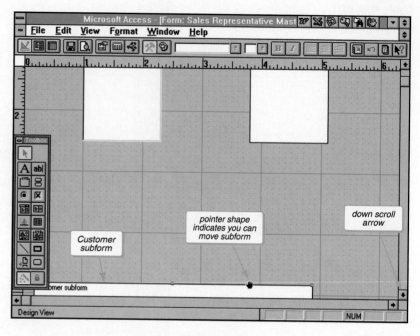

FIGURE 2-49

STEP 2 ▶

Drag the subform to the position shown in Figure 2-50.

The subform is now in the correct position.

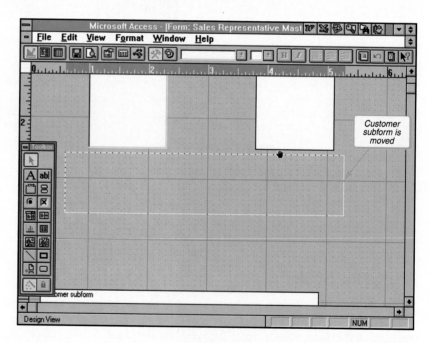

FIGURE 2-50

Returning to the Main Form from the Subform

If you inadvertently double-click the left mouse button on the subform, the design of the subform will display as shown in Figure 2-51. To return to the main form, select the Window menu (Figure 2-52). Choose the 2 Form: Sales Representative Master Form command. Access will then return to the main form.

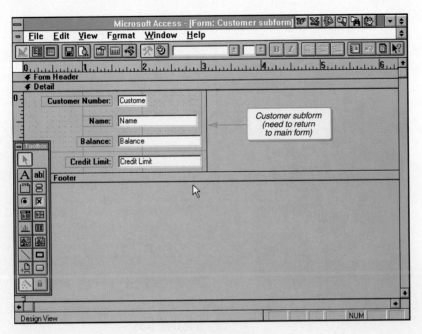

FIGURE 2-51

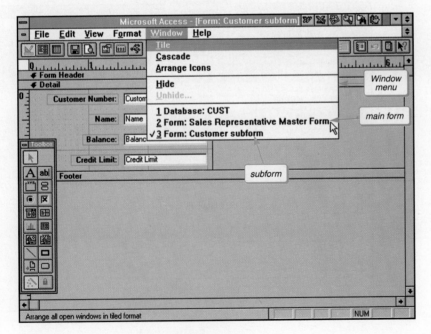

FIGURE 2-52

Viewing Data Using the Form

To view data from the table using the form, click the Form View button. Perform the following steps to display data using the form.

STEP 1 ▶

Point to the Form View button (Figure 2-53).

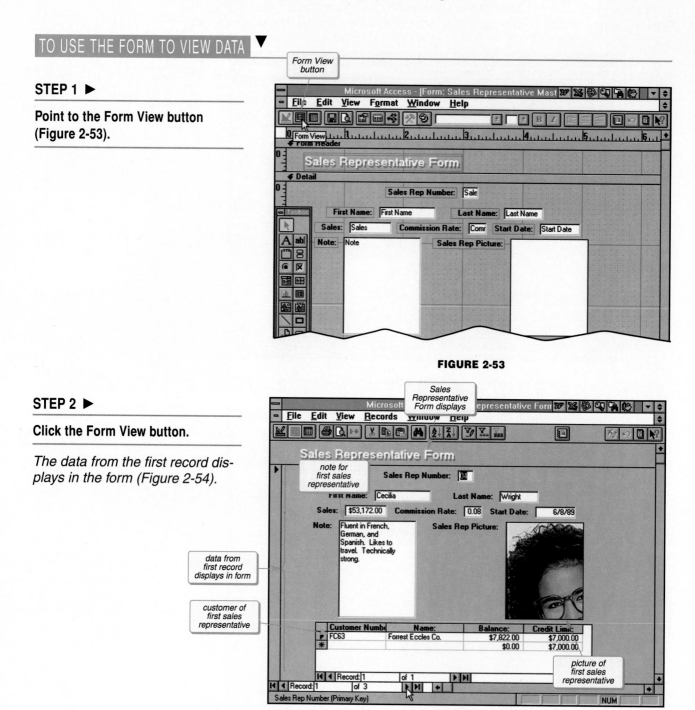

FIGURE 2-53

STEP 2 ▶

Click the Form View button.

The data from the first record displays in the form (Figure 2-54).

FIGURE 2-54

STEP 3 ▶

Click the main form's Next Record button to move to the second sales rep.

*The data from the second record displays (Figure 2-55). Because there are more customers than will fit in the subform at a single time, Access automatically adds a **vertical scroll bar**. You can use the scroll bar or the navigation buttons to move between customers.*

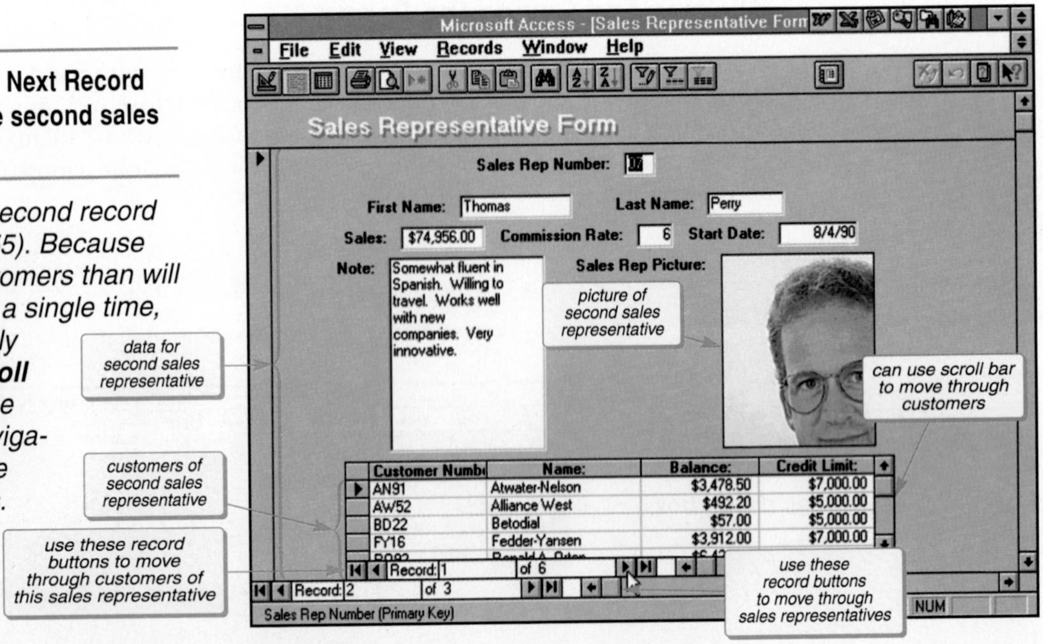

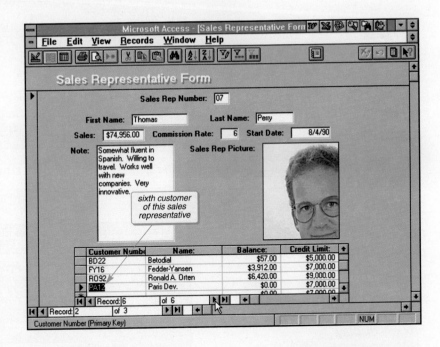

FIGURE 2-55

STEP 4 ▶

Click the subform's Next Record button five times.

The data from the sixth customer of sales rep 07 displays in the subform (Figure 2-56).

FIGURE 2-56

The previous steps illustrated the way you work with a main form and subform. Clicking the navigation buttons for the main form moves to a different sales rep. Clicking the navigation buttons for the subform moves to a different customer represented by the given sales rep; that is, the sales rep who displays in the main form.

Closing and Saving the Form

To save a form without closing it, use the Save command on the File menu. To save a form and close it at the same time, simply close it. If any changes have been made to the form, Access will ask if you want to save the changes. By choosing the Yes button, the changes will be saved. Perform the following steps to close and save the form.

TO CLOSE AND SAVE THE FORM ▼

STEP 1 ▶

Click the form's Control-menu box.

The Microsoft Access dialog box displays (Figure 2-57).

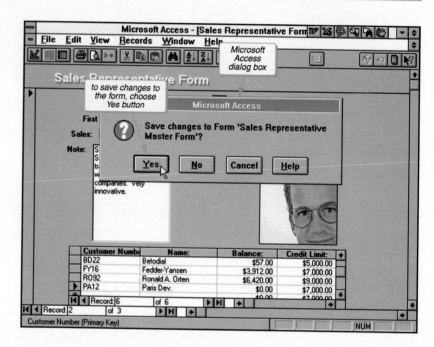

FIGURE 2-57

STEP 2 ▶

Choose the Yes button to save changes to the master form.

If you have made any changes involving the subform (Figure 2-58), the Microsoft Access dialog box will display.

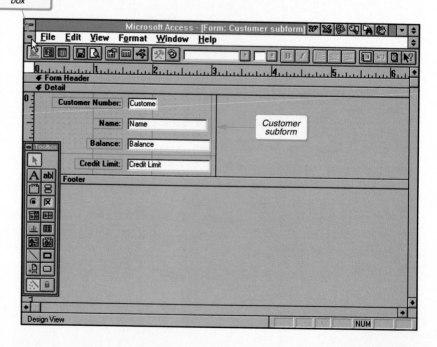

FIGURE 2-58

STEP 3 ▶

If the Microsoft Access dialog box displays, choose the Yes button to save changes to the subform.

The changes are saved and the Database window once again displays (Figure 2-59).

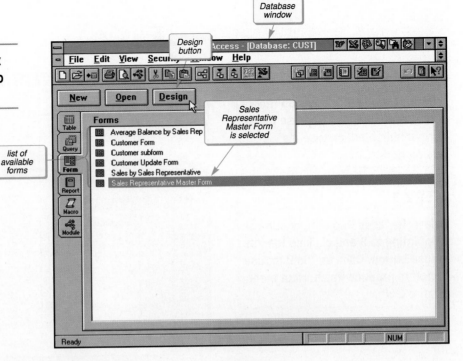

FIGURE 2-59

The next time the form is used, it will have the new modifications.

Changing the Size Mode of a Picture

The amount of a picture that displays, as well as the way that picture displays, is determined by the **size mode**. The possible size modes are as follows:

1. Clip — Only display the portion of the picture that will fit in the space allocated to it.
2. Stretch — Expand or contract the picture to fit the precise space allocated on the screen. For photographs, this is usually not a good choice because fitting a photograph to the allocated space can distort the image, giving it a stretched appearance.
3. Zoom — Do the best job of fitting the picture to the allocated space without changing the look of the picture. The entire picture will display and will look as it should. There may be some white space either above or to the right of the picture, however.

Currently, the size mode is Clip and that is why only a portion of the picture displayed. To see the whole picture, use the shortcut menu for the picture to change the size mode to Zoom, as shown in the steps on the next page.

TO CHANGE THE SIZE MODE OF THE PICTURE ▼

STEP 1 ▶

With the Database window on the screen and the Sales Representative Form highlighted, choose the Design button.

STEP 2 ▶

Select the Sales Rep Picture control by pointing to it and clicking the left mouse button. Click the right mouse button to produce its shortcut menu (Figure 2-60).

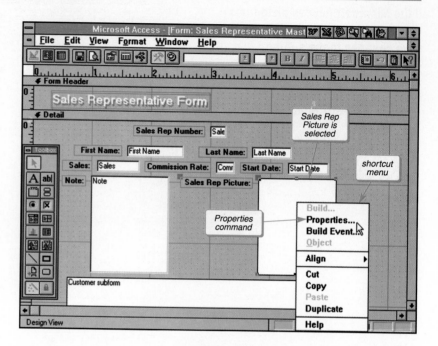

FIGURE 2-60

STEP 3 ▶

Choose the Properties command from the shortcut menu.

The Bound Object Frame: Sales Rep Picture window displays (Figure 2-61).

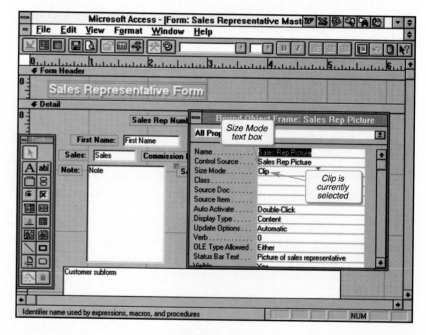

FIGURE 2-61

STEP 4 ▶

Point to the Size Mode text box, click the left mouse button, and then click the down arrow that displays.

The available Size Mode options display (Figure 2-62).

STEP 5 ▶

Select the Zoom option and then close the window by double-clicking its Control-menu box.

The size mode is changed. The entire picture will now display.

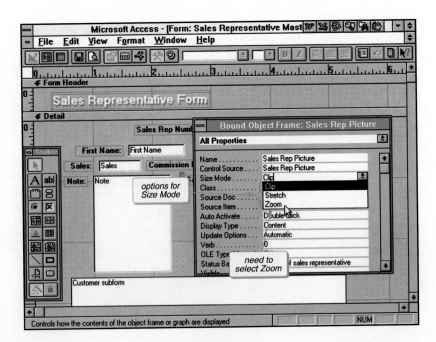

FIGURE 2-62

Changing Border Styles and Colors of Labels

To change characteristics of labels, such as border styles and colors, you first need to select them. Then, click the right mouse button to produce a shortcut menu, select the Properties command, and modify whichever properties you want to change.

In some cases, you will want to make the same change to several objects, for example, to several labels. Instead of making the changes individually, you can select all the objects at once and then make a single change. To select more than one object at a time, press and hold down the SHIFT key as you select the additional objects.

Perform the following steps first to select all the labels and then to change the border styles and colors.

TO CHANGE BORDER STYLES AND COLORS OF LABELS ▼

STEP 1 ▶

Select the Sales Rep Number field by pointing to it and clicking the left mouse button. Select the other fields by pointing to them, pressing and holding down the SHIFT key, and clicking the left mouse button.

All fields are selected (Figure 2-63). The pointer points to the last field selected. (In the figure it is the Sales Rep Picture field.)

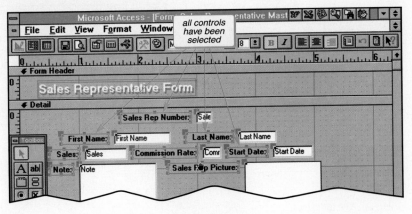

FIGURE 2-63

STEP 2 ▶

With the pointer pointing to one of the selected fields, click the right mouse button.

The shortcut menu for the fields displays (Figure 2-64).

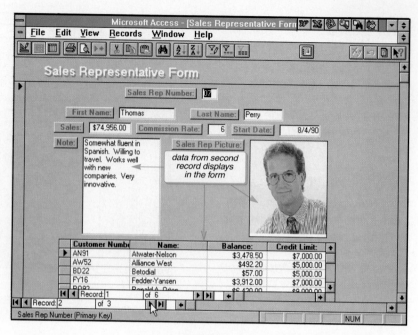

FIGURE 2-64

STEP 3 ▶

Choose the Properties command. Point to the Border Style text box and click the left mouse button.

The Multiple selection dialog box displays (Figure 2-65). An insertion point displays in the Border Style text box and a down arrow displays to the right.

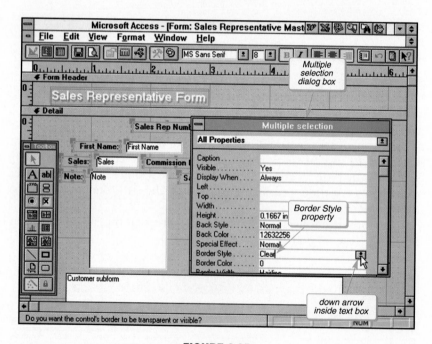

FIGURE 2-65

STEP 4 ▶

Click the down arrow.

A drop-down list of available bor-der styles displays (Figure 2-66).

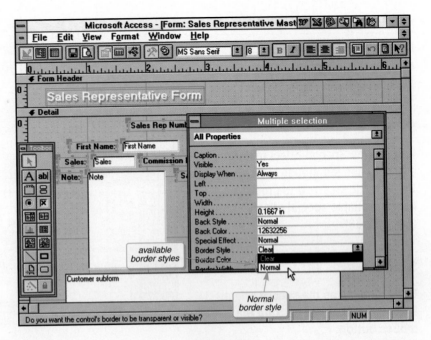

FIGURE 2-66

STEP 5 ▶

Select the Normal border style by pointing to it and clicking the left mouse button.

STEP 6 ▶

Click the down scroll arrow until the Fore Color text box displays, point to the Fore Color text box, and click the left mouse button. A button containing three dots displays. Click the button containing the three dots to produce a color palette and then point to the medium blue color, as shown in Figure 2-67.

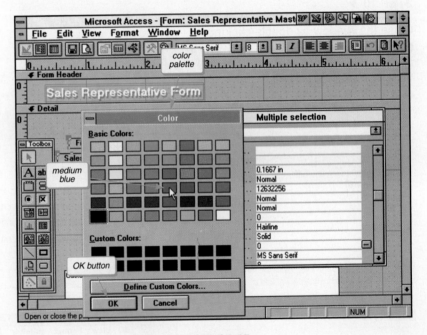

FIGURE 2-67

STEP 7 ▶

Select the medium blue color by clicking the left mouse button and then choose the OK button.

STEP 8 ▶

Point to the Special Effect text box and click the left mouse button. Click the down arrow to produce a list of available special effects (Figure 2-68).

STEP 9 ▶

Select Raised as the special effect by pointing to it and clicking the left mouse button.

STEP 10 ▶

Close the window by double-clicking the Control-menu box.

The changes to the labels have now been made.

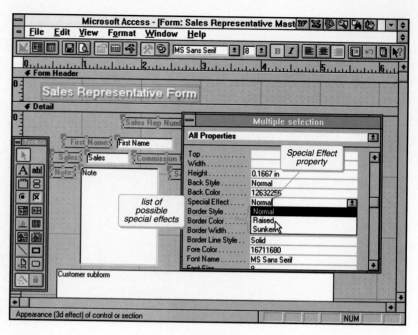

FIGURE 2-68

Saving the Changes

To save the changes without closing the form, use the Save command on the File menu. The form will still be open, and you can make further changes to it. You can also test the changes by switching to Form view to view the form with data in it. Perform the following step to save the form without closing it.

TO SAVE THE CHANGES ▼

STEP 1 ▶

Select the File menu and choose the Save command (Figure 2-69).

The changes have been saved.

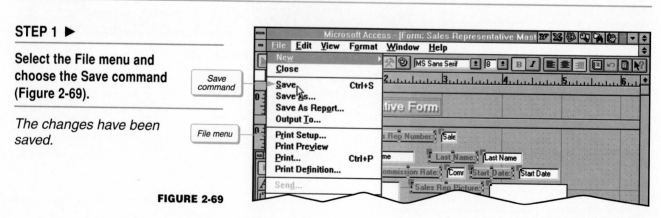

FIGURE 2-69

Testing the Changes

The simplest way to test the effect of the changes is to view the form with data from the database. To do so, click the Form View button to transfer to Form view. Perform the following steps to test the changes to the form.

TO TEST THE CHANGES ▼

STEP 1 ▶

Point to the Form View button (Figure 2-70).

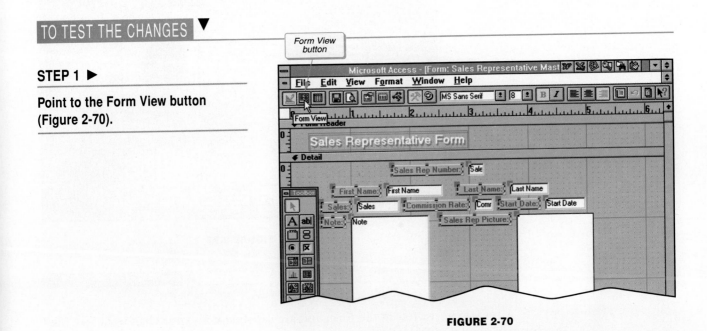

FIGURE 2-70

STEP 2 ▶

Click the Form View button.

The first record displays in the newly modified form (Figure 2-71).

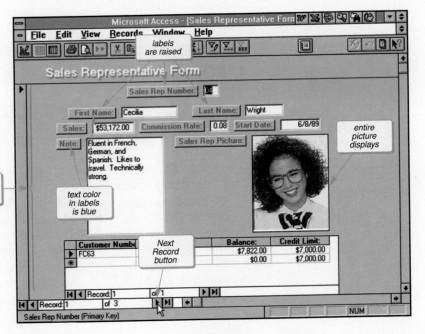

FIGURE 2-71

STEP 3 ▶

Click the Next Record button in the main form.

The second record displays in the form (Figure 2-72).

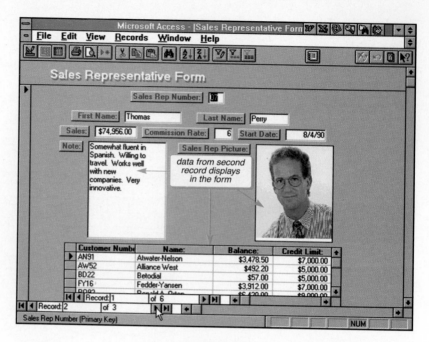

FIGURE 2-72

After you have viewed the form and are satisfied with your changes, close the form, as shown in the following step.

TO CLOSE THE FORM

Step 1: Double-click the form's Control-menu box to close the form.

The form is removed from the screen. To use it at any time in the future, select it in the Database window and then choose the Open button.

▶ USING DATE AND MEMO FIELDS IN A QUERY

To use date fields in queries, simply type the dates (including the slashes). To search for records with a specific date, type the date. You can also use comparison operators. To find all the sales representatives whose start date was prior to January 1, 1990, for example, enter the criterion <1/01/90

You can also use memo fields in queries. Typically, you will want to find all the records on which the memo field contains a specific word or phrase. To do so, use wild cards. For example, to find all the sales representatives who have the word Spanish in the Note field, enter the criterion Like *Spanish*

Perform the following steps to create and run queries that use date and memo fields.

TO USE DATE AND MEMO FIELDS IN A QUERY ▼

STEP 1 ▶

With the Database window on the screen, choose the Query button.

The list of available queries displays (Figure 2-73).

FIGURE 2-73

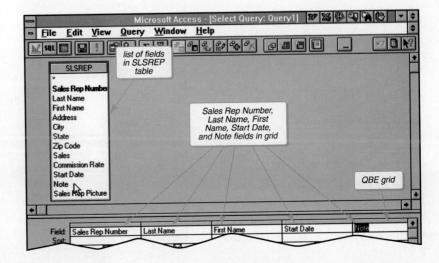

STEP 2 ▶

Choose the New button, choose the New Query button, select the SLSREP table, choose the Add button, and choose the Close button. Resize the two portions of the Microsoft Access - [Select Query: Query1] window to the sizes shown in Figure 2-74. Resize the SLSREP field list to the one shown in the figure.

FIGURE 2-74

STEP 3 ▶

Include the Sales Rep Number, Last Name, First Name, Start Date, and Note fields in the query by pointing to them in the SLSREP field list and double-clicking the left mouse button. Click the Criteria row under the Note field and type the criterion `Like *Spanish*` (Figure 2-75).

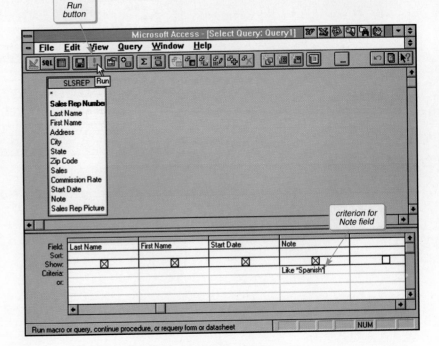

FIGURE 2-75

STEP 4 ▶

Click the Run button to run the query.

The results display in Datasheet view (Figure 2-76). Two records are included in the dynaset produced.

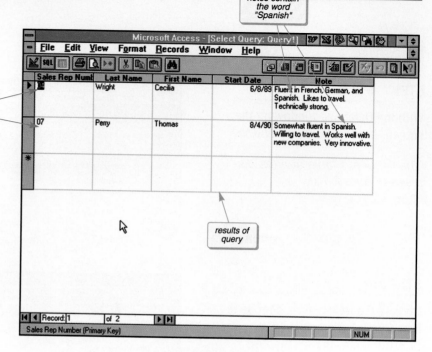

FIGURE 2-76

STEP 5 ▶

Click the Design View button to return to the Select Query window. Point to the Criteria row under the Start Date field, click the left mouse button, and type <1/01/90 **(Figure 2-77).**

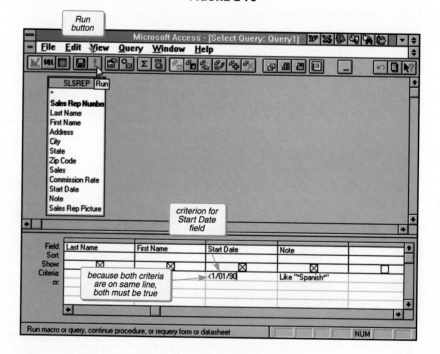

FIGURE 2-77

STEP 6 ▶

Click the Run button to run the query.

The result only contains a single row (Figure 2-78), because there is one sales representative who was hired before January 1, 1990, and whose Note contains the word Spanish.

STEP 7 ▶

Close the Select Query window by clicking its Control-menu box. When asked if you want to save the query, choose the No button.

The results of the query are removed from the screen and the Database window once again displays.

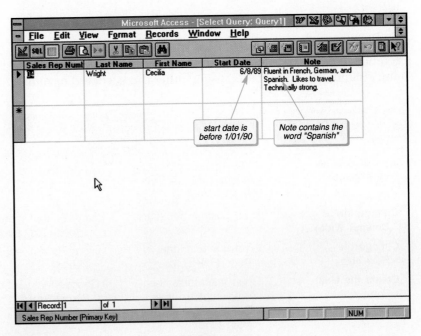

FIGURE 2-78

▶ **PROJECT SUMMARY**

Project 2 introduced you to some additional field types. You learned how to create and work with date, memo, and OLE fields. You also learned how to use such fields in a form. You also learned how to build a form on a one-to-many relationship in which you had several records from one of the tables appearing on the screen at the same time. Finally, you learned how to use date and memo fields in queries.

▶ **KEY TERMS AND INDEX**

In Access, you can accomplish a task in a number of different ways. The following table provides a quick reference to each task presented in this project with its available options. The commands listed in the Menu column can be executed using either the keyboard or mouse.

Task	Mouse	Menu	Keyboard Shortcuts
Add Data to an OLE Field	Click the right mouse button, choose Insert Object	From Edit menu, choose Insert Object	
Change the Column Width	Drag column boundary in Field Selector bar	From Format menu, choose Column Width	
Change the Row Size	Drag row boundary in Record Selector box	From Format menu, choose Row Height	
Create the Main Form with a Subform	Open main form, then drag subform from Database window into main form	Choose Main/Subform Form Wizard	
Move or Resize an Object on a Form	Click object to select, drag object to move it or drag handles to resize it		
Return from Subform to Main Form During Design		From Window menu, choose main form	
Save the Table Properties	Double-click Control-menu box, choose Yes	From File menu, choose Save Table	Press CTRL+S
Update an OLE Field	Click the right mouse button, choose name of object	From Edit menu, choose name of object	
Use the Date Field in a Query			Type comparison operator, then type date, including slashes
Use the Memo Field in a Query			Type character string (including any necessary wildcard symbols)
Use the Shortcut Menu	Click the right mouse button		
Use Zoom Box	Click the right mouse button, choose Zoom		Press SHIFT+F2

STUDENT ASSIGNMENT 1
True/False

Instructions: Circle T if the statement is true or F if the statement is false.

T   F   1. The term OLE means Object Linking and Encoding.

T   F   2. The easiest way to enter data for a memo field is to select the field, click the right mouse button, and select Magnify to produce a box with plenty of room to type the memo.

T   F   3. Once an OLE field is entered in a record, you cannot update the object at any point in the future.

T   F   4. To change the size of a column, position the pointer on the right boundary of the column in the field selector bar and drag the boundary.

T   F   5. To insert data into an OLE field, select the field, click the right mouse button to produce the shortcut menu, and choose the Insert OLE command from the shortcut menu.

T   F   6. You can import pictures from files on disk and place them in an OLE field.

T   F   7. To create a form that shows a one-to-many relationship, use the Main/Subform Form Wizard.

T   F   8. When you create a form/subform, the subform contains data from the one table in a one-to-many relationship.

T   F   9. To save table properties permanently, choose the Save command from the Properties menu.

T   F   10. When you save a form of the form/subform type, you must save and assign a name to both the main form and the subform.

T   F   11. You cannot resize OLE fields on a form.

T   F   12. To change the color of a field label, select the object, click the right mouse button, and choose Color from the shortcut menu.

T   F   13. To select more than one object at a time, press and hold down the CTRL key as you select additional objects.

T   F   14. To use a date field in a query, enclose the date in single quotes.

T   F   15. You cannot use comparison operators with date fields.

T   F   16. To save changes without closing a form, choose Save from the File menu.

T   F   17. To change the border style of a field label, select the label, click the right mouse button, choose Properties from the shortcut menu, and then point to and click the Border Style text box.

T   F   18. To find all records where the word German is included in a memo field, enter "German" in the Criteria row of the Query window.

T   F   19. When you enter date fields in a record, you do not need to enter the slashes.

T   F   20. To return from a subform to a main form during design, choose the main form from the Window menu.

STUDENT ASSIGNMENT 2
Multiple Choice

Instructions: Circle the correct response.

1. The term OLE means _____.
    a. Object Linking and Encoding
    b. Object Linking and Embedding
    c. Object Locking and Encoding
    d. Object Locking and Embedding

(continued)

STUDENT ASSIGNMENT 2 (continued)

2. To easily update a memo field, select the field, click the right mouse button, and select _____ from the field's shortcut menu to display a box large enough to type the data for the memo field.
   a. Magnify
   b. Enlarge
   c. Zoom
   d. View

3. In a table, the row containing the list of field names is called the _____.
   a. field selector bar
   b. field label bar
   c. column selector panel
   d. column label panel

4. The box at the beginning of a record that you can click to select a record is called the _____.
   a. row selector box
   b. record selector box
   c. row identifier box
   d. record identifier box

5. To insert data in an OLE field, select the field, click the right mouse button, and choose the _____ command from the field's shortcut menu.
   a. Insert OLE
   b. OLE
   c. Insert Object
   d. Object

6. A sales rep may represent many customers, but a customer can be represented by only one sales rep. This is a _____ relationship.
   a. one-to-none
   b. one-to-one
   c. one-to-many
   d. many-to-many

7. To select all field objects on a form, select the first object by clicking the left mouse button and then press and hold down the _____ key as you select each of the others.
   a. left CTRL
   b. right CTRL
   c. SHIFT
   d. ALT

8. To change the color of a field label, select the field, click the right mouse button, choose _____ from the field's shortcut menu, and then click the Fore Color text box.
   a. Color
   b. Properties
   c. Label
   d. Image

9. The SLSREP table contains a Start Date field that contains the date a sales rep began with the organization. To find all sales reps who started after 1989, enter the criterion _____ in the Criteria row of the Start Date field in the Query window.
   a. >'12/31/89'
   b. >=12/31/89
   c. >12/31/89
   d. >='12/31/89'

10. The SLSREP table contains a Note field that contains notes describing important characteristics of the sales representatives. To find all sales reps who have technical capabilities, enter the criterion _____ in the Criteria row of the Note field in the Query window.
   a. Like ?technical
   b. Like *technical
   c. Like ?technical?
   d. Like *technical*

STUDENT ASSIGNMENT 3
Understanding Table Properties

Instructions: Figure SA2-3 shows the Datasheet view for the Vendor table in the Soft database on the Student Diskette that accompanies this book. Two additional fields, Order Date and Notes, have been added to the table. Use this figure to answer the following questions.

1. What is the easiest way to enter data in the Notes field?

   _____

   _____

2. How do you change the column widths in Datasheet view?

   _____

   _____

3. How do you change the row spacing in Datasheet view?

_____

_____

_____

_____

_____

FIGURE SA2-3

4. How do you save table properties?

_____

_____

STUDENT ASSIGNMENT 4
Memo and OLE Fields

Instructions: Figure SA2-4 shows the structure for the Vendor table in the Soft database. Use this figure and Figure SA2-3 to answer the following questions.

1. Explain how to add the phrase, No telephone orders accepted, to the record for Vendor LS.

_____

_____

_____

FIGURE SA2-4

2. Each vendor has a drawing that identifies the company. This drawing needs to be added to the Vendor table. Give the steps necessary to add this field to the Vendor table. Use the name Logo for the field.

_____

_____

3. The drawings can be imported from the Microsoft Draw program. Give the steps necessary to add the actual drawings to the Logo field.

_____

_____

STUDENT ASSIGNMENT 5
Understanding Forms

Instructions: Figure SA2-5 shows a partially completed form for the Vendor table. Use this figure to answer the following questions.

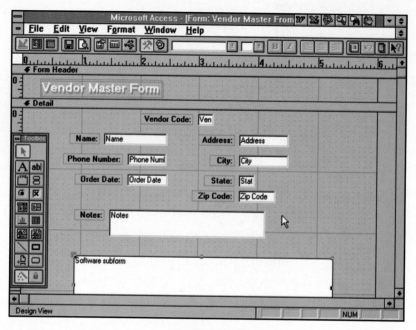

FIGURE SA2-5

1. How can you select more than one field object at a time?

_____

_____

2. How would you change the color of the field labels on the form?

_____

_____

3. The vendor form includes the software subform. What is a subform?

_____

_____

STUDENT ASSIGNMENT 6
Understanding the Soft database

Instructions: In Figure SA2-6, arrows point to various fields in the Vendor table in the Soft database. Identify the field types for these fields in the spaces provided. Answer the following questions about the Soft database.

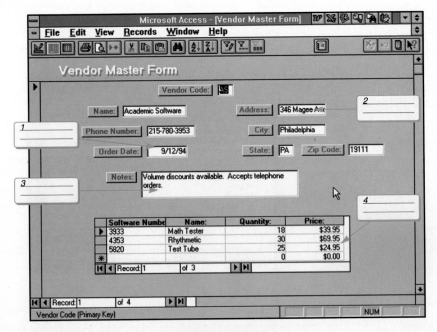

FIGURE SA2-6

1. The Vendor Master Form depicts a one-to-many relationship between the Vendor table and the Software table. What is a one-to-many relationship?

_____

_____

2. Assume the highlight is on the first field of the record shown in Figure SA2-6. How would you add the phrase, Provides excellent technical support, to the Notes field?

_____

_____

3. Figure SA2-6 displays information on three software packages distributed by the vendor. Assume two additional records are added to the Software table and that these records also have a Vendor Code of AS. What would you need to do to display the information for the fifth software package?

_____

_____

_____

COMPUTER LABORATORY EXERCISES

COMPUTER LABORATORY EXERCISE 1
Using the Help Menu

Instructions: Perform the following tasks:

1. Start Microsoft Access.
2. Open the Soft database.
3. Choose the Contents command from the Help menu.
4. Choose Search.

(continued)

COMPUTER LABORATORY EXERCISE 1 (continued)

5. Type memo in the Search dialog box and click the Show Topics button, as shown in Figure CLE2-1.

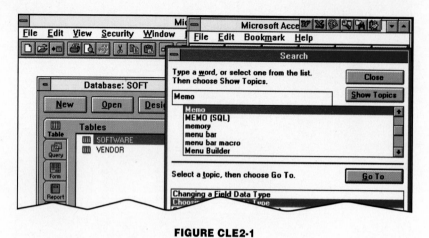

FIGURE CLE2-1

6. Go to the Choosing a Field Data Type topic, read the information, and answer the following questions.
   a. How many characters can you store in a memo field?

   _____

   b. How many characters can you store in a text field?

   _____

   c. What is a counter data type?

   _____

7. Place the cursor on the terms linked and embedded (the cursor will change to a hand), read the descriptions for these terms, and answer the following questions.
   a. Explain the difference between a linked object and an embedded object.

   _____

   b. How do you embed objects in Microsoft Access?

   _____

8. Exit the Help window and close the Soft database.
9. Exit Access.

COMPUTER LABORATORY EXERCISE 2
Creating and Using Date and Memo Fields

Instructions: Perform the following tasks:

1. Start Access and open the Soft database.
2. Select the Vendor table and choose Design.
3. Add the fields Order Date and Notes to the Vendor table. Order date is a Date/Time data type and Notes is a Memo data type. Enter last Order Date as the description for the Order Date field. Enter information on Ordering Procedures as the description for the Notes field
4. Add the data shown in Figure CLE2-2a to the Vendor table.
5. Print the table. Close the table. Choose Query, New, and then New Query.
6. Add the Vendor table to the query and display the fields as shown in Figure CLE2-2b.

▶ **TABLE CLE 5-2a**

Vendor Code	Order Date	Notes
AS	9/12/94	Volume discounts available. Accepts telephone orders
CC	10/3/94	No discounts. Minimum order requirements
EI	9/24/94	Volume discounts available. Minimum order required
LS	10/7/94	

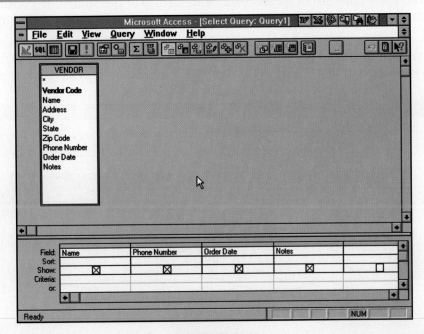

FIGURE CLE2-2b

7. Query the Vendor table for all records with order dates before October 1, 1994.
8. Print the results.
9. Query the Vendor table to find all vendors who give volume discounts.
10. Print the results.
11. Query the Vendor table to find all vendors who either have minimum order requirements or who have order dates after September 30, 1994.
12. Print the results.
13. Close the query without saving it.
14. Exit Access.

COMPUTER LABORATORY EXERCISE 3
Creating a Form/Subform for the Vendor Table

Instructions: Perform the following tasks:

1. Start Microsoft Access.
2. Open the Soft database, choose the Form button and then choose the New button.
3. Use the FormWizard to create a form/subform for the Vendor table that includes all the data from the Vendor table and the Software Number, Name, Quantity, and Price from the Software table. Name the form Vendor Master Form.
4. Modify the form design to create the form shown in Figure SA2-6 on page A105.
5. Print the form.
6. Close and save the form.
7. Close the database and exit Access.

COMPUTER LABORATORY ASSIGNMENT 1
Improving the Items Database

Purpose: To provide practice in using date, memo, and OLE fields and to create forms containing subforms.

Instructions: Use the Items database in the Access2 subdirectory of the Student Diskette that accompanies this book for this assignment. Execute each task on the computer and print the results.

1. Start Microsoft Access and open the Items database.
2. Highlight the Product table and choose the Design button.
3. Add the fields Reorder Date and Reorder Notes to the table structure as shown in Figure CLA2-1a.

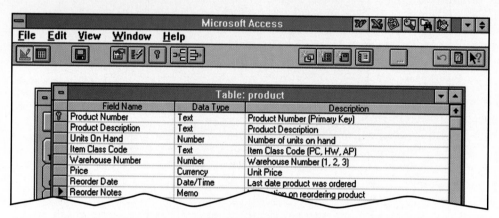

FIGURE CLA2-1a

4. Save the changes to the structure.
5. Add the data shown in Figure CLA2-1b to the Product table. If necessary, adjust the row and column spacing for the table.

Product Number	Reorder Date	Reorder Notes
AD29	7/12/94	Father's Day item. Call in order to EJZ Mfr.
AK13	7/24/94	Summer item. Order from ABC Supplies.
AY83	9/17/94	Call in order to PC Unlimited. Minimum order required.
BE24	9/15/94	Blanket Purchase Order. Call in order to EJZ Mfr.
BL07	8/9/94	Can single order. Requires written Purchase Order. Order from Whirlwind or ABC Supplies.
BX55	6/30/94	Call in order to PC Unlimited. Minimum order required.
CB03	10/1/94	Can single order. Requires written Purchase Order. Order from Whirlwind or ABC Supplies.
CC04	8/28/94	Graduation item. Replenish stock in early April. Call in order to PC Unlimited.
CX22	9/21/94	Requires written Purchase Order. Order from PC Unlimited or ABC Supplies.
CZ81	9/19/94	Blanket Purchase Order. Call in order to EJZ Mfr.

FIGURE CLA2-1b

6. Close the Product table.
7. Create the form shown in Figure CLA2-1c for the Class table. The form includes all the fields from the Class table and the Product Number, Product Description, Units On Hand, and Price fields from the Product table.

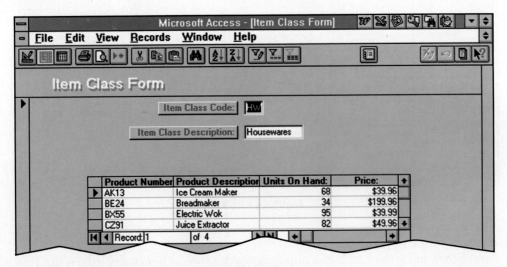

FIGURE CLA2-1c

8. Print the form.
9. Save the form as Item Class Master Form.
10. Close the form and create a new query for the Product table.
11. Query the Product table to find all records where products were ordered after August 31, 1994. Display the Product Number, Product Description, Units On Hand, Price, and Reorder Date fields.
12. Print the results.
13. Query the Product table to find all records where the product can be ordered from ABC Supplies. Display the Product Number, Product Description, Price, and Reorder Notes fields.
14. Print the results.
15. Query the Product table to find all records where products were ordered before September 1994 and the number of units on hand is less than 20. Display the Product Number, Product Description, Units On Hand, Price, Reorder Date, and Reorder Notes fields.
16. Print the results.
17. Close the query without saving it.
18. Close the database and exit Access.

COMPUTER LABORATORY ASSIGNMENT 2
Improving the Employee Database

Purpose: To provide practice in using date, memo, and OLE fields and to create forms containing subforms.

Instructions: Use the Emp database in the Access2 subdirectory of the Student Diskette that accompanies this book for this assignment. Execute each task on the computer and print the results.

1. Start Microsoft Access and open the Emp database.
2. Highlight the Employee table and choose the Design button.
3. Add the fields Start Date, Notes, and Employee Picture to the table structure as shown in Figure CLA2-2a on the next page.

(continued)

COMPUTER LABORATORY ASSIGNMENT 2 (continued)

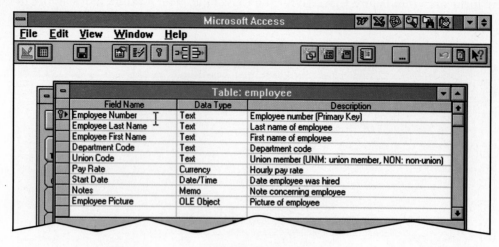

FIGURE CLA2-2a

4. Save the changes to the structure.
5. Add the data shown in Figure CLA2-2b to the Employee table. If necessary, adjust the row and column spacing for the table.

Employee Number	Start Date	Notes
0011	7/01/88	Employee of the Year 1991.
0023	6/15/90	Won safety award. Had CPR training.
0036	6/01/89	Union representative.
0047	2/15/91	Eligible for promotion in 1995.
0120	8/15/91	Excellent computer skills. Trains co-workers.
0122	1/02/90	Had CPR training. Speaks Spanish.
0225	4/01/90	Excellent telephone skills. Trains co-workers.
0226	1/15/92	Expert in distribution channels.
0229	7/16/92	Employee of the Month June 1993.
0337	1/01/93	Eligible to sit for the CPA exam in 1994.
0441	6/01/93	Quality Assurance skills.
0756	9/01/93	Contract negotiation skills.
0787	3/01/94	Marketing intern.
0866	4/01/94	General Business intern.
0909	4/01/94	Marketing intern.

FIGURE CLA2-2b

6. Add the Employee Pictures for the employees in the Accounting department. Use the same picture files that you used for the SLSREP table in this project.
7. Close the Employee table.

8. Create the form shown in Figure CLA2-2c for the Department table. The form includes all the fields from the Department table and the Employee Number, Employee Last Name, Employee First Name, and Pay Rate fields from the Employee table.

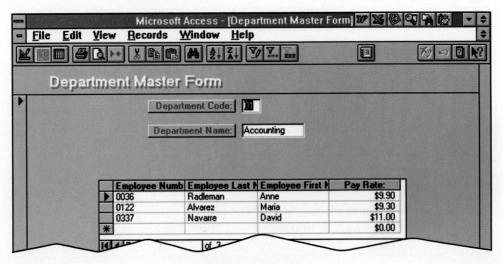

FIGURE CLA2-2c

9. Print the form.
10. Save the form as Department Master Form.
11. Close the form and create a new query for the Employee table.
12. Query the Employee table to find all employees who started after 1990. Display the Employee Number, Employee Last Name, Employee First Name, Start Date, and Pay Rate fields.
13. Print the results.
14. Query the Employee table to find all employees who have had CPR training. Display the Employee Number, Employee Last Name, Employee First Name, and Notes fields.
15. Print the results.
16. Query the Employee table to find all employees who started before 1991 and who have a pay rate greater than 9.00. Display the Employee Number, Employee Last Name, Employee First Name, Department Name, and Pay Rate fields. (Hint: You will have to join the Employee and Department tables.)
17. Print the results.
18. Close the query without saving it.
19. Close the database and exit Access

COMPUTER LABORATORY ASSIGNMENT 3
Improving the Movie Database

Purpose: To provide practice in using date, memo, and OLE fields and to create forms containing subforms.

Instructions: Use the Mov database in the Access2 subdirectory of the Student Diskette that accompanies this book for this assignment. Execute each task on the computer and print the results.

1. Start Microsoft Access and open the Mov database.
2. Highlight the Director table and choose Design.
3. Add the fields Birth Date, Notes, and Director Picture to the table structure, as shown in Figure CLA2-3a on the next page.

(continued)

COMPUTER LABORATORY ASSIGNMENT 3 (continued)

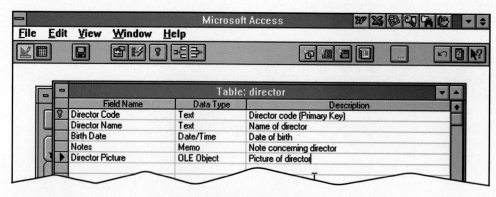

FIGURE CLA2-3a

4. Save the changes to the structure.
5. Add the data shown in Figure CLA2-3b to the Director table.

Director Code	Birth Date	Notes
01	12/12/25	Won two Academy Awards. Comfortable with all types of movies. Won an award at Cannes film festival.
02	10/21/13	Combines excellent photography with wonderful music.
03	3/4/22	Excels at Westerns. Won American Film Institute Award.
04	5/14/38	Youngest director to ever win an Academy Award.

FIGURE CLA2-3b

6. Add director pictures for three of the directors in the Director table. Use the same pictures that you used for the SLSREP table in this project.
7. Close the Director table.
8. Create the form shown in Figure CLA2-3c for the Director table. The form includes all the fields in the Director table and the Movie Number, Movie Title, Year Made, and Movie Type fields from the Movie table.
9. Print the form
10. Save the form as Director Master Form.
11. Close the form and create a new query for the Director table.
12. Query the Director table to find all records where the director was born before 1930. Display the Director Code, Director Name, and Birth Date fields.
13. Print the results.
14. Query the Director table to find all records where the Director won an award at the Cannes film festival. Display the Director Code, Director Name, Birth Date, and Notes fields.
15. Print the results.
16. Query the Director table to find all records where the Director was born after 1930 and won an Academy Award. Display the Director Code, Director Name, Birth Date, and Notes fields.
17. Print the results.
18. Close the query without saving it.
19. Close the database and exit Access.

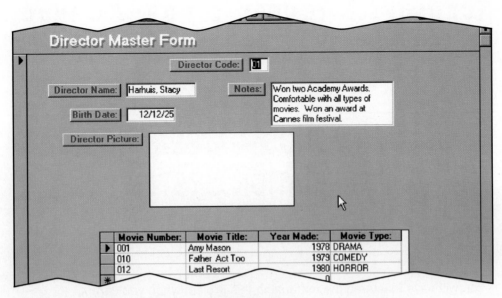

FIGURE CLA2-3c

COMPUTER LABORATORY ASSIGNMENT 4
Improving the Book Database

Purpose: To provide practice in using date, memo, and OLE fields and to create forms containing subforms.

Problem: The bookstore owner has asked you to make some improvements to the Book database. She has sent you a memo outlining the improvements.

Instructions: Use the Books database in the Access2 subdirectory of the Student Diskette that accompanies this book for this assignment. Provide the following:

1. Add fields to the Publisher table to store data on the date when the most recent order was placed with the publisher and to store ordering information. The data for these fields shows in Figure CLA2-4.

Publisher Code	Order Date	Notes
BB	9/24/94	Will fill single orders and special requests.
FR	9/3/94	Will fill single orders. Ships twice a week.
PB	8/18/94	Will fill single orders on emergency basis only. Ships twice a week.
SI	8/31/94	Has minimum order requirement of 10 books. Ships orders when needed.
SS	9/27/94	Has minimum order requirement of 25 books. Ships weekly.
VN	10/3/94	Will fill single orders and special requests. Ships daily.

FIGURE CLA2-4

2. Each publisher has an agent with whom the owner will now contact. She would like to include the agent's picture in the Publisher table. Use the same pictures that you used for the SLSREP table in this project.
3. A form that shows information about the publisher and all the publisher's books. The only items she needs from the Book table are Book Code, Title, Author, and Price.
4. Two lists – one showing orders placed before September 1, 1994 and the other showing orders placed after September 1, 1994.
5. A list of all publishers who fill single orders.

▼

USING MACROS – CREATING AN APPLICATION SYSTEM

OBJECTIVES You will have mastered the material in this project when you can:

- ▸ Create a macro
- ▸ Add actions and comments to a macro
- ▸ Modify arguments in a macro
- ▸ Run a macro
- ▸ Add a combo box to a form
- ▸ Modify the properties of a combo box
- ▸ Add a Paintbrush picture to a form

- ▸ Create an application system
- ▸ Add an option group to a form
- ▸ Modify the properties of an option group
- ▸ Add a command button to a form
- ▸ Include conditions in macros
- ▸ Use an application system

▸ INTRODUCTION

I n previous projects, you created tables, forms, and reports. Each time you want to use any of these, the correct series of steps must be followed. To open the Customer Update Form in a maximized window, for example, you first choose the Forms button in the Database window, then you select the correct form. Once you have done so, you choose the Open button. Finally, you choose the Maximize button for the window containing the form.

All these steps are unnecessary if you create your own menu, such as the one shown in Figure 3-1. Although this menu includes only two tables and two reports, the same techniques could be used to produce menus that include a large number of tables, reports, and queries.

By using the form in Figure 3-1, you can use any of the tables, forms, or reports simply by choosing the appropriate buttons. Thus, the buttons are effectively options in a menu. Such a menu, together with its associated tables, forms, and reports, is called an **application system**.

In this project, you will create the application system represented in Figure 3-1. You will begin by creating **macros**, which are collections of **actions** designed to carry out specific tasks. You will use a macro to enhance the Customer Update Form you created earlier by including a feature that allows users to search for customers by name (Figure 3-2). You will then create the form shown in Figure 3-1. In the process, you will associate the macros you created earlier with the buttons on the form.

A114

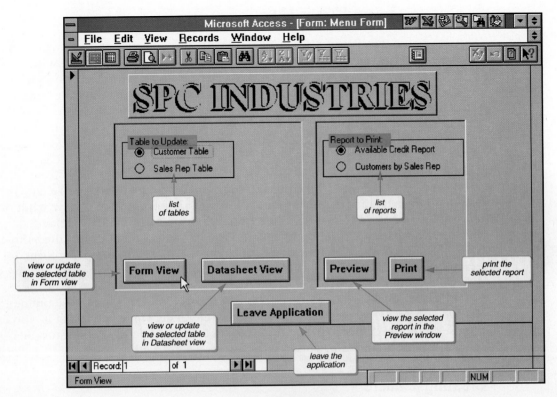

FIGURE 3-1

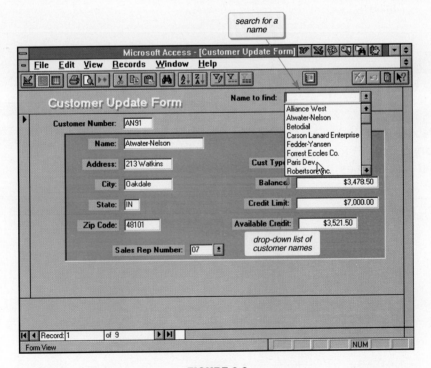

FIGURE 3-2

▶ CREATING AND USING MACROS

A macro consists of a series of actions that Access will perform when the macro is run. To create a macro, enter the actions in a special window called a **Macro window**. Once a macro is created, you can run it from the Database window by selecting it and then choosing the Run button. Macros can also be associated with objects on forms, such as buttons. These macros will then execute automatically in response to some action. For example, a macro assigned to a button will run automatically whenever the button is clicked. In either case, by allowing you to combine several actions, macros provide great flexibility.

In this project, you will create macros to open a form and maximize its window; to open a table in datasheet mode; to open a report in the Preview window; to print a report; and to search for a customer whose name matches a name selected by the user. As you enter actions, you will select them from a drop-down list. The names of the actions are self-explanatory. The action to open a form, for example, is OpenForm. Thus, there is no need to memorize the specific actions that are available.

If you are curious about other actions not covered in this book, use online Help to search for the general topic: actions: reference. Once you select it, you can then select either Actions Grouped by Task or Actions Reference. Either topic should provide all the information you need to use the action.

Creating a Macro

To create a macro, choose the Macro button in the Database window and then choose the New button. The following steps begin the process of creating a macro.

TO CREATE A MACRO ▼

STEP 1 ▶

Open the CUST database from the Access2 subdirectory on the Student Diskette that accompanies this book.

The Database window displays (Figure 3-3).

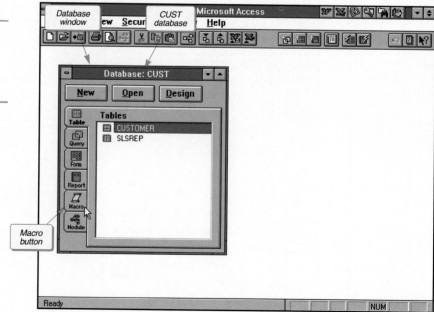

FIGURE 3-3

STEP 2 ▶

Click the Macro button.

The list of previously created macros displays (Figure 3-4). Currently there are no previously created macros.

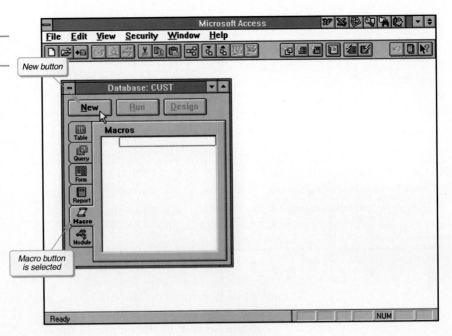

FIGURE 3-4

STEP 3 ▶

Choose the New button.

The Macro window displays (Figure 3-5).

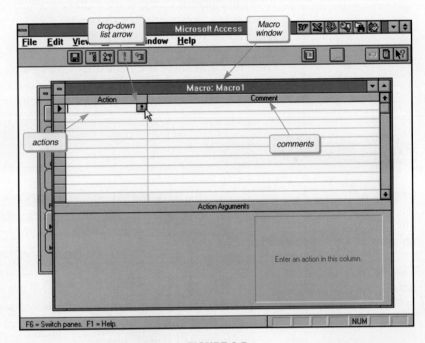

FIGURE 3-5

The Macro Window

You enter the actions for the macro in the first column in the Macro window (Figure 3-5). To enter an action, click the drop-down list arrow and select the action from the list that displays. Many actions require additional information, called the arguments of the action. If you select such an action, the arguments will display in the lower portion of the Macro window, and you can make any necessary changes to them.

▶ **TABLE 3-1**

Action	Argument to Change	New Value for Argument	Comment
Echo	Echo On	No	Turn echo off to avoid screen flicker
Hourglass			Turn on hourglass
OpenForm	Form Name	Customer Update Form	Open Customer Update Form
Hourglass	Hourglass On	No	Turn off hourglass
Echo			Turn echo on to display customer form

The second column in the Macro window is for **comments**; that is, brief descriptions of the purpose of the corresponding action. The actions, the arguments requiring changes, and the comments for the first macro you will create are shown in Table 3-1.

The macro begins by turning off the "echo." This will eliminate the screen flicker that can be present when a form is being opened. The second action changes the pointer to an hourglass to indicate that the some process is currently taking place. The third action opens the form called Customer Update Form. The fourth action turns off the hourglass, and the fifth turns the echo back on so the Customer Update Form will display.

(Turning on and off the echo and the hourglass are not absolutely necessary. On computers with faster processors, you might not notice a difference between running a macro that included these commands and one that did not. For slower processors, however, they can make a difference, and that is why they are included here.)

To create this macro, enter the actions. For each action, fill in the action and comment and make the necessary changes to any arguments. Once the actions have been entered, close the macro, choose the Yes button to save the changes, and assign the macro a name. The following steps create and save the macro.

TO ADD ACTIONS TO A MACRO ▼

STEP 1 ▶

Click the drop-down list arrow in the first row of the Action column.

The list of possible actions displays (Figure 3-6).

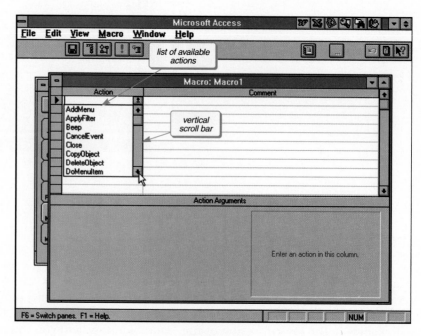

FIGURE 3-6

STEP 2 ▶

Click the down scroll arrow until the Echo action displays (Figure *3-7*).

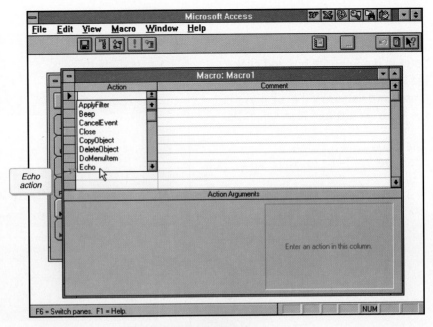

FIGURE 3-7

STEP 3 ▶

Select the Echo action.

The arguments for the Echo action display (Figure 3-8).

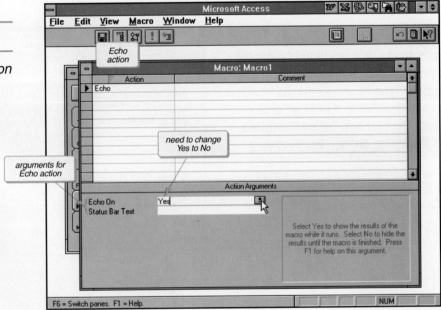

FIGURE 3-8

STEP 4 ▶

Point to the Echo On box and click the left mouse button. Click the drop-down list arrow that displays in the Echo On box and then select No.

The Echo On argument is changed from Yes to No (Figure 3-9).

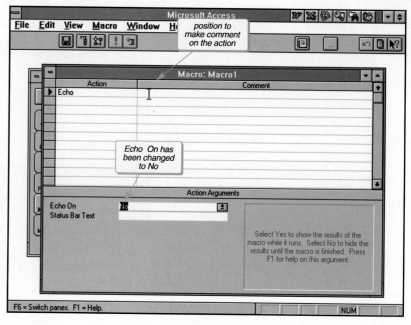

FIGURE 3-9

STEP 5 ▶

Point to the first row in the Comment column and click the left mouse button. Type Turn echo off to avoid screen flicker **and press the TAB key. Select Hourglass as the action on the second row.**

The comment for the first action is entered, and the second action is selected (Figure 3-10).

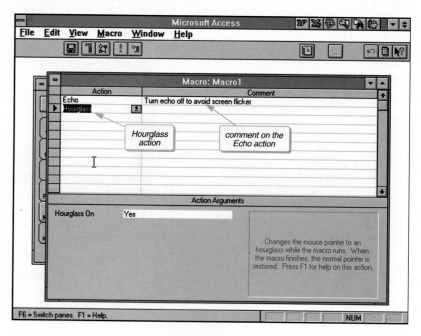

FIGURE 3-10

STEP 6 ▶

Press the TAB key, type `Turn on hourglass` as the comment on the second row, press the TAB key, and select OpenForm as the third action.

STEP 7 ▶

Point to the box for the Form Name argument, click the left mouse button, and then click the drop-down list arrow that displays.

A list of available forms displays (Figure 3-11).

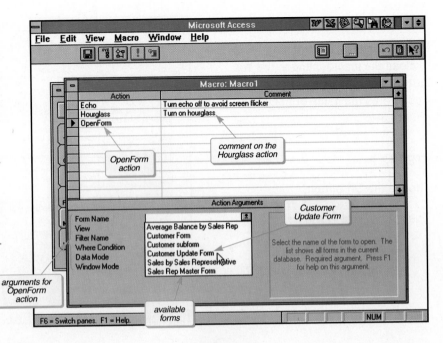

FIGURE 3-11

STEP 8 ▶

Select Customer Update Form, point to the third row in the Comment column, click the left mouse button, and type `Open Customer Update Form` as the comment.

STEP 9 ▶

Select Hourglass as the fourth action, change the Hourglass On argument to No, and type `Turn off hourglass` as the comment.

STEP 10 ▶

Select Echo as the fifth action. Type `Turn echo on to display customer form` as the comment (Figure 3-12).

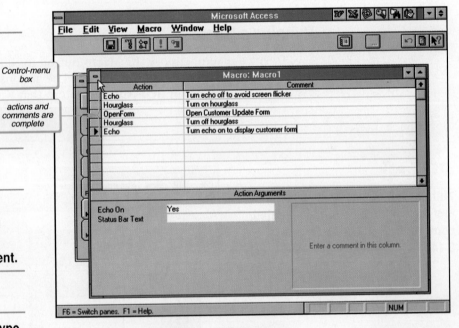

FIGURE 3-12

STEP 11 ▶

Double-click the Control-menu box to close the macro, choose the Yes button, and type Open Form for Update as the name of the macro (Figure 3-13).

STEP 12 ▶

Choose the OK button.

The macro is created.

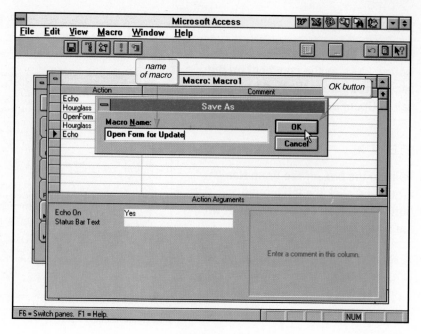

FIGURE 3-13

Running a Macro

To run a macro, choose the Macro button in the Database window, select the macro, and then choose the Run button. The actions in the macro will then be executed. The following steps run the macro that was just created.

TO RUN A MACRO ▼

STEP 1 ▶

With the list of macros displaying and the macro to be run highlighted, point to the Run button (Figure 3-14).

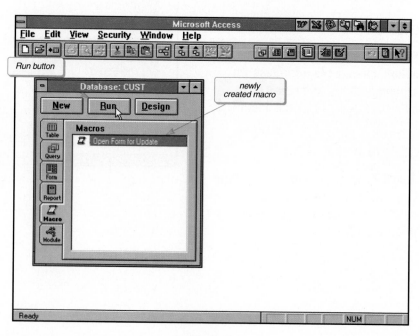

FIGURE 3-14

STEP 2 ▶

Choose the Run button.

The macro runs and the Customer Update Form displays (Figure 3-15). The form is not maximized.

STEP 3 ▶

Close the Customer Update Form.

The form no longer displays.

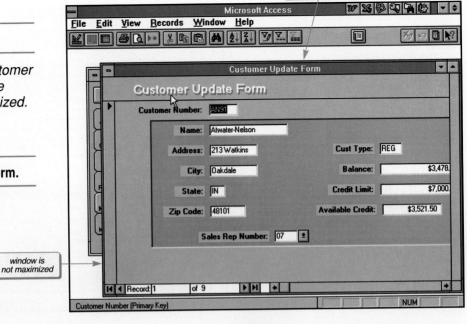

FIGURE 3-15

Modifying a Macro

To modify a macro, first select the macro in the Database window, click the Design button, and then make the necessary changes. To insert a new action, select the position for the action. If the action is to be placed between two actions, press the INSERT key to insert a new blank row. Then, enter the new action, change the values for any necessary arguments, and enter a comment.

The following steps modify the macro just created, adding a new step to automatically maximize the form.

TO MODIFY A MACRO ▼

STEP 1 ▶

With the list of macros displayed and the macro to be run highlighted, point to the Design button (Figure 3-16).

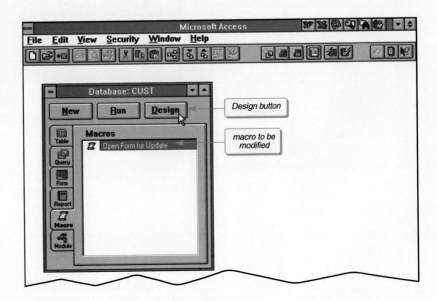

FIGURE 3-16

STEP 2 ▶

Choose the Design button.

The macro displays in the Macro window (Figure 3-17).

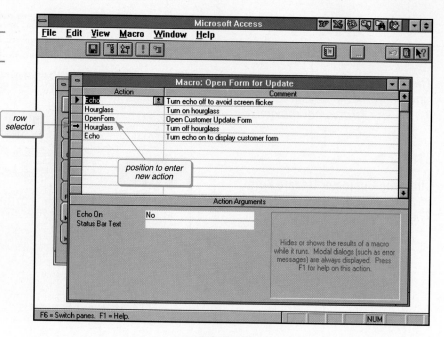

FIGURE 3-17

STEP 3 ▶

Point to the row selector in the fourth row (the small square directly to the left of the second Hourglass action), click the left mouse button to select the row, and then press the INSERT key to insert a new row.

A blank row is inserted between the OpenForm action and the second Hourglass action (Figure 3-18).

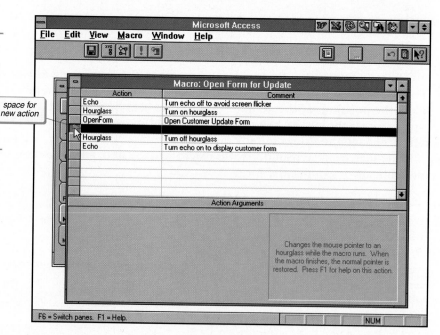

FIGURE 3-18

STEP 4 ▶

Select Maximize as the action on the new row and type `Maximize the window` as the comment (Figure 3-19).

STEP 5 ▶

Double-click the Control-menu box and then choose the Yes button to save the changes.

The macro has been changed.

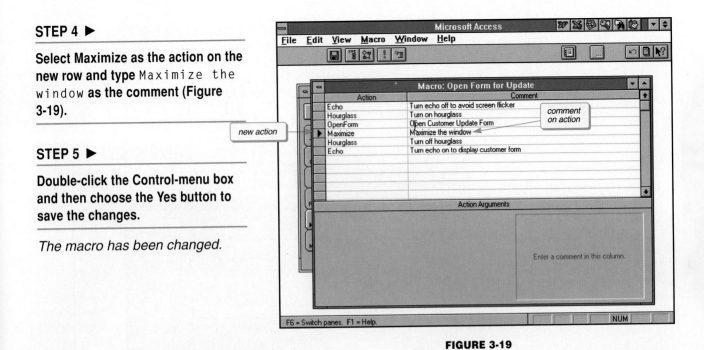

FIGURE 3-19

The next time the macro is run, the form will not only be opened, but the window containing the form will also be maximized.

Errors in Macros

Macros can contain errors. For example, if you typed the name of the form in the Form Name argument of the OpenForm action instead of selecting it from the list, you might type it incorrectly. Access would then be unable to execute the desired action. In that case, it displays an error message (Figure 3-20).

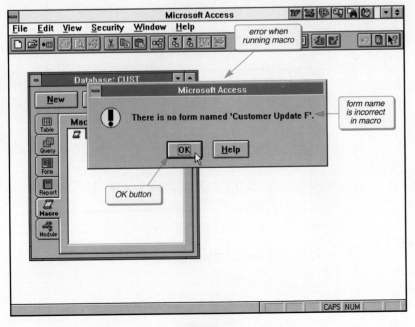

FIGURE 3-20

If such an error message displays, choose the OK button. The Action Failed dialog box then displays (Figure 3-21). It indicates the macro that was being run, the action that Access was attempting to execute, and the arguments for the action. This information tells you which action needs to be corrected. To make the correction, choose the Halt button and then modify the design of the macro.

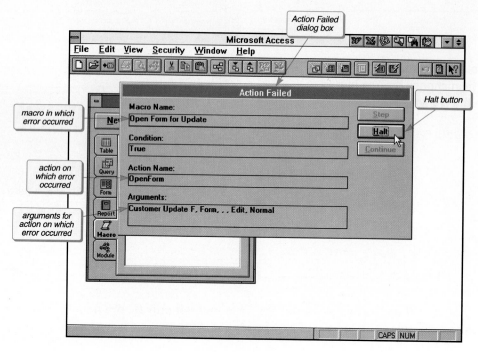

FIGURE 3-21

Creating Additional Macros

Create additional macros by using the same steps you used to create the first macro. The following steps create three additional macros: Open Table as Datasheet, Open report for printing, and Open report for preview.

TO CREATE ADDITIONAL MACROS ▼

STEP 1 ▶

Create a macro with the single action: OpenTable. For the Table Name argument, select the CUSTOMER table. For the comment, type Open table in Datasheet view. Close the macro by double-clicking its Control-menu box. Choose the Yes button to save the macro. Type the name Open Table as Datasheet (Figure 3-22).

FIGURE 3-22

STEP 2 ▶

Create a macro with the single action: OpenReport. For the Report Name argument, select the Available Credit Report. For the View argument, click the drop-down list arrow.

The list of available views displays (Figure 3-23).

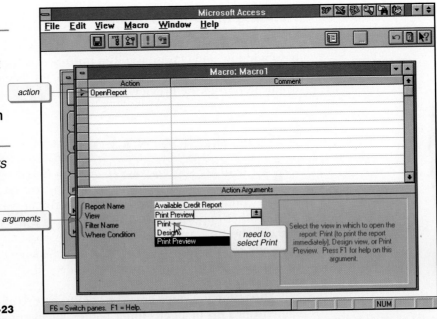

FIGURE 3-23

STEP 3 ▶

Select Print as the view. **Type** Open Available Credit Report and print **as the comment. Close and save the macro, giving it the name** Open report for printing **(Figure 3-24).**

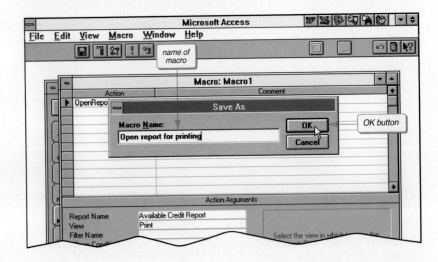

FIGURE 3-24

STEP 4 ▶

Create another macro. The first action is OpenReport. For the Report Name argument, again select the Available Credit Report. The View argument does not need to be changed. Type the comment for the **action:** Open report in Preview window. **The second action should be Maximize. Type the second comment:** Maximize the window. **Close and save the macro. Type the name** Open report for preview **(Figure 3-25).**

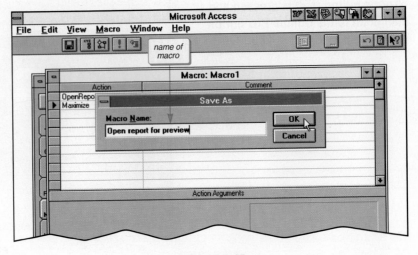

FIGURE 3-25

Running the Other Macros

To run any of the other macros, highlight the appropriate macro in the Database window and choose the Run button — just as you ran the first macro. Running the OpenReport for Preview macro, for example, would display the Available Credit Report in the Preview window.

▶ USING MACROS ON A FORM

There are several ways to use macros on forms. Later in this project, you will assign the running of macros to buttons on forms. When one of the buttons is chosen, the corresponding macro will automatically run.

Another important way to use a macro is in connection with a combo box. The **combo box** can request the user to select an item from a list and then automatically run the macro once the user has made a selection. To use a macro in this fashion, change the After Update property of the combo box to the name of the macro to be run.

The following steps create a combo box to allow a user to select a customer name from a list of all customer names. In a later series of steps, the After Update property of this combo box will be modified to run a macro that will search the Customer table for a customer whose name matches the selected name.

Adding a Combo Box

To add a combo box, use the Combo Box button in the toolbox. The following steps place a combo box for customer names on the form.

TO ADD A COMBO BOX ▼

STEP 1 ▶

Open the Customer Update Form in Design view and maximize the window. Make sure the Control Wizards button (⬚) is pressed and then point to the Combo Box button in the Toolbox (Figure 3-26).

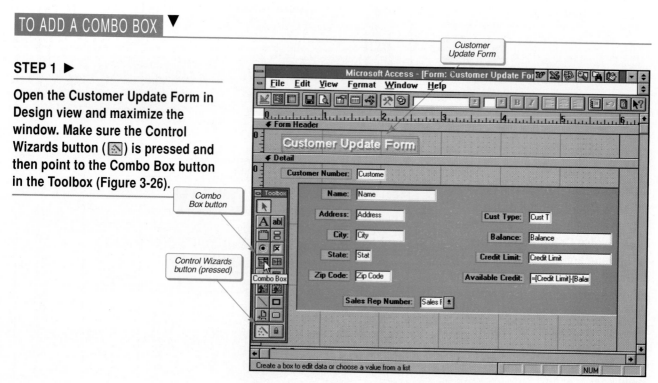

FIGURE 3-26

STEP 2 ▶

Click the Combo Box button and then move the pointer, whose shape has changed to a small plus sign with a combo box (⁺▤), to the position shown in Figure 3-27.

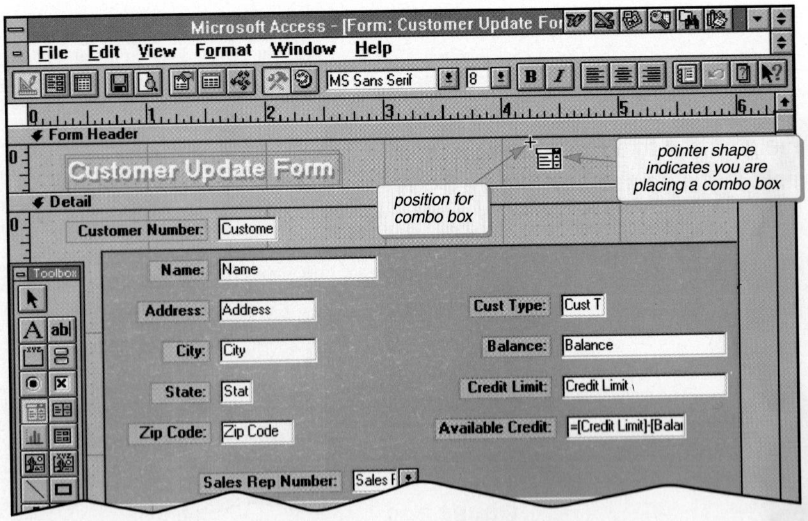

FIGURE 3-27

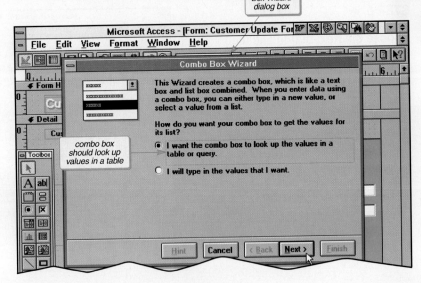

STEP 3 ▶

Click the left mouse button to place a combo box.

The Combo Box Wizard dialog box displays, instructing you to indicate how the combo box is to obtain values for the list (Figure 3-28).

FIGURE 3-28

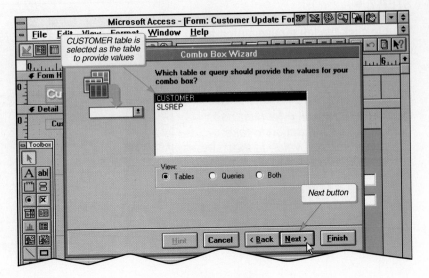

STEP 4 ▶

Choose the Next button in the Combo Box Wizard dialog box, select the CUSTOMER table, and then point to the Next button.

The CUSTOMER table is selected as the table to provide values for the combo box (Figure 3-29).

FIGURE 3-29

STEP 5 ▶

Choose the Next button, select the Name field, and then click the Add Field button to add the Name as a field in the combo box (Figure 3-30).

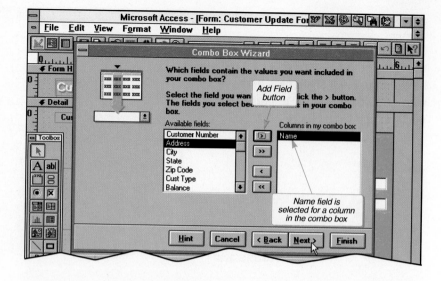

FIGURE 3-30

STEP 6 ▶

Choose the Next button and then point to the boundary after column 1 (Col1:).

The mouse pointer, whose shape has changed to a dark plus sign with two arrowheads (✚) is positioned on the border after the first column (Figure 3-31).

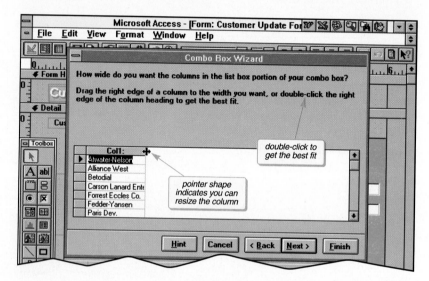

FIGURE 3-31

STEP 7 ▶

Double-click the left mouse button to cause Access to select the best fit for the column. Choose the Next button.

Remember the value for later use. is selected as the action to take when you select a value in the combo box (Figure 3-32).

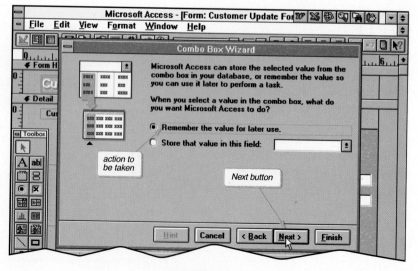

FIGURE 3-32

STEP 8 ▶

Choose the Next button. Type Name
to find: as the label for the
combo box (Figure 3-33).

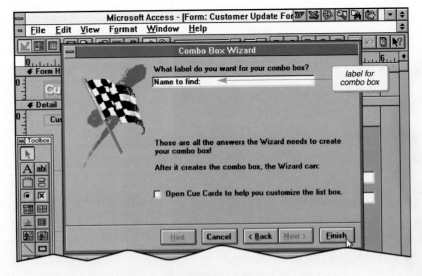

FIGURE 3-33

STEP 9 ▶

Choose the Finish button. Select the
label for the combo box. Point to the
handle on the left-hand edge of the
label.

*The pointer changes to a double
arrow, indicating you can drag the
left-hand edge (Figure 3-34).*

STEP 10 ▶

Double-click the left mouse button
so the entire label (Name to find:)
displays.

*The combo box is added and the
label has been resized.*

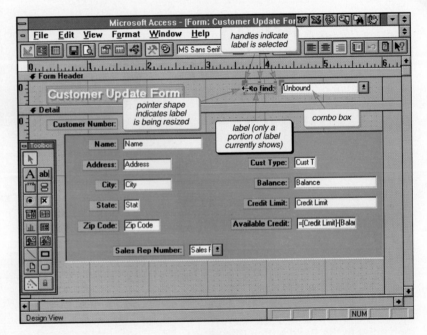

FIGURE 3-34

Three properties of the combo box need to be changed. The Name property
needs to be changed to a name that you will then use in the macro that searches
for a customer. The After Update property needs to be changed to the name of a
macro that is to be run after the contents of the combo box are updated. In the
process, you can use an existing macro or create a new one. Finally, the Row
Source property needs to be changed to indicate that the names in the list are to
be sorted. Without this change, the names would display in the order in which
they occur in the table.

The steps on the next page change the Name property to Name to find,
change the After Update property to Name Search, create a macro called Name
Search, and change the Row Source property so that the names in the list are to be
sorted.

The Name Search macro uses a name selected by the users. The selected name will be stored in Name to find. The macro searches for a customer whose name matches the one in Name to find. To indicate which field is to be used in the search, use the GoToControl command and change the value in the Control Name argument to the name of the field (in this case Name).

TO MODIFY THE PROPERTIES OF A COMBO BOX ▼

STEP 1 ▶

Point to the combo box and click the right mouse button. Choose the Properties command from the shortcut menu that displays. Type Name to find as the Name property.

The Combo Box property window displays (Figure 3-35). The Name property has been changed to Name to find.

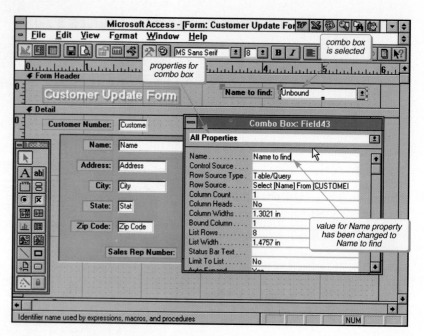

FIGURE 3-35

STEP 2 ▶

Click the down scroll arrow to move down through the properties until the After Update property displays. Select the After Update property and then point to the Build button (the button containing the three dots) (Figure 3-36).

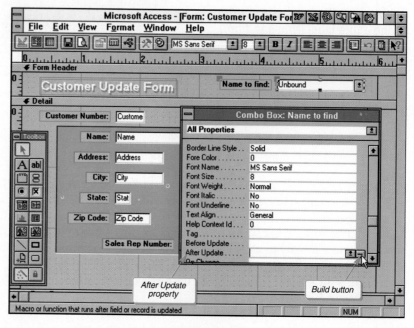

FIGURE 3-36

STEP 3 ▶

Click the Build button.

The list of available builders displays (Figure 3-37).

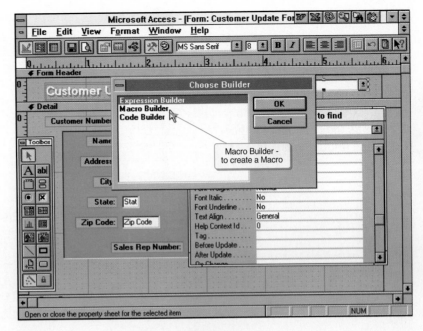

FIGURE 3-37

STEP 4 ▶

Select Macro Builder and then choose the OK button. Type Name Search **as the name of the macro.**

The Macro window displays (Figure 3-38). The Save As dialog box displays and the name of the macro is entered.

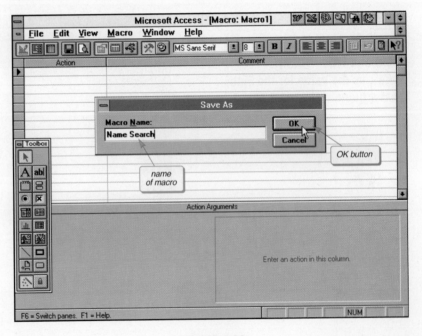

FIGURE 3-38

STEP 5 ▶

Choose the OK button. Select GoToControl as the first action, type `Name` as the value for the Control Name argument, and then type `Go to customer name for search` as the comment for the first action (Figure 3-39).

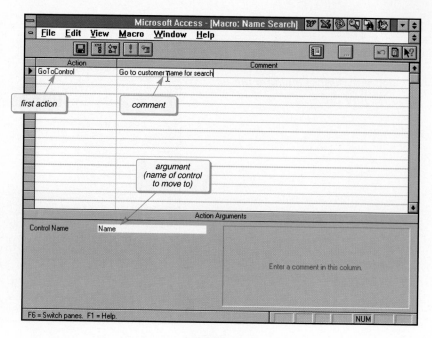

FIGURE 3-39

STEP 6 ▶

Select FindRecord as the second action and type `=[Name to find]` as the value for the Find What argument (Figure 3-40).

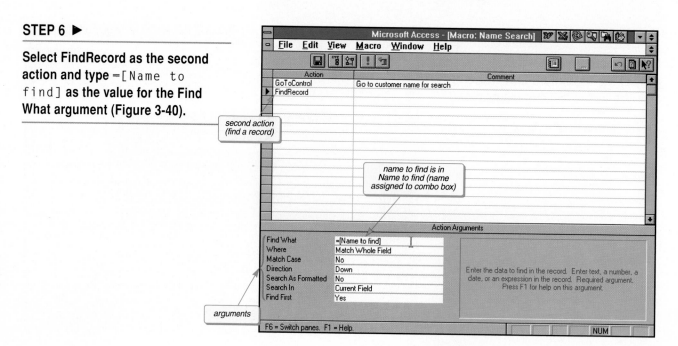

FIGURE 3-40

STEP 7 ▶

Type Find the record on which the name is equal to the name to find **as the comment for the second action. Close the Macro window by clicking its Control-menu box and then choose the Yes button to save the macro.**

STEP 8 ▶

Select the Row Source property (Figure 3-41).

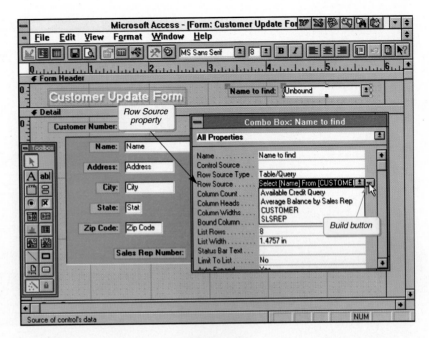

FIGURE 3-41

STEP 9 ▶

Click the Build button.

The Microsoft Access - [Query Builder: SQL Statement] window displays (Figure 3-42). You can make changes on this screen just as you did when you created queries in Project 2.

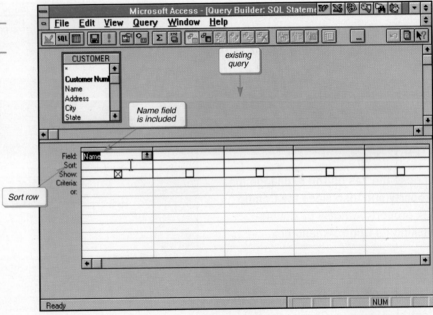

FIGURE 3-42

STEP 10 ▶

Point to the Sort row in the first column, click the left mouse button, click the drop-down list arrow, and select Ascending (Figure 3-43).

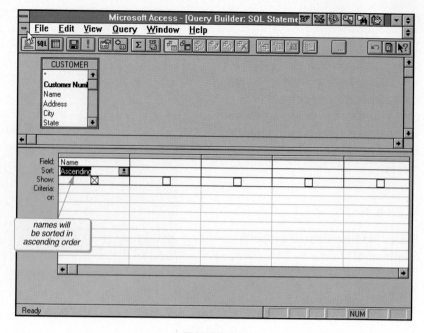

FIGURE 3-43

STEP 11 ▶

Close the Query Builder window by double-clicking its Control-menu box.

The Microsoft Access dialog box displays (Figure 3-44).

STEP 12 ▶

Choose the Yes button to change the property and then close the Combo box property window by double-clicking its Control-menu box.

STEP 13 ▶

Close the form by double-clicking its Control-menu box. Choose the Yes button to save the changes.

The form is closed and the changes are saved.

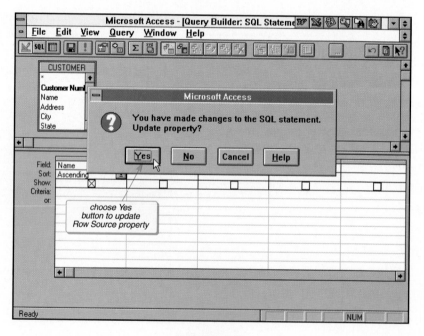

FIGURE 3-44

Using the Combo Box

Two ways to use the combo box exist to search for a customer. You can click the drop-down list arrow to display a list of customer names and then select the name from the list by pointing to it and clicking the left mouse button. Alternatively, you can begin typing the name. As you type, Access will automatically display the first name that begins with the letters you have typed. Once the correct name is displayed, select the name by pressing the TAB key. Regardless of the method used, the data for the selected customer displays in the form once the selection is made.

The following steps search for Paris Dev. by clicking the drop-down list arrow and selecting it from the list.

TO USE THE COMBO BOX TO SEARCH FOR A CUSTOMER ▼

STEP 1 ▶

Run the Open Form for Update macro.

The Customer Update Form displays in a maximized window (Figure 3-45a).

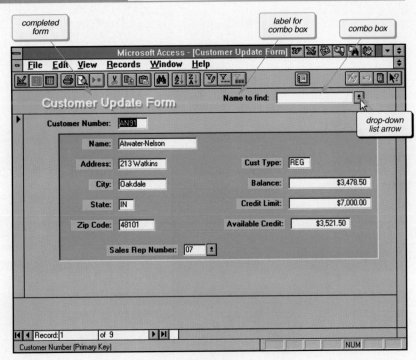

FIGURE 3-45a

STEP 2 ▶

Click the drop-down list arrow in the Name to find combo box.

A drop-down list of customer names displays (Figure 3-45b).

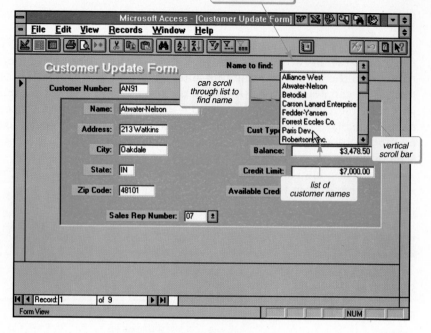

FIGURE 3-45b

STEP 3 ▶

Point to Paris Dev. and click the left mouse button.

Customer PA12 (Paris Dev.) displays in the form (Figure 3-45c).

STEP 4 ▶

Close the form by double-clicking its Control-menu box.

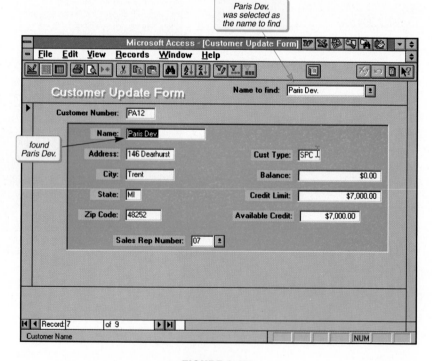

FIGURE 3-45c

▶ CREATING AND USING THE APPLICATION SYSTEM

T
he reports and forms for the application system have already been created. To combine them into a single application system, create a blank form instead of a form that includes data from a table or query. Then, add buttons for the various options you want to include on the form. The buttons will be associated with macros that cause Access to take the appropriate action.

To run the application system, open the form. To take an action, choose the corresponding button. If the option uses a form or datasheet, the form or datasheet will display. If the option is to preview a report, the report will display in the Preview window. If the option prints a report, the report will print.

Creating the Initial Form

To create the initial form for the application system, choose the Form button in the Database window and then choose the New button. Choose the Blank Form button to display a blank form in Design view. The application title can be added as text by using the Text button in the toolbox. To include graphics or special effects, such as shadowed letters, you need to insert an object. To do so, select the Object Frame button in the toolbox and then select the object type.

The following steps create an initial blank form and begin placing an object on the form. The object type is Paintbrush Picture.

TO CREATE THE INITIAL FORM ▼

STEP 1 ▶

With the Database window displaying, choose the Form button and then choose the New button.

The New Form dialog box displays (Figure 3-46).

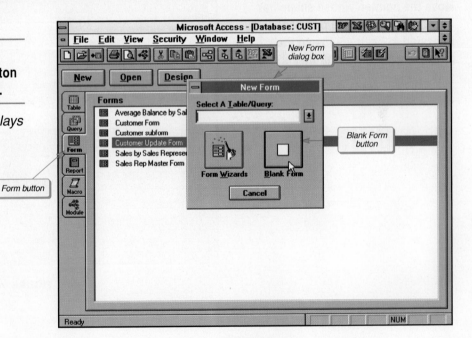

FIGURE 3-46

STEP 2 ▶

Choose the Blank Form button.

A blank form displays in Design view (Figure 3-47).

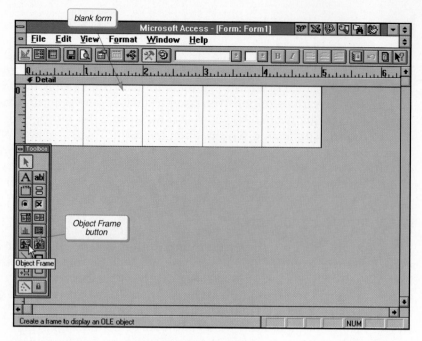

FIGURE 3-47

STEP 3 ▶

Click the Object Frame button (▣). Move the pointer, whose shape has changed to ⁺▣, to the position indicated in Figure 3-48 and then click the left mouse button.

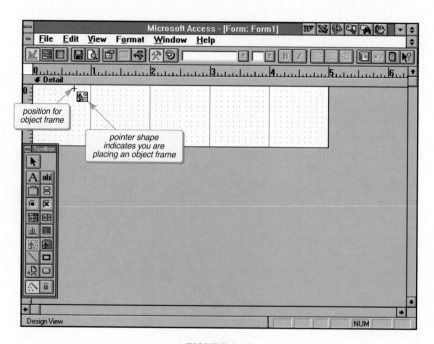

FIGURE 3-48

STEP 4 ▶

Use the down scroll arrow to move
through the list of object types until
Paintbrush Picture displays.

*The Insert Object dialog box dis-
plays (Figure 3-49). Paintbrush
Picture displays in the Object Type
list box.*

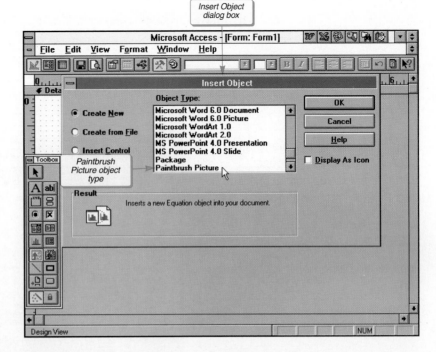

FIGURE 3-49

STEP 5 ▶

Select Paintbrush Picture and then
choose the OK button.

*The Paintbrush window displays
(Figure 3-50).*

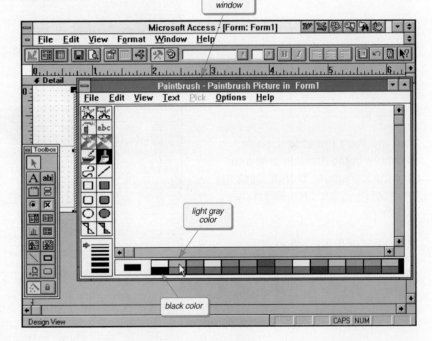

FIGURE 3-50

Entering the Application Title

Before entering the application title, change the color of the drawing area to
light gray (the color that will be used for the form) by changing the color scheme
and then using the Paint Roller tool. To enter the title, select the Text tool, change
the font, and choose Shadow as a special effect. Once you have done so, position
the mouse pointer where the text is to begin, click the left mouse button, and
then type the title.

The following steps create the title for the application system.

TO ENTER THE APPLICATION TITLE ▼

STEP 1 ►

Point to the light gray color (Figure 3-50) and click the left mouse button. Point to the black color and click the right mouse button.

STEP 2 ►

Point to the Paing Roller tool (Figure 3-51).

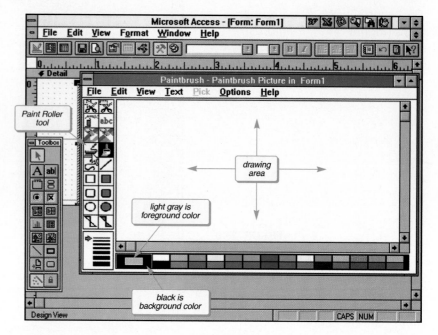

FIGURE 3-51

STEP 3 ►

Click the Paint Roller tool, point anywhere in the drawing area and click the left mouse button. Click the Text tool (abc) and then select the Text menu.

The color of the drawing area changes from white to light gray (Figure 3-52). The Text tool is selected and the Text menu displays.

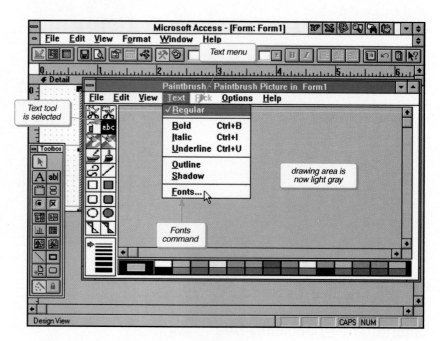

FIGURE 3-52

STEP 4 ▶

Choose the Fonts command. Select
Times New Roman as the font and
select a size of 36 (Figure 3-53).

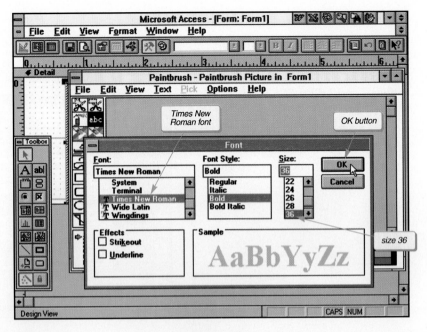

FIGURE 3-53

STEP 5 ▶

Choose the OK button. Select the
Text menu again and choose the
Shadow command.

STEP 6 ▶

Point to the position for the text
(Figure 3-54). Click the left mouse
button.

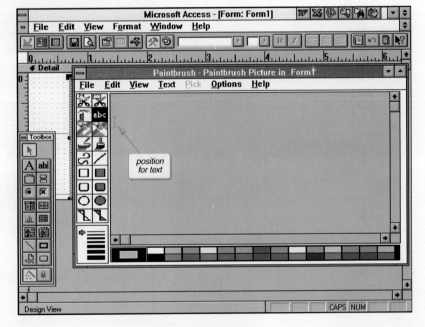

FIGURE 3-54

STEP 7 ▶

Type SPC INDUSTRIES **and then select the File menu.**

The text is entered and the File menu displays (Figure 3-55).

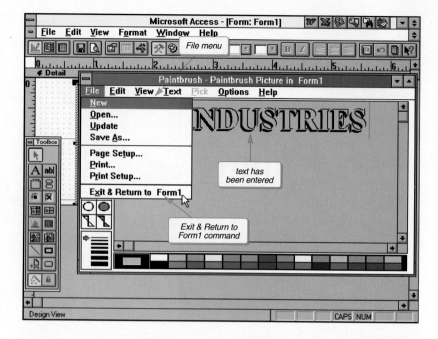

FIGURE 3-55

STEP 8 ▶

Choose the Exit & Return to Form1 command.

The Paintbrush dialog box displays (Figure 3-56). The message asks if you want to update the open embedded object; that is, the form.

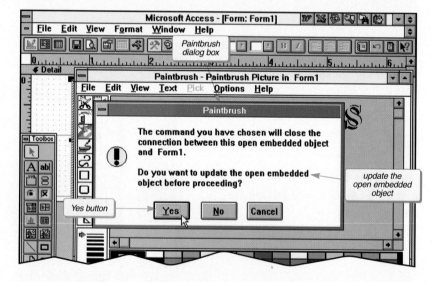

FIGURE 3-56

STEP 9 ▶

Choose the Yes button.

The object displays on the form (Figure 3-57). It is incorrectly sized.

FIGURE 3-57

STEP 10 ▶

Move the mouse pointer to the handle in the middle of the bottom boundary of the object so its shape changes to (↕), indicating you can drag the boundary. Drag the lower boundary to the position in Figure 3-58. Move the mouse pointer to the handle in the middle of the right edge of the boundary and drag it to the position shown in Figure 3-58.

FIGURE 3-58

STEP 11 ▶

Move the mouse pointer to any position in the white space of the form but outside of the object containing SPC INDUSTRIES. Click the right mouse button and choose the Properties command from the shortcut menu that displays. Select the Back color property and use the color palette to change the background color to light gray. Click the OK button. Close the Section: Detail0 dialog box.

The entire form is light gray (Figure 3-59).

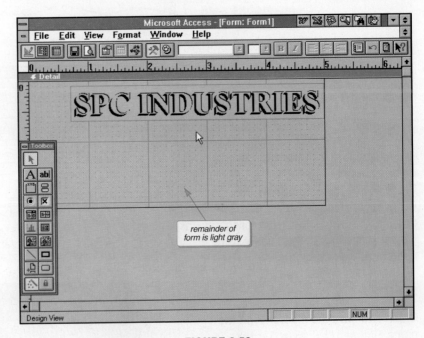

FIGURE 3-59

STEP 12 ▶

Close the form by double-clicking its Control-menu box. Choose the Yes button to save the changes, type Menu Form as the name of the form, and choose the OK button.

The basic form is now saved.

Creating Macros to Start and End the Application

To make it easy to start the application, create a macro to open and maximize the menu form. Although you can exit the system by closing the menu form in the usual manner (double-clicking its Control-menu box), this process can be simplified by adding a button to the form. The button can execute a macro that closes the menu form and restores the Database window to its original size when the menu form is closed.

The following steps create the macro that will start the application and the macro that will be executed when the button to leave the application is clicked.

TO CREATE MACROS FOR STARTING AND ENDING THE APPLICATION ▼

STEP 1 ▶

Create a macro with the actions and comments in Figure 3-60. For the OpenForm action, type the value `Menu Form` **for the Form Name argument. The Maximize action has no arguments.**

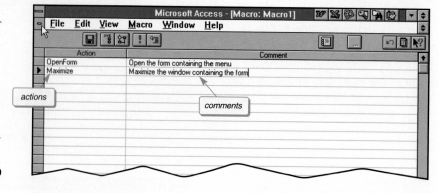

FIGURE 3-60

STEP 2 ▶

Close and save the macro. Type the name `Begin Application System.`

STEP 3 ▶

Create a macro with the actions and comments in Figure 3-61. For the Close action, select Form as the value for the Object Type argument and Menu Form as the value for the Object Name argument. The Restore action has no arguments.

STEP 4 ▶

Close and save the macro. Type the name `End Application System.`

The macros for starting and ending the application are now created.

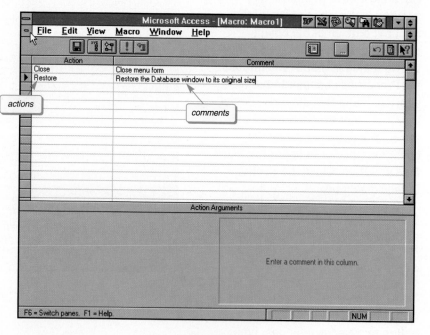

FIGURE 3-61

Adding Option Groups to the Application

The buttons in front of Customer Table, Sales Rep Table, Available Credit Report, and Customers by Sales Rep in Figure 3-1 on page A115 are called **option buttons**. A collection of option buttons is called an **option group**. There are two option groups in Figure 3-1. One is called Table to Update and contains the Customer Table and Sales Rep Table option buttons. The other is called Report to Print and contains the Available Credit Report and Customers by Sales Rep option buttons.

To create an option group, use the Option Group button in the toolbox. The Option Group Wizard will then assist in the creation of the option group. As part of the process, you will specify the option buttons. The following steps create the option groups for the application system.

TO ADD OPTION GROUPS TO THE APPLICATION ▼

STEP 1 ▶

Open the Menu Form in Design view and maximize the window. Make sure the Control Wizards button is pressed and then click the Option Group button ( ) in the Toolbox. Move the pointer, whose shape has changed to a small plus sign in an option group ( ), to the position shown in Figure 3-62.

pointer shape indicates you are placing an option group

position for option group

Option Group tool is selected

FIGURE 3-62

STEP 2 ▶

Click the left mouse button to place an option group. Type Customer Table **as the first label name, press the DOWN ARROW key, type** Sales Rep Table **as the second label name, and press the DOWN ARROW key again.**

The Option Group Wizard dialog box displays, instructing you to enter the labels for the options (Figure 3-63). The labels are entered.

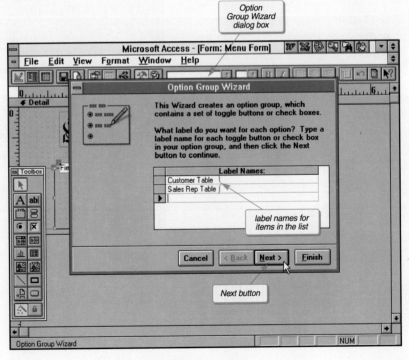

Option Group Wizard dialog box

label names for items in the list

Next button

FIGURE 3-63

STEP 3 ▶

Choose the Next button.

The Option Group Wizard dialog box displays, asking if there is to be a default option (Figure 3-64). The Customer Table option, which is already selected, is to be the default option.

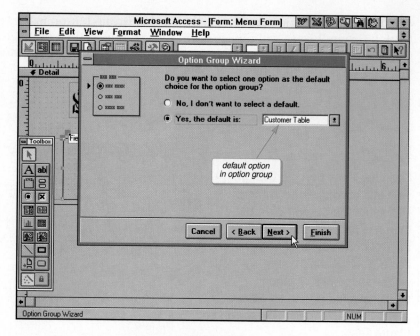

FIGURE 3-64

STEP 4 ▶

Select the Yes, the default is: option button and then choose the Next button.

The Option Group Wizard dialog box displays, requesting values for the labels (Figure 3-65). The values that display are acceptable.

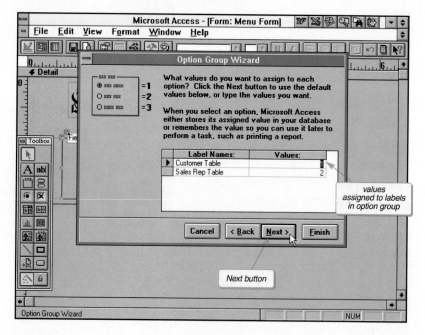

FIGURE 3-65

STEP 5 ▶

Choose the Next button.

The Option Group Wizard dialog box displays (Figure 3-66), requesting a style and a button type. The selections in the dialog box are acceptable.

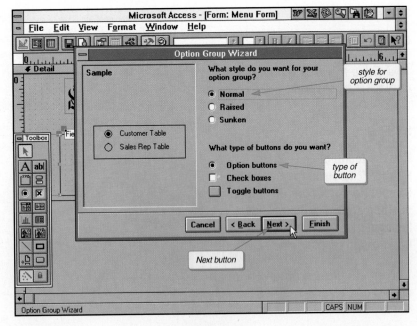

FIGURE 3-66

STEP 6 ▶

Choose the Next button. Type `Table to Update:` **as the label for the option group.**

The Option Group Wizard dialog box displays (Figure 3-67), requesting a label for the entire option group.

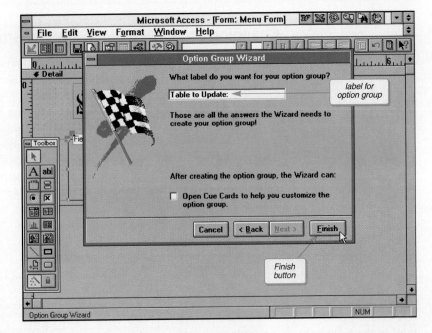

FIGURE 3-67

STEP 7 ▶

Choose the Finish button.

The Table to Update option group is placed on the form.

STEP 8 ▶

Use the techniques in Steps 1 through 7 to place the Report to Print option group on the form in the position shown in Figure 3-68. Indicate that the Available Credit Report is to be the default option.

The option groups have now been created and positioned on the form.

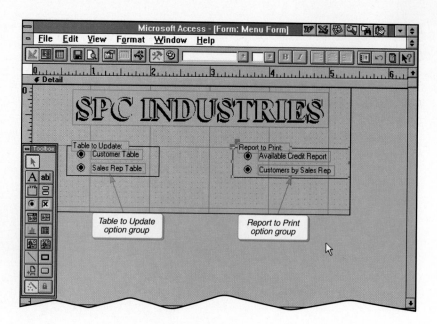

FIGURE 3-68

Changing Properties of the Option Groups

The buttons on the form (Form View, Datasheet View, Preview, and Print) all use values selected in the option groups. To do so, the option groups must be assigned names. Assign a name to an option group by selecting the option group, clicking the right mouse button, choosing the Properties command from the shortcut menu, and then changing the Name property.

In selecting the option group, be sure to point to the *boundary* of the option group; that is, the rectangle surrounding the object group. If you point anywhere else, the wrong menu will display. (If this happens, point somewhere outside the menu and click the left mouse button. The menu will disappear and you can begin the process again.)

The following steps change the name of the option groups.

TO CHANGE THE PROPERTIES OF THE OPTION GROUPS ▼

STEP 1 ▶

Point to the boundary of the Table to Update option group (Figure 3-69).

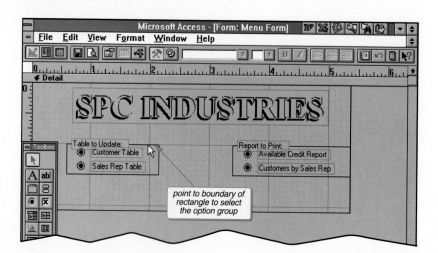

FIGURE 3-69

STEP 2 ▶

Click the right mouse button.

The shortcut menu for the option group displays (Figure 3-70).

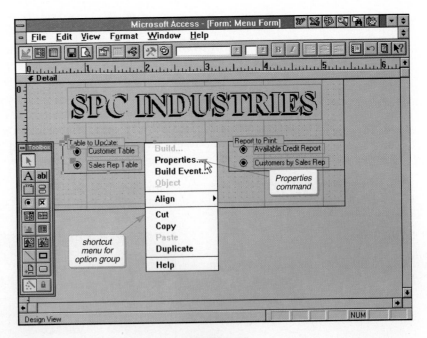

FIGURE 3-70

STEP 3 ▶

Choose the Properties command. Change the Name property by typing `Table to Update` **(Figure 3-71).**

STEP 4 ▶

Close the Option Group window by double-clicking its Control-menu box.

STEP 5 ▶

Use the techniques in Steps 1 through 4 to change the Name property for the Report to Print option group by typing `Report to Print`.

The properties of the option groups have now been changed.

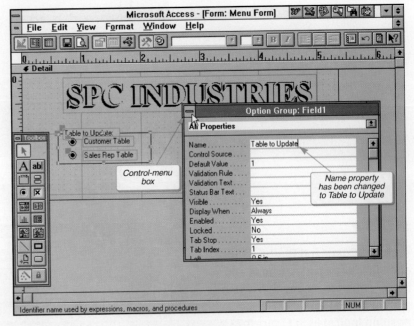

FIGURE 3-71

Adding Command Buttons to the Application

A **command button** executes a command when clicked. Command buttons can be added to a form by using the Command Button button in the toolbox. The Command Button Wizard then requests the action that should be taken when the button is clicked. There are several categories of actions. The action that gives the most flexibility is Run Macro, an action found in the Miscellaneous category. You then specify the text or picture that will appear on the button.

The following steps place the command buttons for viewing a form, viewing a datasheet, previewing a report, printing a report, or quitting the application.

TO ADD COMMAND BUTTONS TO THE APPLICATION ▼

STEP 1 ▶

Point to the Command Button button (▢) in the Toolbox (Figure 3-72).

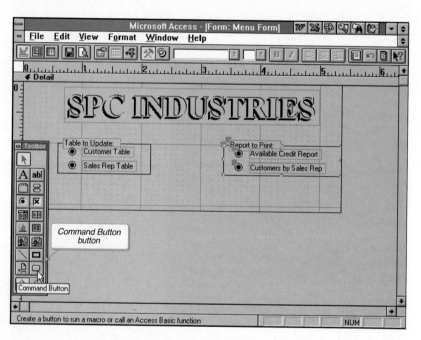

FIGURE 3-72

STEP 2 ▶

Click the Command Button button and move the pointer, whose shape has changed to a plus sign with a picture of a button (⁺▢), to the position indicated in Figure 3-73.

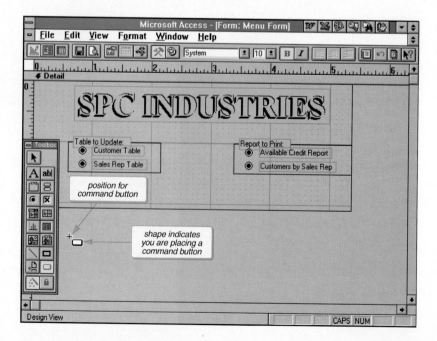

FIGURE 3-73

STEP 3 ▶

Click the left mouse button. Select Miscellaneous as the category in the Command Button Wizard dialog box.

The Command Button Wizard dialog box displays (Figure 3-74), requesting a category and an action to take place when the button is clicked. The Miscellaneous category is selected. The actions in the Miscellaneous category display.

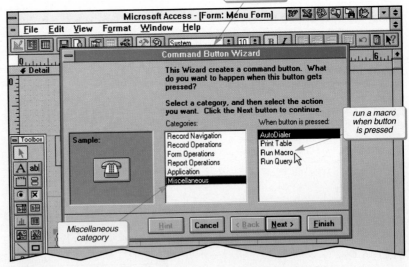

FIGURE 3-74

STEP 4 ▶

Select Run Macro as the action by pointing to it and clicking the left mouse button. Then choose the Next button.

The Command Button Wizard dialog box displays (Figure 3-75). It contains a list of macros currently in the CUST database.

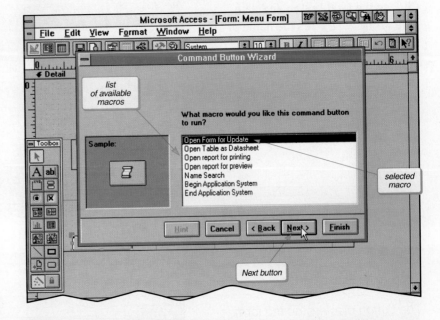

FIGURE 3-75

STEP 5 ▶

Because the macro for this button, Open Form for Update, is already selected, no special action needs to be taken. (For any other macro, you would select the macro by pointing to it and clicking the left mouse button.) Choose the Next button.

The Command Button Wizard dialog box displays, asking what to display on the button (Figure 3-76). The button can contain either text or a picture.

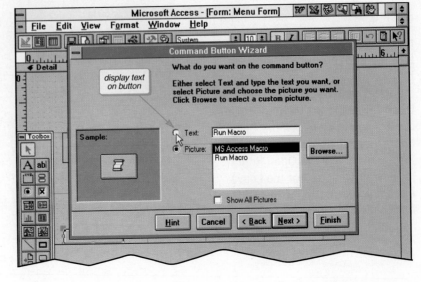

FIGURE 3-76

STEP 6 ▶

Select the Text option button by pointing to it and clicking the left mouse button. Change the entry in the Text box by typing Form View (Figure 3-77).

FIGURE 3-77

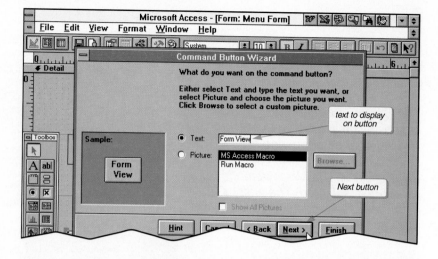

STEP 7 ▶

Choose the Next button and then type Form View as the name of the button (Figure 3-78).

FIGURE 3-78

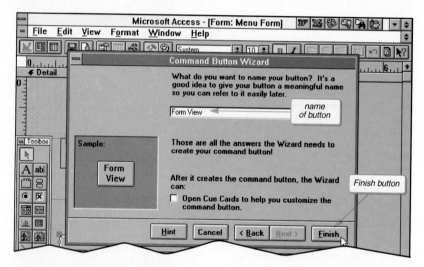

STEP 8 ▶

Choose the Finish button.

The button displays on the form.

STEP 9 ▶

Use the techniques in Steps 1 through 8 to place the additional buttons shown in Figure 3-79. For the Datasheet View button, use the Open Table as Datasheet macro. For the Preview button, use the Open Report for Preview macro. For the Print button, use the Open Report for Printing macro. For the Leave Application button, use the End Application System macro.

All the buttons are placed on the form.

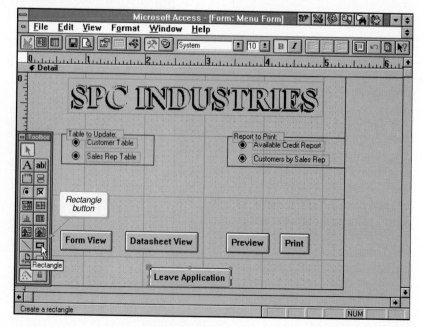

FIGURE 3-79

Placing Boxes on the Application System Form

To place boxes on the form, use the Rectangle button in the toolbox, just as you did in the form in Project 1. After placing the rectangle, you will need to choose the Send to Back command in order to make the objects covered by the rectangle visible.

The following step places two boxes on the form. One encloses the options and buttons associated with the table options. The other encloses the options and buttons associated with the report options.

TO PLACE BOXES ON THE FORM ▼

STEP 1 ▶

Use the Rectangle button in the toolbox (Figure 3-79) and the techniques in Project 1 on pages Axxx-Axxx to place rectangles in the positions shown in Figure 3-80. Choose the Send to Back command from the Format menu so the fields display. Use the Properties command from the shortcut menus of the rectangles to change the Special Effect property to Sunken and to change the Back Color to light gray. Select the title and change its Special Effect property to Raised.

The rectangles enclosing the two groups of options and buttons display. The rectangles are sunken and the title is raised.

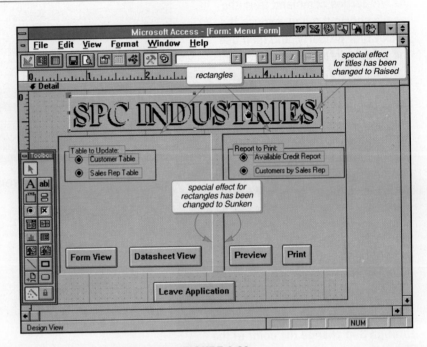

FIGURE 3-80

Changing Colors

One way to emphasize the labels of the option group (Table to Update and Report to Print) is to change their color. To do so, select the labels and change the Back Color property. The steps on the next page change the color of the labels to light blue.

TO CHANGE THE COLOR OF THE OPTION GROUP LABELS ▼

STEP 1 ▶

Select the Table to Update label (Figure 3-80). (The handles should appear only around the label.)

STEP 2 ▶

Click the right mouse button, choose the Properties command from the label's shortcut menu, choose the Back Color property, and then use the color palette to select the light blue color (Figure 3-81).

STEP 3 ▶

Choose the OK button in the color palette and then close the window containing the label's properties by double-clicking its Control-menu box.

The color of the label is changed to light blue.

STEP 4

Use the techniques in Steps 1 through 3 to change the color of the Report to Print label to light blue.

The colors of both labels are changed.

STEP 5

Close the form and save the changes.

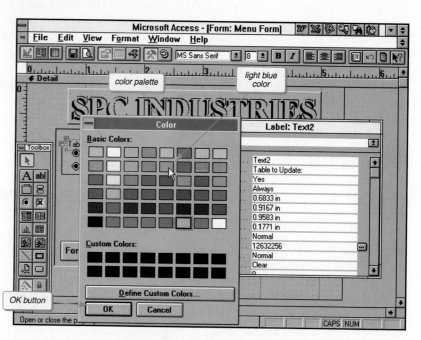

FIGURE 3-81

▲

Including Conditions in Macros

In the macros created earlier in this project, the actions were unconditional; that is, every time the macro is run, the same actions will all take place. It is possible to make the actions conditional. For example, the Open Table as Datasheet macro could open the Sales Rep Table in the event the user selected Sales Rep Table in the option group and the Customer Table in the event the user selected the Customer Table.

To include **conditions** in a macro, click the Conditions button. A column for
the conditions then appears. Just as with field names in expressions, any names
that represent items the user must enter (such as Table to Update) must be
enclosed in square brackets. For example, the expression to test whether Table to
Update is equal to 1 (the value for the Customer Table option button) would be
[Table to Update]=1.

The following steps add conditions to the Open Form for Update, Open Table
as Datasheet, Open Report for Printing, and Open Report for Preview macros.

TO INCLUDE CONDITIONS IN MACROS ▼

STEP 1 ▶

Choose the Macro button, select the
Open Form for Update macro, and
then choose the Design button.

*The Macro window displays
(Figure 3-82).*

FIGURE 3-82

STEP 2 ▶

Choose the Conditions button (⌨).

*The Condition column displays
(Figure 3-83).*

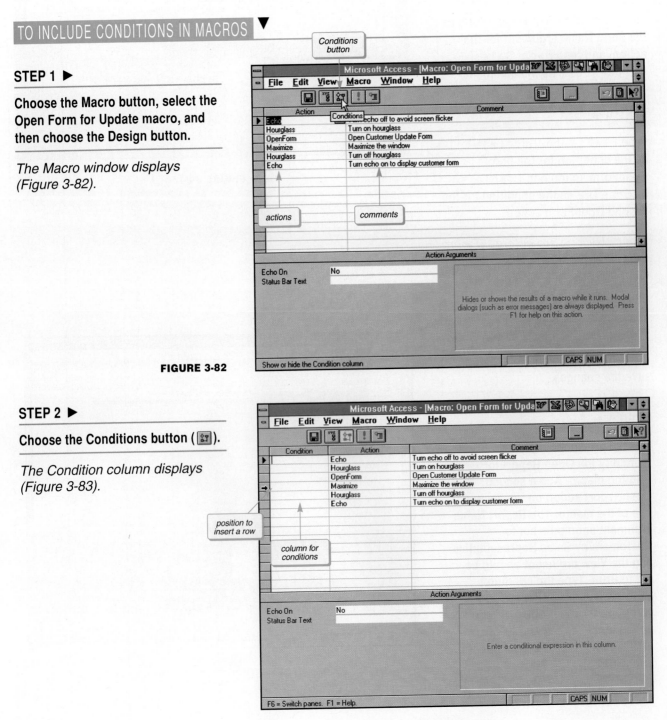

FIGURE 3-83

STEP 3 ▶

Point to the row selector for the row containing the Maximize action, click the left mouse button to select the row, and press the INSERT key to insert a blank row. For the new row, assign the action OpenForm, select the Sales Rep Master Form as the Form Name argument for the action, and type Open Sales Rep Master Form as the comment.

STEP 4 ▶

Type [Table to Update]=1 as the condition for the first OpenForm action and [Table to Update]=2 as the condition for the second OpenForm action.

The conditions are entered (Figure 3-84). The final portions of both conditions do not display.

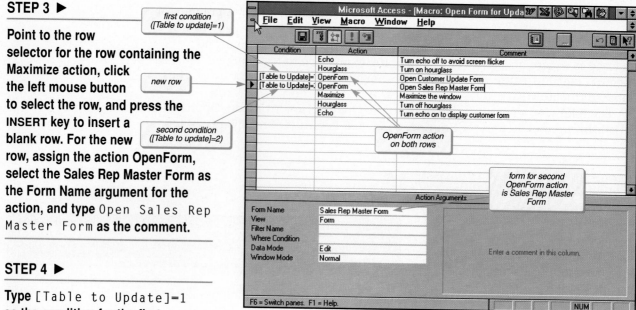

FIGURE 3-84

STEP 5 ▶

Close the macro and save the changes.

STEP 6 ▶

Use the previous steps to modify the Open Report for Printing macro. Add a second OpenReport action on the second line of the macro. The Report Name argument should be set to Customers by Sales Representative and the View argument should be set to Print. Type the condition [Report to Print]=1 as the condition for the first OpenReport action and [Report to Print]=2 as the condition for the second (Figure 3-85).

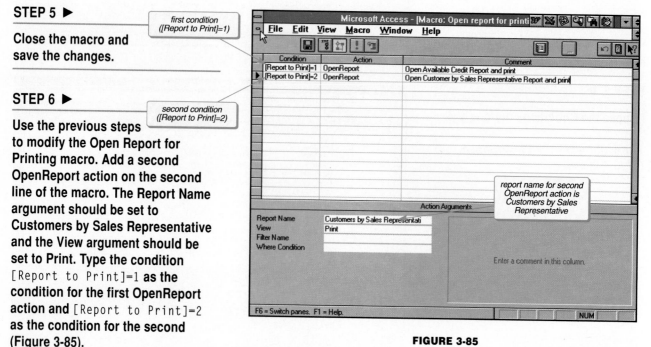

FIGURE 3-85

STEP 7

Close the macro and save the changes.

STEP 8

Make the same changes as in Step 7 to the Open Report for Preview macro. The only difference is that the new OpenReport action should have its View argument left as Preview, instead of changed to Print. Close the macro and save the changes.

STEP 9

Modify the Open Table as Datasheet macro. Add a second OpenTable action with the Table Name argument set to SLSREP. Type `[Table to Update]=1` as the condition for the first OpenTable action and `[Table to Update]=2` as the condition for the second. Close the macro and save the changes.

The modifications to the macros are complete.

Using the Application System

To use the application system, run the Begin Application System macro. The menu form will then display. To take any action, choose the appropriate option from the menu. The following steps illustrate the use of the application system.

TO USE THE APPLICATION SYSTEM ▼

STEP 1 ▶

Run the Begin Application System macro from the Database window.

The menu for the application system displays (Figure 3-86).

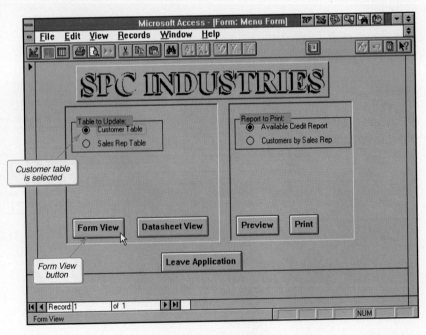

FIGURE 3-86

STEP 2 ▶

To view or update the Customer Table using a form, make sure Customer Table is selected and choose the Form View button.

The form for the Customer Table displays.

STEP 3 ▶

When you have finished working with the form, close the form.

The Application System menu once again displays (Figure 3-87).

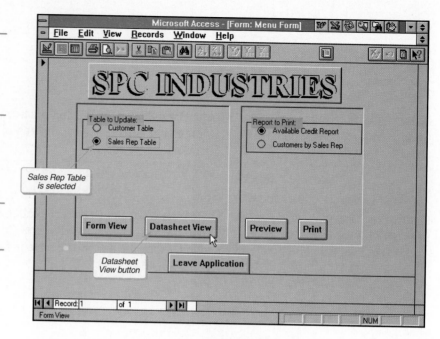

FIGURE 3-87

STEP 4 ▶

To view or update the Sales Rep Table using Datasheet view, make sure the Sales Rep Table is selected and choose the Datasheet View button.

The Sales Rep Table displays in Datasheet view.

STEP 5 ▶

When you have finished working with the datasheet, close it.

The Application System menu once again displays (Figure 3-88).

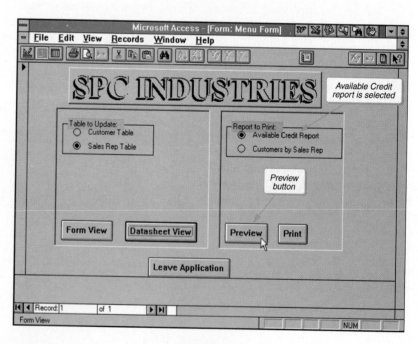

FIGURE 3-88

STEP 6 ▶

To preview the Available Credit Report, make sure the report is selected and choose the Preview button.

The report displays in the Preview window.

STEP 7 ▶

When you have finished previewing the report, close the Preview window.

The Application System menu once again displays (Figure 3-89).

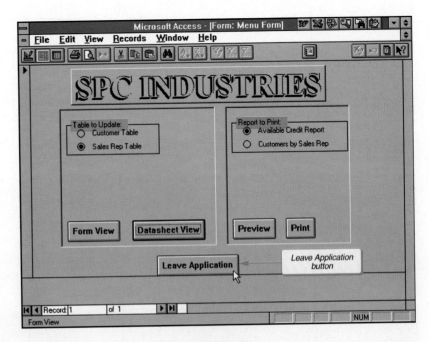

FIGURE 3-89

STEP 8 ▶

To leave the application, choose the Leave Application button.

The Application System menu is removed from the screen and the Database window displays (Figure 3-90). It has been restored to its original size.

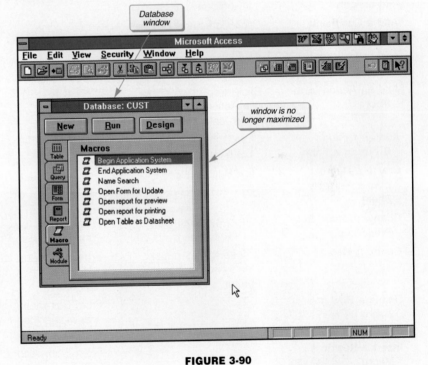

FIGURE 3-90

▶ PROJECT SUMMARY

Project 3 introduced you to creating and using macros. From the Database window, steps and techniques showed you how to create and run macros. You also learned how to use macros on a form in connection with combo boxes and command buttons. You learned how to create option groups and option buttons. Finally, you learned how to include conditions in macros.

▶ KEY TERMS AND INDEX

action *(A114)*
application system *(A114)*
combo box *(A128)*
command button *(A152)*
comment *(A118)*

condition (in a macro) *(A157)*
macro *(A114)*
Macro window *(A116)*
option button *(A146)*
option group *(A146)*

QUICK REFERENCE

In Access, you can accomplish a task in a number of different ways. The following table provides a quick reference to each task presented in this project with its available options. The commands listed in the Menu column can be executed using either the keyboard or the mouse.

Task	Mouse	Menu	Keyboard Shortcuts
Add a Combo Box to a Form	Click Combo Box button in toolbox		
Add a Command Button to a Form	Click Command Button button in toolbox		
Add a Paintbrush Picture to a Form	Click Object Frame button in toolbox	From Edit menu, choose Insert Object	
Add an Action to a Macro	Click drop-down arrow in Actions column, then select action		Type the action
Add an Option Group to a Form	Click Option Group button in toolbox		
Create a Macro from a Property Sheet	Click Build button		
Change Combo Box Properties	Double-click combo box	From combo box's shortcut menu, choose Properties	
Create a Macro	Choose Macro button, then choose New button	From File menu, choose New and then choose Macro	
Delete a Row in a Macro		From Edit menu, choose New and then choose Macro	Press DELETE
Insert a Row in a Macro		From Edit menu, choose INSERT row	Press INSERT
Modify a Macro	Select macro, then choose Design button		
Run a Macro	Select macro, then choose Run button	From File menu, choose Run Macro	

STUDENT ASSIGNMENT 1
True/False

Instructions: Circle T if the statement is true or F if the statement is false.

T   F   1. Macros are collections of actions designed to carry out some specific task.

T   F   2. To create a macro, choose the Macro button in the Database window and then choose the Create button.

T   F   3. Many actions that you enter in the Macro window require additional information called the parameters of the action.

T   F   4. Setting the Echo action to No eliminates screen flicker.

T   F   5. To run a macro, choose the Macro button in the Database window, select the macro, and then choose the Execute button.

T   F   6. To modify a macro, select the macro in the Database window and click the Design button.

T   F   7. To insert a new macro action between two existing actions, select the row beneath where you want to insert the action, and press CTRL+I.

T   F   8. A combo box allows a user to select entries from a list.

T   F   9. When you create a combo box to list values, you can use the Row Arrange property to indicate that the names in the list are to be sorted.

T   F   10. To combine forms and reports into a single application system, create a blank form, add buttons for the various options, and associate the buttons with macros.

T   F   11. To create an initial form for an application system, choose the Form button in the Database window, choose New, and then choose the Blank Form button.

T   F   12. To include graphics or special effects on a form, use the Graphics Frame button in the toolbox.

T   F   13. To change the background color of an object, select the object, click the right mouse button, choose Properties from the shortcut menu that displays, and select the Background property.

T   F   14. A collection of option buttons is called an option frame.

T   F   15. A command button is a button that will execute a command when pressed.

T   F   16. When you create a command button, you can specify that either text or a picture appear on the button.

T   F   17. To place boxes on a form, click the Box button in the toolbox.

T   F   18. To make objects covered by a rectangle visible, choose the Send to Back command from the View menu.

T   F   19. To include conditions in a macro, click the Conditions button in the Macro window.

T   F   20. To assign a macro to a command button, select Miscellaneous as the category in the Command Button Wizard dialog box and then select Run Macro.

STUDENT ASSIGNMENT 2
Multiple Choice

Instructions: Circle the correct response.

1. In Access, a(n) _____ is a collection of actions designed to carry out some specific task.
   a. script
   b. button
   c. macro
   d. option group

(continued)

STUDENT ASSIGNMENT 1 (continued)

2. Many actions require additional information called the _____ of the action.
   a. arguments
   b. parameters
   c. properties
   d. options

3. To run a macro, choose the Macro button in the Database window, select the macro, and then choose the _____ button.
   a. Execute
   b. Perform
   c. Do
   d. Run

4. To insert a new macro action between two existing actions, select the row beneath where you want to insert the action, and press _____.
   a. INSERT
   b. CTRL+N
   c. CTRL+I
   d. CTRL+INSERT

5. When you create a combo box to list values, you can use the _____ property to indicate that the names in the list are to be sorted.
   a. Row Arrange
   b. Row Source
   c. Row Sort
   d. Sort

6. To include graphics or special effects on a form, use the _____ button in the toolbox.
   a. Object
   b. Object Frame
   c. Graphics
   d. Graphics Frame

7. To change the background color of an object, select the object, click the right mouse button, choose Properties from the shortcut menu that displays, and select the _____ property.
   a. Background
   b. Color
   c. Back Color
   d. Desktop

8. To place boxes on a form, use the _____ button in the toolbox.
   a. Box
   b. Frame
   c. Border
   d. Rectangle

9. To make objects covered by a rectangle visible, use the Send to Back command from the _____ menu.
   a. View
   b. Edit
   c. Window
   d. Format

10. To assign a macro to a command button, select _____ as the category in the Command Button Wizard dialog box and then select Run Macro.
    a. Miscellaneous
    b. Application
    c. Record Operations
    d. Table Operations

STUDENT ASSIGNMENT 3
Understanding Macros

Instructions: In Figure SA3-3, arrows point to various items in the Macro window. Identify these items in the spaces provided and use this figure to answer the following questions.

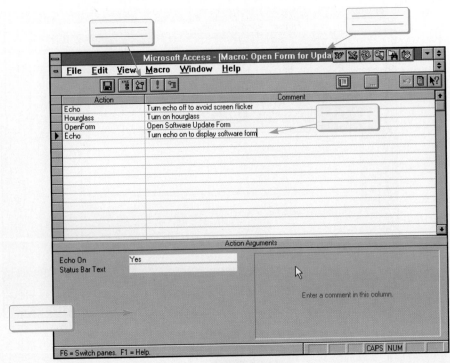

FIGURE SA3-3

1. The Hourglass action to turn off the hourglass should be inserted between the OpenForm and Echo action. How can you insert a new action?

   _____

   _____

2. What value would you assign to the argument for this new action?

   _____

   _____

3. How can you maximize the form when it is opened?

   _____

   _____

4. How do you execute a macro?

   _____

   _____

STUDENT ASSIGNMENT 4
Understanding the Toolbox

Instructions: In Figure SA3-4, arrows point to various buttons in the Toolbox. Identify these options in the spaces provided and use this figure to answer the following questions.

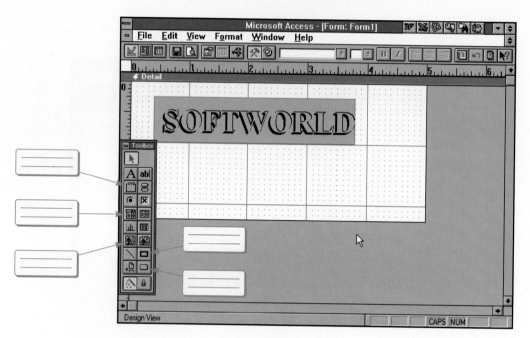

FIGURE SA3-4

1. The title for this application was created in Paintbrush. What toolbox button was used to create this graphic?

_____

_____

2. What is the purpose of the Rectangle toolbox button?

_____

_____

3. When do you place a combo box on a form?

_____

_____

STUDENT ASSIGNMENT 5
Understanding Properties

Instructions: Figure SA3-5 shows a partial Property Sheet for the Name to Find combo box on the Software Update Form. Use this figure to answer the following questions.

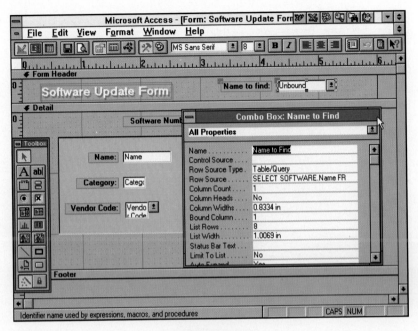

FIGURE SA3-5

1. What is the purpose of the Row Source property?

_____

_____

2. When would you use the Special Effect property?

_____

_____

3. When would you use the Back Color property?

_____

_____

STUDENT ASSIGNMENT 6
Understanding Applications

Instructions: Figure SA3-6 shows an application system created for the SOFT database. Use this figure to help answer the following questions.

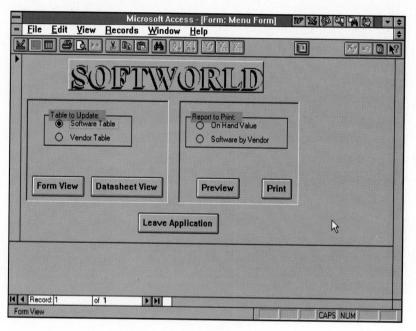

FIGURE SA3-6

1. What is an application system?

_____

_____

_____

2. How would you display the Vendor table in Datasheet view?

_____

_____

_____

3. What is a command button? How do you assign the Run Macro action to a command button?

_____

_____

_____

4. What is an option group? Name the option groups in Figure SA3-6.

_____

_____

_____

COMPUTER LABORATORY EXERCISE 1
Using the Help Menu

Instructions: Perform the following tasks.

1. Start Microsoft Access.
2. Open the SOFT database.
3. Choose the Contents command from the Help menu.
4. Choose Search.
5. Type `Toolbox` in the Search dialog box and click the Show Topics button.
6. Go to the Toolbox topic.
7. The Help window shown in Figure CLE3-1 will display. You can click a tool to learn more about it and to answer the following questions.

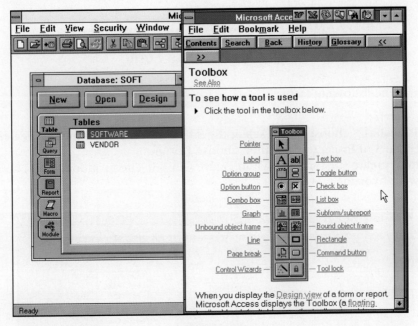

FIGURE CLE3-1

a. Explain the difference between the Bound object frame tool and the Unbound object frame tool.

_____

_____

b. Explain the difference between the List box tool and the Combo box tool.

_____

_____

c. When would you use the Line tool?

_____

_____

8. Exit the Help window and close the SOFT database.
9. Exit Access.

COMPUTER LABORATORY EXERCISE 2
Creating and Using Macros

Instructions: Perform the following tasks.

1. Start Microsoft Access and open the SOFT database.
2. Choose Macro and then choose New.
3. Create a macro to open the Software Update Form you created in Computer Laboratory Exercise 3 of Project 1. The macro should automatically maximize the form when it is opened.
4. Save the macro as Open Form for Update.
5. Create a macro to print the Software by Vendor report you created in Computer Laboratory Exercise 2 of Project 1.
6. Save the macro as Open Report and Print.
7. Run the Open Report and Print macro to print the Software by Vendor report.
8. Close the database and exit Access.

COMPUTER LABORATORY EXERCISE 3
Using Macros on a Form

Instructions: Perform the following tasks.

1. Start Microsoft Access.
2. Open the SOFT database, choose Form, select the Software Update Form you created in Computer Laboratory Exercise 3 of Project 1, and then choose Design.
3. Modify the form to create the form shown in Figure CLE3-3. The form includes a combo box to search for software by name.

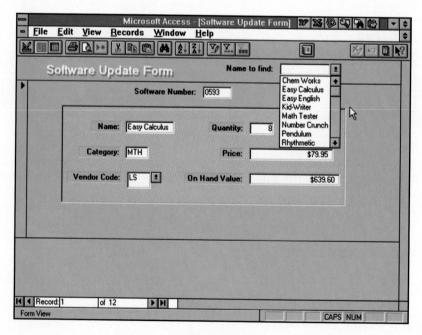

FIGURE CLE3-3

4. Print the form. To print the form, view the form with data, click the Print button, and select Selection as the Print Range.
5. Close and save the form.
6. Close the database and exit Access.

COMPUTER LABORATORY ASSIGNMENT 1
Creating an Application System for the Items Database

Purpose: To provide practice in creating and using macros and application systems.

Instructions: Use the database created in Computer Laboratory Assignment 1 of Project 1 for this assignment. Execute each task on the computer and print the results.

1. Start Microsoft Access and open the ITEMS database.
2. Create macros that will perform the following tasks:
   a. open the Product Update Form you created in Project 1.
   b. open the Product table in Datasheet View.
   c. preview the Product Master Report you created in Project 1.
   d. print the Product Master Report you created in Project 1.
3. Print the Product Master Report using the macro you created in Step 2d above.
4. Modify the Product Update Form to create the form shown in Figure CLA3-1a. The form includes a combo box to search for products by description.

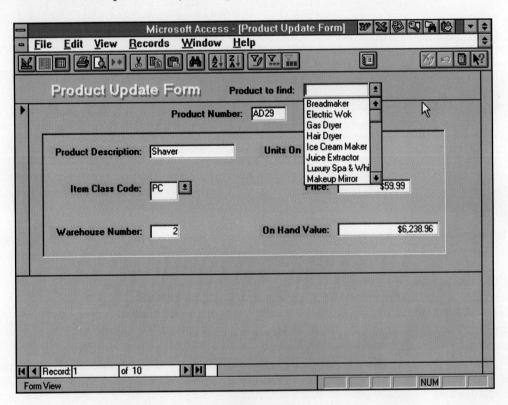

FIGURE CLA3-1a

5. Save and print the form. To print the form, view the form with data, click the Print button, and select Selection as the Print Range.

(continued)

COMPUTER LABORATORY ASSIGNMENT 1 (continued)

6. Create the application system for the ITEMS database shown in Figure CLA3-1b.

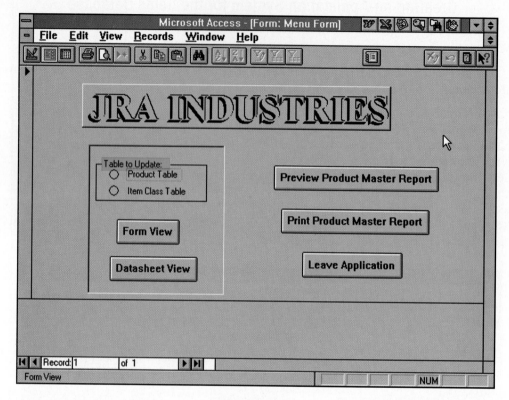

FIGURE CLA3-1b

The application system should do the following:

    a. display the Product table in Datasheet view.
    b. display the Class table in Datasheet view.
    c. open the Product Update Form you created in Project 1.
    d. open the Item Class Master Form you created in Project 2.
    e. print the Product Master Report you created in Project 1.
    f. preview the Product Master Report you created in Project 1.
    g. return to the ITEMS database window.
7. Save the application system menu design as Menu Form.
8. Run your application and correct any errors.
9. Print the application system menu. To print, begin the application to display the menu form, then click the Print button and select Selection as the Print Range.
10. Exit the application.
11. Close the database and exit Access.

COMPUTER LABORATORY ASSIGNMENT 2
Creating an Application System for the Employee Database

Purpose: To provide practice in creating and using macros and application systems.

Instructions: Use the database created in Computer Laboratory Assignment 2 of Project 1 for this assignment. Execute each task on the computer and print the results.

1. Start Microsoft Access and open the EMP database.
2. Create macros that will perform the following tasks:
    a. open the Employee Update Form you created in Project 1.
    b. open the Employee table in Datasheet view.
    c. preview the Employees by Department report you created in Project 1.
    d. print the Employees by Department report you created in Project 1.
3. Print the Employees by Department report using the macro you created in Step 2d above.
4. Modify the Employee Update Form to create the form shown in Figure CLA3-2a. The form includes a combo box to search for employees by last name.

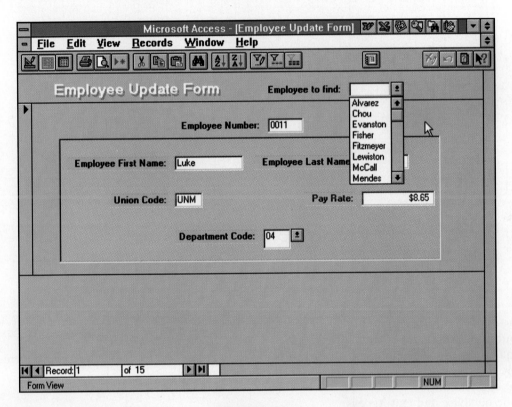

FIGURE CLA3-2a

5. Save and print the form. To print the form, view the form with data, click the Print button, and select Selection as the Print Range.
6. Create the application system for the EMP database shown in Figure CLA3-2b on the next page. The application system should do the following:
    a. display the Employee table in Datasheet view.
    b. display the Department table in Datasheet view.
    c. open the Employee Update Form you created in Project 1.
    d. open the Department Master Form you created in Project 2.
    e. print the Employees by Department report you created in Project 1.
    f. preview the Employees by Department report you created in Project 1.
    g. return to the EMP database window.

(continued)

COMPUTER LABORATORY ASSIGNMENT 2 (continued)

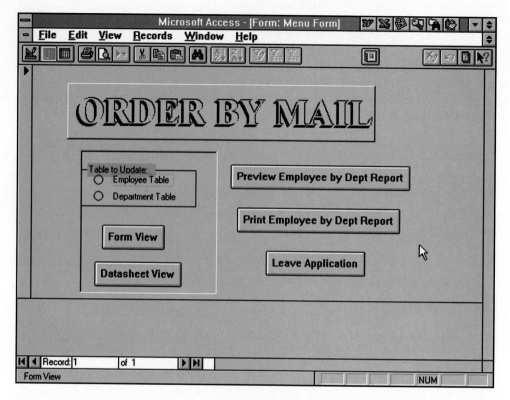

FIGURE CLA3-2b

7. Save the application system menu design as Menu Form.
8. Run your application and correct any errors.
9. Print the application system menu. To print, begin the application to display the menu form, then click the Print button and select Selection as the Print Range.
10. Exit the application.
11. Close the database and exit Access.

COMPUTER LABORATORY ASSIGNMENT 3
Creating an Application System for the Movie Database

Purpose: To provide practice in creating and using macros and application systems.

Instructions: Use the database created in Computer Laboratory Assignment 3 of Project 1 for this assignment. Execute each task on the computer and print the results.

1. Start Microsoft Access and open the MOV database.
2. Create macros that will perform the following tasks:
   a. open the Movie Update Form you created in Project 1.
   b. open the Movie table in Datasheet view.
   c. preview the Movie Report you created in Project 1.
   d. print the Movie Report you created in Project 1.
3. Print the Movie Report using the macro you created in Step 2d above.
4. Modify the Movie Update Form to create the form shown in Figure CLA3-3a. The form includes a combo box to search for movies by title.

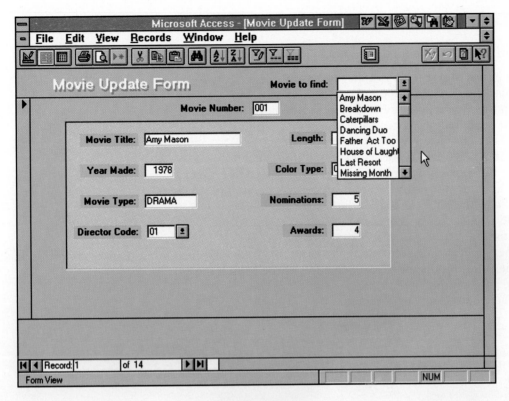

FIGURE CLA3-3a

5. Save and print the form. To print the form, view the form with data, click the Print button, and select Selection as the Print Range.
6. Create the application system for the MOV database shown in Figure CLA3-3b.

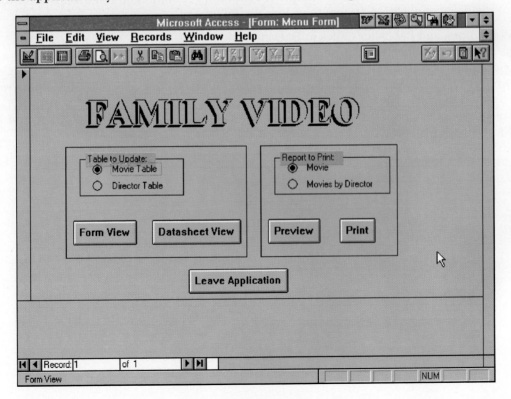

FIGURE CLA3-3b

(continued)

COMPUTER LABORATORY ASSIGNMENT 3 (continued)

The application system should do the following:

    a. display the Movie table in Datasheet view.
    b. display the Director table in Datasheet view.
    c. open the Movie Update Form you created in Project 1.
    d. open the Director Master Form you created in Project 2.
    e. print the Movie report you created in Project 1.
    f. preview the Movie report you created in Project 1.
    g. print the Movies by Director report you created in Project 1.
    h. preview the Movies by Director report you created in Project 1.
    i. return to the MOV database window.

7. Save the application system menu design as Menu Form.
8. Run your application and correct any errors.
9. Print the application system menu. To print, begin the application to display the menu form, then click the Print button and select Selection as the Print Range.
10. Exit the application.
11. Close the database and exit Access.

COMPUTER LABORATORY ASSIGNMENT 4
Creating an Application System for the Book Database

Purpose: To provide practice in creating and using macros and application systems.

Problem: The bookstore owner has asked you to create an application system for the Book database. She has sent you a memo outlining the improvements.

Instructions: Use the database created in Computer Laboratory Assignment 4 of Project 1 for this assignment. Provide an application system that does the following:

1. Displays the Book and Publisher tables in Datasheet view.
2. Displays update forms for the Book and Publisher tables. Users should be able to use the forms to search books by book title and publishers by publisher name.
3. Prints a report of all books in the database, a report of books grouped by publisher, and a report of books grouped by book type.
4. Previews a report of all books in the database, a report of books grouped by publisher, and a report of books grouped by book type.

PRESENTATION GRAPHICS

USING MICROSOFT POWERPOINT 4 FOR WINDOWS

MICROSOFT POWERPOINT 4 FOR WINDOWS

PROJECT ONE

▼

EMBEDDED VISUALS

OBJECTIVES You will have mastered the material in this project when you can:

▶ Import an outline created in another application
▶ Create a title slide with a special background
▶ Scale objects
▶ Resize objects
▶ Send objects to the bottom of a stack
▶ Embed an organization chart

▶ Ungroup clip art
▶ Embed an Excel chart
▶ Group objects
▶ Layer objects
▶ Add a picture
▶ Create a black closing slide

▶ INTRODUCTION

Bulleted lists and simple graphics are the starting point for most presentations; but, they can become boring. Advanced PowerPoint users want exciting presentations — something to impress their audiences. With PowerPoint, it is easy to develop impressive presentations by creating special backgrounds, embedding organization charts, creating new graphics by combining objects, and inserting pictures.

One problem you may experience when developing a presentation is finding the proper graphic image to convey your message. One way to overcome this obstacle is to create an image by

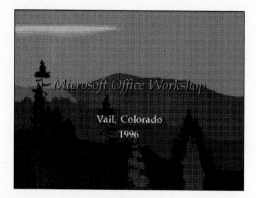

FIGURE 1-1a

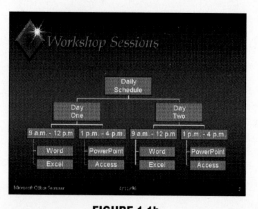

FIGURE 1-1b

combining multiple images from the Microsoft ClipArt Gallery. Another solution is to modify clip art or combine clip art and an embedded object, thereby creating a graphic to best convey the message. Because the PowerPoint templates offer a limited number of slide backgrounds, PowerPoint allows you to create your own background from a picture or a clip art image.

This project introduces several techniques to make your presentations more exciting.

▶ PROJECT ONE – MICROSOFT OFFICE WORKSHOP

Project 1 expands on PowerPoint's basic presentation features by importing existing files and inserting special objects. The presentation created in this project is used in the orientation session of the Microsoft Office Workshop. This workshop provides intense training sessions on four Microsoft Office software applications. The project begins by building the presentation from an outline created in another application and saved as a Rich Text Format (RTF) file. Then, special objects are inserted to customize the presentation. These special objects include a special background, modified clip art, an organization chart, and a picture.

Slide Preparation Steps

The following slide preparation steps summarize how to create the slides shown in Figures 1-1a through 1-1e. If you are creating these slides on a personal computer, read these steps without doing them.

1. Start PowerPoint.
2. Import the PROJ1.RTF outline from the Student Diskette that accompanies this book.
3. Format the presentation using the Pick a Look Wizard.
4. Save the presentation on your data diskette as PROJ1.PPT.
5. Create a title slide using the Mountain View clip art image as the background (see Figure 1-1a).
6. Embed an organization chart on Slide 2 to identify the seminar schedule (see Figure 1-1b).
7. From the Student Diskette, embed the Excel chart and worksheet CLE1-2.XLS into the Group Meeting clip art image on Slide 3 (see Figure 1-1c).
8. From the Student Diskette, import the HORSES.PCX picture into the object placeholder on Slide 4 (see Figure 1-1d).
9. Create a black closing slide by changing slide background options (see Figure 1-1e).
10. Save the presentation on your data diskette.
11. Exit PowerPoint.

FIGURE 1-1c

FIGURE 1-1d

FIGURE 1-1e

▶ IMPORTING OUTLINES CREATED IN ANOTHER APPLICATION

S omeday, you may be asked to present the findings of a research paper. Instead of typing the presentation outline, you can import the outline from the research paper. If you did not create an outline for the research paper, you can create it by first saving the research paper document as an RTF file, removing all text except topic headings, and then saving the RTF file again. Once the research paper outline is saved as an RTF file, you can import the outline into PowerPoint.

You can also create a presentation by opening an outline created in Microsoft Word or another word processor. The advantage of using an outline saved as a Microsoft Word document or as an RTF file is the text attributes and outline heading levels are maintained. Documents saved as plain text files (TXT) can be opened in PowerPoint but do not maintain text attributes and outline heading levels. Consequently, each paragraph becomes a slide title.

To create a presentation using an existing outline, select Outlines from the List Files of Type box in the PowerPoint Open dialog box. When you select Outlines, PowerPoint displays a list of file extensions it recognizes. Table 1-1 identifies these file extensions. Next, you select the file that contains the outline you want. PowerPoint then creates a presentation using your outline. Each major heading in your outline becomes a slide title and sub-headings become a bulleted list on that slide.

▸ **TABLE 1-1**

FILE EXTENSION	FILE EXTENSION DESCRIPTION
.doc	Microsoft Word document, other word processor
.xls	Microsoft Excel 5.0 worksheet
.xlw	Microsoft Excel 4.0 workbook, workspace
.xl5	Microsoft Excel 5.0 workbook
.wri	Microsoft Write document
.rtf	Rich Text Format document
.mcw	Word for Macintosh document
.txt	Plain text document saved without formatting

When the Microsoft Office seminar organizing team planned the training seminar, the members created an outline using Microsoft Word. They used this outline to develop their sales literature and publication advertisements. They have asked you to develop the orientation session presentation. You will use the existing seminar outline to create your presentation.

Opening an Existing Outline Created in Another Application

After starting PowerPoint, the first step in this project is to open an outline created in another application. PowerPoint can produce slides from an outline created in Microsoft Word or another word processor if the outline was saved in a format that PowerPoint can recognize (see Table 1-1 above). The outline created by the seminar organizing team was saved as an RTF file.

Opening an outline created in another application consists of two steps. First, you must tell PowerPoint you are opening an existing presentation. Then, in order to open the outline saved as an RTF file, you need to select the proper file type from the List Files of Type box. The following steps explain how to open an outline created in another application.

TO OPEN AN OUTLINE CREATED IN ANOTHER APPLICATION ▼

STEP 1 ▶

Insert the Student Diskette that accompanies this book into drive A. With the PowerPoint startup dialog box displaying on the screen, select the Open an Existing Presentation option button. Choose the OK button to display the Open dialog box. If necessary, click the Drives box arrow and select drive A in the Drives box. Then, point to the List Files of Type box arrow.

PowerPoint displays the Open dialog box (Figure 1-2).

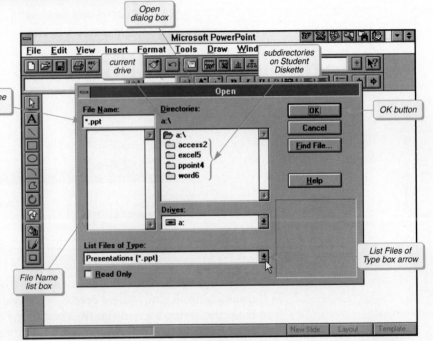

FIGURE 1-2

STEP 2 ▶

Click the List Files of Type box arrow and point to Outlines (*.doc; *.mcw; *.rft;*.wri; *.xls;*.xlw;*.xl5; *.rtf;*...).

A drop-down list of available file types displays (Figure 1-3). Your list may be different, depending on the software installed on your computer.

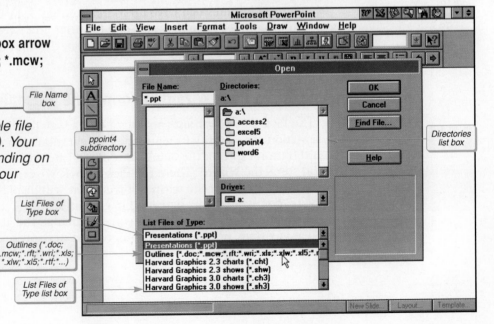

FIGURE 1-3

STEP 3 ▶

Click Outlines (*.doc;*.mcw;
.rft;.wri;*.xls;*.xlw;*.xl5;
.rtf;...). Double-click the ppoint4
subdirectory in the Directories list
box. Then, double-click proj1.rtf in
the File Name list box.

*PowerPoint opens PROJ1.RTF
and displays it in Outline view
(Figure 1-4).*

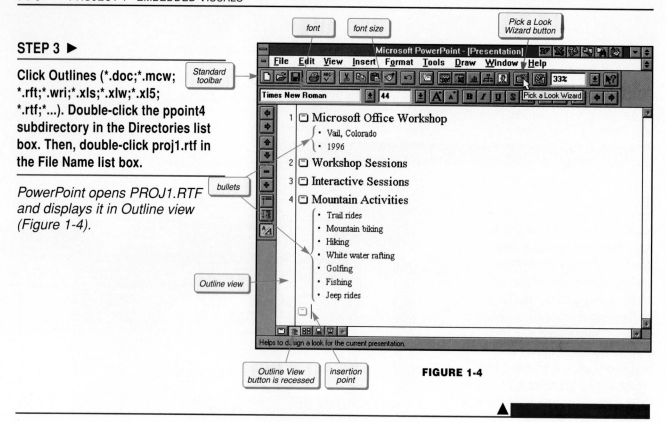

FIGURE 1-4

When opening a file created in another presentation graphics program, such as Harvard Graphics or Aldus Persuasion, PowerPoint picks up the outline structure from the styles used in the file (heading 1 becomes a title, heading 2 becomes the first level of text, and so on). If the file does not contain heading styles, PowerPoint uses paragraph indents to create the outline. For plain text files, which are files saved without formatting, PowerPoint uses the tabs at the beginning of paragraphs to define the outline structure.

Imported outlines can have up to nine indent or heading levels, whereas PowerPoint outlines have only six (one for titles and five for text). When you import an outline, all text in heading levels six through nine is treated as heading level five text.

Using Pick a Look Wizard to Format the Presentation

The Pick a Look Wizard provides a quick way to format the look of your presentation. To simplify formatting a presentation, you may use the Pick a Look Wizard button ( ) on the Standard toolbar. Clicking the Pick a Look Wizard button starts the wizard. Then, the Pick a Look Wizard's multiple dialog boxes prompt you to choose the master objects that will display on each slide, such as template, company name, date, and page number.

Using the Pick a Look Wizard, you can change the appearance of your presentation at any time, not just when you create a new presentation. For example, you can organize the topics for your presentation and then let the Pick a Look Wizard help you design the look.

The following steps summarize how to format the presentation using the Pick a Look Wizard.

TO FORMAT THE PRESENTATION

Step 1: Click the Pick a Look Wizard button on the Standard toolbar.

Step 2: When the Pick a Look Wizard - Step 1 of 9 dialog box displays, choose the Next button.

Step 3: If not already selected, select the On-Screen Presentation option button. Choose the Next button in the Pick a Look Wizard - Step 2 of 9 dialog box.

Step 4: When the Pick a Look Wizard - Step 3 of 9 dialog box displays, choose the More button.

Step 5: Drag the File Name scroll bar elevator down until twinkles.ppt displays. Double-click twinkles.ppt in the File Name list box.

Step 6: When the Pick a Look Wizard - Step 3 of 9 dialog box displays again, choose the Next button.

Step 7: When the Pick a Look Wizard - Step 4 of 9 dialog box displays, remove the x in the Speaker's Notes check box, the x in the Audience Handout Pages check box, and the x in the Outline Pages check box by pointing to each check box and clicking the left mouse button. Choose the Next button.

Step 8: When the Pick a Look Wizard - Slide Options dialog box displays, select the check boxes for Name, company, or other text; Date; and Page Number. If a name displays in the Name, company, or other text box, select it. Type `Microsoft Office Seminar` in the Name, company, or other text box. Choose the Finish button.

PowerPoint applies the twinkles.ppt template, inserts the text, date, and page number on the Slide Master, and returns to Outline view (Figure 1-5).

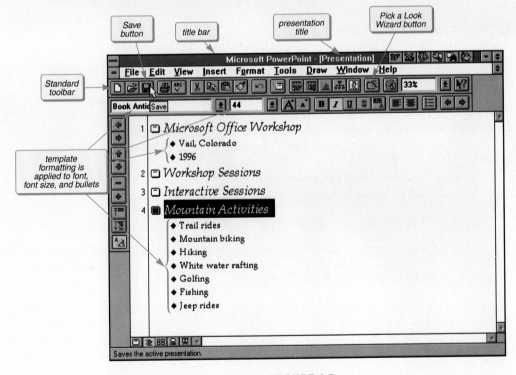

FIGURE 1-5

The template formatting is applied as indicated by the change to the font and bullets. If you compare Figure 1-4 to Figure 1-5, you see that the font changed from Times New Roman to Book Antiqua and the bullets changed from dots to diamonds.

Saving the Presentation

It is wise to frequently save your presentation on a diskette. Because you have created all the text for your presentation, you should save your presentation now. The following steps summarize how to save a presentation.

TO SAVE A PRESENTATION

Step 1: Insert a formatted diskette into drive A.
Step 2: Click the Save button on the Standard toolbar.
Step 3: Type proj1 in the File Name box. Do not press the ENTER key.
Step 4: If drive A is not selected, click the Drives box arrow and select a:.
Step 5: Choose the OK button in the Save As dialog box.
Step 6: If you desire, revise the information in the Summary Info dialog box, and choose the OK button.

The presentation is saved to drive A with the name PROJ1.PPT. The presentation title, PROJ1.PPT, displays in the title bar.

PowerPoint automatically appends the extension PPT to the filename PROJ1. The information in the Summary Info dialog box assists you in documenting the presentation when you include the presentation title, the presentation subject, the author's name, and keywords to associate with the presentation when using the Find File command in the File menu or any comments pertinent to the presentation.

▶ CREATING A TITLE SLIDE WITH A SPECIAL BACKGROUND

PowerPoint has more than fifty templates in each of its three template subdirectories. Suppose, however, the background you want for your presentation is not in one of the templates, such as the mountains in Figure 1-1a on page PP2. Using clip art, you can create that background. The clip art is embedded on the slide and then resized to cover the template.

To create a title slide background using clip art, you perform several steps. Begin by changing the slide layout to the Title Slide layout. Next, you embed the clip art image. Once the clip art image displays on the slide, modify the size of the image to cover or hide the template. Finally, place the clip art image behind the text.

The next several sections explain how to create a slide background using clip art.

Changing Slide Layout to Title Slide

When you import an outline to create a presentation, PowerPoint assumes the text is bulleted text. Because Slide 1 is the title slide for this presentation, you want to change the slide layout to the Title Slide layout. You cannot change the slide layout in Outline view, however. Therefore, you want to change to Slide view and then change the layout.

The steps below summarize how to change to Slide view and change the layout of Slide 1 to the Title Slide layout.

TO CHANGE THE SLIDE LAYOUT TO TITLE SLIDE

Step 1: Click the Slide View button at the bottom of the PowerPoint screen.

Step 2: Drag the vertical scroll bar elevator up until Slide 1 displays in the slide indicator box (Slide 1), which indicates the slide you are about to display.

Step 3: Click the Layout button (Layout...) on the status bar.

Step 4: Double-click the Title Slide layout, the first layout in the Reapply the current master styles box, in the Slide Layout dialog box.

Slide 1 displays in Slide view with the twinkles.ppt template (Figure 1-6).

PowerPoint provides two alternative methods to double-clicking the slide layout in Step 4. The first alternative is to type the layout number of one of the twenty-one slide layouts and press the ENTER key. The second alternative is to type the layout number and choose the Apply button. PowerPoint interprets the number you type as the corresponding slide layout and applies it when you press the ENTER key, in alternative one, or choose the Apply button, in alternative two. For example, the title slide layout is layout number one. When the Layout dialog box displays, you can type 1 and press the ENTER key instead of double-clicking the Title Slide layout.

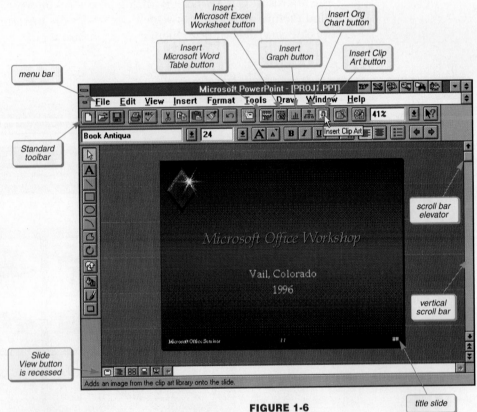

FIGURE 1-6

The twinkles.ppt template format determines the slide attributes of the Slide Master. For example, the text Microsoft Office Workshop displays shadowed and italicized. The slide attributes change when you select a different template.

Inserting Clip Art for a Special Background

The next step in creating the title slide is inserting clip art to create a special background. Because this presentation is the first organized session of the seminar, you want to stress the relaxed learning atmosphere by emphasizing the mountains surrounding Vail, Colorado. PowerPoint does not have a template that is suitable for your opening slide. To create the desired effect, you decide to insert a mountain clip art image to cover the twinkles.ppt template.

PowerPoint provides you with several ways to insert an object into your presentation. One method is to click one of the object placeholders, which opens an auxiliary application such as Microsoft Graph. Another method is to select the Insert menu and select the Object command. Still another method is to click one of the five object buttons on the Standard toolbar. Those buttons are **Insert Microsoft Word Table** ( ), **Insert Microsoft Excel Worksheet** ( ), **Insert Graph** ( ), **Insert Org Chart** ( ), and **Insert Clip Art** ( ) (see Figure 1-6 on page PP9). This project uses the Insert Clip Art button for the special background on Slide 1, and again later in the project on Slide 3.

Using the ClipArt Gallery Find Feature

Instead of searching the various ClipArt Gallery categories to locate a clip art image, you can locate an image quickly by clicking the **Find button** (Find...) in the Microsoft ClipArt Gallery dialog box. Clicking the Find button displays the Find Picture dialog box in which you select the criterion to search for an image by its category, description, filename, or picture type.

TO USE THE CLIPART GALLERY FIND FEATURE ▼

STEP 1 ▶

Click the Insert Clip Art button on the Standard toolbar. When the Microsoft ClipArt Gallery - Picture in PROJ1.PPT dialog box displays, point to the Find button.

The Microsoft ClipArt Gallery - Picture in PROJ1.PPT dialog box displays (Figure 1-7).

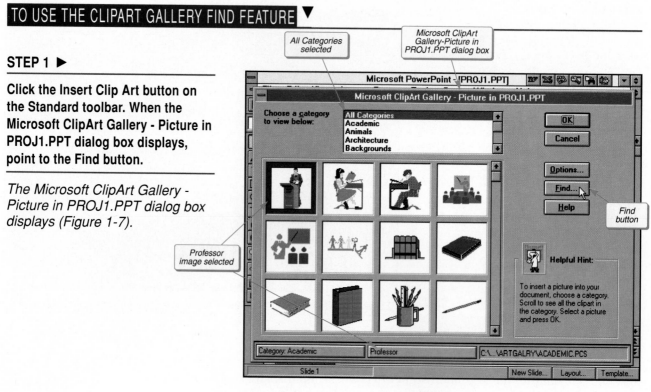

FIGURE 1-7

STEP 2 ▶

Choose the Find button. When the Find Picture dialog box displays, click the With a Description containing option button. Type `mountain` **and point to the OK button.**

When you click the With a Description containing option button, the insertion point displays in the text box (Figure 1-8). The description may be a word or part of a word. The description you type is used to search the ClipArt Gallery for images that contain this description in whole or in part. The description is not case-sensitive, meaning any uppercase or lower-case character is valid.

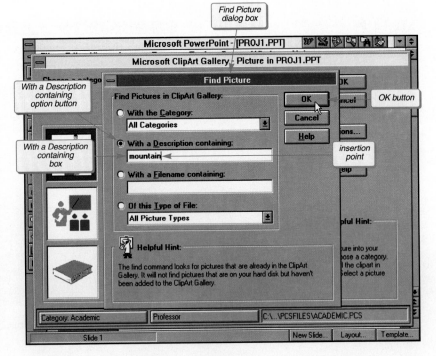

FIGURE 1-8

STEP 3 ▶

Choose the OK button.

The ClipArt Gallery displays images that match your description (Figure 1-9). Depending on the clip art installed on your computer, your clip art images may be different from those in Figure 1-9. The selected image name displays at the bottom of the Microsoft ClipArt Gallery - Picture in PROJ1.PPT dialog box. The name of the category containing the selected image also displays at the bottom of the dialog box. The first image is selected by default. If not already selected, click the Mountain View image to verify you have selected the correct image.

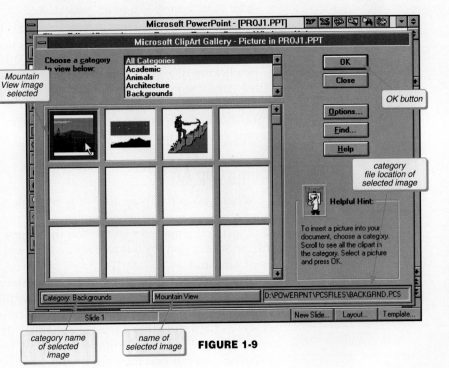

FIGURE 1-9

STEP 4 ▶

Double-click the Mountain View image.

The Mountain View image displays on Slide 1 (Figure 1-10).

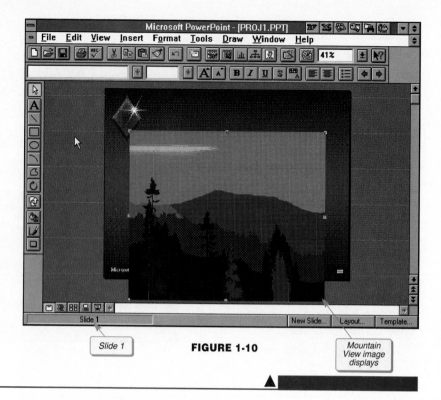

Slide 1   **FIGURE 1-10**   Mountain View image displays

The Find feature is a quick way to find specific clip art images. In the Find Picture dialog box, however, you can specify only one search criterion at a time (see Figure 1-8 on page PP11). To search by category, click the With the Category option button, click the With the Category box arrow, select a category from the list by clicking it, and then choose the OK button. To search by filename, click the With a Filename containing option button, type a ClipArt Gallery filename or part of a filename, and then choose the OK button. To search by type of file, click the Of this Type of File option button, click the Of this Type of File box arrow, select a file type from the list by clicking it, and then choose the OK button.

Scaling Clip Art

When you add clip art to a slide without first selecting an object placeholder, such as the Sub-title placeholder, the clip art object displays on the slide at the size the object was originally saved. You then must resize the object and move it to the location where you wish it to display. One way to resize the object is to use the Scale command.

The **Scale command**, located on the Draw menu, allows you to enlarge or reduce an object by very precise amounts while retaining its original proportions. **Proportions** are relationships between an object's height and width such that if one varies then the other varies in a manner dependent on the first. For example, a rectangle one-inch high and two-inches wide has proportions of one to two (1:2). Therefore, if you increase the rectangle's height by one inch, its width must increase by two inches to maintain the original proportions. The original rectangle scale is 100 percent. The change in the rectangle's height and width increases the scale of the rectangle by 100 percent. Therefore, the rectangle is now 200 percent of its original size (see Figure 1-11). Specify the scale percentage in the Scale To box in the Scale dialog box.

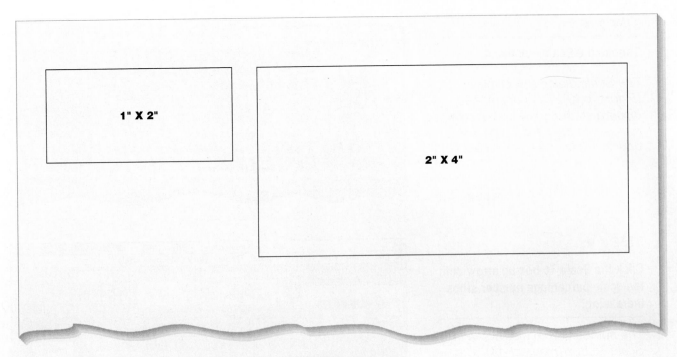

FIGURE 1-11

The following steps explain how to scale a clip art object.

TO SCALE CLIP ART ▼

STEP 1 ►

With the Mountain View image selected, select the Draw menu and point to the Scale command (Figure 1-12).

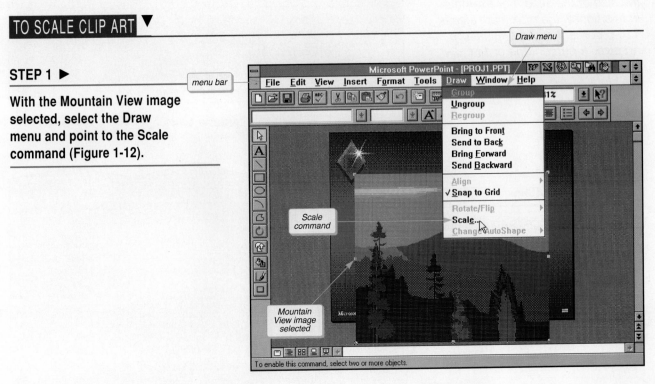

FIGURE 1-12

STEP 2 ▶

Choose the Scale command.

The Scale dialog box displays (Figure 1-13). The number 100 displays in the Scale To box, which represents the percentage the original object has been scaled.

FIGURE 1-13

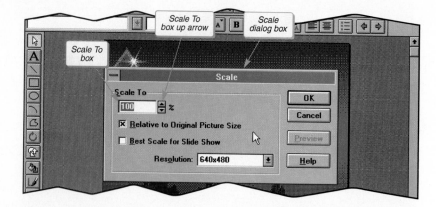

STEP 3 ▶

Click the Scale To box up arrow until the scale percentage number stops increasing.

The number 110.6 displays in the Scale To box (Figure 1-14). The number displaying in your Scale To box may be different depending on the resolution of your screen. You can scale an object only to a percentage equal to or less than the size of the slide. For example, in this figure, the maximum size is 110.6 percent of the original clip art size. A percentage of 111 would be larger than the size of the slide.

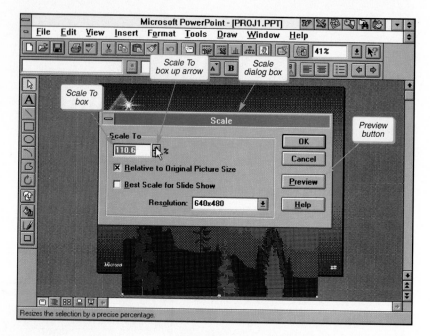

FIGURE 1-14

STEP 4 ▶

Choose the OK button.

The scaling change is applied and the clip art displays at the maximum size of the slide height (Figure 1-15). The scaled clip art displays 10.6% larger than the original.

Mountain View image is scaled to maximum size of slide height

FIGURE 1-15

The Preview button in the Scale dialog box allows you to view the object's new size without applying it (see Figure 1-14). When you want to make an object larger, enter a number greater than 100 in the Scale To box. To make an object smaller, enter a number less than 100.

The Best Scale For Slide Show check box in the Scale dialog box is used to scale videos for optimal viewing in a slide show.

Moving Clip Art

Once the Mountain View clip art object is scaled, you move it to the center of the slide. To move clip art, select the clip art image, and then, using the mouse pointer, drag the clip art to its new position on the slide. The steps below summarize moving clip art.

TO MOVE CLIP ART

Step 1: Point to the center of the Mountain View clip art object. Then, press and hold down the left mouse button.

Step 2: Drag the Mountain View clip art object up until the top and bottom edges are even with the top and bottom edges of Slide 1.

Step 3: Release the left mouse button.

FIGURE 1-16

When you press and hold down the left mouse button, a dotted box outlines the clip art. As you drag the clip art, the outline box follows your mouse pointer to show you where the clip art object will be placed when you release the mouse button. When you release the mouse button, PowerPoint drops the clip art object into place on Slide 1 (Figure 1-16).

Mountain View image is moved to center of slide

The procedure for moving an object with the mouse is called dragging and dropping.

Turning Off the Grid when Resizing Clip Art

Even though the clip art object was scaled to the maximum height of the slide, it still does not cover the width of the slide. You can resize an object by dragging one of the resize handles that displays when the object is selected. For precise placement of objects on a slide, you can use the **grid,** a series of invisible, crisscrossing lines, called **gridlines.** Gridlines are spaced about one-twelfth of an inch apart on the grid. When you move an object close to one of the invisible gridlines, it jumps to it as though it were a magnet. Using the grid, however, can prevent you from placing an object exactly where you would like it if a gridline is not positioned on that same location. You can turn the grid on or off by selecting the **Snap to Grid command** from the Draw menu. The following two sections explain how to turn off the grid and how to resize clip art.

TO TURN OFF THE GRID ▼

STEP 1 ▶

Select the Draw menu and point to the Snap to Grid command.

The check mark in front of the Snap to Grid command indicates the command is active (ON) and that objects will jump to the closest gridline (Figure 1-17). This command toggles on and off. Thus, the command is not active (OFF) when no check mark displays.

STEP 2

If a check mark displays, choose the Snap to Grid command.

The Snap to Grid command is no longer active.

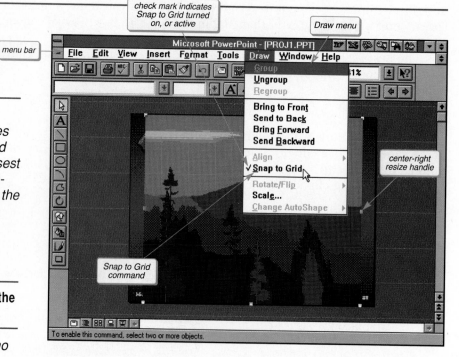

FIGURE 1-17

When the grid is on, you can temporarily turn it off by holding down the ALT key as you drag the object.

Resizing Clip Art

The next step is to change the size of the clip art object to completely cover the slide and the template. In a previous step, you scaled the clip art to the maximum height of the slide. Because scaling maintains the object's proportions, the clip art object's width is less than the width of the slide. Resize the clip art object by dragging one of its resize handles.

PowerPoint allows you to **constrain,** or control, the resizing of an object from its center by holding down the CTRL key while dragging a resize handle. This method of constraining is called **resizing about center**. The following steps explain how to resize the Mountain View clip art about center.

TO RESIZE CLIP ART ▼

STEP 1 ▶

Position the mouse pointer on the center-right resize handle.

When the mouse pointer is positioned on a resize handle, its shape changes to a two-headed arrow (Figure 1-18). The two-headed arrow changes to a cross-hair pointer when you click the left mouse button.

FIGURE 1-18

STEP 2 ▶

While holding down the CTRL key, drag the mouse pointer to the right edge of the slide. When the cross-hair pointer reaches the edge of the slide, release the left mouse button. Release the CTRL key.

Holding down the CTRL key when dragging the cross-hair pointer resizes an object evenly from its center (Figure 1-19).

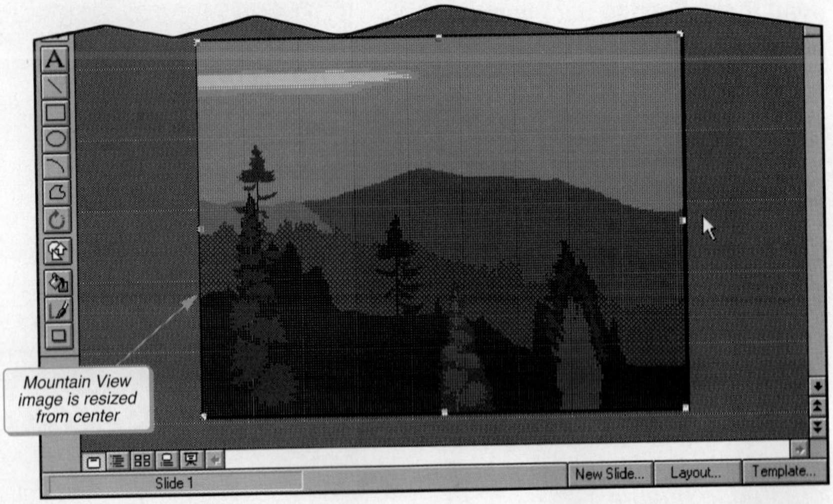

FIGURE 1-19

Caution should be exercised when resizing an object about center. In Step 2 above, releasing the CTRL key before releasing the left mouse button does not resize about center; it resizes only the right side of the clip art. To correct this error, click the Undo button on the Standard toolbar and resize the image again, making certain to first release the left mouse button and then release the CTRL key.

PowerPoint has other methods of constraining objects when resizing. Table 1-2 explains the various constraining methods.

▶ **TABLE 1-2**

METHOD	CONSTRAINING WHEN RESIZING AN OBJECT
SHIFT+drag	Resizes an object vertically, horizontally, or diagonally from one corner. Diagonal resizing maintains the height-to-width relationship
CTRL+drag	Resizes an object from the center outward.
CTRL+SHIFT+drag	Resizes an object vertically, horizontally, or diagonally from the center outward.

To restore a resized picture or clip art image to its original proportions, select the object, choose the Scale command, type 100 in the Scale To box, select the Relative to Original Picture Size check box in the Scale dialog box, and then choose the OK button.

Sending Clip Art to the Background

Now that the Mountain View clip art is sized to fill the slide and hide the twinkles.ppt template, you can no longer read the title and sub-title text. To display the text on top of the Mountain View clip art, send, or place, the clip art behind the text using the **Send to Back command**. The following steps explain how to send clip art behind the text objects so it displays in the background.

TO SEND CLIP ART TO THE BACKGROUND ▼

STEP 1 ▶

With the Mountain View image selected, select the Draw menu and point to the Send to Back command (Figure 1-20).

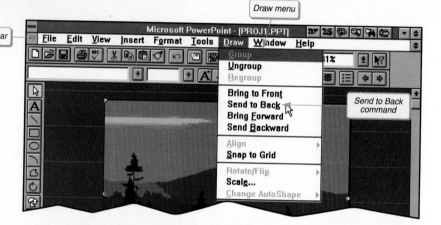

FIGURE 1-20

STEP 2 ▶

Choose the Send to Back command.

The clip art displays in the background and the text displays in the foreground (Figure 1-21).

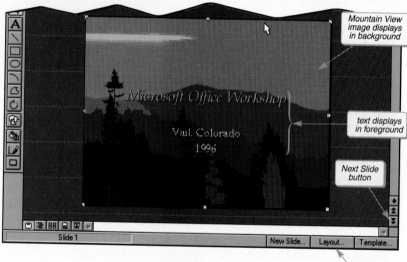

FIGURE 1-21

PowerPoint has four commands to help you manipulate objects that have been layered. **Layered objects** are objects that have been positioned on top of each other like a stack of cards (see Figure 1-22). The object at the bottom of the stack is the **background object**. Only a portion of the background object is visible because it is covered by the objects layered on top. Each layer hides a portion of the object on which it is overlaid. The top layer, or **foreground object**, is the part of slide closest to the audience and is fully visible.

In the previous steps, you used the Send to Back command to move a selected object, the Mountain View clip art, to the bottom of a stack of objects. Because Slide 1 has only two layers, clip art and text, you can achieve the same result by moving the clip art back one layer. When you are working with several layered objects and want to move one object back just one layer in the stack, use the **Send Backward command**. You can also move an object to the top of the stack or up just one layer. To send a selected object to the top of the stack, use the **Bring to Front command**. To move a selected object one layer up toward the top of the stack, use the **Bring Forward command**.

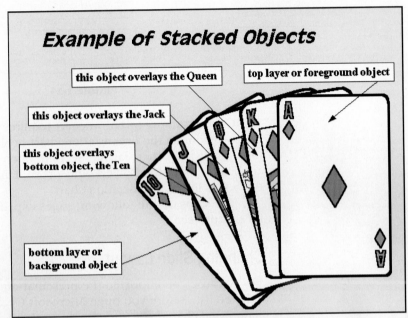

FIGURE 1-22

▶ EMBEDDING AN ORGANIZATION CHART

Slide 2 contains a chart that elaborates on the daily schedule for the Microsoft Office Workshop as shown in Figure 1-23. This type of chart is called an organization chart. An **organization chart** is a hierarchical collection of elements depicting various functions or responsibilities that contribute to an organization or to a collective function. Typically, an organization chart is used to show the structure of people or departments within an organization, hence the name, organization chart. Figure 1-24 illustrates how a company uses an organization chart to describe the relationships between the company's departments. In the information sciences, organization charts are often used to show the decomposition of a process or program. When used in this manner, the chart is called a **hierarchy chart**.

PowerPoint contains a supplementary application called **Microsoft Organization Chart** that allows you to create an organization chart. When you open Microsoft Organization Chart, its menus, buttons, tools, and so on, are available to you directly in the PowerPoint window. Microsoft Organization Chart is an object linking and embedding (OLE) application. The organization chart you will create for Slide 2 (see Figure 1-23) is an embedded object because it is created in an application other than PowerPoint.

FIGURE 1-23

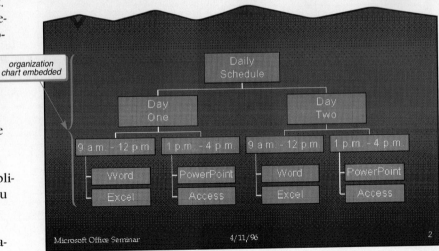

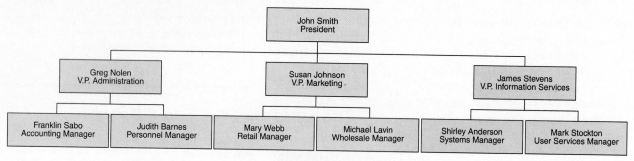

FIGURE 1-24

Creating an organization chart requires several steps. First, display the slide that will contain the organization chart in Slide view and change the slide layout to the organization chart layout. Second, open the Microsoft Organization Chart application onto the PowerPoint screen. Finally, enter and format the contents of the boxes in the organization chart.

The steps on the following pages explain how to create the organization chart for this project.

Changing Slide Layout

Because you imported the presentation outline, the current slide layout is a bulleted list. Before you open Microsoft Organization Chart, you need to display Slide 2 and change the slide layout to the Org Chart layout.

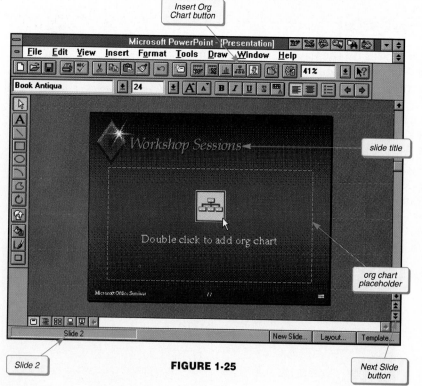

FIGURE 1-25

TO DISPLAY SLIDE 2 AND CHANGE SLIDE LAYOUT

Step 1: Click the Next Slide button.

Step 2: Click the Layout button.

Step 3: When the Slide Layout dialog box displays, double-click the sixth layout, Org Chart (⬛).

Slide 2 displays the organization chart placeholder and the slide title (Figure 1-25).

Slide 2 now displays the placeholder for the organization chart. The next section explains how to open the Microsoft Organization Chart application.

Opening the Microsoft Organization Chart Application into the PowerPoint Window

In order to create the organization chart in Slide 2, you first must open the Microsoft Organization Chart application, which is included with PowerPoint. Recall that this supplementary application opens into the PowerPoint window and makes the menus, buttons, tools, and so on, in the Microsoft Organization Chart application available in the PowerPoint window. Once open, Microsoft Organization Chart displays a sample, four-box organization chart in a work area in the middle of the PowerPoint window, as explained in the following step.

TO OPEN THE MICROSOFT ORGANIZATION CHART APPLICATION INTO THE POWERPOINT WINDOW ▼

STEP 1 ►

Double-click the organization chart placeholder (see Figure 1-25) in the middle of Slide 2.

The Microsoft Organization Chart - [Object in PROJ1.PPT] window displays in a work area in the PowerPoint window (Figure 1-26). Notice the sample organization chart is composed of four boxes connected by lines. When Microsoft Organization Chart opens, the top box is automatically selected and displays with a black background.

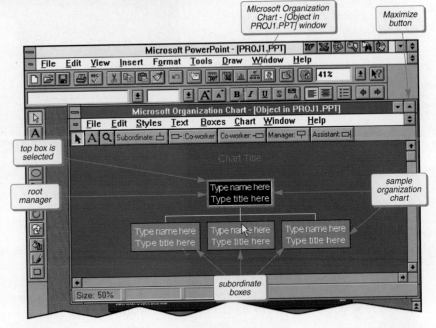

FIGURE 1-26

Microsoft Organization Chart displays a sample organization chart to help you create your organization chart. The sample is composed of one **manager box**, located at the top of the chart, and three **subordinate boxes**. A manager box is one that has one or more subordinates. The topmost manager is called the **root manager**. A subordinate box is located at a level lower than its manager. A sub-ordinate box has only one manager. When a lower level subordinate box is added to a higher level subordinate box, the higher level subordinate box becomes the manager of the lower level subordinate box.

Maximizing the Microsoft Organization Chart Window

When Microsoft Organization Chart opens into the PowerPoint window, the Microsoft Organization Chart window is not maximized. Maximizing the Microsoft Organization Chart window makes it easier to create your organization chart because it displays a larger area in which to view the chart.

TO MAXIMIZE THE MICROSOFT ORGANIZATION CHART WINDOW ▼

STEP 1 ▶

Click the Maximize button in the upper right corner of the Microsoft Organization Chart window.

The Microsoft Organization Chart window fills the desktop (Figure 1-27). Choosing the Restore button returns the Microsoft Organization Chart window to its original size.

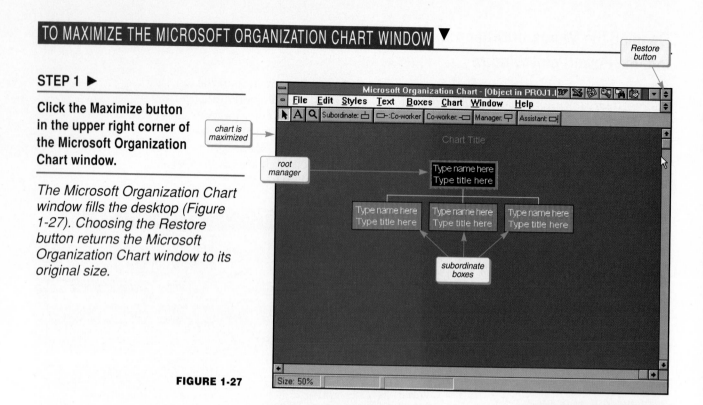

FIGURE 1-27

Creating the Title for the Root Manager

In this presentation, the organization chart is used to communicate the daily workshop schedule. The topmost box, the root manager, will identify the primary focus of this organization chart: Daily Schedule. Recall that when Microsoft Organization Chart opened, the root manager box was selected. The following steps explain how to create the title for the root manager box.

TO CREATE THE TITLE FOR THE ROOT MANAGER ▼

STEP 1 ▶

Type Daily and press the ENTER key.

STEP 2 ▶

Type Schedule

Daily Schedule displays in the root manager box (Figure 1-28). Comment 1 and Comment 2 prompts display below the root manager box title.

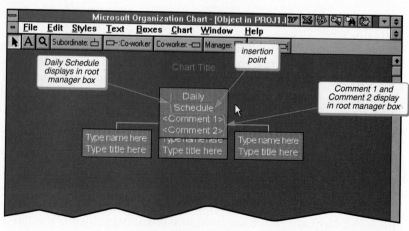

FIGURE 1-28

Deleting Subordinate Boxes

The organization chart in this presentation has two boxes on the level immediately below the root manager. Because the schedule for Day One and Day Two are the same, you will create the schedule for Day One, copy it, and modify it for Day Two. Before proceeding with the remaining boxes for Day One, you will want to delete unnecessary boxes as shown in the steps below.

TO DELETE SUBORDINATE BOXES ▼

STEP 1 ▶

Click the middle subordinate box located directly under the root manager box.

STEP 2 ▶

While holding down the SHIFT key, click the right subordinate box.

The middle and right subordinate boxes are selected (Figure 1-29). Comment 1 and Comment 2 do not display because text was not entered at their prompts. Name and Title prompts will display without entering text at their prompts. The technique of selecting more than one object by holding down the SHIFT key while clicking the objects is called SHIFT+Click.

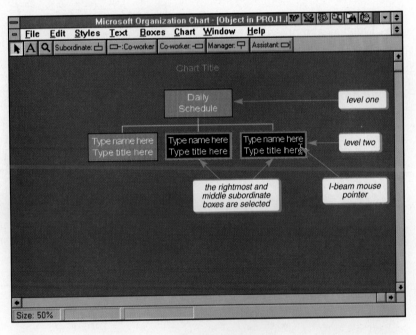

FIGURE 1-29

STEP 3 ▶

Press the DELETE key.

Microsoft Organization Chart displays two boxes: the root manager and one subordinate (Figure 1-30).

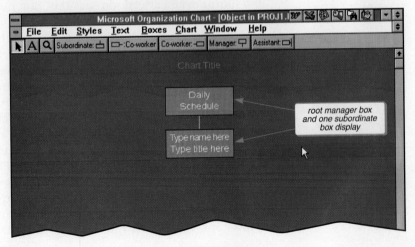

FIGURE 1-30

Titling a Subordinate Box

The process of adding a title to a subordinate box is the same as adding the title to the root manager, except that you first must select the subordinate box. The following step explains how to title a subordinate box.

TO TITLE A SUBORDINATE BOX ▼

STEP 1 ▶

Click anywhere on the subordinate box. Type Day **and press the ENTER key. Type** One

Day One displays as the title for the subordinate box (Figure 1-31).

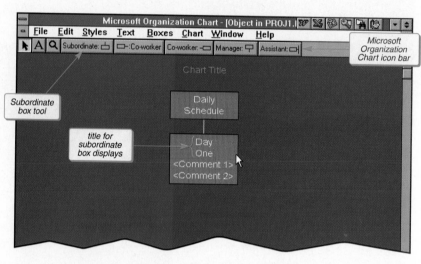

FIGURE 1-31

Adding Subordinate Boxes

Microsoft Organization Chart has five types of boxes you can add to a chart. Each box type has a corresponding box tool on the Microsoft Organization Chart icon bar. Because the daily activities for the workshop in this project are divided into morning and afternoon sessions, you need to add two subordinate boxes to Day One.

To add a single subordinate box, click the Subordinate box tool (Subordinate: ⬦) and then click the box on the organization chart to which the subordinate reports. On the occasions when you wish to add several subordinate boxes, you can hold down the SHIFT key and click the Subordinate box tool. This keeps the Subordinate box tool active so you do not have to keep clicking it before you click the manager box to which you are adding the subordinates. When you hold down the SHIFT key, you can click a box tool once for each box you want to add to the organization chart. For example, if you want to add two subordinate boxes, hold down the SHIFT key and click the Subordinate box tool two times. As long as the box tool is active, you can add the same number of boxes repeatedly without selecting the box tool again. Once activated, the Subordinate box tool stays recessed on the icon bar until you deselect it. Deselect the Subordinate box tool by clicking the Arrow tool (▐) on the Microsoft Organization Chart icon bar or pressing the ESC key.

The following steps explain how to use the SHIFT key and the Subordinate box tool to add two subordinate boxes to Day One.

TO ADD MULTIPLE SUBORDINATE BOXES ▼

STEP 1 ▶

Hold down the SHIFT key and click the Subordinate box tool on the Microsoft Organization Chart icon bar two times. Release the SHIFT key. Then, point to the Day One box.

The Subordinate box tool is recessed. The status bar displays the number of subordinate boxes Microsoft Organization Chart is creating. The mouse pointer displays as the subordinate box icon in the Day One box (Figure 1-32).

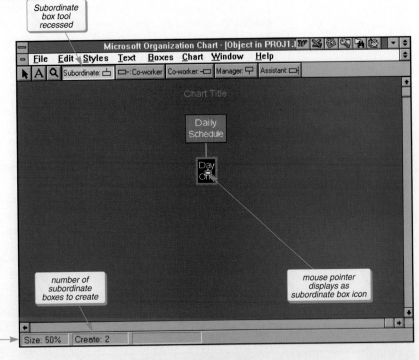

FIGURE 1-32

STEP 2 ▶

Click the Day One box.

Two subordinate boxes display beneath the Day One box (Figure 1-33). The new subordinate boxes display one level lower than the box to which they are attached. Day One is now the manager to the new subordinate boxes. The Subordinate box tool is still recessed indicating that it is still active.

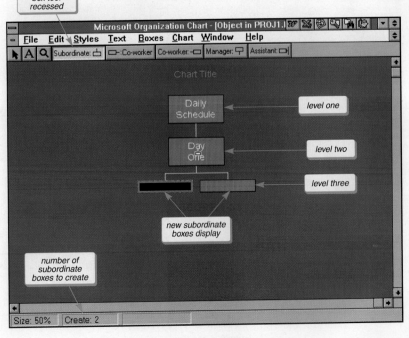

FIGURE 1-33

Adding Another Level of Subordinate Boxes

To further develop the organization chart in this project, you need to add a fourth level of subordinate boxes for the workshop sessions. This workshop will present two classes during the morning session and two classes during the afternoon session. Workshop participants must decide which three-hour class they wish to attend. For example, a participant could attend the Word session the morning of Day One and then attend the Excel session the morning of Day Two. The same decision can be made for the afternoon sessions.

The following steps summarize adding multiple subordinate boxes to a higher level box.

TO ADD ANOTHER LEVEL OF SUBORDINATE BOXES

Step 1: With the Subordinate box tool still active, click the left subordinate box on level three.

Step 2: Click the right subordinate box on level three.

Two subordinate boxes display under each level three subordinate box (Figure 1-34).

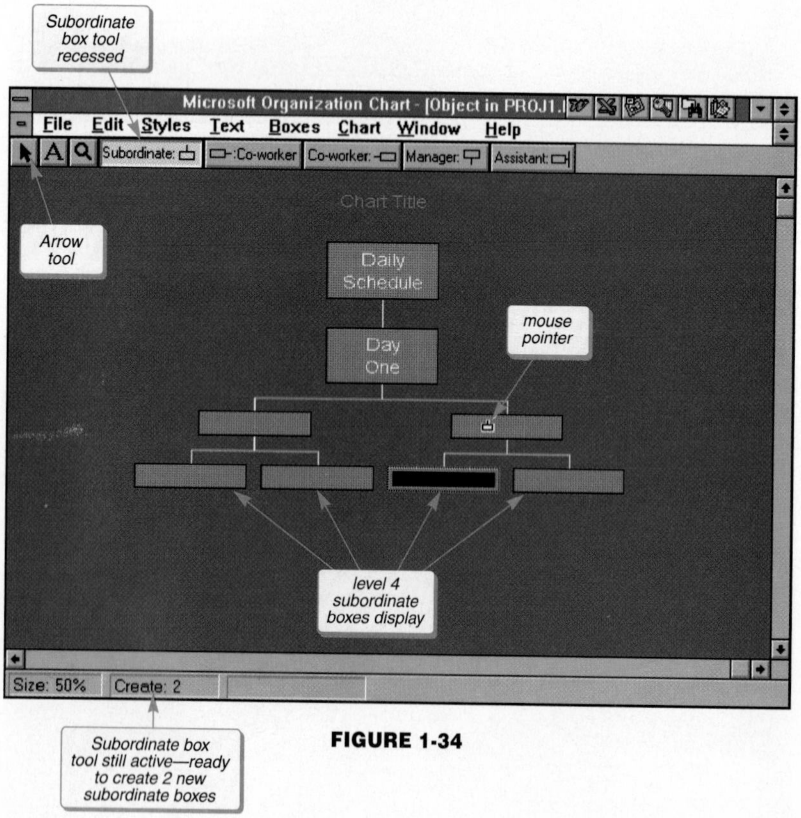

FIGURE 1-34

The structure of the organization chart is complete. The next step is to add titles to the boxes in the chart.

Adding Names to the Subordinate Boxes

To complete the organization chart, add names to all boxes subordinate to the Day One box. Before you can add names, however, you must deactivate the Subordinate box tool and activate the Arrow tool. When the **Arrow tool** is active, the mouse pointer displays as a left-pointing block arrow. Because the subordinate boxes in this project have names, but do not have titles, the Title, Comment 1, and Comment 2 prompts display in brackets under the box name when the box is selected. The brackets indicate the label is optional and it displays only when and if replaced by text.

Use the Arrow tool to select a subordinate box before you type its title. The following steps summarize how to activate the Arrow tool and add a title to each subordinate box.

TO ADD NAMES TO THE SUBORDINATE BOXES

Step 1: Click the Arrow tool on the Microsoft Organization Chart icon bar.

Step 2: Click anywhere on the left subordinate box under Day One. Type
9 a.m. - 12 p.m.

Step 3: Click anywhere on the right subordinate box under Day One. Type
1 p.m. - 4 p.m.

Step 4: Click the left subordinate box under 9 a.m. - 12 p.m. Type Word

Step 5: Click the right subordinate box under 9 a.m. - 12 p.m. Type Excel

Step 6: Click the left subordinate box under 1 p.m. - 4 p.m. Type PowerPoint

Step 7: Click the right subordinate box under 1 p.m. - 4 p.m. Type Access

All subordinate boxes under Day One display with their names (Figure 1-35).

Changing Organization Chart Styles

Now that the boxes for Day One are labeled, you want to change the way the organization chart looks. With the addition of each new box, the chart expanded horizontally. Before you add the schedule for Day Two, you will change the style of selected boxes from horizontal to vertical.

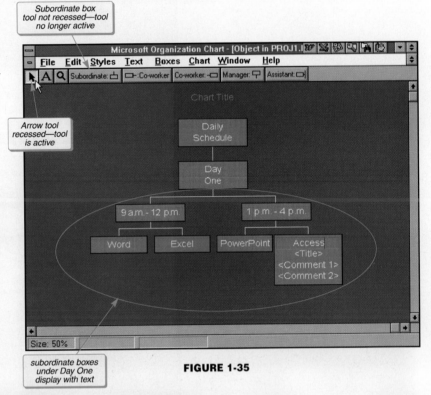

FIGURE 1-35

TO CHANGE ORGANIZATION CHART STYLE ▼

STEP 1 ▶

While holding down the SHIFT key, click the four lowest level boxes: Word, Excel, PowerPoint, and Access.

The four lowest level boxes are selected (Figure 1-36).

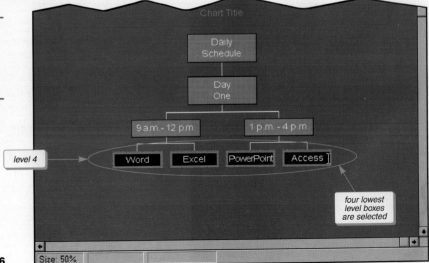

FIGURE 1-36

STEP 2 ►

Select the Styles menu and point to the vertical style box, which is the second box from the left in the top row of the Group styles menu.

By default, the horizontal style box is currently selected (Figure 1-37).

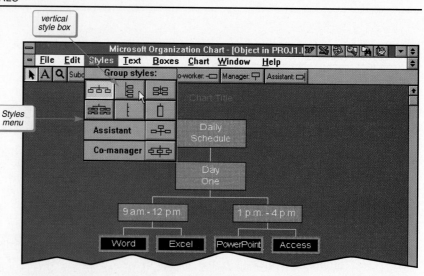

FIGURE 1-37

STEP 3 ►

Click the vertical style box.

The organization chart vertically displays the two morning sessions and the two afternoon sessions (Figure 1-38). The 9 a.m. - 12 p.m. box and the 1 p.m. - 4 p.m. box still display horizontally under the Day One box because the style changes only the selected boxes.

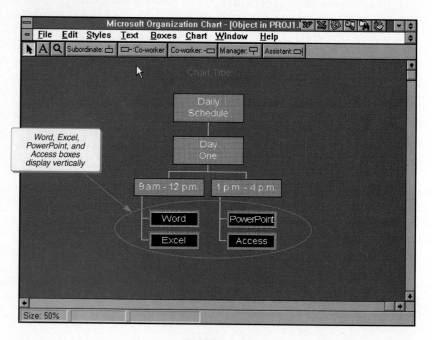

FIGURE 1-38

If you select the wrong style box or want to return to the previous style, choose the Undo Chart Style command from the Edit menu.

Copying a Leg of the Organization Chart

The Day One schedule is complete. Day Two follows the same schedule so that participants can attend a workshop session they missed on Day One. Rather than create the Day Two schedule by adding and labeling boxes, you copy the Day One schedule and add it under the Daily Schedule box. Working with a whole section of an organization chart is referred to as working with a **leg**, or an appendage, of the chart. The steps on the next two pages explain how to copy a leg of the chart.

TO COPY A LEG OF THE ORGANIZATION CHART ▼

STEP 1 ►

Select the Edit menu and point to the Select Levels command (Figure 1-39).

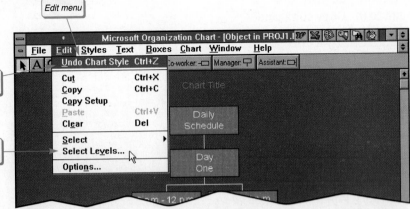

FIGURE 1-39

STEP 2 ►

Choose the Select Levels command.

The Select Levels dialog box displays (Figure 1-40). By default, all boxes in the chart are selected as indicated by the Select all boxes at levels: 1 through 4. The number 1 is selected.

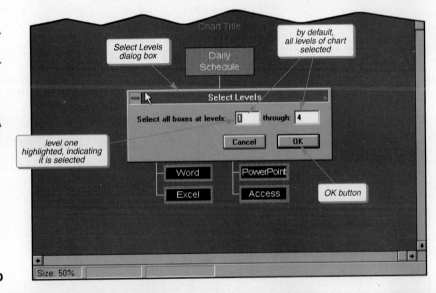

FIGURE 1-40

STEP 3 ►

With the number 1 still selected, type 2 and choose the OK button.

Boxes on levels 2 through 4 are selected (Figure 1-41).

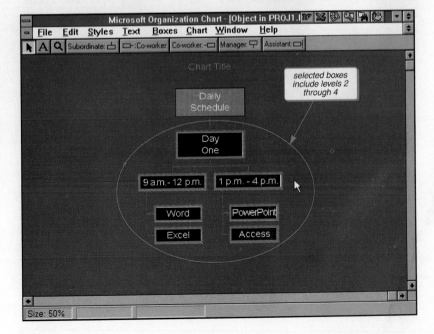

FIGURE 1-41

STEP 4 ▶

Select the Edit menu and point to the Copy command (Figure 1-42).

STEP 5 ▶

Choose the Copy command.

Microsoft Organization Chart copies the Day One leg of the organization chart to the Clipboard. Recall that the Clipboard is a temporary Windows storage area.

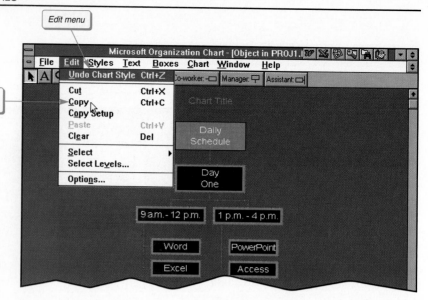

FIGURE 1-42

The next section explains how to paste the Day One leg of the organization chart to another location on the chart.

Pasting a Leg of the Organization Chart

Now that a copy of the Day One leg of the organization chart is on the Clipboard, the next step is to paste it from the Clipboard to the Daily Schedule slide.

TO PASTE A LEG OF THE ORGANIZATION CHART ▼

STEP 1 ▶

Click the root manager box (labeled Daily Schedule). Then, select the Edit menu and point to the Paste Boxes command.

The Daily Schedule box is selected (Figure 1-43).

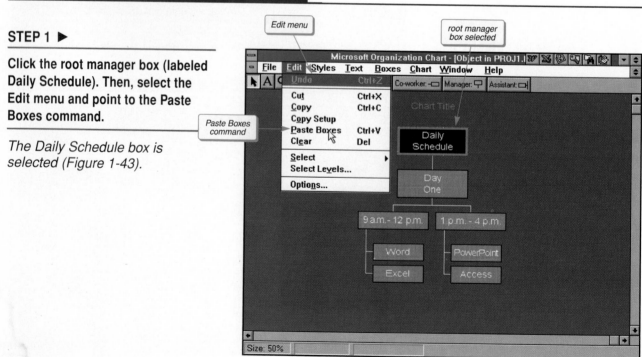

FIGURE 1-43

STEP 2 ▶

Choose the Paste Boxes command.

The organization chart displays with two legs, both labeled Day One (Figure 1-44).

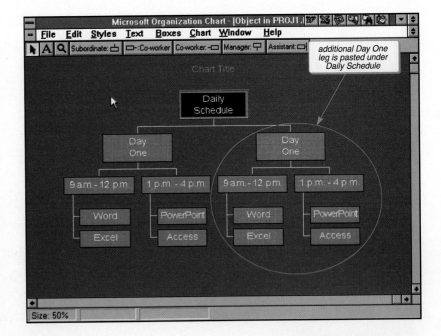

FIGURE 1-44

Editing Text

After you have copied and pasted a leg of the organization chart, you need to edit the title of the first subordinate level so that it displays as Day Two. Editing a box requires you to first select the box and then make your edits.

TO EDIT TEXT IN AN ORGANIZATION CHART ▼

STEP 1 ▶

Click the Day One box located at the top of the right leg of the organization chart. Then, drag through the word One.

The word One is selected (Figure 1-45).

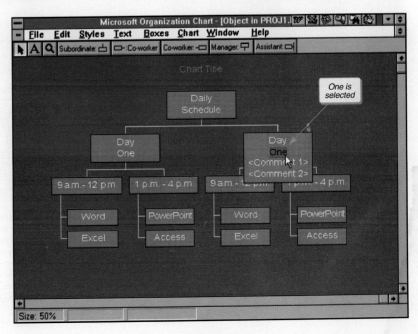

FIGURE 1-45

STEP 2 ▶

Type Two

The word Two replaces the word One (Figure 1-46).

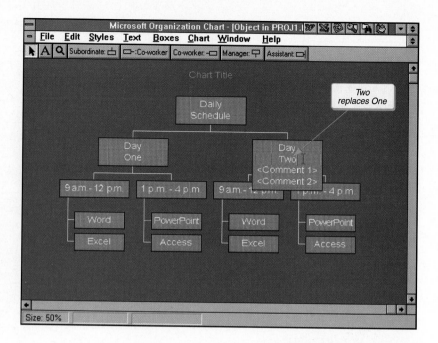

FIGURE 1-46

The text on the organization chart is complete. The next section explains how to format an organization chart.

Formatting an Organization Chart

Microsoft Organization Chart allows you to format the contents of a box simply by selecting it. To make your organization chart look like Figure 1-23 on page PP19, increase the font size of text in every box. The following sections explain how to quickly select all boxes in the chart and change the text font size.

TO SELECT ALL BOXES IN THE ORGANIZATION CHART ▼

STEP 1 ▶

Select the Edit menu and choose the Select command. Point to the All command (Figure 1-47).

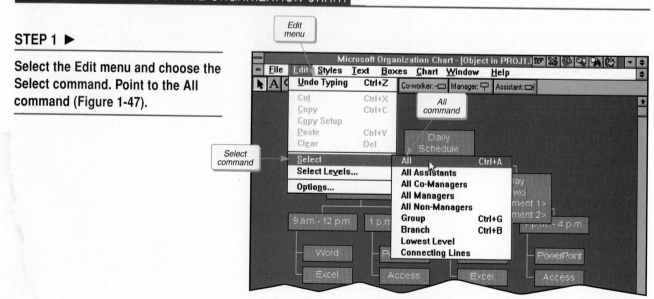

FIGURE 1-47

STEP 2 ▶

Choose the All command.

Microsoft Organization Chart selects all boxes in the chart (Figure 1-48).

all boxes are selected

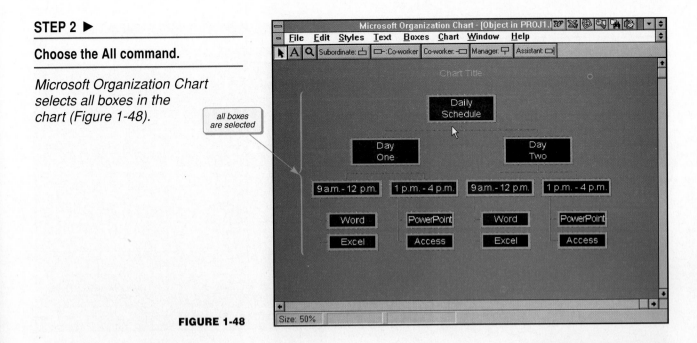

FIGURE 1-48

Changing the Font Size of the Text in an Organization Chart

Now that all the boxes are selected, change the font size for all text in the organization chart. The following steps explain how to change font size in an organization chart.

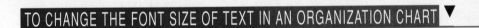

TO CHANGE THE FONT SIZE OF TEXT IN AN ORGANIZATION CHART ▼

STEP 1 ▶

With all the boxes in the organization chart still selected, select the Text menu and choose the Font command. Point to 22 in the Size list box.

The Font dialog box displays (Figure 1-49). The default settings are Arial font, Regular style, and 14 points. A sample of the settings displays in the Sample box in the Font dialog box.

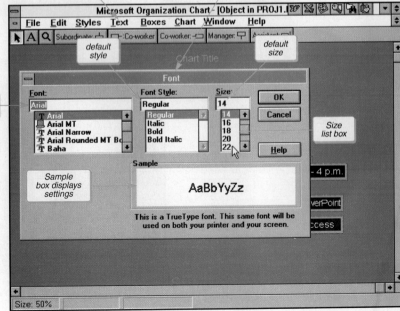

FIGURE 1-49

STEP 2 ▶

Click 22 and choose the OK button.

The font size changes from 14 to 22 points and the Font dialog box closes (Figure 1-50). Because of the font size change, only the Day One leg of the organization chart displays in the work area. Use the horizontal scroll bar to view the Day Two leg of the chart.

FIGURE 1-50

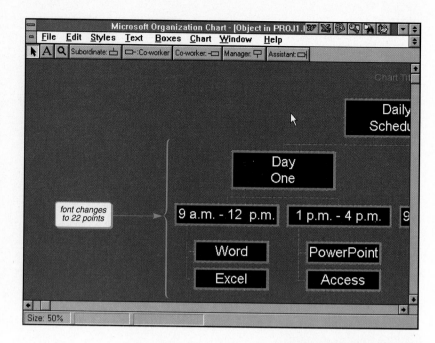

The organization chart is now complete. The next step is to return to PowerPoint.

Exiting Microsoft Organization Chart and Returning to PowerPoint

After you create and format an organization chart, exit Microsoft Organization Chart and return to the PowerPoint window. The following steps explain how to return to PowerPoint.

TO EXIT MICROSOFT ORGANIZATION CHART AND RETURN TO POWERPOINT ▼

STEP 1 ▶

Select the File menu and point to the Exit and Return to PROJ1.PPT command (Figure 1-51).

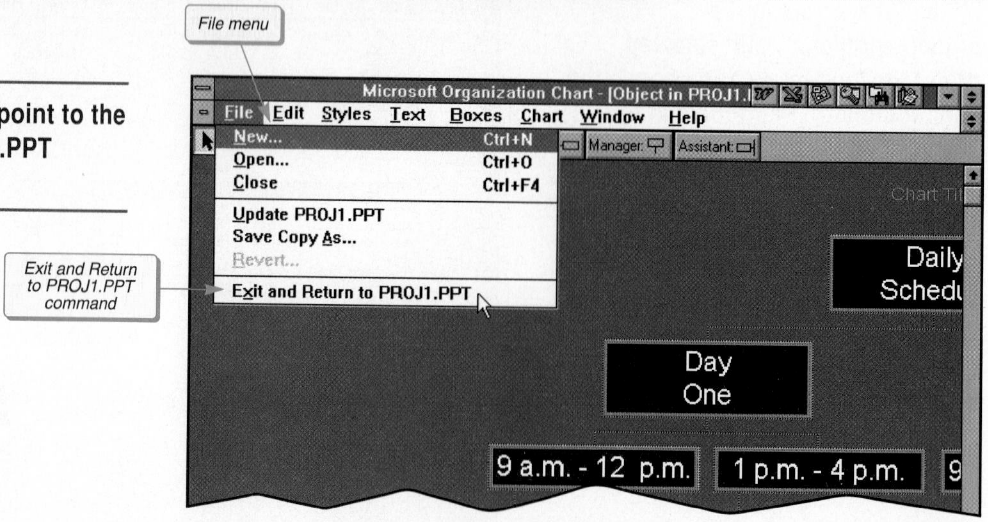

FIGURE 1-51

STEP 2 ▶

Choose the Exit and Return to PROJ1.PPT command. When the Microsoft Organization Chart dialog box displays, point to the Yes button.

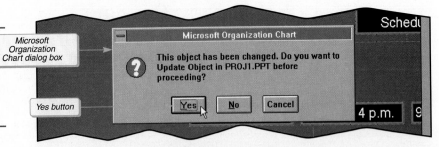

The Microsoft Organization Chart dialog box warns you that the organization chart object has changed and asks you if you want to update the object in the PowerPoint presentation, PROJ1.PPT, before proceeding (Figure 1-52).

FIGURE 1-52

STEP 3 ▶

Choose the Yes button. When the next Microsoft Organization Chart dialog box displays, point to the No button.

Microsoft Organization Chart updates the organization chart object and then displays another dialog box asking if you want to save the large Clipboard copied from Object in PROJ1.PPT (Figure 1-53). The Clipboard object in question is the Day One leg you copied to create the Day Two leg of the organization chart in Step 4 on page PP30.

FIGURE 1-53

STEP 4 ▶

Choose the No button.

Microsoft Organization Chart closes and the PowerPoint window displays with the organization chart displayed on Slide 2 (Figure 1-54).

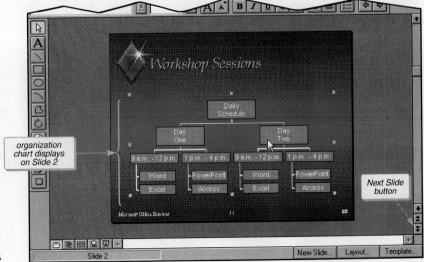

FIGURE 1-54

In Step 4, you chose the No button because you did not have a reason to keep the Day One Clipboard object. If, for some reason, you wanted to save the Clipboard object, you would choose the Yes button. The Clipboard object would remain on the Clipboard until it was replaced by a copy or cut command.

▶ UNGROUPING CLIP ART

FIGURE 1-55

igure 1-55 contains the Group Meeting image from the Microsoft ClipArt Gallery. This image has been modified by inserting an Excel chart onto the screen. The reasons to modify clip art are numerous. Many times you cannot find clip art to precisely illustrate your topic. For example, you want an image of a man and a woman shaking hands but the only available clip art image has two men and a woman shaking hands. From time to time you want to remove or change a portion of a clip art image. For example, you are presenting to a group of people who do not believe in wearing jewelry and you want to delete all jewelry from the clip art image. Sometimes you want to combine two or more clip art images. For example, you choose to use one clip art image for the background and another image as the foreground. Still other times, you may want to combine clip art with another type of object. Table 1-3 identifies the types of objects you can combine with clip art.

Because clip art objects are composed of many objects grouped together to form one object, PowerPoint allows you alter clip art by ungrouping the objects. **Ungrouping** a clip art object separates the grouped object into multiple objects. Once ungrouped, you can manipulate the individual objects as needed to form a new object.

Modifying the clip art image on Slide 3 requires several steps. First, before you can ungroup the Group Meeting clip art, you must insert it onto the slide. Next, resize the clip art to cover most of the slide. Then, ungroup the clip art. Once the clip art is ungrouped, embed an Excel chart onto the screen.

▶ **TABLE 1-3**

AutoSketch	Freelance Presentation
Lotus Annotator Note	Lotus Media
Lotus Sound	Media Clip
Microsoft ClipArt Gallery	Microsoft Drawing
Microsoft Equation 2.0	Microsoft Excel 5.0 Chart
Microsoft Excel 5.0 Worksheet	Microsoft Excel Chart
Microsoft Excel Macrosheet	Microsoft Graph 5.0
Microsoft Organization Chart 1.0	Microsoft Project
Microsoft Word 2.0	Microsoft Word 6.0 Document
Microsoft Word 6.0 Picture	Microsoft WordArt 1.0
Microsoft Work Sheet	MS PowerPoint 4.0 Presentation
MS PowerPoint 4.0 Slide	Package
Paintbrush Picture	Sound

The steps on the following pages explain in detail how to insert, resize, ungroup clip art, and embed an Excel chart on this slide.

Inserting Clip Art

The first step in manipulating a clip art image is to insert the image on a slide. You will insert the Group Meeting clip art from the Microsoft ClipArt Gallery. In a later step, you will modify the clip art by combining it with another object. The following steps summarize how to insert the Group Meeting clip art onto Slide 3 of this presentation.

TO INSERT CLIP ART ON SLIDE 3

Step 1: Click the Next Slide button.

Step 2: Click anywhere within the text placeholder to select it.

Step 3: Click the Insert Clip Art button on the Standard toolbar.

Step 4: Choose the Find button in the Microsoft ClipArt Gallery - Picture in PROJ1.PPT dialog box.

Step 5: Select the With a Description containing option button in the Find Picture dialog box. Type group meeting

Step 6: Choose the OK button in the Find Picture dialog box.

Step 7: Choose the OK button in the Microsoft ClipArt Gallery - Picture in PROJ1.PPT dialog box.

Slide 3 displays the Group Meeting clip art image (Figure 1-56).

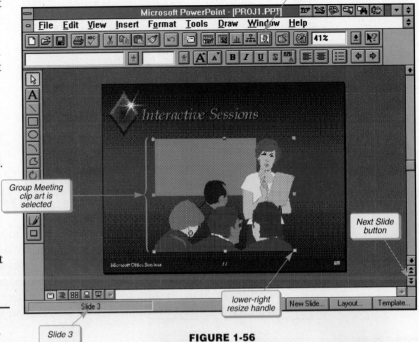

FIGURE 1-56

Resizing Clip Art

Now that the clip art image is inserted onto Slide 3, you will resize it. Changing the size of the object can be done simply by dragging a resize handle. This resizes the image in the direction in which you drag. Dragging a resize handle, however, changes the proportions of the image. Recall that evenly resizing the object from its center point is called resizing about center. This method of resizing the clip art image maintains the object's proportions.

The following steps summarize how to resize clip art about center.

TO RESIZE CLIP ART ABOUT CENTER

Step 1: If not still selected, click the Group Meeting clip art image. Next, while holding down the CTRL key, position the mouse pointer over the lower right resize handle of the image.

Step 2: While still holding down the CTRL key, drag the lower right resize handle down to the right until the center bottom resize handle touches the top of the two slashes that indicate the date. Then, release the left mouse button. Finally, release the CTRL key.

The Group Meeting clip art image is resized (Figure 1-57 on the next page).

FIGURE 1-57

Recall, that if you release the CTRL key before you release the left mouse button, the object is not resized about center. Instead, it is resized in the direction the resize handle was dragged. To correct this error, click the Undo button and resize the image again, making certain to first release the left mouse button and then release the CTRL key.

Using the View Menu to Display the Drawing+ Toolbar

In order to modify the clip art on Slide 3, use the Ungroup button (🔲) on the Drawing+ toolbar. The Drawing+ toolbar contains special tools for modifying visuals, such as changing fill color or altering the width of a line. Display the Drawing+ toolbar by selecting the View menu and choosing the Toolbars command. The following steps explain in detail how to display the Drawing+ toolbar. If the Drawing+ toolbar already displays in the PowerPoint window, read the next three steps without doing them and then proceed to the next section: Ungrouping Clip Art.

TO DISPLAY THE DRAWING+ TOOLBAR ▼

STEP 1 ▶

Select the View menu and point to the Toolbars command (Figure 1-58).

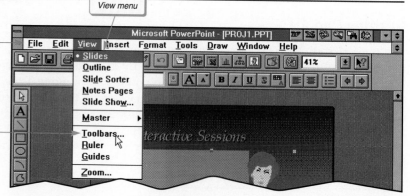

FIGURE 1-58

STEP 2 ▶

Choose the Toolbars command. When the Toolbars dialog box displays, click the Drawing+ check box. Then, point to the OK button.

When a Toolbars check box contains an x, the toolbar is selected to display in the PowerPoint window (Figure 1-59).

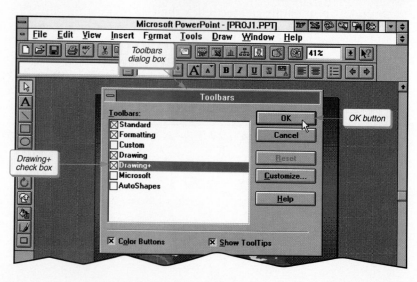

FIGURE 1-59

STEP 3 ►

Choose the OK button.

The Drawing+ toolbar displays in the PowerPoint window (Figure 1-60). The Ungroup button displays on the Drawing+ toolbar.

Ungroup
button

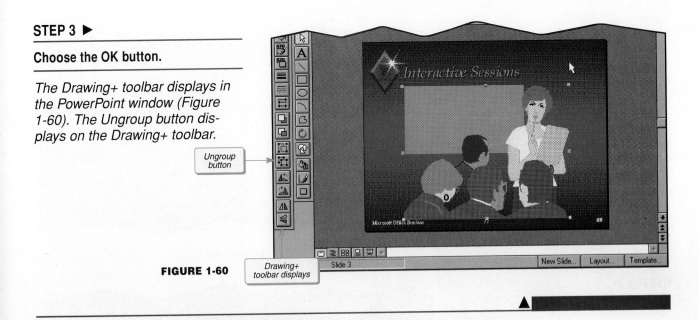

FIGURE 1-60

Drawing+
toolbar displays

You can also display the Drawing+ toolbar from a shortcut menu by pointing to any toolbar in the PowerPoint window, clicking the right mouse button, and choosing the Drawing+ command. This method, however, allows you to select only one toolbar, whereas the Toolbars command from the View menu allows you to choose more than one toolbar at one time because the Toolbars dialog box displays. Additionally, you can use the toolbar shortcut menu and select the Toolbars command to display the Toolbars dialog box.

Ungrouping Clip Art

The next step is to ungroup the Group Meeting clip art image on Slide 3. When you ungroup a clip art image, PowerPoint breaks it into its component objects. These new groups can be repeatedly ungrouped until they decompose into individual objects. Depending on the clip art image, it may be composed of a few individual objects or several complex groups of objects.

The following steps explain how to ungroup clip art.

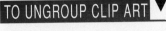

STEP 1 ►

With the Group Meeting clip art image selected, point to the Ungroup button on the Drawing+ toolbar (Figure 1-61)

Ungroup
button

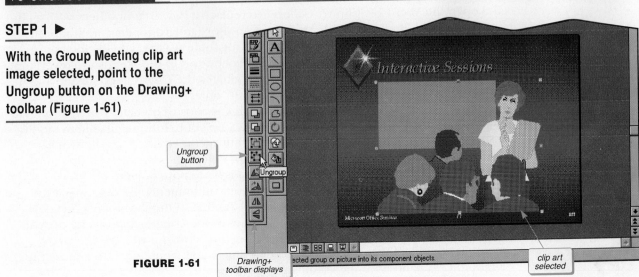

FIGURE 1-61

Drawing+
toolbar displays

...ected group or picture into its component objects.

clip art
selected

STEP 2 ▶

Click the Ungroup button. Point to the OK button.

A Microsoft PowerPoint dialog box displays explaining that this clip art object is an imported object and that converting it to a PowerPoint object permanently discards any embedded data or linking information it contains (Figure 1-62). Finally, you are asked if you want to convert the object to a PowerPoint object.

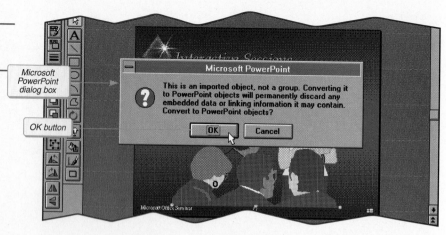

Microsoft PowerPoint dialog box

OK button

FIGURE 1-62

STEP 3 ▶

Choose the OK button.

The clip art now displays as several objects (Figure 1-63). Selection rectangles display around the ungrouped objects. Recall that a selection rectangle is the box framed by the resize handles when a graphic is selected.

selection rectangles display around the ungrouped object

clip art displays as several objects

FIGURE 1-63

When you ungroup a clip art object and choose the Yes button in the Microsoft PowerPoint dialog box (Steps 2 and 3 above), PowerPoint converts the clip art object to a PowerPoint object. A **PowerPoint object** is an object *not* associated with a supplementary application, such as Word, Excel, or the Microsoft ClipArt Gallery. As a result, you lose the ability to double-click the clip art image and open the Microsoft ClipArt Gallery. To replace a PowerPoint object with a clip art object, click the Insert Clip Art button on the Standard toolbar or choose the Clip Art command from the Insert menu. If, for some reason, you decide not to ungroup the clip art object, choose the Cancel button in the Microsoft PowerPoint dialog box. Choosing the Cancel button terminates the Ungroup command and the clip art object displays on the slide as a clip art object.

Because clip art is a collection of complex groups of objects, you may need to ungroup a complex object into a less complex object before being able to modify a specific object. For example, in the clip art image in Figure 1-62, the woman on the left is wearing an earring. To modify or delete the earring, you first must further ungroup the clip art until her earring is a separate object.

If you accidentally ungroup an object, you can immediately **regroup** it by choosing the Group button on the Drawing+ toolbar. If, however, only one composite object is selected, or you made changes to the composite objects, you can regroup the composite objects using the **Regroup command** from the Draw menu. If the object was ungrouped several times, you would need to choose the Regroup command until the command was **ghosted**, or disabled on the menu.

You can stop regrouping anytime before the command is disabled. The Regroup command also is available from a shortcut menu. To display the shortcut menu, point somewhere within the ungrouped object and click the right mouse button. Then, choose the Regroup command from the shortcut menu.

Recall that a clip art object is imported from the Microsoft ClipArt Gallery. Ungrouping imported, embedded, or linked objects eliminates the embedding data or linking information the object contains that ties it back to its original source.

Caution should be used when objects are not completely regrouped. Dragging or resizing affects only the selected object, not the entire collection of objects.

Deselecting Clip Art Objects

All of the ungrouped objects in Figure 1-63 are selected. Before you can manipulate an individual object, you must **deselect** all selected objects to remove the selection rectangles, and then select the object you want to manipulate. For example, in this project you want to modify the light blue screen. The following step explains how to deselect objects.

TO DESELECT A CLIP ART OBJECT ▼

STEP 1 ▶

Point anywhere in the PowerPoint window that is not within a selected object and click the left mouse button.

Slide 3 displays without selection rectangles around the clip art images (Figure 1-64).

FIGURE 1-64

The Group Meeting clip art image is now ungrouped into many objects. The next section explains how to embed an Excel chart into the presentation and display it on the light blue screen of the Group Meeting clip art image.

▶ EMBEDDING AN EXISTING EXCEL CHART

PowerPoint allows you to embed many types of objects into a presentation. In this project, you want to embed an existing Excel chart onto the screen in the Group Meeting clip art image. This Excel chart is on the Student Diskette that accompanies this book.

Embedding an existing Excel chart is similar to embedding other objects. Because the Excel chart already exists, however, you retrieve it from the file in which it was saved, rather than opening the supplementary application and creating the object. Additionally, to make placing and sizing the Excel chart less difficult, you move the screen object away from the other ungrouped objects. Once the screen object is fully visible, you embed and resize the Excel chart.

The next two sections explain how to move an ungrouped clip art object and embed an Excel chart.

Moving an Ungrouped Clip Art Object

To make working with the screen object easier, move it away from the other clip art objects to the upper left corner of the PowerPoint window. The following steps explain how to move an ungrouped clip art object.

TO MOVE AN UNGROUPED CLIP ART OBJECT ▼

STEP 1 ►

Select the screen object by clicking it.

The selection rectangle displays around the screen object (Figure 1-65). If you inadvertently select a different object, point to the center of the screen object and click the left mouse button.

screen object is selected

FIGURE 1-65

STEP 2 ►

Drag the screen object to the upper left corner of Slide 3 (Figure 1-66)

clip art objects in original position

screen object displays in upper left corner

FIGURE 1-66

The reason you move the screen object away from the other objects is to avoid placing the Excel chart on top of the other screen objects. Later in this project, you will combine the screen object and the Excel chart. Moving the screen object now makes this process less complicated.

Embedding an Excel Chart

The next step to modifying the clip art image for Slide 3 is to embed an Excel chart. The Excel chart is already created and saved in the Excel5 subdirectory on the Student Diskette that accompanies this book. The following steps explain how to embed an existing Excel chart.

TO EMBED AN EXCEL CHART ▼

STEP 1 ▶

Select the Insert menu and choose the Object command.

The Insert Object dialog box displays (Figure 1-67). Depending on your installation, the list of object types on your computer may look different from the one in this figure.

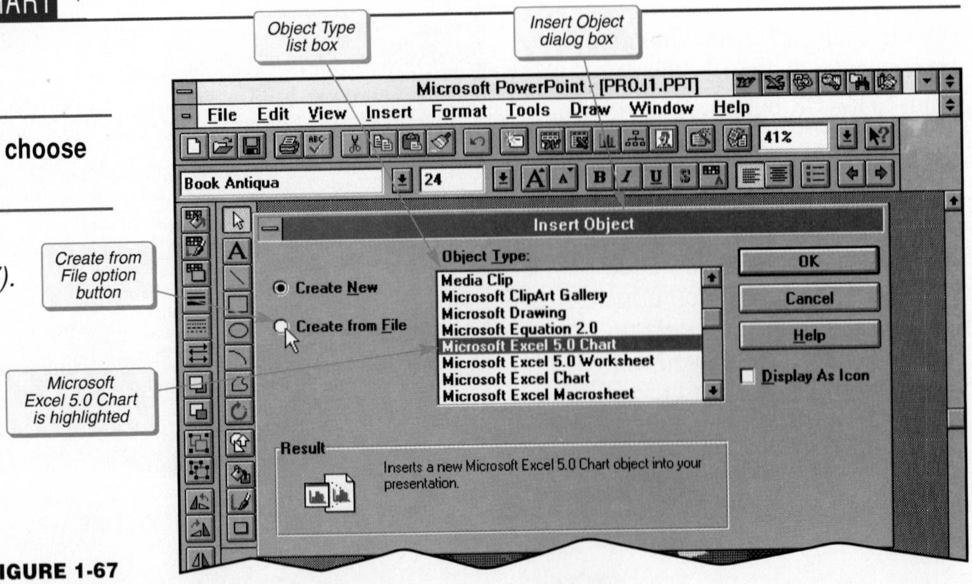

Object Type list box

Insert Object dialog box

Create from File option button

Microsoft Excel 5.0 Chart is highlighted

Insert Object

Object Type:

Media Clip
Microsoft ClipArt Gallery
Microsoft Drawing
Microsoft Equation 2.0
Microsoft Excel 5.0 Chart
Microsoft Excel 5.0 Worksheet
Microsoft Excel Chart
Microsoft Excel Macrosheet

○ Create New
○ Create from File

OK
Cancel
Help

☐ Display As Icon

Result — Inserts a new Microsoft Excel 5.0 Chart object into your presentation.

FIGURE 1-67

STEP 2 ▶

Click the Create from File option button.

The Insert Object dialog box now displays the File box (Figure 1-68). Drive A is the current drive and ppoint4 is the current subdirectory. If your current drive is not drive A, type a:.

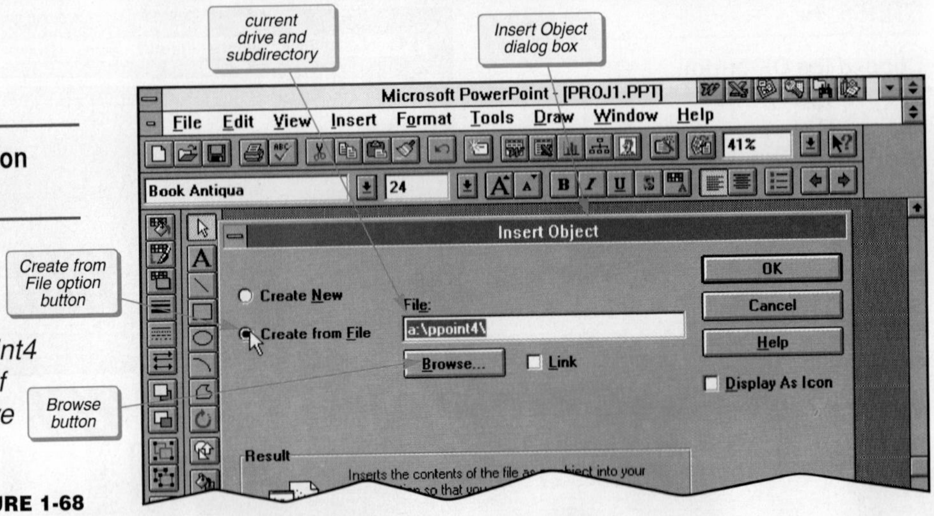

current drive and subdirectory

Insert Object dialog box

Create from File option button

Browse button

Insert Object

○ Create New
○ Create from File

File:
a:\ppoint4\

Browse...   ☐ Link

OK
Cancel
Help

☐ Display As Icon

Result — Inserts the contents of the file as an object into your ... so that you ...

FIGURE 1-68

STEP 3 ▶

Choose the Browse button. When the Browse dialog box displays, double-click a:\ in the Directories box to select the root directory, double-click excel5 in the Directories box, and point to cle1-2.xls in the Source list box.

The Browse dialog box displays the files in the excel5 subdirectory (Figure 1-69).

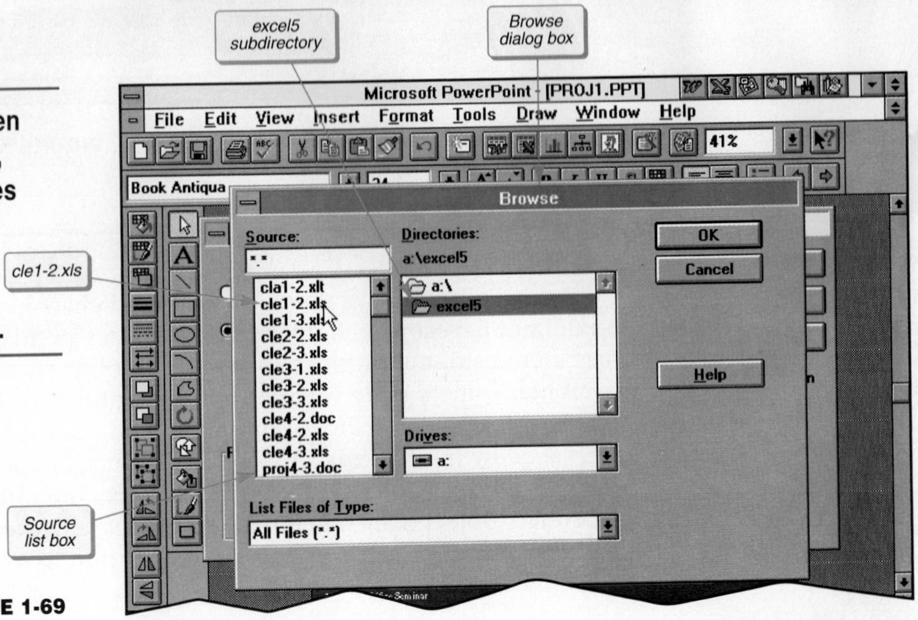

excel5 subdirectory

Browse dialog box

cle1-2.xls

Source list box

Browse

Source:
.

cla1-2.xlt
cle1-2.xls
cle1-3.xls
cle2-2.xls
cle2-3.xls
cle3-1.xls
cle3-2.xls
cle3-3.xls
cle4-2.doc
cle4-2.xls
cle4-3.xls
proj4-3.doc

Directories:
a:\excel5

📁 a:\
📁 excel5

Drives:
💾 a:

OK
Cancel

Help

List Files of Type:
All Files (*.*)

FIGURE 1-69

STEP 4 ▶

Double-click cle1-2.xls. When the Insert Object dialog box displays, point to the OK button.

The Insert Object dialog box now displays Microsoft Excel 5.0 above the File box and the name in the File box is a:\excel5\cle1-2.xls (Figure 1-70). When you double-clicked cle1-2.xls, you selected it as the file from which you will embed the Excel chart onto Slide 3.

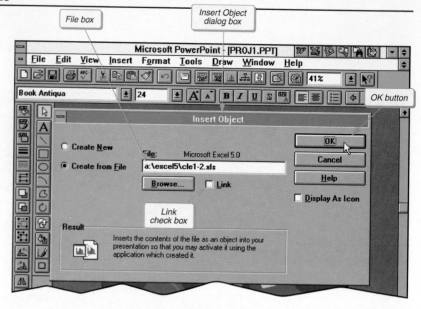

FIGURE 1-70

STEP 5 ▶

Choose the OK button.

After a short time, Slide 3 displays the King's Computer Outlet worksheet and chart in the middle of the slide (Figure 1-71).

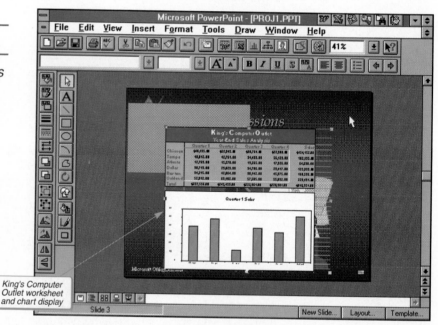

FIGURE 1-71

PowerPoint displays the worksheet and chart in the middle of Slide 3 because you did not have a placeholder selected. Later in this project, you will resize the chart and position it on the clip art screen object.

When you click the Create from File option button in the Insert Object dialog box, the dialog box changes (Figure 1-68 on page PP43). The Object Type list box is replaced by the File box. Another change to the dialog box is the addition of the Link check box. The **Link check box** inserts the object as a linked, rather than an embedded, object. Like an embedded object, a **linked object** also is created in another application but maintains a connection to its source. If the original object is changed, the linked object on the slide also changes. The linked object itself is stored in the source file where it was created. For example, the Excel chart you inserted onto the screen is stored in the cle1-2.xls file on the Student Diskette. If you linked the cle1-2.xls file to your presentation, every time the cle1-2.xls file was changed in Excel, the changes would display on the chart on Slide 3. Your PowerPoint presentation stores a representation of the original cle1-2.xls file and information about its location. Therefore, if you later move or delete the source file, the link will be broken and the object will not be available. Hence, if you make a presentation on a computer other than the one on which the presentation was created, and the presentation contains linked objects, be certain to include a copy of the source files. The source files must be stored in the exact location as originally specified when you linked them to your presentation.

When you select a source file from the Browse dialog box, PowerPoint associates the file with a specific application based on the file extension. For example, if you select a source file with the file extension of DOC, PowerPoint recognizes the file to be a Word file. Additionally, if you select a source file with the file extension of XLS, PowerPoint recognizes the file to be an Excel file.

Scaling an Embedded Object

The Excel chart is too large to place on the clip art screen in Figure 1-71. Before you position the Excel chart on the screen, you need to resize it. Resizing the chart before you move it helps to center the chart both vertically and horizontally. Resize the Excel chart using the Scale command from the Draw menu.

The following steps summarize how to resize an object using the Scale command.

TO SCALE AN EMBEDDED OBJECT

Step 1: With the Excel chart selected, select the Draw menu and choose the Scale command.

Step 2: With the number 100 highlighted, type 40 in the Scale To box.

Step 3: Choose the OK button.

Excel chart and worksheet resized to 40%

FIGURE 1-72

The Excel chart is scaled to 40% of its original size (Figure 1-72).

If you do not know the number to type in the Scale To box in Step 2 above, you can type a number and then click the Preview button. Then see if you need to increase the number in the Scale To box to increase the size of the object, or decrease the number in the Scale To box to decrease the size of the object. You can continue to change the number in the Scale To box and click the Preview button until the object displays at the desired scale. An alternative to scaling the Excel chart is to resize the chart about center.

▶ GROUPING OBJECTS

The next step in creating Slide 3 requires you to move the Excel chart onto the clip art screen and to combine the two objects into one object. Combining two or more objects into one object is called **grouping**. Grouping objects allows you to move the combined objects at the same time. If the objects are not grouped, you must move them one object at a time. This is inefficient and does not take advantage of PowerPoint tools that help you quickly create presentations. To make grouping objects more efficient, use the **Group button** (▦) on the Drawing+ toolbar. After selecting the objects you want to group, click the Group button.

Finalizing Slide 3 requires several steps. First, layer the Excel chart over the clip art screen and then group the chart and the screen into one object. Then, move the grouped screen and chart to the screen's original position in the Group Meeting clip art image. Because the Group Meeting clip art image is composed of multiple layered objects, you will send the grouped screen and chart to the bottom of the stack of clip art images so that it displays behind the speaker's shoulder. Finally, group all the objects in the Group Meeting clip art image into one object.

The next sections explain how to create a layered object, group two layered objects into one modified screen object, return the modified screen object to the Group Meeting clip art image, send the modified screen object to the background of the Group Meeting clip art image, and combine the ungrouped objects of the clip art image into one new clip art image.

Overlaying Objects

A layered object is created by overlaying one or more objects. An **overlay** is something that is laid over or covers something else. You will create a layered object by overlaying the Excel chart on the screen object. The following steps summarize how to overlay the Excel chart on the clip art screen to create the layered object.

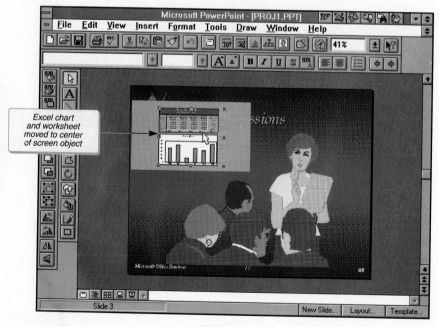

Excel chart and worksheet moved to center of screen object

FIGURE 1-73

TO OVERLAY OBJECTS

Step 1: Point to the Excel chart and hold down the left mouse button.

Step 2: While holding down the left mouse button, drag the Excel chart to the center of the screen object, which you previously moved to the upper left corner of the slide.

Step 3: Drop the Excel chart onto the center of the screen object by releasing the left mouse button.

The Excel chart is moved to the center of the screen object (Figure 1-73). The Excel chart overlays the screen image.

Grouping the Two Layered Objects into One Modified Screen Object

Now that the chart has been overlaid onto the screen, group the two objects into one. The following steps explain how to select the objects and then use the Group button to combine them into one object.

TO GROUP LAYERED OBJECTS INTO ONE OBJECT ▼

STEP 1 ►

With the Excel chart still selected, hold down the SHIFT key and click the screen object image. Point to the Group button on the Drawing+ toolbar.

A selection rectangle displays around each of the two objects (Figure 1-74).

Group button

Drawing+ toolbar

selected objects

FIGURE 1-74

STEP 2 ►

Click the Group button.

The two objects become one object (Figure 1-75). One selection rectangle displays around the grouped objects.

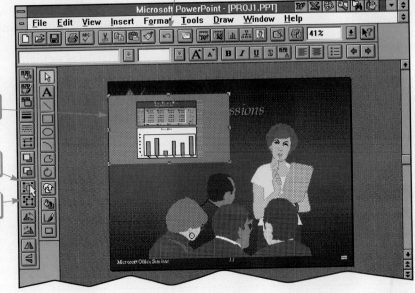

Undo button

two objects grouped into one

Group button

Ungroup button

FIGURE 1-75

If you make an error and do not want the objects grouped, you can click the Undo button on the Standard toolbar or click the Ungroup button on the Drawing+ toolbar.

Returning the Modified Screen Object to the Clip Art Image

The next step in creating Slide 3 is to return the modified screen object to the Group Meeting clip art image. The following steps summarize moving an object.

TO RETURN THE MODIFIED SCREEN OBJECT TO THE CLIP ART IMAGE

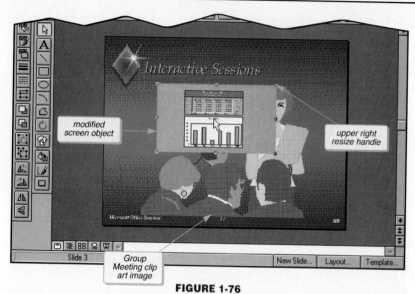

FIGURE 1-76

Step 1: Point to the modified screen object and hold down the left mouse button.

Step 2: Drag the modified screen object down to the right until the upper right resize handle is positioned at the top and center of the speaker's head.

Step 3: Release the left mouse button to drop the modified screen object on top of the Group Meeting clip art image.

The modified screen object overlays the clip art objects that form the Group Meeting image (Figure 1-76).

Sending an Object to the Background

The modified screen object hides portions of the objects beneath it because it overlays the stack of clip art objects that constitute the Group Meeting image. To make the hidden portions visible, send the modified screen object to the bottom of the stack of objects.

The steps below summarize sending an object to the background.

FIGURE 1-77

TO SEND AN OBJECT TO THE BACKGROUND

Step 1: With the modified screen object selected, select the Draw menu.

Step 2: Choose the Send to Back command.

The modified screen object displays behind the speaker's shoulder at the bottom of the stack of clip art objects (Figure 1-77).

Selecting Objects

Before you can group all the clip art objects into a new Group Meeting clip art image, you first must select the objects to be grouped. When you have a few objects to select, you can use the SHIFT+Click method. However, when you have many objects to select, it is easier to use the Select All command from the Edit menu. When the Select All command is chosen, every object on the slide is selected. For example, if you select all objects on Slide 3, you will select all of the clip art objects and the title object.

If you select objects you do not want included in the object you are grouping, you must deselect those objects. The following steps explain how to select all the objects on Slide 3 and then deselect the title object.

TO SELECT ALL OBJECTS ▼

STEP 1 ▶

Select the Edit menu and point to the Select All command (Figure 1-78).

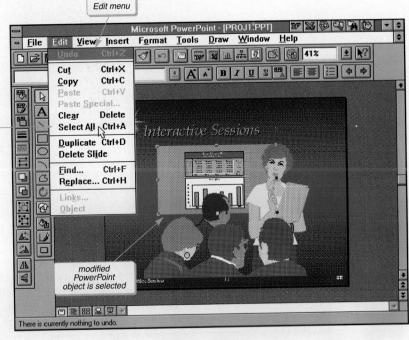

FIGURE 1-78

STEP 2 ▶

Choose the Select All command.

All objects on Slide 3 are selected (Figure 1-79). A selection rectangle displays around each object.

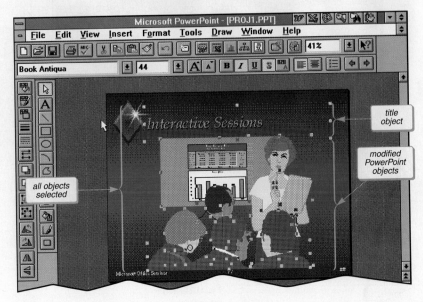

FIGURE 1-79

STEP 3 ▶

Point to one of the words in the title. SHIFT+Click in the title text.

The title text is not selected (Figure 1-80). All clip art objects on Slide 3 are still selected.

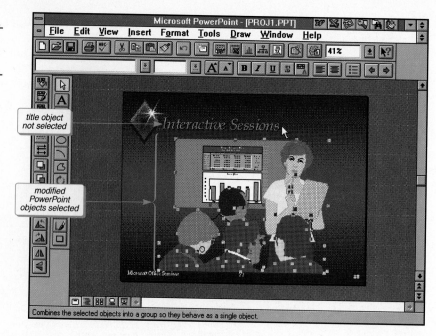

FIGURE 1-80

Grouping Selected Objects

Now that the clip art objects that form the Group Meeting image are selected, the final step in creating Slide 3 is to group those objects into one object. The step below summarizes how to group selected objects.

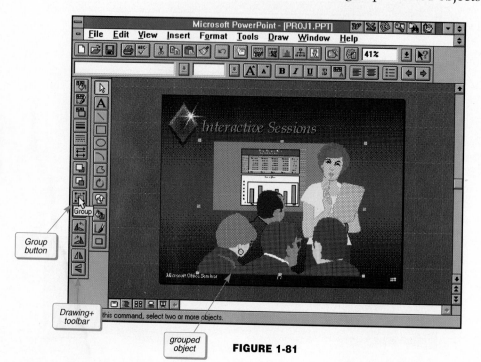

FIGURE 1-81

TO GROUP SELECTED OBJECTS

Step 1: Click the Group button on the Drawing+ toolbar.

The selected objects are grouped into one object (Figure 1-81). Notice only one selection rectangle displays.

Slide 3 is now complete. The next section introduces you to inserting a picture onto a slide.

ADDING A PICTURE TO A SLIDE

A nother graphic object often inserted onto a slide is a picture. In PowerPoint, a **picture** is any graphic image from another application (see Table 1-3 on page PP36). Pictures usually are saved as one of two **graphic formats**: bit-mapped or vector.

A **bit-mapped graphic** is a piece of art that has been stored as a pattern of spots called **pixels**. A pixel, short for **picture element**, is one spot in a grid. Thousands of such spots are individually "painted" to form an image that is produced on the computer screen or on paper by a printer. Just as a bit is the smallest unit of information a computer can process, a pixel is the smallest element that display or print hardware and software can manipulate in creating letters, numbers, or graphics. For example, the letter A in Figure 1-82 is actually made up of a pattern of pixels in a grid.

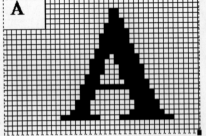

FIGURE 1-82

Bit-mapped graphics are created in paint programs such as Microsoft Windows Paintbrush. Bit-mapped graphics also can be produced from **digitizing** art, pictures, or photographs by passing the artwork through a scanner. A **scanner** is a hardware device that converts lines and shading into combinations of the binary digits 0 and 1 by sensing different intensities of light and dark. The scanner shines a beam of light on the image being scanned. The beam passes back and forth across the image sending a digitized signal, which resembles a bit-mapped graphic, to the computer's memory. A **digitized signal** is the conversion of input, such as the lines in a drawing, into a series of discrete units represented by the binary digits 0 and 1. **Scanned images** are bit-mapped images and have jagged edges. The jagged edges are caused by the individual pixels that create the image. Bit-mapped graphics also are known as **raster images**. Additionally, bit-mapped files cannot be ungrouped into smaller object groups.

A **vector graphic** is a piece of art that has been created by a draw program such as CorelDRAW! or AutoCAD. Vector graphic objects are created as collections of lines, rather than as patterns of individual spots (pixels), as is the case with bit-mapped graphics. Vector graphic files store data as image descriptions, or calculations. These files describe an image mathematically as a set of instructions for creating the objects in the image. These mathematical descriptions determine the position, length, and direction in which lines are to be drawn. These calculations allow the draw program to re-create the image on-screen as necessary. Because vector graphic objects are described mathematically, they also can be layered, rotated, and magnified relatively easily. Vector graphics also are known as object-oriented images. Clip art images in the Microsoft ClipArt Gallery that have the file extension PCS or WMF are examples of vector files. Vector files can be ungrouped and manipulated by their component objects.

PowerPoint allows you to insert either bit-mapped or vector files because it uses **graphic filters** to convert the various graphic formats into a format PowerPoint can use. These filters are installed with the initial PowerPoint installation or can be added later by running the Setup program.

 PRESENTATION TIP

Use a picture when you want to achieve an emotional response. For example, if you are making a presentation to raise funds for building a homeless children's shelter in your community, create one of the slides with just a picture of a homeless child. The picture of the homeless child will appeal to the compassion of the audience more than the words that describe the homeless child's plight.

Changing Slide Layout to Text and Object

PowerPoint slide layouts are designed to help you quickly create your presentations. Because Slide 4 contains both text and a picture, you want to change the slide layout on Slide 4 to the Text and Object slide layout. Remember that PowerPoint automatically resizes objects to fit the layout placeholders. Changing to the Text and Object layout will resize the bulleted list automatically. Then, when you insert the picture, PowerPoint will adjust the picture to fit the size of the placeholder.

The following steps summarize how to display Slide 4 and change the slide layout.

TO DISPLAY SLIDE 4 AND CHANGE SLIDE LAYOUT TO TEXT & OBJECT

Step 1: Click the Next Slide button.
Step 2: Click the Layout button.
Step 3: When the Slide Layout dialog box displays, double-click the eleventh layout, Text & Object.

Slide 4 displays the Text & Object layout (Figure 1-83). The bulleted list is resized to fit the text placeholder. The object placeholder will hold the picture object.

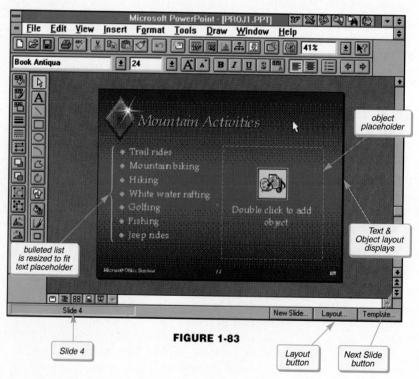

FIGURE 1-83

Inserting a Picture

Slide 4 is included in this presentation to encourage prospective seminar attendees to combine educational activities with recreational activities. Inserting a picture reinforces that message. The picture you will insert on Slide 4 is a scanned image that has been stored as a bit-mapped graphic and saved as a PCX file. The file is on the Student Diskette that accompanies this book. Perform the following steps to insert this picture.

TO INSERT A PICTURE ▼

STEP 1 ►

Select the object placeholder. Next, select the Insert menu and point to the Picture command.

The object placeholder is selected (Figure 1-84).

FIGURE 1-84

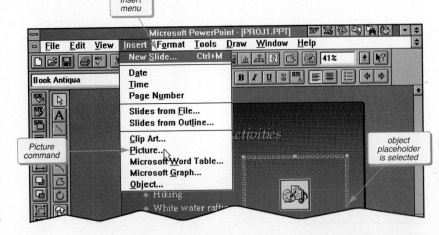

STEP 2 ►

Choose the Picture command. When the Insert Picture dialog box displays, point to horses.pcx in the File Name list box. If drive A is not the current drive, click the Drives box arrow to display the list of available drives and select drive A from the list.

The Insert Picture dialog box displays horses.pcx in the File Name list box (Figure 1-85).

FIGURE 1-85

STEP 3 ►

Double-click horses.pcx.

PowerPoint displays a dialog box stating it is importing the HORSES.PCX file from the PPOINT4 subdirectory on drive A (Figure 1-86). The dialog box also indicates the percent completed of the file importation. Once the file is imported, the HORSES.PCX file displays in the object placeholder (Figure 1-87 on the next page).

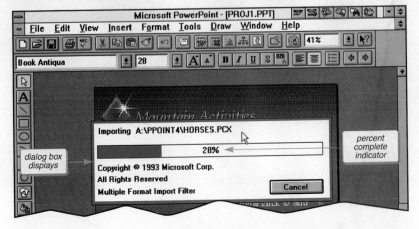

FIGURE 1-86

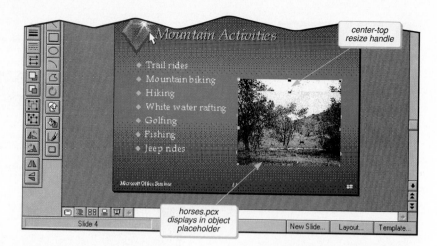

FIGURE 1-87

When the Insert Picture dialog box displays, PowerPoint does not require that you specify which format your artwork is in. The default includes all the formats installed on your system that PowerPoint recognizes.

Notice that the object placeholder size changed to fit the size of the picture. This change occurred because PowerPoint maintains the proportions of the original 3" x 5" picture. The next section explains how to increase the picture's proportions in the object placeholder.

Resizing a Picture

PowerPoint automatically adjusted the height of the object placeholder to fit the original proportions of the picture. In doing so, it makes the slide look **out-of-balance**, meaning that the slide lacks a harmonious or satisfying arrangement of its objects. To correct the slide's balance, change the proportions of the picture.

The following steps explain how to increase the height of a picture.

TO INCREASE THE HEIGHT OF A PICTURE ▼

STEP 1 ▶

With the picture of the horses selected, point to the top-middle resize handle.

The mouse pointer shape changes to a two-headed arrow when on a resize handle (Figure 1-88).

FIGURE 1-88

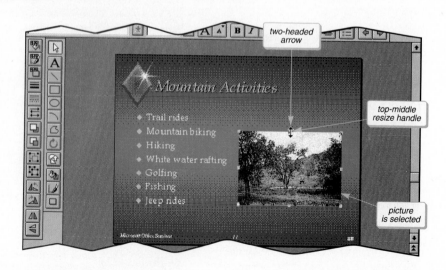

STEP 2 ▶

While holding down the CTRL key, drag the mouse pointer up until the top edge of the picture aligns with the top of the text in the bulleted item Trail rides. Release the left mouse button. Release the CTRL key.

The picture is resized about center (Figure 1-89). Recall that resize about center means changing the size of an object proportionally from its center.

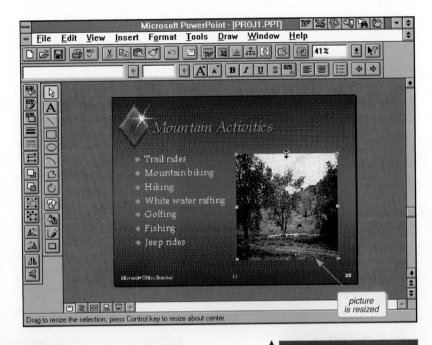

FIGURE 1-89

Changing Line Spacing

Previously you changed the size of the picture in an attempt to balance the slide. This change improved the appearance of the slide but did not balance it. Changing the line spacing in the bulleted list will balance the slide.

The steps below summarize how to change line spacing.

TO CHANGE LINE SPACING

Step 1: Select the text object by clicking anywhere on the bulleted text or on one of the bullets.

Step 2: Select all the text in the bulleted list by dragging the mouse pointer from the words Trail rides through the words Jeep rides.

Step 3: Select the Format menu and choose the Line Spacing command.

Step 4: In the Line Spacing dialog box, change the After Paragraph line spacing to .2 Lines.

Step 5: Choose the OK button.

PowerPoint displays the bulleted list with line spacing set at .2 lines after paragraph (Figure 1-90). Slide 4 is now balanced.

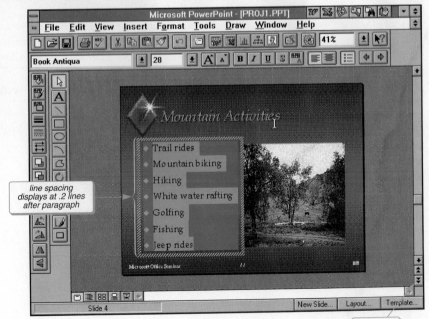

FIGURE 1-90

Slide 4 is now complete. The next section introduces you to another option for gracefully closing an on-screen slide show.

▶ CREATING A BLACK CLOSING SLIDE

PowerPoint returns to the PowerPoint window when you advance beyond the last slide in your slide show. Using a black slide to end an on-screen slide show gives the presentation a clean ending and prevents the audience from seeing the PowerPoint window. Creating a black closing slide requires hiding all objects that normally display on the slide master and changing the color of the closing slide to black.

The following steps explain how to advance to Slide 5 and create a black closing slide.

TO CREATE A BLACK CLOSING SLIDE ▼

STEP 1 ▶

Click the Insert New Slide button on the Standard toolbar. When the New Slide dialog box displays, choose the OK button. Point to the edge of the slide outside all placeholders and click the right mouse button. When a shortcut menu displays, point to the Slide Background command.

A shortcut menu displays (Figure 1-91). When you added the new slide, you chose the OK button, which applied the same slide layout as Slide 4. Because this slide will display as a black slide, the slide layout does not matter. Any layout will work.

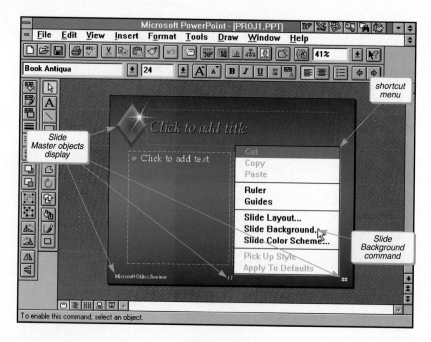

FIGURE 1-91

STEP 2 ▶

Choose the Slide Background command. Point to the Display Objects on This Slide check box.

The Slide Background dialog box displays (Figure 1-92). An x displays in the Display Objects on This Slide check box, indicating it is selected.

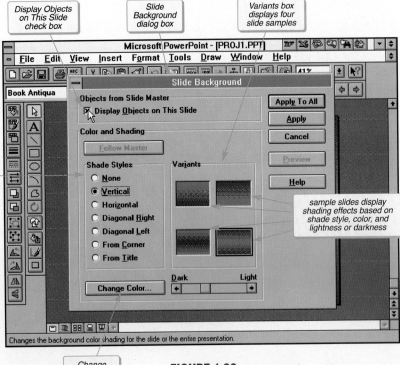

FIGURE 1-92

STEP 3 ▶

Click the Display Objects on This Slide check box. Then, point to the Change Color button at the bottom of the Slide Background dialog box.

The x no longer displays in the Display Objects on This Slide check box (Figure 1-93). Removing the x tells PowerPoint not to display Slide Master objects on this slide.

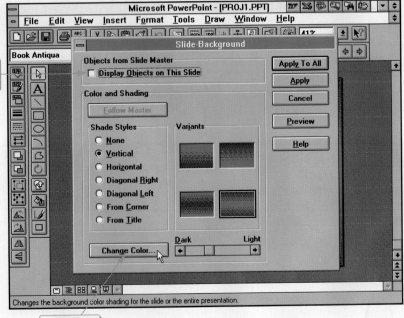

FIGURE 1-93

STEP 4 ▶

Select the Change Color button. When the Background Color dialog box displays, point to the black color sample, which is at the bottom right of the Color Palette.

The Color Palette displays 90 color samples (Figure 1-94). The current background color is the color of the template background: a purple and pink pattern. The current background color is designated by the black box surrounding the color sample.

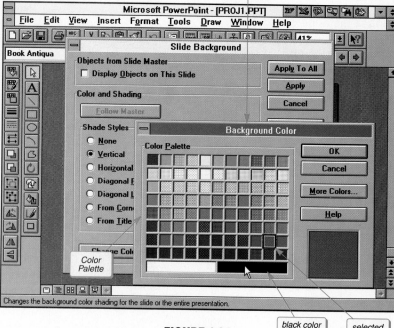

FIGURE 1-94

STEP 5 ▶

Double-click the black color sample. When the Slide Background dialog box displays, point to the Apply button.

Double-clicking the black color sample selects black for the background color, closes the Background Color dialog box, and displays the Slide Background dialog box (Figure 1-95).

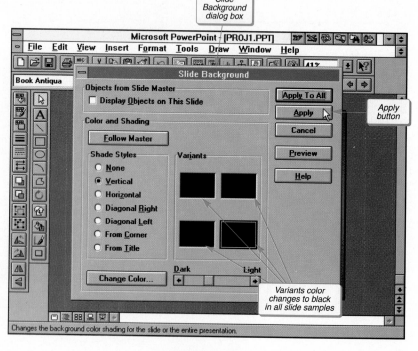

FIGURE 1-95

STEP 6 ▶

Choose the Apply button.

PowerPoint changes the background color of Slide 5 to black and no longer displays the twinkle or the diamond in the upper left corner of the slide (Figure 1-96).

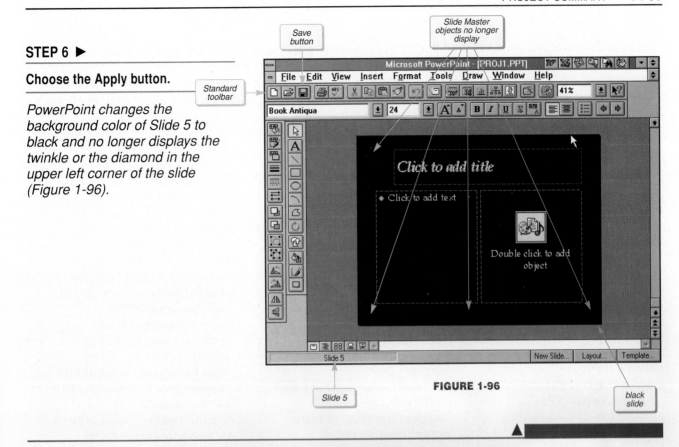

FIGURE 1-96

In addition to the Apply button, the Slide Background dialog box has an Apply To All button. Choosing the Apply To All button causes the changes to be made to all slides in the presentation. Be careful when changing a slide background so that you change only the slide you want. If you inadvertently choose the Apply To All button, you can click the Undo button on the Standard toolbar to reverse the background change on all slides. Recall that clicking the Undo button reverses the last action. If any other action was performed, you must use the Slide Background command to make your corrections.

PRESENTATION TIP

Use a black slide between sections of a large presentation or when you want to pause for discussion. The black slide focuses the audience's attention on you, the speaker, and away from the screen display.

Saving and Printing the Presentation

Project 1 is complete. Because several changes have been made since your last save, you should save the presentation again with the same filename by clicking the Save button on the Standard toolbar. Print the presentation using the Black & White and the Scale to Fit Paper options.

▶ PROJECT SUMMARY

Project 1 introduced you to several methods of enhancing a presentation with embedded visuals. You began the project by creating the presentation from an outline that was created in another application. Then, you learned how to create a special slide background using a clip art image. In creating the background, you learned how to scale an object using the Scale command, how to resize an object about center using the CTRL key, and how to send an object to the bottom of a stack of objects using the Send to Back command.

Slide 2 introduced you to embedding an organization chart using the supplementary application Microsoft Organization Chart. When you created Slide 3, you learned how to ungroup objects, embed an existing Excel chart, create a layered object, group a layered object, and then group several objects to create a new PowerPoint object. You then learned how to embed a picture on Slide 4 and how to create a black closing slide for Slide 5.

KEY TERMS AND INDEX

QUICK REFERENCE

In PowerPoint, you can accomplish a task in a number of ways. The following table provides a quick reference to each task in this project with its available options. The commands listed in the Menu column can be executed using either the keyboard or the mouse.

Task	Mouse	Menu	Keyboard Shortcuts
Bring Object Foward One Layer	Click Bring Forward button on Drawing+ toolbar	From Draw menu, choose Bring Forward	
Bring Object to Top of Stack	Click Bring Forward button on Drawing+ toolbar until object is at top of object stack	From Draw menu, choose Bring to Front	
Exit PowerPoint	Double-click Control-menu box in title bar	From File menu, choose Exit	CTRL+Q or ALT+F4
Grid On/Off		From the Draw menu, choose Snap to Grid	
Group Objects	Click Group button on Drawing+ toolbar	From Draw menu, choose Group	CTRL+SHIFT+G

Task	Mouse	Menu	Keyboard Shortcuts
Insert Clip Art	Click Insert Clip Art button on Standard toolbar	From Insert menu, choose Clip Art	
Insert Graph	Click Insert Graph button on Standard toolbar	From Insert menu, choose Microsoft Graph	
Insert Microsoft Excel Worksheet	Click Insert Microsoft Excel Worksheet button on Standard toolbar	From Insert menu, choose Object and then select Microsoft Excel 5.0 Worksheet	
Insert Microsoft Word Table	Click Insert Microsoft Word Table button on Standard toolbar	From Insert Menu, choose Microsoft Word Table	
Insert Organization Chart	Click Insert Org Chart button on Standard toolbar	From Insert menu, choose Object and then select Microsoft Organization Chart 1.0	
Insert Picture		From Insert menu, choose Picture	
Open a File to Create a Presentation	Click Open button on Standard toolbar	From File menu, choose Open	CTRL+O
Regroup Object		From Draw menu, choose Regroup	CTRL+SHIFT+J
Resize an Object	Drag resize handle of selected object		
Resize an Object About Center	Hold down CTRL key and drag resize handle of selected object		
Restore Picture to Original Size	Hold down CTRL key and double-click resize handle of selected object		
Restore Picture to Proportional Size	Hold down SHIFT key and double-click resize handle		
Scale an Object		From Draw menu, choose Scale	
Select All Objects	Hold down left mouse button and drag selection rectangle	From Edit menu, choose Select All	CTRL+A
Send Object Backward One Layer	Click Send Backward button on Drawing+ toolbar	From Draw menu, choose Send Backward	

(continued)

QUICK REFERENCE (continued)

Task	Mouse	Menu	Keyboard Shortcuts
Send Object to Background	Click Send Backward button on Drawing+ toolbar until object is at bottom of object stack	From Draw menu, choose Send to Back	
Ungroup Object	Click Ungroup button on Drawing+ toolbar	From Draw menu, choose Ungroup	CTRL+SHIFT+H

S T U D E N T   A S S I G N M E N T S

STUDENT ASSIGNMENT 1
True/False

Instructions: Circle T if the statement is true or F if the statement is false.

T   F   1. A presentation can be created by opening an outline that was created using Microsoft Word or another word processor.

T   F   2. Layered objects are objects that have been positioned on top of each other like a stack of cards.

T   F   3. The object at the bottom of a stack of objects is the foreground object.

T   F   4. The top layer in a stack of objects is the background object and is the part of the slide farthest away from the audience and is partially visible.

T   F   5. A scanner is a software device that converts lines and shading into combinations of the binary digits 0 and 1 by sensing different intensities of light and dark.

T   F   6. Microsoft Organization Chart is an OLE application supplementary to PowerPoint.

T   F   7. In Microsoft Organization Chart, the bottommost manager box is called the root manager.

T   F   8. Turning on the Snap to Grid from the Draw menu allows for precise placement of objects on a slide.

T   F   9. Vector graphic objects are created as collections of pixels and are stored as image descriptions or calculations.

T   F   10. To resize an object about center, hold down the SHIFT key and drag one of the object's resize handles.

T   F   11. To quickly regroup an object that is ungrouped accidentally, choose the Regroup button on the Draw menu.

T   F   12. If an object is ungrouped down to its composite objects, you must choose the Regroup command until the command is ghosted on the menu.

T   F   13. Before you can manipulate an individual object, you must deselect all selected objects and then select the object you want to manipulate.

T   F   14. The Scale command enlarges or reduces an object by very precise amounts while maintaining the object's proportions.

T   F   15. Combining two or more objects into one object is called grouping.

T   F   16. The Group button is on the Drawing toolbar.

T   F   17. An overlay is something that is laid over or covers something else.
T   F   18. In PowerPoint, a picture is any graphic image from another application.
T   F   19. Pictures usually are saved as one of two graphic formats: bit-map or vector.
T   F   20. A vector graphic is a piece of art that has been stored as a pattern of spots called pixels.

STUDENT ASSIGNMENT 2
Multiple Choice

Instructions: Circle the correct response.

1. An outline saved as a(n) _____ or as a(n) _____ maintains its text attributes and outline heading levels.
   a. Microsoft Word document, RTF file
   b. PowerPoint format file, plain text file
   c. rich text format file, plain text file
   d. Excel format file, plain text file

2. To quickly locate a clip art image, click the _____ button in the Microsoft ClipArt Gallery dialog box.
   a. Options   b. Search   c. Find   d. Locate

3. PowerPoint allows you to alter clip art after _____ the object.
   a. cutting   b. ungrouping   c. pasting   d. rearranging

4. Constraining an object from its center point is called _____.
   a. expanding around center
   b. sizing around center
   c. resizing about center
   d. all of the above

5. The object at the bottom of a stack of objects is the _____.
   a. midground object
   b. background object
   c. foreground object
   d. all of the above

6. A _____ is a series of invisible, crisscrossing lines about one-twelfth of an inch apart.
   a. grid   b. ruler   c. guide   d. none of the above

7. A(n) _____ chart is a hierarchical collection of elements depicting various functions or responsibilities that contribute to an organization or to a collective function.
   a. responsibility
   b. organization
   c. Microsoft Excel
   d. Microsoft Word

8. Grouping objects together to create one object is accomplished by _____.
   a. clicking the Group button on Drawing+ toolbar
   b. choosing the Group command on the Draw menu
   c. choosing the Group command from the shortcut menu
   d. all of the above

9. A(n) _____ object is created in another application and maintains a connection to its source so that if the original object changes, so does this object.
   a. embedded   b. inserted   c. pasted   d. linked

10. Scanned images are _____ images and have jagged edges.
    a. bit-mapped   b. vector   c. grouped   d. all of the above

STUDENT ASSIGNMENT 3
Finding Clip Art Images

Instructions: Assume you are in Slide view. Write the step numbers below to indicate the sequence necessary to insert the clip art image shown in Figure SA1-3 using the Find button.

Step ____: Type train

Step ____: Click the Insert Clip Art button on the Standard toolbar.

Step ____: Double-click the train image that matches the image in Figure SA1-3.

Step ____: When the Find Picture dialog box displays, click the With a Description containing option button.

Step ____: Click the OK button.

Step ____: Click the Find button.

FIGURE SA1-3

STUDENT ASSIGNMENT 4
Understanding PowerPoint Menus and Commands

Instructions: Identify the menu and the command that carry out the listed operation or cause the dialog box to display and allow you to make the indicated changes.

	MENU	COMMAND
Ungroup selected object		
Select all objects on slide		
Insert a picture		
Turn off Snap to Grid		
Change slide background to black		
Resize an object to 130 percent		
Embed an Excel chart		
Insert an organization chart		
Regroup selected objects		
Insert clip art		

STUDENT ASSIGNMENT 5
Short Answer

Instructions: Answer the following questions.

1. How do you hide all objects that normally display on the slide master to prevent them from displaying on a slide? _____

    _____

2. How do you display the Drawing+ toolbar using a shortcut menu? _____

    _____

3. Which menu contains the Scale command? _____

4. How do you find the clip art image for a farm? _____

    _____

    _____

5. What are the three methods for ungrouping a selected object? _____

    _____

    _____

6. How do you turn off the Snap to Grid? _____

7. What menu and command allow you to insert a Microsoft Excel chart? _____

8. How is a raster graphic stored? _____

9. How is a vector graphic stored? _____

10. How do you resize an object about center? _____

    _____

C O M P U T E R   L A B O R A T O R Y   E X E R C I S E S

COMPUTER LABORATORY EXERCISE 1
Using Microsoft Organization Chart Help Index

Instructions: Start PowerPoint. Open a blank presentation and choose the Org Chart AutoLayout. Perform the following tasks.

1. Double-click the organization chart placeholder. When the Microsoft Organization Chart window displays, select the Help menu and choose the Index command.
2. From the Microsoft Organization Chart Help Index, select the Menu commands and icons topic. When the Menu commands and icons Help window displays, select the Styles menu topic. When the Styles menu Help window displays, read the information about the Styles menu. From the File menu, choose the Print Topic command.

(continued)

COMPUTER LABORATORY EXERCISE 1 (continued)

3. Jump to Rearranging boxes by clicking the topic name at the bottom of the Styles menu Help window. When the Rearranging boxes Help window displays, read the information. Next, click each of the four underlined topics—manager, assistant, subordinates, and group style—and read the related information. Then, print the Rearranging boxes information.

4. Click the Back button on the Help toolbar two times to display the Menu commands and icons Help window. Select The icon bar topic.

5. When The icon bar Help window displays, read and print the information.

6. Jump to the General purpose tools topic. Read and print the information. Click the Back button.

7. Jump to the Box tools topic. Read and print the information. Click the Back button.

8. Jump to the Custom drawing tools topic. Read and print the information.

9. From the Microsoft Organization Chart Help File menu, choose the Exit command. From the Microsoft Organization Chart - [Object in Presentation] File menu, choose the Exit and Return to Presentation command. When the Microsoft Organization Chart dialog box displays, choose the No button.

10. When the PowerPoint window displays, exit PowerPoint without saving the presentation.

COMPUTER LABORATORY EXERCISE 2
Ungrouping, Modifying, and Regrouping Clip Art

Instructions: Start PowerPoint. Open a blank presentation using the twentieth layout, Title Only. Perform the following tasks to modify the clip art object in Figure CLE1-2.

1. Click the Template button an apply the sidebars.ppt template from the sldshow template subdirectory. Type your name for the slide title.

2. If not already displayed, display the Drawing+ toolbar by pointing to any toolbar and clicking the right mouse button. When a shortcut menu displays, choose Drawing+.

3. Click the Insert Clip Art button on the Standard toolbar. When the Microsoft ClipArt Gallery - Picture in Presentation dialog box displays, click the Find button. When the Find Picture dialog box displays, click the With a Description containing option button. Then, type pencil and choose the OK button.

FIGURE CLE 1-2

4. When the Microsoft ClipArt Gallery - Picture in Presentation dialog box displays, double-click the large pencil image located in the Household category as identified at the bottom of the dialog box.

5. When the pencil displays on the PowerPoint slide, click the Ungroup button on the Drawing+ toolbar. When the Microsoft PowerPoint dialog box displays, choose the OK button. Click the Ungroup button again.

6. Click away from the pencil, anywhere on the slide background, to deselect the composite pencil objects.
7. Select the pencil lead by clicking its upper-left side. Press the DELETE key to remove the pencil lead.
8. Point to the pencil barrel and click the right mouse button to display a shortcut menu. Choose the Regroup command. Click the right mouse button again on the pencil barrel to display a shortcut menu. Choose the Regroup command to group the entire pencil.
9. Save the presentation with the filename CLE1-2 on your data diskette. Print the presentation slide using the Black & White option.
10. Exit PowerPoint.

COMPUTER LABORATORY EXERCISE 3
Changing a Slide Background

Part 1 Instructions: Start PowerPoint. Perform the following tasks to open the outline CLE1-3.RTF and use the Pick a Look Wizard to format the presentation in Figure CLE1-3a.

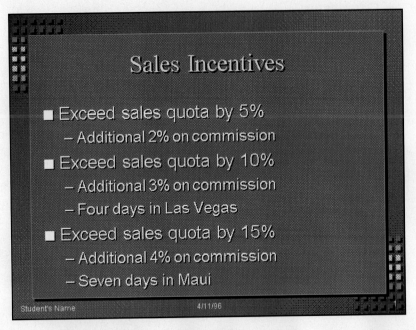

FIGURE CLE1-3a

1. Open the outline CLE1-3.RTF from the subdirectory PPoint4 on the Student Diskette that accompanies this book. Recall that you need to change the List Files of Type to Outlines.
2. Click the Pick a Look Wizard button on the Standard toolbar. When the Pick a Look Wizard - Step 1 of 9 dialog box displays, choose the Next button.
3. When the Pick a Look Wizard - Step 2 of 9 dialog box displays, click the On-Screen Presentation option button and then choose the Next button.
4. When the Pick a Look Wizard - Step 3 of 9 dialog box displays, choose the More button. When the Presentation Template dialog box displays, scroll until multboxs.ppt displays in the File Name list box. Then, double-click multboxs.ppt. When the Pick a Look Wizard - Step 3 of 9 dialog box redisplays, choose the Next button.
5. When the Pick a Look Wizard - Step 4 of 9 dialog box displays, remove the x in the Speaker's Notes check box, the x in the Audience Handout Pages check box, and the x in the Outline Pages check box. Then, choose the Next button.
6. When the Pick a Look Wizard - Slide Options dialog box displays, select the text in the Name, company, or other text box. Then, type your first and last names. Next, select the Date check box and the Page Number check box. Choose the Finish button.
7. Save the presentation with the filename CLE1-3A on your data disk.
8. Print the presentation slide using the Pure Black & White option.

(continued)

COMPUTER LABORATORY EXERCISE 3 (continued)

Part 2 Instructions: Change slide background to create the slide shown in Figure CLE1-3b.

Sales Incentives

Student's Name

- Exceed sales quota by 5%
  - Additional 2% on commission
- Exceed sales quota by 10%
  - Additional 3% on commission
  - Four days in Las Vegas
- Exceed sales quota by 15%
  - Additional 4% on commission
  - Seven days in Maui

FIGURE CLE1-3b

1. Click the Slide View button. From the Format menu, choose the Slide Background command.
2. When the Slide Background dialog box displays, remove the x in the Display Objects on This Slide check box. Next, click the None option button in the Shade Styles box. Choose the Change Color button.
3. When the Background Color dialog box displays, double-click the red-orange color sample in column two, row six.
4. When the Slide Background dialog box displays, choose the Apply button.
5. Add a text box by clicking the Text Tool on the Drawing toolbar, positioning the mouse pointer far enough from the upper right corner of the slide to fit your name, and clicking the left mouse button. Type your first and last names. If the text box exceeds the width of the slide, drag the text box left so that that your name displays on the slide.
6. Triple-click your name in the box. Change the font size of your name to 18 points by clicking the Decrease Font Size button on the Formatting toolbar two times.
7. Use the Save As command to save the presentation with the filename CLE1-3B on your data diskette.
8. Click the Print button on the Standard toolbar.
9. Exit PowerPoint.

COMPUTER LABORATORY ASSIGNMENTS

COMPUTER LABORATORY ASSIGNMENT 1
Opening an Existing Outline and Creating a New Clip Art Image

Purpose: To become familiar with creating a presentation from an existing outline and grouping clip art images to create a new image.

Problem: You have written a satire on life in the Navy. Your literature instructor has asked you to present your work to the English department at its monthly meeting. You are using the outline you created for your satire. You need to add graphics, but you cannot find a caricature of a man in naval attire. You create the caricature shown in Figure CLA1-1.

Instructions: Perform the following tasks.

1. Start PowerPoint. Use the Open an Existing Presentation option to open the CLA1-1.RTF outline from the subdirectory PPoint4 on the Student Diskette that accompanies this book.
2. Use the Pick a Look Wizard to create an on-screen presentation, apply the bubbles.ppt template, select the Full-Page Slides check box, and include your name, the date, and page number. Click the Slide View button. When the title slide displays, change the slide layout to Text & Clip Art.
3. Select the bulleted list and click the Increase Font Size button four times so that the Font Size box displays 40+.
4. Insert the clip art image, Man with Too Many Hats, from the Cartoons category in the Microsoft ClipArt Gallery, onto the clip art placeholder. Ungroup the clip art image until the hats display as individual objects.
5. Delete all hats except the sailor's cap. Then, delete the group of curved lines, which indicate motion.
6. Drag the sailor's cap onto the man's head to just above his eyebrows. Next, increase Zoom Control to 100%. Then, bring the cap to the foreground using the Bring to Front command.
7. Scroll to display the image of the man. Next, select the pants object by clicking the man's right foot. Then, change the color of the pants to white using the Fill Color button on the Drawing+ toolbar.

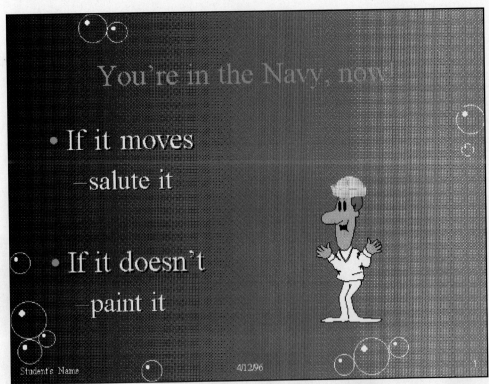

FIGURE CLA1-1

8. Select the sweater object and change its color to white. Next, select the neckline with pink tie object and change its color to white. Then, ungroup the neckline with tie object by clicking the Ungroup button one time.
9. Delete the tie object by clicking on the tie knot to select it and then pressing the DELETE key.
10. Group all the individual objects in the clip art image into one object.
11. Save the presentation with the filename CLA1-1 on your data diskette. Then, print the presentation using the Pure Black & White option.
12. Exit PowerPoint.

COMPUTER LABORATORY ASSIGNMENT 2
Embedding an Organization Chart, Inserting a Picture, and Creating a Black Closing Slide

Purpose: To become familiar with embedding an organization chart, inserting a picture, and creating a black closing slide.

Problem: You are the administrative assistant for Solar Technology and Radiant Energy Storage Systems. Your boss wants a few slides to familiarize the employees in the four regional sales offices with the senior management team and the newly hired vice president of research. You decide to use PowerPoint to create the organization chart shown in Figure CLA1-2a, the fact sheet shown in Figure CLA1-2b, and the black closing slide.

Instructions: Perform the following tasks.

1. Start PowerPoint, choose a blank presentation. Choose the Org Chart slide layout. Then, apply the TABLETS.PPT template.
2. Type Solar Technology and Radiant Energy Storage Systems for the slide title.
3. Create the organization chart shown in Figure CLA1-2a. Type your name in the Admin. Asst. box.
4. Change the font of all text in the organization chart to Times New Roman, 48 points, bold.
5. Change the box color for the president (level one) to yellow.
6. Change the box color for the administrative assistant and vice presidents (level two) to light blue-green (cyan).
7. Change the box color for the engineers, supervisors, and managers (level three) to green.
8. Exit Microsoft Organization Chart and return to Slide 1.

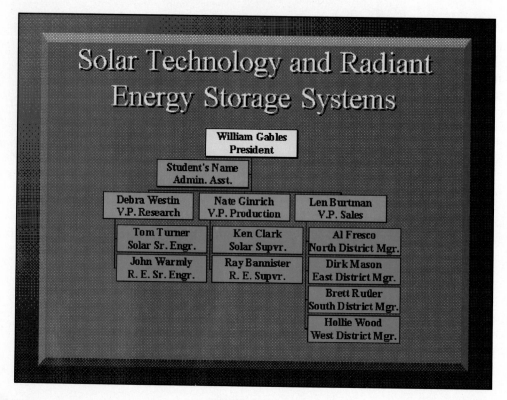

FIGURE CLA1-2a

9. Insert a new slide with the Object & Text slide layout. Type the bulleted list shown in Figure CLA1-2b.
10. Insert the picture shown in Figure CLA1-2b using the file PICT1.PCX from the subdirectory Access2 on the Student Diskette that accompanies this book.
11. Insert a new slide with the same slide layout as the current slide. Then change the slide background to create a black closing slide.
12. Save the presentation with the filename CLA1-2 on your data diskette.
13. Print the presentation using the Pure Black & White option.
14. Exit PowerPoint.

FIGURE CLA1-2b

COMPUTER LABORATORY ASSIGNMENT 3
Creating a Special Background

Purpose: To become familiar with creating special backgrounds.

Problem: You are the marketing manager for a new time-share development. As part of your sales training presentation, you want to create a title slide with a picture of the resort as the background. Unfortunately, your pictures were lost. Consequently, you decide to create a special background from images in the ClipArt Gallery (Figure CLA1-3).

(continued)

COMPUTER LABORATORY ASSIGNMENT 3 (continued)

Instructions: Perform the following tasks.

1. Start PowerPoint, choose a blank presentation, and then choose the Title Only AutoLayout.
2. Change the slide background color to light blue-green (column eight, row two of the Color Palette in the Background Color dialog box).
3. Type Polynesian Princess Resort for the slide title. Then, change the font to Algerian or a similar font if your computer does not have Algerian.
4. Insert the Resort Hotel clip art image from the Microsoft ClipArt Gallery.

FIGURE CLA1-3

5. Turn off the Snap to Grid. Resize the clip art image about center so that the clip art covers the width of the slide.
6. Ungroup the Resort Hotel image two times. Next, select the blue water object. Then, drag the middle-bottom resize handle down to the edge of the slide so that the water object covers the bottom portion of the slide. Change the fill color of the water object to dark blue (column nine, row six of the Color Palette in the Other Color dialog box).
7. Regroup the clip art.
8. Save the presentation with the filename CLA1-3 on your data diskette.
9. Print the presentation using the Pure Black & White option.
10. Exit PowerPoint.

COMPUTER LABORATORY ASSIGNMENT 4
Creating a Presentation with Embedded Objects

Purpose: To become familiar with creating a special background, embedding and modifying clip art, embedding a picture, embedding an organization chart, and creating a black closing slide.

Problem: You are responsible for conducting the orientation seminar for all new freshmen at your school. Design and create a slide show presentation. Select an appropriate template. The presentation should consist of at least five slides, four of which should consist of a title slide with a special background, a picture (which may be from the Microsoft ClipArt Gallery or any other picture you have available), an organization chart, and a black closing slide. The additional slide must support the orientation topic. Research your school's student orientation program to obtain ideas for your presentation. Be certain to include your name on each slide. Submit a copy of the slide show on a diskette saved as CLA1-4 along with printouts of the slides.

CUSTOMIZING A PRESENTATION

OBJECTIVES You will have mastered the material in this project when you can:

- ▸ Select a color scheme
- ▸ Draw an object
- ▸ Rotate an object
- ▸ Create a graphic image with text
- ▸ Add a border to a picture
- ▸ Create a "drill down" document
- ▸ Link a PowerPoint presentation

- ▸ Add a caption to an object
- ▸ Hide a slide
- ▸ Create speaker notes
- ▸ Use the PowerPoint Viewer to run a slide show with a hidden slide and "drill down" documents

▸ INTRODUCTION

Because every presentation is created for a specific audience, subsequent deliveries of the same presentation may require you to make changes. These changes are necessary to accommodate the knowledge base or interest level of the audience. Sometimes you want to branch into another application to show the audience the effect of change. For example, when presenting next year's projected sales, you might want to perform a "what if" analysis with the figures during the slide show without leaving PowerPoint. PowerPoint allows you to do so using "drill down" documents. A **"drill down" document** is a file created in an object linking and embedding (OLE) application such as Microsoft Word or Microsoft Excel. Other times you might want to refrain from showing one or more slides because they are not applicable to a particular audience. PowerPoint has the capability to hide slides. As the presenter, you decide whether to display them. Occasionally, you will need to change the look of your presentation by adding special graphics, such as a company logo, adding borders to objects and text, or changing the overall color scheme. This project explains how PowerPoint helps you quickly customize a presentation.

▶ PROJECT TWO — MICROSOFT OFFICE WORKSHOP CUSTOMIZED

P roject 2 customizes the Microsoft Office Workshop presentation created in Project 1 (see Figures 1-1a - 1-1e on pages PP2-3). After reviewing the Microsoft Office Workshop orientation presentation, the organizing team decides to embellish it. They want to change templates, but they cannot find one that uses the colors associated with their company logo. Therefore, they decide to change templates and select a new color scheme. They use PowerPoint to draw their company logo and then insert text to create a graphic image. They insert the logo onto the Slide Master so that it displays on every slide. They also decide to add a border around the horse picture. Finally, the team decides to add a slide to demonstrate the four Microsoft Office applications featured in the workshop. They decide to display that slide only if time permits, however.

Slide Preparation Steps

The following slide preparation steps summarize how to create the slides shown in Figures 2-1a through 2-1k. If you are creating the slides on a personal computer, read these steps without doing them.

1. Start PowerPoint.
2. Open an existing presentation and save it with a new filename.
3. Apply the marbles.ppt template to the presentation.
4. Select a new color scheme.
5. Create a company logo.
6. Create a graphic image using Microsoft WordArt.
7. Add a border to the horse picture.
8. Add a new slide and create a "drill down" document.
9. Link a PowerPoint presentation.
10. Add captions to the "drill down" document icons.
11. Hide a slide.
12. Create speaker notes.
13. Save the presentation on your diskette.
14. Exit PowerPoint.
15. Run the slide show to display the hidden slide and activate the "drill down" documents.

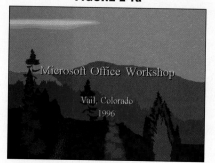

FIGURE 2-1a

FIGURE 2-1b

FIGURE 2-1c

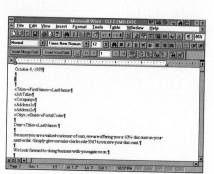

FIGURE 2-1d

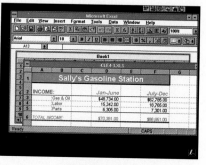

FIGURE 2-1e

FIGURE 2-1f

FIGURE 2-1g

FIGURE 2-1h

FIGURE 2-1i

FIGURE 2-1j

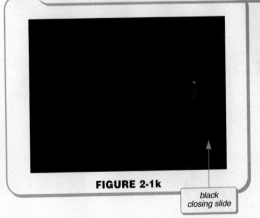

FIGURE 2-1k

black closing slide

▶ CUSTOMIZING AN EXISTING PRESENTATION

Because you are customizing the Microsoft Office Workshop presentation created in Project 1, the first step in this project is to open PROJ1.PPT. To ensure that the original Project 1 remains intact, you save PROJ1.PPT with a new filename: PROJ2.PPT. Later in this project, you modify the new project's slides by changing templates, selecting a new color scheme, adding a border to a picture, and adding one new slide. The steps on the following pages illustrate these procedures.

Opening a Presentation and Saving It with a New Filename

After starting PowerPoint, the first step in this project is to open the Microsoft Office Workshop presentation saved in Project 1 and save it with the filename PROJ2.PPT. This procedure should be done immediately to prevent inadvertently saving Project 2 with the original filename, thus losing Project 1. The following steps summarize how to open an existing presentation and save it with a new filename. If you did not complete Project 1, see your instructor for a copy of the presentation.

TO OPEN A PRESENTATION AND SAVE IT WITH A NEW FILENAME

Step 1: Insert the diskette containing the file PROJ1.PPT into drive A.

Step 2: Select the Open an Existing Presentation option button in the PowerPoint startup dialog box.

Step 3: Choose the OK button.

Step 4: If necessary, click the Drives box arrow and select drive A in the Drives box. Select proj1.ppt so that its name displays in the File Name box. Choose the OK button.

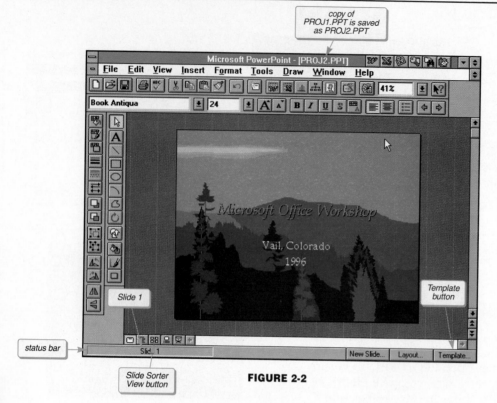

copy of PROJ1.PPT is saved as PROJ2.PPT

Template button

Slide 1

status bar

Slid., 1

Slide Sorter View button

FIGURE 2-2

Step 5: From the File menu, choose the Save As command.

Step 6: Type `proj2` in the File Name box. Do not press the ENTER key.

Step 7: With drive A set as the default drive, choose the OK button in the Save As dialog box.

Step 8: If necessary, revise the information contained in the Summary Info dialog box by selecting the text and typing the new information. Choose the OK button.

The presentation is saved to drive A with the filename PROJ2.PPT (Figure 2-2).

Changing Templates

One of the changes requested by the Microsoft Office seminar organizing team is the template. The template used in Project 1 was twinkles.ppt; the template requested for Project 2 is marbles.ppt. Perform the steps below to change the template.

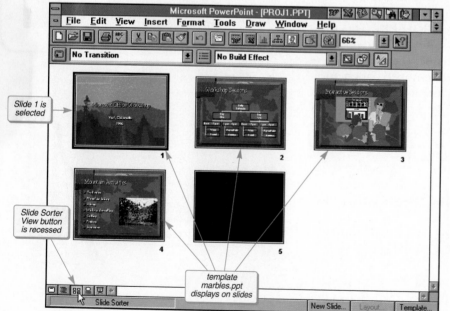

Slide 1 is selected

Slide Sorter View button is recessed

template marbles.ppt displays on slides

Slide Sorter

New Slide...   Layout...   Template...

FIGURE 2-3

TO CHANGE TEMPLATES

Step 1: Click the Slide Sorter View button.

Step 2: Click the Template button on the status bar.

Step 3: If not already open, open the sldshow subdirectory in the Directories box of the Presentation Template dialog box. Drag the File Name scroll bar elevator until marbles.ppt displays.

Step 4: Double-click marbles.ppt.

PowerPoint displays the message, Charts are being updated with the new color scheme. After several seconds, the slides display with the new template, marbles.ppt (Figure 2-3). Slide 1 is selected.

▶ SELECTING A NEW COLOR SCHEME

S ometimes it is difficult to find a template that has all the attributes your presentation requires. For example, you may find a template with background objects you want, but you may not like the color it uses for text and lines. Fortunately, you are not limited to the default color schemes associated with the PowerPoint templates. A **color scheme** is the set of eight colors assigned to a slide. It consists of background color, text and line color, title text color, shadow color, fill color, and three different accent colors. Table 2-1 explains the components of a color scheme. Changing a color scheme can change the look of your slides dramatically.

▶ **TABLE 2-1**

COMPONENT	DESCRIPTION
Background color	The background color is the fundamental color of a PowerPoint slide. For example, if your background color is white, you can place any other color on top of it, but the fundamental color remains white. The white background shows everywhere you don't add color or other objects. Any other background color on a slide works the same way.
Text and line color	The text and line color contrasts with the background color of the slide. Together with the background color, the text and line color sets the tone for a presentation. For example, a gray background with black text and line color sets a dreary tone. In contrast, a red background with yellow text and line color sets a vibrant tone.
Title text color	Similar to text and line color, the title text color contrasts with the background color. Title text displays in the title placeholder on a slide.
Shadow color	When you shadow an object, the shadow color is applied. This color is usually a darker shade of the background color.
Fill color	The fill color contrasts with both the background color and the text and line color. The fill color can be used for graphs and charts.
Accent colors	Accent colors are designed as colors for secondary features on a slide. Additionally, accent colors are used as colors on graphs.

PRESENTATION TIP

To help the audience distinguish between related topics, color-code sections of the presentation by applying different color schemes to groups of slides. For example, in a presentation with three distinct sections, such as past history, current trends, and future projections, you could use three different color schemes to uniquely identify each section.

Selecting Slides for a New Color Scheme

The color scheme can be changed on all slides in the presentation or on just selected slides. This project applies a new color scheme to Slide 2, Slide 3, and Slide 4. The organizing team likes Slide 1 in its present form and Slide 5 is a black closing slide. Therefore, the color scheme for those two slides will not change. Perform the step on the next page to select the slides to be changed.

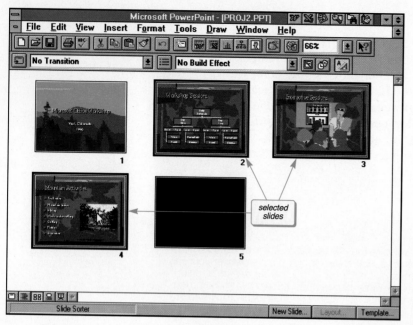

FIGURE 2-4

**TO SELECT SLIDES FOR
A NEW COLOR SCHEME**

Step 1: Hold down the SHIFT key and click Slide 1 (to deselect it), Slide 2, Slide 3, and Slide 4. Release the SHIFT key.

Slide 1 is no longer selected (Figure 2-4). Slide 2, Slide 3, and Slide 4 are selected.

Recall from Project 1, holding down the SHIFT key and clicking an object is called the SHIFT+Click method. This allows you to select multiple objects. When multiple objects are selected, holding down the SHIFT key and clicking one of the selected objects deselects that object.

Selecting a Color Scheme

Selecting a color scheme begins with selecting the background color and then selecting the text and line color. PowerPoint then suggests four color schemes. Choose one of the four color schemes. Perform the following steps to select a new color scheme.

TO SELECT A COLOR SCHEME ▼

STEP 1 ▶

With Slides 2, 3, and 4 still selected, select the Format menu and point to the Slide Color Scheme command (Figure 2-5).

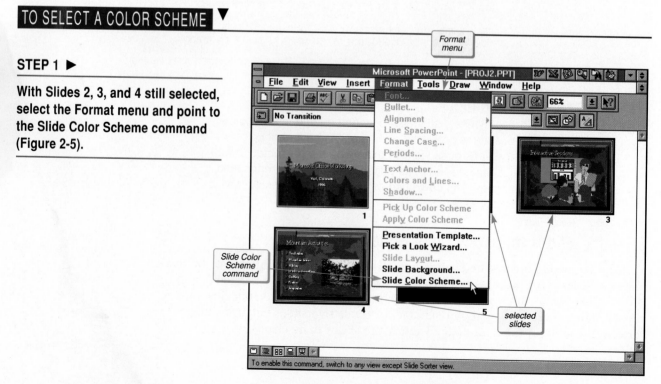

FIGURE 2-5

STEP 2 ▶

Choose the Slide Color Scheme command.

The Slide Color Scheme dialog box displays (Figure 2-6). The current color scheme displays in the preview box. The eight colors that constitute the current color scheme display in the color sample boxes in the Change Scheme Colors box.

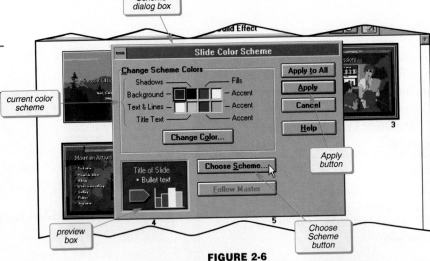

FIGURE 2-6

STEP 3 ▶

Choose the Choose Scheme button in the Slide Color Scheme dialog box.

The Choose Scheme dialog box displays (Figure 2-7). By default, the white background color sample is selected.

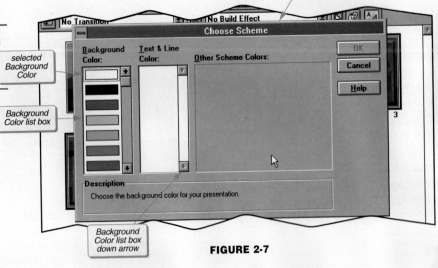

FIGURE 2-7

STEP 4 ▶

Click the down arrow in the Background Color list box to scroll to the dark green color sample (57th color sample). Use the position of the Background Color scroll bar elevator in Figure 2-8 to help locate the dark green color sample. The two color samples that display after the dark green color sample are blackish-green and lime green, respectively.

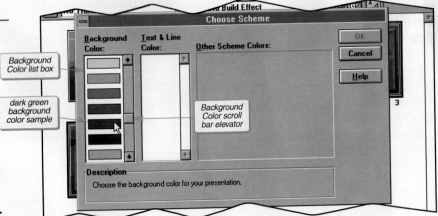

FIGURE 2-8

STEP 5 ►

Select the dark green color sample by clicking it. Then, select the light yellow color sample currently displayed at the bottom of the Text & Line Color list box (7th color sample).

Four color schemes display in the Other Scheme Colors box (Figure 2-9). By default, the upper left color scheme is selected.

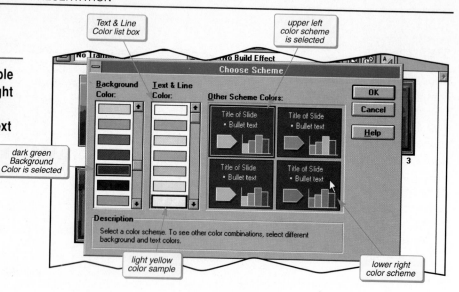

FIGURE 2-9

STEP 6 ►

Double-click the color scheme located in the lower right corner of the Other Scheme Colors box.

The Slide Color Scheme dialog box displays (Figure 2-10). The eight colors that constitute the new color scheme display in the color sample boxes in the Change Scheme Colors box. The new color scheme displays in the preview box.

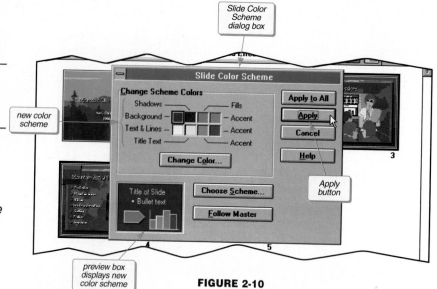

FIGURE 2-10

STEP 7 ►

Choose the Apply button in the Slide Color Scheme dialog box.

PowerPoint displays the message, Charts are being updated with the new color scheme. PowerPoint applies the new color scheme to Slides 2, 3, and 4 (Figure 2-11).

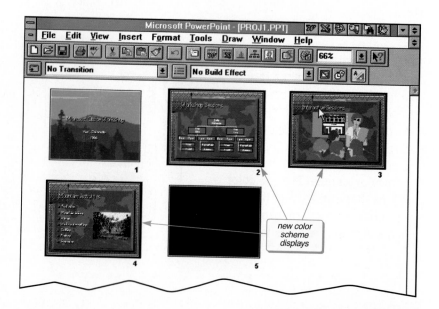

FIGURE 2-11

Choosing the Apply button in the Slide Color Scheme dialog box, as described in Step 7, applies the new color scheme to selected slides. Choosing the Apply to All button applies the new color scheme to every slide, not just selected slides. If you choose the Apply to All button by mistake, you can correct the error immediately by clicking the Undo button on the Standard toolbar.

Saving Project 2 Again

Because you have made several changes to this project, save your presentation now by clicking the Save button on the Standard toolbar.

▶ CREATING A LOGO

Many companies establish presentation standards to which every presentation must adhere. Very often, a company logo is part of those standards. The Microsoft Office seminar organizing team is following The Software Institute standards by displaying the institute logo (Figure 2-12) on all slides except the title and closing slides.

Displaying The Software Institute logo requires several steps. First, open a new presentation. Then, draw the logo. Next, apply attributes such as fill color and lines. Then use the company name to create a graphic text image. The drawing and graphic text image then are combined into one logo object. Finally, after copying the logo object onto the Clipboard, paste it on the Microsoft Office Workshop slide master. The next several sections explain how to create The Software Institute logo.

FIGURE 2-12

Opening a New Presentation

Because you may want to reuse The Software Institute logo in other presentations, you create it in a new presentation. The following steps summarize opening a new presentation.

TO OPEN A NEW PRESENTATION

Step 1: Click the New button (◫) on the Standard toolbar.

Step 2: When the New Presentation dialog box displays, select the Blank Presentation option button if it is not already selected.

Step 3: Choose the OK button.

Step 4: When the New Slide dialog box displays, type 21 to select the Blank slide layout.

Step 5: Choose the OK button.

Step 6: Click the Maximize button if the PowerPoint window is not already maximized.

Slide 1 displays the Blank slide layout in a new presentation titled Presentation (Figure 2-13 on the next page).

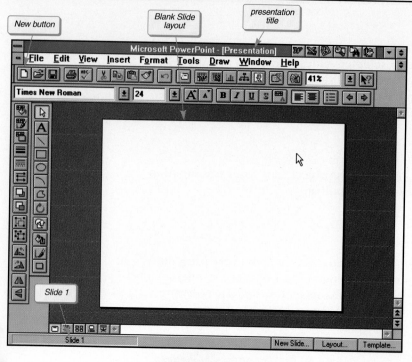

FIGURE 2-13

Drawing the Logo

The Software Institute's logo resembles a flower in an ellipse (see Figure 2-12 on the previous page). Draw the logo using PowerPoint's drawing tools. Drawing the logo requires several steps. To help you draw the logo, first display the horizontal and vertical rulers. Then, display the horizontal and vertical guides to assist in aligning the objects. Next, increase Zoom Control to see the detail of small objects better. Then, draw the outline of the logo with the Ellipse tool. Once the outline of the logo is drawn, rotate it into the proper position. Add a border and change its line style. Next, draw the diamond shape that resembles a flower, the straight line that resembles a flower stem, and two arcs that resemble leaves. After drawing the logo objects, add shaded fill color to the diamond shape. The logo objects then are grouped into one object. The next several sections explain how to draw the logo object shown in Figure 2-12.

Displaying Rulers

To help you align objects, PowerPoint provides two **rulers**: one horizontal ruler and one vertical ruler. The **horizontal ruler** displays on the top of the slide window. The **vertical ruler** displays on the left side of the slide window. **Tick marks** on the rulers identify 1/8 inch segments. When you move the mouse pointer, a **pointer indicator** traces the position of the pointer and displays its exact location on both rulers. You will use the rulers and pointer indicator later in this project when you draw The Software Institute logo. In preparation for drawing the logo, display the rulers now. Perform the following steps to display the horizontal and vertical rulers.

TO DISPLAY THE RULERS ▼

STEP 1 ▶

Point anywhere on the blank slide and click the right mouse button. When a shortcut menu displays, point to the Ruler command.

A shortcut menu displays (Figure 2-14).

STEP 2 ▶

Choose the Ruler command.

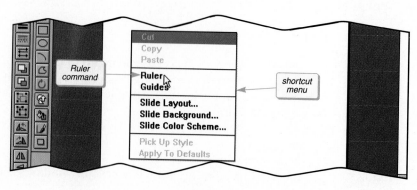

FIGURE 2-14

An alternative method for displaying the rulers is to select the View menu and choose the Ruler command. When the Ruler command is active, a check mark displays in front of the Ruler command in both the shortcut menu and the View menu. When you want to prohibit the rulers from displaying on the PowerPoint window, hide them. To hide the rulers, click the right mouse button anywhere on the PowerPoint window, except on an object, and choose the Ruler command.

Displaying the Guides

PowerPoint has a Guides tool to help you align objects. The **guides** are two straight lines, one horizontal and one vertical, used for aligning objects. When an object is close to a guide, its corner or its center (whichever is closer) snaps to or attaches itself to, the guide. The guides can be moved to meet your alignment requirements. Because you are preparing the slide window to draw the logo, perform the step below to display the guides.

TO DISPLAY THE GUIDES ▼

STEP 1 ▶

Point anywhere on the blank slide and click the right mouse button. When the shortcut menu displays, choose the Guides command.

*The horizontal and vertical guides intersect in the middle of the slide window (Figure 2-15). The horizontal guide aligns with the zero tick mark on the horizontal ruler. The vertical guide aligns with the zero tick mark on the vertical ruler. The intersection of the vertical guide and horizontal guide is the **center** of the slide.*

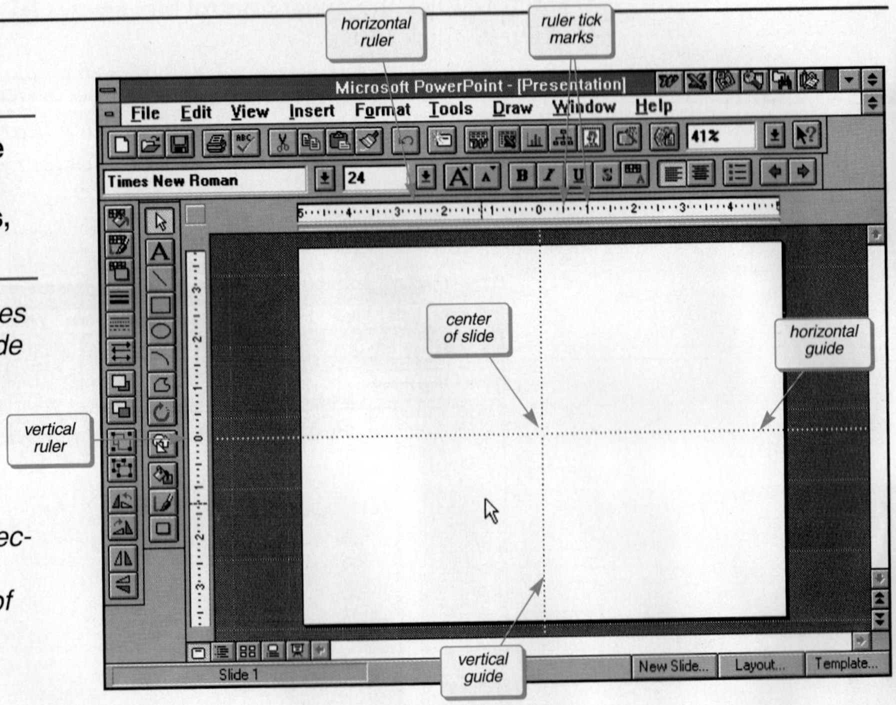

FIGURE 2-15

An alternative method for displaying the guides is to select the View menu and choose the Guides command.

When the shortcut menu displayed in Step 1 above, a check mark displayed in front of the Rulers command because you turned on the rulers in the previous section. Recall that a check mark displays when a command is active, or turned on. Similarly, when the Guides command is active, a check mark displays in front of the Guides command on both the shortcut menu and the View menu.

When you no longer want the guides to display on the screen or want to control the exact placement of objects, hide the guides. To hide the guides, click the right mouse button anywhere on the PowerPoint window except on an object, and choose the Guides command.

Increasing Zoom Control

By default, Zoom Control is 41% in Slide view. This displays an editing view equivalent to the size of a slide, which is 10" by 7 1/2". Increasing Zoom Control reduces the editing view of the slide. For example, increasing Zoom Control to 100% decreases the editing view to 5 1/2" by 3 3/4". Increase Zoom Control when you want to enlarge the display and make working with detailed objects or small objects easier. In this project, you will increase Zoom Control to 150% because it allows you to display an edit view approximately 4" by 2". The following steps summarize how to increase Zoom Control.

TO INCREASE ZOOM CONTROL

Step 1: Click the Zoom Control box arrow (⬇) on the Standard toolbar.
Step 2: Click 150%.

Zoom Control changes to 150% (Figure 2-16). Compare Figure 2-16 to Figure 2-15 on the previous page. Notice that when you increase the Zoom Control, the ruler tick marks display farther apart.

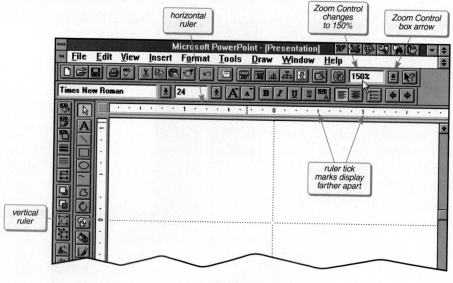

FIGURE 2-16

Drawing an Ellipse

Creating The Software Institute logo begins with drawing an ellipse. An **ellipse** is a symmetrical oval-like object. Draw an ellipse with the Ellipse Tool button on the Drawing toolbar. To draw an ellipse from a point on its circumference, click the Ellipse Tool button and drag the mouse pointer. To draw an ellipse from a point in its center, click the Ellipse Tool button, press and hold down the CTRL key, and drag the mouse pointer as shown in the following steps.

TO DRAW AN ELLIPSE ▼

STEP 1 ▶

Click the Ellipse Tool button on the Drawing toolbar. Press and hold down the CTRL key and position the cross-hair pointer at the intersection of the horizontal and vertical guides.

The Ellipse Tool button displays recessed, which indicates it is selected (Figure 2-17).

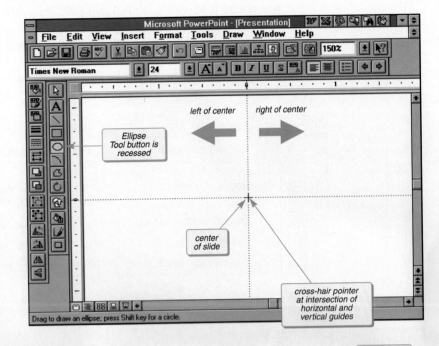

FIGURE 2-17

STEP 2 ▶

While holding down the CTRL key, press and hold down the left mouse button and drag the cross-hair pointer to the right of center until the horizontal pointer indicator is on the 1" horizontal tick mark, and drag upward until the vertical pointer indicator is slightly below the 7/8" vertical tick mark. Release the left mouse button and then the CTRL key.

The ellipse displays with the PowerPoint default attributes: blue fill color and black lines (Figure 2-18). A selection rectangle displays around the ellipse to designate it is selected.

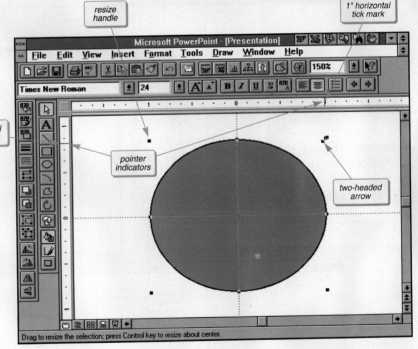

FIGURE 2-18

The ellipse in Figure 2-18 is slightly wider than it is tall. The ellipse in the logo in Figure 2-12 on page PP81 is taller than it is wide. To make the ellipse drawn in Step 2 above look like the one in Figure 2-12, rotate the horizontal axis 90°. The next section explains how to rotate the ellipse.

Rotating an Ellipse

When drawing objects, you sometimes want to see how the object looks if you rotate it vertically or horizontally. PowerPoint has five buttons to help you rotate objects. The Drawing+ toolbar contains four buttons for rotating objects: the Rotate Left button, the Rotate Right button, the Flip Horizontal button, and the Flip Vertical button. The Drawing toolbar contains the Free Rotate Tool button. Table 2-2 explains the function of each button.

▶ **TABLE 2-2**

ICON	NAME	FUNCTION
	Rotate Left button	Rotates the selected object to the left, counterclockwise, in 90° increments each time you choose the button.
	Rotate Right button	Rotates the selected object to the right, clockwise, in 90° increments each time you choose the button.
	Flip Horizontal button	Flips the selected object horizontally 180°.
	Flip Vertical button	Flips the selected object vertically 180°.
	Free Rotate Tool button	Rotates the selected object to an exact position.

Perform the step below to rotate the ellipse 90°.

TO ROTATE AN ELLIPSE ▼

STEP 1 ▶

With the ellipse selected, click the Rotate Right button on the Drawing+ toolbar.

The ellipse rotates 90° to the right (Figure 2-19). The ellipse is now taller than it is wide.

FIGURE 2-19

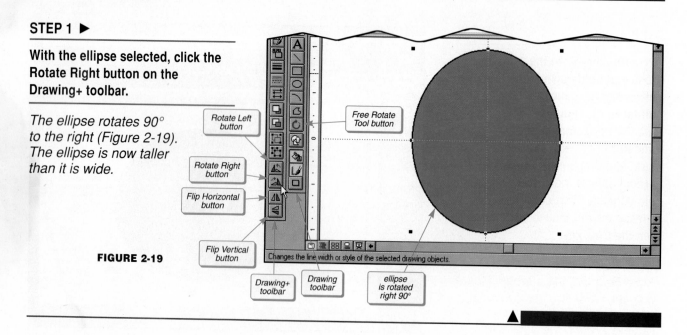

Because you needed to rotate the ellipse 90°, in this case you could have used the Rotate Left button instead of the Rotate Right button and achieved the same result.

Adding a Border to the Logo

The next step is to add a border to the ellipse. A **border** is the visible line around the edge of an object. The border draws attention to the object by defining its edges. A border is composed of three attributes: line style, line color, and fill color. The **line style** determines the line thickness and line appearance of the border. For example, you could choose a thick, solid line for your border. **Line color** determines the color of the line that forms the border. For example, you will use black for the line color on The Software Institute logo. Fill color determines the interior color of the selected object. The ellipse in Figure 2-19 has a single-line border. Perform the steps below to add a three-line border.

TO ADD A BORDER TO THE LOGO ▼

STEP 1 ▶

Click the Line Style button on the Drawing+ toolbar. When the Line Style drop-down list displays, point to the three-line style (narrow, wide, narrow) at the bottom of the list.

The Line Style drop-down list displays (Figure 2-20). By default, the thinnest line is selected.

FIGURE 2-20

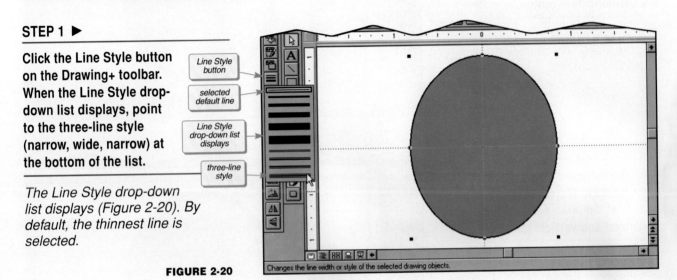

STEP 2 ▶

Select the three-line style (narrow, wide, narrow).

A three-line border displays around the ellipse (Figure 2-21).

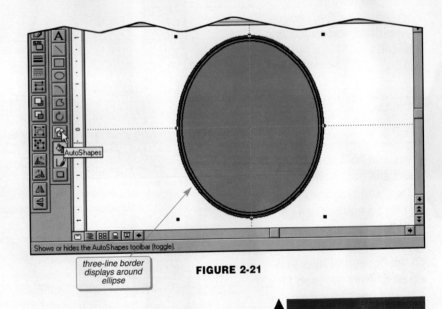

three-line border displays around ellipse

FIGURE 2-21

Drawing a Diamond Shape

Now that the ellipse is drawn, the next step is to draw the diamond shape that resembles a flower in the logo. To assist in positioning the diamond shape, use the guides. Recall that when an object is close to a guide, its corner or its center (whichever is closer) snaps to or attaches itself to, the guide. Perform the steps on the next page to draw the diamond shape.

TO DRAW A DIAMOND SHAPE ▼

STEP 1 ▶

Click the AutoShapes button (🖉) on the Drawing toolbar. When the AutoShapes toolbar displays, point to the Diamond Tool button.

The AutoShapes toolbar displays (Figure 2-22). The AutoShapes button is recessed.

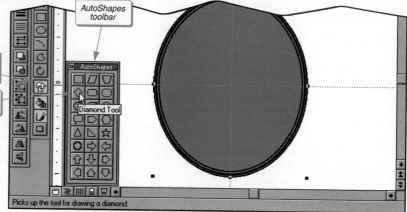

FIGURE 2-22

STEP 2 ▶

Click the Diamond Tool button. Then, position the cross-hair pointer at the intersection of the horizontal and vertical guides.

The cross-hair pointer is positioned at the center of the ellipse (Figure 2-23). The Diamond Tool button is recessed, indicating it is selected.

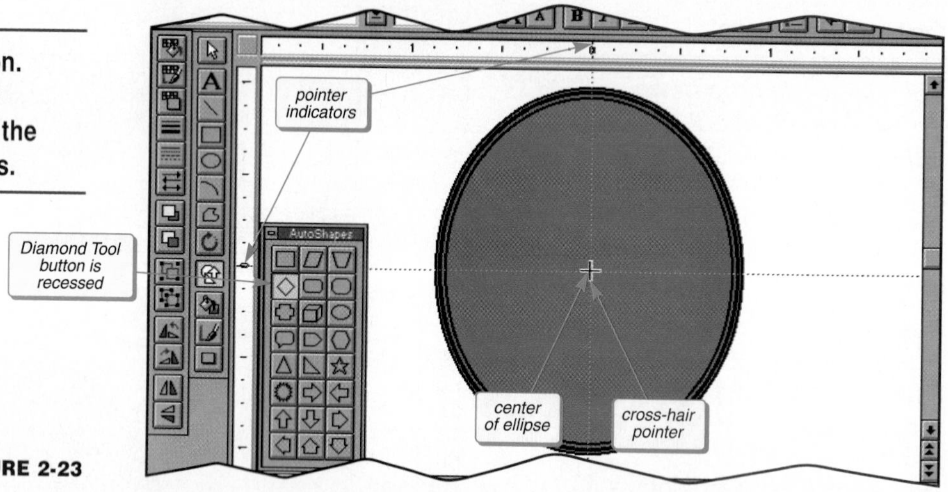

FIGURE 2-23

STEP 3 ▶

Press and hold down the CTRL key, press and hold down the left mouse button, and drag the cross-hair pointer up and to the right of center until the pointer indicator is approximately on the 3/8" tick mark on the horizontal ruler and about halfway between the 1/4" and the 3/8" tick marks on the vertical ruler (approximately 5/16"). Release the left mouse button and then the CTRL key.

The diamond object displays in the center of the ellipse (Figure 2-24). A selection rectangle displays around the diamond object.

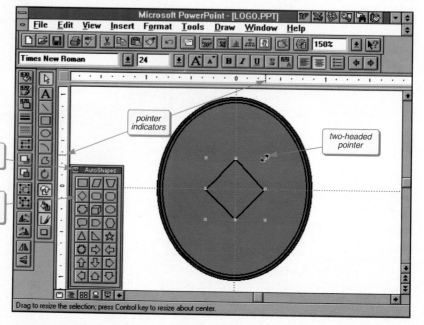

FIGURE 2-24

STEP 4 ▶

Click the AutoShapes Control-menu box to hide the AutoShapes toolbar. Drag the diamond object up toward the top of the slide until the bottom of the diamond object snaps to the horizontal guide.

The bottom of the diamond object aligns with the horizontal guide (Figure 2-25). The AutoShapes toolbar no longer displays.

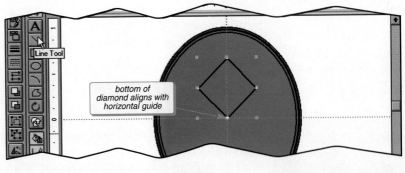

FIGURE 2-25

Drawing a Straight Line

The next object to add to The Software Institute logo is a straight line. PowerPoint allows you to constrain the angle of a line to by holding down the SHIFT key while you draw. Recall from Project 1 that constraining means to control the shape of the object. When you hold down the SHIFT key while using the Line Tool button to draw a line, the line can be drawn only at 45° angles. Perform the following steps to draw a straight line.

TO DRAW A STRAIGHT LINE ▼

STEP 1 ▶

Click the Line Tool button ( ) on the Drawing toolbar. Then, position the cross-hair pointer on the intersection of the horizontal and vertical guides at the bottom of the diamond object.

The Line Tool button is recessed, indicating it is selected (Figure 2-26).

FIGURE 2-26

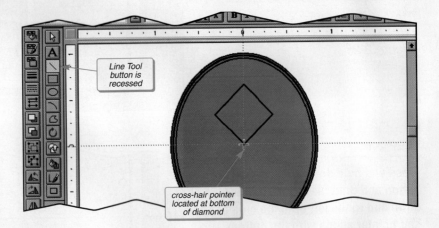

STEP 2 ▶

To constrain the angle of the line, press and hold down the SHIFT key, press and hold down the left mouse button, then drag the cross-hair pointer down the vertical guide 1/2" on the vertical ruler. Release the left mouse button and then release the SHIFT key.

A straight line displays beneath the diamond object (Figure 2-27). The Line Tool button no longer is recessed.

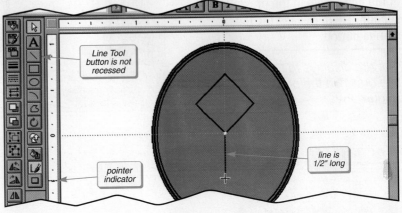

FIGURE 2-27

To draw a straight line when the guides are not displaying, click the Line Tool button, press and hold down the SHIFT key, press and hold down the left mouse button, and drag the mouse pointer. Release the left mouse button and then the SHIFT key.

Drawing an Arc

The next step is to add two arcs to the logo. Use the guides to help you draw the arcs. Before drawing the arcs, you will need to move the vertical guide. To move the vertical guide, position the mouse pointer on the guide and then drag it to its new position in the PowerPoint window. Perform the following steps to relocate the verticle guide and draw an arc.

TO DRAW AN ARC ▼

STEP 1 ▶

Drag the vertical guide to the 1/2" tick mark right of center. Click the Arc Tool button ( ) on the Drawing toolbar and position the cross-hair pointer on the intersection of the horizontal and vertical guides.

The Arc Tool button is recessed, indicating that it is selected (Figure 2-28).

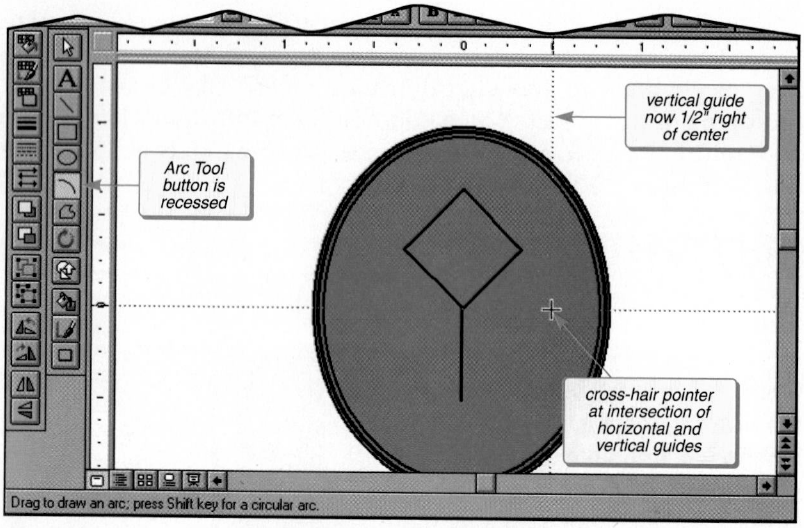

FIGURE 2-28

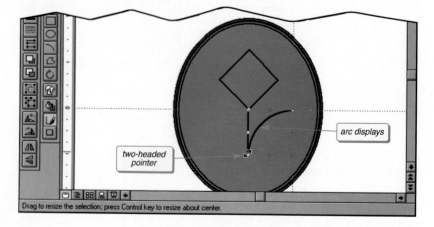

STEP 2 ▶

Press and hold down the left mouse button and drag the mouse pointer down and to the left until the cross-hair pointer aligns with the bottom of the line drawn in the previous section. Then, release the left mouse button.

The arc displays to the right of the line drawn in the previous section (Figure 2-29).

FIGURE 2-29

Drawing the Second Arc

The logo has two arcs — one on the right side of the line and one on the left side of the line. The first arc is drawn. Follow the steps below to draw the second arc.

TO DRAW THE SECOND ARC

Step 1: Drag the vertical guide to the 1/2" tick mark left of center.

Step 2: Click the Arc Tool button. Position the cross-hair pointer on the intersection of the horizontal and vertical guides.

Step 3: Drag the mouse pointer down and to the right until the cross-hair pointer aligns with the bottom of the line in the logo.

The arc displays to the left of the line in the logo (Figure 2-30).

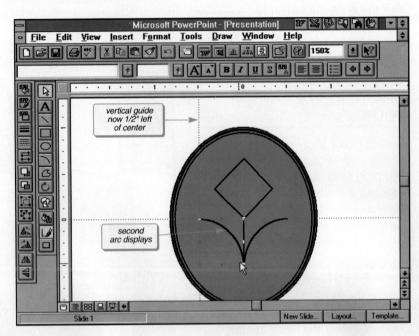

FIGURE 2-30

Saving the Presentation

The drawing of the logo is complete. Because the logo is being created in a separate presentation and has not yet been saved, save it to your data diskette with the filename LOGO.PPT.

Adding Shaded Fill Color

The diamond object in The Software Institute logo in Figure 2-12 on page PP81 has a light-blue shaded fill color. **Shaded fill** gives an object a three-dimensional look by gradually lightening or darkening the fill color. Choose a shaded fill by selecting a shade style, a color, and then a variant. A **variant** is one of the shading variations that display in the Variants box on the Shaded Fill dialog box. PowerPoint has six shade styles from which to choose: Vertical, Horizontal, Diagonal Right, Diagonal Left, From Corner, and From Center. The shade style determines the direction of the shading effect. For example, the Vertical shade style creates shading variations that change from the top of an object through the bottom of the object. The Horizontal shade style creates shading variations that change from one side of the object through the opposite side of the object. The Color box on the Shaded Fill dialog box displays the current shade color. The degree of shading is controlled by moving the Shaded Fill scroll bar box to the left for darker shading or move it to the right for lighter shading. Perform the steps on the next two pages to add shaded fill color.

TO ADD SHADED FILL COLOR ▼

STEP 1 ►

Click the diamond object to select it. Click the Fill Color button (▨) on the Drawing+ tool bar. Then, point to the Shaded command on the Fill Color drop-down list.

The Fill Color drop-down list displays (Figure 2-31). The light-blue color sample is selected because it is the default fill color when a template is not selected.

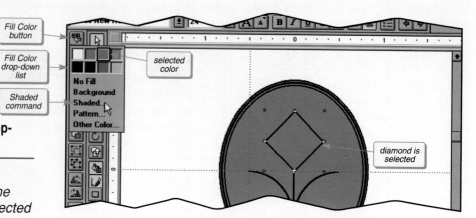

FIGURE 2-31

STEP 2 ►

Choose the Shaded command. When the Shaded Fill dialog box displays, select the From Center option button in the Shade Styles box. Then, point to the right variation in the Variants box.

The Shaded Fill dialog box displays (Figure 2-32). The From Center shade style option button is selected. By default, the left variation is selected in the Variants box.

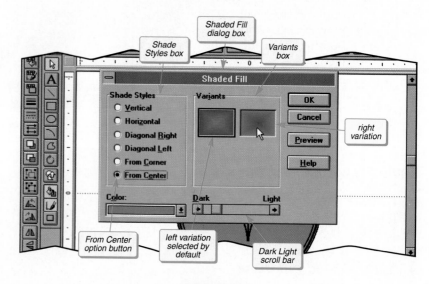

FIGURE 2-32

STEP 3 ►

Click the right variation. Then, drag the scroll bar box to the extreme right of the Dark Light scroll bar.

As you move the Dark Light scroll bar box, the variations in the Variants box reflect the changes in lightness (Figure 2-33).

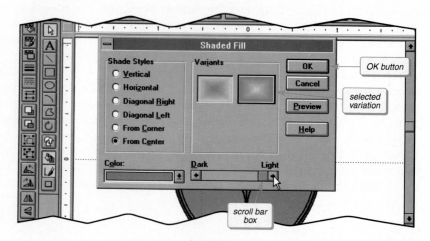

FIGURE 2-33

STEP 4 ▶

Choose the OK button.

The diamond object's fill color displays shaded from center (Figure 2-34).

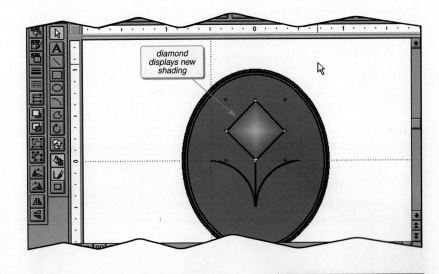

FIGURE 2-34

Grouping the Logo Objects

Before continuing with the logo, group the objects together to form one object. This prevents the individual objects that compose the logo from being moved out of position. Recall from Project 1 that you group objects together with the Group button on the Drawing+ toolbar. Perform the following steps to group the logo objects.

TO GROUP OBJECTS

Step 1: Select the Edit menu and choose the Select All command.

Step 2: Click the Group button on the Drawing+ toolbar.

The logo objects are grouped into one object (Figure 2-35). A selection rectangle displays around the grouped object.

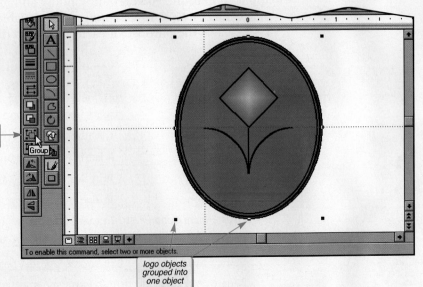

FIGURE 2-35

▶ CREATING A GRAPHIC IMAGE WITH TEXT

The Software Institute logo contains text that has been manipulated into a graphic image using Microsoft WordArt. **Microsoft WordArt**, a supplementary application that comes with PowerPoint, allows you to create graphic images with text. Because Microsoft WordArt is an object linking and embedding (OLE) application, its menu bar and toolbar display in the PowerPoint window when you open the Microsoft WordArt application. The next several sections explain how to use Microsoft WordArt to create the graphic text image shown in Figure 2-12 on page PP81.

Decreasing Zoom Control

Before you begin to work in Microsoft WordArt, you want to reduce the size of the object displayed. By reducing Zoom Control, you will be able to see the logo and the Microsoft WordArt window. The following steps summarize how to reduce Zoom Control.

FIGURE 2-36

Zoom Control displays as 66%

Zoom Control box arrow

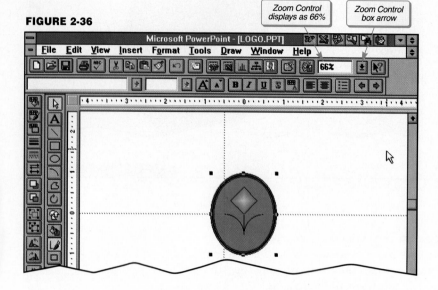

TO DECREASE ZOOM CONTROL

Step 1: Click the Zoom Control box arrow.

Step 2: Select 66%.

Zoom Control changes to 66% (Figure 2-36).

Opening the Microsoft WordArt Application into the PowerPoint Window

To create the graphic text image in The Software Institute logo, you first must open the Microsoft WordArt application. OLE brings this supplementary application to the PowerPoint window and makes the menus, buttons, and toolbar in the Microsoft WordArt application available in the PowerPoint window. Table 2-3 explains the purpose of each button on the Microsoft WordArt toolbar.

▸ **TABLE 2-3**

ICON	NAME	FUNCTION
—Plain Text ⬦	Shape box	A list from which you choose a shape
Arial ⬦	Font box	A list from which you choose a font
Best Fit ⬦	Size box	A list from which you choose a font size
B	Bold button	To make Microsoft WordArt text thick
I	Italic button	To add a slight slant to Microsoft WordArt letters
Ee	Even Height button	To make all letters the same height regardless of capitalization
◁	Flip button	To turn letters on their sides
ᴬ	Stretch button	To stretch out text both horizontally and vertically
ᵉ≣	Align button	Left justify, right justify, center, stretch justify, word justify, or letter justify text
AV↔	Spacing Between Characters button	To display options for adjusting spacing between text characters
C	Rotation button	To display options for rotating text
▨	Shading button	To display options for adding patterns and colors to text
▢	Shadow button	To display options for adding shadow to text
≡	Border button	To display options for choosing a border thickness to text

Once open, Microsoft WordArt displays a window and a box as explained in the following steps.

TO OPEN THE MICROSOFT WORDART APPLICATION INTO THE POWERPOINT WINDOW ▼

STEP 1 ▶

From the Insert menu, choose the Object command. When the Insert Object dialog box displays, scroll through the Object Type list until Microsoft WordArt 2.0 displays.

The Insert Object dialog box displays (Figure 2-37). By default, the Create New option button is selected.

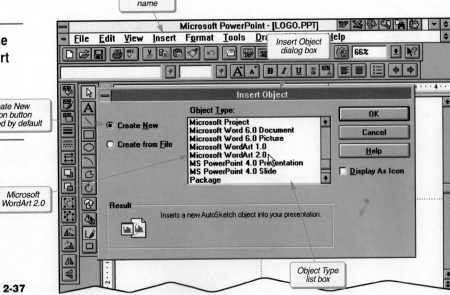

FIGURE 2-37

STEP 2 ▶

Double-click Microsoft WordArt 2.0.

The Microsoft WordArt application opens and displays its menus and toolbar (Figure 2-38). The Enter Your Text Here dialog box displays. The selected text inside the Enter Your Text Here box displays in the Microsoft WordArt window.

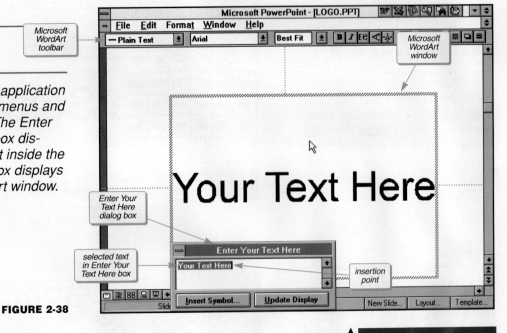

FIGURE 2-38

Entering Text

When you create a graphic image in Microsoft WordArt, you enter the text for your graphic image in the Enter Your Text Here dialog box. By default, Microsoft WordArt highlights the words Your Text Here in the Enter Your Text Here box. When you type the text for your graphic image, it replaces the highlighted text. Press the ENTER key each time you want to start a new line. Perform the steps on the next page to type the text for the graphic image on the logo.

TO ENTER TEXT ▼

STEP 1 ▶

With the text in the Enter Your Text Here box still selected, type The Software **and press the ENTER key two times. Type** Institute

Three text lines display in the Enter Your Text Here box: (1) The Software text line, (2) a blank text line, and (3) Institute text line (Figure 2-39). Microsoft WordArt updates the text in the Microsoft WordArt window when you click the Update Display button in the Enter Your Text Here dialog box, or when you click one of the buttons on the Microsoft WordArt toolbar, or when you click a menu name.

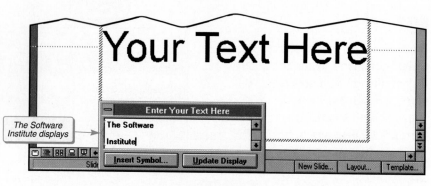

FIGURE 2-39

STEP 2 ▶

Click the Shape box arrow on the Microsoft WordArt toolbar. When the Shape list displays, point to the Button (Pour) shape ( ) (column 4, row 3).

The Shape list displays (Figure 2-40). By default, Plain Text is the selected shape. When you click a button on the Microsoft WordArt toolbar, the text in the Enter Your Text Here box displays in the Microsoft WordArt window.

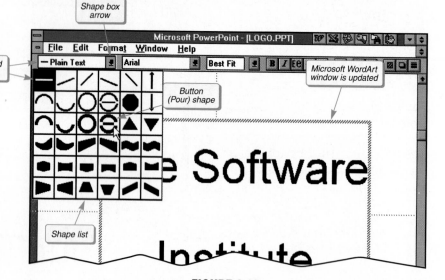

FIGURE 2-40

STEP 3 ▶

Click the Button (Pour) shape.

WordArt applies the Button (Pour) shape to the text in the Microsoft WordArt window (Figure 2-41).

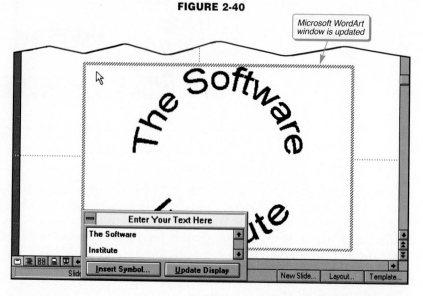

FIGURE 2-41

The Microsoft WordArt toolbar does not have a Copy button or a Paste button. Nor does the Edit menu contain a Copy command or a Paste command. To use Microsoft WordArt to create a graphic image with text created in an application that supports the Copy command, copy the text in the original application and paste it into the Enter Your Text Here box by pressing the CTRL+V keys.

Changing Fonts

In Microsoft WordArt, the default font is Arial. You want to change the Microsoft WordArt font to Arial Rounded MT. Perform the following steps to change the font.

TO CHANGE FONTS ▼

STEP 1 ▶

Click the Font box arrow on the Microsoft WordArt toolbar. When the Font list displays, point to Arial Rounded MT. If Arial Rounded MT is not available on your computer, point to a similar font.

The Font list displays available fonts (Figure 2-42).

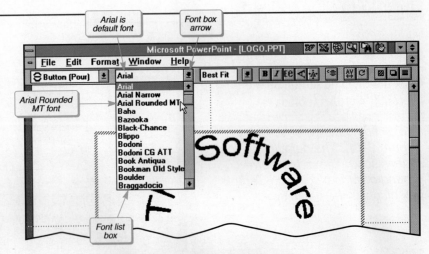

FIGURE 2-42

STEP 2 ▶

Select Arial Rounded MT or a similar font.

The font of the text in the Microsoft WordArt window changes to Arial Rounded MT (Figure 2-43).

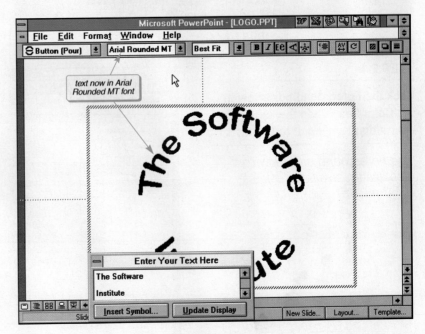

FIGURE 2-43

Changing Font Color

Microsoft WordArt has a Shading button to give you options for adding color and patterns to your Microsoft WordArt text. The Shading dialog box contains three boxes: a Style box, a Color box, and a Sample box. The **Style box** displays twenty-four pattern styles. The **Color box** contains a drop-down list box for the text foreground color and another drop-down list box for the text background color. Select a new foreground color by clicking the box arrow in the Foreground drop-down list box. Select a new background color by clicking the box arrow in the Background drop-down list box. The **Sample box** displays a preview of the selected pattern and colors.

In this project, you change the Microsoft WordArt text to solid yellow. Follow the steps below to change font color.

TO CHANGE FONT COLOR ▼

STEP 1 ▶

Click the Shading button on the Microsoft WordArt toolbar.

The Shading dialog box displays (Figure 2-44). The default shading style is solid. The default foreground color is black. The Sample box displays the defaults.

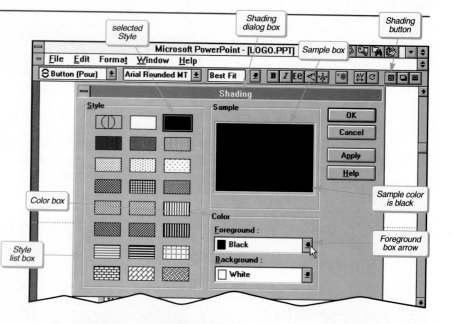

FIGURE 2-44

STEP 2 ▶

Click the Foreground box arrow in the Color box. When the list of colors displays, point to Yellow.

The Foreground drop-down list displays the available colors (Figure 2-45).

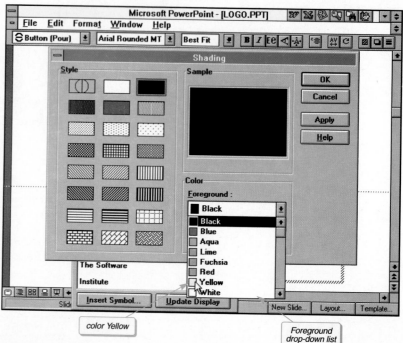

FIGURE 2-45

STEP 3 ▶

Select Yellow. Then, point to the OK button in the Shading dialog box.

The Sample box displays the solid style and the yellow foreground color (Figure 2-46). The background color is not visible because the style is solid.

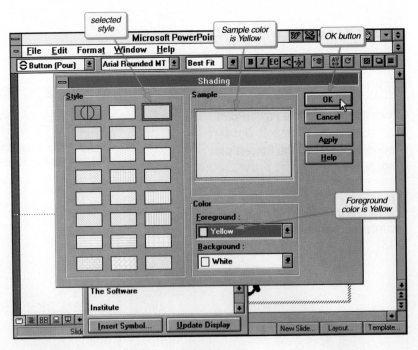

FIGURE 2-46

STEP 4 ▶

Choose the OK button.

Microsoft WordArt applies the solid style and yellow foreground color to the text in the Microsoft WordArt window (Figure 2-47).

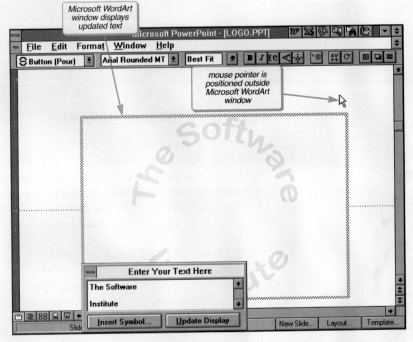

FIGURE 2-47

Exiting the Microsoft WordArt Application

The graphic image is complete. You now must exit the Microsoft WordArt application and update the logo. Perform the step on the next page to exit Microsoft WordArt.

TO EXIT MICROSOFT WORDART ▼

STEP 1 ▶

Click anywhere on the PowerPoint slide outside the Microsoft WordArt window to return to the PowerPoint window.

The PowerPoint window displays. The Microsoft WordArt object is centered around the logo (Figure 2-48).

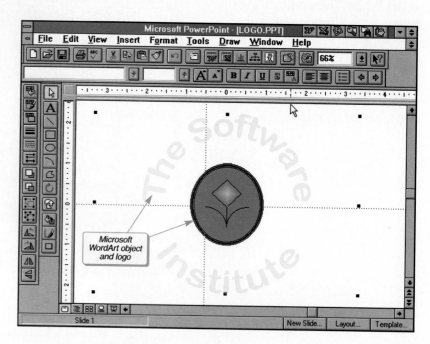

FIGURE 2-48

Turning Off the Snap to Grid

Because you want to control the exact placement of the graphic image created in Microsoft WordArt, you turn off the Snap to Grid. Recall from Project 1 that when you move an object close to one of the invisible gridlines, it jumps to it as though the gridline was a magnet. Therefore, if the Snap to Grid is turned on, it can prevent you from placing an object exactly where you would like. Follow the steps below to turn off the Snap to Grid.

TO TURN OFF THE SNAP TO GRID

Step 1: Select the Draw menu.
Step 2: Choose the Snap to Grid command.

PowerPoint turns off the Snap to Grid Command.

To move an object to a precise location, you can temporarily turn off the grid by pressing the ALT key as you drag the object. This method also works when drawing an object.

Scaling a Graphic Image

The graphic image created in Microsoft WordArt is too large to fit inside the ellipse. To reduce the size of the graphic image, use the Scale command. Scaling the graphic image to 36% of its original size will reduce it to fit inside the logo. The following steps summarize how to scale an object.

TO SCALE THE GRAPHIC IMAGE

Step 1: Select the graphic image created in Microsoft WordArt by clicking it.

Step 2: Select the Draw menu and choose the Scale command.

Step 3: When the Scale dialog box displays, type 36

Step 4: Choose the OK button.

The graphic image is scaled to 36% (Figure 2-49).

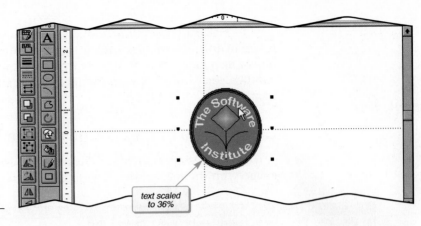

FIGURE 2-49

Recall from Project 1 that if you do not know the number to type in the Scale To box in Step 3 above, you can type a number and then click the Preview button. This allows you to see if you need to increase the number to increase the size of the object or decrease the number to decrease the size of the object. Continue to change the number in the Scale To box and click the Preview button until the object displays at the proper scale. An alternative to scaling the Microsoft WordArt text is to resize it about center.

Changing the Shape of the Graphic Image

The shape of the graphic image created in Microsoft WordArt is a circle. The shape of the logo is an ellipse. In order to change the shape of the graphic image from a circle to an ellipse, you will vertically resize the image about center. Recall from Project 1 that you resize an object about center by holding down the CTRL key while dragging a resize handle. Holding down the CTRL key constrains the direction of an object when you resize it.

Additionally, when you resize the graphic image in this project, you create a margin between the graphic image and the border of the logo. A **margin** is the blank space around an object. Perform the following step to change a circle to an ellipse.

TO CHANGE A CIRCLE TO AN ELLIPSE ▼

STEP 1 ▶

With the graphic image selected, press and hold down the CTRL key, and drag the center-bottom resize handle down until the pointer indicator on the vertical ruler displays near the 7/8" tick mark. Release the mouse button and then the CTRL key.

The graphic image displays as an ellipse within the border of the logo object (Figure 2-50).

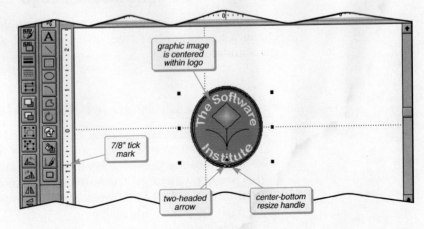

FIGURE 2-50

To resize an object horizontally, hold down the CTRL key and drag one of the resize handles on the left side or the right side of the selection box. To resize an object diagonally, hold down the CTRL key and drag one of the corner resize handles. Resizing an object diagonally maintains the object's height-to-width relationship.

Grouping the Graphic Image with the Logo Object

The final step in creating The Software Institute logo is to group the graphic image with the logo object. The following steps summarize how to group objects.

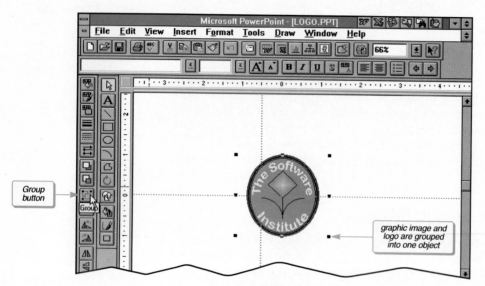

TO GROUP THE GRAPHIC IMAGE WITH THE LOGO OBJECT

Step 1: From the Edit menu, choose the Select All command.

Step 2: Click the Group button on the Drawing+ toolbar.

The graphic image and logo object are grouped into one object (Figure 2-51).

FIGURE 2-51

Grouping the graphic image with the logo object converts the graphic image into a PowerPoint object. The link is lost between the graphic image and the Microsoft WordArt application, so that if you double-click the graphic image created in Microsoft WordArt, the Microsoft WordArt application will not start automatically. If you ungroup the logo, however, you can once again double-click the graphic image and automatically start Microsoft WordArt.

Saving The Software Institute Logo

The Software Institute logo now is complete. Because you have made several changes since your last save, save LOGO.PPT again by clicking the Save button on the Standard toolbar.

▶ ADDING A LOGO TO A PRESENTATION

O nce a logo is created, it can be added to any new or existing presentation. Add a logo by copying a logo object from its presentation and then pasting it into the presentation in which you want it to display. For example, in this project, you copy The Software Institute logo object from LOGO.PPT and paste it into the PROJ2.PPT presentation. If you want the logo to display on every slide, paste it to the Slide Master.

Perform the following steps to add The Software Institute logo to the Slide Master in Project 2.

TO ADD A LOGO TO A PRESENTATION ▼

STEP 1 ▶

With The Software Institute logo still selected, click the Copy button (⧉) on the Standard toolbar.

A copy of The Software Institute logo is placed on the Clipboard.

STEP 2 ▶

Select the Window menu and point to PROJ2.PPT (Figure 2-52).

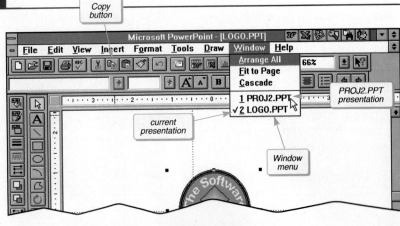

FIGURE 2-52

STEP 3 ▶

Choose PROJ2.PPT.

PowerPoint displays the PROJ2.PPT presentation (Figure 2-53). LOGO.PPT is still open, but it does not display.

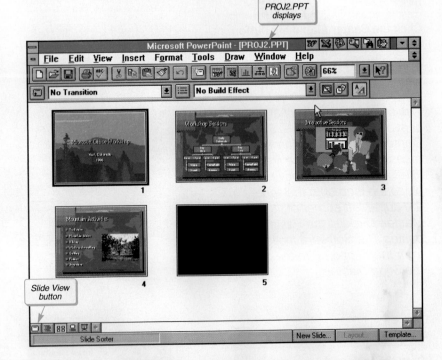

FIGURE 2-53

STEP 4 ▶

Press and hold down the SHIFT key and click the Slide View button. Release the SHIFT key.

PowerPoint displays the Slide Master for PROJ2.PPT (Figure 2-54).

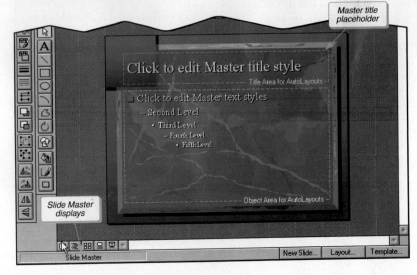

FIGURE 2-54

STEP 5 ▶

Click anywhere on the Slide Master Title Area to edit the Master title style.

The Master title placeholder is selected (Figure 2-55). The Left Alignment button is recessed because the marbles.ppt template Master title style is left-aligned.

FIGURE 2-55

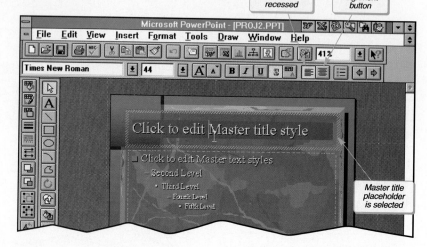

STEP 6 ▶

Click the Center Alignment button on the Formatting toolbar. Click the Paste button on the Standard toolbar.

The Master title style changes to center aligned (Figure 2-56). The Center Alignment button is recessed. Because the Master title is centered, you have room to place the logo onto the square in the upper left corner of the Slide Master. Clicking the Paste button pastes The Software Institute logo from the Clipboard to the center of the Slide Master.

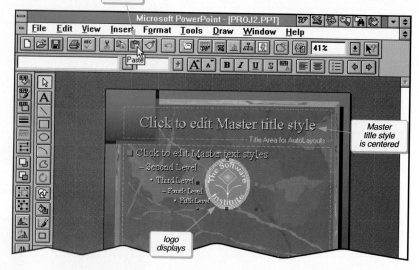

FIGURE 2-56

STEP 7 ▶

Drag the logo to the upper left corner of the Slide Master.

The logo displays in the upper left corner of the Slide Master (Figure 2-57).

FIGURE 2-57

Adjusting the Size and Placement of the Logo

To position the logo in the middle of the square in the upper left corner of the Slide Master, you first must scale the logo and then drag it to the center of the square. Recall that scaling changes the size of an object while maintaining the proportions of the object. Because you want to create a margin between the logo and the edges of the square in the upper left corner of the Slide Master, you scale the logo to 75%. After you scale the logo, drag it to the center of the square. The following steps summarize how to scale and position the logo.

TO ADJUST THE SIZE AND PLACEMENT OF THE LOGO

Step 1: With the logo still selected, select the Draw menu and choose the Scale command.

Step 2: Type 75 in the Scale dialog box and choose the OK button.

Step 3: Drag the logo to center it vertically and horizontally in the box in the upper left corner of the Slide Master.

The logo displays in the center of the square in the upper left corner of the Slide Master (Figure 2-58).

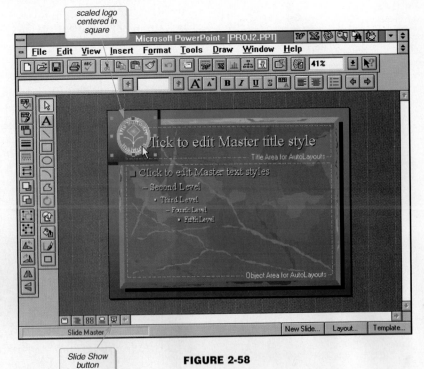

FIGURE 2-58

If you want to make small adjustments in the position of the logo, select the logo and press the arrow keys on the keyboard that correspond to the direction in which you wish to move.

To inspect the logo and color scheme, click the Slide Show button. Notice the logo does not display on the title slide because the Mountain View clip art object overlays all objects on the slide. (For more information on clip art object overlays, see page PP18 in Project 1.) Also notice that the logo uses the color scheme of the slide.

▶ ADDING A BORDER TO A PICTURE

Recall from Project 1, that Slide 4 encourages prospective workshop attendees to integrate educational activities with recreational activities. To emphasize the picture on Slide 4 in this project, you will add a three-line border with dark green lines and rose fill color.

Earlier in this project, when you applied the marbles.ppt template, PowerPoint returned the picture to its original size. Before adding the border, resize the picture to match the height of the bulleted list; thus, balancing the slide. Perform the steps on the next page to resize and add a border to the horse picture on Slide 4.

TO RESIZE AND ADD A BORDER

Step 1: Click the Slide View button to return to Slide view. Click the Next Slide button twice to display Slide 4.

Step 2: Select the picture object. Press and hold down the CTRL key and drag the middle-top resize handle to resize the picture about center so that its height is the same as the bulleted list in Figure 2-59. Release the left mouse button. Release the CTRL key.

Step 3: Click the Line Style button (▤) on the Drawing+ toolbar. When the Line Style list box displays, choose the bottom line style (three lines).

Step 4: Click the Line Color button (▤) on the Drawing+ toolbar. When the Line Color list box displays, choose the dark green color sample (column 2, row 1).

Step 5: Click the Fill Color button (▤) on the Drawing+ toolbar. When the Fill Color list box displays, choose the rose color sample (column 3, row 2). If the rose color is not in the list box, select the Other Color option, select the rose color box, and choose the OK button.

A border displays around the picture of the horses (Figure 2-59).

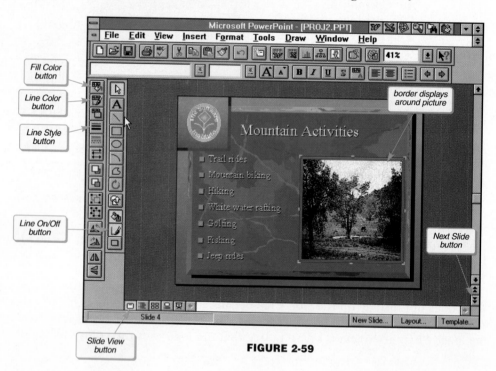

FIGURE 2-59

When you add a border, it becomes part of the object. When you apply a fill color to an object with a border, it is applied to the object and its border. The fill color is not visible behind the picture object in Figure 2-59 because the picture hides it. Fill color is visible, however, when the object contains white space, such as the space between the lines in the border. Recall that white space is blank space added for the purpose of directing the attention of the audience to specific text or graphics. The fill color is visible inside the border because the border has white space. Hence, the visibility of fill color depends on the chosen line style and the contents of the object.

To remove a border from an object, select the object and click the Line On/Off button on the Drawing toolbar. Alternatively, you can remove a border from a selected object by clicking the Line Color button on the Drawing+ toolbar and selecting the No Line option.

Saving Project 2 Again

Because you have made several changes since your last save, save your presentation now.

▶ CREATING A "DRILL DOWN" DOCUMENT

T he next step in customizing the Microsoft Office Workshop presentation is to add a slide to demonstrate the four Microsoft Office applications featured in the workshop. You will add the new slide after Slide 2. Figure 2-60 illustrates the new Slide 3, which contains four icons to reference each of the four Microsoft Office applications presented at the Microsoft Office Workshop. An **icon** is a graphic representation of a command. For example, the picture on the face of the Copy button is an icon. When you click the button, you actually execute the Copy command.

In this project, an icon represents a "drill down" document.
Recall that a **"drill down"
document** is a file created in an
object linking and embedding (OLE)
application such as Microsoft Word
or Microsoft Excel. When you run
the presentation, clicking one of
the icons activates the associated
application and loads the designated file. For example, if you click
the Microsoft Word icon on Slide 3,
PowerPoint opens the Microsoft
Word 6.0 application and loads
the Microsoft Word document
CLE2-2MD.DOC. For a "drill down"
document to function properly, the
application used to create the OLE
object must be installed on the
computer used to run the presentation. The applications required for
Slide 3 are Microsoft Word 6,
Microsoft Excel 5, Microsoft
PowerPoint 4, and Microsoft
Access 2.

FIGURE 2-60

"Drill down" documents give you the ability to run an application during a slide show without leaving PowerPoint. Once a "drill down" document displays, you can make changes to the source document. A **source document** is the file or document in which a linked object is created. A **linked object** is similar to an embedded object, in that it is created in another application. The difference between a linked object and an embedded object is the linked object maintains a connection to its source. Whenever the original object changes, the linked object also changes. A linked object is stored in its source document. The PowerPoint presentation stores a representation of the original document and information about its location. PowerPoint is a container document for the linked object. A **container document** is the receiver of a linked object.

When you create a "drill down" document, you can display either the document object or an icon that represents the document object. With either choice, you click the document object or the icon to activate the source document when running the slide show.

Creating the slide shown in Figure 2-60 on the previous page requires several steps. First, add a new slide to your presentation. Next, apply the new color scheme. Then, create a "drill down" document for each of the four applications featured in the workshop; after which, you scale the icons that represent the "drill down" documents. Finally, add captions to the icons. The next several sections explain how to create Slide 3.

Adding a New Slide

The first step in creating Slide 3 in this project is to add a new slide. The following steps summarize how to add a new slide.

TO ADD A NEW SLIDE

Step 1: Click the Slide Sorter View button.
Step 2: Position the insertion point between Slide 2 and Slide 3 by pointing to the location and clicking the left mouse button.
Step 3: Click the New Slide button on the status bar.
Step 4: When the New Slide dialog box displays, type 19 to select the 4 Objects slide layout.
Step 5: Choose the OK button.

The new Slide 3 displays the 4 Objects slide layout (Figure 2-61). Slide 3 has the original color scheme of the marbles.ppt template because the new color scheme was applied to only selected slides. PowerPoint automatically renumbers the original Slide 3, Slide 4, and Slide 5 as Slide 4, Slide 5, and Slide 6, respectively.

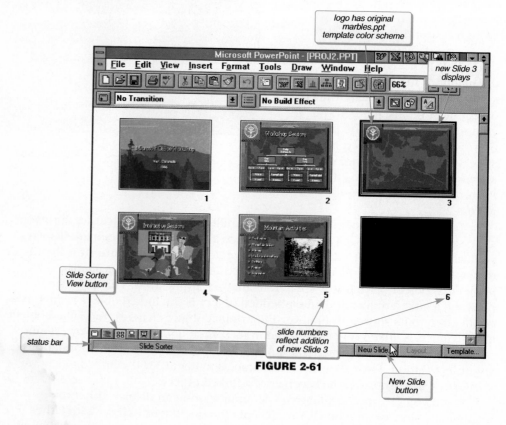

FIGURE 2-61

Copying and Applying a Color Scheme

When you added Slide 3, it maintained the color scheme of the marbles.ppt template. Before continuing the development of Slide 3, apply the color scheme selected earlier in this project. PowerPoint has a Pick Up Color Scheme command to copy the color scheme of a slide quickly so you can later apply it to another slide. Perform the following steps to pick up the color scheme from Slide 2 and apply it to Slide 3.

TO COPY AND APPLY A COLOR SCHEME ▼

STEP 1 ▶

Point to Slide 2 and click the right mouse button.

A shortcut menu displays (Figure 2-62).

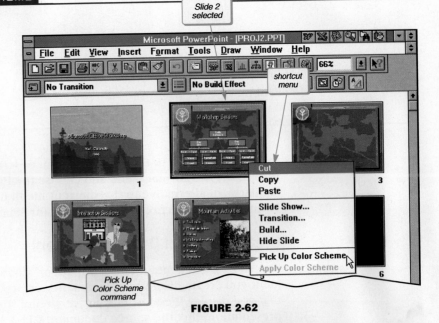

FIGURE 2-62

STEP 2 ▶

Choose the Pick Up Color Scheme command.

PowerPoint copies the attributes of the color scheme on Slide 2.

STEP 3 ▶

Point to Slide 3 and click the right mouse button.

A shortcut menu displays (Figure 2-63).

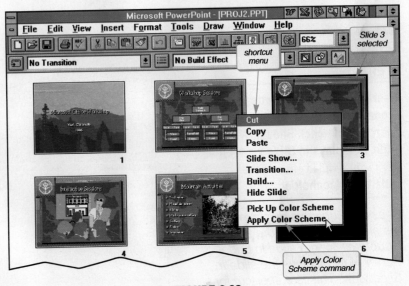

FIGURE 2-63

STEP 4 ▶

Choose the Apply Color Scheme command.

PowerPoint applies the color scheme attributes of Slide 2 to Slide 3 (Figure 2-64).

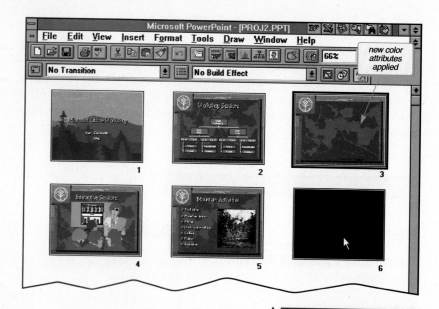

FIGURE 2-64

An alternative to the shortcut menu described in Step 2 on the previous page, is to select the Format menu and choose the Pick Up Color Scheme command. Similarly, an alternative to the shortcut menu described in Step 4, is to select the Format menu and choose the Apply Color Scheme command.

Creating a "Drill Down" Document

Slide 3 will contain four "drill down" documents. The first "drill down" document you create illustrates a form letter created in Microsoft Word. To be certain that you display the most current version of this form letter when you run the presentation, link the source document CLE2-2MD.DOC. The next section explains how to create a "drill down" document.

TO CREATE A "DRILL DOWN" DOCUMENT ▼

STEP 1 ▶

Insert the Student Diskette that accompanies this book into drive A. Then, double-click Slide 3. When Slide 3 displays in Slide view, type Session Highlights **in the slide title placeholder.**

Session Highlights displays as the slide title text (Figure 2-65). Double-clicking a slide in Slide Sorter view displays the slide in Slide view. This is a shortcut for selecting the slide in Slide Sorter view and then clicking the Slide View button.

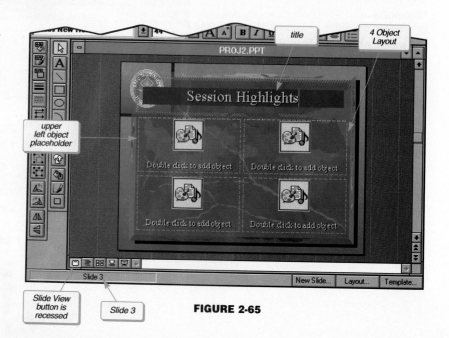

FIGURE 2-65

STEP 2 ▶

Double-click the upper left object placeholder. When the Insert Object dialog box displays, select the Create from File option button. Then, point to the Browse button.

The Insert Object dialog box displays (Figure 2-66). The Create from File option button is selected.

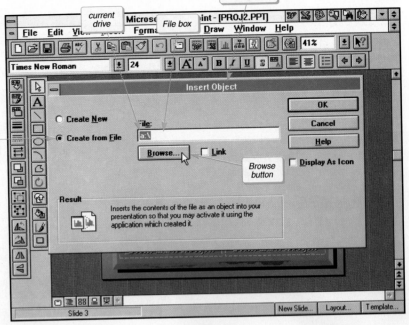

FIGURE 2-66

STEP 3 ▶

Choose the Browse button. When the Browse dialog box displays, double-click word6 in the Directories list box. Then, point to cle2-2md.doc in the Source list box.

The Browse dialog box displays (Figure 2-67). Drive A is the current drive as designated in the Drives box. If drive A is not the current drive, click the Drives box arrow and select drive A. The files contained in the word6 subdirectory display in the Source list box.

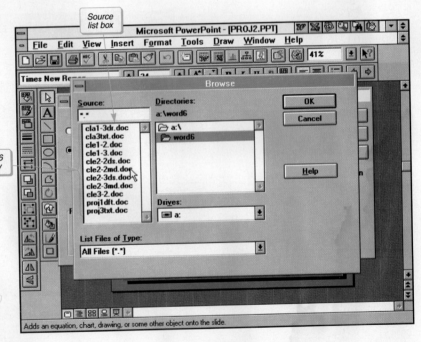

FIGURE 2-67

STEP 4 ▶

Double-click cle2-2md.doc. When the Insert Object dialog box displays, click the Link and the Display As Icon check boxes.

The Insert Object dialog box displays again (Figure 2-68). The File box identifies the selected file. The Link and the Display As Icon check boxes are selected. PowerPoint displays a preview of the "drill down" document icon.

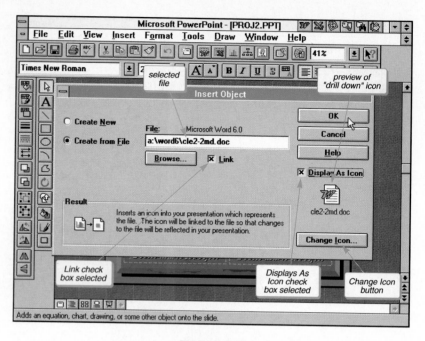

FIGURE 2-68

STEP 5 ▶

Choose the OK button.

The Word "drill down" icon displays in the upper left object placeholder (Figure 2-69).

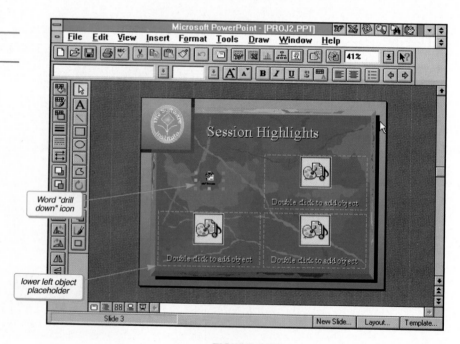

FIGURE 2-69

If you wanted to select a different icon for the "drill down" document, you would select the Change Icon button in the Insert Object dialog box (see Figure 2-68). When the Change Icon dialog box displays, select a new icon from the From File box. The icon label can be changed by typing a new label name in the Label box in the Change Icon dialog box. After making your icon changes, choose the OK button. When the Insert Object dialog box displays, choose the OK button.

Adding a Spreadsheet to a Presentation as a "Drill Down" Document

Because Microsoft Excel is an OLE application, it too, can be added to the presentation as a "drill down" document. When the slide show is running, you can activate the Microsoft Excel application and edit the CLE4-3.XLS spreadsheet and chart. The following steps summarize adding a Microsoft Excel spreadsheet as a "drill down" document.

TO ADD A SPREADSHEET TO A PRESENTATION AS A "DRILL DOWN" DOCUMENT

Step 1: Double-click the lower left object placeholder on Slide 3.

Step 2: When the Insert Object dialog box displays, select the Create from File option button. Choose the Browse button.

Step 3: When the Browse dialog box displays, double-click the root directory in the Directories list box. Double-click excel5. Double-click cle4-3.xls in the Source list box.

Step 4: When the Insert Object dialog box displays, select the Link and the Display As Icon check boxes.

Step 5: Choose the OK button.

The Excel "drill down" icon displays in the lower left object placeholder (Figure 2-70).

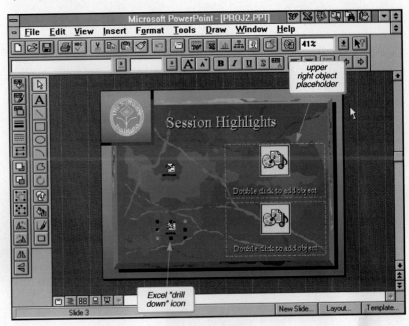

FIGURE 2-70

▶ LINKING A POWERPOINT PRESENTATION

L inking a PowerPoint presentation is the same as creating a "drill down" document. The difference between all other "drill down" documents and a linked PowerPoint presentation is obvious only when you run the presentation. When you activate any other "drill down" document, the application window associated with the document displays so you can edit the source document. When you activate a linked presentation, the PowerPoint window does not display. Instead, the linked presentation runs in Slide Show view.

The process for linking a PowerPoint presentation is the same as creating a "drill down" document. The source file is a PowerPoint presentation, however. Perform the steps on the next page to link a PowerPoint presentation.

TO LINK A POWERPOINT PRESENTATION

Step 1: Double-click the upper right object placeholder on Slide 3.

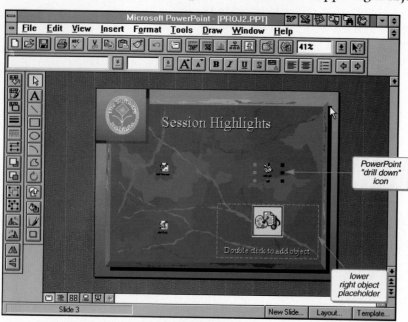

Step 2: When the Insert Object dialog box displays, select the Create from File option button. Choose the Browse button.

Step 3: When the Browse dialog box displays, double-click the root directory in the Directories list box. Double-click ppoint4. Double-click rally.ppt in the Source list box.

Step 4: When the Insert Object dialog box displays, select the Link and the Display As Icon check boxes.

Step 5: Choose the OK button.

The PowerPoint "drill down" icon displays in the upper right object placeholder (Figure 2-71).

FIGURE 2-71

▶ EMBEDDING A "DRILL DOWN" DOCUMENT

There may be times when you do not want to maintain the links to the source documents from your presentation; such as when you are the only user of the source documents or the source documents do not change frequently. In these cases, you may choose to embed, rather than link, your "drill down" document. Recall that an embedded object is created in another application and only a copy of that object is inserted into your presentation. Changes made to the original object, the source document, are not reflected in the embedded object. In other words, the embedded object is static; it does not change. In this project, the Microsoft Access "drill down" document will be embedded into the presentation. The process for embedding a "drill down" document is the same as creating a linked "drill down" document except you do not select the Link check box in the Insert Object dialog box. Perform the following steps to embed a "drill down" document.

TO EMBED A "DRILL DOWN" DOCUMENT

Step 1: Double-click the lower right object placeholder on Slide 3.

Step 2: When the Insert Object dialog box displays, select the Create from File option button. Choose the Browse button.

Step 3: When the Browse dialog box displays, double-click the root directory in the Directories list box. Double-click access2. Double-click cust.mdb in the Source list box.

Step 4: When the Insert Object dialog box displays, select only the Display As Icon check box.

Step 5: Choose the OK button.

The Access "drill down" icon displays in the lower right object placeholder (Figure 2-72). The customer database icon displays without a label because the database is embedded and not linked.

Scaling Icons

The icons on Slide 3 are too small for the audience to see (see Figure 2-72). Recall that the audience cannot easily read a font size less than 18 points. Currently, the icon label font size is approximately six points. Because the icon label is part of the icon, scale the four icons to 350% to increase the size of each icon three and one-half times. Consequently, you increase the label font size to approximately 21 points. Perform the following steps to scale the four icons simultaneously.

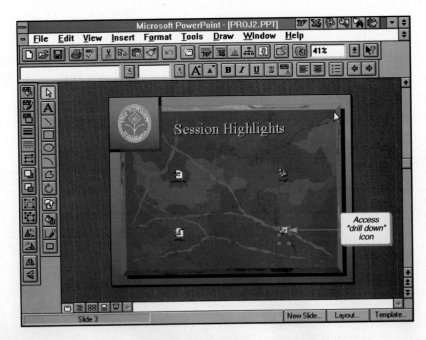

FIGURE 2-72

TO SCALE ICONS

Step 1: Press and hold down the SHIFT key and click each of the four icons on Slide 3. Release the SHIFT key.

Step 2: From the Draw menu, choose the Scale command. When the Scale dialog box displays, type 350 in the Scale To box.

Step 3: Choose the OK button.

All four "drill down" icons are resized (Figure 2-73).

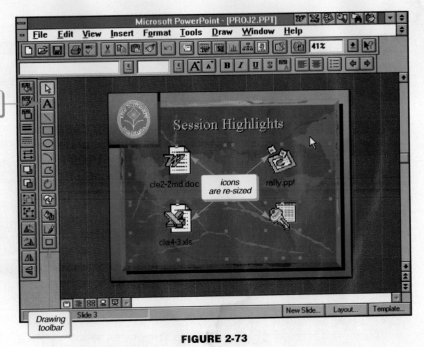

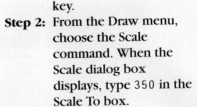

FIGURE 2-73

Adding a Caption to an Object

PowerPoint automatically assigns text attributes to the icon labels. To change the look of the icon label, you must create a caption to hide the icon label. A **caption** is a title, short narrative, or description that accompanies an object. Create a caption using the Text Tool button on the Drawing toolbar.

Because the Microsoft PowerPoint icon is the longest of all the icon captions in Figure 2-60 on page PP107, create this caption first. In a later step, you duplicate the Microsoft PowerPoint caption so all captions look the same except for the text. Perform the steps below to create the Microsoft PowerPoint caption.

TO ADD A CAPTION TO AN OBJECT ▼

STEP 1 ▶

Click the Text Tool button (A) on the Drawing toolbar. Position the text pointer under the PowerPoint "drill down" icon and about the width of one character to the left of the letter r in rally.ppt. Then, click the left mouse button.

A selection box displays in front of the PowerPoint "drill down" icon label rally.ppt (Figure 2-74).

FIGURE 2-74

STEP 2 ▶

Type Microsoft PowerPoint

The Microsoft PowerPoint caption displays in the selection box (Figure 2-75).

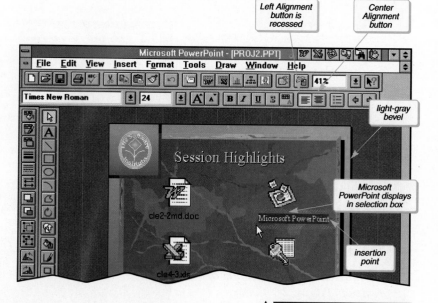

FIGURE 2-75

Adding White Space to the Caption

Because you add a border to the caption in a later step, you want to add white space before and after the text. The added white space prevents the caption from looking crowded. Without the added white space, the borders would display immediately before the letter M in Microsoft and immediately after the letter t in PowerPoint. Add white space by increasing the size of the selection box surrounding the caption. Then, center the text in the caption to evenly distribute the white space using the Center Alignment button on the Formatting toolbar. Perform the following steps to add white space to the caption.

TO ADD WHITE SPACE
TO THE CAPTION

Step 1: Click the fuzzy line of the selection box to display the resize handles.

Step 2: While holding down the CTRL key, drag the middle-right resize handle to the right until it touches the left side of the light-gray bevel. Release the CTRL key.

Step 3: Click the Center Alignment button on the Formatting toolbar.

The text is centered in the caption (Figure 2-76).

FIGURE 2-76

Adding Shaded Fill to the Caption

Because you want to hide the "drill down" icon label, add fill color to the caption. To further enhance the caption, shade the fill color. Recall that shaded fill gives an object a three-dimensional look. Earlier in this project, you applied the From Center shade style to the diamond shape in The Software Institute logo (see page PP91). For the caption, use the Vertical shade style to give the it a three-dimensional, convex appearance. After you add shaded fill, the caption will look like a rounded button bar. Perform the step below to add shaded fill to the caption.

TO ADD SHADED FILL TO THE CAPTION ▼

STEP 1 ▶

With the Microsoft PowerPoint caption still selected, click the Fill Color button on the Drawing+ toolbar. When the Fill Color list box displays, choose the Shaded command. Double-click the lower right variant box, which displays light-red in the middle and increases darkness toward the top and bottom.

By default, the caption displays the red shaded fill (Figure 2-77). If your computer displays a different color, the color scheme is not correct. Re-apply the color scheme (see pages PP77-80).

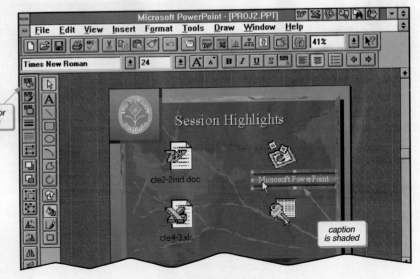

FIGURE 2-77

The caption is created and shaded. The next step is to define its edges by adding a border.

Adding a Border to a Caption

To give the caption added depth, define its edges by adding a border. The following steps summarize how to add a border.

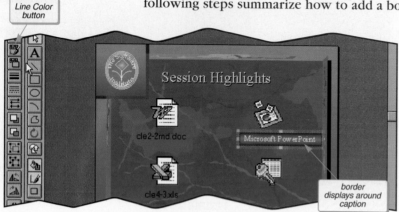

Line Color button

border displays around caption

FIGURE 2-78

TO ADD A BORDER TO A CAPTION

Step 1: With the Microsoft PowerPoint caption still selected, click the Line Color button on the Drawing+ toolbar.

Step 2: Select the dark-green color sample (column 2, row 1).

A border is added to the caption (Figure 2-78).

Duplicating a Caption

Rather than creating a new caption for each "drill down" icon on Slide 3, you can save time and maintain consistency by duplicating a previously created caption. Once you duplicate a caption, move it to overlay the icon text, and then replace the caption text with the new application name. You will move and edit the caption later in this project. Perform the following steps to duplicate the Microsoft PowerPoint caption.

TO DUPLICATE A CAPTION ▼

STEP 1 ▶

With the Microsoft PowerPoint caption selected, select the Edit menu and point to the Duplicate command (Figure 2-79).

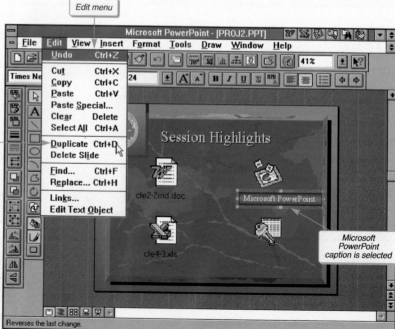

Edit menu

Duplicate command

Microsoft PowerPoint caption is selected

FIGURE 2-79

STEP 2 ▶

Choose the Duplicate command.

A copy of the Microsoft PowerPoint caption cascades over the original (Figure 2-80).

FIGURE 2-80

duplicate caption cascades over original

Making Additional Duplicate Captions

Because you need to create a total of four captions, one for each application "drill down" icon on Slide 3, you want to create two more duplicates of the Microsoft PowerPoint caption. The following steps summarize how to duplicate a caption.

TO MAKE ADDITIONAL DUPLICATE CAPTIONS

Step 1: With the caption duplicated in the previous steps still selected, select the Edit menu. Choose the Duplicate Again command.

Step 2: Select the Edit menu. Choose the Duplicate Again command.

Four Microsoft PowerPoint captions display under the PowerPoint "drill down" icon.

Moving Captions

In PowerPoint, you move a caption by dragging it to a new location on the slide using the drag and drop method. The following steps summarize how to move an object.

TO MOVE A CAPTION

Step 1: Drag the selected Microsoft PowerPoint caption and center it under the Excel "drill down" icon.

Step 2: Select the foreground Microsoft PowerPoint caption under the PowerPoint "drill down" icon. Drag the caption and center it under the Word "drill down" icon.

Step 3: Select the foreground Microsoft PowerPoint caption under the PowerPoint "drill down" icon. Drag the caption and center it under the Access "drill down" icon.

All four "drill down" icons have a Microsoft PowerPoint caption (Figure 2-81).

FIGURE 2-81

captions display under icons

Aligning Captions

To aid in aligning objects horizontally and vertically, PowerPoint has an Align command. The Align command allows you to select objects and then align them horizontally by their left edges, by their centers, or by their right edges. Objects can be aligned vertically by their top edges, by their middles, or by their bottom edges. Objects are aligned by their selection rectangles, not by the object's actual shape. To be certain the captions display vertically on the same plane, align the left edges of the Microsoft Access caption and the Microsoft PowerPoint caption selection rectangles. Then, vertically align the right edges of the selection rectangles of the Microsoft Word and the Microsoft Excel captions. To be certain the captions display horizontally on the same plane, you align the bottom edges of the Microsoft Excel caption and the Microsoft Access caption selection rectangles and then the bottom edges of the selection rectangles of the Microsoft Word caption and the Microsoft PowerPoint caption. Later in this project, you align the captions horizontally. Perform the following steps to vertically align the captions.

TO ALIGN CAPTIONS VERTICALLY ▼

STEP 1 ▶

With the caption under the Access "drill down" icon still selected, press and hold down the SHIFT key and select the caption under the PowerPoint "drill down" icon by clicking it. Release the SHIFT key. Then, select the Draw menu and choose the Align command. When the Align submenu displays, point to the Lefts command.

The Align submenu displays (Figure 2-82). The top three alignment commands control the vertical alignment. The bottom three alignment commands control the horizontal alignment.

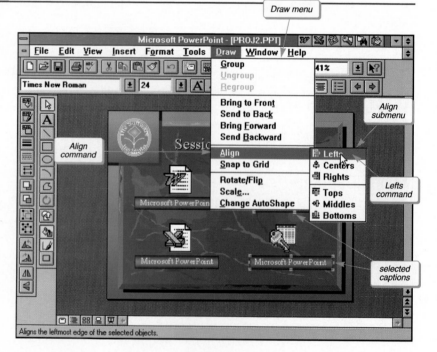

FIGURE 2-82

STEP 2 ▶

Choose the Lefts command.

The left edges of the captions are aligned (Figure 2-83).

FIGURE 2-83

Aligning the Remaining Captions Vertically

To complete the vertical alignment of the captions on Slide 3, you must select the captions under the Word and Excel "drill down" icons. The following steps summarize how to align captions vertically.

TO ALIGN THE REMAINING CAPTIONS VERTICALLY

Step 1: Select the caption under the Word "drill down" icon. Press and hold down the SHIFT key and click the caption under the Excel "drill down" icon. Release the SHIFT key.

Step 2: Select the Draw menu and choose the Align command. When the Align submenu displays, choose the Rights command.

The right edges of the captions are aligned (Figure 2-84).

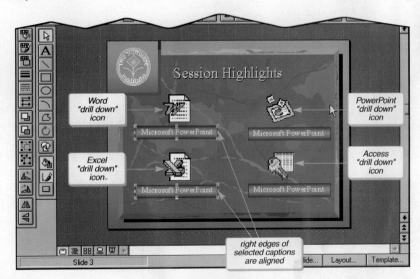

FIGURE 2-84

Aligning Captions Horizontally

The captions are aligned vertically. Next, you want to be certain the captions are in horizontal alignment. The process for horizontal alignment is much the same as vertical alignment. In this project, all captions on Slide 3 are horizontally aligned with the bottom of the caption selection rectangles. The steps on the next page summarize how to align captions horizontally.

TO ALIGN CAPTIONS HORIZONTALLY

Step 1: Press and hold down the SHIFT key and click the caption under the Word "drill down" icon (to deselect it) and the caption under the Access "drill down" icon. Release the SHIFT key.

Step 2: Select the Draw menu and choose the Align command. When the Align submenu displays, choose the Bottoms command.

Step 3: Select the caption under the Word "drill down" icon. Press and hold down the SHIFT key and click the caption under the PowerPoint "drill down" icon. Release the SHIFT key.

Step 4: Select the Draw menu and choose the Align command. When the Align submenu displays, choose the Bottoms command.

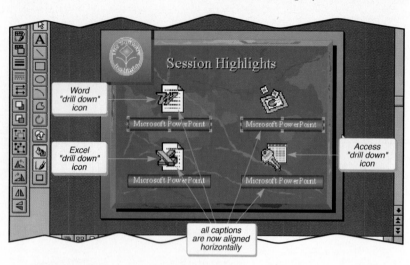

FIGURE 2-85

The Access "drill down" icon and the Excel "drill down" icon captions align horizontally, and the Word "drill down" icon and PowerPoint "drill down" icon captions align horizontally (Figure 2-85).

Editing Captions

The captions almost are complete. You now must edit the captions to change the application name to match the application icon. For example, change the text in the caption under the Word "drill down" icon from Microsoft PowerPoint to Microsoft Word. Editing the text in a caption is accomplished the same way text is edited in any PowerPoint object. Double-click the word you want to edit and then type your change. The following steps summarize editing a caption.

TO EDIT THE CAPTIONS

Step 1: Click anywhere in the PowerPoint window to deselect the selected captions.

Step 2: Double-click the word PowerPoint in the caption under the Word "drill down" icon. Type Word

Step 3: Double-click the word PowerPoint in the caption under the Excel "drill down" icon. Type Excel

Step 4: Double-click the word PowerPoint in the caption under the Access "drill down" icon. Type Access

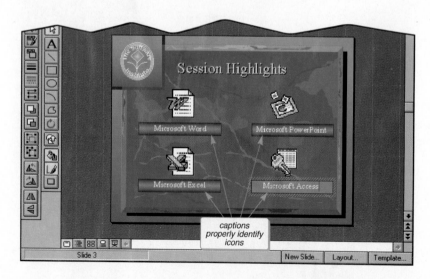

The captions properly identify the "drill down" icons (Figure 2-86).

FIGURE 2-86

The captions now are complete. Because you made several changes to your presentation since your last save, you should now save again.

Setting the "Drill Down" Document Play Setting

Before a "drill down" document can function properly during a slide show, you must tell PowerPoint how and when to play the document. **Playing the document** is using the OLE features of Microsoft Windows to open the application in which the "drill down" document was created and to open the specified file. The contents of the file display as if you were running the application outside of PowerPoint.

Two choices are available to start playing the "drill down" document. One choice is manually: clicking a "drill down" document icon. This method is useful when you want to control the play of a "drill down" document. The other choice is automatically. If you choose to play the "drill down" document automatically, you must tell PowerPoint when to play it. The start of play is based on the slide transition. The When Transition Starts option button in the Play Settings dialog box is used to start the play of the "drill down" document as soon as the slide transition begins. The When Transition Ends option button is used to set the starting time of the "drill down" document to a specified number of seconds after transition ends. Also, you must specify how long to wait after transition ends before starting play by entering the number of seconds in the Ends Plus box in the Play Settings dialog box.

Perform the following steps to establish the play settings for each "drill down" document on Slide 3.

TO SET THE "DRILL DOWN" DOCUMENT PLAY SETTINGS ▼

STEP 1 ▶

Select the Word "drill down" icon on Slide 3. Select the Tools menu and point to the Play Settings command.

The Word "drill down" icon is selected (Figure 2-87). The Tools menu displays.

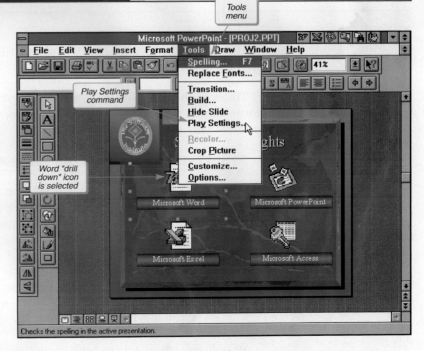

FIGURE 2-87

STEP 2 ▶

Choose the Play Settings command. When the Play Settings dialog box displays, select the When Click on Object check box.

The Play Settings dialog box displays (Figure 2-88). The When Click on Object check box is selected. PowerPoint determines the "drill down" document object to be a document. PowerPoint selects the Other Category option button because it interprets the document is not a Sound object or a Movie object.

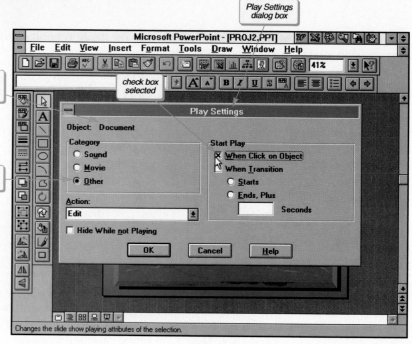

FIGURE 2-88

STEP 3 ▶

Choose the OK button.

Slide 3 displays. The Play Setting for the Microsoft Word "drill down" document is complete.

Setting the Play Settings for the Remaining "Drill Down" Documents

The remaining "drill down" document play settings must be established before running the slide show. The following steps summarize setting "drill down" document play settings.

TO SET THE PLAY SETTINGS FOR THE REMAINING "DRILL DOWN" DOCUMENTS

Step 1: Select the Excel "drill down" icon.

Step 2: Select the Tools menu and choose the Play Settings command. When the Play Settings dialog box displays, select the When Click on Object check box, if it is not already selected.

Step 3: Choose the OK button.

Step 4: Select the PowerPoint "drill down" icon.

Step 5: Select the Tools menu and choose the Play Settings command. When the Play Settings dialog box displays, select the When Click on Object check box, if it is not already selected.

Step 6: Choose the OK button.

Step 7: Select the Access "drill down" icon.

Step 8: Select the Tools menu and choose the Play Settings command. When the Play Settings dialog box displays, select the When Click on Object check box, if it is not already selected.

Step 9: Choose the OK button.

Slide 3 displays. All Play Settings now are set.

HIDING SLIDES

A **supporting slide** provides detailed information to supplement another slide. For example, in a presentation to department chairpersons about the increase in student enrollment, one of the slides displays a graph representing the current year and the previous three years enrollment. In this example, the supporting slide displays a table of student enrollment by department for each year in the graph.

When running a slide show, you do not always want to display the supporting slide. You display the supporting slide when you want to show the audience more detail about a topic. The supporting slide is inserted after the slide you anticipate might warrant more detail. Then, you use the Hide Slide command to hide the supporting slide. The **Hide Slide command** hides the supporting slide from the audience during the normal running of a slide show. When you want to display the supporting, hidden slide, move the mouse pointer to display an icon on the slide that precedes the hidden slide. Then, click the icon. The icon on the preceding slide is visible only if you move the mouse pointer.

Hiding a Slide

Slide 3 is a slide that supports the session information discussed in Slide 2. If time permits, or if the audience needs more information, you can display Slide 3. As the presenter, you decide to show, or not to show, Slide 3. Hide a slide in Slide Sorter view so you can see the slashed square that surrounds the slide number that indicates the slide is hidden. Perform the following steps to hide Slide 3.

TO HIDE A SLIDE ▼

STEP 1 ▶

Click the Slide Sorter View button.

The presentation displays in Slide Sorter view. Slide 3 is selected.

STEP 2 ▶

With Slide 3 still selected, click the Hide Slide button ( ) on the Slide Sorter toolbar.

A square with a slash surrounds the slide number to indicate Slide 3 is a hidden slide (Figure 2-89). The Hide Slide button is recessed.

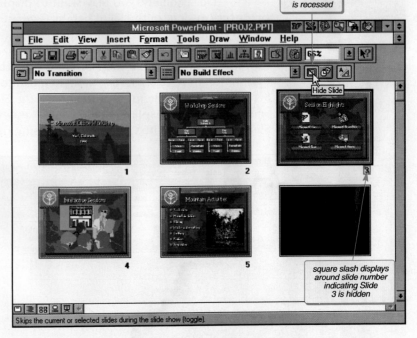

FIGURE 2-89

The Hide Slide button is a toggle; it either applies or removes a square with a slash surrounding the slide number. When a slide is selected in Slide Sorter view, you click the Hide Slide button to mark the slide as a hidden slide. When you no longer want to hide the slide, you change views to Slide Sorter view, select the slide, and click the Hide Slide button. This removes the square with a slash surrounding the slide number.

An alternative to hiding a slide in Slide Sorter view is to hide a slide in Slide view, Outline view, or Notes Pages view. In these views, however, there is no visible indication that a slide is hidden. To hide a slide in Slide view or Notes Pages view, display the slide you want to hide, select the Tools menu, and choose the Hide Slide command. To hide a slide in Outline view, select the slide icon of the slide you want to hide, select the Tools menu, and choose the Hide Slide command.

When you run your presentation, the hidden slide does not display unless you click the hidden slide icon (🔲) at the bottom of the slide preceding the hidden slide. For example, Slide 3 does not display unless you click the hidden slide icon at the bottom of Slide 2. When the slide preceding the hidden slide displays, you can see the hidden slide icon by moving the mouse. Display the hidden slide by clicking the hidden slide icon. You can also display the hidden slide by typing an H when the slide preceding the hidden slide displays. Continue your presentation by clicking the left mouse button or by pressing any of the keys associated with running a slide show. You may skip the hidden slide by ignoring the hidden slide icon and advancing to the next slide.

▶ CHANGING THE SLIDE SETUP

By default, PowerPoint slides display horizontally, or in **landscape orientation,** where the slide width is greater than its height. Occasionally, you may want to display a slide vertically, or in **portrait orientation**, where the slide height is greater than its width. PowerPoint allows you to change the slide orientation from landscape to portrait by changing Slide Setup. Slide Setup controls how slides are sized, their width, their height, how they are numbered, and their orientation. Additionally, Slide Setup controls the orientation of speaker notes, audience handouts, and outlines. To change the Slide Setup, select the File menu and choose the Slide Setup command. When the Slide Setup dialog box displays, make your changes by clicking the down arrow on the Slides Sized for list box, and then choosing the size you want; by selecting an Orientation option button; or by clicking the arrows on the Width, Height, or Number Slides From boxes. After you make your changes to the Slide Setup, choose the OK button. Figure 2-90 identifies the components of the Slide Setup dialog box.

PowerPoint uses the Slide Setup for the entire presentation. To display two different orientations within the same presentation, you "drill down" to the presentation with the different Slide Setup. For example, if you want to display a slide with portrait orientation in the middle

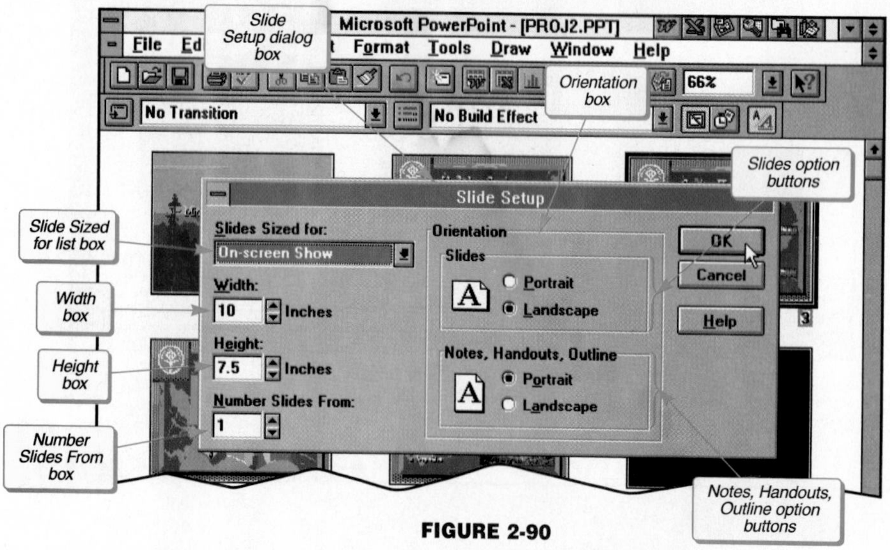

FIGURE 2-90

of a slide show in landscape orientation, you create a "drill down" document that consists of a one slide presentation. You would create the "drill down" source presentation and change the Slide Setup to portrait orientation. When you run the slide show, your presentation displays in landscape orientation until you display the "drill down" slide. The slide with the portrait orientation displays and then the remainder of the presentation displays in landscape orientation.

▶ USING NOTES PAGES VIEW

T o help you remember the key points that you want to communicate to the audience, PowerPoint provides you with notes pages. Each slide in a PowerPoint presentation has an accompanying **notes page**, which includes a smaller version of the slide, and an area where you can type your speaker notes. Create the notes pages in **Notes Pages view**. You can create notes pages for all the slides in the presentation or for just those you want. Print the notes pages and use them to prompt you through the presentation. To provide pages on which the audience can make notes, leave the notes area blank when you print them.

By default, Notes Pages Zoom Control is 33%. This makes it difficult to see the notes as you are typing them. Therefore, you begin creating your notes pages by increasing Zoom Control to 100%. To easily format your notes pages, create them using Microsoft Word. Create the notes pages in Microsoft Word by inserting the Microsoft Word document in the notes area as explained in the following steps.

TO CREATE NOTES PAGES ▼

STEP 1 ▶

Point to the Notes Pages View button (▤) on the status bar (Figure 2-91).

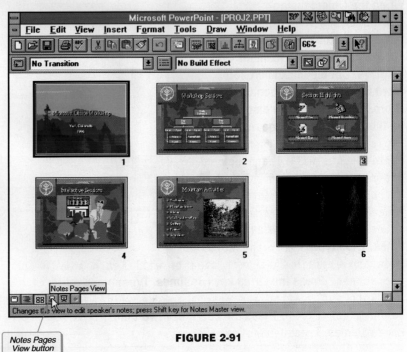

FIGURE 2-91

Notes Pages
View button

STEP 2 ▶

Click the Notes Pages View button. When Slide 3 displays in Notes Pages view, click the Zoom Control down arrow and select 100%.

PowerPoint displays Slide 3 in Notes Pages view because it was selected when you hid it earlier in this project (Figure 2-92). A smaller version of Slide 3 displays at the top of the page and an area to type your notes displays below. The status bar indicates Notes 3 instead of Slide 3 because you are in Notes Pages view.

FIGURE 2-92

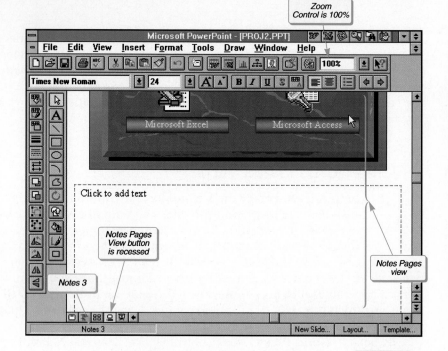

STEP 3 ▶

Select the notes area by clicking it. Select the Insert menu and choose the Object command. When the Object dialog box displays, scroll down the Object Type list box until Microsoft Word 6.0 Document displays. Double-click Microsoft Word 6.0 Document. When the Microsoft Word window displays on the Slide 3 notes page, type: Explain that the workshop participants will learn how to use Microsoft Word 6, Microsoft Excel 5, Microsoft PowerPoint 4, and Microsoft Access 2. **Press the ENTER key two times. Then type:** Click the Word icon and explain that participants will learn how to create form letters as shown on the screen. **Press the ENTER key two times. Type:** Double-click the Control Menu box to exit the Word application and return to the slide. **Press the ENTER key two times. Type:** Demonstrate Excel. **Press the ENTER key two times. Type:** Demonstrate PowerPoint. **Press the ENTER key two times. Type:** Demonstrate Access.

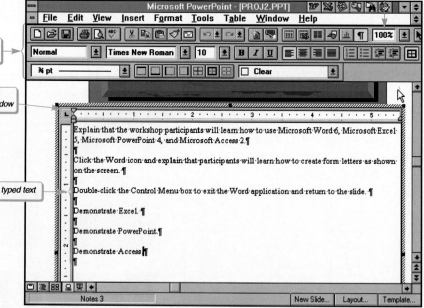

FIGURE 2-93

The text displays in the Microsoft Word window in PowerPoint Notes Pages view (Figure 2-93).

STEP 4 ▶

Click outside the Microsoft Word window to exit Microsoft Word and return to PowerPoint Notes Pages view.

The notes display in the notes area of Notes 3 (Figure 2-94).

text displays in Notes Pages view

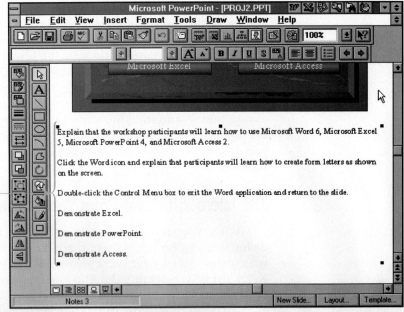

FIGURE 2-94

The look of the notes pages can be designed using the Notes Master. The **Notes Master** is similar to the Slide Master. It is here that you add the objects you want to display on every notes page. For example, if you wanted to display the date, the time, and the page number on every notes page, you would add them to the Notes Master. To display the Notes Master, press and hold down the SHIFT key and click the Notes Pages View button. Then, release the SHIFT key. To exit Notes Master and return to Notes Pages view, click the Notes Pages View button.

To print the notes pages, select the File menu and choose the Print command. When the Print dialog box displays, click the Print What box down arrow. Select Notes Pages and choose the OK button.

Checking Spelling and Saving the Presentation

The presentation is complete. You should now spell check the presentation by clicking the Spelling button (🔤) on the Standard toolbar, and save the presentation.

▶ RUNNING A SLIDE SHOW WITH A HIDDEN SLIDE AND "DRILL DOWN" DOCUMENTS USING THE POWERPOINT VIEWER

PowerPoint comes with an application called the **PowerPoint Viewer** that allows you to run an electronic slide show without installing the PowerPoint application. For example, if you are presenting a slide show using a computer that does not have PowerPoint installed, install the PowerPoint Viewer, and run your presentation. The PowerPoint Viewer only runs an existing presentation. It does not allow you to create or edit a presentation. Because of this, Microsoft has licensed the PowerPoint Viewer to be distributed freely. Therefore, you can give a copy of the PowerPoint Viewer to someone running your slide show who does not have a licensed copy of the PowerPoint application. The computer running the PowerPoint Viewer, however, must have Microsoft Windows 3.1 or later installed.

When you run a slide show, the freehand annotation icon () displays when you move the mouse pointer. Use it to temporarily mark your slide with lines, circles, or, with practice, words. To turn on the freehand annotation feature, click the freehand annotation icon near the lower right coner of the slide. The mouse pointer displays as a pencil. To draw a straight line on your slide during a slide show, click the freehand annotation icon, press and hold down the SHIFT key, click and hold down the left mouse button, and drag the mouse pointer. Release the left mouse button and then the SHIFT key. To turn the freehand annotation feature off, click the freehand annotation icon. The annotation on the slide disappears when you display another slide. You can erase annotations without changing slides by pressing the letter E key.

The Microsoft PowerPoint Viewer Dialog Box

When you start the PowerPoint Viewer, the Microsoft PowerPoint Viewer dialog box displays. It is there that you choose the drive and subdirectory in which you placed your presentation. Then, you select your presentation in the File Name list box. Selecting the Run Continuously Until 'Esc' check box tells the PowerPoint Viewer to repeat the slide show until you press the ESC key. This allows you to repeatedly run a slide show without human intervention, such as one that explains the features of a product you are selling at a trade show. Selecting the Use Automatic Timings check box tells PowerPoint to run the slide show using the slide timings set using the Rehearse Timings button on the Slide Sorter toolbar. Choosing the Show button begins the slide show. Depending on the size of the presentation, it may take several seconds before the slide show begins. You can shorten the time it takes to load the presentation by installing the presentation on the hard drive prior to running the PowerPoint Viewer. Choosing the Quit button exits the PowerPoint Viewer. Perform the following steps to use the PowerPoint Viewer to run the presentation created in this project.

PRESENTATION TIP

Install and run your slide show on the computer you will be using before presenting it before an audience. This gives you the opportunity to correct any problems so that your presentation runs without any surprises.

TO RUN A SLIDE SHOW USING THE POWERPOINT VIEWER ▼

STEP 1 ▶

With the data diskette that contains the file PROJ2.PPT in drive A, point to the PowerPoint Viewer program-item icon in the Microsoft Office window (Figure 2-95).

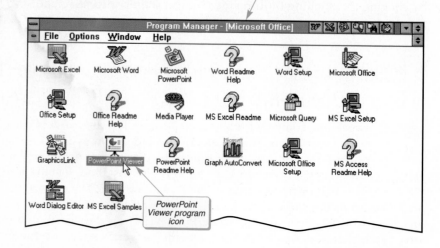

FIGURE 2-95

STEP 2 ▶

Double-click the PowerPoint Viewer program-item icon. When the Microsoft PowerPoint Viewer dialog box displays, select drive A, if it is not already selected. Select proj2.ppt in the File Name list box. Then, point to the Show button.

The PowerPoint Viewer dialog box displays (Figure 2-96). Slide 1 of PROJ2.PPT displays in the preview box.

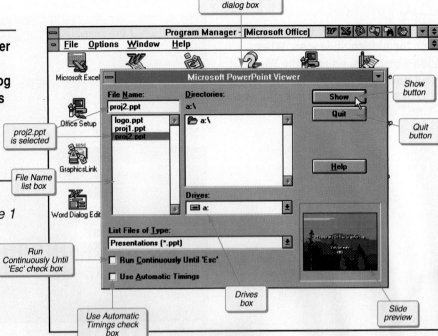

FIGURE 2-96

STEP 3 ▶

Choose the Show button.

After several seconds, Slide 1 displays in Slide Show view.

STEP 4 ▶

Click the left mouse button to display Slide 2. Move the mouse pointer to display the hidden slide icon in the lower right corner of the slide.

Slide 2 displays the hidden slide icon (Figure 2-97). The freehand annotation icon displays. Clicking the freehand annotation icon displays a pencil icon that allows you to temporarily mark the slide.

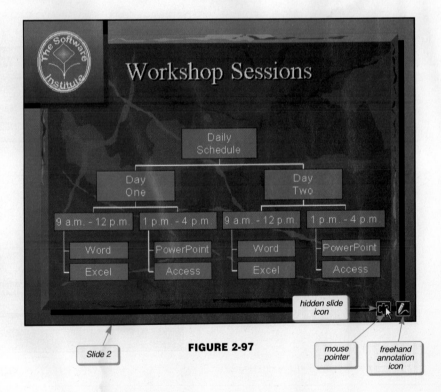

FIGURE 2-97

STEP 5 ▶

Click the hidden slide icon. When Slide 3 displays, point to the Word "drill down" icon.

Slide 3 displays (Figure 2-98).

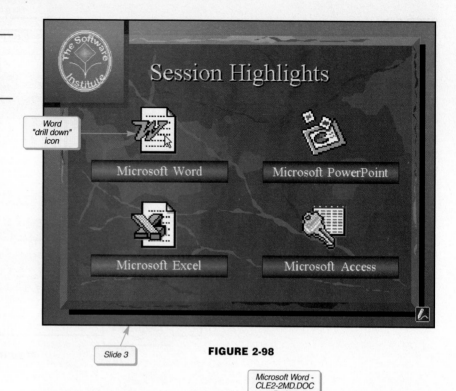

FIGURE 2-98

STEP 6 ▶

Remove the data diskette from drive A and insert the Student Diskette that accompanies this book. Click the Word "drill down" icon.

After a short time, the Microsoft Word 6 application opens and loads the file CLE2-2MD.DOC (Figure 2-99).

STEP 7 ▶

Double-click the Control-menu box to exit Microsoft Word and return to Slide 3.

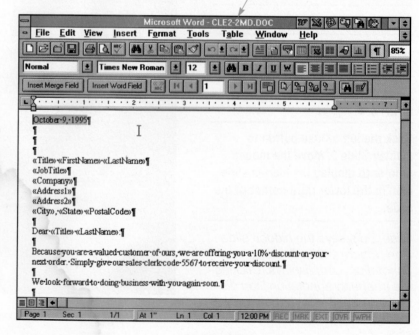

FIGURE 2-99

You changed diskettes in Step 6 above because the PowerPoint Viewer does not establish the link to a "drill down" document until you try to run it. This is different from running the slide show within the PowerPoint application, which establishes the links when you open the presentation.

The slide show is still running. You need to finish running the slide show to display the other three "drill down" documents on Slide 3 and display Slides 4, 5, and 6 as described in the steps below.

TO FINISH RUNNING THE SLIDE SHOW

Step 1: Click the Excel "drill down" icon.

Step 2: Double-click the Control-menu box to exit Microsoft Excel and return to Slide 3.

Step 3: Click the PowerPoint "drill down" icon.

Step 4: When the rally.ppt slide show begins, click the left mouse button to display the second slide. Click the left mouse button to end the presentation and return to Slide 3 in the PROJ2.PPT slide show.

Step 5: Click the Access "drill down" icon. When the MS Access Cue Cards window displays, double-click the Control-menu box on its title bar.

Step 6: If not already selected, select CUSTOMER in the DATABASE window by clicking it. Click the Open button.

Step 7: When the window displays Table: CUSTOMER, double-click the Control-menu box on the Microsoft Access title bar to return to Slide 3.

Step 8: Point to the slide title, or anywhere away from the "drill down" icons, and click the left mouse button to display Slide 4. Click the left mouse button to display Slide 5. Click the left mouse button to display Slide 6.

Step 9: Click the left mouse button to return to the Microsoft PowerPoint Viewer dialog box.

Step 10: Exit the PowerPoint Viewer by choosing the Quit button.

The Microsoft Office group window displays.

When you advance past the last slide, Slide 6, the Microsoft PowerPoint Viewer dialog box displays. When using the PowerPoint Viewer to run a presentation with "drill down" documents, you must supply the source documents in the same directories as those in which they were created. Recall that when you run a presentation containing linked documents, PowerPoint loads the source document. Therefore, you must place the source document exactly where you told PowerPoint to find it. For more information, refer to the section titled Creating a "Drill Down" Document on page PP107.

▶ PROJECT SUMMARY

Project 2 customized the Microsoft Office Workshop presentation created in Project 1. The first step was to save the presentation with a new name to preserve the Project 1 presentation. You then changed templates. Because the colors in the new template did not satisfy The Software Institute standards, you selected a new color scheme. Next, you used the drawing tools to create a company logo. You then added shaded fill color to objects in the logo.

After drawing the logo, you created a graphic image from text. To create the graphic image, you used Microsoft WordArt. Then, you grouped the graphic image with the logo to create a single logo object. The logo object was pasted to the Slide Master of the Microsoft Office Workshop presentation so that it would display on every slide in the presentation, except the title and closing slides. Next, you added a border to a picture. Then, you created a slide containing "drill down" documents to demonstrate the four Microsoft Office applications featured in the workshop; after which, you added captions to the "drill down" icons. Next, you hid the slide to display during the slide show if time permitted. Then, you created speaker notes in Notes Pages view and exited PowerPoint. Finally, you ran the slide show using the PowerPoint Viewer.

▶ KEY TERMS AND INDEX

Q U I C K   R E F E R E N C E

In PowerPoint, you can accomplish a task in a number of ways. The following table provides a quick reference to each task in this project with its available options. The commands listed in the Menu column can be executed using either the keyboard or mouse.

Task	Mouse	Menu	Keyboard Shortcuts
Add Text Box	Click Text Tool button on Drawing toolbar		
Align Objects		From Draw menu, choose Align	
Apply Fill Color	Click Fill Color button on Drawing+toolbar	From Format menu, choose Colors and Lines, click Fill arrow, and choose color	
Apply Style/Scheme		From Format menu, choose Apply Style	
Change Color Scheme		From Format menu, choose Slide Color Scheme	
Change Line Color	Click Line Color button on Drawing+toolbar	From Format menu, choose Colors and Lines. Then click Line box arrow and select color	
Change Line Style	Click Line Style button on Drawing+toolbar	From Format menu, choose Colors and Lines, Then select Line Style	
Display Rulers		From Edit menu, choose Ruler	
Display Movable Guide Lines		From View menu, choose Guides	

Task	Mouse	Menu	Keyboard Shortcuts
Display Notes Pages View	Click Notes Pages View button on status bar	From View menu, choose Notes Pages	
Draw a Line	Click Line Tool button on Drawing toolbar		
Draw an Arc	Click Arc Tool button on Drawing toolbar		
Duplicate an Object		From Edit menu, choose Duplicate	Press CTRL+D
Flip an Object	Click Flip Horizontal or Flip Vertical button on Drawing+ toolbar	From Draw menu, choose Rotate/Flip	
Hide a Slide	Click Hide Slide button on Slide Sorter toolbar	From Edit menu, choose Hide Slide	
Pick Up Style/Scheme		From Format menu, choose Pick Up Color Scheme	
Rotate an Object	Click Rotate Right or Rotate Left button on Drawing+ toolbar	From Draw menu, choose Rotate/Flip	
Set Slide Show Playing Attributes for an OLE Object		From Tools menu, choose Play Settings	
Switch to a Different Open Presentation		From Window menu, choose presentation from list	
Turn Line On/Off	Click Line On/Off button on Drawing toolbar	From Format menu, choose Colors and Lines, then click Line box arrow, and select color or No Line	

S T U D E N T   A S S I G N M E N T S

STUDENT ASSIGNMENT 1
True/False

Instructions: Circle T if the statement is true or F if the statement is false.

T   F   1. A color scheme is a set of eight colors assigned to a slide.
T   F   2. PowerPoint provides two rulers: one horizontal and one vertical.
T   F   3. Segments on the rulers are identified as tick marks.
T   F   4. The guides are two straight lines, one horizontal and one vertical, used for aligning objects.
T   F   5. The visible line around the edge of an object is a border.
T   F   6. The line thickness of a border is determined by the line color.

(continued)

STUDENT ASSIGNMENT 1 (continued)

T   F   7. The color of the line that forms a border is determined by the line style.
T   F   8. A border is composed of five attributes.
T   F   9. A picture is a graphic representation of a command.
T   F   10. The Color box in the Microsoft WordArt Shading dialog box contains a drop-down list box for the text foreground color and another drop-down list box for the text background color.
T   F   11. The file in which a linked object is created is the source document.
T   F   12. A linked object is similar to an embedded object in that it is created in a supplementary application.
T   F   13. A "drill down" document is a file created in an OLE application.
T   F   14. The difference between a linked object and an embedded object is the linked object maintains a connection to its source.
T   F   15. A variant is one of four shading variations that displays in the Color box.
T   F   16. Playing the document is using the OLE features of Microsoft Windows to open the application in which the "drill down" document was created and opening the specified file.
T   F   17. A container document is the originator of the linked object.
T   F   18. Shaded fill gives an object a three-dimensional look.
T   F   19. The vertical ruler displays on the top of the slide window.
T   F   20. The horizontal ruler displays on the left side of the slide window.

STUDENT ASSIGNMENT 2
Multiple Choice

Instructions: Circle the correct response.

1. Tick marks on the rulers identify _____.
   a. 1 inch segments
   b. 1/8 inch segments
   c. 1/4 inch segments
   d. 1/64 inch segments
2. A set of eight colors assigned to a slide is called a _____.
   a. color layout
   b. background color
   c. color scheme
   d. slide color
3. A border is composed of _____.
   a. line style
   b. line color
   c. fill color
   d. all of the above
4. When you do not want to maintain the link to a source document, you _____ the "drill down" document.
   a. embed
   b. insert
   c. place
   d. all of the above
5. When running a slide show, a hidden slide displays when you click the hidden slide icon on the _____.
   a. title slide
   b. hidden slide
   c. slide preceding the hidden slide
   d. slide following the hidden slide

6. In the Insert Object dialog box, selecting the _____ inserts the object as a linked object.
   a. Create New option button
   b. Link check box
   c. Display As Icon check box
   d. Create from File option button

7. Like an embedded object, a _____ is also created in another application but maintains a connection to its source.
   a. pasted object
   b. linked object
   c. copied object
   d. all of the above

8. The fundamental color of a PowerPoint slide is _____.
   a. text and line color
   b. accent color
   c. background color
   d. fill color

9. The _____ are two straight lines, one horizontal and one vertical, used for aligning objects.
   a. grids
   b. indicators
   c. rulers
   d. guides

10. The _____ command gives an object a three-dimensional look.
    a. Line Fill
    b. Fill
    c. Shaded Fill
    d. Line Color

STUDENT ASSIGNMENT 3
Understanding the Microsoft WordArt Shading Dialog Box

Instructions: Arrows in Figure SA2-3 point to the major components of the Microsoft WordArt Shading dialog box. Identify the various parts of the window in the spaces provided.

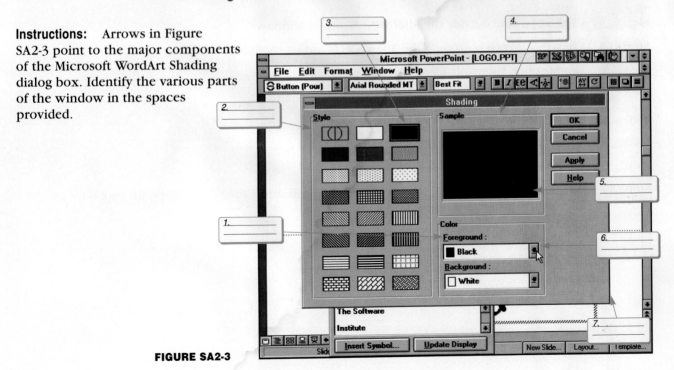

FIGURE SA2-3

STUDENT ASSIGNMENT 4
Understanding How to Embed a Microsoft WordArt Graphic Object

Instructions: You are revising a presentation. Assume you are in Slide view displaying Slide 1 of your presentation. You want to use Microsoft WordArt to change the title slide. Fill in the step numbers below to indicate the sequence necessary to embed the graphic object shown in the title placeholder in Figure SA2-4.

FIGURE SA2-4

Step ____: Click anywhere outside the Microsoft WordArt window.

Step ____: Click the Stretch button on the Microsoft WordArt toolbar.

Step ____: Double-click Microsoft WordArt 2.0.

Step ____: Select the Insert menu and choose the Object command.

Step ____: Select the Title placeholder on Slide 1.

Step ____: Select the Wave1 style in the Styles list box.

Step ____: Type Surfing the Internet

Step ____: When the Insert Object dialog box displays, scroll down the Object Type list box until Microsoft WordArt 2.0 displays.

STUDENT ASSIGNMENT 5
Understanding Color Scheme

Instructions: Answer the following questions.

1. What color scheme component is used for graphs and charts as well as contrasts with both the background color and text and line color?_____

2. What is background color?_____

3. How do text and line color work together with background color?_____

4. What color scheme component is applied when you shadow an object?_____

5. How many accent colors are in a color scheme?_____

6. What color scheme component is designed for secondary features on a slide, such as a graph?

_____

7. What color scheme component is applied to title text?_____

8. What happens when you choose the Apply to All button in the Slide Color Scheme dialog box?

_____

9. Which color scheme color do you select first in the Choose Scheme dialog box?_____

10. What box, in the Choose Scheme dialog box, displays four color schemes?_____

STUDENT ASSIGNMENT 6
Understanding the PowerPoint Drawing Tools

Instructions: Answer the following questions.

1. PowerPoint provides two rulers to help you align objects. What is the name of each ruler and where does it display on the PowerPoint window?

    a. _____

    b. _____

2. What two methods display the rulers on the PowerPoint window?

    a. _____

    b. _____

3. What two methods display the guides on the PowerPoint window?

    a. _____

    b. _____

4. Which toolbar contains the Free Rotate Tool button? _____

5. What button do you click to rotate a selected object counterclockwise in 90° increments?

_____

(continued)

STUDENT ASSIGNMENT 6 (continued)

6. What button do you click to vertically flip a selected object 180°? _____

7. What is a border? _____

8. How do you draw a straight line when the guides are not displaying? _____
   _____

   _____

9. What button do you click to remove the border around a selected object? _____
   _____

10. What button do you click to change the color of a line? _____

COMPUTER LABORATORY EXERCISES

COMPUTER LABORATORY EXERCISE 1
Using the Help Menu to Understand Drawing

Instructions: Start PowerPoint, open a blank presentation, and perform the following tasks using a computer.

1. Select the Help menu and choose the Search for Help on command. Type draw in the Search dialog box and choose the Show Topics button.
2. Click About Drawing Objects in PowerPoint in the list at the bottom of the Search dialog box. Choose the Go To button. Read the information displayed. Print the information displayed by selecting the Help window File menu and choosing the Print Topic command.
3. Click the Search button at the top of the Help window. If the word draw is not displaying in the Search dialog box, type draw and choose the Show Topics button.
4. Click About Drawing Rectangles, Ellipses, and Other AutoShapes in the list at the bottom of the Search dialog box. Choose the Go To button. Read and print the information displayed.
5. Click Changing the shape of an AutoShape in the See also section of the Help window. Read and print the information displayed. Click the Tip button. Read the tip. Click anywhere on the Help window to exit the tip.
6. Click the Search button at the top of the Help window. If the word draw is not displaying in the Search dialog box, type draw and choose the Show Topics button. Click About Drawing Lines, Arcs, and Freeforms in the list at the bottom of the Search dialog box. Choose the Go To button. Read and print the information displayed.
7. Exit Help by double-clicking the Control-menu box in the Help window.

COMPUTER LABORATORY EXERCISE 2
Adding a Caption with Shaded Fill and a Border

Instructions: Start PowerPoint. Open a blank presentation using the twentieth layout, Title Only. Perform the following tasks to create the clip art caption shown in Figure CLE2-2.

1. Type Congratulations in the title placeholder.
2. Click the Template button on the status bar. Double-click the cheerss.ppt template in the sldshow subdirectory.
3. Point anywhere on the slide except the title and click the right mouse button to display a shortcut menu. Choose the Guides command.
4. Click the Insert Clip Art button on the Standard toolbar. Choose the Find button in the Microsoft ClipArt Gallery - Picture in Presentation dialog box. When the Find Picture dialog box displays, type At the Top in the With a Description containing box. Choose the OK button. Double-click the At the Top image in the gallery of images list box. Scale the clip art image to 60%. Drag the clip art image up to the middle of the slide.

FIGURE CLE2-2

5. Click the Text Tool button on the Drawing toolbar. Position the pointer near the bottom of the slide and click the left mouse button. Type You've made it to the top!
6. Click the selection box to display the resize handles. Increase the font size to 36 points.
7. Click the Line Color button on the Drawing+ toolbar. Choose the dark maroon (almost black) color sample (column 2, row 1).
8. Click the Fill Color button on the Drawing+ toolbar. Choose the Shaded command. When the Shaded Fill dialog box displays, click the down arrow in the Color box. Choose the medium rose color sample (column 4, row 2). If not already selected, select the Vertical option button in the Shade Style box. Double-click the lower right shading variation in the Variants box.
9. Drag the caption to the center of the slide, below the clip art image as shown in Figure CLE2-2.
10. Save the presentation to your data diskette with the filename CLE2-2.
11. Print the slide using the Black & White option.
12. Exit PowerPoint.

COMPUTER LABORATORY EXERCISE 3
Editing a WordArt Object and Changing the Color Scheme

Instructions: Start PowerPoint. Insert the data diskette containing The Software Institute logo, created in Project 2 and saved with the filename LOGO.PPT, into drive A. Open LOGO.PPT. If you did not create The Software Institute logo in Project 2, ask your instructor for a copy. Perform the tasks on the next page to modify the logo to look like Figure CLE2-3 on the next page.

(continued)

COMPUTER LABORATORY EXERCISE 3 (continued)

1. Select the File menu and choose the Save As command. Save the presentation with the filename CLE2-3.
2. Select the logo object by clicking it. Click the Ungroup button on the Drawing+ toolbar two times. Click outside the logo object to deselect the ungrouped objects.
3. Select the border around the ellipse by clicking it. Click the Line Style button on the Drawing+ toolbar. Choose the third line style from the top of the list in the Line Style list box.
4. Press the TAB key to select the Microsoft WordArt object. Double-click the Microsoft WordArt object to the open the Microsoft WordArt application. Select the words The Software. Type your name in place of The Software. Click the Font box arrow. Scroll down the list of fonts and choose Times New Roman.

FIGURE CLE2-3

5. Click outside the logo object to return to the PowerPoint window. Select the Edit menu and choose the Select All command. Click the Group button on the Drawing+ toolbar.
6. Point outside the logo and click the right mouse button to display a shortcut menu.
7. Choose the Slide Color Scheme command. Choose the Choose Scheme button in the Slide Color Scheme dialog box. When the Choose Scheme dialog box displays, click the first color sample in the Background Color list box, white. When the colors display in the Text & Line Color box, click the fourth color sample from the top of the list, bright blue. Double-click the upper left color scheme in the Other Scheme Colors box. When the Slide Color Scheme dialog box displays, choose the Apply button.
8. Save the logo object again by clicking the Save button on the Standard toolbar.
9. Print the logo slide using the Black & White and Scale to Fit Paper options.

COMPUTER LABORATORY ASSIGNMENTS

COMPUTER LABORATORY ASSIGNMENT 1
Creating a Title Slide Containing a Logo

Purpose: To become familiar with changing slide orientation, changing color scheme, drawing objects, adding a border, adding shaded fill color, inserting Microsoft WordArt, and pasting the logo object to the slide master.

Problem: You are a student at Western State University enrolled in an introductory computer literacy course. Your assignment is to create the title slide for the Western State University Freshman Orientation presentation. The title slide contains a school logo in portrait orientation, using the school colors; blue and yellow, the school's name, a border, and a graphic. You create the title slide shown in Figure CLA2-1c on page PP144.

Part 1 Instructions: Perform the following tasks to create the title slide in Figure CLA2-1a.

1. Open a blank presentation and apply the Title Slide AutoLayout (layout number 1).
2. Apply the metlbars.ppt template from the sldshow subdirectory.
3. Type the text for the title slide as shown in Figure CLA2-1a.
4. Check your presentation for spelling errors by clicking the Spelling button on the Standard toolbar.
5. Save the presentation on your data diskette with the filename CLA2-1.
6. Print the title slide using the Black & White Only and Scale to Fit Paper options. Label your printout as Part 1.

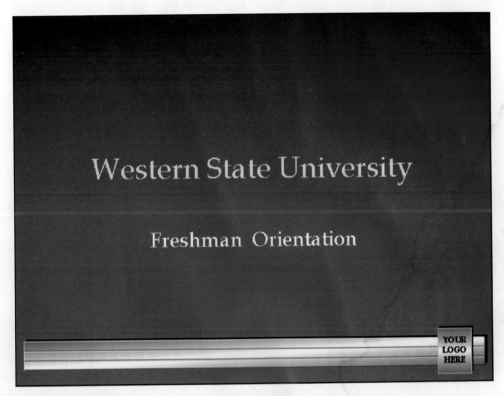

FIGURE CLA2-1a

Part 2 Instructions: Perform the following tasks to create the logo in Figure CLA2-1b.

1. Open a new blank presentation and apply the Blank AutoLayout (layout number 21).
2. Apply a new color scheme by selecting the first bright yellow color sample from the top of the Background Color box and the second color sample from the top of the Text & Line Color box (bright blue) in the Choose Scheme dialog box. Choose the lower right color scheme in the Other Scheme Colors box.
3. Apply shaded fill color to the slide background with the attributes in the table.
4. Insert the Microsoft WordArt object shown in Figure CLA2-1b using the attributes in the table.
5. In PowerPoint, scale the Microsoft WordArt object to 150%.
6. Save the Western State University WordArt logo on your data diskette with the filename CLA2-1b.
7. Print the title slide using the Black & White and Scale to Fit Paper options. Label your printout as Part 2.

ATTRIBUTE	SELECTION
Shade Style	Diagonal Right
Color	Default, yellow
Variant	Lower-Right variation
Dark Light scroll	Lighten the default by four clicks on the right arrow

WORD ART ATTRIBUTE	SELECTION
Shape	Inflate ◼
Font	Impact, or a similar

(continued)

COMPUTER LABORATORY ASSIGNMENT 1 (continued)

FIGURE CLA2-1b

Part 3 Instructions: Perform the following tasks to paste the logo into the Western State University Freshman Orientation shown in Figure CLA2-1c.

1. Change the view of the Western State University WordArt logo presentation to Slide Sorter view. Click the Copy button on the Standard toolbar.
2. Select the Window menu and choose the presentation CLA2-1.PPT.
3. Press and hold down the SHIFT key and click the Slide View button to display the Slide Master. Click the Paste button on the Standard toolbar.
4. Add a border with the attributes in the table.
5. Scale the logo to 25%.
6. Drag the logo to the lower right corner of Slide Master to overlay the object labeled YOUR LOGO HERE so it looks like Figure CLA2-1c.

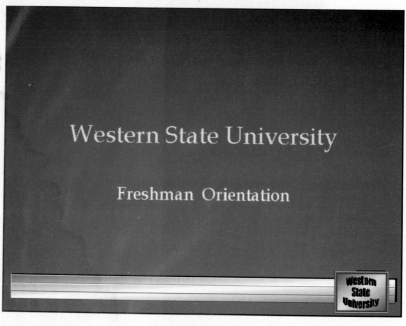

FIGURE CLA2-1c

ATTRIBUTE	SELECTION
Line Style	Two lines, third line style from bottom in the Line Style list
Line	Dark blue (row 1, column 2 in the Color list box)
Fill Color	Yellow (row 2, column 2 in the Color list box)

7. Save the presentation on your data diskette again with the filename CLA2-1.
8. Print the title slide using the Black & White and Scale to Fit Paper options. Label your printout as Part 3.

COMPUTER LABORATORY ASSIGNMENT 2
Linking PowerPoint Presentations and Running the PowerPoint Viewer

Purpose: To become familiar with linking PowerPoint presentations, creating captions, and running a slide show using the PowerPoint Viewer.

Problem: You are a volunteer at a local hospital. The state organ procurement organization has requested that all hospitals educate the community about the need for organ and tissue donors. Because of the difficulty in speaking to family members about organ and tissue donation when a loved one is dying, the nursing staff suggests that someone create an interactive presentation. This presentation would educate family members about organ donation. The person watching the presentation could click a button to display answers about specific questions relating to organ donation. Because you know how to create linked PowerPoint presentations, you volunteer to develop the presentations shown in Figures CLA2-2a through CLA2-2f.

Part 1 Instructions: Perform the following tasks to create the presentation in Figure CLA2-2a and CLA2-2b.

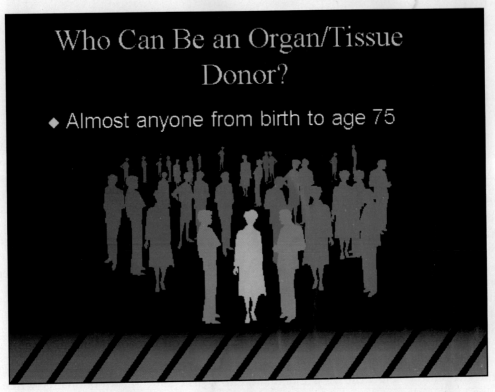

FIGURE CLA2-2a

1. Open a blank presentation and apply the Bulleted List AutoLayout (layout number 2). Apply the linsblus.ppt template from the sldshow subdirectory.
2. Type the slide title and bulleted list shown in Figure CLA2-2a. Insert the Crowd image from the People category in the Microsoft ClipArt Gallery by clicking the Insert Clip Art button on the Standard toolbar.

(continued)

COMPUTER LABORATORY ASSIGNMENT 2 (continued)

3. Create the bulleted list slide shown in Figure CLA2-2b. Increase the line spacing of the demoted paragraph to .5 Lines After Paragraph. Check the spelling of your presentation by clicking the Spelling button on the Standard toolbar.

Who Can Donate?

- ◆ In general, anyone wishing to donate
  - − Some age limitations may apply for specific organs and tissues

- ◆ Children under 18 can donate with consent of parent or guardian

FIGURE CLA2-2b

4. Click the Slide Sorter View button. Select Slide 1. Click the Transition button on the Slide Sorter toolbar. When the Transition dialog box displays, select Blinds Vertical in the Effect box and type 8 in the Seconds box. Choose the OK button. Select Slide 2. Click the Transition button. When the Transition dialog box displays, select Blinds Vertical in the Effect box and type 15 in the Seconds box. Choose the OK button. Click the Build Effects down arrow on the Slide Sorter toolbar and select Fly From Left. Select the View menu and choose the Slide Show command. When the Slide Show dialog box displays, select the Use Slide Timings option button. Choose the Show button. Press the ESC key.
5. Save the presentation to your data diskette with the filename CLA2-2A.PPT. Print the presentation slides using the Black & White option. Close the presentation.
6. Open a new presentation and select the Current Presentation Format option button in the New Presentation dialog box. Change slide layout to 2 Column Text (slide layout number 4). Display the slide in Slide view. Create the slide shown in Figure CLA2-2c. Check the spelling of your presentation.
7. Click the Slide Sorter View button. Click the Transition button on the Slide Sorter toolbar. When the Transition dialog box displays, select Blinds Vertical in the Effect box and type 15 in the Seconds box. Choose the OK button. Select the View menu and choose the Slide Show command. When the Slide Show dialog box displays, select the Use Slide Timings option button. Choose the Show button. Press the ESC key.

What Can Be Donated?

◆ Organs
- Kidneys
- Heart
- Lungs
- Liver
- Pancreas

◆ Tissues
- Corneas
- Skin
- Heart Valves
- Bones
- Tendons

FIGURE CLA2-2c

Can I Sell My Organs?

◆ No!

◆ Federal law prohibits the sale of organs or tissues.

◆ All anatomical donations are an extraordinary gift...a gift of life!

FIGURE CLA2-2d

8. Save the presentation to your data diskette with the filename CLA2-2B.PPT. Print the presentation slides using the Black & White option. Close the presentation.

9. Open a new presentation and choose the Current Presentation Format option button in the New Presentation dialog box. Change slide layout to Bulleted List (slide layout number 2). Display the slide in Slide view. Create the slide shown in Figure CLA2-2d. Increase the line spacing for all three paragraphs to .5 Lines After Paragraph. Check the spelling of your presentation.

(continued)

COMPUTER LABORATORY ASSIGNMENT 2 (continued)

10. Click the Slide Sorter View button. Click the Transition button on the Slide Sorter toolbar. When the Transition dialog box displays, select Blinds Vertical in the Effect box and type 20 in the Seconds box. Choose the OK button. Click the Build Effects down arrow on the Slide Sorter toolbar and choose Fly From Left. Select the View menu and choose the Slide Show command. When the Slide Show dialog box displays, select the Use Slide Timings option button. Choose the Show button. Press the ESC key.

11. Save the presentation to your data diskette with the filename CLA2-2C.PPT. Print the presentation slides using the Black & White option. Close the presentation.

12. Open a new presentation and select the Current Presentation Format option button in the New Presentation dialog box. Apply the Bulleted List AutoLayout (slide layout number 2). Display the slide in Slide view. Create the slide show in Figure CLA2-2e. Check the spelling of your presentation. Increase the line spacing to .5 Lines After Paragraph for both paragraphs.

FIGURE CLA2-2e

13. Click the Slide Sorter View button. Click the Transition button on the Slide Sorter toolbar. When the Transition dialog box displays, select Blinds Vertical in the Effect box and type 20 in the Seconds box. Choose the OK button. Click the Build Effects down arrow on the Slide Sorter toolbar and choose Fly From Left. Select the View menu and choose the Slide Show command. When the Slide Show dialog box displays, select the Use Slide Timings option button. Choose the Show button. Press the ESC key.

14. Save the presentation to your data diskette with the filename CLA2-2D.PPT. Print the presentation slides using the Black & White option. Close the presentation.

Part 2 Instructions: Perform the following tasks to create the presentation in Figure CLA2-2f.

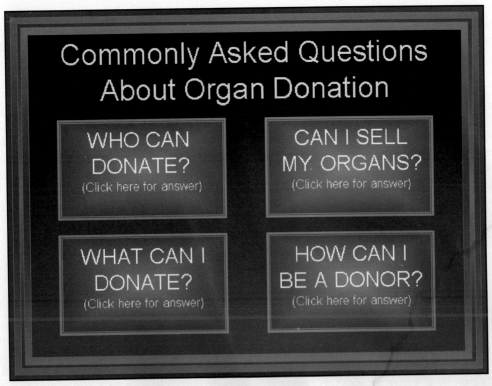

FIGURE CLA2-2f

1. Open a new presentation and select the Blank Presentation Format option button in the New Presentation dialog box. Apply the 4 Objects AutoLayout (slide layout number 19). Apply the blueboxs.ppt template from the sldshow subdirectory. Type the slide title as shown in Figure CLA2-2f.
2. Double-click the upper left object placeholder. Link the PowerPoint presentation CLA2-2A.PPT, created in Part 1 and saved to your data diskette, and display it as an icon. Select the Tools menu and choose the Play Settings command. Select the When Click on Object check box in the Start Play box. Select the Hide While not Playing check box. Choose the OK button.
3. Double-click the lower left object placeholder. Link the PowerPoint presentation CLA2-2B.PPT from your data diskette and display it as an icon. Select the When Click on Object and Hide While not Playing check boxes in the Play Settings dialog box.
4. Double-click the upper right object placeholder. Link the PowerPoint presentation CLA2-2C.PPT from your data diskette and display it as an icon. Select the When Click on Object and Hide While not Playing check boxes in the Play Settings dialog box.
5. Double-click the lower right object placeholder. Link the PowerPoint presentation CLA2-2D.PPT from your data diskette and display it as an icon. Select the When Click on Object and Hide While not Playing check boxes in the Play Settings dialog box.
6. SHIFT+Click to select the four icons. Scale the icons to 300%. Add shaded fill to the icons using the From Center shade style, the light green color sample (row 1, column 4), and the default variation in the Variants box. Apply a border around the icons by changing line color to the light-green color sample (row 1, column 4). Change the border line style to the second line style from the bottom in the Line Style list box.
7. Save the presentation to your data diskette with the filename CLA2-2.PPT.
8. Click the Text Tool button on the Drawing toolbar. Place the insertion point in the middle of the icon in the upper left object placeholder. Click the Center Alignment button on the Formatting toolbar. Type the text for the button as shown in Figure CLA2-2f. Increase the font size of WHO CAN DONATE to 32 points and decrease the font size of (Click here for answer) to 18 points.

(continued)

COMPUTER LABORATORY ASSIGNMENT 2 (continued)

9. Use Figure CLA2-2f to label the remaining three buttons. Increase the font size of the words in all capitalized letters to 32 points. Decrease the font size of the words in parentheseis to 18 points.
10. Select the View menu and choose the Slide Show command. When the Slide Show dialog box displays, select the Run Continuously Until 'Esc' check box. Choose the Show button. Press the ESC key
11. Save the presentation again. Print the slide using the Pure Black & White option. Exit PowerPoint.
12. Start the PowerPoint Viewer and select the Run Continuously Until 'Esc' and Use Automatic Timings check boxes. Start the slide show. Click the WHO CAN DONATE? button to display the linked presentation. When the linked presentation returns, click the WHAT CAN I DONATE? button. When the linked presentation returns, click the CAN I SELL MY ORGANS? button. When the linked presentation returns, click the HOW CAN I BE A DONOR? button. When the linked presentation returns, press the ESC key to end the slide show. Quit the PowerPoint Viewer.

COMPUTER LABORATORY ASSIGNMENT 3
Drawing a Company Logo

Purpose: To become familiar with drawing objects, adding shaded fill color, rotating an object, flipping an object, duplicating an object, creating a caption, and changing line style.

Problem: You are the national sales manager of a new company called The hOle in One cOmpany. The company manufactures golfing apparel. The company name uses all lowercase letters in its name except for the letter O. The letter O is capitalized to resemble a golf ball. Every employee has been asked to submit an idea for the company logo. You create the logo shown in Figure CLA2-3.

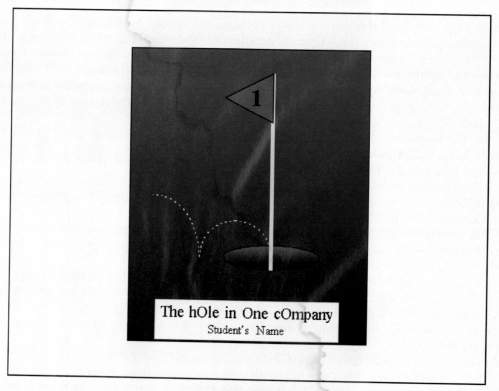

FIGURE CLA2-3

Part 1 Instructions: Perform the following tasks to create the drawing in Figure CLA2-3

1. Open a blank presentation and apply the Blank AutoLayout (layout number 21).
2. Display the Guides and Rulers.
3. At the intersection of the vertical and horizontal guides, draw a rectangle, about center, using the Rectangle Tool button on the Drawing toolbar so that it is five inches wide and six inches high.
4. Apply shaded fill color to the rectangle using the attributes in the table.

ATTRIBUTE	SELECTION
Shade Style	Vertical
Color	Gray (row 2, column 3 in the Color list box)
Variant	Upper-Left variation
Dark Light scroll bar	Lighten the default by three clicks on the right arrow

5. Increase Zoom Control to 50%. Drag the vertical guide to .50 inch right of center on the horizontal ruler. Drag the horizontal guide to 1.25 inches below center on the vertical ruler. At the intersection of the vertical and horizontal guides, draw an ellipse about center so it is one inch wide and .50 inch high. Change the fill color of the ellipse using the attributes in the table.

ATTRIBUTE	SELECTION
Shade Style	Vertical
Color	Gray (row 2, column 3 in the Color list box)
Variant	Upper-Left variation
Dark Light scroll bar	Lighten the default by three clicks on the right arrow

6. Draw a straight line down the vertical guide by clicking the Line Tool button, pressing and holding down the SHIFT key, and dragging the mouse pointer from a point 2.5 inches above center on the vertical ruler to a point at the bottom of the ellipse, approximately 1.50 inches below center on the vertical ruler. Release the left mouse button and the SHIFT key.
7. Change the line style of the straight line by selecting the third line style from the top of the list in the Line Style list box.
8. Change the color of the straight line to yellow by clicking the Line Color button on the Drawing+ toolbar, choosing the Other Color command, and double-clicking the yellow color sample (row 1, column 5 in the Other Color dialog box).
9. Drag the horizontal guide to 1.5 inches above center. Draw the flag object by clicking the AutoShapes button on the Drawing toolbar, clicking the Isosceles Triangle Tool button, positioning the mouse pointer at the intersection of the horizontal and vertical guides, clicking the left mouse button, and dragging the mouse pointer up and to the left to a point 2.5 inches above center on the vertical ruler and a point .5 inch left of center on the horizontal ruler. Release the left mouse button.
10. Rotate the triangle 90° to the left so it looks like the flag in Figure CLA2-3. Type 1 and do not press the ENTER key. Select the number 1. Click the Increase Font Size button on the Formatting toolbar three times to 36 points. Click the Bold button on the Formatting toolbar. Hide the AutoShapes toolbar.
11. Drag the horizontal guide to 1.25 inches below center on the vertical ruler. Drag the vertical guide to 2 inches left of center on the horizontal ruler. Click the Arc Tool button on the Drawing toolbar. Position the mouse pointer on the vertical guide at the center point (zero tick mark) of the vertical ruler. Draw the arc by dragging the mouse pointer down to the horizontal guide and to the right of the 1 inch tick mark left of center on the horizontal ruler.
12. Drag the vertical guide to .25 inch left of center on the horizontal ruler. Click the Arc Tool button and position the mouse pointer on the vertical guide at .5 inch below center on the vertical ruler. Press and hold down the SHIFT key and drag the mouse pointer down to the horizontal guide and to the right of the straight line. Select the Edit menu and choose the Duplicate command. Click the Flip Horizontal button on the Drawing+ toolbar. Drag the duplicated arc to the left to create a half-circle as shown in Figure CLA2-3.

(continued)

COMPUTER LABORATORY ASSIGNMENT 3 (continued)

13. SHIFT+Click all three arcs. Click the Group button on the Drawing+ toolbar. Click the Dashed Lines button on the Drawing+ toolbar. Select the third line in the Dashed Lines list box. Click the Line Color button on the Drawing+ toolbar and click the white color sample.
14. Save the presentation on your data diskette with the filename CLA2-3.PPT.

Part 2 Instructions: Perform the following tasks to create the caption in Figure CLA2-3.

1. Drag the horizontal guide to 2.5 inches below center on the vertical ruler. Drag the vertical guide to the center (zero tick mark) of the horizontal ruler. Click the Text Tool button on the Drawing toolbar. Position the horizontal line of the Text Tool pointer at the intersection of the horizontal and vertical guides. Click the left mouse button.
2. Click the Center Alignment button on the Formatting toolbar. Type The hOle in One cOmpany and press the ENTER key.
3. Type your name in place of the Student's Name in Figure CLA2-3 on the previous page.
4. Select your name by triple-clicking it. Click the Decrease Font Size button on the Formatting toolbar two times to 18 points.
5. Click the Line Color button and select the yellow color sample.
6. Click the Fill Color button and select the white color sample.
7. Save the presentation on your data diskette again by clicking the Save button on the Standard toolbar.
8. Print the slide using the Black & White and Scale to Fit Paper options.
9. Exit PowerPoint.

COMPUTER LABORATORY ASSIGNMENT 4
Designing, Creating, and Running a Slide Show with a "Drill Down" Document and a Hidden Slide

Purpose: To provide practice in designing, creating, and running a slide show that contains a "drill down" document and a hidden slide.

Problem: You are the Director for the 1996 Student Senate election. You are responsible for designing a presentation to introduce the three candidates at next month's student assembly.

Instructions: Design and create a slide show presentation to highlight three students running for Student Senate. Use Microsoft WordArt to create the title slide. Create a logo for the 1996 Student Senate election and place it on every slide. Create at least one "drill down" document that displays when you click its icon during the running of the slide show. Create and hide a supporting slide that displays when you click its icon during the running of the slide show. Use all the customizing features presented to you in this project. Use the three files from the subdirectory Access2 on the Student Diskette that accompanies this book labeled PICT1.PCX, PICT2.PCX, and PICT3.PCX for pictures of the student candidates or use pictures that you have scanned. Add borders and captions to the pictures. Be sure to follow good presentation design techniques. Run the presentation using the PowerPoint Viewer.